SPECIAL EDITION

# USING®

# WordPerfect® 12

*Laura Acklen*

*Read Gilgen*

800 East 96th Street
Indianapolis, Indiana 46240

## CONTENTS

# SPECIAL EDITION USING® WORDPERFECT® 12

**Copyright© 2005 by Que® Corporation.**

International Standard Book Number: 0-7897-3243-2

Library of Congress Catalog Card Number: 2001093933

Printed in the United States of America

First Printing: August 2004

07  06  05  04       4  3  2  1

## Trademarks

## Warning and Disclaimer

## Bulk Sales

Que Publishing offers excellent discounts on this book when ordered in quantity for bulk purchases or special sales. For more information, please contact

**U.S. Corporate and Government Sales**
**1-800-382-3419**
corpsales@pearsontechgroup.com

For sales outside of the U.S., please contact

**International Sales**
international@pearsoned.com

**Associate Publisher**
Greg Wiegand

**Acquisitions Editor**
Stephanie J. McComb

**Development Editor**
Kevin Howard

**Managing Editor**
Charlotte Clapp

**Project Editor**
Sheila Schroeder

**Copy Editor**
Kate Givens

**Indexer**
Mandie Frank

**Proofreader**
Juli Cook

**Technical Editors**
Cyndy Zook
Charles Girard

**Team Coordinator**
Sharry Lee Gregory

**Interior Designer**
Anne Jones

**Cover Designers**
Anne Jones

**Page Layout**
Julie Parks

# CONTENTS

## III  Organizing Information

## V  Integrating Information from Other Sources

# About the Authors

**Laura Acklen** first encountered WordPerfect 4.2 in early 1988 when she developed custom courseware and trained law offices that were converting from Wang systems to Novell LANs. In 1990, she began teaching classes for the international training company, Productivity Point International (PPI), and progressed into courseware development for its corporate headquarters. Her student and instructor manuals were distributed internationally and used in all PPI training centers.

In 1993, Laura wrote her first book for Que called *Oops! What to Do When Things Go Wrong with WordPerfect*. Her second book, *WordPerfect 6.0 SureSteps*, was written that same year. Since that time, she has authored or co-authored eleven other books for Que, including five editions of the *Special Edition Using WordPerfect* books (for versions 6, 6.1, 7, 9, and 10) and three editions of the *Absolute Beginner's Guide to WordPerfect* (for versions 10, 11, and 12).

Laura was a contributing editor for the *WordPerfect for Windows Magazine* for four years. She wrote the monthly "Basics" column for the first year before switching over to the "Troubleshooting" column, which also appeared in every issue. Laura is currently writing articles and tutorials for Corel's WordPerfect.com site and its monthly e-newsletter, "The WordPerfect Expert."

Laura enjoys scuba diving, cooking, reading, swimming, and biking. She lives in Austin, Texas with her husband, Jeff, and their three children.

The WPWriter.com Web site was created after the release of *Special Edition Using WordPerfect 9* and now boasts the largest collection of WordPerfect tips on the Web. There are also articles, links to other WP resources, and a page containing updates and patches for virtually every version of WordPerfect.

**Read Gilgen** completed his B.A. at Brigham Young University, and his M.A. and Ph.D. in Latin American Literature and Linguistics at the University of California, Irvine. He taught Spanish at the University of North Carolina, Chapel Hill and at the University of Wisconsin before becoming director of UW's L&S Learning Support Services (the language labs) in 1981.

His professional interests include instructional technology in higher education, especially in foreign language education. He recently concluded a term as president of the International Association for Language Learning Technology.

He has taught and written extensively on DOS, Windows, and WordPerfect since the early 1980s. He is author of Que's *WordPerfect for Windows Hot Tips*, contributing author to several Que books including the Special Editions of *Using WordPerfect* (both *DOS* and *Windows 5.1, 5.2, 6.0, 6.1, 7*), co-author of *Using Corel WordPerfect Suite 8*, and co-author of *Special Edition Using WordPerfect 9*. He also recently wrote *Absolute Beginner's Guide to Microsoft PowerPoint 2003* for Que.

Most of his spare time is spent with family (especially his grandkids) and church leadership, but when he can find the time he also enjoys singing and acting.

# DEDICATION

From Laura:

> *To my children, Ben, Lindsey, and Sarah, who help me remember*
> *that some days are meant to be spent at a park.*

From Read:

> *To my wife, Sue, a talented woman in her own right,*
> *for her unending and loving support.*

From Laura and Read:

> *To all the loyal and new WordPerfect users*
> *who refuse to follow the uneducated masses,*
> *insisting instead on using the best*
> *word processing program available.*
> *We hope this book helps you confidently keep the faith.*

# ACKNOWLEDGMENTS

Read and I would like to thank everyone who helped bring this book to fruition. Stephanie McComb, our Acquisitions Editor, is such a pleasure to work with that we actually enjoyed the process of negotiating contracts and submission dates. She cheerfully fielded our many questions and made every effort to put together the best team possible for this book.

We want to thank the folks at Corel who helped us sort through the questions we had about WordPerfect 11 and 12. A special thanks goes to Mark Rathwell and Cindy Howard (Program Managers for WordPerfect Office) who acted as our point people, and who never failed to provide the answers and information we asked for.

We also gratefully acknowledge the kind and generous support of the Corel C-Techs and other volunteers on the Corel newsgroups. They spend countless hours answering questions and troubleshooting problems. They don't quit until they find a solution, or track down the source of the difficulty, and they should all be commended for their patience and perseverance.

Last, but not least, we want to extend a warm thanks to our friends on WordPerfect Universe. The talent pool on that site is nothing short of amazing. For the first time, we were able to tap into that talent and recruited two of the best to do the technical edit on this book. Thanks to Cyndy Zook and Charles Girard for their attention to detail, and for the friendly and helpful comments they made. Thanks also to Ian McCreath for his important feedback on WordPerfect's implementation of XML.

*From Laura:*

I could not ask for a more understanding and supportive family. They try not to roll their eyes when I promise that this project won't be as time-consuming as the last one. I especially want to thank my husband, Jeff, for doing more than his share of the chores, and for entertaining the children on the weekends so I could hide in my office and work. I also want to extend my warmest thanks to my writing partner, Read. We're a great team and I'm thrilled we were able to work together again on this revision. I hope we are still doing this when WordPerfect Office 2010 comes out!

*From Read:*

No acknowledgment would be complete without thanking those closest to you who support you when you've gone into hiding to write. My wife, Sue, is always supportive, recognizing when it's time to yank me out of the basement to watch a movie (or mow the lawn!). I probably should also acknowledge my grandkids who made taking on this project necessary (so I can retire closer to them). Finally, I was delighted to have the chance to work once again with Laura on this revision project. Not only is she a great team leader, but she's also as excited about WordPerfect as I am.

# WE WANT TO HEAR FROM YOU!

As the reader of this book, *you* are our most important critic and commentator. We value your opinion and want to know what we're doing right, what we could do better, what areas you'd like to see us publish in, and any other words of wisdom you're willing to pass our way.

As an associate publisher for Que Publishing, I welcome your comments. You can email or write me directly to let me know what you did or didn't like about this book—as well as what we can do to make our books better.

*Please note that I cannot help you with technical problems related to the topic of this book. We do have a User Services group, however, where I will forward specific technical questions related to the book.*

When you write, please be sure to include this book's title and author as well as your name, email address, and phone number. I will carefully review your comments and share them with the author and editors who worked on the book.

**Email:**   feedback@quepublishing.com

**Mail:**   Greg Wiegand
Associate Publisher
Que Publishing
800 East 96th Street
Indianapolis, IN 46240 USA

For more information about this book or another Que Publishing title, visit our Web site at www.quepublishing.com. Type the ISBN (excluding hyphens) or the title of a book in the Search field to find the page you're looking for.

# INTRODUCTION

## In this chapter

If you're looking at this book, it means you've either purchased WordPerfect Office, or you're seriously thinking about it. Good for you! WordPerfect is without a doubt the most powerful, customizable, and easy-to-use program that you can get your hands on. Period. WordPerfect lets you work the way you want to work, not the way the programmers want you to work.

File compatibility with Microsoft Word and other Microsoft applications has been enhanced to the point where document migration is virtually seamless, so it no longer matters what your clients and associates are using. What does matter is that you have a choice. WordPerfect Office 11 and 12 are the most cost-effective office application suites available, delivering more features, more flexibility, and more compatibility than any other suite on the market.

Don't let the size of the book intimidate you. We won't bore you with minute details of every little feature. Who has time for that? No, this book is crammed full of tips, tricks, and practical examples that you won't find anywhere else. We explain what a feature is, but more importantly, we tell you why you want to use it. What's in it for you? How can it save you time? What features can be used together to achieve a higher level of productivity? All this and more...just waiting for you to start turning the pages.

# WHO SHOULD BUY THIS BOOK?

If you've used a word processor before, and you want to learn how to take advantage of all that WordPerfect has to offer, this book is for you. We made a few assumptions about our audience when we developed the outline for this book. We decided that most of you already know the basics of creating and formatting documents, even if you've done the work in another application. Many of you have used a previous version of WordPerfect, so your interest lies not only in the new features, but also in how you might use the familiar features more effectively.

# WHY TWO VERSIONS IN ONE BOOK?

You might be wondering why we are covering two different versions of WordPerfect in one book. That's a good question! We decided that since the release of WordPerfect Office 11 and WordPerfect Office 12 were only a year apart, we could better serve both audiences by combining the coverage into one book. In addition, the enhancements and new features in WordPerfect 12 are almost exclusively focused on compatibility issues, so it was a simple matter to point out the differences as we went along.

You'll see a "New" icon next to the paragraphs that cover new features in WordPerfect 11 and 12, so you won't miss out on any of the exciting changes. The next two sections highlight the new features and the enhancements that were made in WordPerfect 11 and those that were made in WordPerfect 12, so no matter which version you are using, you'll be able to quickly pinpoint the new features in your version.

# New Features and Enhancements in WordPerfect 11

This version of WordPerfect includes some very exciting new features and some welcome improvements that speed up navigation and formatting. You might notice that the list of new features isn't as lengthy as it has been in previous versions. Corel decided to focus instead on addressing known issues, improving on the existing feature set and producing a reliably stable product. Who can argue with that? Here are some highlights:

- Although WordPerfect's file format hasn't changed since version 6.1, other applications' file formats change like the weather. WordPerfect Office 11 includes updated conversion drivers to make the transfer of documents between WordPerfect and Microsoft Word cleaner than ever. You can even set the default file save format to Microsoft Word (.doc) so that the user doesn't have to intervene at all.

- WordPerfect Office 11 includes a copy of Adobe Acrobat Reader version 5.0. The Publish to PDF feature has been significantly enhanced—WordPerfect can export files to PDF with graphics (including watermarks) and hyperlinks intact. WordPerfect 11 now supports symbols, which means your graphics-laden documents will have smaller file sizes when published in PDF format. Furthermore, page numbering has been improved so that it is consistent between the WordPerfect file and the PDF file. Note that similar capability, using Adobe Acrobat, costs about $250 per workstation.

- WordPerfect Office offers two different sets of XML tools for two varying degrees of users. WordPerfect 11 adds the quick "Publish to XML" on the File menu for users who simply need to get text and information out of a propriety file format and into XML quickly. The WordPerfect Office XML Layout Designer and Editor are the full-featured tools for users who create templates for XML documents and want their users to have a layout representation within WordPerfect.

- In response to thousands of user requests, Corel has given you the option of working in the classic WP 5.1 mode—an easy-on-the-eyes blue screen with light gray text. The toolbar and property bar are turned off so you get a cleaner screen to work in. The WPDOS 5.1 keyboard is automatically selected so you can use all of your favorite 5.1 keyboard shortcuts.

- Corel's RealTime Preview shows you what a formatting change will look like, before you make it. For example, as you highlight fonts in the Font drop-down list, the document text is reformatted in that font, on-the-fly. RealTime Preview works for fonts, font sizes, zoom, justification, lines, borders, shading, and color, just to name a few. In WordPerfect 11, the RealTime Preview feature has been enhanced to include QuickFonts, underline, drop caps, and other formatting options.

- A new file conversion utility that will convert entire folders of files in one step has been added. The utility includes file filters for newer versions of competing products.

- The Variables feature has been enhanced to enable you to save variables to the default template so you can reuse them in other documents. Also, you'll be prompted if there are unused variables in the document.

- The new Document Map feature is the perfect companion to the table of contents, table of authorities, index, and list features. Although you might not create many tables of contents or indexes, I bet you'll review some documents with these elements in them. If you do, you'll love this feature.

- If you can't beat 'em, join 'em. Corel has incorporated Microsoft Word 97 menus and toolbars that you can display in place of the WordPerfect default menus and toolbar, so if you are migrating from Microsoft Word, these items will put features where you expect to find them. This simple tool can be invaluable during the transition. There is even a Microsoft Word Help item on the Help menu that takes you to a page with links to notes for converting files between the two programs, and a side-by-side comparison of their features.

- Reveal Codes is a feature that sets WordPerfect apart from competing products. In WordPerfect 11, an important enhancement was made. You can now print the contents of the Reveal Codes window.

- The Envelope feature has a couple of enhancements. First, a preview window was added so you can see how your envelope will look before you print it. Second, you can now include 11-digit delivery point bar codes, in addition to the 9-digit or 5-digit ZIP codes.

- Outline and bullets and numbering styles functionality has been improved so that they are easier to create and preview. There are also new watermark templates to work with.

- A new Layout Preview button was added to the Print dialog box so you can preview the settings you have made in that dialog box before you send the document to the printer.

- The Ruler can now be turned on in Two Page view mode so you can adjust the tabs, margins and indents while previewing your document.

- The new AutoScroll feature, which was previously only available in Quattro Pro, lets you quickly scroll through a document using the mouse. It gives you the same functionality as the Microsoft Intellimouse with a regular mouse.

- A new collaborative review feature enables you to route documents via Microsoft Outlook to a list of reviewers in a specific order. When each reviewer is finished and closes the document, it is automatically sent to the next person on the distribution list.

- WordPerfect 11 has the capability to use the Microsoft Outlook address book. If you've been using Outlook as your contact information manager, you will be pleased to know that you can use that information in a mass mailing, to print labels and envelopes, and to route documents for review.

- A new collaborative review feature uses the Outlook integration to enable you to send a copy of a document to multiple reviewers in a specified routing order.

- The Master Document/Subdocument feature has been improved so that you can use documents that were created in Microsoft Word, or any other file format that is supported by WordPerfect 11, as a subdocument.

- The Pleading Wizard that was included in the Legal editions of WordPerfect has now been incorporated into WordPerfect 11. The wizard guides you through creating cases and generating pleading documents.

- Macros written in previous versions of WordPerfect can be recompiled and in many cases, will run without any modifications. If the macro happens to contain an obsolete command, a warning message will appear explaining that the command might be removed in future versions.

- Support for Microsoft Visual Basic for Applications (VBA) version 6.3 is included, so now you have a very powerful alternative to the PerfectScript macro language. WordPerfect is the only mainstream word processor to offer two powerful programming languages that can be used separately or in combination.

- Unlike the latest release of Microsoft Word, WordPerfect Office 11 will run on Windows 98 SE systems.

# New Features and Enhancements in WordPerfect 12

This latest version of WordPerfect focuses on enhanced compatibility with Microsoft products. The good news is the changes that consumed the majority of the development resources are invisible. The bad news is that because they are invisible to most users, it's easy to get the impression that not much has changed in this new release. I can tell you that some of these changes are significant and will greatly improve round-tripping documents between WordPerfect and Microsoft Word. Here are some of the most notable changes:

- For the first time, you can upgrade an existing version of WordPerfect, migrate your custom settings, and remove the previous version, all in one step. The upgrade install will transfer the templates and macros that you created, user word lists, QuickWords, address books created in WordPerfect 11, and if you upgraded the Pocket Oxford English Dictionary, the upgraded dictionary files are copied over. The upgrade install options will only appear if WordPerfect Office 2002 or WordPerfect Office 11 is already installed on your computer.

- You can now work with Microsoft Word 2002 menus and toolbars instead of the WordPerfect default menus and toolbar, so if you are migrating from Microsoft Word, these items will put features where you expect to find them. This simple tool can be invaluable during the transition. There is even a Microsoft Word Help item on the Help menu that takes you to a page with links to notes for converting files between the two programs, and a side-by-side comparison of their features.

- The Workspace Manager enables you to switch back and forth between different working environments. There are four modes to choose from: WordPerfect mode, with the WordPerfect 12 menus and toolbars displayed; Microsoft Word mode, with the Microsoft Word 2002 menu, keyboard (shortcuts) and toolbar all selected and the default file save format set to Microsoft Word 97/2000/2002/2003 format; the popular WordPerfect Classic mode, with the WP 5.1 interface and keyboard shortcuts; and the WordPerfect Legal mode, which turns on the Legal toolbar.

- There is a new Microsoft Word Compatibility toolbar that lets you can save a file in Word, PDF, XML, or HTML formats with just one click. There is also a button to open Microsoft Word Help, which displays information about the compatibility of WordPerfect with Microsoft Word.

- There have been some very specific changes made to WordPerfect to include features that are available in Microsoft Word. Some enhancements were also made so that certain elements could be matched up during document conversions. See the next section for specifics.

- WordPerfect Wireless Office—Powered by ZIM is an exciting new addition to WordPerfect Office. ZIM SMS Office enables two-way communication so you can stay on top of changing situations when you (or your associates) are on the go. It will forward e-mail from a POP3 client to your cell phone when you are not at your desk. ZIM SMS Mail is a wireless e-mail offering that works with any POP3 e-mail account, regardless of what e-mail client software you use. ZIM SMS Chat enables instant two-way chats between computer and cell phone users via SMS text messaging.

- The WordPerfect OfficeReady Browser enables you to browse, preview, and launch WordPerfect OfficeReady templates. The product ships with 40 new templates that can be used in WordPerfect, Quattro Pro, and Presentations. More templates are available for free download; others can be purchased.

- Enhancements were made to the Publish to PDF feature so that the default settings provide for truer rendering, compatibility with more recent versions of Adobe Acrobat, and significantly smaller file sizes.

- There is a new option in the Header/Footer, Footnote/Endnote, and Watermark dialog boxes that lets you align the item with the document margins. In the past, you had to set the margins for these elements separately from the body text margins, and if this wasn't done, the margins were mismatched.

- Unlike the latest release of Microsoft Word, WordPerfect Office 12 will run on Windows 98 SE systems.

# COMPATIBILITY ENHANCEMENTS IN WORDPERFECT 11/12

You've probably been reading about how the compatibility enhancements in WordPerfect 12 focus on better document conversions between WordPerfect and Microsoft Word. What you might not realize is that some of these enhancements were introduced in the first service pack for WordPerfect 11. These enhancements were carried over to WordPerfect 12 and served as the basis for the improvements that were made in version 12.

The following compatibility improvements were made in Service Pack 1:

- Word conversion filters were updated to include Word 2002.
- Conversions of Word 97 documents were improved.
- Improved bullet import from Microsoft Word.
- You can open Word documents containing nested tables.
- Paragraph alignment when opening Word documents in WordPerfect was corrected.
- Improvements were made to background compatibility issues when opening documents created in previous versions of WordPerfect that include macros for headers/footers, footnotes/endnotes, and watermarks.

The following compatibility improvements were made in WordPerfect 12:

- The same footnote and endnote numbering styles are found in Word and WordPerfect, but the names are different ("Numbers" in WordPerfect and "1,2,3" in Word). The styles have been matched up and "mapped" so that they convert into the correct style.
- Horizontal and vertical positioning options for images were revised to match the options in Word.
- In Word, you can apply attributes to a specific table cell, not just an entire column or row. You can now do the same in WordPerfect.
- In tables, a new minimum row height feature was added to match the capability in Word. Here is how it works: When you type text into the cell, it expands; if you take the text back out, the row will go down only as far as the minimum height. If you use tables in your forms, you will agree that this is a notable improvement.
- Enhancements were made to the Publish to PDF feature to decrease file sizes and to update compatibility with Adobe Acrobat 6.0. For example, the default setting was changed from High to the Acrobat 6.0 standard dpi setting, which eliminates file bloat in PDF files. You can manually switch it back if you need to preserve the details. Also, the dpi thresholds for image resampling (1-bit, grayscale, and color) were changed to match Acrobat 6.0 settings.

# HOW THIS BOOK IS ORGANIZED

*Special Edition Using WordPerfect 12* is designed for users who have some experience using a word processor and want to learn how to use WordPerfect's more advanced features. The book is divided into sections to help you focus on the areas that you are particularly interested in. The first section is a good place to start because some fundamental concepts are covered, but beyond that, you are free to jump around and read about what interests you.

## PART I: LEARNING THE BASICS

Chapters 1 through 6 cover the fundamentals of using WordPerfect to create, edit, save, and print documents. A short basic formatting chapter covers the features that you need to use right away, such as changing fonts, applying bold, italic, and underline, and adjusting the margins. The file management chapter is in this first section because managing files is such an integral part of what you do every day. After all, what good is all your hard work if you can't find a file when you need it? In the other chapters, you learn how to use the writing tools and how to print, fax, and e-mail your documents. If you're tempted to skip this part because you've already used a word processor, don't. It's loaded with tips and practical advice on how to use the basic features to be more productive.

## PART II: FORMATTING DOCUMENTS

Chapters 7, 8, and 9 focus on formatting documents. Chapter 7 sticks to formatting lines and paragraphs, so you learn how to align and indent text, set tabs, keep text together, and add line numbers and borders. Chapter 8 tackles formatting page elements: page numbers, paper size, headers and footers, subdividing the page, columns, borders, and Make It Fit. Chapter 9 explains how to create and implement styles for consistency and speedier formatting. Bet you didn't know that if you modify a style, the text that is formatted with that style is automatically updated, every bit, all at once.

## PART III: ORGANIZING INFORMATION

Chapters 10 and 11 cover organizing information into tables, lists, and outlines. You'll learn everything you need to know about creating and formatting tables, and you'll discover why WordPerfect is the champion when it comes to tables. Bulleted and numbered lists are used in all types of documents to present (sequential and nonsequential) pieces of information in an easy-to-read list. Obviously, the Outline feature can be used to create outlines that show the structure of a document or an idea. The outline styles can also be used to create numbered sections of text where the numbers are automatically updated as you rearrange the text.

## PART IV: WORKING WITH GRAPHICS

In this section, Chapters 12, 13, and 14 teach you how to incorporate graphics images and effects in your documents. You'll learn how to insert clip art and other types of images, such those that you download from your digital camera. You'll learn how to create custom graphics lines and borders and how to insert the new shapes. Chapter 13 shows you how to customize graphics and Chapter 14 focuses on the Draw and TextArt features. In Chapter 14, you'll also learn how to customize WordPerfect graphics and bitmap graphics in Presentations.

## PART V: INTEGRATING INFORMATION FROM OTHER SOURCES

Chapters 15 and 16 show you how to use information from other applications. You'll learn how to use the Windows Clipboard and WordPerfect's new Clipbook to copy information between applications. We'll show you how to use OLE to create a link so that the information is automatically updated in the document anytime it's been modified in the originating program. You'll learn how to import documents, spreadsheets, and databases from other applications. The conversion drivers have improved dramatically so that the transport between WordPerfect and Microsoft Word is virtually seamless. Chapter 16 focuses on creating data charts and organizational charts.

## PART VI: PUBLISHING DOCUMENTS

This section has some very weighty chapters in it. Chapter 17 covers the document collaboration features, such as document comments, reviewing and comparing documents, adding a digital signature to validate a document, and routing documents with Microsoft Outlook. Chapter 18 talks about the features geared toward long documents, such as bookmarks, footnotes, endnotes, cross references, and the Master Document feature. Chapter 19 covers the creation of tables of contents, tables of authorities, indexes, and lists. The new Document Map feature is covered here because it uses these reference markers to help you navigate through long documents. Chapter 20 presents information on creating interactive and multimedia documents with hypertext links, links to Web pages, and embedded video and sounds. Chapter 21 covers WordPerfect's Web publishing features and is packed with practical advice on how to publish your documents on the Internet or your company intranet. Chapter 22 helps you understand XML and how to use it in a shared environment.

## PART VII: AUTOMATING EVERYDAY TASKS

This last section discusses ways that you can use WordPerfect's automation tools to speed up repetitive tasks. Chapter 23 covers templates, from using the project templates that come with WordPerfect to creating your own templates (both from existing documents and from scratch). You'll learn how to insert prompts that guide the user through the template and how to link fields in a template to address book fields. Chapter 24 covers the Merge feature. A complete set of steps for a typical mail merge is given, but the focus is on using other sources for names and addresses and creating documents other than form letters during a merge. Chapter 25 covers using the WordPerfect and Microsoft Outlook address books with some excellent tips on importing and exporting data. Chapter 26 shows you how to use the PerfectExpert panel to create and edit documents without searching through the menus for an elusive command. The bulk of this chapter focuses on macros—running macros that others have developed (including the shipping macros), and creating your own macros with the Macro Recorder. The steps to assign macros to toolbars, keystrokes, and menus are included, as well as information about using macros from previous versions and whether or not you need to install VBA support.

# CONVENTIONS USED IN THIS BOOK

Que, as well as all of Pearson Technology Group's various imprints, has more than 10 years' experience creating the most popular and effective computer reference books available. From trainers to programmers, Que's authors have invaluable experience using and—

most importantly—explaining computer and software concepts. From basic to advanced topics, Que's publishing experience, and its authors' expertise and communication skills, combine to create a highly readable and easily navigable book.

**TIP FROM**

*Read Gilgen*

Liberally sprinkled throughout the text, tips are places where we share insights that we've gained after using, teaching, and writing about WordPerfect for the past 15 years.

**NOTE**

Notes contain extra information or alternative techniques for performing tasks that we feel will enhance your use and/or understanding of the current topic.

**CAUTION**

If we want to warn you about a potential problem, you'll see that information in a caution note. Believe me, after years in a classroom, we know all about the pitfalls!

 *This element is designed to call your attention to areas where you are likely to get into trouble. When you see a Troubleshooting note, you can skip to the Troubleshooting section at the end of the chapter to learn how to solve (or avoid) a problem.*

→ Cross-references are used whenever possible to direct you to other sections of the book that give complementary or supportive information. If you want to learn how to use WordPerfect features together, pay close attention to the cross-references.

## BUTTONS

Whenever a button is referred to in an explanatory paragraph or step-by-step procedure, the button will appear in the left margin, next to the paragraph or step that mentions it. This visual reminder helps you quickly locate the button on the toolbar so that you can remember it for future use.

## KEYBOARD SHORTCUTS

Whenever a combination of keys can be pressed to execute a command, they'll appear paired by a plus sign, as in Ctrl+Home (to move to the top of a document) or Ctrl+P (to open the Print dialog box). When using a keyboard shortcut, press the first key, and while that key is depressed, tap the second key, and then release the first key.

## TYPEFACES

Throughout this book, a variety of typefaces is used, each designed to draw your attention to specific text:

| Typeface | Description |
| --- | --- |
| Monospace | Screen messages, text you type, and Internet addresses appear in this special typeface. |
| *Italic* | New terminology and emphasized text will appear in italic. |

## END-OF-CHAPTER EXAMPLES

Every chapter ends with a Troubleshooting section, where you'll find answers to frequently encountered problems. We've addressed more than just the simplest problems and solutions here—we cover the pitfalls you're likely to encounter when you push WordPerfect to the limit.

The Project element is designed to complement the information presented in the chapter. In some chapters, you'll see "before and after" shots that illustrate how features can be used to enhance a document. In others, there will be a practical and real-world example of how you can implement the features covered in the chapter. And in one or two chapters, we've shown you how to prepare information for use with a particular feature.

# LEARNING THE BASICS

# CHAPTER 1

# GETTING COMFORTABLE WITH WORDPERFECT

**In this chapter**

*by Laura Acklen*

When you sit down to your computer, you're probably going to be creating more than just letters and memos. Downsizing has virtually eliminated support staff and home/small office users don't have that luxury, so it's likely that you are solely responsible for generating your own documents. Well, you can relax because WordPerfect can help you accomplish any task, from typical correspondence to complex mail merges to tables with spreadsheet formulas to desktop publishing to document collaboration to Web publishing.

The challenge becomes uncovering the features and shortcuts that *you* need. That's where this book comes in. Written by two WordPerfect professionals who've been involved with the program since the early days of the DOS versions, we show you the best ways to harness the power of WordPerfect. Along the way, we share tips, tricks, and shortcuts that we've gained from years of using the program, and from teaching the program to others.

This chapter covers the basics of creating and saving documents, so if you've used WordPerfect before, you might think you can just skip it. Don't. You'll find lots of useful information and some great shortcuts that you can use every day.

# STARTING WORDPERFECT

The quickest way to start WordPerfect is to have a *shortcut* on the desktop. Double-click it, and away you go! If you don't have the shortcut, using the Start menu is easy—it just takes a few more mouse clicks:

1. Click the Start button.
2. Highlight Programs.
3. Highlight WordPerfect Office 11 or WordPerfect Office 12 to open the submenu (see Figure 1.1).
4. Click WordPerfect.

 In WordPerfect 12, you might see a dialog box that asks you which mode you want to start in (see Figure 1.2). This is the Workspace Manager, a new feature that helps you switch back and forth between three different WordPerfect interfaces: regular, classic, and legal. You can also switch to a Microsoft Word interface that helps users making the transition from Word to WordPerfect. Leave the selection set to WordPerfect Mode and choose OK to clear the dialog box.

> **NOTE**
>
> Word users: the Workspace Manager gives you an easy way to switch to Microsoft Word keyboards, menus and toolbars. There is no change in the way a document is put together. WordPerfect users: the Workspace Manager let's you quickly switch between the regular interface, 5.1 classic mode, and the legal mode (which is basically activating the legal tools).

→ For more information, **see** "Using the Workspace Manager," **p. 58.**

You're now ready to start working in WordPerfect.

**Figure 1.1**
You can start
WordPerfect 11/12
from the Start menu
with two clicks.

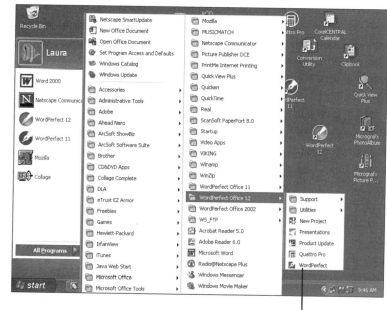

Click here to start WordPerfect

**Figure 1.2**
The Workspace
Manager dialog box
enables you to select
a different interface
quickly.

 *If you can't find the WordPerfect Office 11 or WordPerfect Office 12 folder on your Start menu, see "Having Trouble Starting WordPerfect" in the Troubleshooting section at the end of this chapter.*

1

# TOURING THE WORDPERFECT SCREEN

All Windows applications look essentially the same. They all have title bars, menus, tool-bars, and control buttons. This gives you a distinct advantage because using one Windows application prepares you to learn another.

**TIP FROM**

*Laura Acklen*

In WordPerfect 11 and 12, as in WordPerfect 8, 9, and 10, you can click anywhere in a document and move the insertion point to that place. No more pressing Enter or Tab until the insertion point is where you want it. Just click and start typing.

When you start WordPerfect, a blank document appears (see Figure 1.3), so you can start typing immediately. The insertion point shows you where the text will appear when you start typing. The shadow cursor shows you where the insertion point will be if you click the mouse button.

**Figure 1.3**
The WordPerfect screen includes elements that you have seen in other Windows applications.

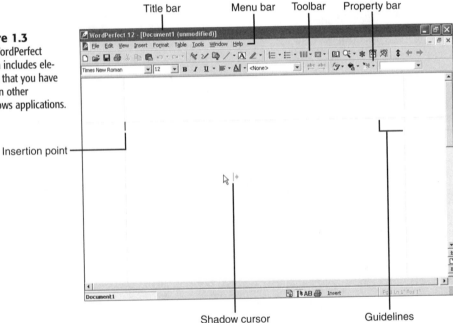

Title bar     Menu bar    Toolbar    Property bar

Insertion point

Shadow cursor        Guidelines

**TIP FROM**

*Laura Acklen*

The Shadow Cursor On/Off button on the application bar shows whether the shadow cursor is turned on (the button appears pressed in). Click the button to turn the shadow cursor on and off.

The gray lines you see onscreen are called *guidelines*. They help you see the text area of your page by marking the top, bottom, left, and right margins. Clicking and dragging the guidelines is a quick way to change the margins. If you find the guidelines distracting, you can turn them off by opening the View menu and selecting Guidelines. In the Guidelines dialog box, remove the check mark next to Margins, and then click OK.

→ To learn more about changing the margins with guidelines, **see** "Changing Margins by Using Guidelines," **p. 79.**

# SAVING TIME WITH TOOLBARS

The property bar is like a shape-shifter from a sci-fi story; it changes depending on where the insertion point is or what you have selected (refer to Figure 1.3). You start out with the text property bar, but as soon as you create a table, it switches to the table property bar. When you move the insertion point into an outline, you get the outline property bar, and so on. It's handy because the buttons you need magically appear, and you get your work done twice as fast because you aren't hunting around in the menus for a command.

**TIP FROM**

*Laura Acklen*

If you point to a button on any of the toolbars and pause, a QuickTip appears that describes the function of that button.

The toolbar is different from the property bar—it doesn't change unless you tell it to. The one you see in Figure 1.3 is called the WordPerfect 12 toolbar and has buttons for general editing tasks. There are more than 20 other toolbars to choose from, including toolbars from WordPerfect versions 7, 8, 9, 10, and 11. In WordPerfect 11, you can select a Microsoft Word 97 toolbar; in WordPerfect 12, you can select a Microsoft Word 2002 or a Microsoft Compatibility toolbar. Other toolbars contain buttons for working with tables, graphics, outlines, fonts, macros, and so on.

To begin working with toolbars, follow these steps:

1. Right-click the toolbar to open the toolbar QuickMenu (see Figure 1.4). Notice that the WordPerfect 11 (or 12) toolbar already has a check mark next to it. A check mark next to the name means the toolbar is already displayed. To see a complete list of available toolbars, choose More.

**NOTE**

In Windows 95, Microsoft introduced the concept of right-clicking an object to display a pop-up menu of context-sensitive commands. These menus are called *QuickMenus* in WordPerfect. There's one for just about everything you do. Start right-clicking on things and discover how much time these menus can save you.

Toolbar QuickMenu

**Figure 1.4**
You can right-click the toolbar to open a QuickMenu, where you can switch to another toolbar or turn the toolbar(s) off.

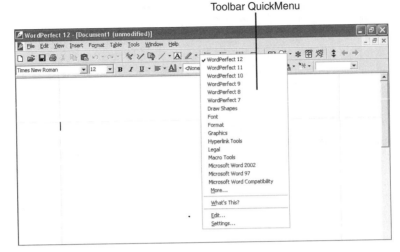

2. Click the toolbar you want to turn on (clicking an *unchecked* toolbar name turns it on; clicking a *checked* toolbar name turns it off).

**NOTE**

You might change your mind and decide not to use a QuickMenu. Just click in the document window to clear it.

*If you can't find the toolbar or the property bar, see "The Missing Property Bar and Toolbar" in the Troubleshooting section at the end of this chapter.*

*If the QuickTips aren't showing up, see "QuickTips Don't Appear" in the Troubleshooting section at the end of this chapter.*

# CREATING DOCUMENTS

With WordPerfect, you can start typing as soon as the program is loaded. A blank document, with all the standard settings in place, stands ready for you. Table 1.1 lists some of WordPerfect's default settings. Others are discussed in later chapters.

| TABLE 1.1 | WORDPERFECT'S DEFAULT SETTINGS |
| --- | --- |
| **Element** | **Default Setting** |
| Margins | 1 inch at the top, bottom, left, and right |
| Line spacing | Single-spaced |
| Font | Times New Roman 12 point |
| Tabs | Every $\frac{1}{2}$ inch |

| TABLE 1.1 CONTINUED | |
|---|---|
| **Element** | **Default Setting** |
| Paper size | 8 ½ inches × 11 inches |
| Automatic backup | Every 10 minutes |

→ To learn how to change the margins, **see** "Changing Margins by Using Guidelines," **p. 79.**

→ To learn how to change line spacing, **see** "Adjusting the Spacing Between Lines and Paragraphs," **p. 212.**

→ To learn how to change the font, **see** "Choosing the Right Font," **p. 72.**

→ To learn how to change tab settings, **see** "Setting Tabs," **p. 205.**

→ To learn how to change the paper size, **see** "Choosing Different Paper Sizes," **p. 238.**

→ To learn how to change the automatic backup interval, **see** "Saving Documents," **p. 25.**

→ To learn more about setting up your own default settings, **see** "Editing Styles," **p. 277.**

→ To learn more about creating documents with templates, **see** "Using WordPerfect's Templates," **p. 712** and "Creating New Templates," **p. 722.**

**TIP FROM**

*Laura Acklen*

> Templates are documents with formatting and *form text* already in place. All you have to do is fill in the blanks and print (or e-mail, or fax). There are templates for fax cover sheets, newsletters, certificates, business cards, calendars, labels, and more.

**NOTE**

> When you first use a program, there are settings already in place for you. These are called *default* settings. As you read through this book, you'll see this term often when a new feature is introduced. For example, in the section on changing margins, it's explained that the default margins are one inch on each side. You can set up your own default settings, which define how you want your documents formatted in most cases. This way, you make only minor adjustments, which saves you loads of time in the long run.

## TYPING TEXT

One of the coolest features in WordPerfect is the capability to click anywhere in a document, and then start typing. No pressing Enter or Tab or any of that—just click and type!

To type text in a WordPerfect document, do the following:

1. Click anywhere in the document area. The insertion point moves to the new place.
2. Begin typing text.

As you type along, you may occasionally notice that things are happening automatically. For example, if you forget to capitalize the first word in a sentence, WordPerfect corrects it for you. When you type ordinal numbers, WordPerfect changes the two letters to superscript text so the number has the proper format (such as 1$^{st}$, 2$^{nd}$, 3$^{rd}$). This is the Format-As-You-Go feature working for you. Format-As-You-Go corrects common mistakes as you type.

→ To learn how to customize the Format-As-You-Go feature, **see** "Customizing Format-As-You-Go," **p. 157.**

**NOTE**

If you are already working on one document and you want to create a new one, click the New Blank Document button on the toolbar.

## ERASING TEXT

We all make mistakes when we're typing—especially when we're thinking faster than our fingers can move. The problem is, if you stop and correct every little mistake, you lose your train of thought. A better idea is to correct only those mistakes that you notice right away, and then go back later and fix the rest.

There are three ways to erase text:

- If you make a mistake and you notice it right away, press the Backspace key to backspace over and erase the mistake.

- Click to the left of the word(s) you want to delete and press the Delete key repeatedly until the text has been erased.

- Select the text and then press Delete.

*If you've been a little heavy-handed with the Delete key and you've accidentally deleted too much text, see "Heavy-Handed Deletions" in the Troubleshooting section at the end of this chapter.*

## INSERTING TODAY'S DATE

You might be surprised at how many times a day you type out the date. With just one keystroke, you can insert today's date anywhere in a document.

1. Click in the document where you want the date to appear.

2. Press Ctrl+D.

WordPerfect gets the date and time from the Windows Date/Time Properties dialog box, so if the date or time you insert is wrong, you need to reset the clock. Double-click the time on your taskbar to open the Date/Time Properties dialog box, where you can make the necessary changes.

You can also insert the current time into a document. Choose Insert, Date/Time to open the Date/Time dialog box (see Figure 1.5). Select the 12-hour format or the 24-hour format (scroll down the list), and then click Insert.

**Figure 1.5**
You can choose a format for the date and time in the Date/Time dialog box.

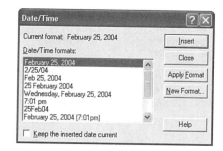

**TIP FROM**

> There is a different type of date for those documents that you use over and over again. This date is automatically updated every time you open or print the document. Consider using it in fax cover sheets, memos, press releases, invoices, receipts, and so on. To insert this type of date, press Ctrl+Shift+D or select Keep the Inserted Date Current in the Date/Time dialog box.

## UNDERSTANDING WORDPERFECT'S AUTOMATIC PROOFREADING FEATURES

As you type, you might notice that red squiggly underlines appear under some words. The Spell-As-You-Go feature has marked these words as possible misspellings. Spell-As-You-Go is one of the two automatic proofreading features in WordPerfect—the other is Grammar-As-You-Go, which checks for grammatical errors. If Grammar-As-You-Go is activated instead of Spell-As-You-Go, you might see blue dashes in the text as well. The theory behind these two features is that it's faster to correct errors while you are typing than to go back and fix them later.

 *Have you incorrectly spelled a word, but don't see the red, wavy line under it? See "Spell-As-You-Go Gone" in the Troubleshooting section at the end of this chapter.*

To correct a word with Spell-As-You-Go, follow these steps:

1. Right-click an underlined word to display a list of suggested replacement words that you can choose from (see Figure 1.6).

2. Click the correctly spelled word in the list. That's it—you just corrected the misspelled word. Selecting a word from this list automatically replaces the underlined word with the word you chose.

If you find these proofing marks distracting, you can disable the Spell-As-You-Go and Grammar-As-You-Go features by following these steps:

1. Open the Tools menu and select Proofread from the drop-down list. Notice that Spell-As-You-Go has a bullet next to it—this means it's turned on (see Figure 1.7). You can switch to using Grammar-As-You-Go, but both options cannot be selected at the same time. However, because Grammar-As-You-Go includes Spell-As-You-Go, choosing Grammar-As-You-Go turns them both on.

1

Choose a suggested replacement word from this list

**Figure 1.6**
You can right-click an underlined word to choose from a list of suggested replacement words.

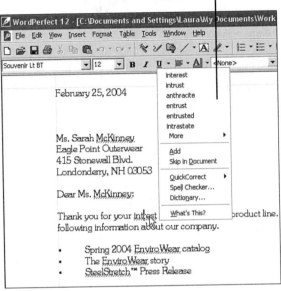

Only one of these features can be selected at a time

**Figure 1.7**
The bullet next to Spell-As-You-Go means it is on.

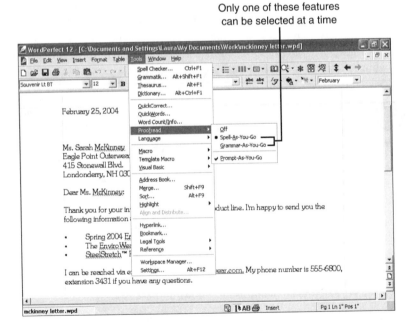

2. Choose Off. Choosing Off turns off both Spell-As-You-Go and Grammar-As-You-Go.

**NOTE**

Have you ever noticed that in menus, some items have a check mark next to them and others have a bullet? Besides showing you which item is currently selected, is there any other difference? Yes! Bullets are there to tell you that only one of the options in that group can be selected at one time. Check marks tell you that more than one option in that group can be selected at one time.

## SAVING DOCUMENTS

When you create a new document, your work is being held in your computer's memory, which is a temporary location. It's temporary because if anything happens to your computer and you have to restart, that memory gets erased. This means that you should make a habit of saving your new documents right away. And then, as you work on them, you should save as often as you can. I've developed a habit of pressing Alt+F, S whenever I stop for a second. Even if you don't expect to work with this document again, you should save it so you'll have a record of it.

Follow these steps to save a document:

1. Click the Save button.

   - If you've already named this document, it will seem like nothing has happened. Because the document has already been named, WordPerfect saves the changes without any intervention from you. The only difference you'll see is (unmodified) after the filename in the title bar—that's how you know a document has been saved.

   - If you haven't named the document yet, the Save File dialog box appears (see Figure 1.8).

**NOTE**

Introduced in WordPerfect 10, the Auto-Suggest Filename feature automatically inserts a suggested filename in the File Name text box when you save a file. You can either accept this name, or type your own.

2. Type a filename and press Enter (or click the Save button).

   - Filenames can be up to 255 characters in length and can contain letters, numbers, and spaces. Some symbols can be used, but not others, so to avoid problems, stick with hyphens (-) and underscores (_).

   - You can include the name of the drive and the *folder* where you want the document to be saved when you type the filename. For example, typing `c:\reports\FY2004` saves the document FY2004 to drive `c:` in the `reports` folder.

   - When you type a filename without selecting a location, the document is saved in the folder that is listed in the Save In text box.

This is where you want the file saved

**Figure 1.8**
You use the Save As dialog box to save your files, giving each a name and a location.

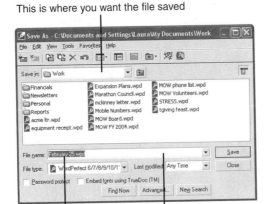

Type the name of the file here

Auto-suggest filename

→ To learn more about how to change to a different folder, **see** "Finding and Opening Documents,"
**p. 42.**

**NOTE**

If you want to preserve an original document, use Save As to save the file under a different name. Do this right away, so you don't accidentally replace the original with your revised version.

**TIP FROM**

*Laura Acklen*

WordPerfect has a Timed Document Backup feature that automatically makes a backup copy of your document while you work. It's already turned on and set to make a backup every 10 minutes. If you aren't able to exit WordPerfect correctly (because of a power failure or system lockup), you'll be able to open the backup file when you restart WordPerfect. However, if you do exit WordPerfect correctly, the backup file will be deleted.

You can adjust the interval and take a look at where your backup files are created in the File Settings dialog box. Choose Tools, Settings, Files. If necessary, click the Document tab. You can adjust the Timed Document Backup interval by typing a new value in the Timed Document Backup text box or by clicking the spinner arrows next to the text box.

# PREVIEWING AND PRINTING DOCUMENTS

Unless you plan to e-mail or fax the document directly from WordPerfect, you'll need to print it. However, before you print a document, you should preview it. Often, the way a document appears onscreen can be quite different from the way it appears when printed.

## SWITCHING TO PRINT PREVIEW

The Print Preview feature shows you exactly what your document will look like when you print it. Use it often. You'll save time, paper, printer resources, and let's not forget—frustration.

Previous versions of WordPerfect included a Print Preview feature, but you couldn't make any changes while in it. Starting with version 10, you can freely edit the text, reposition graphics, change the margins, and so on.

To use the Print Preview feature, follow these steps:

1. Open the File menu and choose Print Preview. The current page is displayed (see Figure 1.9). Using buttons on the Print Preview toolbar, you can switch to a Two Page view, or you can use the Zoom feature to adjust the size of the page. There are other buttons that give you access to the Spell Checker, the Make It Fit feature, and both the Page Setup and the Print dialog boxes.

2. When you are finished, click the Print Preview button to switch back to the document window.

**Figure 1.9**
Print Preview displays a fully editable representation of how the document will look when printed.

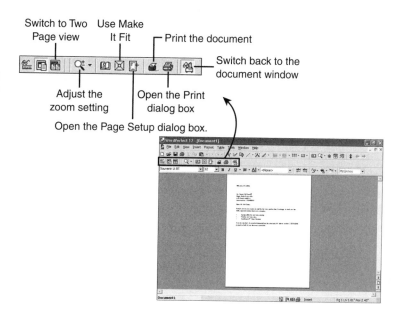

Switch to Two Page view  Use Make It Fit  Print the document  Switch back to the document window  Adjust the zoom setting  Open the Print dialog box  Open the Page Setup dialog box.

→ To learn more about how to change the Zoom setting, **see** "Using the Zoom Settings," **p. 57.**

→ To learn more about the Make It Fit feature, **see** "Using Make It Fit," **p. 255.**

→ To learn more about the options in the Page Setup dialog box, **see** "Changing Margins," **p. 228.**

## PRINTING DOCUMENTS

After you've previewed your document and checked it for accuracy, you're ready to print. If you're printing an envelope, have the envelope ready. (Most printers accept envelopes through a manual feed tray.) Follow these steps to print the document:

1. Press Ctrl+P, or open the File menu and select Print to open the Print dialog box.

2. Press Enter to send the document to the printer. You perform this type of quick print only if you want to print the whole document and you don't need to select another printer.

**TIP FROM**

*Laura Acklen*

 The Print Preview toolbar has a Print Document button that sends the document to the printer, bypassing the Print dialog box.

→ To learn how to set print options, **see** "Using Print Options," **p. 175.**

→ To learn how to fax a document, **see** "Faxing Documents," **p. 192.**

→ To learn how to e-mail a document, **see** "Sending Documents via E-Mail," **p. 194.**

# CLOSING DOCUMENTS

When you've finished working on a document, you clear it off your screen by closing the document window. If you haven't saved it yet, you get the chance to do that now. Follow these steps to close a document:

1. Click the Close button on the menu bar.

   If you haven't made any changes since the last time you saved, WordPerfect closes the document. If you *have* made some changes, you'll be prompted to save the document (see Figure 1.10).

2. Click Yes if you want to save your work; click No if you want to close the document without saving.

   If you click Yes and you haven't yet given this document a name, the Save File dialog box appears (refer to Figure 1.8). This is where you can type a name and location for the file. Otherwise, WordPerfect saves and closes the document.

3. Type the filename and press Enter.

**Figure 1.10**
When you click the Close button, WordPerfect prompts you to save your changes before clearing the document off the screen.

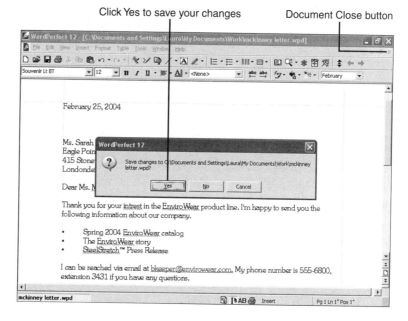

Click Yes to save your changes

Document Close button

# GETTING HELP

WordPerfect 11 and 12 offer an unprecedented level of support to help you become productive as quickly as possible. With so many places to go for help, it's almost like having someone sitting right next to you, telling you which keys to press. Even if you don't know *exactly* what you're looking for, you can still find help when you need it.

## GETTING QUICK AND EASY HELP

WordPerfect 11 and 12 offer an unprecedented level of support to help you become productive as quickly as possible. With so many places to go for help, it's almost like having someone sitting right next to you, telling you which keys to press.

Even if you don't know *exactly* what you are looking for, you can still find help when you need it. Here are the places where you can get help while you are working:

- Find out what a button stands for by pointing to it with the mouse and pausing. A QuickTip appears and gives you either the name or a brief description of the button. You can use this on all types of screen elements, not just toolbar buttons.

- Get descriptions of menu items by pointing to the item and pausing. A QuickTip appears with a description.

 - Press Shift+F1 to change the mouse pointer into a What's This pointer. Then, click on a screen element for a description.

■ In dialog boxes, click the What's This button, and then click the dialog box option you want help on. A QuickTip appears with a description for that option (see Figure 1.11). For more help, click the Help button in the lower-right corner. This opens a Help window with the help topic for that dialog box or feature.

**Figure 1.11**
If a dialog box has a question mark next to the Close button, you can click the question mark, and then click a dialog box component to display a QuickTip on that component.

QuickTip

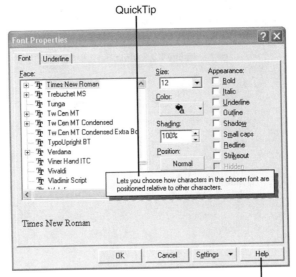

Click here to display the help topic

## CHOOSING FROM THE HELP TOPICS

You can learn a lot about a program when you browse around in the Help screens. There are several ways to access the help topics so you can use whichever method suits your task.

Here are the methods you can use to locate and read the help topics:

■ The Contents section is task-oriented, so you're likely to discover features as they relate to a specific project, such as adding images to your documents or using Internet tools. Choose the Help menu, choose Help Topics, and then click the Contents tab. Double-click the book icons to open more topics. Next to each help page is a question mark icon (see Figure 1.12). You can double-click these icons to display help topics.

■ The Help Index is great when you want to search for a subject and get a list of help topics from which to choose. Choose the Help menu, choose Help Topics, and then click the Index tab. Type a keyword (or just the first few letters) to jump down through the index (see Figure 1.13). Double-click an index entry to display the help topic, or in some cases, a list of possible help topics from which to choose.

Double-click this icon to display a help topic

**Figure 1.12**
The Contents tab of
the Help Topics dialog
box organizes help
topics using a book-
and-chapter model.

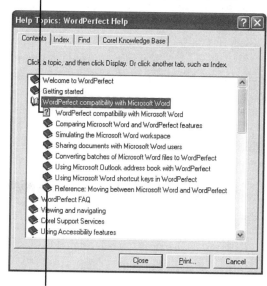

Double-click the book icon to open more topics

Type a keyword here

**Figure 1.13**
The Index tab of the
Help Topics dialog box
organizes help topics
alphabetically in an
index.

Double-click
an entry

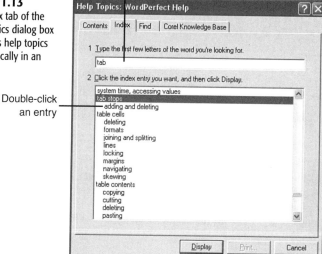

- If you're still having trouble finding what you want, you can try using the Find feature to search through every word in the help topics. Choose Help, Help Topics, and then click the Find tab. The first time you use Find, you'll have to select the type of searches you want to perform, and then wait a few minutes for the index to be created. After that's done, you're ready to go. Type in the word(s) you're searching for, and then click the help topic that you want to view.

■ For the ultimate in point-and-click productivity, choose Help, PerfectExpert. The PerfectExpert panel opens on the left side of the screen, with buttons to help you design virtually every aspect of a document (see Figure 1.14). Rather than searching for the correct command in the menus, you can click buttons from the well-organized lists. (Click the Go Back and Go Forward buttons at the top of the panel to move between lists.)

Click here to start a new document

**Figure 1.14**
The PerfectExpert panel has frequently used features organized so that you don't have to search for items in the menus. All you have to do is click a button and choose from a list.

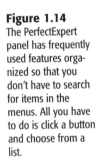
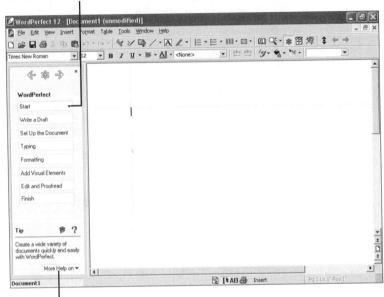

Click here to get help

**NOTE**

Corel took the best of WordPerfect's coaches, guides, templates, and QuickTasks and created PerfectExpert projects. A panel of buttons on the left side of the screen offers choices that automate the creation of all types of documents. You don't have to search through any menus because the commands are grouped together for you.

## GETTING HELP ON THE WEB

If you have an Internet connection, there are several Corel Web sites that can provide support. The advantage of using online resources is that they can be continuously updated so you are always getting the most up-to-date information.

■ Choose Help, Corel on the Web, and then choose an item from the list. WordPerfect launches your browser and then takes you to the selected page. Figure 1.15 shows the Technical Support page, where you'll find links to technical support documents, file downloads (updates, patches, and utilities), and newsgroups.

**Figure 1.15**
Corel's Technical Support page has links to technical support documents, tips and tricks, and updates.

■ Corel also maintains an online searchable knowledge base. Choose Help, Help Topics; then click the Corel Knowledge Base tab. Type in a keyword, and then click Search to search through thousands of technical information documents (TIDs) created by Corel's Technical Support department. You can also go directly to the knowledge base at http://support.corel.com.

## HELPING MICROSOFT WORD USERS MAKE THE TRANSITION

For those making the transition from Microsoft Word, there is a special help section just for you. In WordPerfect 12, choose Help, Microsoft Word Help and then double-click the WordPerfect Compatibility with Microsoft Word book icon to display a list of help topics to help ease the transition from Microsoft Word (see Figure 1.16). In WordPerfect 11, choose Help, Microsoft Word Help to access a list of help topics on Microsoft Word compatibility. From here, click the Help Topics button, and then double-click the Moving Between Microsoft Word and WordPerfect book icon to display the same list of help topics that you see in Figure 1.16.

**Figure 1.16**
A special section in Help assists Word users when they make the transition to WordPerfect.

In this section of help topics, you will learn how to

- Open Microsoft Word documents in WordPerfect.

- Save documents in Microsoft Word format so that you can easily share documents with clients and associates who use Word.

- Convert multiple files from Microsoft Word format to WordPerfect format.

- Turn on the Microsoft Word toolbar so that you can find familiar buttons.

- Compare the Word shortcut keys to WordPerfect shortcut keys so that you can see the differences. A link takes you to a help topic that explains how to customize the shortcut keys to reflect Microsoft Word or WordPerfect settings.

- Use the Microsoft Outlook address book so you can bring your contact information into WordPerfect.

- Compare WordPerfect and Word features so that you can match up similar features.

## GETTING HELP FROM THE PERFECTEXPERT

The PerfectExpert in WordPerfect has a dual purpose. One function is to automate the creation of documents by organizing features and putting them at your fingertips. From start to finish, the PerfectExpert leads you through the process of creating many types of documents. The PerfectExpert is context-sensitive, so if you are working in a blank document, you get a certain list of functions (refer to Figure 1.14). If you are working inside a table, the list changes. You might relate this back to the way the property bar changes depending on what you are working on.

The second function of the PerfectExpert is a unique new way to help you prepare to create different types of documents. In addition to explaining how to use WordPerfect's features, these PerfectExpert help topics give you valuable advice on how to avoid writer's block, how to write and give persuasive speeches, and how to develop interesting documents with a well-organized and attractive appearance.

Let's say you have to put together a brochure. Before you get started, take a look at the list of PerfectExpert help topics for creating a brochure. You'll find information on the essential elements: placing information, adding logos and page borders, and incorporating a questionnaire. There are also brief descriptions of informational, corporate, and product brochures that help clarify the differences between them.

To use the PerfectExpert to help you learn how to prepare different types of documents, do the following:

1. Open the Help menu and choose Help Topics.

2. Scroll down to the bottom of the list and then double-click the book icon next to Reference Information.

3. Double-click the book icon next to Getting the Most Out of the PerfectExpert.

4. Double-click the question mark icon next to Getting the Most Out of the PerfectExpert.

5. In the WordPerfect PerfectExpert Help dialog box, double-click the book icon next to Getting the Most out of PerfectExpert.

6. Scroll down and double-click the book icon next to Creating a Brochure to open a list of help topics (see Figure 1.17).

7. Double-click one of the question mark icons to view the information.

**Figure 1.17**
WordPerfect's PerfectExpert encompasses a set of help topics that were developed to help you plan and prepare many different types of documents.

Double-click a question mark icon to display the help topic

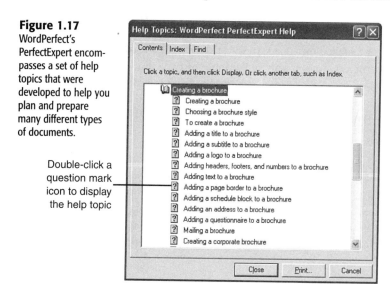

# EXITING WORDPERFECT

The quickest way to exit WordPerfect is to click the application Close button. You'll see two Close buttons in the upper-right corner. Don't let this confuse you—the top one is the application Close button; the bottom one is the document Close button.

When you closed your document, you clicked the bottom Close button. Now, click the top Close button to close the application window and exit WordPerfect.

Exit WordPerfect by doing the following:

1. Click the application Close button. Before closing the program, WordPerfect prompts you to save your changes (in every open document window).

2. If necessary, give filenames to any documents that you have not yet saved and named.

**TIP FROM**

Would you like to be able to pick up *right* where you left off when you start WordPerfect again? Let's say you're working on three documents, and you want to be able to save your place in one of the documents. The next time you start WordPerfect, you want those same three documents open and your insertion point where you left it. No problem—choose the Tools menu and select Settings, and then Environment to open the Environment Settings dialog box. Click the Interface tab. In the Save Workspace section, select Always (to save automatically each time you exit) or Prompt on Exit (to selectively save the workspace). Click OK and then Close to return to the document.

# TROUBLESHOOTING

### HAVING TROUBLE STARTING WORDPERFECT

*I'm trying to start WordPerfect, but I can't find WordPerfect Office 11/12 on my Start menu.*

The program hasn't been installed on your system yet. Insert the WordPerfect CD in the CD drive. If the Setup program doesn't start in a minute or two, choose Start, Run, browse to the CD drive, and then double-click `intro.exe` to start the Setup program.

### THE MISSING PROPERTY BAR AND TOOLBAR

*I don't see the property bar or the toolbar on my screen.*

It's possible that another user has placed these bars somewhere else on the screen. Look on the left and right sides of the document window. Also, look at the bottom of the screen, just above the status bar. The property bar and toolbar might also be positioned as a "floating palette" anywhere in the document window. To move them back, point to a blank section (or the title bar of the palette) and wait for a four-pronged arrow to appear. Click and drag the bar back up to the top of the screen. When the gray guidelines appear as a long rectangle, release the mouse button.

If you don't see the bars at all, they've probably been turned off. Choose View, Toolbars. Place a check mark in the box next to Property Bar or WordPerfect 11 (or WordPerfect 12).

### QUICKTIPS DON'T APPEAR

*When I point to a toolbar button, a QuickTip doesn't appear.*

Perhaps another user turned off QuickTips. Choose Tools, Settings to open the Settings dialog box. Click the Environment icon, and then click the Interface tab. Place a check mark in the QuickTips check box, click OK, and then click Close.

### HEAVY-HANDED DELETIONS

*I got in a big hurry and deleted way too much text. How can I get it back?*

 You mean, you don't remember exactly what you just deleted so you can't just type it back in really fast? Well, no one else does, either. Press Ctrl+Z or click the Undo button to reverse the last action taken on the document. If this doesn't work, you've done something else after you deleted the text. Press Ctrl+Z or click the Undo button until the text comes back.

If you click Undo too many times, you can click Redo to undo the last Undo. It sounds like a tongue twister, but it really does work that way. Seriously.

### SPELL-AS-YOU-GO GONE

*I don't see any red wavy lines onscreen, even if I type a misspelled word.*

The Spell-As-You-Go feature has been turned off. Choose Tools, Proofread, Spell-As-You-Go to turn it back on.

# PROJECT

In the "Saving Documents" section, I talked about the Timed Document Backup feature and how it's turned on and set to make backups of your documents every 10 minutes. In the event of a system crash, the most you stand to lose is 10 minutes of work (or less, if you decrease the backup interval). You might be wondering how you can get to this backup file if your system locks up. Here's how it works:

If you fail to exit WordPerfect properly, the next time you start the program, you'll see a message box, telling you that you have a backup file available (see Figure 1.18). You have to choose one of the three options before you can get into the program.

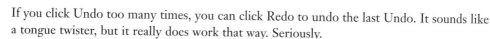

**Figure 1.18**
In the Timed Backup message box, you can open, rename, or delete the backup file.

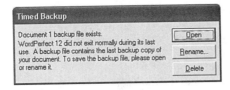

I strongly suggest that you open the backup file so you can see what's in it before you even consider deleting it. When you delete the backup file, it's gone; you can't restore it from the Recycle Bin.

Backup files are named wp{wp}.bk#, where the # stands for the number of the document. If you have four documents open, you'll have four different backup files: wp{wp}.bk1, wp{wp}.bk2, wp{wp}.bk3, and wp{wp}.bk4. Bear in mind that only the active document is backed up when the backup interval comes up, so if you're in document number 3, that document is backed up. If you're in another document when the interval comes up again, that document is backed up. Maybe someday they can engineer a Timed Document Backup feature that backs up all the open documents during the backup interval, but it hasn't happened yet.

Choose Open to open the backup file so that you can take a look. I usually open the named document so that I can do a visual comparison to see which is the most recent version. You can even do a Document Compare to compare the two so you can see the differences. With the backup copy open, choose File, Document, Compare. Type the name of the named document or browse for it. Choose Compare Only to start the comparison.

→ For more information, **see** "Comparing Documents," **p. 552.**

When you've figured out which copy is the most recent, you can save it. If the backup file has changes that the named document doesn't, close the named document, and then save the backup document with that name to overwrite the older file. If the named document has the most recent information, you can close the backup document without saving it.

If you want to take a look at the backup file, but not right now, rename it so you can get back to it later. Choose Rename to open the Rename File dialog box (see Figure 1.19). The original filename is shown. Type the new filename in the New Name text box, and then click OK. The named backup file is saved in the current folder unless you type a different drive and folder name when you name the file. I suggest saving the named backup file to the Backup folder so you know where to find it.

Now, if for some strange reason, you don't get the Timed Backup dialog box, you can go look for the backup files and open them manually. They are stored in the folder that is specified in the Files Settings dialog box. Choose Tools, Settings, and then click Files. If necessary, click the Document tab. The name of the backup folder is shown in the Backup Folder text box. Open the Open File dialog box and move to that folder. The backup files all follow the same naming convention—wp{wp}.bk#. If you aren't sure which one you need, choose View, Details to see the date and time the file was last saved.

The current filename is displayed here

**Figure 1.19**
You can rename a
Timed Document
Backup file so that
you can go back and
look at it later.

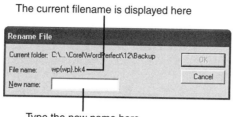

Type the new name here

It's a good idea to do some periodic housekeeping in the Backup folder. Delete the files that you don't need anymore and move the files that you want to keep.

# CHAPTER 2

# OPENING AND EDITING DOCUMENTS

**I**n this chapter

*by Read Gilgen*

# FINDING AND OPENING DOCUMENTS

Although much of what you work on in WordPerfect is new, original material, more often than not you will find yourself modifying and correcting existing documents. That, after all, is the real value and power of the word processing program: It saves you time and energy as you perfect your work.

WordPerfect's Open File dialog box is the easiest way to locate and to open existing files. It's WordPerfect's friendlier equivalent to the Windows Explorer. Simply choose File, Open (or press Ctrl+O or F4) and WordPerfect displays the dialog box shown in Figure 2.1.

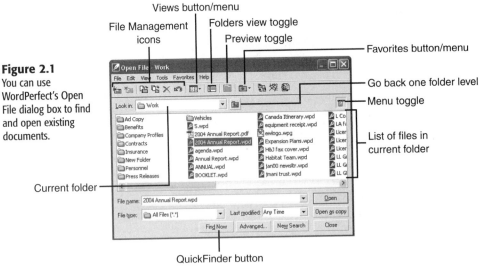

**Figure 2.1**
You can use WordPerfect's Open File dialog box to find and open existing documents.

WordPerfect automatically opens the default, or the most recently opened folder. To open a file in this folder, scroll through the list, click the file you want to open, and click Open. You can also double-click the file to select and open at the same time.

**TIP FROM**

*Read Gilgen*

WordPerfect's *QuickOpen* feature remembers the last nine documents you worked on and lists these at the bottom of the File menu. Simply click File and then click the name of the document you want to open. That's it! WordPerfect opens the document and you're ready to begin editing.

**TIP**

Unfortunately, in WordPerfect when using Windows XP the path (location) to the default folder is horribly long. You can change the default location to something simpler, for example c:\docs, by choosing Tools, Settings, Files, and changing the location and name of the default document folder.

## UNDERSTANDING THE OPEN FILE DIALOG BOX

You'll probably be surprised at how useful WordPerfect's file management system (the Open File dialog box) can be. You'll find yourself here often as you find, open, delete, rename, or copy files. After a quick overview, you'll be able to use this tool much more effectively.

 The Views button determines how WordPerfect displays filenames in the file list. You can click the Views button to choose from the following Views button options:

- *Large Icon* shows each file with a large icon. This isn't terribly useful unless you like large pictures!

- *Small Icon* shows the list of files with small icons, arranged alphabetically by row from left to right.

- *List* is the default view, and files are shown with small icons, arranged alphabetically by column from top to bottom.

- *Details* is perhaps the most useful view (see Figure 2.2). Files are listed with small icons, arranged alphabetically from top to bottom. However, you also see the date and time the file was last modified, and its size relative to other files in the list.

**Figure 2.2**
The Details view of the Open File dialog box offers the most information about files, and also enables you to sort your files.

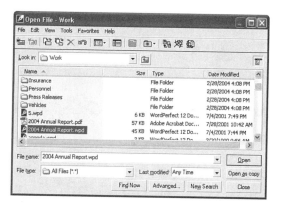

**TIP FROM**

*Read Gilgen*

The column heading buttons in the Details view can do much more than look pretty. Click the Date Modified button, for example, and WordPerfect arranges the list of files in chronological order of when the files were last modified. Click it again to sort in reverse chronological order. Click the Name button and you get an alphabetical listing. This procedure also works in other Windows applications where the files are listed with column headings.

 If you really want to make the WordPerfect Open File dialog box look like Windows Explorer, click the Folders button (see Figure 2.3).

**TIP FROM**

*Read Gilgen*

Don't forget that you can size the Open File dialog box window just as you do most Windows windows. A larger Open File dialog box is particularly useful if you choose the Details view.

**Figure 2.3**
If you toggle the Folders view on, the Open File dialog box looks and works very much like Windows Explorer.

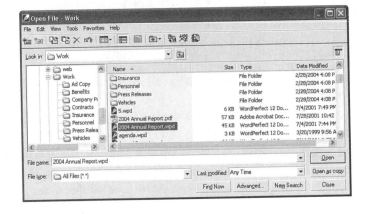

## PREVIEWING FILES

 If you want to preview a file created by WordPerfect Office before opening it, click the Preview button (see Figure 2.4).

**Figure 2.4**
The Preview view shows you a thumbnail sketch of a page of your document.

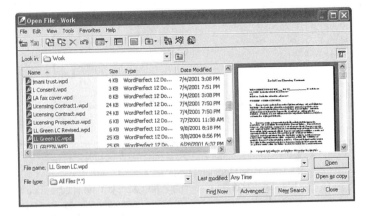

Unfortunately, what you actually see in the Preview window is so small that it's not terribly useful as you try to determine the contents of the file. However, you can remedy this by creating a larger Preview window. Follow these steps:

1. Right-click the Preview window to display a menu of choices.

2. Choose Use Separate Window. WordPerfect displays a separate Previewer window (see Figure 2.5). Alternatively, you can choose View, Preview, Use Separate Window to display the separate Previewer window.

**Figure 2.5**

The Previewer window can be detached from the Open File dialog box and sized larger to make the document more readable.

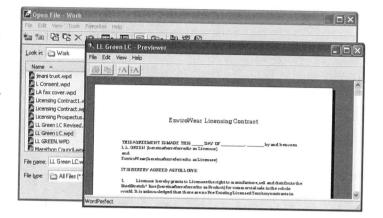

3. Size the Previewer window so that it's large enough to display the document in a readable format.

4. Close the Previewer window to return to the Open File dialog box.

The next time you click the Preview button, WordPerfect displays the document preview in this separate window. To cancel the separate preview window, simply right-click the Previewer window and uncheck Use Separate Window.

> **NOTE**
>
> When you size the Previewer window, WordPerfect remembers that size the next time you click the Preview button in the Open File dialog box. However, if you maximize the Previewer window, the next time you access it WordPerfect once again displays the smaller-size window.

The main limitation in using the Previewer is that it can only display documents or graphics created by recent versions of the WordPerfect Office suite, including WordPerfect, Quattro Pro, or Presentations. Although it is purported to be able to preview ASCII text and Word documents, for these and for other non-WordPerfect files you're likely to use, including .gif or .jpg Internet files, the Previewer does not work.

Previous versions of WordPerfect (WordPerfect 10, in WordPerfect Office 2002, and earlier) included a nifty file viewer called QuickView Plus. If you're lucky, it might already be installed on your system. In the Open dialog box, right-click on a filename and see if

QuickView or QuickView Plus is listed on the QuickMenu. If it isn't, and if you still have the installation CDs for WordPerfect Office 2002 (WordPerfect 10) or earlier, you can install QuickView Plus as a separate program.

## CHANGING TO ANOTHER FOLDER

What happens when you don't see the file you want in the current folder? Assuming that you did save the file, the most likely reason you don't see it is that you saved it in a different folder.

To navigate to another folder, first look in the list of files for other folders that might contain the file. Double-click a folder to open it and to see its contents.

If you don't find the file there, you might have to return to the next level up. Just click (once) the Go Back One Folder Level button (refer to Figure 2.1) and then decide whether to try another folder, or to go back another folder level.

When you finally find the file you want, open it.

**CAUTION**

If you do change folders, the last opened folder becomes the default folder. The next time you access the Open File dialog box, you see a listing of files in that folder. This can be confusing if you're not mindful of which folder you are in.

**TIP FROM**

If you want to always open the same default folder, choose Edit, Change Default Folder (make sure it does *not* have a check beside it). Now, regardless of how often you browse for files in other folders, you'll always return to the default folder when you access the Open File dialog box.

*Still having trouble making the proper default folder come up when you access the Open File dialog box? See "Setting the Default Folder" in the Troubleshooting section at the end of this chapter.*

## USING QUICKFINDER TO LOCATE DOCUMENTS

Sometimes you simply can't remember the name of the document you're looking for. However, you might remember a keyword or phrase that you know is contained in the document itself. WordPerfect's *QuickFinder* feature enables you to search for and find documents based on their contents.

Access the Open File dialog box, and in the File Name text box, type the word you want to find. Then, click Find Now. Do *not* click Open and do *not* press Enter. WordPerfect searches all the documents in the current folder and its subfolders, and returns the results in the QuickFinder Results dialog box. Select the file you want, and click Open.

> If you know the name of the file you're looking for, but just can't seem to find it, don't forget that you can use the Windows Search feature. Click the Start button, choose Search, All Files and Folders, and then search for your file by name.

## OPENING A COPY OF A DOCUMENT

Sometimes you want to edit a copy of a document, but you want to leave the original intact. For example, you need the original for historical purposes or as a reference point. Follow these steps:

1. Access the Open File dialog box (by selecting File, Open).

2. Find and select the file you want to work on.

3. Click the Open As Copy button (not the Open button). WordPerfect opens a copy of the file, which you now can edit.

4. When you finish making changes, choose File, Save. WordPerfect forces you to provide a new filename.

5. Click Save and you now have a modified copy of the original, leaving the original intact.

## CONVERTING DOCUMENTS ON OPEN

Believe it or not, not everyone uses Corel WordPerfect! Even if they do, they don't always use the most recent version. Fortunately, WordPerfect's built-in file conversion feature enables you to open nearly every kind of word processing document.

> If you have a lot of old WordPerfect files, you don't need to worry about losing them when you switch to WordPerfect 12. Just leave them alone until you need them, and *then* open them into WordPerfect 12 just as you open any normal document. WordPerfect converts the older WordPerfect formats to the new WordPerfect 12 format. When you save the converted file, choose the WordPerfect 6/7/8/9/10/11/12 format.

When you save a converted document, WordPerfect asks whether you want to save it in the latest WordPerfect format (WordPerfect 6/7/8/9/10/11/12) or in the original format from which it was converted (see Figure 2.6). If you're returning the document to someone who isn't using WordPerfect, simply select the original format and click OK.

→ To learn how to convert several documents at once using the WordPerfect Conversion Utility, **see** "Using WordPerfect's Conversion Utility," **p. 474.**

**Figure 2.6**
Before saving an edited non-WordPerfect 12 file, WordPerfect asks if you want convert it back to the original file, or keep it in the updated WordPerfect 12 format.

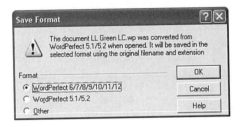

**2**

# GETTING AROUND IN A DOCUMENT

When you have found a document to edit, you need to know the most efficient ways of getting around so you can quickly make changes to the document. Before you can make a change, you must reposition the insertion point (that is, the cursor) at the point at which you want to make the change.

Consistent with the Windows environment, you can move the insertion point by using either the mouse or the keyboard.

**TIP FROM**

*Read Gilgen*

It's easy to get into a rut of using primarily the mouse or the keyboard. Instead, you should become familiar with both methods of moving around your document so that as the need arises, you can use the more appropriate method. For example, if your hands are already on the keyboard, it might make more sense to use the keyboard to move the insertion point instead of moving your hand to the mouse to move the insertion point.

## USING THE MOUSE TO MOVE AROUND

You move the insertion point with the mouse in the following ways:

- Point and click—Position the mouse pointer at the location in the text where you want to place the insertion point. (The mouse pointer will be either an arrow or an I-beam, depending on the Shadow Cursor options you have chosen.)

→ To learn about the Shadow Cursor, and how to enable or disable it, **see** "Touring the WordPerfect Screen," **p. 18.**

- Scrollbar—As in any Windows application, you can scroll bit by bit simply by clicking the up and down arrows at either end of the vertical scrollbar. You can scroll more quickly by clicking and dragging the scroll box found between the two arrows. When you use the scroll box, WordPerfect displays a QuickTip that indicates the page number you see on the screen.

- Browse Buttons—These buttons are located at the bottom of the vertical scrollbar (see Figure 2.7). By default, you browse by page. Click the double up arrow to go to the previous page, and click the double down arrow to go to the next page. To toggle among other methods of browsing, click the Browse By button, located between the double up and down arrows. You can browse by page, heading, table, footnote, endnote, comment, text box, bookmark, graphic, equation, hyperlink, redline text, or strikeout text.

**Figure 2.7**
You can browse your document by page, heading, table, and so on, using the Browse buttons on the vertical scrollbar.

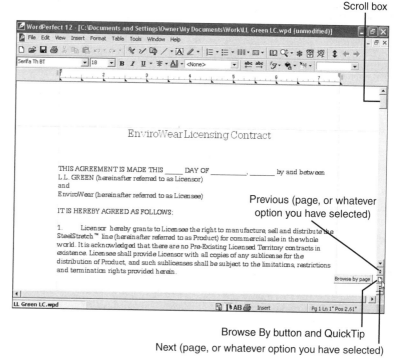

Scroll box

Previous (page, or whatever option you have selected)

Browse By button and QuickTip

Next (page, or whatever option you have selected)

 ■ The AutoScroll feature—You can click the AutoScroll icon on the toolbar to activate automatic scrolling. The mouse pointer automatically positions itself in the middle of the screen, and displays a dot with up and down arrows (see Figure 2.8). As you move the mouse pointer up, the pointer changes to a dot with an upward arrow, and the text scrolls toward the top of the document. Pull the mouse downward to scroll toward the bottom of the document. The closer the mouse pointer is to the center of the screen, the slower the text scrolls. Click the mouse to reposition the insertion point, and at the same time turn off AutoScroll.

**TIP FROM**

*Read Gilgen*

Using the AutoScroll feature, you can read your document as you scroll. Simply move the mouse pointer a short distance downward away from the center of the screen to scroll slowly, thus enabling you to read the text before it disappears from the screen.

AutoScroll mouse pointer

**Figure 2.8**
AutoScroll makes it
easy to scroll through
your document by
moving your mouse
pointer up or down
on the screen.

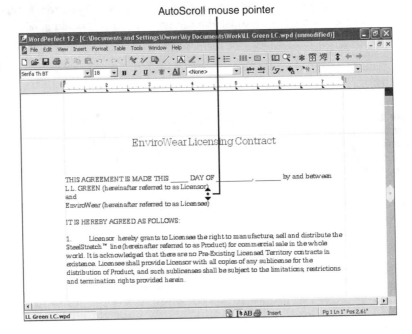

## USING THE KEYBOARD TO MOVE AROUND

Moving the insertion point with the mouse often can be imprecise, and even tedious.
Moving it by using the keyboard can be quicker and more accurate.

**TIP FROM**

*Read Gilgen*

Don't worry if the list of possible keystrokes seems overwhelming. Actually, there are relatively few *different* procedures, each with two or more directions (up or down, for example). Try one or two, and add to your repertoire until you can move around your documents like greased lightning.

Table 2.1 shows keyboard shortcuts for repositioning the insertion point. These keystrokes
are standard in all Windows applications, except as noted (with an asterisk).

| TABLE 2.1 WORDPERFECT'S KEYBOARD SHORTCUTS | |
|---|---|
| **Keystroke(s)** | **Insertion Point Moves** |
| Right arrow | One character to the right |
| Left arrow | One character to the left |
| Down arrow | One line down |
| Up arrow | One line up |

| **TABLE 2.1** | **Continued** |
|---|---|
| **Keystroke(s)** | **Insertion Point Moves** |
| Ctrl+Right arrow | One word to the right |
| Ctrl+Left arrow | One word to the left |
| Ctrl+Down arrow | One paragraph down |
| Ctrl+Up arrow | One paragraph up |
| Home | To beginning of current line |
| End | To end of current line |
| Page Down | To bottom of current screen |
| Page Up | To top of current screen |
| Alt+Page Down* | To top of next physical page |
| Alt+Page Up* | To top of previous physical page |
| Ctrl+End | To end of document |
| Ctrl+Home | To beginning of document |

*\*This keystroke is not standard in other Windows programs.*

# Working with Selected Text

Can you imagine having to format your text or delete whole paragraphs one character at a time? Fortunately, you can select a chunk of text and cut it, delete it, or apply formatting to it.

## Selecting Text

Although typically you use the mouse or the keyboard to select text, you can also use the Edit menu to select the text. Choose Edit, Select to choose these options:

- Sentence—WordPerfect selects the sentence in which the insertion point is found.
- Paragraph—WordPerfect selects the entire paragraph, but not any extra blank spaces between paragraphs.
- Page—WordPerfect selects the entire current page.
- All—WordPerfect selects the entire document.
- Section—WordPerfect enables you to specify a single page or range of pages, secondary pages, chapters, or volumes.

→ To learn about formatting your document using page, chapter, section, or volume numbering, **see** "Setting Page, Chapter, and Volume Numbers," **p. 236.**

None of these options are terribly common, however. Instead, you'll probably end up using the mouse or the keyboard to select text. Let's look first at selecting text using the keyboard. This procedure is simple after you've mastered the cursor control keystrokes in Table 2.1. To select a portion of text, position the insertion point at the beginning of the area you want to select, hold down the Shift key, and use any cursor movement to move to the end of the selection.

For example, to select text one word at a time, hold down the Shift key while pressing Ctrl+Right arrow. To select everything from the cursor to the end of the document, hold down the Shift key and press Ctrl+End.

**NOTE**

> Selecting text using the Shift key along with cursor movement keys or along with repositioning the insertion point with the mouse is standard in all Windows applications.

**TIP FROM**

*Read Gilgen*

> Pressing Shift+End selects the entire line *plus* the hard return, which is a change from previous versions of WordPerfect. If you want to return to the previous WordPerfect default of not including the hard return in the selection, choose Tools, Settings, Environment, and select Use WordPerfect 9 text selection.

Selecting text with the mouse is also easy, although a bit of dexterity and practice might be necessary before you become really good at it.

Table 2.2 shows several methods of using the mouse to select text. Again, these methods are standard in all Windows applications, except as noted (with an asterisk).

**TABLE 2.2 SELECTING TEXT IN WORDPERFECT BY USING THE MOUSE**

| Mouse Action | What It Selects |
| --- | --- |
| Drag across text | One whole word at a time |
| Alt+drag across text | One character at a time |
| Double-click | Entire word |
| Triple-click* | Entire sentence |
| Quadruple-click* | Entire paragraph |
| Single-click in left margin* | Entire sentence |
| Double-click in left margin | Entire paragraph |

*This mouse action is not standard in other Windows programs.*

The methods listed in Table 2.2 are used only for selecting text. The mouse is used differently to select graphics objects or cells of a table.

→ To learn more about selecting graphics objects, **see** "Resizing and Moving Graphics" in Chapter 12, "Adding Graphics to Documents."

→ To learn more about selecting tables and table cells, **see** "Selecting Text and Cells" in Chapter 10, "Working with Tables."

Finally, with text selected, you can further refine your selection by choosing Edit, Select, and selecting one of the following options:

- Tabular Column—If your text is arranged in tabular columns and you want to select the column, select your text from the beginning of the tabular column to the end of the tabular column. WordPerfect initially selects all text, including other columns, but choosing this option changes the selection to include only the desired tabular column.

- Rectangle—If you want to select a specific rectangle of text, first select from the beginning (upper-left corner) of the rectangle to the end (lower-right corner) of the rectangle. WordPerfect initially selects all text. Choosing this option changes the selection to include only the rectangle of text.

- Select Table—With the cursor positioned inside a table, this option selects the entire table.

Although you probably won't use these options frequently, they can be quite useful when you have to edit and reformat text that was poorly formatted to begin with.

## DELETING TEXT

You already know how to delete text by using the Backspace key (erasing to the left of the insertion point) or the Delete key (erasing to the right of the insertion point). However, you can also quickly delete a selected block of text. After selecting the text you want to delete, you can use one of these methods:

- Press Delete.

- Press Backspace.

- Right-click the selection and choose Delete from the QuickMenu.

## MOVING AND COPYING TEXT

So, you've got some text selected. Besides deleting it, what else can you do with it? The "bread and butter" of word processing consists of moving text from one place to another. When you move the text, but leave a copy in the original location, you are *copying and pasting* text. If you move it and delete the original location, you are *cutting and pasting* text.

WordPerfect likes to try to please everyone, so there are several different ways to cut and paste selected text. The basic procedure is this:

1. Select the text you want to move.

2. Copy (or cut) the selected text.

3. Reposition the insertion point at the target location.

4. Paste the text you copied (or cut).

You can paste copied text as many times as you like, until you copy or cut something new.

**NOTE**

> The Windows Clipboard is an area of your computer's memory that stores information that you cut or copy. If you cut or copy another selection, this selection replaces whatever was in your Clipboard. If you turn off your computer, you lose the complete contents of the Clipboard.

The various methods for copying, cutting, and pasting are listed in Table 2.3. Use the method that helps you work the fastest. For example, if your hands are already on the keyboard, try using the keyboard methods. Otherwise, you might want to use the mouse.

**TABLE 2.3    METHODS FOR MOVING TEXT**

| Action | Method |
|---|---|
| Copy | Choose Edit, Copy |
| | Click the Copy toolbar icon |
| | Right-click the selection and choose Copy |
| | Press Ctrl+C |
| | Press Ctrl+Insert |
| Cut | Choose Edit, Cut |
| | Click the Cut toolbar icon |
| | Right-click the selection and choose Cut |
| | Press Ctrl+X |
| | Press Shift+Delete |
| Paste | Choose Edit, Paste |
| | Click the Paste toolbar icon |
| | Right-click and choose Paste |
| | Press Ctrl+V |
| | Press Shift+Insert |

**TIP FROM**

*Read Gilgen*

Typically when you cut or copy material, it replaces anything you previously cut or copied to the Windows Clipboard. You can also cut or copy a series of selections, and append them to the Windows Clipboard. Select the text, and choose Edit, Append. You then paste at once from the Clipboard everything you appended.

**TIP FROM**

*Read Gilgen*

A fast and easy-to-remember sequence for cutting and pasting involves using the Shift key: Shift+cursor to select the text, Shift+Delete to cut the text, and then Shift+Insert to paste the text. If you learn these keystrokes, you can save incredible amounts of time as you cut and paste.

 *Is what you pasted different from what you thought you copied? See "Pasting Things Correctly" in the Troubleshooting section at the end of this chapter.*

WordPerfect also enables you to use the mouse to drag selected text from one location and drop it in another. This Drag and Drop feature can be useful in many situations. To drag and drop text, follow these steps:

1. Use the mouse or the keyboard to select the text you want to move.
2. Position the mouse pointer on the highlighted text. The pointer changes to an arrow.
3. Click and hold down the left mouse button.
4. Drag the mouse to the target location. The mouse pointer changes to an arrow along with a small rectangular box (see Figure 2.9). An insertion point also appears showing you exactly where the text will be pasted when you release the mouse button.

**Figure 2.9**
You can use the mouse to quickly drag and drop text.

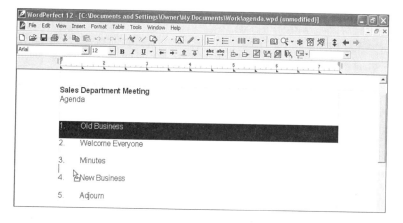

5. Release the mouse button. WordPerfect continues to highlight the text. If you didn't quite hit your target, you can drag again, or you can choose Undo and start over again.
6. When you have the selection where you want it, click the selection to deselect it.

**2**

**TIP FROM**

*Read Gilgen*

> In addition to moving text, you can also copy selected text by holding down the Ctrl key while dragging and dropping the text.

# OOPS (USING UNDO)

When your finger slips and you type the wrong letter, it's no big deal. Backspace quickly zaps the letter and you're back on track. But when you make a change to a large amount of text, reconstructing the original can be tedious and time-consuming. Fortunately, WordPerfect gives you the capability to undo your actions quickly and easily.

You can use any of the following methods to undo an action:

- Choose Edit, Undo.
- Click the Undo icon on the toolbar.
- Press Ctrl+Z.

What's more, WordPerfect remembers up to the last 10 things you did, and enables you to undo them sequentially in reverse order.

If you get carried away and undo too many steps, you can also redo those steps by clicking the Redo icon on the toolbar or choosing Edit, Redo.

**CAUTION**

> Both Undo and Redo operate sequentially. If you need to undo or redo a step or two, do so immediately. Otherwise, you might not be able to back up or move forward without undoing correct steps or redoing incorrect steps.

**TIP FROM**

*Read Gilgen*

> You can click the drop-down menu on the Undo and Redo buttons on the toolbar to display a list of your 10 most recent steps. To Undo or Redo more than one step at a time, just move the mouse pointer to select the number of steps you want to Undo or Redo and click.

By default, WordPerfect does not save Undo information with your document. Thus, if you save your document while still working on it, as you should, or if you close your document, you can no longer undo your most recent actions. You can avoid this by having WordPerfect save Undo information along with the document. Choose Edit, Undo/Redo History, Options and check Save Undo/Redo Items with Document; if you or someone else opens the document later, you can still undo the last 10 steps performed on the document. Note, however, that if you are deleting or moving large quantities of text or graphics, or if you also choose to increase the number of Undo/Redo items, and you save the Undo information, the size of your saved file can increase dramatically.

NOTE

> By default, WordPerfect remembers only your last 10 actions. You can increase this amount, up to 300, by choosing Edit, Undo/Redo History, Options and changing the Number of Undo/Redo Items.

NOTE

> Nearly since its inception, WordPerfect has included an Undelete feature. Longtime WordPerfect users looking for Undelete will find that the feature no longer is available. Instead, use Undo when you delete text accidentally, and use standard cut and paste to move text.

# ZOOMING IN ON YOUR TEXT

No matter where you choose to edit your document—in the document window or in Print Preview—you can adjust the size of the document onscreen making it easier to see what you're working on.

## USING THE ZOOM SETTINGS

By default, WordPerfect displays your document at a zoom ratio of 100%. This simply means that the document onscreen is the same size as it will be when printed. A zoom ratio of 50% displays your document at only half the printed size. Although a smaller zoom ratio enables you to see more of the page, you might find it difficult to read the text or see other fine details.

Adjust the zoom by following these steps:

 1. Click the drop-down arrow on the Zoom button on either the Standard toolbar or the Print Preview toolbar. A menu of zoom settings appears (see Figure 2.10).

**Figure 2.10**
Clicking the drop-down menu of the Zoom button enables you to select a zoom ratio. Hover over any setting for a RealTime Preview.

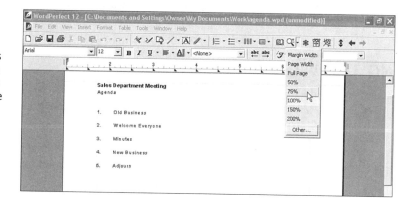

2. Select a zoom setting.

**2**

If you have a Microsoft IntelliMouse or equivalent (a mouse with a scroll wheel between the buttons), you can adjust the zoom ratio by holding down the Ctrl key and rotating the IntelliMouse wheel. WordPerfect zooms in or out at intervals of 10% for each notch on the IntelliMouse wheel.

**NOTE**

You might find that none of the preset sizes look good on your screen. Don't worry—you're not bound by the standard sizes offered. Simply choose Other from the Zoom button menu, or choose View, Zoom. This opens the Zoom dialog box where you can type in a zoom ratio of your own choosing.

**TIP FROM**

*Read Gilgen*

Sometimes it takes a little experimenting to find the right zoom setting for the task. Fortunately, RealTime Preview shows you a preview of each setting before you choose it. Simply point to and hover over any of the zoom settings, whereupon WordPerfect redisplays the document with that setting. When you find the one you want, click to choose it.

## ZOOMING TO SELECTED TEXT

Suppose you really want to get up close and personal with a specific section of your document. With WordPerfect you can magnify selected text by following these steps:

1. Click the Zoom button on the toolbar. WordPerfect displays the mouse pointer as a magnifying glass.

2. Click and drag the area of the document you want to magnify. WordPerfect adjusts the zoom ratio to display the selected text as large as possible.

3. Click the Zoom button again to turn off the magnification feature.

Note that the maximum zoom ratio is 400%. Click the Zoom button drop-down menu to choose a normal zoom ratio once again.

# USING THE WORKSPACE MANAGER

Since the introduction of WordPerfect for Windows with version 5.1, users have clamored to get back the blue screen with white text so familiar in WordPerfect for DOS. Other users, new to WordPerfect, want instead to see menus and buttons that are familiar to them.

WordPerfect 12 introduces the Workspace Manager, which enables you to customize quickly and easily WordPerfect's look, including menus, buttons, and screen colors.

To activate the Workspace manager, choose Tools, Workspace Manager. WordPerfect displays the Workspace Manager dialog box (see Figure 2.11).

This is the same dialog box that appears by default when you first start WordPerfect 12. If don't want to be bothered by the Workspace Manager upon startup, just uncheck the Show at Startup check box.

**Figure 2.11**
The Workspace Manager helps create a customized working environment by changing menus, toolbars, or colors.

CAUTION

Changing the workspace does *not* change how WordPerfect features work. Further, if you inadvertently change the workspace, you might find it difficult to locate and use features you're already familiar with.

## WORKING IN THE MICROSOFT WORD MODE

The primary reason for switching to the Microsoft Word mode is to make it easier to find features that are similar in both programs, but that are located differently on menus or toolbars in each program.

If you choose Microsoft Word mode from the Workspace Manager, WordPerfect displays differently organized menus and toolbars, a PerfectExpert box to assist you, and a floating toolbar with WordPerfect/Word-specific options (see Figure 2.12).

The three most significant features in this mode are

- Menus—Although WordPerfect's features function the same as always, the location of the menu items required to select certain features have been moved to reflect their location on Word menus. For example, in WordPerfect, the Outline/Bullets & Numbering feature is located under the Insert menu. In Word, it's called Bullets and Numbering, and it's located under the Format menu. In Word mode, WordPerfect uses its own feature name, Outline/Bullets & Numbers, but you'll find it under the Format menu.

- PerfectExpert—Targeted to those not very familiar with WordPerfect, the PerfectExpert dialog box guides you through the basic elements of creating, editing, formatting, and finishing a WordPerfect document. It suggests when rather than how to use WordPerfect features, although buttons at the bottom of the dialog box link to tips, help, and tutorials at the Corel Web site.

- Microsoft Word Compatibility toolbar—The buttons on this floating toolbar help you quickly convert documents to or from Word, to PDF, XML, or HTML, and to access specific help about WordPerfect for Word users.

Microsoft Word Compatibility toolbar    Microsoft Word menus and toolbars

**Figure 2.12**
The Microsoft Word
mode assists those
familiar with Word as
they create and edit
WordPerfect docu-
ments.

PerfectExpert
dialog box

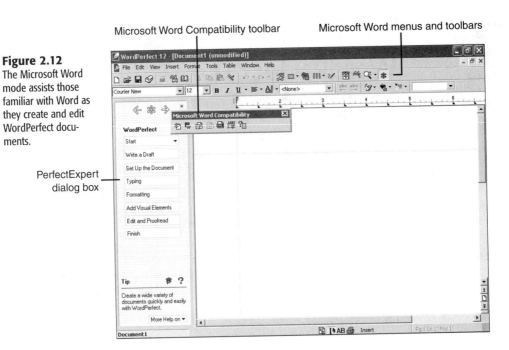

The Microsoft Word mode is intended for the most part as a transition tool until one becomes more familiar with WordPerfect's features. For example, quite likely you'll soon close the PerfectExpert dialog box. However, you might still want to use Word-type menus or toolbars until you become more familiar with how WordPerfect does things.

## SWITCHING TO 5.1 CLASSIC MODE

Back in the day when nearly everyone used WordPerfect, the DOS-based version was particularly identifiable by its blue screen with white text. Windows-based versions of current-day word processing programs typically try to emulate white paper and black printing, which some feel is hard on the eyes.

Beginning with WordPerfect 11, you now have the option of working in WordPerfect "Classic" mode, which emulates to a certain degree the workspace of a WordPerfect 5.1 document. You switch to this mode by choosing Tools, Workspace Manager, and selecting WordPerfect Classic Mode (version 5.1), shown in Figure 2.13.

In WordPerfect 11, you do not have the Workspace Manager, so in order to access the Classic mode you must choose Tools, Settings, Display, and on the Document tab, click the Classic mode check box. Then click OK and Close.

The primary characteristics of this mode include the following:

■ A blue background, with white text and guidelines.

■ The absence of toolbars, rulers, or horizontal scroll bars, which also provides more workspace.

- The use of version 5.1's keystrokes, including F3 for the Help key, F7 to exit, Shift+F7 to print, and so on. Many feel that a more keyboard-based approach to word processing is faster and more efficient.

- A few features long since absent in Windows versions of WordPerfect, such as Undelete (F1), become available.

- The menu does not change, but includes all the features of WordPerfect 12, arranged the same as in recent WordPerfect for Windows versions.

**Figure 2.13**
The Classic Mode emulates DOS-based WordPerfect 5.1's keyboard and uncluttered blue screen.

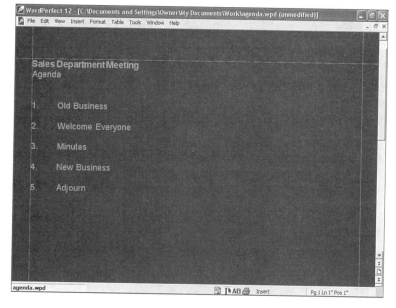

If you've longed for the good old days when the mouse was still a Macintosh curiosity, you'll love this workspace option. If you've never before used WordPerfect 5.1, it's unlikely you'll want to learn the keystrokes associated with it. However, if you still like the clean screen and blue background, you can customize the classic workspace. For example, you can:

- Add toolbars by choosing View, Toolbars, and selecting those you want to see.

- Add the Ruler by choosing View, Ruler.

- Change back to the WordPerfect 12 keyboard by choosing Tools, Settings, Customize, and then clicking the Keyboards tab and selecting a more recent keyboard, such as WPWin 12 Keyboard.

For detailed information on the keystrokes and features of the Classic mode, choose Help, Help Topics, Using WordPerfect Classic Mode.

## CHANGING TO THE LEGAL MODE

The Legal workspace is more like WordPerfect 12 than the Word or Classic modes. All that really happens when you choose Tools, Workspace, Legal Mode is that WordPerfect displays an additional Legal toolbar (see Figure 2.14). This option is not available in WordPerfect 11.

Outline, numbering tools buttons

Pleadings button                    Watermark button

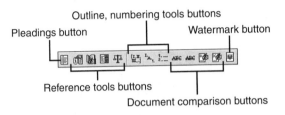

**Figure 2.14**
The Legal toolbar provides several WordPerfect options that assist in preparing legal documents in one convenient location.

Reference tools buttons

Document comparison buttons

All the features made available through the Legal toolbar are also available in the menus or elsewhere in WordPerfect. However, the buttons on this toolbar make it easier to access those features you'll likely need as you prepare legal documents. For example, the toolbar includes the following:

■ A Pleadings button, which opens a dialog box that helps you select formatting options, such as vertical lines, margins, spacing, font, and so on (see Figure 2.15).

**Figure 2.15**
The Pleadings dialog box helps set lines, numbering, fonts, margins, and other settings required in legal pleading documents.

■ Reference tools, such as Tables of Contents or Authorities.

■ Outline, paragraph, and line numbering tools.

■ Redline, strikeout, and document comparison tools.

■ A Watermark button for creating a graphic watermark.

Details for using these features can be found in various chapters throughout this book. For example, Chapter 12 covers graphic lines, whereas Chapter 13 "Customizing Graphic Shapes and Images," talks about watermarks. Chapter 7, "Formatting Lines and Paragraphs," describes the use of line spacing and paragraph formatting.

→ For information on setting margins or adding page numbers, see Chapter 8, "Formatting the Page."

→ For information on reference tools such as tables of contents or of authorities, see Chapter 19, "Generating Tables, Indexes, and Lists."

→ For information on line spacing and line numbering, see Chapter 7, "Formatting Lines and Paragraphs."

→ For information on redline, strikeout, or comparing documents, see Chapter 17, "Collaborating on Documents."

→ For information on inserting vertical lines or graphic watermarks, see Chapter 12, "Adding Graphics to Documents."

→ For information on adding text-based watermarks, **see** "Watermark Text Boxes," **p. 412.**

→ For information on using automatic outlining, see Chapter 11, "Organizing Information with Lists and Outlines."

# WORKING WITH REVEAL CODES

The capability to look behind the scenes and to see how specific codes control the flow of the WordPerfect document is called Reveal Codes (see Figure 2.16). For many, this is the single most important distinguishing feature between WordPerfect and other word processing programs. Some people love using the feature, whereas others don't. But even the critics have to admit that Reveal Codes does give you detailed control over your document.

**Figure 2.16**
The Reveal Codes screen enables you to view what's controlling the format of your document.

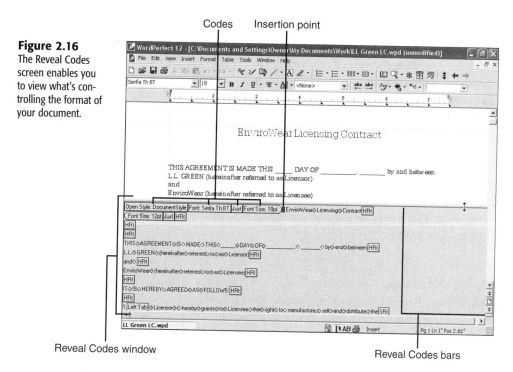

Codes    Insertion point

Reveal Codes window

Reveal Codes bars

You can use any of the following methods to turn on Reveal Codes:

- Choose View, Reveal Codes.
- Press Alt+F3.
- Right-click the editing screen and choose Reveal Codes from the QuickMenu.
- Drag the Reveal Codes bar located at the bottom of the vertical scrollbar (refer to Figure 2.16).

Control codes appear in the Reveal Codes screen as buttons mixed in with the text. The insertion point is shown as a small red box. You can reposition the insertion point by clicking the mouse in the Reveal Codes window, in addition to using the usual mouse and keyboard methods.

**NOTE**

> When Reveal Codes is off, Delete and Backspace remove text but don't necessarily delete formatting codes. In Reveal Codes, WordPerfect assumes that you see the codes, and that you intend to delete them when you use Delete or Backspace. If you accidentally delete a formatting code, just use Undo to restore it.

Generally, when you make a change in your WordPerfect document, you do so at the insertion point. Sometimes you make changes that you don't even see but that cause problems with the document's formatting. Using Reveal Codes enables you to find errant codes and delete them. Simply position the insertion point before or after the code and press Delete or Backspace as appropriate.

WordPerfect's AutoCode Placement feature also places certain codes at more appropriate locations. For example, codes that clearly affect paragraphs, such as margin or tab settings, are placed at the beginning of the paragraph in which the insertion point is resting. Codes that pertain to pages, such as page numbering or headers, are placed at the beginning of the current page.

You can also use the mouse in the Reveal Codes screen to delete or edit codes:

- You can delete codes by clicking and dragging them out of the Reveal Codes screen (see Figure 2.17).
- You can edit many format settings by double-clicking their codes in the Reveal Codes screen. This opens the appropriate dialog box, which enables you to make changes in the code setting.

Some WordPerfect aficionados prefer to work all the time with the Reveal Codes screen on. However, it's also quite easy to toggle Reveal Codes back off again. Simply press Alt+F3; choose View, Reveal Codes; right-click the Reveal Codes window, and choose Hide Reveal Codes; or drag the Reveal Codes separator bar all the way to the bottom of the screen.

Code button being dragged

**Figure 2.17**
You can use the
mouse to drag codes
out of the Reveal
Codes screen to
delete them.

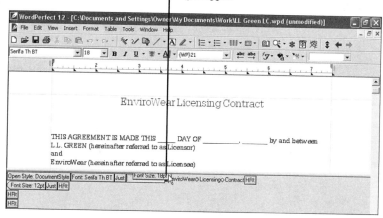

Having trouble seeing a Reveal Codes window? See *"Sizing the Reveal Codes Window"* in the
Troubleshooting section at the end of this chapter.

# EDITING MORE THAN ONE DOCUMENT

If your desk looks anything like mine, you realize that we rarely work on just one thing at a
time. While we're correcting the annual report, someone calls and asks for the action list
from last week's board meeting.

Fortunately, WordPerfect makes it easy for us to work this way by giving us up to nine separate document windows.

To open a document in another WordPerfect window, access the Open File dialog box and
then open the document. If you want to open more than one file at a time, simply access the
Open File dialog box, and then while holding down the Ctrl key, click each file you intend
to open and click Open. However, don't forget that WordPerfect cannot open more than
nine documents at once.

To open a new window, with a blank document, click the New Blank Document icon on the
toolbar. You can also choose File, New, or press Ctrl+N.

When you have more than one document open, you have to remember what documents you
have open and learn to jump quickly from one document to another. WordPerfect's title bar
displays the name of the currently active document window, whereas the application bar displays the titles of all open documents (see Figure 2.18).

**Figure 2.18**
Tabs on the application bar display each open WordPerfect document. Clicking a document enables you to switch to that document.

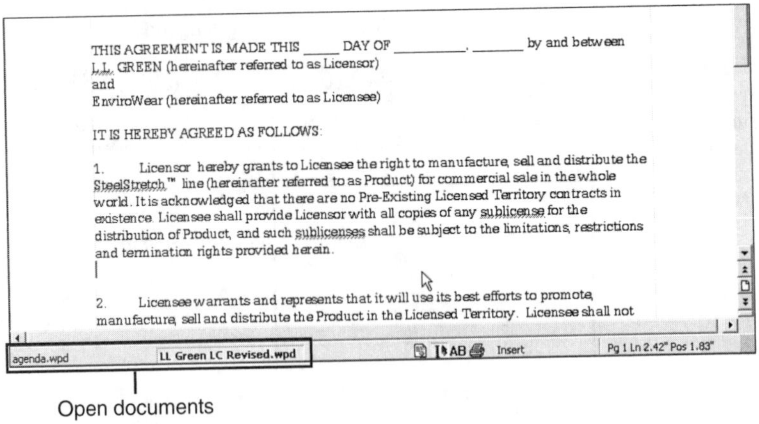

THIS AGREEMENT IS MADE THIS _____ DAY OF _____, _____ by and between
L.L. GREEN (hereinafter referred to as Licensor)
and
EnviroWear (hereinafter referred to as Licensee)

IT IS HEREBY AGREED AS FOLLOWS:

1. Licensor hereby grants to Licensee the right to manufacture, sell and distribute the SteelStretch.™ line (hereinafter referred to as Product) for commercial sale in the whole world. It is acknowledged that there are no Pre-Existing Licensed Territory contracts in existence. Licensee shall provide Licensor with all copies of any sublicense for the distribution of Product, and such sublicenses shall be subject to the limitations, restrictions and termination rights provided herein.

2. Licensee warrants and represents that it will use its best efforts to promote, manufacture, sell and distribute the Product in the Licensed Territory. Licensee shall not

agenda.wpd | LL Green LC Revised.wpd | AB Insert | Pg 1 Ln 2.42" Pos 1.83"

Open documents

You can switch from one document to another by using any of the following methods:

- On the application bar, click the name of the document you want to work on and WordPerfect opens that window for you.
- Choose Window and then click the document you want.
- Press Ctrl+F6 repeatedly until WordPerfect displays the document you want to work on.

**TIP FROM**

*Read Gilgen*

Remember that you can copy and paste from one document to another. Simply cut or copy while viewing one document, and then switch to another document and paste.

→ To learn more details about moving information from one WordPerfect document to another, including Drag and Drop, or information about WordPerfect's Clipboard program, **see** Chapter 15, "Importing Data and Working with Other Programs."

# TROUBLESHOOTING

## PASTING THINGS CORRECTLY

*Sometimes when I paste, I get something other than what I wanted to copy.*

The Windows Clipboard remembers the last thing you copied or cut. When you paste something you previously copied or cut, this is because you didn't cut or copy correctly. Simply undo what you pasted, and then go back and cut or copy the selection again.

### SETTING THE DEFAULT FOLDER

*When I open the Open File dialog box, I can't seem to make the default folder what I want it to be.*

Even if you turn off Change Default Folder, WordPerfect still remembers the last folder you were in. Access the Open File dialog box, toggle the menu on if necessary, and then choose Edit, Change Default Folder (make sure there is a check mark beside this menu item). Next, browse to the folder you want to become the default folder, and then click Close. Access the Open File dialog box again and choose Edit, Change Default Folder to turn off this feature, and choose Close. Now, each time you open the Open File dialog box, you'll find yourself in the correct default folder. Note that after you exit WordPerfect, the Open File dialog box opens to the default folder (for example, c:\My Documents) specified in your settings.

### SIZING THE REVEAL CODES WINDOW

*Even if I choose View, Reveal Codes, I still don't see a Reveal Codes window.*

If you dragged the Reveal Codes bar to size the Reveal Codes window, you might have sized it so small that you don't realize the window is still open. When you turn on Reveal Codes, if you see a solid gray bar at the bottom of the document window, you must drag this bar up to make a larger Reveal Codes window. You can also drag the bar completely to the bottom of the screen to turn off the Reveal Codes window.

# PROJECT

Selecting text and moving it by using cut and paste is the heart and soul of word processing. All programs let you cut and paste standard selections of text, but WordPerfect enables you to select nonstandard selections.

Suppose, for example, that someone has sent you a file that contains text arranged in columns. However, they formatted the text using spaces or tabs instead of using the column feature. Arranging the text into one long sequential column is a snap using WordPerfect. Follow these steps:

1. Begin by selecting the second column from the beginning of the column to the end of the column. WordPerfect selects all text between the beginning and ending points (see Figure 2.19).

2. Choose Edit, Select, Rectangle to select only the material in a rectangle defined by the beginning and the end of the selection (see Figure 2.20).

3. Use the cut feature to remove only the rectangle.

4. Position the cursor after the first column and then paste the rectangle. You now have a single, sequential column of text (see Figure 2.21).

**Figure 2.19**
If you try to select a column of text, WordPerfect first selects all text.

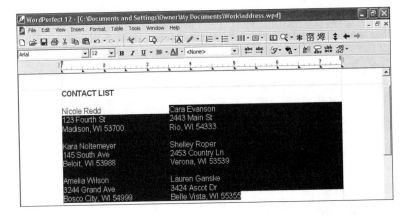

**Figure 2.20**
WordPerfect can refine a selection to select only a rectangle.

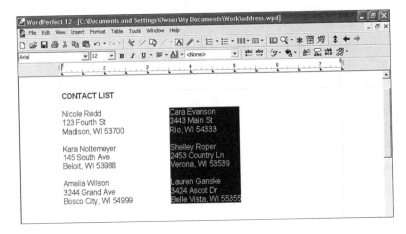

Before formatting the new single column (for example, into newspaper-style columns), you might have to remove extra spaces or tabs following the lines from the original first column.

**Figure 2.21**
Cutting and pasting a rectangular selection enables you to move columns of text.

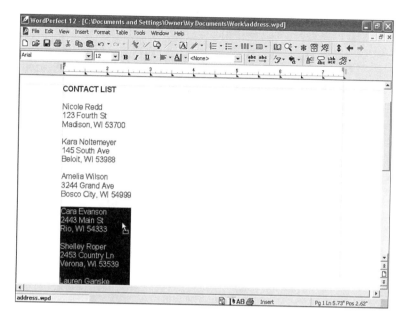

# UNDERSTANDING THE BASICS OF FORMATTING

**I**n this chapter

*by Laura Acklen*

# CHOOSING THE RIGHT FONT

You've tirelessly researched the facts and figures. You've chewed your nails down to the quick trying to think of *just the right* words. You're almost done, when your co-worker stops by and expresses concern that your document won't get the attention it deserves if it isn't easy to read. "Wonderful," you think. You have three seconds to finish this document and *now* you have to worry about making it easy to read!

What can you do? Choose attractive fonts to generate interest in your subject. Make the titles and headings larger than the body text so that they really stand out. It only takes a few minutes, and the results are well worth your effort.

**CAUTION**

As you format your document, remember to always, always, always position the insertion point first. As a general rule, your changes take effect at the insertion point, which may or may not be where you want them. If you forget and get some unexpected results, you've got a safety net: You can click the Undo button to reverse the last action (or continue clicking to reverse the last several actions).

**NOTE**

Corel offers 1,000 fonts in WordPerfect 11 and 600 in WordPerfect 12—plenty to satisfy even the most discriminating fontmeisters. Of these, 24 are the character set fonts, which contain the symbols and foreign language alphabets. During a typical installation, a default set of fonts is installed. The rest can be installed separately, using either the Install Wizard or the options in the Fonts folder. To use the Fonts folder, choose File, Install New Font and follow the prompts.

## SELECTING FONTS

The quickest way to choose a different font is to click the Font Face drop-down arrow on the property bar. A drop-down list of fonts appears, and a large preview window pops up at the top of the document (see Figure 3.1). As you point to a font in the list, the sample text in the preview window morphs into that font. Thanks to Real Time Preview, the text in the document does the same thing. You don't have to play guessing games, trying to figure out how a font will look from a tiny piece of sample text—you can see how a whole page of text will look. When you find the font that you want, click it.

**TIP FROM**

*Laura Acklen*

WordPerfect keeps a list of the six most recently used fonts at the top of the Font Face drop-down list.

**Figure 3.1**
As you hover over fonts in the drop-down list, the sample text in the preview window and the text in the document morph into that font.

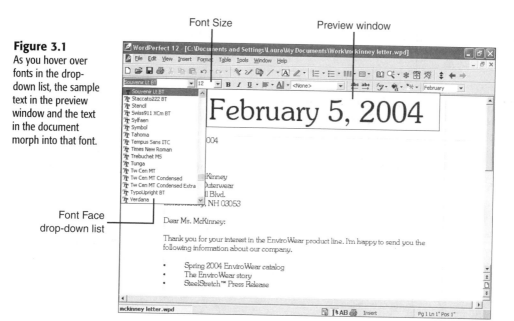

Font Size

Preview window

Font Face
drop-down list

**NOTE**

The sample text you see in the preview window varies depending on where the insertion point is. If the insertion point is at the top of the document, a small snippet of text from the beginning of the document is shown. If the insertion point is in a word, that word is used. If the insertion point is in blank space, four letters (A, B, Y, Z) are used. Finally, if you've selected text, a short section of that text appears.

**CAUTION**

When you're changing the font (or font size) for existing text, such as a title or heading, select it first. Otherwise, the new font (or size) takes effect at the insertion point and stays in effect for the rest of the document (unless, of course, you change the font or size again later).

## SELECTING FONT SIZES

Choosing a different font size works essentially the same way as choosing a different font. Click the Font Size drop-down arrow on the property bar to open a drop-down list of sizes. If you click the scroll arrows, you'll see that the list has sizes ranging from 6 points to 72 points. A *point* is a unit of measurement used to describe the size of a font. A 72-point character is 1" tall; a 36-point character is 1/2" tall, and so forth.

A preview window with sample text opens next to the list. As you move the mouse down through the list, the sample text and the document text expand and contract to show the new size.

**TIP FROM**

*Laura Acklen*

> If you want to use a font size that isn't in the list, click the Font Size box (to select the current size) and then type the size you want.

When you've decided which font you want to use for the body text, set that as the default font for the document. Likewise, if you select a font that you want to use for most, if not all, your documents, set that as the default for all *new* documents. Choose Format, Font to open the Font Properties dialog box. Make your selections, and then choose Settings. Choose Set Face and Point Size As Default for This Document or Set Face and Point Size As Default for All Documents.

**TIP FROM**

*Laura Acklen*

> Have you ever been stuck making last-minute changes to a document on a machine that didn't have the same fonts installed? What was once a logistical nightmare is now completely painless, thanks to font-embedding technology. You can save fonts with a document so they go where the document goes. When you save a file, choose Embed Fonts using TrueDoc™ in the Save File dialog box. WordPerfect compresses the fonts and saves them with the file.

**TIP FROM**

*Laura Acklen*

> Ever wish you had a "font catalog" that you could flip through? Call me old-fashioned, but I'll take a printout over an onscreen sample *any day*. WordPerfect includes a nifty macro that prints out a sample of the fonts on your system. Choose Tools, Macro, Play, and then double-click the Allfonts icon. Bear in mind that if you have hundreds of fonts on your system (and who doesn't) it will take a while to build the document. It will also take a while to print and may overload your printer, depending on how much printer memory you have. If you are unable to print the entire font document, try breaking it up in to several pieces.

→ To find a list of all the macros that ship with WordPerfect, along with the steps to create your own macros, **see** "Running the Shipping Macros," **p. 818**

## SELECTING RECENTLY USED FONTS BY USING QUICKFONTS

Say you're formatting a lengthy report. You're finished experimenting, so you know which fonts you want to use for your headings and key terms. Even with the Font Face and Font Size drop-down lists, reselecting the same fonts and sizes over and over is tedious.

 QuickFonts to the rescue! The last 10 fonts (with sizes and effects) you selected are kept in the QuickFonts list for fast access. Click the QuickFonts button on the property bar (see Figure 3.2), and then click the font you want to reuse. Sorry—no Real Time Preview here.

Click here to open the Font Properties dialog box.

QuickFonts button

**Figure 3.2**
Click the QuickFonts button to select from the 10 most recently used fonts.

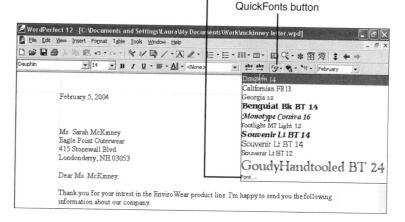

# EMPHASIZING IMPORTANT TEXT

When you speak, you use inflection for emphasis. To get an important point across, you might raise your voice and enunciate each word slowly and clearly. This gets the audience's attention and it gives a point of reference.

You can do the same thing with your printed document. Judicious use of bold, italic, underline, and other effects can guide a reader through the text and draw attention to key points. You have to be careful not to use these elements too much or you risk distracting the reader.

**NOTE**

Don't get carried away with all the different fonts and font effects that you can choose from! A light touch is all you need. Too many fonts, too many effects, or too much color only frustrates the reader.

Try to keep things simple: Don't use more than three or four fonts on a page, don't apply bold *and* italic *and* underline (all at once), don't apply color to long passages of text, don't use a bunch of different font sizes, and choose a font that suits the subject matter.

## USING BOLD, ITALIC, AND UNDERLINE

Before there were gazillions of fonts to play with, the only way you could vary the look of the text was with bold, italic, and underline. These old standbys still have their place. The designers for the *Special Edition Using* books decided to use italic to point out important terms and to emphasize words. Titles and headings are bold so they really stand out. Screen shots illustrate WordPerfect's use of underlines for hotkeys. All of these things make it easier for you to understand the information being presented.

To apply bold, italic, or underline, select the text, and then click the Bold, Italic, or Underline button (or any combination of the three).

*If you can't figure out why your bold, italic, and underline disappear after you change the font, see "Disappearing Act" in the Troubleshooting section at the end of this chapter.*

## ADDING COLOR

I can't remember the last time I printed a document for someone to read. Like many others, I use e-mail most of the time. I just attach the file to an e-mail message. The recipient opens it in his word processing program and reads it onscreen.

This method of reviewing documents gave me the excuse I needed to start adding color to my documents. I began using it to draw attention to titles and headings, and progressed to using it for key terms, statistics, quotes, references, headers and footers, and so on.

I'm not too ashamed to admit that I really get a kick out of it. It's fun! I also like to think that if the finished product gets your attention, you're more likely to *read* it, rather than *skim* it.

**NOTE**

> By the time you read this chapter, no fewer than six people have reviewed and edited the electronic text. Proofreaders, tech editors, development editors, and production staff have all added their two cents. We would all go crazy if we didn't have a good method for keeping everyone's comments separate. Our solution? We let everyone use a different color (hopefully one that's easy to read).

To add color to your text, follow these steps:

1. If you've already typed some text to which you want to add color, select the text you want to add color to. Otherwise, position the insertion point where you want to start typing the colored text.

**CAUTION**

> When you finish typing the colored text, you'll have to switch the color back to black. For this reason, it's easier to type the text, select it, and then choose the color.

2. Click the Font Color button on the property bar (see Figure 3.3).
3. Click one of the color boxes to choose one of the standard colors.

Click here to create your own custom colors ⌐

Most recently
chosen colors

**Figure 3.3**
Clicking the Font
Color button on the
property bar is the
fastest way to open
the color palette. This
palette is also available in the Font
Properties dialog box.

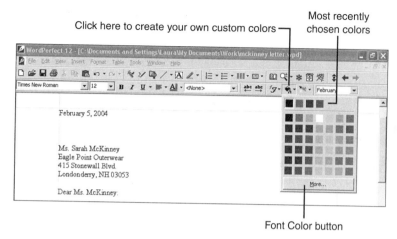

Font Color button

**TIP FROM**

So, 42 colors aren't enough for you? When you've got to have just the right shade of blue/green (and you have a few minutes to play), choose More from the color palette to open the Select Color dialog box. Click anywhere on the color wheel to move the little selection box and display the color you've created in the New Color section. Now, click and drag the selection box on the vertical luminosity bar to the desired color intensity. You can then make minor adjustments by tweaking the numbers in the Color Values section.

**TIP FROM**

If you use the same colors over and over, you'll love this! WordPerfect places the last seven colors you've selected on the top row of the palette. I really appreciate this with the custom colors because I don't have to reselect them each time.

→ To learn how to use the highlighter to accentuate sections of text, **see** "Using the Highlight Tool," **p. 544.**

## USING OTHER FONT EFFECTS

Bold, italic, underline, and color all have buttons on the property bar, so they are the easiest font effects to add. The other effects, also called *attributes*, are found in the Font Properties dialog box. First, position the insertion point where you want the effects to start (or select some existing text). Choose Format, Font or press F9 to open the Font Properties dialog box (see Figure 3.4).

Choose color here

Choose attributes here

Choose a font size here

**Figure 3.4**

You can use the Font Properties dialog box if you need to set multiple font options or if you want to preview your changes first.

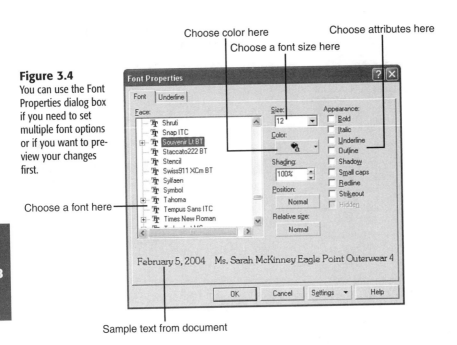

Choose a font here

Sample text from document

The font attributes are listed in the Appearance section. As you select attributes, the sample text in the lower-left corner shows you how the attributes will look when applied to the text. The Real Time Preview feature pops up again here—WordPerfect pulls in a short section of text from your document and uses it as the sample text. (If you're working in a blank document, the sample text is the name of the currently selected font.) Click OK when you're done choosing effects.

You should use the Font Properties dialog box any time you need to set more than a couple of font options at once. For example, if you need to choose a different font and size, and apply bold and italic, it's faster to do it all at once in the Font Properties dialog box than to choose each one separately from the property bar.

**NOTE**

If you skipped WordPerfect 9 and 10, you haven't seen Real Time Preview yet. How many times have you changed a format only to discover that it wasn't exactly what you wanted? You might reselect three or four times before finding just the right one. No more—now you can preview a formatting change before you ever apply it to the text! Real Time Preview works on borders, columns, color fills, fonts, font attributes, frames, justification, outlines, and zoom. In many cases, the change is reflected in the text in the document window. In other situations, the preview text in the dialog box is a portion of text from your document.

**TIP FROM**

If you use font attributes a lot, consider adding buttons for them to the toolbar. Or, create a new toolbar and add *all* your favorite buttons to it. Choose Tools, Settings, Customize. You can add to an existing toolbar, or you can create a new toolbar. To add a button to an existing toolbar, select the toolbar, and then choose Edit. Open the Feature Categories drop-down list and choose Format. Select the feature in the list, and then choose Add Button. When you are finished adding buttons, click OK to save your changes. To create a new toolbar, choose Create, type a name for the toolbar, and then click OK. Add buttons as previously described.

*If you received an error message during setup saying that you had too many fonts selected, see "Too Many Fonts" in the Troubleshooting section at the end of this chapter.*

*If you're selecting options in the Appearance section of the Font Properties dialog box and the sample text isn't changing to reflect your changes, see "Disappearing Act" in the Troubleshooting section at the end of this chapter.*

# CHANGING MARGINS BY USING GUIDELINES

Believe it or not, you can make your document easier to read by adjusting the margins. A wider margin creates more whitespace around the text and limits the number of words on a line. The shorter the line, the less likely the reader is to lose her place.

On the other hand, if you're trying to keep the number of pages down, you might want to make the margins smaller so you can fit more on a page. For example, if you plan to use headers and footers, you might want to cut the top and bottom margins down to 1/2 inch. By default, the margins are set to 1 inch on all sides (see Table 1.1 on pages 20-21).

To adjust the margins, position the mouse pointer over a guideline and wait until the pointer changes into a double-arrow. Click and drag the guideline. As you click and drag, you'll see a dotted guideline and a bubble. The dotted guideline shows you where the new margin will be, and the bubble tells you what the new margin will be (in inches) when you release the mouse button (see Figure 3.5).

**CAUTION**

If you don't see the guidelines (as shown in Figure 3.5), someone might have turned them off on your system. Choose View, Guidelines, place a check mark next to Margins, and then choose OK.

*If you accidentally drag a margin guideline and end up with wacky margins, see "Bad Dragging" in the Troubleshooting section at the end of this chapter.*

**NOTE**

If you're not a big fan of clicking and dragging, or if you just want to be more precise, you can make your changes in the Margins dialog box. Choose Format, Margins, and then either type the measurements in the text boxes or click the spinner arrows to bump the value up or down—in this case, 0.1 inch at a time.

**Figure 3.5**
Clicking and dragging guidelines is the fastest way to adjust the margins. The dotted guideline and bubble show you what the new margins will be when you release the mouse button.

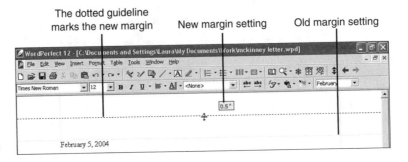

The dotted guideline marks the new margin

New margin setting

Old margin setting

**CAUTION**

Many printers (such as inkjet and laser printers) aren't capable of printing to the edge of the paper. This area is called the *unprintable zone*. The size of this zone varies from printer to printer, so the information is kept in the printer's setup. What does this mean? If you try to set a margin within the unprintable zone, WordPerfect automatically adjusts it to the printer's minimum margin setting.

# JUSTIFYING TEXT

*Justification* controls how text flows between the left and right margins. The most obvious example of this is centering text on a line. WordPerfect does the math, and you get the same amount of space on the left and right sides. No matter what you do to the left and right margins, that text stays centered.

The default setting in WordPerfect is left justification, which creates a smooth left margin and a ragged right margin. The result is an open, informal appearance that is accessible and easy to read. For that reason, this book has been formatted with left justification.

There are four other justification options that you might be interested in, especially if you work with columns, newsletters, and formal documents (see Figure 3.6).

Justification button

**Figure 3.6**
This sample document illustrates the different justification settings.

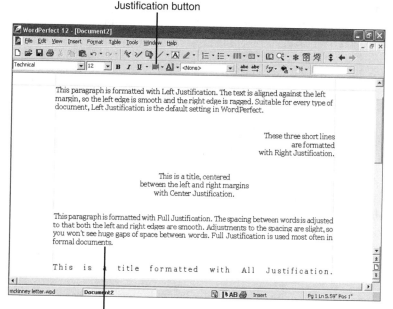

The last line isn't justified

3

WordPerfect offers the following justification options:

- **Left**—Text is aligned against the left margin so the left margin is smooth and the right is ragged. It's suitable for almost every type of document, especially those with long passages of text. To apply left justification, choose Format, Justification, Left, or press Ctrl+L.

- **Right**—Text is aligned against the right margin so the right side is smooth and the left is ragged. The unique placement draws attention, but because it's hard to read, you might not want to use it on more than three or four lines. To apply right justification, choose Format, Justification, Right, or press Ctrl+R.

- **Center**—Text is centered between the left and right margins. It's common practice to center titles and headings to differentiate them from the rest of the text. To apply center justification, choose Format, Justification, Center, or press Ctrl+E.

- **Full**—Text is aligned against the left and right margins, so both edges are smooth. How? WordPerfect makes slight adjustments to the spacing between words so that each line extends from the left to the right margin. Full justification gives documents a more formal and organized appearance. To apply full justification, choose Format, Justification, Full, or press Ctrl+J.

- **All**—This type of justification stretches lines of text between the left and right margins, regardless of their length. Whereas full justification adjusts the spacing between words, all justification adjusts the spacing between letters as well. This setting is used for letterhead, informal titles and headings, and special effects. To apply all justification, choose Format, Justification, All.

Before you choose which type of justification you want to use in your document, decide where you want the justification to take effect, and then move the insertion point there. This may be at the top of the document, the top of a column, or the beginning of a paragraph. If you want to apply justification to a section of text, such as a multiline title, select the text first.

 Instead of using the menus, you can click the Justification button on the property bar, and then choose the justification setting from the pop-up list. This method offers an advantage over the others in that you get a Real Time Preview of each justification setting when you hover over it.

**CAUTION**

With justification set to full, the last line in a paragraph won't be justified if it doesn't extend to the right margin (or pretty close to it). Refer to Figure 3.6 for an example of how this looks.

**TIP FROM**

*Laura Acklen*

Have you noticed that articles in the newspaper are formatted into columns with smooth left and right margins? When the column edges are well-defined, side-by-side columns don't look cluttered or disorganized. You can achieve the same result by setting justification to full. This can be done before or after you type the text into columns.

→ To learn how to define columns, **see** "Setting Up Columns," **p. 250.**

# USING QUICKBULLETS

I use lists in all sorts of documents. They're easier to follow than long, drawn-out explanations, so readers really appreciate them. WordPerfect's QuickBullets feature makes it easy for you to create a bulleted list on-the-fly. Simply type a symbol, and then press Tab—WordPerfect converts the symbol to a bullet. Table 3.1 lists the QuickBullets symbols.

Inserting QuickBullets is easy when you use the following steps:

1. Choose the Tools menu and select QuickCorrect, Format-As-You-Go. If necessary, place a check mark next to the QuickBullets option.
2. Type one of the QuickBullets symbols, and then press Tab. As soon as you press Tab, WordPerfect converts the symbol to a bullet.

**NOTE**

If you type more than one line of text next to the bullet, you'll notice that the text automatically wraps under the text, not under the bullet. WordPerfect actually converts the tab to an indent so the list has the proper format.

3. Type the text, and then press Enter. Notice that you automatically get another bullet when you press Enter (see Figure 3.7).

4. When you are finished with the list, press Enter and then backspace to delete the bullet.

**Figure 3.7**
You can use the QuickBullets feature to create bulleted lists with just one or two keystrokes.

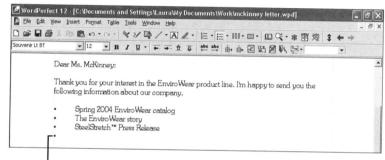

A new bullet is inserted when you press Enter

**TIP FROM**

If for some reason you don't like the QuickBullets feature, you can easily turn it off. Choose the Tools menu and select QuickCorrect, Format-As-You-Go. Deselect (that is, remove the check mark from) the QuickBullets option.

Table 3.1 lists the six bullet symbols you can create with symbols on the keyboard. You can also refer to the help topic on this for a quick reminder.

**TABLE 3.1   QUICKBULLET SYMBOLS**

| Press This | To Get This |
|---|---|
| + then Tab | ☆ |
| ^ then Tab | ◊ |
| o or * then Tab | • |
| O then Tab | ● |
| > then Tab | → |
| — then Tab | — |

→ To learn how to indent text, **see** "Indenting Text," **p. 209.**

→ To learn how to insert bullets with the Bullets and Numbers dialog box, **see** "Working with Bulleted or Numbered Lists," **p. 335.**

# INSERTING SPECIAL CHARACTERS

Special characters, or symbols, are one of the many areas where WordPerfect distinguishes itself from the competition. WordPerfect has more than 1,500 special characters, including entire foreign language alphabets, that you can insert anywhere in your document.

**NOTE**

> Not all special characters are available in every font. Depending on the font you have selected, you may see empty boxes instead of special characters, which means that those characters aren't available. On the other hand, certain fonts, such as Wingdings, are composed entirely of special characters.

To insert special characters, follow these steps:

1. Click in the document where you want the special character to appear.

2. Press Ctrl+W or choose Insert, Symbols to open the Symbols dialog box (see Figure 3.8). You might need to scroll down to see the symbol you want.

Click here to switch to another set of special characters

**Figure 3.8**
Through the Symbols dialog box, you can insert more than 1,500 symbols and characters from foreign language alphabets.

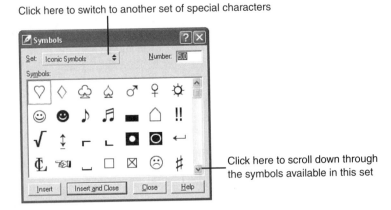

Click here to scroll down through the symbols available in this set

3. If you don't see the character you need, click the Set button, and then select a different character set from the list.

4. Select the symbol, and then choose Insert, or double-click a symbol in the list to insert it. The dialog box stays open to make it easier for you to insert other symbols. (If you want to move it, click and drag the title bar.) Choose Close when you are finished. If you only need to insert one symbol, choose Insert and Close instead.

*If you see empty or black boxes instead of the special characters in the Symbols dialog box, see "Symbols Display As Empty or Black Boxes" in the Troubleshooting section at the end of this chapter.*

**TIP FROM**

*Laura Acklen*

If you insert the same symbols over and over, you'll appreciate this shortcut. The next time you select a symbol, look for the two numbers in the Number text box. Then, when you need to insert that character again, press Ctrl+W, type the two numbers (separated by a space or a comma), and then press Enter. For example, to insert the heart symbol shown in Figure 3.8, press Ctrl+W, type **5,0**; then, press Enter.

The QuickCorrect feature is designed to automatically correct common spelling errors and typos while you type. There are five common symbols that you can insert with QuickCorrect (see Table 3.2).

**TABLE 3.2    CREATING SYMBOLS WITH QUICKCORRECT**

| To Get This | Type This |
| --- | --- |
| Copyright symbol | (c) |
| Registered trademark symbol | (r) |
| $\frac{1}{2}$ | 1/2 |
| en dash (–) | -- or n- |
| em dash (—) | --- or m- |

If you don't want QuickCorrect making these automatic replacements, you can take these symbols out of the list. Choose Tools, QuickCorrect. Select the symbol you want to remove, and then choose Delete Entry.

# TROUBLESHOOTING

### TOO MANY FONTS

*During a custom installation, I got the error message "Too Many Fonts Selected" after I marked the fonts I wanted to install. The installation continued, but now I'm not sure which fonts were installed.*

All the fonts you marked were copied to your hard drive, but not all of them were registered. There is a limit to the number of fonts that can be registered in the Windows Registry. When you exceed this limit, all sorts of problems can crop up—from fonts not displaying correctly to buttons showing symbols instead of text. I've seen conflicting reports on what the actual limitation is, but most technicians recommend that you keep a maximum of 300 fonts registered at one time. This number includes any fonts that you already had on your system (such as Windows fonts and fonts installed with other applications). I would suggest that you run a typical installation so that the character set fonts and default fonts are safely installed before you attempt to install additional fonts.

To see the fonts that are currently registered on your system, open the Fonts folder by choosing Start, Control Panel, Fonts. To make room for the WordPerfect fonts, select and delete the fonts that you don't use. Then choose File, Install New Font to add fonts that were copied to the hard drive but not registered during setup.

### BAD DRAGGING

*I accidentally grabbed a margin guideline with the mouse and before I knew what was happening, half my page had new margins. How do I fix this?*

It's really faster to undo the change than to try to drag the guideline back to its original position. Either click the Undo button, choose Edit, Undo, or press Ctrl+Z.

If you save the document before trying Undo, you won't be able to undo the margin change because by default, the Undo information isn't saved. You can still reverse the margin change though. Simply position the insertion point where the margin change begins, turn on Reveal Codes and delete the margin code. To delete the code, click and drag it out of the Reveal Codes window.

### DISAPPEARING ACT

*After spending 15 minutes selecting text and applying italics, I decided to change the font. Now all the text I italicized is back to normal. How do I restore the italics I originally had?*

Sometimes changing the font causes your bold, italic, underline, or other font effects to disappear. Why? Because the new font doesn't support those effects. This doesn't happen very often—it occurs mostly with the more decorative fonts—but when it does, it's disconcerting. You can either switch to another font and see whether it supports them, or you can just forget about the effects.

### SYMBOLS DISPLAY AS EMPTY OR BLACK BOXES

*When I open the Symbols dialog box, I don't see the special characters that are shown in Figure 3.8. I see black boxes instead. How can I get the special characters back?*

Sometimes the registry entries for the WP character font files get corrupted and you have to re-create them. To force Windows to rewrite the entries, you'll need to delete the files (send them to the Recycle Bin), and then restore them. Click Start, Control Panel, Fonts. In the Fonts folder, select all the fonts that begin with WP (everything between WP Arabic Sihafa and WP TypographicSymbols). Delete the files. Restart the computer. Double-click the Recycle Bin icon, and then select all the WP fonts. Choose File, Restore.

If the characters are still displayed as black boxes, you might need to delete and reinstall the fonts. Follow the steps given in the previous paragraph to delete the fonts. Run the

WordPerfect Office setup program to install the fonts again. You'll have to restart the computer after you update the install. The characters should then display correctly in WordPerfect.

# PROJECT

It's easy to become overwhelmed by all the formatting choices you have with WordPerfect. You can spice up a plain vanilla document with interesting fonts and font effects. You might even find yourself getting carried away with all the colors you can use.

Unfortunately, there are few hard-and-fast rules for formatting documents. Other than the unspecific rule of thumb to try to avoid too many fonts on a page, you'll be hard pressed to find a good set of guidelines.

Because, as they say, "a picture is worth a thousand words," here are two examples for you. Figure 3.9 illustrates a newsletter where some common mistakes were made:

- There are too many font changes on the page.
- The font for the date in the masthead is difficult to read.
- Bold, italic, and underline are not applied well.
- The two title fonts are dissimilar.
- A sans-serif font is used for the body text, and a serif font is used for the headings. It's harder on your eyes to read long passages of text in a san serif font.
- This list is difficult to read both because the first line is indented and because of the font used.
- The margins of the newsletter text leave too much white space on each side.

Figure 3.10 shows the same newsletter with some small, vital corrections:

- The same font is used for both titles and the newsletter text.
- The masthead font is easy to read and blends well with the title text.
- A wider font was chosen so the title stretches completely across the line.
- A serif font is used for the body text whereas a sans serif font was chosen for the headings.
- The margins for the body text line up with the newsletter masthead.
- Bold and italic are applied to the headings for subtle emphasis.

This font is difficult to read    These two fonts don't have much in common

**Figure 3.9**
This newsletter illustrates common mistakes that are made when applying fonts, font effects, and margin formatting.

Underline isn't a very attractive font effect

Serif font

Sans-serif font

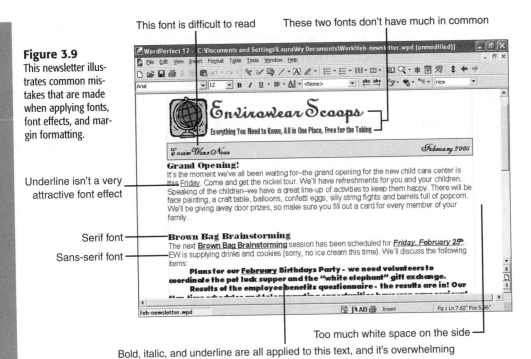

Too much white space on the side

Bold, italic, and underline are all applied to this text, and it's overwhelming

**Figure 3.10**
This newsletter illustrates ways to correct the problems shown in Figure 3.9.

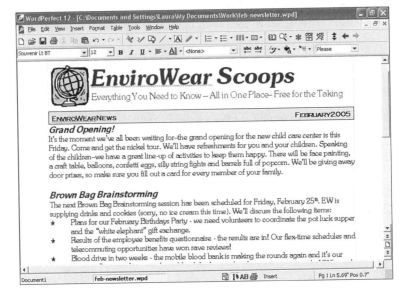

# 4

# MANAGING YOUR FILES AND FOLDERS

**I**n this chapter

*by Laura Acklen*

# ORGANIZING FILES AND FOLDERS

One of the most valuable skills you can learn is how to properly organize your files. Our increasing dependence on electronic copies of files has made it a matter of survival—you must be able to locate important information quickly.

Creating an electronic filing system is very similar to creating a system with manila folders, hanging folders, and filing cabinets. You decide how you want to group files (such as by client, project, department, or case number), and then you create a folder for those files. Existing files can be copied into the folder and new files can be saved there.

Every bit of this can be done within WordPerfect, so you don't even have to start My Computer or Explorer to get the job done. In every situation where you need to choose a file, you can do it in a file management dialog box. The figures in this chapter show the Open File dialog box, but no matter which file management dialog box you're in (it could be Save File, Insert File, Insert Image, Play Macro, or any other), you have the same capabilities.

## SELECTING FILES TO WORK WITH

You probably already know how to select a file—you just click it. And you might know how to select a group of files with the Ctrl and Shift keys. What you might not know is that you can rearrange the list to make it easier to group files together.

Here are two methods for selecting multiple files:

- To select a group of files that are listed one right after the other, click the first file, hold down the Shift key, and then click the last file. Everything between the first click and the second click is selected (see Figure 4.1).

**Figure 4.1**
By using the Shift key, you can select a list of files in just two clicks.

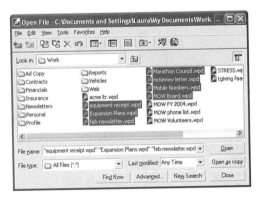

- To select a group of files that are scattered throughout the list, click the first file, hold down the Ctrl key, and then click the other files, one at a time. While you're selecting, you can scroll up or down through the list, but you can't switch to another folder.

TIP FROM

*Laura Acklen*

> If you accidentally select the wrong files, you don't have to start over. Just hold down the Ctrl key and click the offending files.

 *If you're having a hard time selecting multiple files, see "Can't Select Multiple Files" in the Troubleshooting section at the end of this chapter.*

The following are methods for grouping files:

- To group files with similar names, type all or part of the name in the File Name text box. For example, to display only files that begin with "west", type **west***, and then press Enter. The resulting list of files contains only files that begin with "west" (regardless of what follows "west" in the filename). The asterisk is a *wildcard*, like a one-eyed jack in poker: You can use it to represent one or more characters in a filename.

- To arrange files differently, choose View, Arrange Icons By. Choose Name to arrange files in alphabetical order. Choose Type to arrange files by type (such as documents, presentations, and spreadsheets). Choose Size to arrange files from smallest to largest. Choose Modified to arrange files from the most recently edited to the least recently edited. To return to the default arrangement, choose Name.

-  To view additional file details, choose View, Details or click the Views button and then click Details (see Figure 4.2). In the Details view, you can click a column heading to sort the list by that item. Click the column heading once to sort in ascending order; click again to sort in descending order.

- To view a particular type of file, click the File Type drop-down list arrow and select a file type from the list. Choose All Files (*.*) to reset the file list.

- To view files that were modified within a specific time frame, click the Last Modified drop-down list arrow and select a time frame from the list.

CAUTION

> Any changes you make in the Details view are "sticky," which means they remain in effect even after you switch to another view. For example, if you sort the files by date, and then switch back to List view, the files remain grouped by date, even though you can't see the file dates in the list.

TIP FROM

*Laura Acklen*

> After you've grouped your files, you can print a list for future reference (or just because you want to be able to put a check mark next to each one when you're finished with it). Choose File, Print File List, select the options you want in the Print File List dialog box, and then click OK. If you've selected files and you want to print a list of only those files, make sure you select the Print List of Selected Entries option in the Listing Options section.

4

Select a specific View option

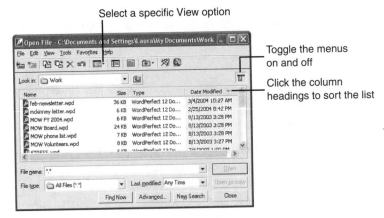

Toggle the menus on and off

Click the column headings to sort the list

**Figure 4.2**
Grouping files makes it easy to sort by a specific criterion.

## ADDING ITEMS TO THE FAVORITES FOLDER

When I first started surfing the Net, it didn't take long before I wanted to bookmark my favorite sites so I didn't have to remember, and type in, the exact addresses. You can do the same thing with folders—you can create a list of frequently used files and folders so you don't have to navigate through the labyrinth of drives and folders every time you want to grab a file.

Windows has a special place to put your favorite stuff—it's called the Favorites folder. It's a Windows feature, so it's not specific to WordPerfect. This is important because you're likely to see items in the Favorites folder that have been added in other applications (such as your Internet browser).

You can add items to the Favorites folder from any file management dialog box. Here are the steps for adding folders, drives, and files:

- To add a drive, open it in the list, and then choose Favorites, Add, Add Favorite Folder. Alternatively, click the Favorites button on the toolbar and choose Add Favorites Folder. A shortcut to the drive is added to the Favorites folder.

- To add a folder, open it in the file list. Choose Favorites, Add, Add Favorite Folder. Alternatively, click the Favorites button on the toolbar and choose Add Favorites Folder. WordPerfect displays a message stating that *.* is the current filter, and asks if you want to save the Favorite with that filter. Choose Yes. A shortcut to the folder is added to the Favorites folder.

**CAUTION**

In the previous two items, the steps won't work if you *select* the drive or folder, rather than *open* it. Just make sure you read the items in the Add menu carefully before you select one.

■ To add a file, select it in the list, and then choose Favorites, Add, Add Favorite Item. Alternatively, click the Favorites button on the toolbar and choose Add Favorites Item. A shortcut to the file is added to the Favorites folder.

After you've added a bunch of items to the Favorites folder and you're ready to use them, click the Favorites button and choose Go To Favorites, or choose Favorites, Go To/From Favorites. The file list displays the contents of the Favorites folder (see Figure 4.3).

**Figure 4.3**
The Favorites folder contains shortcuts to frequently used items such as drives, folders, and files, as well as items that have been added in other Windows applications.

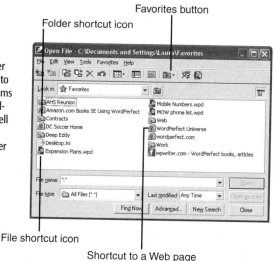

There are three different types of icons: folders, shortcuts to folders, and shortcuts to files. You double-click a folder shortcut to switch to that folder and double-click a file shortcut to open that file. If Windows doesn't know which application to use to open the file, it prompts you to pick one (this shouldn't be a problem with WordPerfect documents). In the case of shortcuts to Web documents, Internet Explorer is launched and the Web page is opened inside the file management window.

 *If you can't get one of your shortcuts to work, see "My Shortcut Stopped Working" in the Troubleshooting section at the end of this chapter.*

After a while, you'll have quite a collection of shortcuts in the Favorites folder, and finding the one you want will take a little longer. At that point, you should create some folders for related shortcuts. You might already be familiar with this concept if you've been keeping URLs for your favorite Web sites organized into folders in your Web browser's Favorites or bookmarks list. I have a folder for financial documents, one for shopping, one for kid stuff, and so on.

You can create folders and move shortcuts by using the same techniques that are described in the next section, so read on for more information.

# MANAGING FILES AND FOLDERS

Now that you can select and group files, you're ready to roll up your sleeves and get some things done. Most of the commands you'll need are on the File menu and the QuickMenu. To open a QuickMenu, right-click a file or folder (see Figure 4.4).

**Figure 4.4**
The file QuickMenu has all the commands you need to effectively manage your files from within WordPerfect.

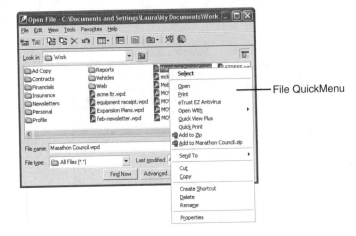

File QuickMenu

**NOTE**

Depending on what you have selected, the options on a QuickMenu (and the File menu) change. For example, the file QuickMenu has Rename and Print; the folder QuickMenu has Explore and Search. Also, if you've toggled the menu bar off (by clicking the Toggle Menu On/Off button), you can still get to the file commands with the QuickMenu.

## MOVING FILES AND FOLDERS

Occasionally, a file (or folder) gets saved to the wrong folder and you need to move it. You don't want to copy it because then you'll have two copies of the same file (or folder). To move a file (or folder), follow these steps:

1. Right-click the file (or folder) and choose Cut; or select it and then click the Cut button.

2. Switch to the folder where you want to store the file (or folder).

3. Right-click anywhere in the file list, and then choose Paste; or, just click the Paste button.

TIP FROM

Depending on your operating system, you might have a couple of extra commands on your File or Edit menu. Move to Folder is used to move files and folders (a file must be selected for this item to appear). Rather than switch to the destination folder, you can choose it from the Select Destination Folder for Move dialog box. This way, you don't have to navigate back to the original folder after you've pasted the file (or folder). While we're on the subject, there is a Copy to Folder command that you can use as well–it works the same way as the Move to Folder command. These two commands are not available in Windows 98. They are both available in Windows 2000 on the File menu, and in Windows XP/NT/ME on the Edit menu.

 *If you can't find a file that you just moved, see "Misplaced Files" in the Troubleshooting section at the end of this chapter.*

## COPYING FILES AND FOLDERS

Network administrators implement security measures so that your co-workers can't get into your folders and accidentally delete or modify your files. If you want to share your files, you can usually copy them to someone else's folder or to a shared area on the network. Because you do the copying, you maintain control over who has access to your files.

→ To learn more about sharing documents, **see** Chapter 17, "Collaborating on Documents."

To copy a file (or folder), follow these steps:

 1. Right-click the file (or folder) and then choose Copy. Or, you can select the file (or folder) and click the Copy button.

2. Switch to the folder where you want to store the file (or folder).

 3. Right-click anywhere in the file list, and then choose Paste; or, click the Paste button.

**CAUTION**

If you select a second file, a group of files, or a folder, and choose Cut or Copy before you paste, you'll lose the information for that item. You have to go back to the folder where the original items were located and cut or copy the file(s) again.

**TIP FROM**

The best way to ensure the integrity and accuracy of your documents is to keep a copy of every file you share. If a person using one of your documents makes any changes, either accidentally or on purpose, you're protected because you still have a clean copy.

**4**

## RENAMING FILES AND FOLDERS

When you create a folder or save a file, you try to give it a descriptive name. Later, however, that name might no longer seem appropriate. To rename a file or folder, select it and then choose File, Rename. You can also right-click the file or folder, and then choose Rename. An editing box appears around the file (or folder) name, and the name is selected (see Figure 4.5). Type the new name and then press Enter.

**Figure 4.5**
You can always change a file or folder name later.

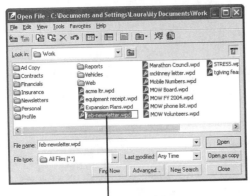

An editing box appears around the name

There is one other method for renaming files and folders that doesn't require selecting from a menu. Click the filename or folder name (not the icon), pause, and then click the name again. The editing box should appear. Type the new name and then press Enter.

CAUTION

You can't rename a file that is currently open, either in your application or in someone else's (if you're working on a networked computer).

*If you're clicking a file twice and you can't get the editing box to appear, see "Can't Click Twice to Rename" in the Troubleshooting section at the end of the chapter.*

## DELETING FILES AND FOLDERS

Periodic housekeeping is an important part of managing your files. One method for keeping your drives uncluttered is to archive folders and files that you no longer use. You might decide to move these onto floppy disks, zip disks, or CDs. The important thing is that you aren't getting rid of them permanently—if the need arises, you can always get to the archive copy.

If you decide that you'll never, ever, ever need a file or folder again, you can delete it from the drive. Select the file(s) or folder(s) in the list and either press the Delete key or click the Delete button. Alternatively, you can right-click the file or folder and then choose Delete from the QuickMenu. If necessary, choose Yes to confirm the deletion.

CAUTION

Be extremely careful about removing folders. Deleting a folder removes all the subfolders and files within that folder.

When you delete files and folders from a local drive, Windows moves them to the Recycle Bin (see Figure 4.6). (Files deleted from a floppy disk or removable drive aren't moved to the Recycle Bin.) The good news is that you can get an accidentally deleted file or folder back. To restore a file or folder, open the Recycle Bin, select the file(s) or folder(s) you didn't really mean to throw away, and choose File, Restore.

The bad news about the Recycle Bin is that when you delete a file or folder and it goes to the Recycle Bin, you haven't actually freed up any disk space. To physically remove deleted files and folders, open the Recycle Bin and choose File, Empty Recycle Bin. Just make sure you look them over carefully, because after you empty the Recycle Bin, they are gone for good!

**Figure 4.6**
The Recycle Bin is the ultimate safety net. If you accidentally delete files or folders, you can restore them to their original locations from the Recycle Bin.

Click to arrange files
by their original location

Click to sort
files by name

Click to sort files
by date deleted

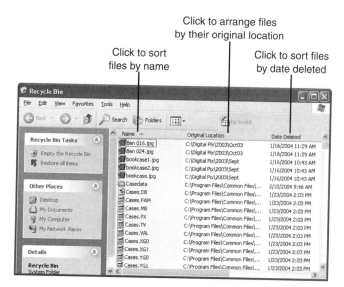

## COPYING FILES TO A FLOPPY DISK/CD/DVD

Electronic mail has revolutionized our capability to share files with one another. Unfortunately, not everyone has an e-mail address, so sometimes you share files the old-fashioned way: You copy the files to a disk and send the disk to the person who needs the file or folder. To copy a file to a floppy disk, CD, or DVD, select it and then choose File, Send To (or right-click it and choose Send To). Choose 3 1/2 Floppy, the CD drive, or the DVD drive in the list.

**TIP FROM**

*Laura Acklen*

I don't need to give you a speech about how important it is to back up your files. Sooner or later, you'll find out for yourself. What I can tell you is this: Copy important files to removable media, such as a floppy disk, CD, DVD or memory stick, at the end of the day. You'll sleep better at night. You can use the Send To command on the QuickMenu to copy files (and folders, if necessary) so it only takes a minute.

## SENDING FILES VIA E-MAIL

If you have e-mail capabilities, you can send a file directly from a file management dialog box. The Mail Recipient command in a file management dialog box works the same way as the Mail Recipient command in the document window. The difference is that in a file management dialog box, you can only send selected text, or a file as an attachment; you can't send the file as a message.

To send a file, right-click it and then choose Send To, Mail Recipient (or select the file and choose File, Send To, Mail Recipient). If the Choose Profile dialog box appears, select a profile from the drop-down list. WordPerfect switches you to your mail program and attaches the document to an e-mail message (see Figure 4.7). You can type your message text, and then address and send the message as you normally would.

**Figure 4.7**
You can send files as attachments to e-mail messages from within a file management dialog box.

Attached file

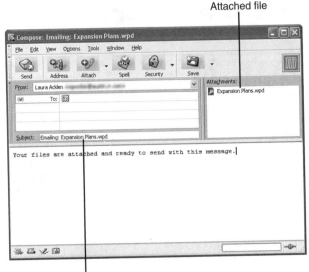

The filename is inserted as the subject

**TIP FROM**

*Laura Acklen*

Downloading large files can really be a pain. Be nice and zip up your files with a file compression utility. One of the most popular is WinZip, a shareware program that you can download from http://www.winzip.com. After you install it, you'll see an option on the QuickMenu to add the file(s) or folder(s) to a zip file. Do you need another good reason to zip up files? Some Internet service providers (ISPs) can't handle more than one file at a time. If you want to send multiple files to someone on one of these services, you can either create a message for each file or you can zip up the files into one file.

→ To learn more about sending files, **see** "Sending Documents via E-Mail," **p. 194.**

## CONNECTING TO NETWORK DRIVES

 If you're connected to a network, you can map to a network drive from within a file management dialog box. Choose Tools, Map Network Drive, or if your menus are turned off, click the Map Drive button. In the Map Network Drive dialog box (see Figure 4.8), select a drive from the Drive list box, and then type the path in the Folder text box. (Don't forget to start the pathname with \ \.)

**Figure 4.8**
You can use the Map Network Drive dialog box to map a drive letter to any drive on the network that you have rights to.

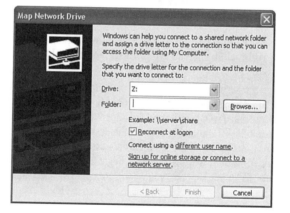

When you're ready to disconnect from this drive, choose Tools, Disconnect Network Drive, or click the Disconnect button. Select the drive, and then click OK.

**CAUTION**

If the drive doesn't map to the path you've typed, you might not have rights to that area of the network. Consult your network administrator.

## CREATING SHORTCUTS ON THE DESKTOP

My Programs menu became so full that I needed another monitor just to see it all. That's when I decided to create some shortcuts to the programs that I use often. Now all I have to do is double-click the shortcut icon to start the application.

There is a shared folder on my network where anyone can copy files for others to use. I open that folder a dozen times a day to retrieve all sorts of files. I can't access it from within an application because I don't always know what type of file I'll be getting—it could be a spreadsheet, a document, or a presentation. So, I created a shortcut to that folder on my desktop. Now all I have to do is open the folder and double-click the file that I need. If all goes well, the originating application loads and opens the file for me.

To create a shortcut to a folder, select the folder, and then choose File, Send To, Desktop (create shortcut). You can also right-click the file and choose Send To, Desktop (create shortcut).

Now let's turn to those files that you open over and over during the day: lists of mobile phone numbers, account numbers for shipping services, timesheets, project tracking tables—any file that you use often. Normally, you would load an application and then open the file. With a shortcut to the file on the desktop, all you have to do is double-click the shortcut icon to load the application and open the file.

To create a shortcut to a file, select the file, and then choose File, Send To, Desktop (create shortcut). You can also right-click the file and choose Send To, Desktop (create shortcut).

**CAUTION**

> When you double-click a file in Explorer or My Computer, Windows loads the application that is associated with that file and then opens the file. The same thing happens when you double-click a shortcut to a file on the desktop. This might seem like magic, but it really boils down to how file extensions are associated with applications in the Windows Registry. For various reasons, Windows might not know which application to load for a particular file. If this happens, you will be prompted to select an application from a list.

When WordPerfect creates shortcuts on the desktop, it uses the name of the file or folder for the shortcut. You can assign a more descriptive name by using the same technique you use for renaming files (discussed in the "Renaming Files and Folders" section earlier in this chapter).

 *If one of your shortcuts has mysteriously stopped working, see "My Shortcut Stopped Working" in the Troubleshooting section at the end of this chapter.*

## VIEWING AND OPENING INTERNET PAGES

You can view Web pages on the Internet, or your company's intranet, from within a file management dialog box. When you find the page you want, you can open it directly into WordPerfect. You must have an Internet browser, such as Netscape Navigator, Microsoft Internet Explorer, or Opera, already installed on your system for this to work.

To view Internet pages, click the Corel Web Site button. An Internet connection is initiated and the Corel Web page is displayed in the list box. Type the URL for the Web site or Web page that you want to view, and then press Enter. The toolbar has some new browser buttons that you can use (see Figure 4.9).

**Figure 4.9**
You can view and open Internet (and intranet) pages from within WordPerfect's file management dialog boxes.

Corel Web Site button

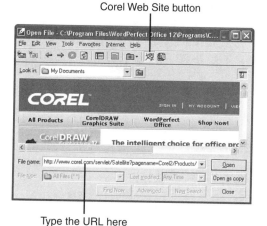

Type the URL here

 You can use the Back, Forward, Stop, and Refresh buttons to navigate through the site. If you find a page that you want to open in WordPerfect, click Open. In the HTML Import dialog box, choose Yes to download and import the images, or No if you just want the text.

 When you're ready to return to the default file management dialog box, click the Corel Web Site button.

**TIP FROM**

If you haven't already maximized the dialog box, you'll definitely want to do it here so you can view the Web page without scrolling back and forth. You can also click and drag a border to resize the dialog box. How? Point to a border and pause—the pointer changes to a double-headed arrow. Click and drag the border; the guideline shows you how large the box will be when you release the mouse button.

# PROTECTING SENSITIVE FILES

With the increasing popularity of flexible work hours and job-sharing, you might have to share your computer with a co-worker. Or, if someone else has rights to your folders on the network, you might want to protect sensitive files.

There are two levels of security in WordPerfect: read-only and password-protected. If you specify a file as read-only, someone else can open the file, but he or she can't save it back under the original name. In other words, the person can't save any changes to the file. The drawback to this approach is that a savvy user could edit the properties for a file and remove the read-only attribute.

Follow these steps to specify a file as read-only:

1. In a file management dialog box, select the file.

2. Choose File, Properties or right-click the file and choose Properties. The Properties dialog box for that file appears (see Figure 4.10).

3. Place a check mark next to Read-only in the Attributes section of the Properties dialog box.

4. Click Apply, and then click OK.

**Figure 4.10**
After you set the read-only attribute, no one (not even you) can save changes to the original file.

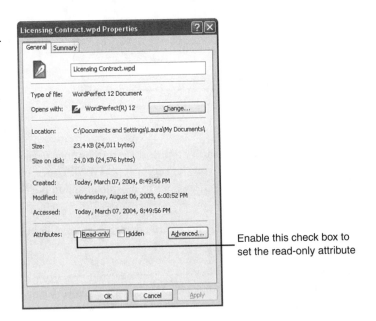

Enable this check box to set the read-only attribute

 The next time you (or anyone else) try to open this file, you'll get a message reminding you that this file is set to read-only (see Figure 4.11). If you attempt to save the file by clicking the Save button (or by using the File, Save command), the Save As dialog box opens, and you are forced to type a new filename before you can save the file.

The second level of security is setting a password for a file. The advantage of this approach is that when you save a file with a password, no one can open it unless he or she knows the password. The disadvantage is that if you forget the password, you can't get to the file. At least that's the way it's supposed to work. There are programs that can crack WordPerfect passwords. Admittedly, some people use these programs to get into documents that they shouldn't see, but realistically speaking, these programs are invaluable to system administrators when employees forget their passwords.

**Figure 4.11**
WordPerfect reminds you with this message that a file has been set to read-only.

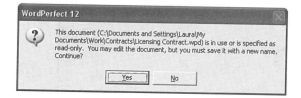

If you can safely assume that the people you are trying to keep away from your sensitive files don't know about those programs, you can use password protection with confidence. Otherwise, save those files on a floppy disk or a CD and lock them up! Follow these steps to password protect a file:

1. With the file open in the document window, choose File, Save As to open the Save As dialog box (see Figure 4.12).

**Figure 4.12**
After you save a document with a password, you must know the password to open the file from then on.

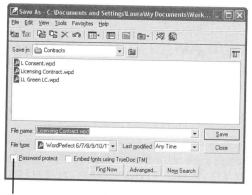

Enable this check box to set a password

2. If necessary, type a name for the file in the File Name text box.
3. Place a check mark in the Password Protect check box.
4. Click Save. The Password Protection dialog box opens (see Figure 4.13).
5. Type the password in the Type Password for Document text box.
6. Retype the password in the Retype Password to Confirm text box.
7. Choose the type of password protection you want to use and then click OK.

**NOTE**

If you opt for Enhanced Password Protection, the password is case-sensitive. In other words, you must type the password in the same case that you used when you assigned it. Original Password Protection is not case-sensitive, so if you think you'll have trouble remembering the case, choose this option instead.

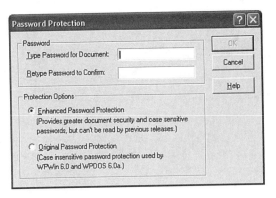

**Figure 4.13**
If you'll be sharing this file with someone who has WordPerfect 6.x, make sure you choose Original Password Protection in the Password Protection dialog box.

If you change your mind and want to "unprotect" a file, you can simply remove the password protection. The steps to remove password protection from a file are very similar. Follow these steps to remove a password:

1. Open the password protected file as you normally would.
2. Choose File, Save As to display the Save As dialog box (refer back to Figure 4.12).
3. Remove the check mark next to Password Protect.
4. Choose Save.
5. When you see the message saying that file already exists, choose Yes to replace it.

**CAUTION**

> I spent some time online researching programs that can crack WordPerfect passwords. I found several Web sites offering password-cracking programs and services, so consider yourself warned. WordPerfect's passwords are not 100% guaranteed to prevent prying eyes.

# SAVING WORDPERFECT FILES IN A DIFFERENT FORMAT

WordPerfect products have always shipped with the most comprehensive and powerful file filters that can be written for other products. WordPerfect 12 takes file compatibility to a whole new level with feature set additions and enhancements geared to creating better matches to comparable Microsoft Word features. For this reason, many businesses are turning to WordPerfect Office 11/12 for a more cost-effective office suite, without worrying about compatibility with their clients.

When you save a file to another application's format, you lose the elements that aren't supported in that application. Thankfully, WordPerfect conversion drivers do an excellent job of translating WordPerfect features into comparable features in other applications.

If someone opens your WordPerfect 11/12 file in a previous version of WordPerfect, document features (in the form of codes) that are not supported in that version won't work, so they are converted to Unknown codes. The codes are preserved so that when you open the document again in WordPerfect 12, everything is still in place.

To save a file in a different format, follow these steps:

1. With the file open in the document window, choose File, Save As. The Save As dialog box appears.

2. Click the File Type drop-down list arrow. A list of available save formats appears (see Figure 4.14).

**Figure 4.14**
When you save a file, you can choose a different file format from the File Type drop-down list.

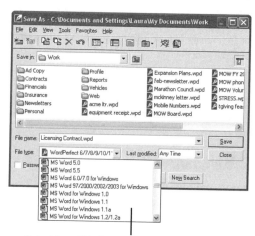

Select from this list to save in a different format

3. Scroll through the list and choose a format.

4. If necessary, type a name (and location) for the document in the File Name text box and then click Save.

**TIP FROM**

*Laura Acklen*

When saving files to another format, it might be helpful to include an abbreviation of the name of that format in the filename, so that you don't confuse that file with the one in WordPerfect format. For example, a file in Word 2003 format might be called `jmani trust-w03`.

**NOTE**

WordPerfect really shines when it comes to importing and exporting files. You can convert files from many different file formats, including word-processor, text, graphics, spreadsheet, and database formats. You can export WordPerfect documents to more than 80 file formats. What does this mean to you? Essentially, it means that it doesn't matter what applications your clients and associates are using—you can open their files in WordPerfect and then save them back to their native format.

*continues*

*continued*

> For more information, choose Help, Help Topics. Click the Index tab and type `import`. Double-click Import File Formats to open the help topic.

**TIP FROM**

*Laura Acklen*

> The file format for WordPerfect documents hasn't changed since version 6.0, so the default save format in WordPerfect 11 is WordPerfect 6/7/8/9/10/11. Likewise, the default save format in WordPerfect 12 is WordPerfect 6/7/8/9/10/11/12. Anyone with WordPerfect version 6 or later can open files created in the more recent versions directly. If you need to send a file to someone with WordPerfect 4.2 or 5.x, choose that format from the File Type list when you save the file.

 *If you're getting an error message when you try to open a file in a different format, see "How Do I Get the Rest of the Conversion Filters?" in the Troubleshooting section at the end of this chapter.*

# USING DOCUMENT SUMMARIES

One of the lesser known, but incredibly powerful, file management features is the *document summary*. Some people don't even know it exists, but those of us who depend on full-text search and retrieval techniques can't live without it. Document summary information can be viewed from the file management dialog boxes, so you can learn a lot about a file without opening it first.

Document summaries go hand-in-hand with QuickFinder because you can narrow a search from the entire document to the document summary. This not only speeds up the process, but it also enables you to search for information that isn't included in the document text, such as an author's name, a client's account number, and so on. The last section discusses searching for files with WordPerfect's QuickFinder.

## FILLING OUT A DOCUMENT SUMMARY

Before you start thinking that you don't have time to fill out a document summary, think of all the time you'll save later, when you need to locate and organize related files. There's no rush—a document summary can be completed whenever you want, as long as you have the document open.

To fill out or edit a document summary, with the document open, choose File, Properties. The Properties dialog box appears (see Figure 4.15). Some of this information might already be filled in for you, such as the creation date, the author, and the typist. WordPerfect grabs the author/typist name from the User Information section of the Environment Settings (which you get to by choosing Tools, Settings, Environment).

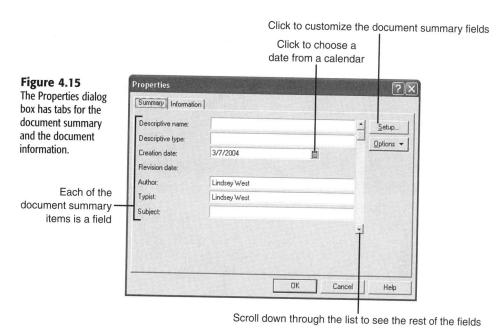

**Figure 4.15**
The Properties dialog box has tabs for the document summary and the document information.

Each of the document summary items is a field

Click to customize the document summary fields

Click to choose a date from a calendar

Scroll down through the list to see the rest of the fields

To enter information in a field, click in the field and type. You can also press Tab to move to the next field or Shift+Tab to move back to the previous field. When you're finished, click OK. Now, save the document so that the summary information you just typed is saved.

## CUSTOMIZING DOCUMENT SUMMARY FIELDS

Document summaries can be customized so that they contain only the fields you will use, which speeds up the time it takes to fill it out. Also, users can quickly locate files by narrowing the search to only those fields in the document summary.

To customize document summary fields, choose File, Properties, Setup. The Document Summary Setup dialog box appears (see Figure 4.16). The left side contains a list of all the document summary fields from which you can choose. The right side shows the fields that are currently displayed.

You can customize the document summary by using the following techniques:

- If you want to remove a field from the Fields to Display list, deselect the field in the Select Fields list. Click the check box to remove the check mark.

- If you want to start from scratch, choose Clear All to remove all the fields from the Fields to Display list.

- Click and drag the fields in the Fields to Display list to arrange them in the proper order. For example, you might want to put the most important fields at the top. This way, you're sure to fill in the important fields because you'll see them first.

■ If you want to use the new document summary as the default, click Use As Default, and then click Yes to confirm that you want to save the new configuration as the default. Otherwise, your changes are reflected in the document summary for this document only.

■ If you change your mind and want to return to the default document summary, choose Cancel to close the Document Summary Setup dialog box without saving your changes.

**Figure 4.16**
You can choose from more than 50 fields to create a document summary that captures the exact information that's relevant to you.

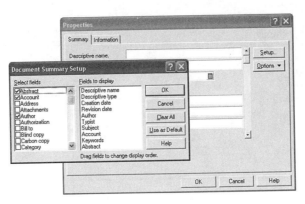

## SETTING DOCUMENT SUMMARY OPTIONS

Now that you've invested the time to get everything set up the way you want it, bear with me for a few more minutes, while I point out some document summary options.

In the Properties dialog box (refer to Figure 4.15), click Options to display a pop-up list with the following options:

■ Print Summary—Choose this option if you want to print the document summary information for future reference. You can also choose Document Summary in the Print dialog box.

■ Delete Summary from Document—Choose this option if you want to delete all the information in the document summary. You can then enter updated information without going to the trouble of erasing the old information first. Keep in mind that if you've customized the document summary, you'll lose those changes. When you delete the summary, WordPerfect replaces it with a blank, default document summary.

■ Extract Information from Document—Choose this option to have WordPerfect pull the first 800 or so characters from your document and place them in the Abstract field (you might have to scroll down the list to see this field). The Extract command can also pull text from the document for the Subject field. The default subject search text is Re: so if the Extract command finds this text in your document, it grabs the information next to Re: and puts it in the Subject field. In Chapter 5, "Using the Writing Tools," you'll learn how to change the default subject search text that Extract looks for.

■ Save Summary As New Document—Choose this option if you want to save the summary information to a file.

## CUSTOMIZING DOCUMENT SUMMARY SETTINGS

WordPerfect has always differentiated itself from other applications by giving you full rein to customize its features. Buried in a dizzying array of customization options is the capability to customize how you use document summaries. The most important one for me is turning on the prompt that reminds me to fill in the document summary when I save a document for the first time.

Choose Tools, Settings, Summary to open the Document Summary Settings dialog box (see Figure 4.17). From here you can do the following:

- Change the default subject search text that the Extract command uses to fill in the Subject field.

- Type a default descriptive type to be used in the Descriptive Type field for all document summaries.

- Turn on a prompt that reminds you to fill in the document summary when you save (or exit) a new document.

- Convert a descriptive filename to a long filename when you open the document.

- Insert the filename in the Descriptive Name field when you save the document.

**Figure 4.17**
You can choose the Create Summary on Save/Exit option if you have trouble remembering to fill in document summaries.

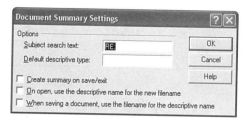

4

**TIP FROM**

*Laura Acklen*

You don't have to change the default subject search text if you use Re: in your documents instead of RE:. The Extract command finds Re:, re:, and RE:.

**NOTE**

Windows 95 introduced long filenames of up to 255 characters, which freed us from the DOS 8-character filename, 3-character extension limitation we were accustomed to. Some of us got around this limitation by creating descriptive filenames in document summaries and setting up our file management dialog boxes so that these filenames displayed as well. If a document created in a previous version of WordPerfect has been saved with a descriptive filename, you can use that name as the new long filename. Furthermore, a macro that ships with WordPerfect Office 11/12, called `longname.wcm`, converts the names of selected documents from the DOS filenames to long filenames.

For more information on playing macros, **see** "Playing Macros," **p. 817.**

# FINDING MISSING FILES BY USING QUICKFINDER

Most new computers ship with at least 40 gigabytes of hard disk space. The number of files you can store on a drive of that size is astounding—it's like trying to get your mind around how much a trillion dollars is. Believe me, you don't want to search through every folder on a 40GB drive "by hand" for a file, and that's assuming you can remember the name of the file you're looking for. No, when it comes to finding files, QuickFinder is the tool you want to reach for.

QuickFinder enables you to search for files based on the filename, content, date modified, or type. You can build a search that is as simple as looking for every file that contains the word "recycle." Or, you can create a complex search designed to display a very narrow selection of documents (which is often the case when searching through legal, scientific, and medical documentation).

For example, with QuickFinder, you can search for all the files on drive E: that contain any form of the word "recycle" and the phrase "#3 plastic" on the same page—but not "#5 plastic" and "glass" in the same paragraph—that were modified within the past week, with 02-1753-4b in the Client field of the document summary.

**TIP FROM**

*Laura Acklen*

> You don't have to be in WordPerfect (or any other application) to use QuickFinder. Choose Start, (All) Programs, WordPerfect Office 11 (or WordPerfect Office 12), Utilities, QuickFinder Searcher.

**NOTE**

> Some Productivity Pack and OEM versions will not include the QuickFinder. Corel pays licensing fees to Novell, Inc. for the QuickFinder technology, so it isn't included in the more economical packages.

## PERFORMING A BASIC SEARCH

I call it a "basic search" but actually you can do quite a bit with the options you have available in the file management dialog boxes. (The next section discusses how to use the options in the Advanced Find dialog box.)

If you've used previous versions of WordPerfect, the new interface is a little disconcerting. Rest assured that the functionality is still here—it has just been reorganized a bit. Before, you had to click the QuickFinder tab or button to switch to another dialog box, where you set the criteria for a search. Now, some of this functionality is incorporated into the file management dialog boxes so you can get to it right away.

For example, in previous versions of WordPerfect, in the QuickFinder dialog box, there was a text box where you could type in a filename (all or part of it), and a separate text box where you could type text that you wanted to search for. In WordPerfect 11/12, the functions of these two text boxes have been combined into one: Now you can type filenames and content in the File Name text box of any file management dialog box (see Figure 4.18).

Click to choose a drive or folder to search

**Figure 4.18**
In WordPerfect 11/12, you can perform a basic search without switching to another dialog box. Some of the QuickFinder tools have been added to file management dialog boxes.

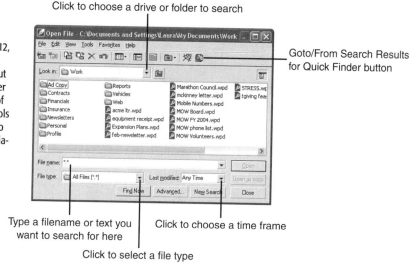

Goto/From Search Results for Quick Finder button

Type a filename or text you want to search for here

Click to choose a time frame

Click to select a file type

The following are the options for creating a basic search in a file management dialog box:

- Choose the drive or folder that you want to search in the Look In text box.

- Type all or part of a filename in the File Name text box. If you don't know the entire name, use the asterisk wildcard to replace one or more characters. For example, type **gateway\*** to locate Gateway Development, Gateway Board, Gateways Center, Gateways PUD, and so on.

- Instead of typing all or part of the filename, you can type the content you want to search for in the File Name text box. This might be a word, part of a phrase, or a combination of both. If you can't remember the exact text, use the asterisk wildcard to replace one or more characters. For example, type **lymph\*** to locate lymph glands, lymphoma, lymphocyte, lymphatic, lymphangial, and so on.

- Select a file type from the File Type text box. The default is to search every file, so if you know you're looking for a WordPerfect document, choose WP Documents from the list. It almost goes without saying, but this really cuts down on the time it takes to find a file.

- Select a time frame from the Last Modified list box. For example, if you want to locate the documents that you've modified in the past month, choose Last Month from the list.

Each of these options can be filled in separately or in combination. When you're finished, click Find Now. When the search is complete, the QuickFinder Search Results folder is displayed, with a list of files (and their locations) that match the criteria (see Figure 4.19).

List of files that matched the search criteria

**Figure 4.19**
When QuickFinder completes a search, the results are placed in the QuickFinder Search Results folder.

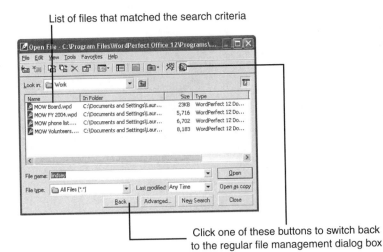

Click one of these buttons to switch back to the regular file management dialog box

If you want to open a file, double-click it. To open a group of files, select them and then click Open. Otherwise, use the same techniques you learned earlier in this chapter to manage the files.

 When you're ready to return to the "regular" file management dialog box, click the Goto/From Search Results for Quick Finder button or the Back button. Use the Goto/From Search Results for QuickFinder button to toggle back and forth between the two file lists.

## PERFORMING AN ADVANCED SEARCH

If you're ready to take your searches one step further, you're ready for Advanced Find. From the Advanced Find dialog box, you can search through document summary fields (didn't I tell you this would come up again?) and you can refine your content searches by using operators. WordPerfect old-timers, this is where you'll find the options you're used to seeing when you click the QuickFinder tab of a file management dialog box.

After you've entered the criteria you want in the file management box, choose Advanced to open the Advanced Find dialog box (see Figure 4.20). From here, you can build on those criteria by adding operators and limitations on where QuickFinder can search.

Criteria entered into the file management dialog box

Double-click to edit the existing content search

**Figure 4.20**
In the Advanced Find dialog box, you can search through document summary fields and add operators to your content search.

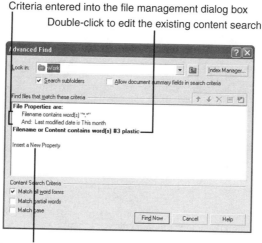

Double-click to create a new property

The following are ways you can create a more complex search:

- Double-click the filename or content search criteria to edit the existing criteria in the Find Files That Match These Criteria list box.

- Double-click the Insert a New Property item in the Find Files That Match These Criteria list box to create a new search criterion.

Follow these steps to create a new search criterion:

1. Choose the And or Or operator from the first drop-down list (see Figure 4.21).

2. Click the second drop-down list arrow and choose where you want QuickFinder to search (such as Content, Filename, Both). The document summary fields will appear if you have selected Allow Document Summary Fields in Search Criteria (see Figure 4.22).

3. Click the third drop-down list arrow and select the proximity criteria you want to use for the content search (see Figure 4.23).

4. Type the content in the text box on the far right.

4

**Figure 4.21**
The first drop-down list contains the And and Or operators so that you can create word combinations in a content search.

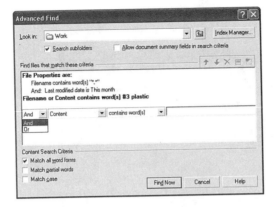

Click to add document summary fields

**Figure 4.22**
Click the second drop-down list arrow to specify a filename or content search. You can also choose from a list of document summary fields if you choose Allow Document Summary Fields in Search Criteria.

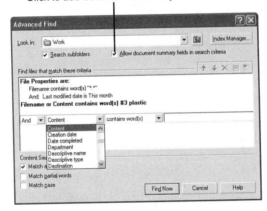

**Figure 4.23**
Click the third drop-down list arrow to choose the proximity limitation you want to impose on the content search.

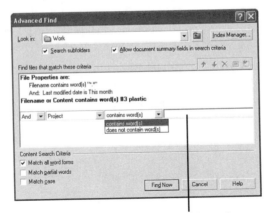

Type the search text here

In the Content Search Criteria section of the Advanced Find dialog box, you can select from the following options:

- Choose Match All Word Forms if you want QuickFinder to look for all the different forms of a word. For example, if you search for `recycle`, QuickFinder finds the words recycle, recycled, recycles, and recycling.

- Choose Match Partial Words if you want QuickFinder to search for the content text even if it's in the middle of another word. For example, searching for `sulfur` locates the following: sulfuric, sulfurous, sulfuryl, and sulfurate.

- Choose Match Case if you want QuickFinder to look for the content by using the exact case that you've typed in. For example, you might want QuickFinder to locate the word "Water," but only if it's capitalized.

**TIP FROM**

*Laura Acklen*

The Advanced Find options are sticky, which means they stay in effect until you close the File Management dialog box. To clear the Advanced Find options, click New Search in the File Management dialog box.

**NOTE**

As you can see, QuickFinder is capable of performing complex searches that put it one step below dedicated full-text search and retrieval programs. The true beauty of QuickFinder lies in the fact that because it is built into WordPerfect, you don't have to learn another program. Besides that, *you* name your files. You don't have a program name your files for you with cryptic filenames that no one but the program can decipher.

4

 *Are you getting frustrated because you're searching for a file that you know is in a folder and you know it contains the text you're searching for, but QuickFinder won't find it? See "QuickFinder Doesn't Find the File" in the Troubleshooting section at the end of this chapter.*

## CREATING A FAST SEARCH

There is one more important aspect of QuickFinder that you should know about. It's called the QuickFinder Manager, and you use it to create files that contain a list of every word in a series of documents. Rather than search through the text of every file, QuickFinder searches through the fast search file.

The most obvious advantage is the significant decrease in the amount of time it takes to locate files. A less obvious advantage is that you can combine text from documents in different folders and drives and search it all at once (rather than perform a series of QuickFinder searches on each folder or drive).

You create fast searches in the QuickFinder Manager (see Figure 4.24). You can click Index Manager in the Advanced Find dialog box or you can choose Start, Programs, WordPerfect Office 11 (or WordPerfect Office 12) Utilities, QuickFinder Manager.

**Figure 4.24**
In the QuickFinder Manager, you can create two types of fast search files, each geared toward saving you time as you search for information in your files.

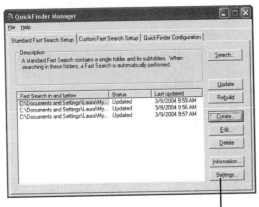

Click to set defaults for all fast search files

### CREATING A STANDARD FAST SEARCH

There are two types of fast searches: standard and custom. A *standard fast search* searches through only one folder (and all its subfolders); a *custom fast search* can search through multiple folders (with or without their subfolders). The following steps show you how to create a standard fast search:

1. If necessary, click the Standard Fast Search Setup tab in the QuickFinder Manager dialog box.

2. Click Create. The QuickFinder Standard Fast Search dialog box appears (see Figure 4.25).

**Figure 4.25**
A standard fast search can only search through one folder, so it's pretty straightforward to set up.

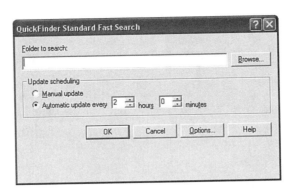

3. Type the path for the folder you want to search or click the Browse button to look for the folder.

4. Select one of the update options:

- If you choose Manual Update, you have to remember to update the file when you add, remove, or edit files in the folder.

- If you choose Automatic Update, QuickFinder updates the fast search at the specified interval (provided your computer is on and Windows is running).

5. Click the Options button to open the QuickFinder Fast Search Options dialog box (see Figure 4.26), where you can finish configuring the fast search. The options that you choose here override the settings you make in the QuickFinder Settings dialog box (click the Settings button in the QuickFinder dialog box shown in Figure 4.24).

**Figure 4.26**
You can fine-tune a fast search with options in the QuickFinder Fast Search Options dialog box.

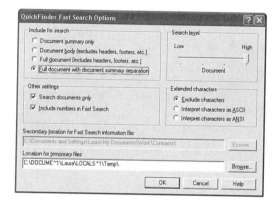

6. Click OK twice to return to the QuickFinder Manager dialog box, where the new fast search appears in the list. When the status is Updated, the fast search file has been created and is ready for use.

**TIP FROM**

If you don't want to include the subfolders of a folder in a standard fast search, create a custom fast search instead. A custom fast search can be created to search through a folder with or without the subfolders.

**NOTE**

By default, QuickFinder creates the fast search file, which has the .idx extension, in the folder that you selected for the standard fast search.

## CREATING A CUSTOM FAST SEARCH

A custom fast search is more flexible than a standard fast search because you're free to build a list of folders to search in one pass; you don't have to conduct a separate QuickFinder search for each folder. You can select folders from different drives (including network drives), and you can exclude certain subfolders when necessary. Follow these steps to create a custom fast search:

1. Click the Custom Fast Search Setup tab in the QuickFinder Manager dialog box.

2. Click Create. The QuickFinder Custom Fast Search dialog box appears (see Figure 4.27).

**Figure 4.27**
With a custom fast search, you can build a list of multiple folders to search through. The folders can all reside on the same drive, or they can be scattered across multiple drives.

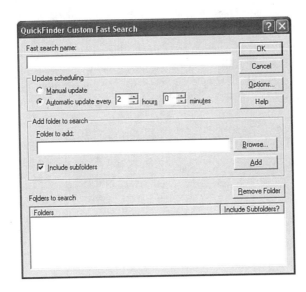

3. Type a name for the fast search in the Fast Search Name text box.

4. Select one of the update options:

   - If you choose Manual Update, you have to remember to update the file when you add, remove, or edit files in the folder.

   - If you choose Automatic Update, QuickFinder updates the fast search at the specified interval (provided your computer is on and Windows is running).

5. Type a folder name in the Folder to Add text box or click the Browse button to look for the folder.

**CAUTION**

Unless your system has gobs of memory and tons of free disk space, resist the urge to create a fast search for huge sections of your hard drive. Instead, create fast searches for folders that have a common thread (such as projects, clients, customers, suppliers, and distributors).

6. Select or deselect the Include Subfolders option to either include or exclude the subfolders for the folder you specified in step 5.

7. Click Add to insert this folder in the Folders to Search list box.

TIP FROM

*Laura Acklen*

> If you accidentally add the wrong folder to the list, or if you forget to select/deselect the Include Subfolders option, you can remove a folder from the list. Select the folder, and then click the Remove Folder button.

8. Repeat steps 5–7 to include all the folders that you want in the fast search.

9. Choose Options to open the QuickFinder Fast Search Options dialog box (refer back to Figure 4.26), where you can finish configuring the fast search. The options you choose here override the settings you make in the QuickFinder Settings dialog box (click the Settings button in the QuickFinder dialog box shown in Figure 4.24).

10. Click OK twice to return to the QuickFinder Manager dialog box, where the new fast search appears in the list. When the status reads Updated, the fast search file has been created and is ready for use.

NOTE

> The fast search file for a custom fast search is created in `\Program Files\WordPerfect Office 11\Programs\` or `\Program Files\WordPerfect Office 12\Programs\`.

CAUTION

> Take care not to accidentally delete a fast search information file (with the .idx extension). The name of the file is cryptic and can easily be mistaken for a misplaced temporary file.

TIP FROM

*Laura Acklen*

> On some networks, it's up to the network administrator to create fast search files for the network drives. These can be distributed across the network and imported into the individual user's custom fast search list. In a file management dialog box, right-click the .idx file and choose Add to Custom Search List. Use the same steps if a co-worker has created a large fast search file and you want to use it. Occasionally, when you import an .idx file, it comes in without a name. You can still see it in the list, with Imported in the Status column. Select it and choose Edit to type a fast search name.

## SELECTING A FAST SEARCH IN QUICKFINDER

Now that you've got a nice, neat list of fast search files, you're probably wondering how to tell QuickFinder *which* fast search to use. The answer is: by selecting them from a custom indexes list in the Advanced Find dialog box.

The first step is to add your fast searches to the list. To do this, you have to locate the search file so that you can select it and add it to the list. You can do this in one of two ways: You can look in the Properties dialog box for each fast search, or you can search for all the fast search files at once.

To look at the properties for a fast search, select it in the QuickFinder Manager dialog box (refer to Figure 4.24), and then click Information. The QuickFinder Fast Search Information dialog box appears (see Figure 4.28). The path for the index file is shown in the dialog box. Jot this down—this is where you need to go to find the file. Switch back to the Open File dialog box and navigate to that folder. The index filename starts with ~QF. Right-click the file, and then choose Add to Custom Search List.

**Figure 4.28**
The path for the fast search file is shown in the QuickFinder Fast Search Information dialog box.

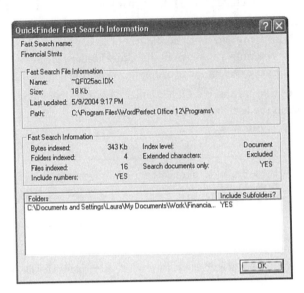

You can also search for all the index files at once and then selectively add them to the Custom Indexes list. In the Open File dialog box, select a drive from the Look In drop-down list. Type ~QF in the File Name text box, and then choose Find Now. When the search results appear, right-click the files you want to add and choose Add to Custom Search List.

Now you have the files in the list. To select a fast search, click the Look In drop-down list arrow in the Advanced Find dialog box. Scroll up to the top of the list. You should see Custom Indexes at the very top. Click the plus sign to open the list (see Figure 4.29). Select the fast search that you want to use, and then fill out the rest of the search criteria.

**NOTE**

You won't be able to choose a QuickFinder fast search from the Look In drop-down list in the Open File dialog box (or any other file management dialog box, for that matter). You must be in the Advanced Find dialog box to get to that option.

*Does QuickFinder find some, but not all, the files you are searching for? See "QuickFinder Doesn't Find All the Files" in the Troubleshooting section that follows.*

**Figure 4.29**
You can choose a fast search in the Look In drop-down list of the Advanced Find dialog box.

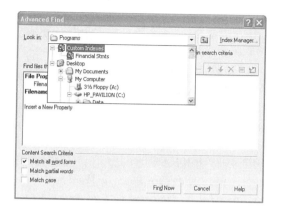

# TROUBLESHOOTING

### CAN'T SELECT MULTIPLE FILES

*I can't seem to select more than one file from my file list. When I try to select the second file, the first is deselected.*

Selecting multiple files can be tricky. You have to remember to hold down the Ctrl key when you select the second and subsequent files. If the files are one after the other, you can select them all at once: Click the first one, hold down the Shift key, and then click the last one.

### MISPLACED FILES

*I just moved (or copied) a file to another folder, but now I can't find it.*

Maybe you are looking for the wrong filename. Or, you could be looking in the wrong folder. Either way, the fastest way to find the file is to use QuickFinder to search for it. You can either search for the filename, or if you are unsure about the filename, you can search for text in the file. See the section "Finding Missing Files by Using QuickFinder" in this chapter for more information.

### CAN'T CLICK TWICE TO RENAME

*I'm trying to click twice to rename a file, and I can't get the editing box to appear.*

This method for renaming files and folders is faster than choosing Rename from a menu, but it's a little trickier. You have to be sure to click the name, not the icon. If you click the icon, WordPerfect selects the file, not just the name. Also, make sure you pause a moment between the first and second clicks.

### MY SHORTCUT STOPPED WORKING

*I can't get one of the shortcuts in the Favorites folder to work. When I double-click the shortcut icon, nothing happens.*

If the file (or folder) has been deleted, moved, or renamed, the shortcut won't be able to find it. Try to locate the file (or folder) by browsing through the other folders on your system, or try to find the file by searching for a piece of text in the file (with QuickFinder). When you find the file, delete the old shortcut, and then create a new shortcut for the file.

### INSTALLING THE REST OF THE CONVERSION FILTERS

*I'm trying to open a file that was saved in an early release of Word for Windows and I'm getting an error message. A colleague mentioned that I might not have all the conversion filters installed. Where do I find the rest of the conversion files?*

To install the additional conversion files, insert the WordPerfect Office 11 (or 12) CD to start the Setup program. For WordPerfect 11, choose WordPerfect Office 11, and then choose Modify. For WordPerfect 12, choose WordPerfect Office 12, and then select Change Which Program Features Are Installed. Choose Next.

Click the plus sign (+) next to WordPerfect Office 11 (or 12) to open the list of different components. Click the plus sign (+) next to Filters to open the list of different conversion files. Click the drop-down list button next to the category you are interested in and choose This Feature Will Be Installed on Local Hard Drive. Or, click the drop-down list arrow next to Filters and choose This Feature, And All Subfeatures, Will Be Installed on Local Hard Drive to install all of the conversion filters at once. Choose Next, and then Install. Click Finish to close the installation wizard. The new filters have been installed, and they are ready for use.

### QUICKFINDER DOESN'T FIND THE FILE

*I'm trying to search for a file by using text that is in the file. QuickFinder doesn't find the file. I know it is in the folder somewhere. What am I doing wrong?*

First, make sure you're searching the correct drive or folder. Second, try using the Match All Word Forms option to search for alternative forms of a word or the Match Partial Words option to find the word even if it's embedded inside another word. Third, broaden the search by removing some of the criteria. Remember that if one single criterion doesn't match, QuickFinder won't find the file.

### QUICKFINDER DOESN'T FIND ALL THE FILES

*I'm searching for all the files that contain "watershed ordinance." QuickFinder finds some of the files, but not all of them. Am I doing something wrong?*

Probably not. This type of error sometimes happens when you're running QuickFinder on a network drive. It could also be a corrupt .idx file on the hard drive.

First, try rebuilding the files. Delete all the .idx files from your hard drive. Make sure you search all the drives where you might have created fast searches. Remember that by default, a standard fast search creates the file in the folder you specified for that fast search.

Open QuickFinder to search for all the fast search files on your system (type ~QF in the File Name text box). Select all the files, and then press Delete. Don't worry—this doesn't delete the fast search information! Now, open QuickFinder Manager and rebuild all the fast search files (both standard and custom) by selecting them and clicking the Rebuild button. If you accidentally try to *update* the fast search, you'll get an error because the index file for that fast search doesn't exist.

# PROJECT

Daily backups are incredibly important, but like many other things in life, if it isn't fast and easy to do, it doesn't get done. Lots of backup programs claim to automate the entire backup process, but you still have to remember to load the program and start the backup. By using the Open File dialog box, you can search for all the files that you worked on throughout the day and copy them to a disk.

Start by opening the Open File dialog box. Choose a drive (or folder) from the Look In drop-down list. Open the Last Modified drop-down list and choose Today. If you are interested in only the WordPerfect documents you modified, open the File Type drop-down list and choose WP Documents (*.wpd); otherwise, leave the filter set to All Files (*.*). Choose Find Now to start the search.

When the search results appear, select the files you want to back up. You probably don't want to back up all the files, especially if you searched for All Files. You'll see plenty of temporary files and other system files that are created or modified every day. You can ignore them and concentrate on the documents, spreadsheets, address books, databases, presentations, calendars, and so on.

When you are finished selecting the files, choose File, Send To. Select 3 1/2 Floppy Disk, the Zip drive, the tape drive, the CD drive, or the DVD drive, depending on what you are backing up to.

# CHAPTER 5

# USING THE WRITING TOOLS

**I**n this chapter

*by Laura Acklen*

# SPELL CHECKING A DOCUMENT

Writing thoughtful and original material is enough of a challenge, without having to worry about misspelled words! If you leave misspellings, the reader can be distracted. And, like it or not, some readers question the intelligence level of the author...and your credibility rating drops a notch.

Who would have thought something as simple as a few misspelled words could undermine all your hard work? Save yourself (or your boss) the potential embarrassment by running Spell Checker on every document, no matter how short, before you send it off.

In Chapter 1, "Getting Comfortable with WordPerfect," you learned how to use the Spell-As-You-Go feature to catch misspelled words (and other potential errors) as you type. If you've turned off Spell-As-You-Go, or if you want to check through the entire document all at once, you can run the Spell Checker from the Tools menu.

→ To learn more about using Spell-As-You-Go and Grammar-As-You-Go, **see** "Understanding WordPerfect's Automatic Proofreading Features," **p. 23.**

**TIP FROM**

Call me paranoid, but I've gotten in the habit of saving my documents before starting any of the writing tools. This way, if I make some changes that I decide I don't want to keep, I can always revert to my saved copy. Also, in rare cases, the writing tools can cause your system to freeze, so you'll want to be able to get back to your saved document after you restart.

Here's how to start Spell Checker and correct mistakes in your document:

1. Choose Tools, Spell Checker or click the Spell Checker button. The writing tools dialog box with tabs for Spell Checker, Grammatik, Thesaurus, and Dictionary appears (see Figure 5.1). Spell Checker immediately begins checking the document for misspelled words, duplicate words, and irregular capitalization. A potential error is highlighted, and suggested replacement word(s) appear in the Replacements list box.

2. Choose from the following options to correct the misspelled word, add the word to the dictionary, or skip the word:

   - To correct a misspelled word manually, click in the document window, correct the problem, and then choose Resume to continue spell checking.
   - To replace a misspelled word with the correctly spelled word, select the correctly spelled word in the Replacements list box, and then choose Replace. In the case of duplicate words and irregular capitalization, you can select the single word, or the word with correct capitalization, in the Replacements list box (before choosing Replace).

The potential error is shown here

**Figure 5.1**
Spell Checker, Grammatik, Thesaurus, and Dictionary are all integrated into the same dialog box. Click the appropriate tab to switch to another writing tool.

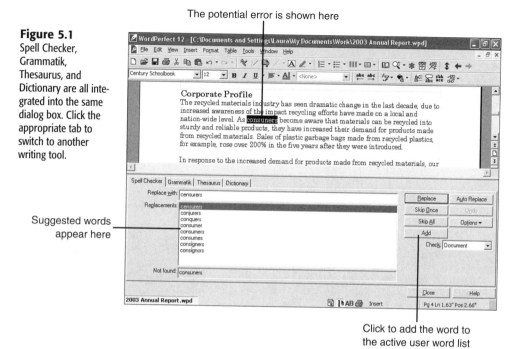

Suggested words appear here

Click to add the word to the active user word list

- If this is a frequently misspelled word, select the correct spelling in the Replacements list box, and then choose Auto Replace to add the combination to the QuickCorrect list. (See "Adding and Removing QuickCorrect Entries" later in this chapter for more information.)

- If the correct spelling doesn't appear in the Replacements list, edit the word manually in the Replace With box, and then choose Replace.

- To skip the word here but have Spell Checker stop if it finds it again, click Skip Once.

- To skip the word here and for the rest of the document, click Skip All.

- To add this word to the active user word list, click Add.

- If you accidentally replace the misspelled word with the wrong replacement word, click Undo.

By default, Spell Checker checks the entire document. If you don't want to check the whole document, you can select just a portion. To specify which portion of the document you want checked, click the Check drop-down list arrow and select an option.

**CAUTION**

If you accidentally add a misspelled word to the user word list, see the section "Editing User Word Lists" later in this chapter for information on removing entries.

TIP FROM

*Laura Achlen*

> The Spell Checker/Grammatik/Thesaurus/Dictionary combo dialog box is a strange beast. It is an integrated dialog box that's anchored to the bottom half of the screen. It doesn't have to stay that way, though, because you can click and drag it wherever you want. Point to the gray area next to the Dictionary tab. The pointer changes to a four-headed arrow. Click and drag the dialog box up into the document window. But be careful—don't go too far, or you'll anchor it to the top half of the screen. Whenever you see the gray rectangular outline, you can drop it. Now it looks like the other dialog boxes—it has a blue title bar and a Close button. To put it back, point to the title bar and wait for the four-headed arrow, and then drag the dialog box down to the bottom of the screen. When you get close to the bottom, the rectangular guideline changes to one that stretches horizontally across the screen. When you see the horizontal guideline, release the mouse button to anchor it at the bottom of the screen.

 *If you are tired of skipping over your name, company name, company address, and so forth, see "My Name Is Not Misspelled" in the Troubleshooting section at the end of this chapter.*

*If you are frustrated because after adding a bunch of words in Spell Checker, it still stops on those words in another document, see "My Words Aren't Being Added" in the Troubleshooting section at the end of this chapter.*

NOTE

> Choosing Skip All adds the word to the document word list, which is saved with the document and doesn't affect other documents. The strength of this feature becomes clear when you work with long documents that are full of technical terminology. It takes only a few mouse clicks, and after you've built the list, Spell Checker runs a lot faster because it isn't stopping on those terms anymore.

## CUSTOMIZING SPELL CHECKER

By default, Spell Checker starts checking the document immediately and looks for misspellings, duplicate words, and irregular capitalization. Phonetically spelled words are included in the Replacements text box to give you more suggested replacement words from which to choose. You can alter these default settings by selectively turning on and off the options that you want to use.

In the Spell Checker dialog box, choose Options to open the pop-up list of options (see Figure 5.2). A check mark next to an option means that it's already turned on. You can choose from the following options:

- Deselect Auto Start if you don't want Spell Checker to start checking the document immediately. You'll have to open the Spell Checker dialog box and click Start to start the spell check.

- Select Beep on Misspelled if you want Spell Checker to beep every time it stops on a word. This is helpful if you want to turn to something else while Spell Checker is running and you want to be notified if Spell Checker stops.

- After you've completed a spell check of the document, the next time you run Spell Checker on the document, it checks only the parts of the document that have been edited or added. If you want to force Spell Checker to recheck the entire document, choose Recheck All Text.

- If you want Spell Checker to check words that contain both letters and numbers, select Check Words with Numbers.

- Deselect Check Duplicate Words if you don't want Spell Checker to stop when it finds duplicate words (that is, two identical words next to each other).

- Deselect Check Irregular Capitalization if you don't want Spell Checker to flag words with irregular capitalization (for example, McKinney, PowerPC, or BestBuy).

- Select Prompt Before Auto Replacement if you want WordPerfect to prompt you before replacing a word that you've added to the user word list with Auto Replace.

- Deselect Show Phonetic Suggestions if you don't want Spell Checker to show you suggestions that are phonetically similar to (that is, they sound like) the word that Spell Checker has stopped on.

**Figure 5.2**
You click Options to customize how Spell Checker operates and to work with the word lists.

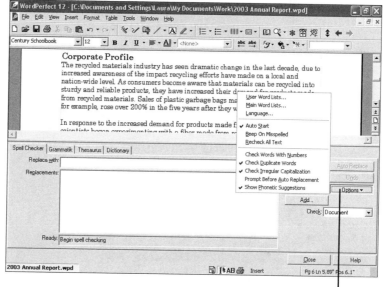

Click to open the pop-up menu

**NOTE**

The settings you make on the Options list are "sticky." In other words, they stay in place until you change them again.

## EDITING USER WORD LISTS

As the capabilities of the Spell Checker program grew, the dictionary files of earlier versions outgrew the term *dictionary* and became *word lists*. Every new document is created with a document word list and the default user word list. You can add entries to the word lists whenever Spell Checker stops on a word. Choosing Add adds the word to the user word list; choosing Skip All adds the word to the document word list.

If you accidentally add a misspelled word to a word list, you have to edit the list to remove the entry (otherwise, Spell Checker thinks that misspelled word is okay). You can edit document word lists and user word lists to add or remove entries.

In the Spell Checker dialog box, choose Options, User Word Lists. The User Word Lists dialog box appears (see Figure 5.3). Select the word list that you want to edit. From here you can do the following:

- If you want to remove an entry, select it in the list box and choose Delete Entry.
- If you want to add an entry, type the word or phrase you want to add in the Word/Phrase text box, and then choose Add Entry.
- If you want to add an entry with a replacement word, type the word or phrase in the Word/Phrase text box, type the replacement word or phrase in the Replace With text box, and then click Add Entry.
- To add multiple replacement words (which will be displayed in the Replacements list box as suggested replacement words), type the word or phrase in the Word/Phrase text box, type the replacement word or phrase in the Replace With text box, and then choose Add Entry. Type that same word or phrase in the Word/Phrase text box, type another replacement word or phrase in the Replace With text box, and then click Add Entry. Repeat for all the replacement words that you want associated with this word or phrase.

**5**

This is the default user word list

**Figure 5.3**
In the User Word Lists dialog box, you can select additional user word lists to use. You can also edit the word lists to add, remove, and replace entries.

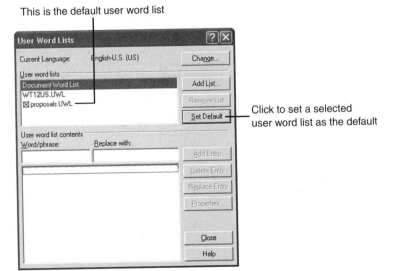

Click to set a selected user word list as the default

- If you want to edit an entry, select the entry in the list box. Edit the word or phrase in the Replace With text box and then click Replace Entry.

**TIP FROM**

*Laura Acklen*

> You can create more user word lists for specific types of documents. The active, or currently selected, word list is the one that Spell Checker adds words to when you choose Add. To create a new user word list, choose Options, User Word Lists, Add List. Type a name for the file, and then choose Open. The new user word list appears in the list, with an X in the box, indicating that it's active for this document. Choose Set Default if you want this user word list to be active in new documents.

**CAUTION**

> If the word list you want to edit doesn't appear in the list, click Add List to browse for .uwl files. When you find the one you need, select it, and then choose Open.

 *If you just realized that you've added a bunch of incorrect entries in the user word list file, see "I Trashed the User Word List" in the Troubleshooting section at the end of this chapter.*

## USING OTHER DICTIONARIES

When you spell check a document, Spell Checker scans two types of word lists: the user word lists and the main word lists. It scans the user word lists first, and if it doesn't find the word, it scans the main word list. If it still doesn't find the word, Spell Checker stops checking the document and flags the word as a possible error.

That's the macro view. The micro view is that you can link up to 10 user word list files and up to 10 main word list files to check your documents. I know, I know, it sounds like overkill—but I've been known to link a few main word lists when I wanted to use several language word list files together. (Each language comes with its own main word list file.) This is how you add specialized third-party dictionaries, such as medical and legal dictionaries, so they can be integrated into Spell Checker.

I've known serious keyboard pounders to create a library of word lists for different types of documents, particularly those of a technical nature. No matter how many word lists you use, Spell Checker checks all the user word lists (including the document word list) before moving to the main word lists.

To add main word lists, choose Options, Main Word Lists, Add List (see Figure 5.4). The name of the file is `wp11xx.mor`, or `wp12xx.mor`, where *xx* is the language code. Select a file from the folder, and then select Open.

5

**Figure 5.4**
When additional language modules are installed, the main word list files are saved in the 11 or 12 subfolder of the Writing Tools folder.

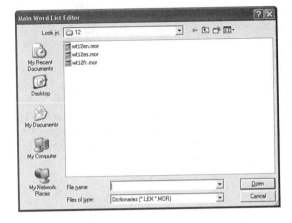

TIP FROM

If you don't see the language file that you need, run Corel's Setup program and install additional language modules.

To add user word lists, choose Options, User Word Lists, Add List. Type a filename for the new list or browse the system to select another word list, and then click Open. After you've created a list of user word lists, you can select and deselect them to make them active or inactive as needed (see Figure 5.5).

This word list is active

This word list is inactive

**Figure 5.5**
You can use up to 10 user word lists together to check your documents, including the default user word list (WT11US.UWL / WT12US.UWL).

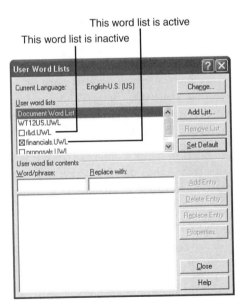

**TIP FROM**

*Laura Acklen*

Spell Checker looks through these files in the order in which they appear in the list, so add the word lists that contain the most relevant words at the top. If necessary, remove the lists and add them back in, in the order that you want them searched.

**TIP FROM**

*Laura Acklen*

If you've been using an earlier release of WordPerfect, you can use the supplementary dictionary files or user word files that you created. In the Spell Checker (or Grammatik), choose Options, User Word Lists, Add List. Open `wt11us.uwl` for version 11, `wt10us.uwl` for version 10, `wt90us.uwl` for version 9, `wt80us.uwl` for version 8, `wt61us.uwl` for version 7, or `wtspelus.sup` for version 6.1 for the U.S. version.

## RUNNING THE SPELL UTILITY

WordPerfect 11 and 12 include a Spell Utility program that you can use to convert word lists and dictionaries from previous versions of WordPerfect. You can also view the contents of a main word list, add and remove words, merge a word list with another word list, and create new main word lists. Start the Spell Utility from the Start menu: Choose Start, (All) Programs, WordPerfect Office 11 (or WordPerfect Office 12), Utilities, and then click the Spell Utility item. The Spell Utility dialog box appears (see Figure 5.6).

**Figure 5.6**
Spell Utility is a separate program that you run outside of WordPerfect.

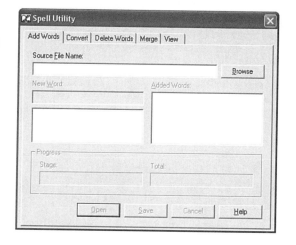

**5**

**NOTE**

The Spell Utility file is called wt11sptlen.exe in version 11 and wt12sptlen.exe in version 12. It is stored in the `\program files\common files\corel\shared\writing tools\11` (or 12) folder on my WinXP Pro system. The location on your system might vary according to the operating system you have. If you are unsure, just search for the file name.

Using the Spell Utility, you can

- *Add words to a main word list*—Click the Add Words tab, and then click the Browse button to select the main word list file (`\program files\common files\corel\shared\writing tools\11\wt11en.mor` [or `\12\wt12en.mor`] is the default main word list file). Choose Open to open the file and activate the rest of the dialog box. Type the word you want to add in the New Word text box, and press Enter. Continue adding words until you've built your list. Choose Save to add the words in the Added Words list.

- *Convert dictionaries and word lists*—Click the Convert tab. Click the Conversion Type drop-down list arrow and choose an item from the list (see Figure 5.7). Choose Browse to select the source file. Specify a name for the word list you are creating in the Destination File Name text box. Choose Convert.

**TIP FROM**

*Laura Acklen*

> If you don't see the item you need on the Conversion Type drop-down list, you might have to do a two-step conversion. Try converting the file to a WordPerfect 11 (or 12) document, and then convert the WordPerfect 11 (or 12) document to a WordPerfect 11 (or 12) Dictionary.

**Figure 5.7**
Using the Convert feature, you can convert dictionaries and word lists from previous versions of WordPerfect to WordPerfect 11 (or 12) word lists.

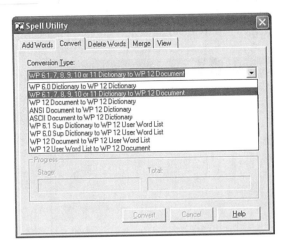

- *Create a new main word list*—Create a list of words in a WordPerfect document, an ANSI text file, or an ASCII text file. In Spell Utility, click the Convert tab. Select the appropriate conversion type, and then browse for the source file. Type a name for the file you are creating in the Destination File Name text box (make sure you use a .mor extension). Choose Convert.

- *Delete words that you've added to a main word list*—Click the Delete Words tab. Choose Browse to select the main word list file (`\program files\common files\corel\shared\writing tools\11\wt11en.mor`, or `\12\wt12en.mor`, is the default main word list file), and then choose Open. A list of words that you've added appears in the User Words list box. Select a word, and then choose Delete. Choose Save when you're done.

- *Merge two main word lists into one list*—Click the Merge tab. Click the Merge Type drop-down list arrow and choose an item from the list. Browse for the source file. Specify a name for the file (or select a target file) that you want to contain both lists in the Target File Name text box. Choose Add Words in Source to Target, and then choose Merge. If you decide later that you want to remove the merged words, follow these same steps, except choose Delete Words in Source from Target.

- *View words in a main word list*—Click the View tab. Click the Browse button to select a main word list file (`\program files\common files\corel\shared\writing tools\11\wt11en.mor`, or `\12\wt12en.mor`, is the default main word list file). Choose Open to open the file and activate the rest of the dialog box. Type the word (or a partial word) that you want to look up in the Word text box. The search results appear in the Results list box. For a more complete list, choose Look Up.

# CHECKING THE GRAMMAR IN A DOCUMENT

Grammatik is a built-in grammar checker that proofs your documents for correct grammar, style, punctuation, and word usage, and thus catches many of the errors that pass by Spell Checker. Interestingly, Spell Checker is integrated into Grammatik, so you only need to run Grammatik in order to run both.

Grammatik follows a strict set of grammatical rules when checking a document for problems. Many good writers, however, often bend these rules to make a point. Don't feel compelled to fix every problem or accept every solution if it changes the meaning of your words. Follow these steps to run Grammatik:

1. Select Tools, Grammatik. If you already have the writing tools dialog box open, click the Grammatik tab. Grammatik immediately starts checking the document and, like Spell Checker, stops and highlights any potential errors (see Figure 5.8).

2. Choose from the following options to correct the error, skip the error, or turn off the rule:

   - To correct a writing error manually, click in the document window, correct the problem, and then click Resume to continue the grammar check.

   - To replace a writing error, select one of the suggestions in the Replacements list box, and then click Replace. If no suggestions are listed, you have to manually correct the text.

   - To skip the writing error here but have Grammatik stop if it finds the error again, click Skip Once.

   - To skip the writing error here and for the rest of the document, click Skip All.

5

The potential error is selected in the document

**Figure 5.8**
Grammatik has many of the same options as Spell Checker to correct a potential problem or move past it.

Suggested replacement text

New sentence

Brief explanation of the problem

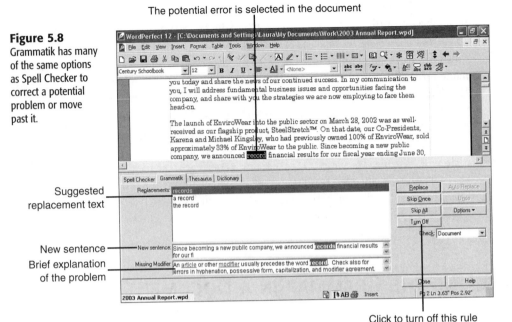

Click to turn off this rule

- The rules by which Grammatik checks your document are organized into *rule classes*. To disable a particular rule class, choose Turn Off. This change is temporary; it affects only the current Grammatik session.

- If you correct a problem, and then change your mind, choose Undo to reverse the last action taken by Grammatik.

By default, Grammatik checks the entire document. If you want to check only a portion of the document, click the Check drop-down list arrow and select an option.

> **NOTE**
> Because Spell Checker is integrated into Grammatik, when you run Grammatik, you also correct errors that are flagged by Spell Checker.

 *If you want Grammatik to stop flagging a certain error, see "My Sentences Are Not Too Long" in the Troubleshooting section at the end of this chapter.*

## SELECTING A DIFFERENT CHECKING STYLE

Different types of documents must conform to particular grammatical rules and require varying levels of formality. To accommodate these differences, Grammatik offers 11 predefined checking styles, and you can create your own. By default, Grammatik uses the Quick Check style to check your documents. You can select another style, change the threshold settings, and choose a formality level. In the Grammatik dialog box, choose Options, Checking Styles to display the Checking Styles dialog box (see Figure 5.9).

**Figure 5.9**
You can select a checking style to match the type of document you are checking.

To choose a checking style, select it in the list, and then click Select. A checking style remains in effect until you choose another one.

To edit a checking style, select it in the list, and then click Edit. The Edit Checking Styles dialog box appears (see Figure 5.10).

Enter threshold settings here

Select and deselect rule classes here

**Figure 5.10**
You can modify any of the predefined checking styles to enable or disable rule classes, modify the threshold settings, or choose a different formality level.

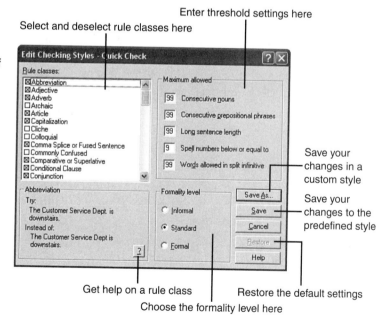

Save your changes in a custom style

Save your changes to the predefined style

Get help on a rule class

Choose the formality level here

Restore the default settings

 *If you're having trouble getting your changes to a checking style to stick, see "My Edits to a Checking Style Aren't Getting Saved" in the Troubleshooting section at the end of this chapter.*

## CUSTOMIZING GRAMMATIK

By default, when you run Grammatik, it starts checking the document immediately, prompts you before an automatic replacement, and suggests spelling replacement words. You can alter these default settings by selectively turning on and off the options that you want to use.

In the Grammatik dialog box, click the Options button to open the pop-up list of options (see Figure 5.11). A check mark next to an option means that it's already turned on. Choose from the following options.

**Figure 5.11**
You can click the Options button to customize how Grammatik operates, to edit checking styles, and to generate statistical reports.

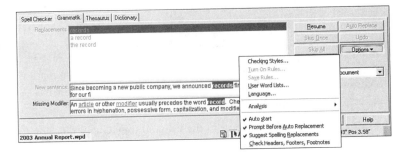

- Choose Checking Styles to open the Checking Styles dialog box, where you can select another style (see the section "Selecting a Different Checking Style" earlier in this chapter).
- Choose Turn On Rules to display a list of the rules that you have turned off during this session. You can select a rule from this list to turn it back on.
- Choose Save Rules to save the rules that you turned off during this session as a new checking style.
- Choose User Word Lists to select, add, and edit user word lists. See the section "Editing User Word Lists" earlier in this chapter for more information.
- Choose Language to open the Language dialog box, where you can select a different language for this session. See the section "Switching to a Different Language" later in this chapter for more information.
- Choose Analysis to generate statistics and readability reports (see "Generating Readability Reports" later in this chapter).
- Deselect Auto Start if you don't want Grammatik to start checking the document immediately. You have to click Start in the Grammatik dialog box to start the grammar check.
- Deselect Prompt Before Auto Replacement if you don't want WordPerfect to prompt you before replacing a word that you've added to the user word list with Auto Replace.
- Deselect Suggest Spelling Replacements if you still want Grammatik to flag spelling errors, but you don't want to see suggested replacement words in the Replacements list box.

- Select Check Headers, Footers, Footnotes if you want to include these elements in the grammar check. Use this option if you've discovered an error in the document and there is a chance that you might have duplicated the error in a header, footer, or footnote.

**NOTE**

> The settings you make on the Options list are "sticky." In other words, they stay in place until you change them again.

## GENERATING READABILITY REPORTS

Grammatik can compile three different statistical reports on your document: a readability report, basic counts, and a flagged list. You can also display a parse tree and a parts of speech diagram. To generate these reports, choose Options, Analysis. Choose from the following options:

- Parse Tree—This diagram identifies the clauses in the sentence where the insertion point lies.

- Parts of Speech—This diagram identifies each word as a noun, a pronoun, an adjective, a verb, an adverb, or another part of speech. This diagram dissects the sentence where the insertion point lies.

- Basic Counts—This is a count of words, sentences, and paragraphs, along with the average number of syllables per word, words per sentence, and sentences per paragraph (see Figure 5.12).

**Figure 5.12**
The Basic Counts report is similar to the Information sheet in the Properties dialog box, but it is more precise.

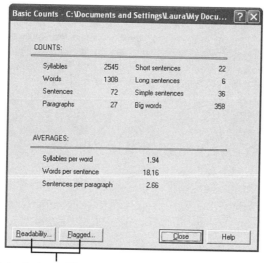

Click to display a different report

5

- Flagged—This report displays a list of errors and the number of times they were flagged during this session.

- Readability—This report compares your document to one of three comparison documents (or a document of your choosing) to give you an idea of the skill required to comprehend the document content (see Figure 5.13).

Click to choose a different comparison document

**Figure 5.13**
The Readability report gives you an idea of how easy or difficult it is to understand the document.

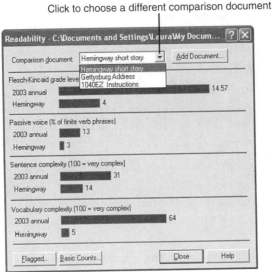

There is a feature that will prompt you with suggestions as you type—it's called Prompt-As-You-Go. You can use Prompt-As-You-Go to replace misspelled words, grammatical errors, and synonyms. There is a Prompt-As-You-Go text box on the property bar that display suggestions in different colors, depending on what the problem is. If the text is red, a word might be misspelled; if the text is blue, there might be a grammatical error; if the text is black, you can choose a synonym to replace a word.

# USING WORDPERFECT'S THESAURUS

A thesaurus helps you find the right words to express your thoughts. Some thoughts and ideas are more complex than others, and most ideas can be expressed in a number of ways. Using the right words enables you to convey exactly the message you want to get across to the reader.

## LOOKING UP WORDS IN THE THESAURUS

WordPerfect's Thesaurus looks up synonyms (that is, words with similar meanings), antonyms, and related words. You can start the Thesaurus from a blank screen, but if you click on a word first, the Thesaurus looks up that word.

Choose Tools, Thesaurus, press Alt+F1, or, if you already have the writing tools dialog box open, click the Thesaurus tab. The Thesaurus looks up the word and, by default, displays a list of synonyms, and if available, a list of antonyms and related words (see Figure 5.14).

**Figure 5.14**
The Thesaurus helps you refine your writing by showing you different words to use.

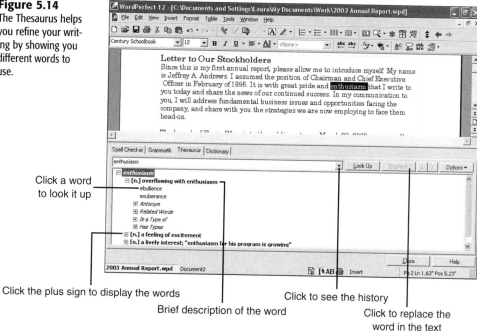

Click a word to look it up

Click the plus sign to display the words

Brief description of the word

Click to see the history

Click to replace the word in the text

If the insertion point is within a word, the Thesaurus looks up synonyms for that word and displays them in the window. Otherwise, you need to type the word you want to look up in the text box and then click Look Up.

To view the list of words within a category, double-click the category, or click the plus sign in the box. You can also use the left and right arrows on your keyboard to open and close categories.

If you double-click a word in the list, a new window opens for that word. Double-clicking a word in the second window causes a third window for that word to open. When you fill more than three windows, new windows are created (to the right). You can click the scroll arrows to move one window to the left or right (see Figure 5.15).

To look up a word in one of the windows, double-click it. To replace the word in the document with the word from the Thesaurus, select the word, and then choose Replace. If you change your mind, click Edit, Undo in the document window to reverse the change.

There is a history list so you can quickly get back to a word that you noticed earlier. Click the drop-down list arrow next to the Look Up button to select from a list of words.

5

Click to move one window to the right ┐ Options
Click to move one window to the left ┐ button

**Figure 5.15**
You can click the Options button to choose the type of words the Thesaurus looks up, to choose a different language, or to activate Spelling Assist.

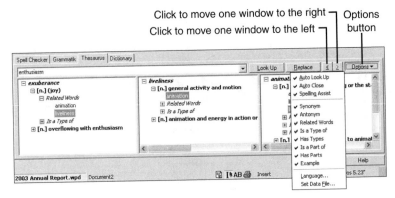

## CUSTOMIZING THE THESAURUS

As with the other writing tools, the Thesaurus is set up to start looking up words immediately, and to compile a list of synonyms and additional categories. You can turn off Auto Look Up and choose the types of words the Thesaurus looks up. In the Thesaurus dialog box, click the Options button to open the pop-up list of options (see Figure 5.15). You can choose from the following options:

- Auto Look Up—Deselect this if you don't want the Thesaurus to look up words right when you start it.

- Auto Close—Select this if you want the Thesaurus to close after you choose a word for the document.

- Spelling Assist—Select this if you want the Thesaurus to give spelling suggestions for misspelled words.

- Language—Select this to select a different language (which has its own Thesaurus data file).

- Set Data File—Select this to set the data file for a language.

- Synonyms—Select this to look up words with the same or similar meaning. For example, if you look up *pretty*, the Thesaurus finds *handsome*, *attractive*, *ravishing*, and so on.

- Antonyms—Select this to look up words with an opposite meaning. For example, if you look up *ugly*, the Thesaurus finds *attractive* and *pretty*.

- Related Words—For example, if you look up *old*, the Thesaurus finds words such as *senior* and *original*.

- Is a Type Of—For example, if you look up *oak*, the Thesaurus lists more general words such as *tree* and *wood*.

- Has Types—For example, if you look up *flower*, the Thesaurus lists specific flower names such as *daisy* and *sunflower*. The Thesaurus also lists specific terms for the verb *to flower*, such as *burst forth* and *effloresce*.

- Is a Part Of—For example, if you look up *leg*, the Thesaurus lists words such as *chair*, *poultry*, and *journey*, because a *leg* is a part of each of these things.

- Has Parts—For example, if you look up *car*, the Thesaurus lists parts of a car, such as *accelerator*, *throttle*, and *gas*.

- Examples—For example, if you look up *city*, the Thesaurus lists examples of cities, such as *New York City*, *Tokyo*, and *Paris*.

- Related Information—Produces a list of words associated to the genus of a word. For example, if you look up *tree*, the Thesaurus finds *plants*, *leaves*, *roots*, and so on.

- Hypernyms—Displays the superordinate of a word. For example, the hypernym of *peach* is *fruit*.

- Hyponyms—Displays the subordinate of a word. For example, a hyponym of *fruit* is *peach*.

- Cross References—Looks up information from other documents.

- Phrases—For example, if you look up *time*, the Thesaurus suggests phrases such as *it's about time* and *time to go now*.

**TIP FROM**

*Laura Acklen*

> Not every lookup option is supported in every language. There is a table in Help that tells you which Thesaurus options each language supports. Choose Help, Help Topics, and then click the Contents tab. Double-click Using Writing Tools, double-click Customizing Look Up Options, double-click Customizing Look Up Options (again), and then click Languages and Support Look Up Options. You can print this out if you want to make it easier to read. In the Help window, choose File, Print Topic.

# USING THE DICTIONARY

Both WordPerfect 11 and 12 include a built-in version of the *Pocket Oxford Dictionary*, so you have definitions for more than 30,000 words at your fingertips. The Dictionary can be used to look up the definition of a selected word in your document, or you can type the word in yourself. You can perform basic searches for a specific word, or using operators, you can perform advanced searches that include and exclude words from the search.

Follow these steps to launch the Dictionary:

1. If you want to look up the definition for a word in your document, select it first.

2. Select Tools, Dictionary or press Ctrl+Alt+F1. Or, if you already have the writing tools dialog box open, click the Dictionary tab to display the Dictionary dialog box (see Figure 5.16).

**NOTE**

> The built-in *Pocket Oxford Dictionary* can be upgraded to the *Oxford Concise Dictionary*, which contains 70,000 definitions. There is an item on the Options menu that takes you to a Corel Web page where you can download the upgrade for a nominal charge.

Type the word you want to look up here

**Figure 5.16**
The built-in Pocket Oxford Dictionary contains definitions for more than 30,000 words.

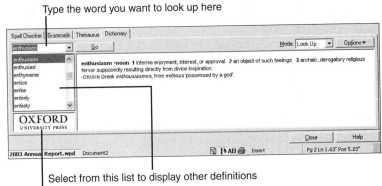

Select from this list to display other definitions

Click to visit the Oxford University Press Web site

## SEARCHING THE DICTIONARY

With a printed dictionary, you have to know what you're looking for. In other words, you must have *some* idea of how to spell the word, or you won't find it. The beauty of an electronic dictionary is that you can locate words by searching through the definitions for a particular word or phrase. For example, you can locate all the terms that have the word *tree* in the definition. Furthermore, if you know how to spell only part of a word, you have a much greater chance of locating it with an electronic search.

Here's how to search through the dictionary:

1. With the Dictionary dialog box displayed, open the Mode drop-down list and choose Search.
2. Type the word that you want to search for in the text box (underneath the writing tools tabs).
3. Choose Go. A list of terms that contain the search word in the definition is shown (see Figure 5.17).

Type the word you want to search for here

Click to search through the definitions

**Figure 5.17**
With an electronic version of a dictionary, it's a simple task to locate words by searching through their definitions.

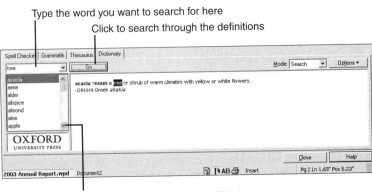

Scroll down through the list to see the rest of the search results

## LIMITING YOUR SEARCH RESULTS

In some cases, searching through the thousands of definitions in the dictionary produces too many search results. You need a way to narrow the scope of the search. This is done through operators, similar to those used to search through files. If you skipped the file management chapter, operators are used to combine or exclude search terms. To display the operators and build an advanced search:

1. With the Dictionary dialog box displayed, open the Mode drop-down list and choose Search.

2. Choose Options and verify that there is a check mark next to Operators.

3. Type the first word that you want to search for, and then press the spacebar. A pop-up palette of operators opens (see Figure 5.18).

Select an operator from this palette

**Figure 5.18**
Using operators, you can include or exclude words from the search criteria.

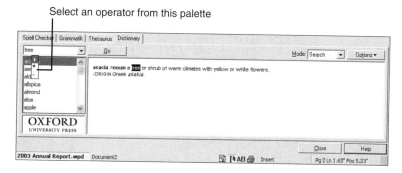

4. Use the Up and Down arrow keys to move through the list of operators. Choose one of the following operators:

   - Plus sign (+)—Lets you include more than one word in the search. For example, searching for tree + flower produces a list of words that have both "tree" and "flower" in the definitions.

   - Minus sign (-)—Enables you to exclude a word from the search. For example, searching for tree - flower results in a list of words with "tree", but not "flower" in the definitions.

   - Asterisk (*)—Enables you to broaden the search with and/or. For example, searching for tree * flo produces a list of words with "tree" and/or words beginning with "flo" or both, in the definitions.

5. Press Enter to insert the highlighted operator in the text box.

6. Press the Spacebar and type the second word (or partial word); then, press Enter to search the Dictionary.

5

TIP FROM

*Laura Acklen*

If you don't know how to spell a word that you want to search for, you can use the first letter, or the first several letters in the word.

## SETTING DICTIONARY OPTIONS

As you could with Spell Checker, Grammatik, and the Thesaurus, you can customize how the Dictionary works. Clicking the Options button opens a list of items that help you control the display, lookup, and language settings. The list of options changes depending on which mode you have selected: Look Up or Search.

In the Dictionary dialog box, choose Options to display a list of menu items. A check mark next to an item means that it's already turned on. Choose from the following options:

- Deselect Auto Look Up if you don't want the Dictionary to look up the selected word in a document when launched.

- Select which version of the English dictionary you want to use: English (US) or English (UK).

- Select Alphabetical if you want to list the closest lookup matches. This option is available when mode is set to Look Up.

- Select Incremental to list only the matches that contain the entire search word. This option is available when mode is set to Look Up.

- Deselect Operators if you prefer to type the operators (+ - *) by hand. Pressing the Spacebar will not open the pop-up palette. This option is available when mode is set to Search.

- Choose Select All to select the text of the definition.

- Choose Copy to copy the selected definition to the Clipboard.

- Choose Display to open the Display Options dialog box where you can assign a certain color to a definition property. This visual aid helps you identify which properties are displayed in the definition. Select the property on the left side; then, choose a color on the right. Notice the brief description for the property underneath the lists.

- Choose Upgrade to launch your default Windows browser and open the Corel Web page where you can purchase and download an upgrade for the Dictionary. After you install the upgrade, you'll have the weightier 70,000-word *Oxford English Concise Dictionary* installed.

NOTE

The *Oxford English Pocket Dictionary* and the *Oxford English Concise Dictionary* are designed to be used with WordPerfect Office 2002/11/12, so they will not work with earlier versions.

# SWITCHING TO A DIFFERENT LANGUAGE

Writing in different languages is more than being able to enter, display, and print non-English characters. You also need to be able to correct spelling, check grammar, and look up terms in the Thesaurus, in addition to using the proper date conventions and currency symbols. WordPerfect supports multiple languages in three ways:

- You can mark an entire document, or just sections of it, as being in one of the more than 30 languages supported by WordPerfect. Additional language modules can be installed that support the Spell Checker, Grammatik, the Thesaurus, the Dictionary, and Hyphenation.

- You can purchase WordPerfect in a different language so that the menus, prompts, messages, dictionaries, and thesauri are all in that language.

- A Language Resource File (LRS file), which comes with the program and each language module, contains the information for formatting numbers and footnote-continued messages, among other things. You can edit this file to customize these options.

If you want to mark only a section of text, select it first. Otherwise, click in the text where you want to switch to a different language (and thus use different writing tools to check the text). Choose Tools, Language, Settings. The Language dialog box appears, with a list of available language modules (see Figure 5.19). Scroll through the list and double-click the language you want.

Make this the default writing tools language

**Figure 5.19**
You can disable the writing tools for sections of text that need to be checked in a different language.

Disable writing tools

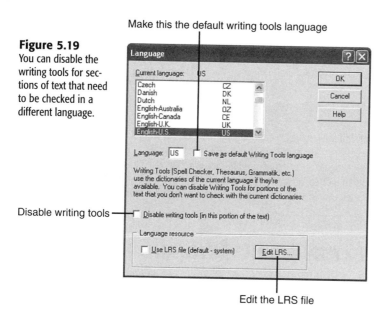

Edit the LRS file

5

TIP FROM

If you frequently switch back and forth between languages, you might be interested in a feature that was introduced in WordPerfect 10. You can now display the current language in the application bar. Right-click the application bar (at the bottom of the screen) and then choose Settings. Scroll down through the list, enable the check box next to Language, and click OK. A new Language button appears on the far-right side of the application bar. Click this button to open the Language dialog box.

You can switch to a different language when you're using any of the writing tools. In Spell Checker, Grammatik, or the Thesaurus, select Options, Language to open the Select Language dialog box (see Figure 5.20). Select Show Available Languages Only to display only those languages that are supported by the current writing tool. Select the language you want and then choose OK.

**Figure 5.20**
Use the Select Language dialog box to switch to a different language when you're using the writing tools.

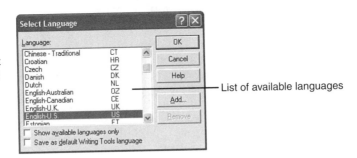

List of available languages

You can add and remove languages in the Select Language dialog box. Click the Add button to add a language. Choose Save As Default Writing Tools Language if you want the setting to be permanent.

**5**

TIP FROM

Help has a list of the languages and the writing tools they support. Choose Help, Help Topics. If necessary, click the Contents tab. Double-click Using Writing Tools, double-click Working with Languages, and then double-click Working with Languages (again). Click Writing Tools supported languages. You can print this out if you want to make it easier to read. In the Help window, choose File, Print Topic or click the Print button.

# SEARCHING FOR TEXT BY USING FIND AND REPLACE

The Find and Replace feature enables you to quickly locate text or codes and replace them if desired. I like to use Find to locate the section of text that I need to work on. (Obviously this isn't necessary for short documents, but for long ones, believe me, WordPerfect can search a lot faster than you can read!)

Here's an example of how you might use the Replace feature with Find: Let's say you accidentally misspelled an important client's name. You can search for all occurrences and replace them with the correct spelling. The same thing goes for codes. If you decide you want to search for a particular font and replace it with another one, you can do it with Find and Replace. To search for (and replace) text, follow these steps:

1. Choose Edit, Find and Replace, or press F2, to open the Find and Replace dialog box (see Figure 5.21).

2. Type the text you want to search for (this might be a complete or partial word, phrase, or number) in the Find text box.

3. Type the replacement text (this should be exact) in the Replace With text box.

4. Click Find Next to start the search.

**TIP FROM**

*Laura Acklen*

You can search for a symbol and replace it with another symbol. Click in the Find text box and press Ctrl+W. Select the symbol from any of the character sets, and then click Insert and Close. Click in the Replace With text box and press Ctrl+W. Select the symbol from any of the character sets, and then click Insert and Close. Choose Find Next. When WordPerfect stops, choose Replace All to do a global replacement.

**TIP FROM**

*Laura Acklen*

If you want to delete all or some instances of the search text, leave <Nothing> in the Replace With text box (or leave it blank). As you go through the search, you can selectively replace (or not replace) the search text with nothing, deleting it from the document.

**Figure 5.21**
You can do complex searches by choosing from the menus in the Find and Replace dialog box.

WordPerfect remembers the last item you searched for

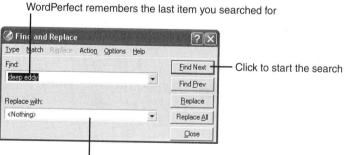

Click to start the search

Type the replacement text here

When WordPerfect locates the search text, you have the following options:

- Click Find Next to continue the search.
- Click Find Prev to move back to the previous instance.
- Click Replace to replace this occurrence of the search text with the replacement text.

- Click Replace All to replace all the rest of the occurrences without further confirmation from you.
- Click Close if you're just using Find to locate your place in a document and you want to get to work.

**N O T E**

]If you've already closed the Find and Replace dialog box, but you need to continue searching, there are two shortcuts that you can use. Press Shift+F2 to find the next occurrence and Alt+F2 to find the previous occurrence. You can also use the QuickFind buttons on the property bar to move to the next or previous instance of the search text.

**TIP FROM**

*Laura Acklen*

Here's a neat trick. You can search for a word without opening the Find and Replace dialog box. First, click on the word you want to search for. Now press Ctrl+Alt+N to search for the next occurrence of that word; press Ctrl+Alt+P to search for the previous occurrence of that word.

## SEARCHING FOR CODES

You can extend a search into the document codes to either locate a particular code so that you can edit or delete it, or to replace the code with another one. For example, if you're cleaning up a converted document, you might want to strip out all the extraneous codes. Or, you might want to search for a symbol and replace it with another symbol. Here's how to search for a code:

1. Choose Edit, Find and Replace or press F2.
2. Choose Match, Codes from the menu in the Find and Replace dialog box. This opens the Codes dialog box (see Figure 5.22).

**Figure 5.22**
Using Find and Replace, you can search for any code in the Codes dialog box.

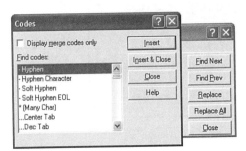

3. When you find the code you want to search for, click it and then click Insert & Close.
4. Click Find Next. When WordPerfect stops, close the Find and Replace dialog box, and then turn on Reveal Codes. The insertion point is right after the code.
5. To delete the code, press Backspace. Otherwise, double-click the code to edit it.

**TIP FROM**

*Laura Acklen*

> If you often work with converted documents, Find and Replace can be your best friend. After you identify the codes you want to get rid of, you can search for the codes and delete them. Some documents are so poorly formatted that it's quicker to clean out the codes and start over. Although this might take numerous find and replace operations, it's still faster than manually deleting each code.

To find and replace a code, follow these steps:

1. Complete the preceding steps 1–3.
2. Click in the Replace With text box.
3. Choose Replace, Codes. The same Codes dialog box shown in Figure 5.22 opens. This time, only the codes that can replace the code you are searching for are available. All the others are grayed out. For example, you can't replace a Center Tab code with a Date Format code.
4. When you find the code you want, click it and then click Insert & Close.
5. Click Find Next. When WordPerfect stops, choose Replace to replace this code and move on to the next one; choose Replace All to replace the rest of the codes without further confirmation.

To find and replace codes with specific settings, follow these steps:

1. Choose Edit, Find and Replace, or press F2.
2. Choose Type, Specific Codes to open the Specific Codes dialog box (see Figure 5.23).

**Figure 5.23**
To search for a code with a specific setting, select the code from the Specific Codes dialog box. This produces a modified Find and Replace dialog box, where you can choose the setting.

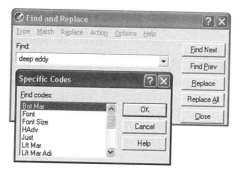

3. Select a code from the list and then click OK. Based on your selection, a modified Find and Replace dialog box appears, with options for you to select the setting that you are searching for. Figure 5.24 shows the dialog box you get after choosing the Font code.

**Figure 5.24**
When you select Font from the Specific Codes dialog box, you get the Find and Replace Font dialog box.

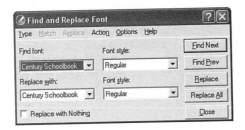

4. Use the Find and Replace Font dialog box options to specify exactly what you want to find (and replace). For example, you could search for Georgia Bold and replace it with Technical, or you could search for all the 14-point text and replace it with 16-point text.

5. Click Find Next to start the search.

**TIP FROM**

In the modified Find and Replace dialog box that you get when you're searching for specific code settings, put a check mark in the Replace with Nothing check box if you want to replace the code with nothing, thus deleting it from the document.

**TIP FROM**

You might not have thought of this yet, but you can combine text and codes in the Find text box to look for text that is followed (or preceded) by a certain code.

## RUNNING CASE-SENSITIVE SEARCHES

When you want to search for a word, but only if it's capitalized, you can narrow a search by making it case-sensitive. You can actually make a case-sensitive replacement, too.

For example, if you want to find the word *Water*, but not *water*, type **Water** in the Find text box, and then choose Match, Case. The text Case Sensitive appears underneath the Find text box. Click Find Next.

Here's another example: Let's say you want to replace all instances of *water quality ordinance* with *Water Quality Ordinance*. However, you don't want to replace *WATER QUALITY ORDINANCE* with *Water Quality Ordinance*. First, enter the exact phrases, with the correct capitalization, in each of the text boxes. Then click in the Find text box and choose Match, Case. Click in the Replace With text box and choose Replace, Case. The text Case Sensitive now appears under both text boxes (see Figure 5.25). Click Find Next.

**Figure 5.25**
When you perform a case-sensitive find and replace, you have to set the Case option for both text boxes.

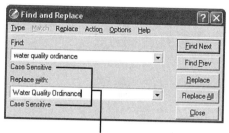

Verify that Case Sensitive appears under both text boxes

CAUTION

The settings that you select in the Find and Replace dialog box are "sticky," which means they will be in place the next time you use Find and Replace. If, for example, you do a case-sensitive search, the next time you open the Find and Replace dialog box, the Case Sensitive option will still be turned on. Furthermore, in order to remove it from both the Find and Replace, you must click in each text box, and then choose Match, Case. In addition, you must perform a Find and a Replace to remove those options from the Find and Replace dialog box. For example, if you choose Match, Case for both the Find and Replace text boxes, but you only select the Find option, the next time you open the Find and Replace dialog box, the Case Sensitive option will still be selected for the Replace text box. Only by doing a Find and a Replace can you truly remove the settings (whatever they may be).

## OTHER FIND AND REPLACE OPTIONS

I could probably write an entire chapter on all the different types of searches you can do by using Find and Replace. Case-sensitive searches and code searches are the most frequently used of the options available, so they get the most coverage. Some other options might prove helpful:

- Choose Type, Word Forms to find all forms of the word you are searching for. For example, if you search for the word *litigate*, you'll locate *litigating*, *litigation*, and *litigated*, as well as *litigate*.

- Choose Match, Whole Word to find the word only if it appears by itself, and not as a part of a larger word.

- Choose Match, Font to open the Match Font dialog box (see Figure 5.26), where you can select a font, font size, and font attributes. WordPerfect finds the search text only if it has been formatted with the font, size, and attributes that you select. (If you click in the Replace With text box and choose Replace, Font, you get the Replace Font dialog box, which is identical to the Match Font dialog box.)

CAUTION

The Word Forms option won't work if you have more than one word or if you have codes in the Find text box.

5

Click to choose a font

**Figure 5.26**
You can use the
Match Font dialog box
options if you want to
locate text in the
selected font, font
size, and attributes.

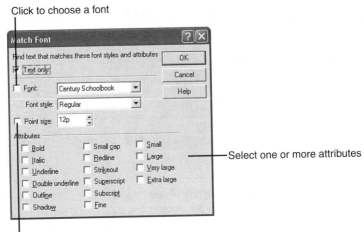

Select one or more attributes

Click to choose a font size

# UNLEASHING THE POWER OF QUICKCORRECT

QuickCorrect automatically corrects common mistakes while you type. QuickCorrect cleans up extra spaces between words, fixes capitalization errors, corrects common spelling mistakes and typos, inserts special symbols, and replaces regular straight quotation marks with typeset-quality curly quotation marks. It also helps you create graphic lines, bulleted lists (recall the discussion of QuickBullets in Chapter 3, "Understanding the Basics of Formatting"), ordinal numbers, and hyperlinks to Internet (or intranet) addresses or to files on your network and local hard drive. QuickCorrect is a robust feature with a lot of tools that do some of your work for you.

Choose Tools, QuickCorrect to open the QuickCorrect dialog box (see Figure 5.27). There are tabs for all the different features that fall under the QuickCorrect umbrella. The QuickWords feature is discussed in the section "Setting Up QuickWords," later in this chapter.

## ADDING AND REMOVING QUICKCORRECT ENTRIES

QuickCorrect includes an extensive list of frequently misspelled words and typos as well as some symbols you can insert by using just a few keystrokes. After you add your own common typos and their corrections to the QuickCorrect list, you'll spend less time proofing your documents with the writing tools.

To add words or phrases to QuickCorrect, type the word or phrase in the Replace text box. Type the replacement word or phrase in the With text box (see Figure 5.28). Click Add Entry.

Current QuickCorrect entries

**Figure 5.27**
In the QuickCorrect dialog box, you can add, remove, and edit the QuickCorrect entries. You can also turn off QuickCorrect so that it doesn't correct words while you type.

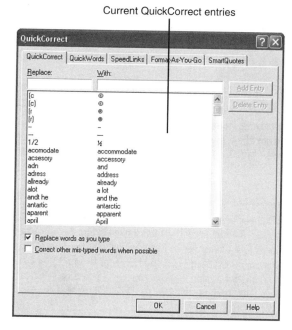

Click to add the entry

**Figure 5.28**
You can add your frequent misspellings and typos to the QuickCorrect list and let WordPerfect fix your mistakes for you as you type.

Click to turn off QuickCorrect

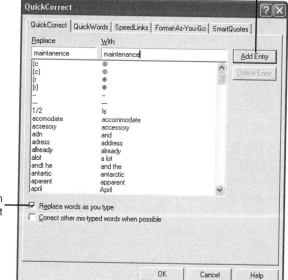

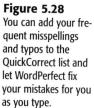

If you don't like QuickCorrect, you can turn it off completely. Choose Tools, QuickCorrect, and deselect Replace Words As You Type (that is, remove the check mark). A better solution might be to remove the entries that you don't like so that you can continue to take advantage of those that are helpful. To remove an entry, select it in the list, and then click Delete Entry, Yes.

**TIP FROM**

*Laura Acklen*

> Think of ways you can use QuickCorrect to insert long or hard-to-type words when you type a few characters. For example, you could add an entry to replace *wpo12* with *WordPerfect Office 12* or *dp* with *diaphoresis*.

**NOTE**

> If you've been using WordPerfect 7/8/9/10/11, you can use the QuickCorrect entries that you created in those versions. You just need to add the user word list file to the list of user word lists. Choose Tools, Spell Checker, Options, User Word Lists, Add List. Open `wt11us.uwl` for version 11, `wt10us.uwl` for version 10, `wt9us.uwl` for version 9, `wt80us.uwl` for version 8 or `wt61us.uwl` for version 7. You might need to substitute your two-letter country code in place of "us" in the filename.

## INSERTING SPEEDLINKS

The SpeedLinks feature creates a hyperlink whenever you type the beginning of an Internet address, such as www, ftp, http, or mailto. For example, when you type the URL www.wordperfect.com, SpeedLinks creates the hyperlink to the Web page. This also works for e-mail addresses such as *yourname@isp.com*. You can then give that hyperlink a friendlier name.

Follow these steps to create a SpeedLink:

1. Choose Tools, QuickCorrect, and then click the SpeedLinks tab (see Figure 5.29).
2. Type the friendlier name that you want to use to activate the hyperlink in the Link Word text box (the @ symbol is inserted automatically).
3. Type the location to link it to in the Location to Link To text box. If necessary, click the Files icon to browse your system (or the network) and select a drive, folder, or file. If you are typing an e-mail address, be sure to precede it with `mailto:`.

To insert a SpeedLinks entry in a document, type the @ symbol followed by the link word. When you press the spacebar or Enter, WordPerfect creates the hyperlink.

**TIP FROM**

*Laura Acklen*

> If you often work with hyperlinks, there is a toolbar that you can turn on. Right-click the toolbar and then click Hyperlink Tools. This toolbar has buttons to help you create and edit hyperlinks, move from the next to the previous hyperlink, activate and deactivate hyperlinks, create bookmarks, and edit the hyperlink style. When you're ready to turn it off, right-click a toolbar, and then click Hyperlink Tools again.

All link words
begin with an @

Click to browse your
system or network

**Figure 5.29**
Using SpeedLinks, you
can create a link word
that automatically cre-
ates a hyperlink to a
Web page, e-mail
address, document,
folder, or drive.

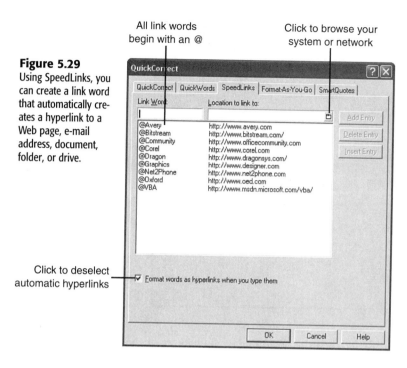

Click to deselect
automatic hyperlinks

 *If you don't want your URLs turned into hyperlinks, see "Please Stop Creating Hyperlinks" in the Troubleshooting section at the end of this chapter.*

## CUSTOMIZING FORMAT-AS-YOU-GO

The Format-As-You-Go feature helps keep your sentence structure accurate by cleaning up extra spaces between words and sentences. I can't get enough of the automatic capitalization at the beginning of a new sentence—I don't have to press that Shift key nearly as often. Format-As-You-Go also fixes most of your capitalization mistakes. For example, if there are two capital letters at the beginning of a word, the second letter is changed to lowercase.

You can choose Tools, QuickCorrect to open the QuickCorrect dialog box, and then click the Format-As-You-Go tab. By default, all the options in the Sentence Corrections section are selected, and End of Sentence Corrections is set to None (see Figure 5.30).

A check mark in the box indicates that a tool is enabled. You can turn these tools on and off by enabling and disabling the check boxes. Choose from the following options:

- CapsFix—Fixes problems with capitalization when Caps Lock is on by mistake and you hold down the Shift key to capitalize the first letter (such as tHIS). CapsFix works only if Caps Lock is on.

- QuickBullets—Helps you quickly create bulleted lists.

  → For more information on using the QuickBullets feature to create bulleted lists, **see** "Using QuickBullets," **p. 82.**

**Figure 5.30**
The Format-As-You-Go feature has six different tools to help you quickly create bulleted lists, graphic lines, ordinal numbers, en dashes, and em dashes.

Enable the check boxes to turn on the tools

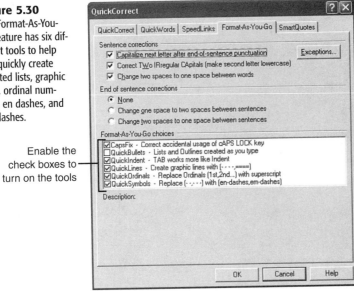

- QuickIndent—Pressing Tab at the beginning of the first and second lines of a paragraph creates a left indent for that paragraph.

- QuickLines—Typing four dashes and then pressing Enter creates a single horizontal line from the left to the right margin; typing four equal signs and then pressing Enter creates a double horizontal line from the left to the right margin.

- QuickOrdinals—Typing ordinal text after a number converts the ordinal text to superscript when you press the spacebar.

- QuickSymbols—Typing two hyphens followed by a space inserts an en dash; typing three hyphens followed by a space inserts an em dash.

## TURNING ON SMARTQUOTES

The mild-mannered SmartQuotes feature converts the regular straight quotation marks to typeset-quality curly quotation marks as you type. It doesn't sound like a big deal, but if you're producing materials that should have a more polished appearance, this is one of those small details that can really help. To turn off SmartQuotes or select different quotation characters:

1. Choose Tools, QuickCorrect, and then click the SmartQuotes tab to display the SmartQuotes options (see Figure 5.31).

2. Deselect the option that you don't want to use.

3. To change the quotation character, click the Open and Close drop-down list arrows and select another character.

Click a drop-down arrow to choose another character

**Figure 5.31**
The SmartQuotes feature replaces straight quotation marks with curly quotation marks for a more polished, professional appearance.

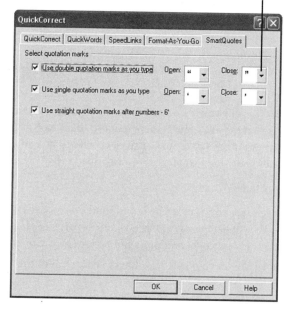

You can insert one of the symbols from the Symbols dialog box in place of a quotation character. Select one of the quotation characters, and then press Delete. Press Ctrl+W to open the Symbols dialog box. Select a symbol, and then click Insert and Close.

5

If you are working on an older document, or a document that was created by someone who did not turn on SmartQuotes, you can convert the regular straight quotation marks to typeset-quality curly quotation marks with the Find and Replace feature. All you have to do is turn on SmartQuotes, and then search for a quotation mark, replacing it with a quotation mark. I know, it sounds like you're searching and replacing the same thing, but since SmartQuotes is activated, the straight quotation marks will be replaced with curly quotation marks during the Find and Replace. This also works with apostrophes, so you can convert all of your single and double straight quotation marks to curly quotation marks in just two find and replace operations. Pretty cool, if you ask me.

*If text is changing automatically and you think your eyes are playing tricks on you, see "The Text Is Changing Right Before My Eyes" in the Troubleshooting section at the end of this chapter.*

# SETTING UP QUICKWORDS

QuickWords simplifies the process of typing frequently used words and phrases. You assign an abbreviation to a word or phrase, use the abbreviation when typing the document, and then expand the abbreviation. QuickWords isn't limited to words or phrases—you can create a QuickWord text with formatting codes, such as font attributes, or graphics that you would use for logos.

Some examples of how you might use QuickWords: create QuickWords for symbols that you use often; assign paragraphs to QuickWords and use them to quickly build documents that consist of form paragraphs (such as wills, leases, contracts, and so on); create a QuickWord for your company logo so you can quickly insert it whenever necessary.

Here's how to create a QuickWords entry:

1. Select the text or graphic you want to assign to QuickWords. If you want to insert a graphic or logo with a QuickWords entry, turn on Reveal Codes and position the red cursor to the left of the box code, and press Shift+right arrow to select the box code.

2. Choose Tools, QuickWords to display the QuickWords tab of the QuickCorrect dialog box (see Figure 5.32).

Select a QuickWords entry in the list to preview the expanded form
Type the abbreviation here

**Figure 5.32**
With QuickWords, you can assign an abbreviation to text or graphics, and then simply type the abbreviation to insert it into a document.

A preview of the text or graphics

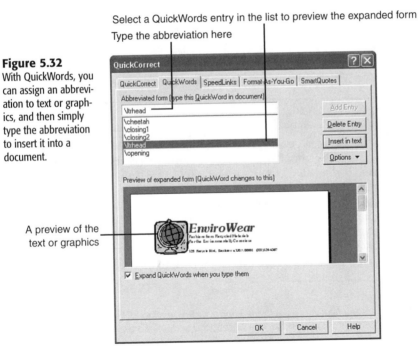

3. Type the abbreviation you want to use in the Abbreviated Form text box. The abbreviation can be a few letters or a one- or two-word phrase.

4. Click Add Entry.

**NOTE**

Try using words that won't normally come up in your documents for QuickWords. For example, you could use *qq* to expand a scientific symbol, *clogo* for the company logo (not just logo), or *will05* for a form paragraph.

**CAUTION**

If you're creating a QuickWords entry for a graphic image, make sure Expand As Text with Formatting is selected on the Options menu. Otherwise, the graphic won't appear in the document.

**TIP FROM**

*Laura Acklen*

The QuickWords feature has been touted as an accessible alternative to creating macros for inserting frequently used sections of text or graphics. You might want to take a closer look. It's faster, more flexible, and it's notably easier to edit a QuickWords entry than it is to edit a macro.

→ For more information on creating and running macros, **see** "Using Macros to Automate Repetitive Tasks," **p. 816.**

You can insert QuickWord entries into documents using one of the following methods:

- Type the abbreviation, and then press the spacebar, Tab, or Enter key. If this method doesn't work, the Expand QuickWords When You Type Them option has been disabled. You can manually expand a QuickWord by pressing Ctrl+Shift+A.

- Open the QuickWords dialog box, select a QuickWord from the list, and then choose Insert in Text.

5

The Options menu has items that control how QuickWords are inserted into a document. By default, QuickWords are expanded as text with formatting. Choose Options, Expand As Plain Text if you want plain text inserted instead.

It's easy to update a QuickWords entry when the form text changes (in the case of form paragraphs) or if you want to insert a different graphic image with a certain QuickWords entry. To replace a QuickWords entry, follow these steps:

1. Select the text or graphic.
2. Choose Tools, QuickWords.
3. Select from the list the QuickWords entry that you want to assign to the selected text or graphic.
4. Click the Options button and choose Replace Entry.
5. Click Yes in the confirmation message box.

You can also rename a QuickWords entry when necessary. On the QuickWords tab of the QuickCorrect dialog box, select the QuickWords entry, and then click Options, Rename Entry. Type the new name, and then click OK.

Every now and then, it's a good idea to go through the QuickWords entries and remove the ones you aren't using anymore. To delete a QuickWords entry, choose Tools, QuickWords. Select the QuickWords entry you want to delete, and then click Delete Entry.

Finally, you can turn off QuickWords if you don't want to expand the QuickWords as you type. In the QuickWords dialog box, deselect Expand QuickWords When You Type Them.

**TIP FROM**

To expand all the QuickWords at once, choose Tools, Macro, Play, and then double-click `expndall`. See "Running the Shipping Macros" in Chapter 24, "Experts and Macros," for more information on the macros that ship with WordPerfect Office 11/12.

*If you're getting an error message when you try to create QuickWords, see "I Can't Create New QuickWord Entries" in the Troubleshooting section at the end of this chapter.*

# USING VARIABLES

One of the cool features that was introduced in WordPerfect 10 is the Variable feature. You can create a variable code that represents a piece of information. You can insert the code in numerous locations, and then update them all at once. For example, in a supplier agreement, you enter the contact's name, payment terms, delivery dates, method of shipment, and so on. During negotiations, these pieces of information need to be updated—a new contact person is taking over, delivery dates have been moved out, the shipper has changed. Instead of conducting multiple search and replace operations, you simply revise the information in each variable and let WordPerfect take care of updating the document.

## CREATING VARIABLES

The Variable feature is the perfect tool for documents where the same information appears multiple times because you can define the Variable once and then insert it as many times as you like. The same thing goes for documents where certain pieces of information change every time you use the document—after you insert the variables, you can update the variable definitions and have those changes immediately reflected in the document. To create a variable in a document, follow these steps:

1. Position the insertion point where you want the information to appear.

2. Choose Insert, Variable. The Variables dialog box appears (see Figure 5.33). If any variables have been defined for this document, you'll see them in the list box.

Existing variables

**Figure 5.33**
Use the Variables feature to insert information that can be edited later and the changes automatically updated in the document.

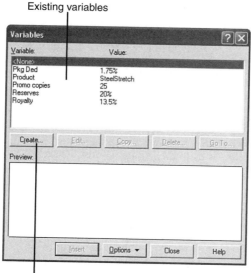

Click to create a new variable

3. Choose Create to open the Variables Editor dialog box (see Figure 5.34). If you've created or edited styles in the Styles Editor, this dialog box should look familiar.

**Figure 5.34**
Revisions to a variable are made in the Variables Editor dialog box, which looks similar to the Styles Editor dialog box.

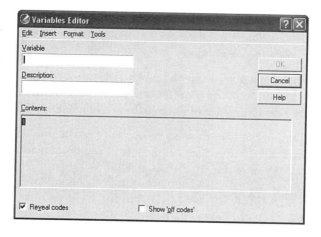

5

4. Type a name for the variable in the Variable text box. A variable name can contain up to 30 characters.

5. Type a description in the Description text box.

6. Click down in the Contents area and type the text that you want to appear in the document. A variable can hold up to 127 characters so keep it short and sweet.

7. Use the menus to format the text the way you want it to appear.

8. Use the menus to insert dates, symbols, graphics, equations, and so on.

9. Choose OK to close the Variables Editor dialog box and return to the Variable dialog box. The Preview section of the dialog box shows you how the variable will look when you insert it.

10. Choose Insert to insert the variable in the document.

After you create a list of variables for the document, you can use the following options in the Variables dialog box:

■ To insert a variable, select it from the list and choose Insert.

■ To edit the content or formatting of a variable, select it from the list and then choose Edit. In the Variables Editor, make the necessary revisions. When you close out of the dialog boxes and return to the document, the document will be updated with your changes. You can also double-click a variable in the document to open the Variables Editor dialog box.

■ If you need to remove a variable from the document, select it in the list and then choose Delete. Choose Including Formatting Codes or Leave Formatting Codes in Document, depending on what you want removed from the document.

## SAVING AND RETRIEVING VARIABLES

Let's say you've just spent the last 15 minutes inserting variables into a document. When you save the document, you save the list of variables with it. So, what happens when you start to edit another document and there are no variables defined yet? Do you have to start from scratch and create them each time?

Thankfully, no—you don't. You can save a list of variables to a file and then retrieve that into any other document. As a matter of fact, you can retrieve variables from multiple files, so you could build a customized list of variables from a library of variable files.

 Starting in WordPerfect 11, you can save a collection of variables to the default template so they are available for all new documents. If there is an additional objects template in use, you'll be able to save them to that template as well.

Here's how to save a list of variables to a file:

1. Choose Insert, Variable, Options, Save As.

2. In the Save File dialog box, type a filename or browse the system and select an existing file.

3. Choose Save.

Here's how to retrieve a list of variables into a document:

1. Choose Insert, Variable, Options, Retrieve.

2. In the Open File dialog box, type the name of the file, or browse the system and select the file.

3. Choose OK.

4. If necessary, confirm the replacement of current variables. You'll see this message if there are two variables with the same name. You have the option of overwriting the existing variable with a new variable from the file, or leaving the existing variable alone.

Finally, you can specify where to save a collection of variables in the Variable Settings dialog box:

1. Choose Insert, Variable, Options, Settings.

2. Select Default Template (or the Additional Objects Template) in the Save New Variables To section.

3. Choose OK.

**TIP FROM**

*Laura Acklen*

> There is a special view option for variables. Choose View, Variables. All the variables in a document will now be shown with blue triangles around them. If you hover over a variable, a QuickTip appears with the name of the variable.

# TROUBLESHOOTING

### MY NAME IS NOT MISSPELLED

*Spell Checker (and Grammatik) stop on my name, company name, company address, and all sorts of other words that are correctly spelled. How can I tell Spell Checker and Grammatik that the word is spelled correctly so that it won't stop on it again?*

In either Spell Checker or Grammatik, you can add correctly spelled words to the user word list so they won't stop on the word again (unless, of course, the word is misspelled). The next time that Spell Checker or Grammatik stops on the word, click Add to add it to the selected user word list. Also, make sure you are adding it to the user word list, not the document word list. Choose Options, User Word Lists, and make sure that WT11US (or WT12US) is selected.

### I TRASHED THE USER WORD LIST

*I wasn't paying attention and I added a bunch of words to the user word list that I should have added to another user word list file. Is there some way I can revert to the default user word list file without manually removing all the entries?*

You can restore the default contents by deleting the file and letting WordPerfect re-create it the next time you start the program. Delete the file WT11XX.UWL or WT12XX.UWL (where XX stands for the language code) in the \my documents\corel user files folder in Windows

98/ME, `\documents and settings\username\my documents\corel user files` in Windows 2000/XP, and the `d:\winnt\profiles\<user name>\my documents\corel` user files in Windows NT4.

This solution also works if you open the QuickCorrect dialog box and the QuickCorrect list is empty.

### MY WORDS AREN'T BEING ADDED

*I just finished spell checking a document, and I see that I added a bunch of words to the word list. Now when I check another document, Spell Checker still stops on those words. What's the deal?*

The words that you added during a spell check were inserted in the document word list, which is available only to this document, not the user word list, which is available to other documents. You need to set the user word list as the default word list. In the Spell Checker dialog box, choose Options, User Word Lists, select `WT11US.UWL` or `WT12US.UWL` in the list, and then click Set Default.

### MY EDITS TO A CHECKING STYLE AREN'T GETTING SAVED

*I made some changes to one of the checking styles, but I can't seem to save the edits.*

Any of the 11 predefined checking styles can be modified, but you must be sure to choose Save or Save As before you exit the Edit Checking Styles dialog box. If you choose Save, the changes are saved to the selected checking style. If you choose Save As, you can specify another name for the checking style. A modified checking style is shown with an asterisk (*) next to it in the Checking Styles dialog box.

### MY SENTENCES ARE NOT TOO LONG

*Grammatik is constantly flagging long sentences in my documents. Is there any way I can change this?*

Each checking style has its own threshold settings in the Maximum Allowed section of the Edit Checking Styles dialog box. You can increase the number of words in the Long Sentence Length text box to change the threshold setting for long sentences. You can set up to a maximum of 99 words.

Choose Tools, Grammatik, Options, Checking Styles. Select the style you are using, and then choose Edit. Adjust the value in the Long Sentence Length text box. Choose Save to save your changes to the selected checking style, or choose Save As to give the checking style a new name.

### THE TEXT IS CHANGING RIGHT BEFORE MY EYES

*I'm typing along and my text is changing automatically. If I type (c) in an outline, it changes into a copyright symbol; if I put two spaces after the end of a sentence, it changes to one; and I've got outlines appearing out of nowhere. What is going on?*

The Format-As-You-Go feature is a great feature…until it starts changing things that you want left alone. One of the most frequently asked questions is how to turn off the automatic outline feature, which can cause problems if a specific type of numbering style is necessary. Here's how to do it: Choose Tools, QuickCorrect and then click the Format-As-You-Go tab. Deselect the QuickBullets and QuickIndent options.

Another problem is the automatic creation of common typographical symbols. As mentioned previously, typing (c) creates the copyright symbol. This is part of the QuickCorrect feature, so open the QuickCorrect dialog box, and, if necessary, click the QuickCorrect tab. Select the entry for (c)—the top entry—and choose Delete Entry. You can go through the QuickCorrect list and selectively delete the entries that are apt to cause you trouble. Or, you can turn QuickCorrect off altogether by removing the check mark next to Replace Words As You Type.

Some people don't want the regular quotation marks changed to curly quotation marks. If you're one of them, open QuickCorrect and click the SmartQuotes tab. Remove the check marks next to the first two options.

Depending on your situation, one or more of the QuickCorrect tools can be a source of irritation! For the most part, it's better to selectively disable the options that you don't want, rather than lose out on all the functionality that QuickCorrect offers.

### Please Stop Creating Hyperlinks

*I'm typing in addresses for Web sites and and I don't want WP to automatically turn into hyperlinks. Is there some way to turn this off?*

Absolutely! This is another aspect of the QuickCorrect feature that can be turned off whenever it becomes inconvenient. First, choose Tools, QuickCorrect and then click the SpeedLinks tab. Remove the check mark from the Format Words As Hyperlinks When You Type Them check box. Choose OK. This will prevent WP from creating hyperlinks while you type. If you already have hyperlinks in the document, and you want them to stop acting like hyperlinks, choose Tools, Settings and then click the Environment tab. On the General tab, remove the check mark from the Activate Hyperlinks check box. Finally, if you want to turn the links into plain text, so they don't display as blue underlined text, turn on Reveal Codes and delete the hyperlink code before or after the text. Remember, the quickest way to delete a code is to click and drag it out of the Reveal Codes window.

### I Can't Create New QuickWord Entries

*I'm trying to create a new QuickWord entry, but when I choose Add Entry, I get an error message and WordPerfect locks up. When I restart WordPerfect, the entries that I had successfully created are gone and all I have is the list of sample entries that are installed with the program. What am I doing wrong?*

You're not doing anything wrong, so just relax. This is a known problem that occurs when QuickCorrect entries are longer than 22 characters. For some reason, this affects QuickWords. Open QuickCorrect and look for entries longer than 20 or so characters and delete them. Try to create a new QuickWord again. If this works, re-create the long QuickCorrect in QuickWords, which does not impose a limit on the number of characters.

# PROJECT

Rather than leave it up to individual employees of your company to add frequently used words to their user word list, you can create a standard user word list and distribute it throughout the company. You can even take things a step further—instead of just adding the company name, company address, names of clients, and technical terms, you can take advantage of the ability to create a custom list of replacement terms when a certain word is encountered. For example, if the word *chairman* is found, suggested replacement words such as *chairperson* or *chair* could be given.

A server installation must be performed first, and then a workstation installation. From this workstation, start WordPerfect and open the user word list by choosing Tools, Spell Checker, Options, User Word Lists. Select WT11US.UWL or WT12US.UWL in the list, and then add entries for your company name and address, clients, key personnel in the company, technical terms, and so on. Leave the Replace With text box blank, so the word is added as a <skip> word.

To add QuickCorrect replacements, type both the word and the replacement. If you add more than one replacement word for the same word, the suggested replacements appear on the Spell-As-You-Go list when a user right-clicks the underlined word. Also, an entry with more than one replacement is not automatically corrected while you type.

When you are finished, use Windows Search to locate this customized user word list file. Search the Windows folder and its subfolders. Make a copy of the file and name it wt11us.sav (or wt12us.sav). Replace the wt11us.sav (or wt12us.sav) file on the server with the customized wt11us.sav (or wt12us.sav) file.

Before you do the rest of the workstation installations, make sure there isn't a user word list file already on the system (from a previous installation). If there is already a wt11us.uwl (or wt12us.uwl) file on the workstation, WordPerfect won't copy the customized wt11us.sav (or wt12us.sav) file (which is renamed wt11us.uwl or wt12us.uwl on the workstation).

CHAPTER

# 6

# PRINTING, FAXING, AND E-MAILING

**In this chapter**

*by Read Gilgen*

# THE BASICS OF PRINTING

Despite predictions of the "paperless office," the end result of most WordPerfect documents is still printed pages. This way of thinking and working might be changing as we move toward publishing documents to the World Wide Web, or as we share documents via e-mail. But the printer continues to be an important part of the office, and printing is one of the essential tasks for any user of WordPerfect.

## SELECTING A PRINTER

WordPerfect is a *WYSIWYG* (what you see is what you get) program. However, to truly see onscreen what your document will look like, WordPerfect has to know what printer you are planning to use so it can display the proper fonts and print attributes. To select a printer, follow these steps:

1. Choose File, Print to display the Print dialog box (see Figure 6.1). The options you see on the Print tab of this dialog box may vary, depending on your printer's features.

**Figure 6.1**
WordPerfect's Print dialog box is the heart and soul of all printing options.

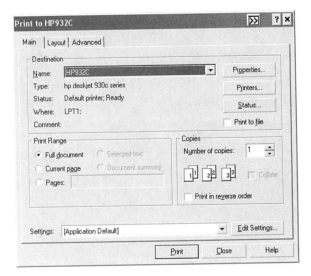

2. In the Destination Name list box, WordPerfect displays the currently selected printer. If the printer name displayed is the printer you will be using, you can click Close to return to your document, or you can proceed to print your document.

3. If the printer is not correct, click the drop-down list that displays the default Windows printer along with any other printers or fax drivers that have been installed in Windows.

4. Select the printer to which you want to print.

5. Click Close to return to your document.

**TIP FROM**

*Read Gilgen*

 You can quickly check which printer is selected by moving the mouse pointer to the printer icon on the application bar. A QuickTip appears that displays the name of the currently selected printer. If this is not the printer you want, click the printer icon to go to the Print dialog box, where you can change the selected printer.

With the proper printer selected, you can create or format your document with confidence, knowing that what you see on the screen will match what your printer can print.

**NOTE**

If you don't have the proper printer selected, you can still change the printer before printing. However, some formatting probably will change, including some printer fonts, line spacing, and so on. If you know the printer you'll use, it's best to choose it before spending too much time on your document.

 *If you get error messages telling you that WordPerfect is unable to access the printer, see "Printer Error Messages" in the Troubleshooting section at the end of this chapter.*

## PREVIEWING PRINTED OUTPUT

If you are working in Page view (which you get to by choosing View, Page), WordPerfect shows you on the screen exactly what you will see on the printed page. However, even if you're working in Draft view, WordPerfect also enables you to preview your printed output quickly and easily.

To preview your document before printing, choose File, Print Preview. Print Preview zooms the document to a full-page view, thus enabling you to see the whole page while at the same time enabling you to edit the document (see Figure 6.2). The Print Preview toolbar also appears, helping you to perform tasks that typically precede printing. These include the following:

 ■ Ruler—Click this icon to display a ruler above the document to help you verify page layout measurements.

 ■ View Page—This default Print Preview view displays a full page of the document. Although the text is usually too small to read, you still can edit or modify the page layout while in Print Preview.

 ■ Two Page View—This option shows two pages, side by side.

 ■ Zoom—If you want to see the document close up, you can zoom in using this option.

 ■ Spell Checker—One of the last things you do before printing is check the document's spelling. This icon makes it easy to access Spell Checker.

 ■ Make It Fit—If after previewing your document you decide you need to squeeze your document into fewer pages, use this icon to access the Make It Fit feature.

**6**

**Figure 6.2**
You can use Print Preview to preview the document layout before printing.

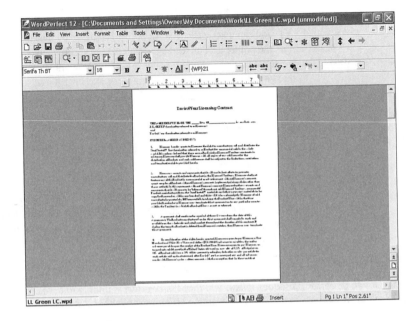

 ■ Page Setup—If you decide to change the paper size or orientation, access the Page Setup dialog box with this icon.

 ■ Print Document—This option sends the document directly to the printer, bypassing the Print dialog box.

 ■ Print—If you want to make changes in the number of copies or which pages to print, access the Print dialog box by clicking this icon.

 ■ Print Preview—Click this icon to turn off Print Preview.

 If you are satisfied with what you see in Print Preview, and if you want to print a single copy of the entire document, you can send the document directly to the printer by clicking the Print Document icon. Otherwise, click the Print icon to proceed to the Print dialog box  (refer to Figure 6.1).

**TIP FROM**

*Read Gilgen*

If you want to bypass the Print dialog box, simply press Ctrl+Shift+P. Unless you have made changes previously in the Print dialog box, this prints a single copy of the entire document.

## PRINTING MULTIPLE COPIES

One of the more commonly used printing options is to specify the number of copies of the document you want to print. To change the number of copies, simply change the number in the Number of Copies text box.

If you choose to print more than one copy, by default WordPerfect groups the copies as illustrated in the Copies area of the dialog box. You can also choose to collate copies by checking the Collate box. Figure 6.3 shows the effect of selecting this option.

**Figure 6.3**
The Print dialog box enables you to choose many options for printing your document, including number of copies, collating options, and even printing only selected text.

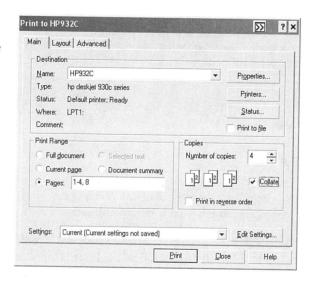

## PRINTING SPECIFIC DOCUMENT PAGES

Although you typically print a full document (WordPerfect's default), you can also print selected pages of the document. The options on the Main tab of the Print dialog box include

- Current Page—This option prints only the page on which the cursor currently resides. This is the quickest way to print a single page in a large document.

- Pages—Using this option you can choose a range of pages, or specific nonsequential pages. For example, if you need to print pages one through four, you type **1-4**. If you also want to print page 15, you type **1-4, 15** in the text box. If you type a page number followed by a dash, WordPerfect prints from that page number to the end of the document. For example, **4-** prints page four and everything that follows it.

**NOTE**

If you click the Advanced tab of the Print dialog box, you see options for printing multiple pages or labels, secondary pages, chapters, and volumes. However, under the Main tab you can indicate only page numbers.

**CAUTION**

The numbers you enter in the Pages text box must be in numeric order; otherwise, all the pages might not print. For example, if you specify **12-15, 4**, only pages 12–15 print. To print these specific pages, you must enter **4, 12-15**.

6

■ Selected text—If you have selected text before accessing the Print dialog box, this option prints only the selected text.

> **NOTE**
>
> When you choose to print selected text, the output appears on the printed page in the same location in which it would have appeared had you printed the surrounding text. For example, if you select the last paragraph on the page, the paragraph prints by itself at the bottom of the page.

 *If you try to print and nothing happens, see "When Nothing Happens" in the Troubleshooting section at the end of this chapter.*

## CONTROLLING PRINT JOBS

When you ask WordPerfect to print something, you create a *print job*. Both WordPerfect and Windows enable you to check the status of any current print jobs and to control multiple print jobs. To control a print job from within WordPerfect, follow these steps:

1. Access the Print dialog box by choosing File, Print (refer to Figure 6.3).
2. Click the Status button. WordPerfect displays the Print History and Status dialog box (see Figure 6.4), which in turn displays information about the various WordPerfect print jobs waiting to be printed, along with a list of recently completed print jobs.

> **NOTE**
>
> If you don't see any print jobs in the Print History and Status dialog box, choose Display, and uncheck Hide Completed Jobs.

**Figure 6.4**
WordPerfect's Print History and Status dialog box provides information about current as well as recent print jobs, and enables you to pause or cancel print jobs in progress.

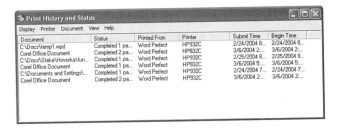

3. Locate and select the print job you want to control.
4. Choose Document, Pause Printing if you want to temporarily pause printing.
5. Choose Document, Cancel Printing to stop the print job, even if it's in progress.
6. Choose Document, Remove to delete a print job from the list.
7. Close the Print History and Status dialog box to return to the Print dialog box.

WordPerfect's Print History and Status dialog box works the same as the Windows Printer dialog boxes, but the Windows dialog box is a bit easier to access. When you begin printing, Windows displays a printer icon on the Windows taskbar (see Figure 6.5). Double-click the icon to display the Printer dialog box (see Figure 6.6). You then can select a print job and pause or cancel it.

**Figure 6.5**
The Windows printer icon on the Windows taskbar appears only when a print job is in progress. You can double-click the icon to access the Windows Printer dialog box.

Windows Printer Control

**Figure 6.6**
The Windows Printer dialog box is similar to the WordPerfect Print History and Status dialog box, but is easier to access, thus enabling you to more quickly cancel a print job.

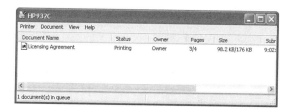

**NOTE**

You can pause or cancel the printing of all documents on a printer that is attached to your computer. If you are using a network printer, you might see other print jobs listed that are not yours. However, you can pause or cancel only your own documents.

**CAUTION**

If you are connected to a network, you might have access to several different printers that are also connected to the network. Be careful, however, to select only those printers where you really want to print. Otherwise, you might end up sending a print job to a printer in a far-flung area of the company or, worse, to someone who shouldn't see your printed output.

# USING PRINT OPTIONS

You now know about some of the most common printing tasks and procedures you are likely to encounter. WordPerfect also offers a wide array of options for printing nearly any kind of document.

6

## MAIN, LAYOUT, AND ADVANCED OPTIONS

On the Main tab of the Print dialog box (refer to Figure 6.1), you can use the following options:

- Print in Reverse Order—Depending on how your printer stacks pages as they're completed, you might want to print the pages in reverse order so that they are stacked in the proper order.

- Printers—In the Destination section, you can add a printer by clicking the Printers button, which is the same as accessing the Windows Start button, and choosing Settings, Printers. Here you can even specify whether this is a fax printer (see the section "Faxing Documents" later in this chapter).

- Properties—The options available in the dialog box that appears when you click the Properties button vary depending on the printer you have selected. For example, Figure 6.7 shows some of the options available for an HP inkjet printer when you choose to print to photo paper.

- Document Summary—This option prints only the document summary but none of the body of the document.

**Figure 6.7**
The Properties dialog box for your currently selected printer enables you to fine-tune your printer's settings for optimal printing.

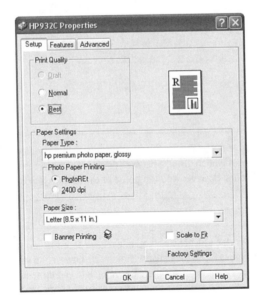

**NOTE**

In earlier versions of WordPerfect, you could specify printer resolution. However, because resolution really is dependent on the printer, WordPerfect now lets you select that and other options in the printer Properties dialog box.

- Print to File—By default, your print job goes to the printer device specified in the printer setup—for example, to a local printer or to a network printer. However, you can also send the output to a file if you choose Print to File. Then when you click Print, WordPerfect asks you for a filename. Use this option if you want to copy a print image directly to a printer—for example, a PostScript file to a PostScript printer.

The Layout Tab offers several options for enlarging or reducing your text, or for double-sided printing. However, two specific options that can be used with all documents are:

- Print File Information—If you select this option, WordPerfect prints the file location of your document in a small font at the lower-left corner of each page of your document.

- Show Crop/Fold Marks—This option is most useful if you print subdivided pages and need to know where to cut or fold the resulting printed pages. However, you can also print crop marks on any document you print.

On the Advanced tab of the Print dialog box (see Figure 6.8), you find the following advanced options:

**Figure 6.8**
The Advanced tab of the Print dialog box enables you to control output options, such as color, graphics, and paper feed.

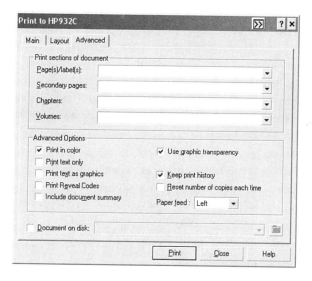

- Document on Disk—You need not open a file before you print it. Instead, simply select this option, and in the text box that appears, enter the name of the document you want to print. WordPerfect then prints the file directly from your disk to the printer.

- Print in Color—Color printing is more often affected by the printer setup than by the WordPerfect setting. If you're having a problem printing in black and white only, try deselecting Print in Color and see if that works. If the document still prints in color, you have to change your printer's setup properties (on the Main tab) in order to print in only black and white. If you have a laser printer that prints only in black and white, the color options are not available.

- Print Text Only—Choose this option if you don't want to print your graphic images (for example, in a draft). WordPerfect still preserves the formatting of the text, leaving blank spaces where the graphics would normally print.

- Print Text As Graphics—If for some reason your printer doesn't print text properly you might try selecting this option. For example, some laser printers don't print white text on a black background (such as in a table heading), or they print text that should be hidden by graphic images. Choosing this option overcomes these limitations.

 *If your graphics don't look good, see "Better Graphics Printing" in the Troubleshooting section at the end of this chapter.*

- Print Reveal Codes—New in WordPerfect 11, you can print the document along with Reveal Codes icons for training or troubleshooting.

- Use Graphic Transparency—Many Internet graphic images, such as transparent GIF images, have a single-color background that displays as a transparent background. By default, WordPerfect does not print such backgrounds. Deselect this option if you want WordPerfect to print solid color graphic backgrounds.

- Keep Print History—If you *don't* want WordPerfect to keep track of your print jobs, deselect this option. Print jobs still appear in the Print History and Status dialog box, but only until the print job is completed, after which they disappear.

- Reset Number of Copies Each Time—If you choose to print more than one copy, on the Main tab of the Print dialog box, WordPerfect remembers that number until you close your document. Choosing this option forces WordPerfect to reset the number of copies to one after you print the document. If you tend to forget that you've changed the number of copies, choosing this option can help you avoid wasting paper for copies you don't want.

- Paper Feed—If you have chosen a paper size that is smaller than the typical 8 1/2 inches by 11 inches, WordPerfect attempts to determine where in that 8 1/2-inch range to print the document. For example, if WordPerfect knows that your printer feeds envelopes along the left side, it prints the text of the envelope there as well. For some paper sizes, you can specify where you want to insert them: at the left, center, or right of the printer tray or manual feed slot. You might have to experiment to get the location just right when using nonstandard paper sizes.

## TWO-SIDED PRINTING

In most cases you'll probably print your documents single-sided. However, if you need to print on both sides—for example, when printing a booklet—WordPerfect can help you. Simply access the Print dialog box and click the Layout tab (see Figure 6.9). Then choose from among these options:

- Use Document Settings—Depending on the type of document you're printing, two-sided printing might already have been chosen for you. If you want to force single-sided printing, choose Off.

**Figure 6.9**
You can use the
Layout tab of the Print
dialog box to print
posters or thumbnails
of your document, or
to scale your docu-
ment pages to differ-
ent paper shapes and
sizes.

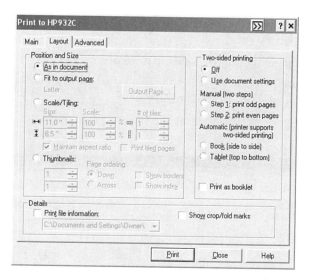

- Manual—If your printer doesn't support automatic two-sided printing (and most don't), you'll have to print all the odd pages, turn the stack of printed pages over, reinsert them in the printer, and then print all the even pages. Choose Step 1 to print the odd pages, and Step 2 to print the even pages.

- Automatic—If your printer does support two-sided printing, you can further choose to print the pages for binding along the side, as in a book, or along the top, as in a tablet. Simply choose Book for side-to-side printing, or Tablet for top-to-bottom printing.

- Print as Booklet—If you format your pages for booklet printing, this option tells WordPerfect to organize the half pages in the sequence required for a folded booklet (see "Printing Booklets," later in this chapter).

## ENLARGING AND REDUCING PRINT OUTPUT

Life would be simple if all you ever had to do was print your documents to standard *portrait* orientation (8 1/2 inches wide by 11 inches tall) or standard *landscape* orientation (11 inches wide by 8 1/2 inches tall). Fortunately, WordPerfect recognizes that you sometimes need to print both larger and smaller versions of documents.

One common printing need is for posters that display larger than one page. For example, if you are making a presentation and want the audience to be able to read a printed page, you could create a poster that consists of up to 10 pages wide and 10 pages tall.

To create a poster, first create the page in WordPerfect as you normally would. Then follow these steps:

1. Access the Print dialog box.

2. Click the Layout tab. WordPerfect displays options for enlarging and reducing your printed output (refer to Figure 6.9).

6

3. Choose Scale/Tiling.

4. Click Print Tiled Pages.

5. Specify the number of tiles you want, up to 10 tiles.

6. Click the Layout Preview button on the title bar of the Print dialog box to preview the layout you have specified (see Figure 6.10).

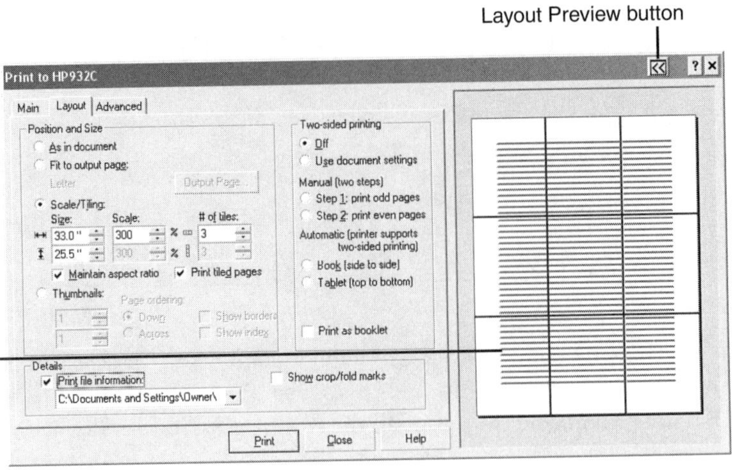

**Figure 6.10**
The Layout Preview box shows how your document is tiled across several pages to enable you to create a poster.

> **NOTE**
> WordPerfect does not display an actual preview of your document, but only a preview of the page layout. Also, the resulting printed pages are complete pages expanded or squeezed to fit the page layout you select.

7. Click Print to print the document. After WordPerfect prints the pages, you must trim and paste the pages together to complete the poster.

You can also specify the exact size of the printed document. For example, if you want to create quarter-page printouts, choose the Scale/Tiling option, and then specify the percentage (for example, 50%). Again, click the Layout Preview box button to display the size of the output (see Figure 6.11).

> **NOTE**
> Remember that 50% is half the height and *also* half the width. You probably need to experiment with size settings until you get a feel for what works best.

If you want to use a smaller (or larger) paper size, but you still want the equivalent of your 8 1/2-inch by 11-inch page on the target paper size, follow these steps:

**Figure 6.11**
The Layout Preview box shows how your reduced pages will appear when printed.

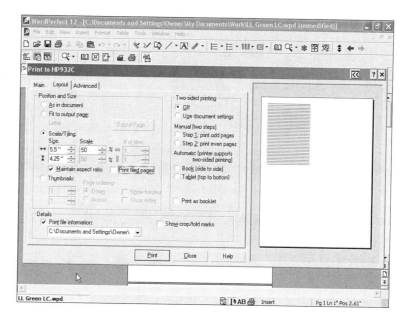

1. While in the Layout tab of the Print dialog box, select Fit to Output Page.
2. Click the Output Page button to display the Page Setup dialog box (see Figure 6.12).

**Figure 6.12**
You can use the Page Setup dialog box to select the paper size you'll be using for your custom print output.

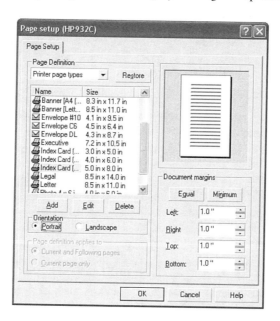

3. Choose the target paper size from the Page Setup list, and click OK.
4. Click Print, and WordPerfect formats the document to fit the target paper size.

> **NOTE**
>
> Although you can squeeze the contents of a regular-size page into another paper size, the result might not be very attractive because WordPerfect has to distort letter spacing and fonts to make things fit.

A *thumbnail* is a small, but complete, view of a page, which gives the reader an idea of what the full-size page contains. Several thumbnails can be included on one full printed page. If you want a thumbnail summary of your document pages, choose the Thumbnails option from the Layout tab. You then can choose the following options (see Figure 6.13 with some options already selected):

**Figure 6.13**
To create a summary of your document, you can print several thumbnail pages on one page.

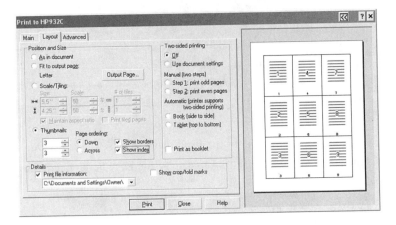

- You can specify how many thumbnails you want per page, up to 10 across and 10 down.
- You can select the order of the thumbnail pages, either across or down.
- You can show borders around each thumbnail, to help set them off and make them appear more like printed pages.
- You can also choose Show Index to display a page number beneath each thumbnail.
- You can select the size and shape of the output page (for example, a landscape page) by clicking the Output Page button, used also for the Fit to Output Page option.

After you determine the options you want, click Print to print the page of thumbnails.

# PRINTING ENVELOPES, LABELS, AND BOOKLETS

Certain documents, such as envelopes, labels, or booklets, must be printed to nonstandard forms. When you set up the page size for these types of documents, WordPerfect automatically knows how to format the output to fit those particular page sizes.

You create content for these types of documents the same as you do for any document. What's different is the shape or size of the document, and how you print it.

## CREATING AND PRINTING ENVELOPES

Despite the capability to fax and e-mail documents from within WordPerfect, some of us still mail them out the old-fashioned way—in an envelope. And why not? With WordPerfect it couldn't be any easier!

To create an envelope, follow these steps:

1. Open the Format menu and choose Envelope. The Envelope dialog box appears (see Figure 6.14).

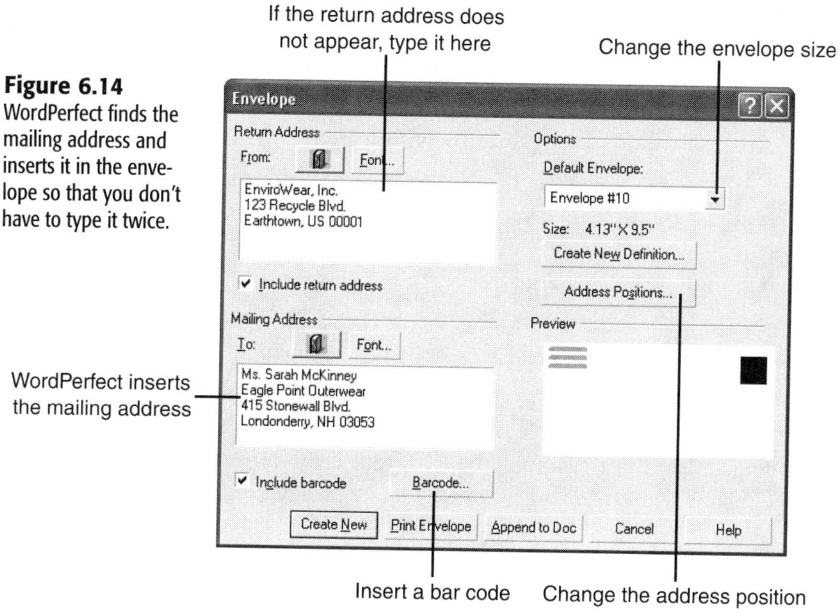

If the return address does not appear, type it here

Change the envelope size

**Figure 6.14**
WordPerfect finds the mailing address and inserts it in the envelope so that you don't have to type it twice.

WordPerfect inserts the mailing address

Insert a bar code    Change the address position

**NOTE**

When you already have a document open that includes an address at the beginning, separated from the body of the text by two hard returns, WordPerfect's envelope feature usually finds that address and automatically places it in the Mailing Address text box. If not you can type it in the Mailing Address box, or click Cancel, select the text of the address from the document, and after choosing Format, Envelope, paste the address into the Mailing Address box.

**CAUTION**

You might see the following message (instead of the Envelope dialog box): "The Template feature allows you to enter information about yourself that will personalize your templates. You need only enter this once."

6

*continues*

*continued*

You have a choice: You can either create a record in the Address Book with your personal information now, in which case WordPerfect will automatically insert your return address, or you can skip this step and type your return address in the envelope manually. Keep in mind if you skip the step of entering your personal information, you'll be prompted to do it every time you try to do something that involves a template.

→ For more information on personalizing templates, **see** "Filling in Personal Information," **p. 716**.

2. If a return address does not appear in the From text box, or if you want to modify the address, you have a couple of options:

- Click in the From text box and enter the information.
- Click the Address Book icon if you want to select an address from any of the available address books (which vary depending on your e-mail capabilities).

3. If necessary, you can do the following:

- Use another mailing address—You can either manually replace the mailing address or click the Address Book icon and choose a mailing address from one of the available address books.
- Click the Font button to change the font and/or font size for the return address and mailing address. For example, the Arial font is often easier to read on an envelope than is Times Roman, or other fonts typically used in text documents.

**NOTE**

If you change the font for either the return or mailing addresses, that font remains in effect the next time you create an envelope. This is sometimes called a *sticky* setting because it doesn't change when you exit WordPerfect.

- Insert a bar code—Click the Bar Code button, and then if WordPerfect hasn't already added the ZIP code from the envelope's address, type the recipient's ZIP code, and choose a position for the bar code.
- Adjust the address positions—Click the Address Positions button, and then adjust the placement of the return and mailing addresses.
- Choose a different envelope size—Click the Default Envelope drop-down list arrow, and then choose a size from the list.

4. When you're finished, choose from the following:

- Click the Create New button if you want to place the envelope in a new document.

- Click the Print Envelope button to send the envelope directly to the printer.
- Click the Append to Doc button if you want to place the envelope at the bottom of the current document.

Figure 6.15 shows a typical envelope, as a separate document, ready to print.

**Figure 6.15**
After you set up your envelope, WordPerfect knows how to print it perfectly on an envelope that's the size you select.

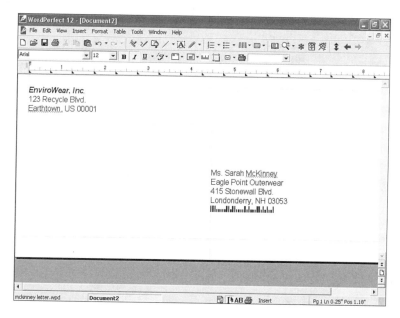

To verify that the page is set up properly, choose File, Page Setup. WordPerfect displays the Page Setup dialog box, shown in Figure 6.16. Note that WordPerfect has selected the Envelope page definition.

NOTE
> WordPerfect chooses a page definition and source based on your currently selected printer. For example, if you are using a laser printer with an envelope bin, WordPerfect automatically selects that source. However, if you don't have an envelope bin, WordPerfect looks for an envelope in the manual feed tray of the laser printer.

6

When you print, WordPerfect automatically selects the proper form and prints the correct size to match that form. Depending on your printer, WordPerfect typically waits for you to insert the proper form if it isn't a standard 8 1/2-inch by 11-inch sheet of paper.

**Figure 6.16**
You can use the Page Setup dialog box to change the envelope (or other page) size before printing.

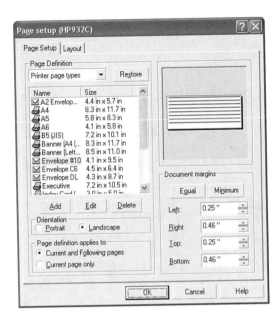

TIP FROM

*Read Gilgen*

If your envelope is appended to a document and you want to print just the envelope, position your cursor on the envelope page. Then choose File, Print, and select Current Page.

*If your envelopes don't seem to be printing correctly, even when you know you have the proper form selected, see "Creating an Envelope Definition" in the Troubleshooting section at the end of this chapter.*

## PRINTING LABELS

Labels are another different-size form, but generally labels come on a standard 8 1/2-inch by 11-inch sheet, or for a dot-matrix printer, on a continuous roll.

Typically, you choose a label layout *before* you create the labels themselves. To set up labels correctly, choose Format, Labels. WordPerfect displays the Labels dialog box (see Figure 6.17). You then can choose from the entire list of label definitions, or just from the Laser-printed, or Tractor-fed labels. The preview box displays the label definition you choose.

If you're printing to a laser printer, WordPerfect prints an entire page of labels (for example, 30 labels on a 3-column-by-10-row page of labels). If you're printing to a dot matrix printer, you can print one label at a time, in a continuous roll.

Assuming you've defined your labels correctly, you simply access the Print dialog box and choose Print.

**Figure 6.17**
WordPerfect formats entire pages of labels, as shown in the preview box of the Labels dialog box.

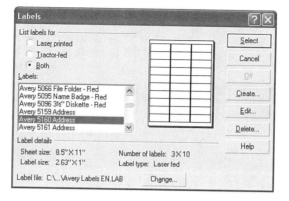

WordPerfect defines each label as a separate page. Thus, if you specify that you want to print only pages 1–15, the first 15 labels print, leaving blank the last 15 labels on a 30-label page.

**TIP FROM**

*Read Gilgen*

If you're using an inkjet printer, you can reuse a partially used sheet of labels by making sure that the first label you want to print corresponds to the first available label on the sheet. For example, to begin with label 16, access the Print dialog box, and choose Print Pages, Beginning at 16.

**CAUTION**

You might be tempted to send a partially used sheet of labels through your laser printer again to print on the unused labels. However, the heat process from printing the sheet the first time can loosen unused labels, causing them to come off in the printer the second time around. Cleaning stuck labels from inside a laser printer is both time-consuming and costly.

➔ For more information on creating labels using WordPerfect's Merge feature, **see** "Merging to Labels," **p. 766**.

## PRINTING BOOKLETS

You can divide pages to print in a booklet style (with pages folded in half). Typically, you use landscape orientation so that each half page ends up 8 1/2 inches tall by 5 1/2 inches wide. Then, using WordPerfect's booklet feature, you can print the pages so that they are numbered and ordered automatically.

**NOTE**

Booklets are like labels in that more than one page is printed on each sheet of paper. However, you can only print booklets that contain two booklet pages per sheet of paper.

To set up booklet printing, follow these steps:

1. Choose File, Page Setup to access the Page Setup dialog box (see Figure 6.18, shown with Landscape selected, and with margins set at 1/2 inch).

**Figure 6.18**
You choose Landscape in the Page Setup dialog box when setting up a typical booklet page.

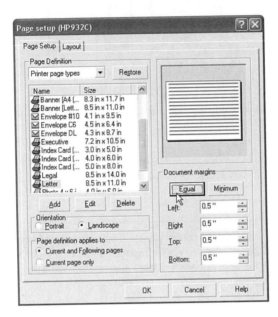

2. Choose the target paper size, typically Letter size (8 1/2 inches by 11 inches).

3. Choose the paper orientation, typically Landscape.

4. Set your margins as desired. In booklets 1-inch margins are too large, so choose something smaller, such as 1/2 inch.

5. Click the Layout tab (see Figure 6.19).

6. In the Divide page section, choose 2 Columns (commonly used with landscape pages), or 2 Rows (often used with portrait pages). Note how the pages look in the preview box and make any adjustments you want.

7. Choose OK to return to your document.

Your pages are now formatted to fit in a half-page–size booklet. However, you also want WordPerfect to organize the printed pages so that they appear in the proper order. Thus, you won't have to cut and paste the pages to prepare them for the duplication.

To illustrate, normally if you print a four-page booklet, WordPerfect prints page 1 on the left side of the first sheet and page 2 on the right side of the first sheet (see Figure 6.20).

**Figure 6.19**
When setting up a booklet, reduce the margins and use Divide Page to specify what type of booklet you want.

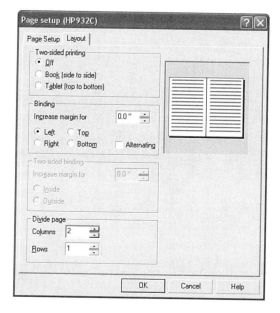

**Figure 6.20**
Normally, WordPerfect prints divided pages sequentially, which is proper for some folded brochures, but doesn't work for folded booklets.

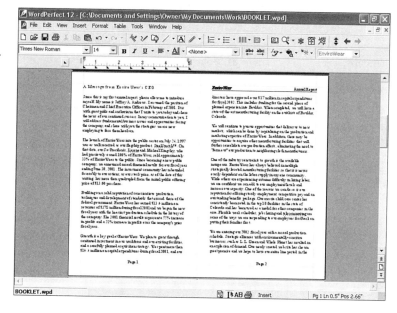

Instead, you want page 4 on the left side of the first sheet, and page 1 on the right side (see Figure 6.21). On the back side, you want page 2 on the left side and page 3 on the right side.

**Figure 6.21**
WordPerfect's booklet printing option organizes divided pages properly so that they appear in proper sequence for a folded booklet.

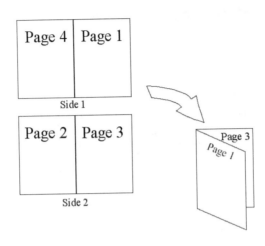

 To print booklet pages in the proper order, first make sure that the booklet pages have been formatted as previously described. Then, access the Print dialog box, click the Layout tab, and check the Print as booklet check box. Also select any two-sided printing options that match your printing situation. Generally, Use Document Settings works for most printers.

Finally, print the document. WordPerfect automatically arranges all the pages correctly and begins to print all of one side of each sheet of paper. If your printer does two-sided printing manually, WordPerfect then prompts you to reinsert the pages to print the second side of the paper (see Figure 6.22).

**Figure 6.22**
Unless you turn two-sided printing off, your printer program typically prompts you when it's time to reinsert pages being printed manually on two sides, such as booklet pages.

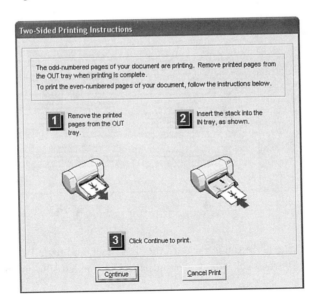

6

**NOTE**

When you save a document formatted for booklet printing, WordPerfect does not remember that setting. If you open such a document, be sure to access the Layout tab of the Print dialog box and select the Print as Booklet option before printing the booklet.

**TIP FROM**

*Read Gilgen*

If you plan to take the printed output to a printer or duplicating service, you do not need to reinsert the pages. Simply click OK when prompted to reinsert a page, and WordPerfect prints the second sides on new sheets of paper. Even easier, you can turn two-sided printing Off on the Layout tab of the Print dialog box. It's easier for a commercial printer to duplicate single-sided sheets than sheets that have been printed on both sides.

**TIP FROM**

*Read Gilgen*

The first time you print double-sided booklets, you might have to experiment with your printer so that the reinserted sheets print properly. Start with a short (for example, four-page) test booklet to try it out before printing a longer booklet.

## USING CUSTOM PRINT SETTINGS

Sometimes you use a customized printing procedure over and over again. WordPerfect lets you save customized settings so that you can recall them quickly when needed.

Suppose, for example, you have a standard report that requires you to print in a booklet format. Follow these steps to save and use a custom print setup:

1. From the Print dialog box, make the various setup changes you need to print exactly what you want (for example, choose Print as Booklet from the Layout tab).

2. Without printing yet, from the Main tab, click Edit Settings. WordPerfect displays the Edit Settings dialog box (see Figure 6.23, which has a new named setting).

3. Change the Name for Current Settings (for example, Annual Report).

4. You can ignore the Settings to Save list because you have already made the changes you want.

5. Uncheck the Use Printer Properties from [System Default] box at the lower-left corner of the dialog box.

6. Click the Save button.

7. Click Close.

6

**Figure 6.23**
You can use the Edit Settings dialog box to save customized print settings for future use.

**NOTE**

The Named Settings dialog box is laid out slightly differently in WordPerfect 11, but the functions are essentially the same. Instead of the Save button, when you're saving a new setup the button is named Add, and when you're saving changes to an existing setup, the button is named Replace.

Now whenever you want to print using your named setting, simply access the Print dialog box, select your named setting from the Settings list box (for example, Annual Report), and WordPerfect modifies the Print dialog box setup. Click Print to print using the new settings.

**TIP FROM**

*Read Gilgen*

When you make changes to the Print dialog box setup, WordPerfect remembers those settings for that document until you close the document. If you want to restore the default print settings quickly without closing the document, access the Print dialog box, click Edit Settings, choose [Application Default], and then choose Retrieve.

## FAXING DOCUMENTS

Printing to paper through a local or network printer is only one method of getting your document out to the world. WordPerfect can also fax your document directly from within WordPerfect to any other location, quickly and painlessly. However, first the following conditions must be met:

- A fax board must be installed in your computer (or connected to your network) and also be connected to a working telephone line. Most modems come with faxing capabilities built in, so if you have a modem, you probably already have the hardware needed to fax. Check your modem manual for more information.

- A Windows-based fax program must be installed on your computer. When fax software is installed, a fax printer appears in your list of available printers. You can check this by clicking the Windows Start button and choosing Settings, Printers (see Figure 6.24), or by accessing the WordPerfect Print dialog box and clicking the drop-down list under Name. Many modems ship with fax software (check your modem documentation for more information), and Windows XP has a built-in Send Fax Wizard.

- The person to whom you send the fax must have a fax machine or a computer-based fax program and a fax/modem to receive the fax.

**Figure 6.24**
If you have a fax printer installed in your Windows system, that printer appears along with other printers in the Windows Printers dialog box.

Assuming that the listed conditions are met and the hardware and software are properly set up, follow these steps to fax a document from WordPerfect:

1. With the document that you want to fax in the active window, choose File, Print, or press F5.

2. Choose the fax printer from the Name drop-down list.

3. Make other changes to the print setup as desired (for example, which pages to print).

4. Click Fax to fax the document. WordPerfect then prepares the document for faxing and hands it off to your fax software for faxing.

5. Your fax software should display a dialog box that enables you to designate where to send the fax. If the dialog box doesn't appear, click the fax software icon on the Windows taskbar or press Alt+Tab to toggle to the fax software.

6. Fill in the destination information in the fax program's dialog box, and then send the fax. Figure 6.25 shows a typical screen from the Windows Send Fax wizard.

6

**Figure 6.25**
Fax software "prints"
your document to
your fax/modem and
sends it to the
fax/phone you spec-
ify. Your Fax dialog
box might be different
than shown, but it
should include
most of the same
information.

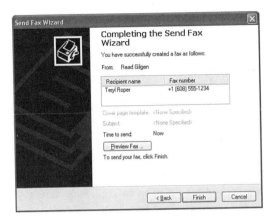

After the document is scheduled for sending, you can use the fax program's software to monitor the fax status, check the fax logs, or even cancel the fax if it hasn't yet been sent.

 *If the recipient of your fax complains about page breaks appearing in the wrong places, see "Fax Has Bad Page Breaks" in the Troubleshooting section at the end of the chapter.*

# SENDING DOCUMENTS VIA E-MAIL

If you use an e-mail program, you can send a selected portion of your document in your messages, or send the entire document as an attachment to a message.

To determine whether your mail program has been installed and is integrated with WordPerfect, choose File, Send To. Supported mail programs are listed on the menu, as is a Mail option (see Figure 6.26).

If you want to send the entire file as an e-mail attachment, simply choose Send to GroupWise Recipient (or whatever e-mail program you're using). Windows switches you to your mail program, which then adds the document as an attachment and enables you to send a message with the attachment (see Figure 6.27).

You can also send just a portion of the document as part of the body of your message. In WordPerfect, select the text you want to mail, choose File, Send To, and choose Mail. Windows starts your mail program and adds the selected text to the body of the message. You then provide an address, edit the text, and send the message.

If your e-mail program does not appear on the WordPerfect File, Send To menu, you still have these options:

- You can enable your mail program so that WordPerfect recognizes it. You can do this on the Windows Control Panel. Find the Mail icon, open it, and follow the procedures listed there for adding a mail program. You can also open the Internet Options icon and, on the Programs tab, specify which mail program should be used.

**Figure 6.26**
If your mail program is installed and recognized by WordPerfect, it appears on the File, Send To menu.

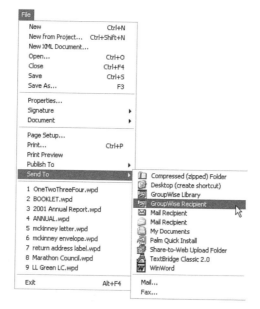

**Figure 6.27**
If you send your document as an attachment, the receiver can then download the attachment and open it in WordPerfect to preserve all the document's formatting.

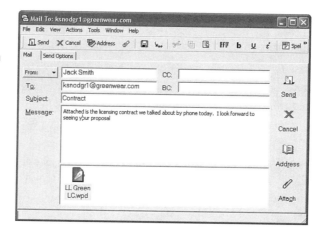

- You can save your document, open your mail program separately, and then add the document as an attachment.

- You can copy text from a WordPerfect document and paste it in the body of the mail message. Using this method removes most, if not all, of WordPerfect's formatting.

**TIP FROM**

*Read Gilgen*

Don't forget that you can also copy text from WordPerfect and paste it into your mail message, even if your mail program isn't integrated with WordPerfect.

6

# TROUBLESHOOTING

### PRINTER ERROR MESSAGES

*When I start WordPerfect, and sometimes at other times, I get an error message saying "Unable to access printer" and it tells me to check the status of the printer in the Printers folder. I do that and everything appears to be normal. What does the message mean?*

Fortunately, when you see this message you still can print. It simply means that the WordPerfect printer engine (Print Server 100) might not be loaded properly. However, the next time you try to print WordPerfect will load it again.

Sometimes, Windows memory gets used up by programs and processes and not enough is left for WordPerfect to load its printer controls. If you open WordPerfect and find only a limited number of fonts available (for example, Courier only), exit WordPerfect and any other programs and restart Windows.

Unfortunately, some early releases of previous versions of WordPerfect had several printing-related bugs. If you encounter these problems with WordPerfect 12, try clicking OK and continue working. However, also make sure you obtain and install from Corel the latest service packs to fix this and any other early release problems. Go to http://www.corel.com and download the Service Pack for WordPerfect 12.

### WHEN NOTHING HAPPENS

*I chose Print from the Print dialog box, but nothing happened. What am I doing wrong?*

First, make sure your printer is on and online. Usually, if a printer is not available or is offline, you get an error message telling you so. Next, make sure you have selected the proper printer. If you're connected to a network, selecting the wrong printer might send your document to someone else's printer.

Finally, check to see if previous Windows or WordPerfect print jobs are stalled and clogging up the print queue. In WordPerfect go to File, Print, Status, and in Windows, go to Start, Printers and Faxes, and double-click the printer you want to check. Delete the offending print job, and then you should be able to start a new print job.

### BETTER GRAPHICS PRINTING

*When I print a document with graphics, the graphic images don't look good even though I'm using a laser printer.*

The problem might be that you haven't selected the best print settings for your printer. Access the Print dialog box and choose Properties. In the Properties dialog box for your currently selected printer, choose the settings that will give you the best graphics printing, such as print quality, graphics dithering, and so on. Text usually isn't affected by a lower-resolution setting.

### CREATING AN ENVELOPE DEFINITION

*I know I selected the correct envelope form, but I still can't get my envelopes to come out right.*

Sometimes it's *not* your fault! You do have everything set correctly, but the envelopes just won't print in the proper location. Often, you can correct this problem by creating a new envelope definition based on the one that should be working. Choose Format, Page, Page Setup, and in the Page Setup dialog box follow these steps:

1. Click the form that should be working—for example, Envelope #10.
2. Click the Add button.
3. In the Add New Form dialog box, give the form a unique name.
4. Do *not* change anything else, and make sure that Current printer only is selected.
5. Click OK twice to return to your document.

The next time you create an envelope, select this new form. If it still doesn't work, follow the preceding steps and in the Add New Form dialog box, try changing the source, or you can experiment with changing other form options.

### FAX HAS BAD PAGE BREAKS

*I sent a fax from WordPerfect, but the person I sent it to says page breaks are in the wrong places.*

Whenever you change printers, small formatting changes often take place, primarily because the fonts and their horizontal and vertical spacing are slightly different for each printer. Before printing, or in this case faxing, go back through your document and check the layout. When you've verified that it's okay, go ahead and send the document to the fax (printer).

# PROJECT

Printing is a pretty mundane task…except when it comes to preparing booklets. Suppose you have a 13-page policy handbook that you want to prepare in a 5 1/2-inch-wide by 8 1/2-inch-high format. You get the whole thing ready, and it looks great in Print Preview, but when you print it and fold it, the pages are all in the wrong places!

WordPerfect makes it easy to set up and print booklet-type pages in the correct order. If you've ever had to cut and paste pages (with scissors and glue!) to arrange them in the right order, you'll appreciate this huge timesaving feature.

To create and print a booklet, follow these easy steps:

1. Prepare the content of the booklet as you normally do and save it (as you should at every step in these procedures).
2. Choose Format, Page, Page Setup to display the Page Setup dialog box.
3. On the Page Setup tab, choose Landscape, using the Letter (8 1/2 inches by 11 inches) page definition.
4. Set all margins equally to .5 inch.

5. On the Layout tab, select 2 in the Columns box. Figure 6.28 shows the Layout tab with these options.

**Figure 6.28**
You can use the Layout tab of the Page Setup dialog box to set options for dividing landscape pages with narrow margins in preparation for booklet printing.

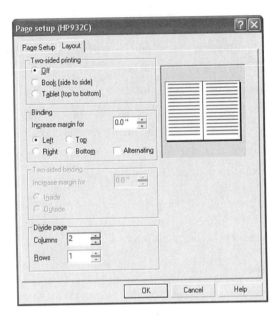

6. Click OK to return to the document. WordPerfect displays half pages, side by side, on the landscape page.

7. Add title pages, headers, footers, page numbering, and other elements that make your document look like a handbook (see Figure 6.29).

**Figure 6.29**
Format each half page as you would a full-size page, including headers, footers, page numbering, and so on.

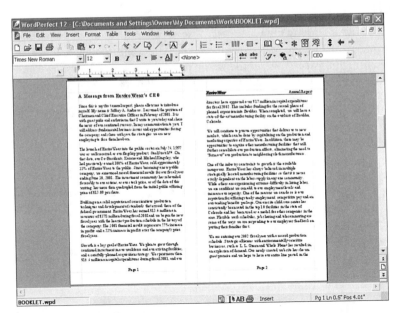

8. Consider whether there should be blank pages. For example, the first page might be a title page, but the inside cover could be blank, followed by the inside title page or table of contents. Insert blank pages (by pressing Ctrl+Enter or selecting Insert, New Page) at the appropriate locations.

9. Use the two-page view of Print Preview to verify that the pages are laid out correctly (see Figure 6.30). Note, however, that the preview shows the sequence of pages, not the final order adjusted for booklet printing.

**Figure 6.30**
The two-page view of Print Preview helps you see how your booklet pages are laid out.

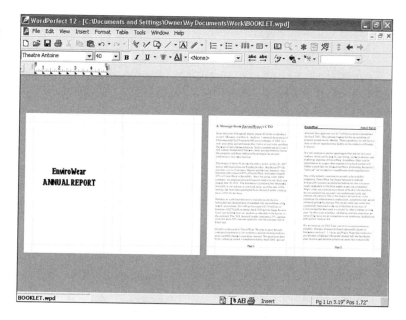

10. Choose File, Print.

11. Click the Layout tab in the Print dialog box and select the Print as Booklet option.

12. WordPerfect assumes that you want to print on both sides of the paper. If this is the case, insert the pages again when prompted by WordPerfect and click OK. Otherwise, just click OK at each prompt and print the second side on a separate sheet of paper. You can also turn off Two-Sided Printing before printing.

WordPerfect calculates the number of pages and organizes them so that each appears in the proper place when the pages are folded. No fuss, no muss!

# FORMATTING DOCUMENTS

CHAPTER

# 7

# FORMATTING LINES AND PARAGRAPHS

**In this chapter**

*by Laura Acklen*

# ALIGNING TEXT WITH CENTER AND FLUSH RIGHT

One of the most common formatting tasks is centering a line. Flush right is a little less common, but it still has an important place, especially in legal documents. In Chapter 3, "Understanding the Basics of Formatting," you learned how to use justification to center and flush-right lines of text. In this chapter, you'll learn how to use the Center and Flush Right features to align text.

What's the difference, you ask? Let me explain. When you change the justification to Center, every line you create from then on is centered, until you change the justification to something else. This is fine for title pages, where you have multiple lines that you want centered, but it's not the most efficient option for single lines. In this situation, the Center feature is the best choice.

- To center a line of text, press Shift+F7 and then type the text. If you've already typed the text, click at the beginning of the line and then press Shift+F7.

- To make a line of text flush right, or align it against the right margin, press Alt+F7, and then type the text. If you've already typed the text, click at the beginning of the line, and then press Alt+F7.

 *If you've accidentally pressed Shift+F7 or Alt+F7 in the middle of a line, see "My Title Is Split in Half" in the Troubleshooting section at the end of the chapter.*

You can also find Center and Flush Right commands in the menus. Choose Format, Line (see Figure 7.1). Note the keyboard shortcuts listed next to the commands.

Keyboard shortcuts

**Figure 7.1**
The Line menu has commands to make lines of text centered and flush right.

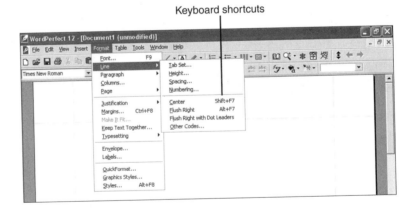

**TIP FROM**

*Laura Acklen*

Here's something you can't do with justification—you can have centered text and flush right text on the same line. Just press Shift+F7, type the centered text, press Alt+F7, and type the flush-right text.

**TIP FROM**

*Laura Acklen*

If you press Shift+F7 twice, you'll get *dot leaders*, periods with spaces between them, leading to the text. Likewise, if you press Alt+F7 twice, you'll get dot leaders across the line to the text. Change your mind? Press Shift+F7 or Alt+F7 again to remove the dot leaders.

# SETTING TABS

Tabs—you either love 'em or you never use 'em. Although they were once the only way to create columns, tabs have fallen out of favor now that we have the Table feature.

Still, tabs have their place, and in some cases, they are easier to set up than a table. For example, if you want to create three columns, one of which is a dollar amount, it's probably faster to turn on the ruler and set two regular tabs and one decimal-align tab than it is to create a table, format the dollar amount column to decimal alignment, and remove the table lines.

There are four types of tabs:

- Left Align—Text flows from the right side of the tab stop. This is the "normal" tab.
- Center—Text is centered over the tab stop.
- Right Align—Text flows from the left side of the tab stop.
- Decimal Align—The numbers are aligned on their decimal points, which rest on the tab stop. You can change the alignment character to something other than a period (decimal point).

Figure 7.2 illustrates the different types of tabs. The Ruler is displayed in the figure so you can see what the different tab markers look like.

**NOTE**

You can add dot leaders to each of the four tab types. Dot leaders are useful when the space between columns is wide because they help the reader's eye travel across the gap. They are especially useful when preparing a table of contents.

If you don't already have the ruler displayed, turn it on by choosing View, Ruler. The default tab settings (every 1/2 inch) are shown with triangles in the tab area of the ruler (see Figure 7.3). The gray area identifies the margin area; the white area is the text area.

7

**Figure 7.2**
The four tab types can be used to align different types of data.

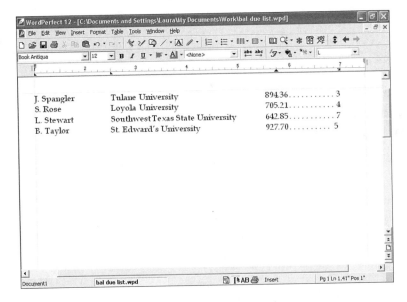

**Figure 7.3**
Using the Ruler, you can set all types of tabs with just a few mouse clicks.

Left margin area     Tab marker     Right margin area

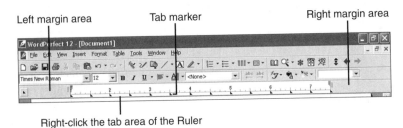

Right-click the tab area of the Ruler
to open the Tab QuickMenu

In most cases, you want to clear the default tabs so that you can create specific tabs. Right-click in the tab area of the ruler (refer to Figure 7.3) or right-click any tab marker to open the Tab QuickMenu (see Figure 7.4). Choose Clear All Tabs to delete the default tabs.

**CAUTION**

> The Indent feature uses the tab settings to indent your text. Changing the default tab settings affects how text is indented. If you plan on indenting text and setting specific tabs in the same document, don't change the tabs at the top of the document. Change them just before you want to type the columnar text. Then, after you've typed the text, restore the default tab settings.

7

Margin icon                    Tab QuickMenu

**Figure 7.4**
Using the Tab
QuickMenu, you can
clear the default tabs,
set specific types of
tabs, and then return
to the default settings.

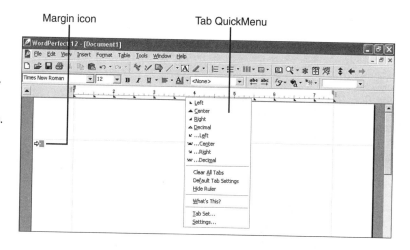

Setting new tabs is easy—just click on the ruler in the tab area where you want the tab stop (this inserts the default tab, which is a left-aligned tab). To remove a tab, drag it off the ruler.

When you set a tab (or modify the default tab settings in any way), a margin icon appears in the left margin area (refer to Figure 7.4). Click the margin icon to display a tab bar, which shows the tab settings for the current paragraph. You can make changes to the tabs on the tab bar using the same methods that you use for the Ruler. Click anywhere in the document to clear the tab bar.

**NOTE**

Because the margin icon is located inside the margin area, you might not be able to see it. Try switching to the Page View mode (choose View, Page) or set Zoom to Page Width by clicking the Zoom button and selecting Page Width.

To move a tab, click and drag the tab marker (on the ruler or on the tab bar). When you do, a bubble appears, telling you where the tab will fall when you release the mouse button, and a guideline appears in the text so that you can see the effect on existing text (see Figure 7.5). The mouse pointer changes, too, whenever you point to a tab marker—it changes to a move pointer (that is, a pointer with a box and a box guideline).

To change the tab type, right-click the tab and choose a tab type from the QuickMenu; then, click on the ruler to set the tab. After you've changed the tab type, it stays selected until you select another tab type. So, if you change the tab type to Decimal, every time you click on the ruler, you'll set a decimal tab.

7

This bubble identifies the tab's position on the page

**Figure 7.5**
If you've already typed the text, you can still move the tabs around. The guideline helps you see where the text will be as you click and drag the tab.

Tab guideline —

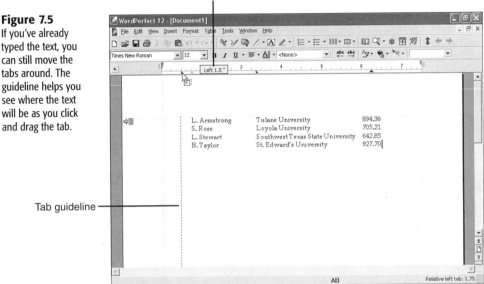

**CAUTION**

When you're working with tabs, it's extremely important to position the insertion point first. Be sure that you're creating new tab settings exactly where you want them, so they don't reformat the wrong text. Furthermore, when you edit your tab settings to adjust the spacing between columns, be sure you click at the beginning of the text. Otherwise, some of the text is formatted with the original tab settings and the rest of the text is formatted with the new tab settings. It's not a pretty sight, believe me. (Remember your old friend—Undo?)

After you've typed the text, you can go back and edit the tab settings. You can click and drag them on the ruler (or the tab bar) to adjust the spacing between columns. You can even switch to a different tab type if necessary. Just be sure you click at the top of the text that you've formatted with tabs before you start making changes.

When you're ready to return to default tab settings (so you can use regular tabs and indent later on in the document), right-click in the document where you want to make the change and choose Default Tab Settings.

It wouldn't be fair not to mention the Tab Set dialog box (see Figure 7.6). Everything you can do from the ruler and more is available in this dialog box. Right-click the ruler, and then choose Tab Set (refer to Figure 7.4). Or choose Format, Line, Tab Set to display the Tab Set dialog box.

Choose either Absolute or Relative tabs

Choose a tab type

**Figure 7.6**
The Tab Set dialog box offers options that aren't available when you use the ruler.

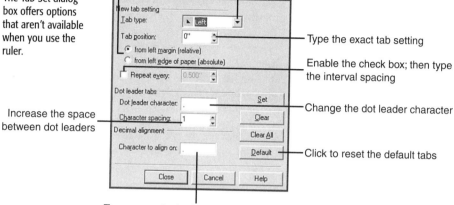

Type the exact tab setting

Enable the check box; then type the interval spacing

Increase the space between dot leaders

Change the dot leader character

Click to reset the default tabs

Type a new decimal alignment character

---

**TIP FROM**

You might be wondering what the difference is between an absolute and a relative tab setting. Absolute tab settings are measured from the left edge of the paper. They stay in the same place no matter what you do to the margins. Relative tabs, on the other hand, move with the tab settings. For example, if you set a tab at 1.5", the actual tab position is the width of the left margin plus the 1.5". Therefore, if the left margin is 1", the actual tab setting is at 2.5". The advantage of relative tabs is that they self-adjust whenever you change the margin settings.

---

If you press Tab, only to have WordPerfect indent the whole paragraph, see "Pressing Tab Indents the Paragraph" in the Troubleshooting section at the end of this chapter.

# INDENTING TEXT

Indentation is often used for quotations, to emphasize text, or to place a paragraph in a subordinate position beneath another paragraph. When you create a bulleted or numbered list, WordPerfect inserts an Indent command after the bullet or number so that the text you type isn't aligned under the bullet or number, but rather under the first word of the text.

→ For more information on creating outlines and bulleted or numbered lists, **see** "Working with Bulleted and Numbered Lists," **p. 335**.

There are four ways to indent text:

- Indent moves every line within a paragraph to the next tab setting (to the left). By default, this moves the text over 1/2 inch every time you choose Indent.

7

- Double Indent moves every line in a paragraph in from the left and right sides, to the next tab setting. By default, this indents the text by 1/2 inch on the left and 1/2 inch on the right.

- Hanging Indent leaves the first line at the left margin—all the other lines are indented (on the left side) by 1/2 inch. Hanging Indent has the opposite effect of Indent.

**CAUTION**

Here's the annoying thing about the Hanging Indent option. If you've cleared all the tabs, the hanging indent will start the first line at the left edge of the paper, which might or might not work, depending on your printer (you might recall that some printers have an unprintable zone, roughly .25" from the edges of the paper). You'll need two tabs: one where the first line should begin and one where the subsequent lines should begin. For example, you might set a tab at 1/2 inch and one at 1 inch for a hanging indent that formats the first line 1/2 inch into the left margin and the subsequent lines at the left margin.

- A Back Tab works like Margin Release on a typewriter (yes, there was a time when everyone used typewriters). It temporarily releases the left margin so the first line of a paragraph starts in the left margin area; the other lines align at the left margin.

To indent a new paragraph, press F7, and then type the text. Press Shift+Ctrl+F7 for a double indent and Ctrl+F7 for a hanging indent. As usual, if you've already typed the text, click in the paragraph before applying an indent style.

You can choose Indent, Double Indent, and Hanging Indent, as well as Back Tab, from the Paragraph menu (see Figure 7.7). Choose Format, Paragraph to open the Paragraph menu.

Indent shortcut keys

**Figure 7.7**
One of the Indent commands on the Paragraph menu, Back Tab, doesn't have a shortcut key assigned to it.

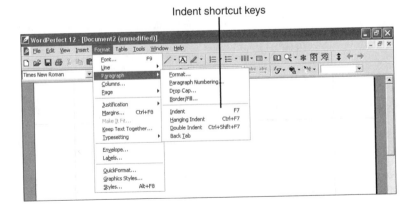

7

**TIP FROM**

*Laura Acklen*

WordPerfect can display symbols for spaces, hard returns, tabs, indent, center, and flush right, as well as a few others. If you want to see these symbols, choose View, Show ¶, or press Ctrl+Shift+F3. You can also choose the symbols that you would rather not have displayed. Choose Tools, Settings, Display and then click the Symbols tab. Deselect the symbols that you don't want to see. Choose OK, and then Close when you are done.

**TIP FROM**

*Laura Acklen*

If the QuickIndent feature is enabled, you can quickly indent paragraphs with the Tab key. When you press Tab at the beginning of the first and second lines, QuickIndent converts those tabs into an indent. You can also quickly create a hanging indent by pressing Tab at the beginning of any line except the first line in a paragraph. Turn QuickIndent on or off by choosing Tools, QuickCorrect. Click the Format-As-You-Go tab, and then enable or disable the check box next to QuickIndent (in the list of Format-As-You-Go choices).

→ For more information on enabling and disabling the QuickIndent feature, **see** "Customizing Format-As-You-Go," **p. 157**.

If you want the first line of every paragraph to be indented automatically (rather than pressing Tab each time), use the First Line Indent option. Choose Format, Paragraph, Format to open the Paragraph Format dialog box (see Figure 7.8). Type the amount that you want the first line indented in the First Line Indent text box. (A tab indents the first line by 1/2 inch.) Click OK. All new paragraphs from this point on will have the first line indented. Set the value back to 0 (zero) inches for no indent.

 *Are you having a hard time sorting paragraphs that have been indented with tabs, indents, or hanging indents? See "Sorting Indented Paragraphs" in the Troubleshooting section at the end of this chapter.*

Type the indent value

**Figure 7.8**
Type the value for the first-line indent in increments of inches. For example, 1/4 inch would be .25".

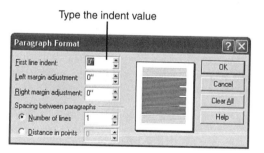

7

# ADJUSTING THE SPACING BETWEEN LINES AND PARAGRAPHS

As you might recall from Chapter 1, "Getting Comfortable with WordPerfect," the default line spacing setting is single-spacing. Some types of documents, such as grants and formal reports, require a certain line-spacing setting. For example, if I'm planning on printing out a document for someone else to review, I'll change to double- or triple-spacing, so that person has room to write comments. After I've incorporated that person's changes, I'll switch the document back to single-spacing.

To change line spacing, click where you want the change to take effect (or select the text you want to change). Choose Format, Line, Spacing to open the Line Spacing dialog box (see Figure 7.9). Either type a value or click the spinner arrows to increase or decrease the value in the Spacing text box. For example, type 1 for single-spacing, 1.5 for one-and-a-half spacing, 2 for double-spacing, and so on.

**Figure 7.9**
You can specify the number of lines that you want between each line by typing the value or clicking the spinner arrows.

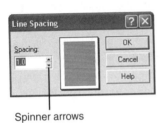

Spinner arrows

The new line-spacing setting takes effect at the beginning of the paragraph where the insertion point is resting, and it remains in effect through the rest of the document, or until you change the line spacing again. For example, in a double-spaced document, it's common to switch to single-spacing for lists or quotations.

> **NOTE**
> The actual amount of space between lines depends on the current font and font size. WordPerfect automatically adjusts the line height to accommodate the tallest character, so if you switch to a line-spacing setting of 1.5 lines, you'll get space equal to one-and-a-half times the height of a line.

The accepted standard is to leave a blank line between paragraphs, so you just press Enter twice after you type a paragraph, right? That's not a problem—until you decide to change the line spacing to double. Now you've got the space of two lines between each paragraph. Furthermore, these extra lines leave space at the top of a page.

Rather than insert extra blank lines, you can adjust the spacing between paragraphs. This way, you always get the same amount of space between each paragraph (no matter what you do to the line spacing), and you don't have extra blank lines floating around. To change the paragraph spacing, click where you want the change to take effect. Choose Format, Paragraph, Format to open the Paragraph Format dialog box (refer to Figure 7.8). In the Spacing Between Paragraphs section, you can enter the number of lines or the number of points that you want between each paragraph. Either type the value or click the spinner arrows to increase or decrease the value.

**NOTE**

> You might be familiar with the term *points* as it relates to font sizes. An inch is 72 points. You probably won't ever use points as a unit of measure, but, just in case you want to, it's there.

# KEEPING TEXT TOGETHER

As you type along, you never have to worry about running out of room—WordPerfect creates a new page for you as soon as you reach the bottom of the current page. It's so transparent that you probably don't even stop to think about it—that is, until you preview the document and realize that you have headings and paragraphs separated by a page break. Some other examples of page formatting problems are page breaks in the middle of a list of numbered paragraphs or a figures separated from the explanatory text.

You can prevent these situations by marking the text that should stay together when a page break is encountered. You can use three features to do this: Widow/Orphan Protection, Block Protect, and Conditional End of Page. Choose Format, Keep Text Together to display the Keep Text Together dialog box (see Figure 7.10).

**Figure 7.10**
The three options in the Keep Text Together dialog box are all designed to keep important information from being separated by a page break.

Enable this check box, then type the number of lines to keep together

## ENABLING WIDOW/ORPHAN PROTECTION

Widow/orphan protection is designed to protect against single lines of a paragraph getting left behind at the bottom of a page or getting pushed to the top of the next page. This improves the document's appearance and makes it easier to read.

7

The first line of a paragraph that gets left behind at the bottom of a page is called an *orphan*. A *widow* is the last line of a paragraph that gets pushed to the top of a page.

Position the insertion point where you want widow/orphan protection to start (usually at the top of the document). In the Keep Text Together dialog box, enable the check box in the Widow/Orphan section.

## USING BLOCK PROTECT

You use the block protect feature when you want to keep a section of text together on the same page. As you edit the document, and the block moves near a page break, WordPerfect decides whether the block will fit on the current page. If it doesn't fit, the entire block gets moved to the top of the next page. Block protect works well for keeping figures or tables and explanatory text together. You can also use it to protect numbered paragraphs and other lists.

To turn on block protect, select the text (and figures or tables) that you want to keep together. In the Keep Text Together dialog box, enable the check box in the Block Protect section.

**CAUTION**

Block-protecting large sections of text can result in big chunks of white space in the middle of a document. If this situation arises, try to find a logical place for a page break so you can separate the text into smaller chunks.

## SETTING A CONDITIONAL END OF PAGE

The Conditional End of Page feature keeps a certain number of lines together when a page break is encountered. You might use Conditional End of Page at the beginning of a heading so you can specify how many lines of the following paragraph you want to keep with the heading.

To turn on Conditional End of Page, position the insertion point at the beginning of the heading. In the Keep Text Together dialog box, choose Number of Lines to Keep Together. In the text box type the number of lines that you want to keep together. Count the heading line as one of the lines, and if there is a blank line between the heading and the paragraph, count that, too.

 *If you're having trouble getting Conditional End of Page to work for you, see "Conditional End of Page Isn't Working Right" in the Troubleshooting section at the end of this chapter.*

# INSERTING LINE NUMBERS

Line numbers are used in certain types of documents (such as legal or scientific documents) to give an easy point of reference. For example, you can tell your client to look for a change that was made on "page 13, line 5." Line numbers can also make it easier to proofread and revise many different types of documents.

To turn on line numbering, click in the line (or paragraph) where you want the line numbers to start. Choose Format, Line, Numbering to open the Line Numbering dialog box (see Figure 7.11). Choose Turn Line Numbering On.

Click to turn on line numbering

Click to choose a numbering style

**Figure 7.11**
In the Line Numbering dialog box, you can turn on line numbers, select a line number style, and specify the position and font for the numbers.

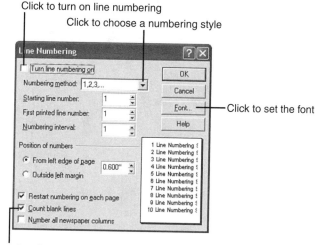

Click to set the font

Disable this check box if you don't want to count blank lines

After you've turned on line numbers, choose from the following options. Notice that as you make changes to the line numbering options, the sample document is updated to reflect the changes.

- Click the Numbering Method drop-down list arrow and choose a style for the numbers.

- Specify the starting line number, the first printed line number, and the numbering interval. (Regardless of the style that you use for the line numbers, you still set these line number options numerically.)

- Change the location of the line numbers by setting the distance between the line numbers and the left edge of the page or the distance between the line numbers and the left margin.

- Deselect Restart Numbering on Each Page if you want the lines numbered consecutively through the end of the document.

7

- Deselect Count Blank Lines if you don't want to skip blank lines in the line number count.

- Select Number All Newspaper Columns if you want to use line numbers in newspaper columns.

- Click Font to open the Line Numbering Font dialog box (see Figure 7.12). Select the font and the font size. If desired, select a color, shading, or appearance attribute to visually separate the numbers from the body text.

Click to choose a color

**Figure 7.12**
You can select the font, font size, color, shading, and text attributes that you want to assign to the line numbers in the Line Numbering Font dialog box.

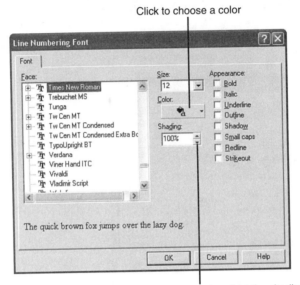

Click the spinner arrows to adjust the shading

WordPerfect has a macro that sets up a blank legal pleading paper, with line numbers and a vertical double line that separates the line numbers from the document text (see Figure 7.13). To run the macro, choose Tools, Macro, Play, and then double-click `pleading.wcm`. You can also click the Pleading button on the Legal toolbar to run this macro.

→ For more information on creating pleading papers with the Pleading Experts, **see** "Using the Pleading Experts," **p. 812**.

7

Vertical line

**Figure 7.13**
The Pleading Paper macro creates a generic legal pleading document.

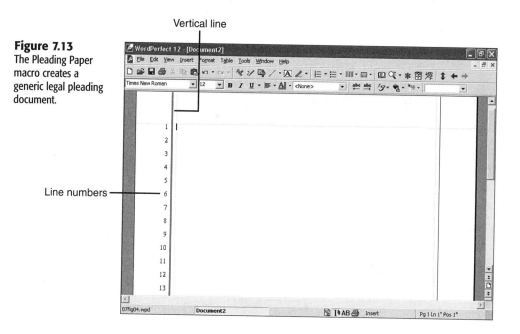

Line numbers

# ADDING BORDERS, DROP SHADOWS, AND FILLS

Strictly speaking, a paragraph is any amount of text followed by a hard return, so a date on a line by itself is treated as a paragraph. You can create a box around any paragraph (or multiple paragraphs) by using the Border feature. A well-chosen border creates a frame around the paragraph, emphasizing it and setting it apart from the rest of the text. You can create a drop shadow behind the box, and you can add a background (fill) to the area inside the border.

**NOTE**

> You can add borders around a page, a column, or a graphics box. The dialog boxes are virtually identical to the Paragraph Border/Fill dialog box, so rather than repeat this discussion in those respective sections, I'll refer you to this section for information on choosing the border, the drop shadow, and the fill.

## ADDING BORDERS

There are 32 different predefined borders from which to choose. Because you can edit these predefined borders to change the color and the line style, there are endless possibilities.

Follow these steps to add a border around a paragraph or selected paragraphs:

1. Click in the paragraph, or select the paragraphs, around which you want to create a border.

7

2. Choose Format, Paragraph, Border/Fill. The Paragraph Border/Fill dialog box opens (see Figure 7.14).

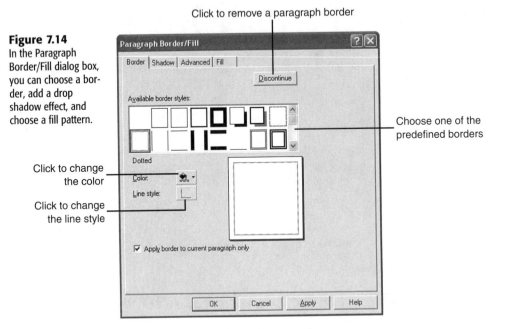

**Figure 7.14**
In the Paragraph Border/Fill dialog box, you can choose a border, add a drop shadow effect, and choose a fill pattern.

Click to remove a paragraph border

Choose one of the predefined borders

Click to change the color

Click to change the line style

3. Click a border in the Available Border Styles list box. Scroll down through the list to see all the predefined borders. After you've chosen a border, you have the following options:
    - To change the color of the border, click the Color button and then click a color on the palette (see Figure 7.15).
    - To change the line style used in the border, click the Line Style button and then click a line style from the palette (see Figure 7.16).

4. Select Apply Border to Current Paragraph Only if you only want the border applied to the current paragraph or selected paragraphs. Otherwise, the border starts with the current paragraph(s) and stops at the end of the document.

To remove a paragraph border, click in the paragraph, choose Format, Paragraph, Border/Fill to open the Paragraph Border/Fill dialog box, and click the Discontinue button.

**TIP FROM**

*Laura Acklen*

If you want to add graphic borders from other programs to the list of available border styles in the Border/Fill dialog box, you must convert the file to WPG format. Open the file in Presentations, and then save it in the `\Program Files\Wordperfect Office 11 (or 12) \graphics\borders` folder in WPG format.

**Figure 7.15**
You can choose any color from this palette to add color to a paragraph border.

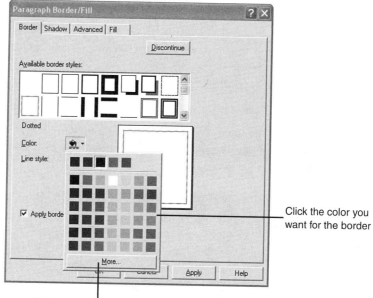

Click the color you want for the border

Click to create custom colors

**Figure 7.16**
You can choose a line style from this palette for the paragraph border.

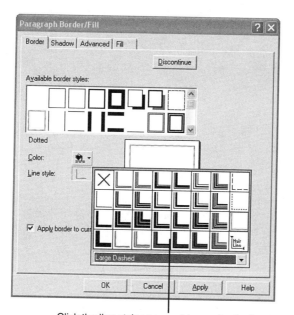

Click the line style you want to use for the border

## ADDING DROP SHADOWS

A drop shadow gives your borders a distinctive look by adding depth behind the frame. You might want to use a drop shadow border for special announcements, advertisements, or important sections of a form. A drop shadow also looks great when applied to a page border for letterhead, a title page, or flyer.

Follow these steps to create a drop shadow:

1. Choose Format, Paragraph, Border/Fill, and then click the Shadow tab. There are 25 different drop shadow effects (see Figure 7.17). Click one of the effects to have it applied to the sample document.

**Figure 7.17**
You can select one of the shadow effects in the Shadow tab of the Paragraph Border/Fill dialog box.

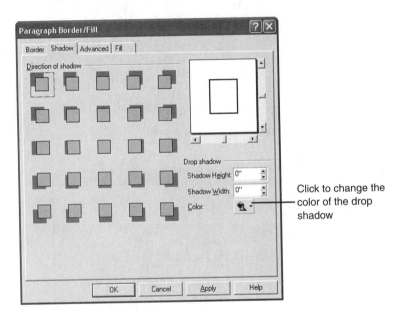

NOTE

If you've been using WordPerfect 7 or 8, you're accustomed to working with only one drop shadow effect in the Advanced tab of the Border/Fill dialog box. Starting with WordPerfect 10, there are now 25 different drop shadow effects. A separate Shadow tab was created so all the effects could have their own area.

*If you're trying to choose a drop shadow and nothing happens, see "I Can't Choose a Drop Shadow" in the Troubleshooting section of this chapter.*

2. (Optional) Enter a value for the height and width of the shadow.

3. (Optional) Click the Color button and select a color for the drop shadow.

4. Choose Apply to apply the drop shadow and leave the Paragraph Border/Fill dialog box open; choose OK to apply the drop shadow and close the dialog box.

## CHOOSING FILL PATTERNS

Borders and fills are independent of each other, so you can apply a fill pattern to a paragraph (or selected paragraphs) without choosing a border first. Although the most common use of fill is to add shading, you can have some fun combining patterns with foreground and background colors.

Here's how to add a fill pattern:

1. Click in the paragraph, or select the paragraphs to which you want to add the fill pattern.

2. Choose Format, Paragraph, Border/Fill, and then click the Fill tab. There are 32 different predefined fill patterns from which to choose.

3. Click a fill pattern to apply it to the sample document. The name of that fill pattern appears under the Available Fill Styles list box (see Figure 7.18).

Name of the selected fill

**Figure 7.18**
After you've selected a fill pattern, you can add color to it by selecting another foreground and/or background color.

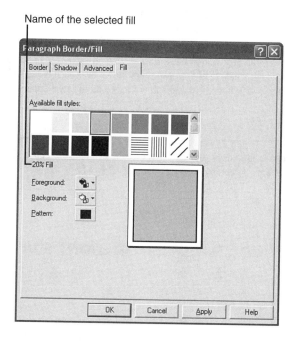

4. After you've selected a fill pattern, you can
   • Click the Foreground button and choose a color for the foreground.
   • Click the Background button and choose a color for the background.
   • Click the Pattern button and choose another fill pattern.

Choose Apply to apply the fill pattern to the paragraph(s) and leave the Paragraph Border/Fill dialog box open; choose OK to apply the fill pattern and close the dialog box.

7

**CAUTION**

You should avoid using a gray fill pattern with more than a 30% shading—your black text will be too hard to read.

# INSERTING DROP CAPS

A drop cap is the first letter in a paragraph, enlarged and positioned so that the top of the letter lines up with the top of the first sentence. The rest of the letter drops down into the text, hence the term "drop cap." Drop caps are used to draw the reader's eye to a specific point in the page, such as to a pull quote or to the beginning of a chapter or section.

 To add a drop cap at the beginning of a paragraph, click in the paragraph, and then choose Format, Paragraph, Drop Cap or click the Drop-Cap Style button to open the Drop Cap dialog box. Select one of the drop cap styles—WordPerfect grabs the first character, enlarges it, and formats the rest of the paragraph around it (see Figure 7.19).

**TIP FROM**

*Laura Acklen*

The Drop-Cap Style button has a "picker" (the arrow next to the button) that you can click to open a palette of drop-cap styles. Hover over each of the styles to see a Real-Time Preview of how the paragraph will look with the style applied.

**TIP FROM**

*Laura Acklen*

You can insert a drop cap character, with the default Drop Cap in Text style, at the beginning of a paragraph by pressing Ctrl+Shift+C.

Drop cap

**Figure 7.19**
You can use a drop cap to decorate the beginning of a page, chapter, or column.

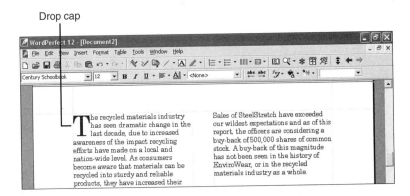

After you're created a drop cap character, click in front of the drop cap to display the Drop Cap property bar with the following buttons:

- Click Drop Cap Font button to choose a font, color, shading, or font attribute for the drop cap.

- Click the Drop Cap Style button to choose a different drop cap style from the palette.

- Click the Drop Cap Size button to choose how tall you want the drop cap to be (in lines). The default is three lines high.

- Click the Drop Cap Position button to place the drop cap in the text or in the margin.

- Click the Drop Cap Border/Fill button to choose a border, drop shadow, or fill pattern.

- Click the Drop Cap Options button to choose how many letters you want in the drop cap. You can choose to have the first word made into a drop cap. You can also choose to adjust for diacriticals and descenders.

- Click the No Drop Cap button to remove a drop cap from the current paragraph.

**NOTE**

> To switch from the Drop Cap Property Bar to the regular Property Bar, click in the body text.

There are some helpful options for customizing drop cap characters in the Drop Caps dialog box (refer to Figure 7.19). You can set the height of the drop cap character and the distance from the rest of the paragraph. You can also specify a different font for the drop cap character in the Font tab. In the Options tab, you can specify the number of characters in the drop cap, adjustments for diacriticals and descenders, and where the drop cap is positioned within the margin and the text.

# TROUBLESHOOTING

### MY TITLE IS SPLIT IN HALF

*I accidentally pressed Shift+F7 in the middle of a title and now the title is split in half. How can I fix this?*

If you accidentally press Shift+F7 or Alt+F7 in the middle of a line, strange things can happen! If the line is short, it just splits the text up, but in a paragraph, it can cause the letters to get all crunched together. If you notice this problem right away, press Backspace to delete the Center or Flush Right code. Next, press Home to move to the beginning of the line so you can try again. If you notice this problem minutes later, turn on Reveal Codes (Alt+F3), click at the beginning of that line, and start looking for the code. When you find it, click and drag it out of the Reveal Codes window to delete it.

### PRESSING TAB INDENTS THE PARAGRAPH

*When I press Tab, the whole paragraph is indented. I want to indent just the first line, not the entire paragraph.*

To indent only the first line of a paragraph, press Tab at the beginning of the first line. If you then press Tab at the beginning of any other line in the paragraph, QuickIndent converts the tab to an indent, which indents the whole paragraph.

Pressing Tab at the beginning of any line in a paragraph except the first line creates a hanging indent. In this case, only the first line of the paragraph is lined up against the left margin, and the remaining lines are indented to the next tab stop (1/2 inch).

To turn off the QuickIndent feature, choose Tools, QuickCorrect. Click the Format-As-You-Go tab, and then deselect QuickIndent.

### SORTING INDENTED PARAGRAPHS

*After painstakingly creating a list of contributors for a fundraising campaign, I can't get the list to sort correctly. I indented each entry so it would be formatted underneath some other text. What am I doing wrong?*

You aren't doing anything wrong—tab and indent codes act as field delimiters in a sort. In other words, they count as fields, moving the first field (the first word) over to the second or third field. In the case of a hanging indent, there are two codes inserted—left indent and back tab—so the first word in the line is actually the third field. The same thing happens if you have flush right, center, and margin release codes at the beginning of a line.

The best thing to do is turn on Reveal Codes and figure out how many codes you have at the beginning of each line. Then, adjust the field number in your sort to skip past the codes.

### CONDITIONAL END OF PAGE ISN'T WORKING RIGHT

*I've used Conditional End of Page to keep the first three lines of a paragraph with a heading, but it isn't working. Only the first line stays with the heading. What am I doing wrong?*

First, be sure you click at the beginning of the heading line before you insert the Conditional End of Page code. Second, when you specify how many lines to keep together, be sure that you count the heading as a line. Furthermore, if there is a blank line between the heading and the paragraph, you have to count that, too. So if you have a heading, a blank line, and then the paragraph, and you want to keep three lines of the paragraph together with the heading, you need to keep five lines together.

### I CAN'T CHOOSE A DROP SHADOW

*I'm in the Shadow tab in the Paragraph Border/Fill dialog box, but whenever I click a drop shadow effect, nothing happens. The sample document doesn't show me the drop shadow effect and nothing is inserted in my document when I click OK.*

You probably forgot to choose a border style first. If you don't choose a border in the Available Border Styles list box, the options in the Shadow tab won't have any effect because they manipulate the borders. The Fill tab still works, without a border selected, because you can add fill to a paragraph without adding a border.

# PROJECT

It's amazing what a difference a few minor changes can make! Take the company newsletter in Figure 7.20, for example. It looks okay, but a few things could be done to improve the appearance. Figure 7.21 shows the same newsletter after a few improvements have been made. The information that you need to make these changes is included in this chapter, so I won't duplicate the steps here.

**Figure 7.20**
Although this newsletter looks pretty good as it is, improvements can be made.

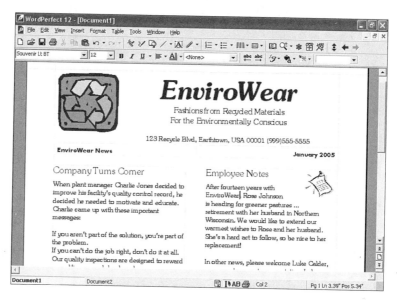

A paragraph border has been added around the last line in the masthead to separate the masthead from the text of the newsletter. A gray fill was added to shade the text and enhance the border's appearance. A drop cap was added at the top of each column. The messages mentioned in the first column were indented on both sides to identify them as quotations. Finally—and this is a change that you won't notice by looking at the document—the graphic image in the second column has been attached to the Employee Notes paragraph with block protect so that the graphic stays with the paragraph.

**Figure 7.21**
With a little formatting and tweaking, the newsletter looks much more attractive.

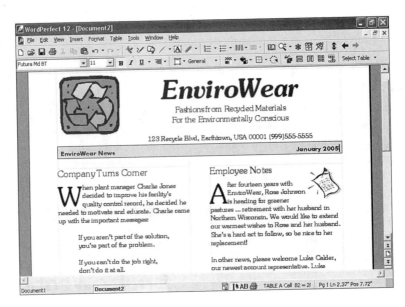

# FORMATTING THE PAGE

In this chapter

*by Laura Acklen*

8

# CHANGING MARGINS

Believe it or not, you can make your document easier to read by adjusting the margins. A wider margin creates more whitespace around the text and reduces the number of words on a line. The shorter the lines, the less likely the reader is to lose his or her place.

On the other hand, if you're trying to reduce the number of pages, you can make the margins smaller so that you can fit more on a page. When you use headers and footers, for example, you might want to set the top and bottom margins to 1/2 inch.

In Chapter 1, "Getting Comfortable with WordPerfect," you learned how to change the margins by clicking and dragging the guidelines. Some people have trouble clicking and dragging these guidelines, so they prefer to use the dialog box, where they can type in the margin settings directly.

To change the margins in a dialog box, choose Format, Margins, or press Ctrl+F8 to open the Page Setup dialog box (see Figure 8.1). You can also choose File, Page Setup. Type the margin settings in the text boxes, or click the spinner arrows to increment/decrement the values.

Click the Layout tab to set up binding and two-sided printing

**Figure 8.1**
The Page Setup dialog box has options for setting and adjusting the margins.

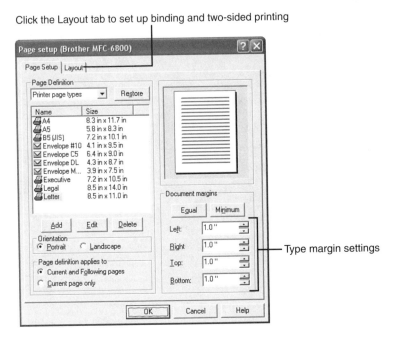

Type margin settings

If you want to set equal margins on all sides, type the margin setting in one of the four text boxes, and then click the Equal button. Click the Minimum button to set the margins according to the minimum margin requirements for the currently selected printer.

By default, the new margin settings take effect on the current and following pages. Choose Current Page Only in the Apply To section to apply the margin change differently.

**TIP FROM**

*Laura Acklen*

> If you type a fraction (such as 1/4, 2/3, 7/8) in the text box, WordPerfect converts it to the decimal equivalent.

 *If you've been trying unsuccessfully to adjust the top and bottom margins to center text on a page, see "Can't Find the Right Margins to Center the Page" in the Troubleshooting section at the end of this chapter.*

*If you notice that margins are changing in the middle of a document and you can't find any margin codes to delete, see "I Have Gremlins Formatting My Document" in the Troubleshooting section at the end of this chapter.*

**NOTE**

> If you need to shift the margins to accommodate book or booklet binding (so the words aren't covered up by the binding), you can set a binding width that functions independently of the margin settings. Click the Layout tab in the Page Setup dialog box. Type the amount of margin space that the binding will require, and then choose Left, Right, Top, or Bottom, depending on where the binding will be placed. To set up alternating pages, place a check mark in the Alternating check box. The sample document in the dialog box shows what the bound pages will look like with the settings you have made. To set the binding for double-sided documents, choose Book or Tablet in the Two-sided printing section, and then choose to increase the binding width on the inside margin or the outside margin (these two options aren't available if Off is chosen).

**TIP FROM**

*Laura Acklen*

> WordPerfect's default margins of 1 inch on all sides might be fine for most folks, but if you prefer to use different margins in your documents, you can alter the settings in the default template. This way, you don't have to set new margins every time you create a new document.

→ To change the settings in the default template, **see** "Editing the Default Template," **p. 718.**

**TIP FROM**

*Laura Acklen*

> Headers, footers, footnotes, endnotes, and watermarks use the margin settings in the DocumentStyle, not the margin settings that you insert in the document. If you have these elements in your document, be sure you change the margins in the DocumentStyle, or you'll have mismatched margins. To edit the DocumentStyle, choose View, Reveal Codes to turn on Reveal Codes. Double-click the DocumentStyle code (at the very top of the document), and then choose Format, Margins from the Styles Editor dialog box to open the Page Setup dialog box, where you can set the margins.

**8**

# INSERTING PAGE BREAKS

No doubt you've noticed that WordPerfect automatically creates a new page for you whenever you fill up the current one. It's transparent, so you don't even have to think about it. For those times when you want to start a new page and you haven't reached the bottom of the current page, you can insert a page break, which is also known as a hard page. Soft page breaks are inserted by WordPerfect as you type; hard page breaks are those that you insert.

To insert a hard page, press Ctrl+Enter. In Draft View mode, a page break displays as a horizontal double line. In Page View mode, you see a space between the two pages (see Figure 8.2).

**Figure 8.2**
In Page view mode, the physical page is displayed, so you can see the space between pages.

Page break

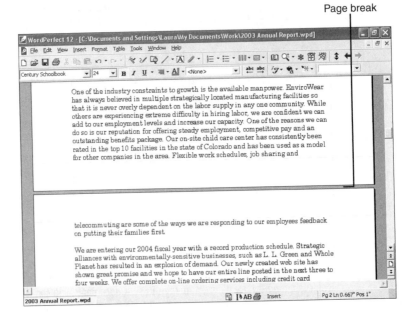

When you insert a page break, a hard page code [HPg] is inserted in the document. To remove a page break, delete the [HPg] code. You can also click at the end of the paragraph, just before a page break, and press Delete. In a style-heavy document, however, you might inadvertently delete a style code with this method. If this happens, choose Undo until things are back to normal or reapply the style.

In a long document, you might decide to precede a major section with a hard page break so that each section begins on a new page. If, during heavy revisions, these hard pages get moved around to the wrong places, use Find and Replace to quickly strip out all the hard page codes (or only the ones that you don't need anymore).

**TIP FROM**

*Laura Acklen*

A hard page break is not the best tool to use if you are trying to keep headings at the top of a page, or if you want to push a few lines of text down to the next page. There are other features that are geared to positioning headings at the top of the next page and for keeping text together. They are grouped together in the Keep Text Together dialog box (choose Format, Keep Text Together).

→ For more information on the features that keep text together, **see** "Keeping Text Together," **p. 213**.

→ To get a refresher on how to search for a code and delete it from the document, **see** "Searching for Codes," **p. 150**.

**TIP FROM**

*Laura Acklen*

In the Reveal Codes window, if the red cursor is to the left of a code, press Delete; if the red cursor is to the right of a code, press Backspace. You can also click and drag a code out of the Reveal Codes window to delete it.

When you're printing on both sides of the paper, you'll want to start new chapters or sections on the right side of facing pages. The simplest way to do this is to use the Force Page feature. First, click in the paragraph where you want to force a new page.

Choose Format, Page, Force Page to open the Force Page dialog box (see Figure 8.3). Choose Current Page Odd to force a new odd-numbered page. (Pick this if you want to start new chapters and sections on the right side.) Choose Current Page Even to force a new even-numbered page. Choose Start New Page to create a new page at the beginning of the current paragraph.

**Figure 8.3**
As with hard page breaks, if further editing moves the new page to an undesirable location, you can turn on Reveal Codes and delete the [Force] code.

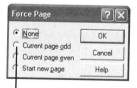

Click to start chapters on the right side

# ADDING PAGE NUMBERS

Numbering pages in WordPerfect can be as simple as printing a page number at the bottom of every page or as complex as numbering chapters individually and choosing different page-numbering styles for various sections of a document. This section follows a logical progression of starting with the simple methods and progressing to the more complicated methods.

8

## INSERTING PAGE NUMBERS AT THE TOP OR BOTTOM OF THE PAGE

You can choose from 10 preset page number positions that place the page number at the top or bottom of the page. If you're printing on both sides of the paper, you might want to place the page numbers at alternating top or bottom corners.

Follow these steps to insert a page number:

1. Click on the page where you want the numbering to start.

2. Choose Format, Page, Numbering to display the Select Page Numbering Format dialog box.

3. Click the Position drop-down list arrow to open the list of positions that you can choose from (see Figure 8.4).

4. Select a page number position from the list.

5. Choose OK to insert the page number.

Choose a page number style

**Figure 8.4**
The quickest way to insert a page number is to choose one of the preset page number positions and page number styles.

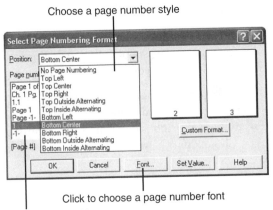

Click to choose a page number font

Choose a page number position

NOTE

> Page numbers are printed on the top or bottom line in the text area of the page, not in the margin space. WordPerfect inserts a blank line to separate the page number from the rest of the document text. This reduces the amount of text that would normally fit on the page by two lines. If you decrease your top or bottom margin (depending on where you put the page numbers) to approximately 2/3 inch, you can regain the lost space, and the page numbers will appear to print in the margin space.

At this point, you can click OK to insert a basic page number that starts on the current page (as page 1) and continues through the rest of the document. Figure 8.5 shows a document with simple page numbers at the bottom center of the page.

8

Page number

**Figure 8.5**
The most common page-numbering scheme is to position the number at the bottom center of every page.

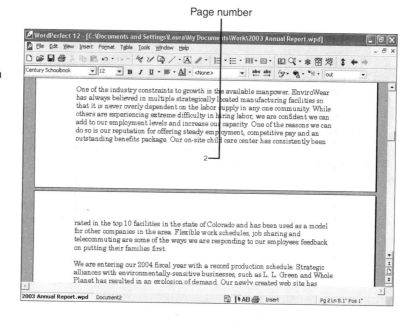

There are other page-numbering options you can choose:

- You can choose a page number format from the Page Numbering Format list box. Scroll down through the list to see the letter and Roman numeral styles.

**TIP FROM**

*Laura Acklen*

A "page x of y" page number tells you the number of the current page (x) and the total number of pages in the document (y). To create a "page x of y" page number, select Page 1 of 1 in the Page Numbering Format list box. Click OK. You may notice that the page number formats are dynamic, so they reflect the page number where the insertion point is located and the total number of pages in the document. Thus this option will only show Page 1 of 1 if the document is only one page long and the insertion point is on the first page.

- You can click the Font button to open the Page Numbering Font dialog box, where you can choose a font, font size, color, or attributes for the page number.

**CAUTION**

WordPerfect uses the font set in the Document Initial Font dialog box for page numbers, which might not match the font that you have set in the document. Either set the font that you want for the body text and the page number in the Document Initial Font dialog box (by choosing File, Document, Default Font) or choose a font in the Page Numbering Font dialog box that matches the one you've used in the document.

8

- You can choose Custom Format to open the Custom Page Numbering dialog box. From here, you can create a combination page number style that can include the volume number, chapter number, or secondary page number. You can also create a customized "page x of y" page number style. See the section "Switching to a Different Page-Numbering Scheme" later in this chapter for more information.

- You can choose Set Value to open the Values dialog box, where you can type the new number to use for any of the page numbering components. This is where you reset page numbering by setting the page number back to 1. See the section "Changing the Page, Chapter, or Volume Numbers" later in this chapter for more information.

**TIP FROM**

*Laura Acklen*

It's common practice to use different numbering styles for the introductory pages, the body of the document, and the closing sections. To accomplish this, select the format for the page numbers at the top of the document, again at the main body, and then again at the closing section. In addition to switching to a different number format, you should restart the page numbering. See the section "Setting Page, Chapter, and Volume Numbers" later in this chapter for more information on restarting page numbers.

## SWITCHING TO A DIFFERENT PAGE-NUMBERING SCHEME

To accommodate long or complex documents, WordPerfect has five types of page numbers that can be used individually or in combination with one another:

- Page and secondary page numbers that increase automatically—Journals and newsletters sometimes use the secondary page numbers in addition to the regular page numbers. One set numbers every page consecutively throughout the year, and the other numbers the pages in the individual issues.

- Chapter and volume numbers that you increase or decrease where appropriate— Chapter numbers are used for different sections in a document; volume numbers are used to number multiple documents. You could also use these with journals and newsletters to provide volume (year) and chapter (issue/month) numbers.

- A total pages number that displays the total number of pages currently in the document—You use this page number in conjunction with the regular page number to create "page x of y" page numbers.

To create a custom page-numbering scheme, move the insertion point to the page where you want the page numbering to start, and then follow these steps:

1. Choose Format, Page, Numbering, Custom Format to open the Custom Page Numbering dialog box (see Figure 8.6).

2. Click a number style in the list box of the page number type that you want to use. For example, to select volume numbering with lowercase Roman numerals, click the fourth item in the Volume list box (see Figure 8.7).

Select a style

**Figure 8.6**
You can create a combination page number style that includes page numbers with chapter numbers, volume numbers, secondary numbers, and a total pages number.

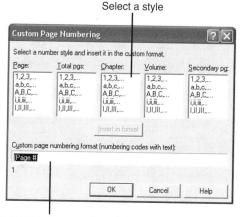

Build the custom page number style

Click for volume numbering in lowercase Roman numerals

**Figure 8.7**
After you've selected a number type and format, you insert it as a code in the list box.

Click to insert the code

3. Click Insert in Format to insert that number style in the Custom Page Numbering Format (Numbering Codes with Text) text box.

4. If necessary, type the text that you want to appear before or after the number. For example, type **Volume** in front of the [Vol #] code.

5. To create a combination page number, insert the other code in the list box and type the necessary accompanying text. One example of the resulting page number appears below the text box (see Figure 8.8).

6. When you're satisfied with the way the page number looks, click OK to return to the Select Page Numbering Format dialog box.

7. Make any necessary adjustments to the font or the placement, and then click OK to insert the page number in the document.

 *If you've just made some adjustments to your custom page numbers and the changes are affecting some of the pages but not others, see "Editing a Custom Page Number" in the Troubleshooting section at the end of this chapter.*

8

**Figure 8.8**
The more complex the document, the more important it is to have accurate and descriptive page numbering.

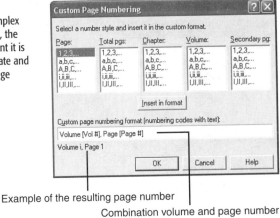

Example of the resulting page number

Combination volume and page number

## SETTING PAGE, CHAPTER, AND VOLUME NUMBERS

Documents with introductory materials often have two sets of page numbers—one for the introductory pages and another for the body text. One common type of formatting uses lowercase Roman numerals (for example, i, ii, iii) for the table of contents and other introductory material, and then Arabic numbers (for example, 1, 2, 3) for the text.

Whether or not you change the format for the page numbers, it's common practice to restart page numbering after the introductory pages. Furthermore, WordPerfect doesn't automatically increment chapter and volume numbers so you have to do that manually.

To change the page number beginning on the current page, follow these steps:

1. In the Select Page Numbering Format dialog box, click the Set Value button to open the Values dialog box (see Figure 8.9).

Type the new page number

**Figure 8.9**
You can set the starting value for page numbers, chapter numbers, and volume numbers in the Values dialog box.

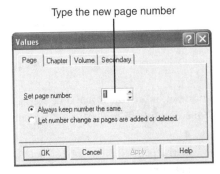

2. If necessary, click the Chapter, Volume, or Secondary tab. Although the options are identical in every tab, the values on each are tied to the corresponding page number codes in your document.

**3.** Type the new number in the Set Page Number text box (or click the spinner arrows).

**4.** Choose one of the following:

- Always Keep Number the Same—Use this option when you don't want the page number to change, no matter how much editing takes place. For example, you might want the first page of the body text to be numbered as page 1, no matter how many introductory pages there are.

- Let Number Change As Pages Are Added or Deleted—Choose this option when you want the page number to be updated as you edit the document.

**TIP FROM**

*Laura Acklen*

If you want the freedom to rearrange chapters, be sure you choose Let Number Change As Pages Are Added or Deleted when you set the chapter number.

## INSERTING PAGE NUMBERS ELSEWHERE IN A DOCUMENT

You're not limited to the 10 predefined page number positions. You can insert a page number anywhere in the document. For example, you might want to refer to the current page, chapter, or volume number within the text. Or, you might want to insert a chapter or volume number directly into a title.

To insert a page number elsewhere in a document, follow these steps:

**1.** Position the insertion point where you want the page number to appear.

**2.** Choose Format, Page, Insert Page Number. The Insert Page Number dialog box has options for inserting primary and secondary page numbers, chapter and volume numbers, and the total pages number (see Figure 8.10).

**Figure 8.10**
You can use the Insert Page Number dialog box to insert a page number in a location other than the predefined page number positions.

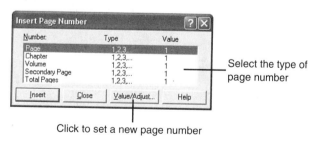

Select the type of page number

Click to set a new page number

**3.** Click the type of number that you want to insert in the list box.

**4.** If necessary, click the Value/Adjust button to open the Values dialog box, where you can change to a different page number method (numbers, letters, or Roman numerals) or set the page number (see Figure 8.11). Click Apply and then OK when you're finished.

**Figure 8.11**
In the Values dialog box, you can choose a different numbering method, and you can set the page, chapter, and volume numbers.

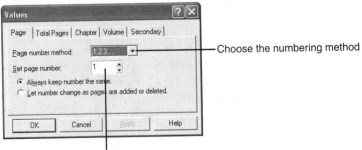

Choose the numbering method

Type the new page number

5. Click Insert (in the Insert Page Number dialog box). The number is inserted at the insertion point.

6. You can continue inserting numbers. Click in the document window and reposition the insertion point, and then click in the dialog box to make it active again. Choose another number type, and then click Insert.

7. Click Close when you're finished inserting page numbers.

**TIP FROM**

You might think that this is the feature you should use to insert page numbers in headers and footers. You're close, but it's actually a little easier than this. When you're working with headers and footers, you can use the Page Numbering button on the Header/Footer property bar to open a drop-down list of numbering types (page, secondary, chapter, volume, total pages).

If you have page numbers cropping up for no apparent reason, see "I Have Gremlins Formatting My Document" in the Troubleshooting section at the end of this chapter.

# CHOOSING DIFFERENT PAPER SIZES

The default paper size in the U.S. version of WordPerfect is 8 1/2 inches by 11 inches (other countries have different standards for paper size). The text is formatted in portrait orientation, which means the paper is taller than it is wide. If all you ever do is create standard business documents, you might never have to change the paper size. However, when the time comes that you have to create an envelope, print on legal-size paper, or rotate a document to landscape orientation, you do so by choosing a different paper size.

Choose Format, Page, Page Setup (or choose File, Page Setup). If necessary, click the Page Setup tab to display the paper sizes that are available for the current printer (see Figure 8.12).

Double-click a page size to select it

**Figure 8.12**
You can choose a different paper size or switch to a different orientation in the Page Setup dialog box.

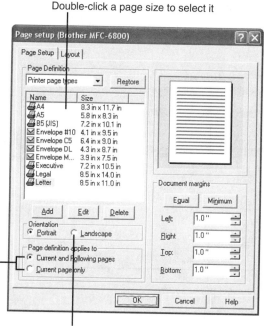

Specify how to apply the changes

Click to switch to landscape orientation

**NOTE**

If you've upgraded from WordPerfect 9, you'll notice right away that the Page Setup dialog box has been redesigned. These improvements were made in response to customer requests for a more organized interface. Most notably, the margin settings have been moved to the Page Setup tab. Items that were available under the Options menu are now shown in the dialog box.

If all you want to do is rotate your text into a landscape orientation (where the page is wider than it is tall), choose Landscape. Select Current Page Only if you want to change the paper size only for the current page, or Current and Following Pages to apply the change to the current page and the rest of the document.

 If your document inexplicably prints on two different types of paper, see "I Have Gremlins Formatting My Document" in the Troubleshooting section at the end of this chapter.

Every printer has a list of paper sizes that it can handle. If you switch to a different printer, or computer, the paper size you chose might not be available. When this happens, WordPerfect makes a best guess and selects a similar paper size. If this doesn't work, you have to edit an existing paper size or create your own.

When you create your own custom paper sizes, you're restricted by the limitations of the printer. In other words, you aren't able to create a paper size that doesn't work with that printer.

It's faster to edit an existing paper size than to create one from scratch, so look for a size in the list that's similar to the size you want to create. Select it in the list, and then click the Edit button. The Edit Page Definition dialog box appears (see Figure 8.13).

**Figure 8.13**
You can edit an existing paper size in the Edit Form dialog box.

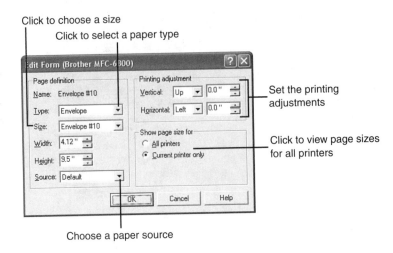

Click to choose a size
Click to select a paper type

Set the printing adjustments

Click to view page sizes for all printers

Choose a paper source

To create a definition from scratch, click the Add button to display the Add New Form dialog box (see Figure 8.14), which is virtually identical to the Edit Page Definition dialog box except that all the options are available. Now you can work with the following options:

- If you're creating a new definition, type a name in the Name text box.
- You can click the Type drop-down list arrow and choose a paper type from the list.
- You can click the Size drop-down list arrow and choose a paper size from the list. If you don't see the size you need, choose User Defined Size.

**Figure 8.14**
You can choose User Defined Size if you don't see the dimensions that you want to use in the list.

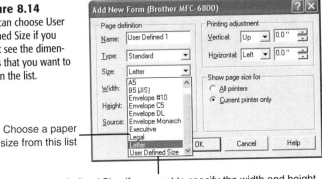

Choose a paper size from this list

Choose User Defined Size if you want to specify the width and height

8

- If you chose User Defined Size, enter the page width in the Width text box and the page height in the Height text box. Or, you can click the spinner arrows to increase or decrease the size.

- You can click the Source drop-down list arrow and choose a source for the paper. For example, unless you have an envelope tray attached to your printer, you need to choose Envelope manual feed so you can insert the envelopes manually.

- If for some reason the text doesn't print using the margins you have set, you can reposition the text on the page with printing adjustments. Click the Vertical drop-down list arrow, choose Up or Down, and then type the amount of adjustment in the text box. Or, click the Horizontal drop-down list arrow, choose Left or Right, and then type the amount of adjustment in the text box.

Click OK when you're finished making your changes. The new paper size appears in the Page Definition list box.

**CAUTION**

Remember that the new definition you've created or the definition that you've edited is not available if you choose another printer. When you switch to a different printer, WordPerfect makes a best-guess match to the paper sizes available on *that* printer. You can, however, create and edit the definitions on that printer to match the definitions on the first printer.

**TIP FROM**

*Laura Acklen*

When you're printing a long letter, usually the first page is on letterhead and the remaining pages are on plainer "second sheets." If you have two paper trays on your printer, you can put letterhead in one and second sheets in the other. I have only one tray, so I either pull out the tray and place the letterhead on top of the second sheets, or I manually feed the letterhead and let the printer pull second sheets from the paper tray. Either way, the trick is to tell the printer where to get the paper. By creating a separate page definition for the letterhead, you can specify where your letterhead paper is. Then you insert a paper size code for the letterhead on the first page and a paper size code for the second sheets on the second page.

You can delete unused paper sizes by selecting them in the list and clicking the Delete button. Keep in mind that the next time you open a document with that paper size, it won't be available and WordPerfect will make a best-guess match from the other sizes.

If you accidentally delete the wrong paper size, you can restore it from the current printer driver. In the Page Setup dialog box, click the Restore button. Note that if you have Standard Page Types selected in the Page Definition drop-down list, only the Windows standard options are restored.

8

TIP FROM

*Laura Achlen*

If you routinely use a paper size other than the default 8 1/2 inches by 11 inches, you can replace the default paper size in the default (`wp11us.wpt` or `wp12us.wpt`) template.

→ For more information on creating and editing templates, **see** "Editing the Default Template," **p. 718.**

# SUBDIVIDING PAGES

A single, physical page can be divided into separate, logical pages. A physical page maintains the original dimensions of the paper. Logical pages are pieces of the physical page, but they are still considered individual pages for purposes of page numbering. For example, if you subdivide a page into six logical pages and then turn on page numbering, the logical pages are numbered 1 through 6. The Labels feature uses the same concept to separate a sheet of paper into individual labels.

In the "Printing Booklets" section of Chapter 6, "Printing, Faxing, and E-Mailing," you learned how to divide the page to create a booklet. Another example of why you would want to subdivide a page is invitations. You can subdivide an 8 1/2-inch by 11-inch piece of paper into four 4 1/4-inch by 5 1/2-inch sections and place four invitations on a page.

To subdivide a page, choose File, Page Setup or choose Format, Margins. Click the Layout tab, and then take a look at the Divide Page section (see Figure 8.15). Choose the number of columns and rows by either typing in the number or clicking the spinner arrows. The sample page illustrates how the paper will be subdivided.

**Figure 8.15**
Using the Divide Page feature, you can divide a physical piece of paper into multiple logical pages.

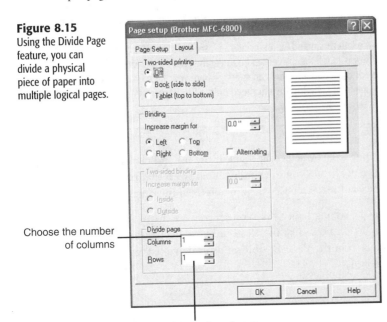

Choose the number of columns

Choose the number of rows

8

Before you click OK, click the Page Setup tab and take a look at the margin settings. WordPerfect uses the current margins for each logical page, so if you keep the default 1-inch margins, you'll have a 1-inch border around each logical page that you won't be able to use. That's a lot of wasted space. Click the Minimum button to quickly set the margins to the minimum allowed by your printer. Figure 8.16 shows the first logical page in a subdivided page. To move to the next page, press Ctrl+Enter.

Finally, when you divide the current page, it dominoes down through the rest of the document. To go back to a full-size page, choose File, Page Setup. Click the Layout tab, and then choose 1 in the Columns text box and 1 in the Rows text box.

Press Ctrl+Enter to move to the next logical page

**Figure 8.16**
Each logical page can be formatted separately with the page formatting options.

Logical page

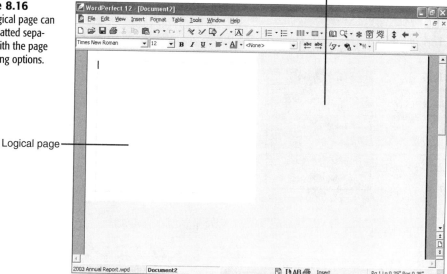

**TIP FROM**

> You can center text on a subdivided page with the Center Page feature. Remember that each section is a logical page, so you format it just as if it were a full-size page. Click in the section (page) that you want to center, and then choose Format, Page, Center. Choose Current Page if you only want to center the current page, or choose Current and Subsequent Pages to center all the pages from this point forward.

# ADDING HEADERS AND FOOTERS

*Headers* hold information that you want printed at the top of every page; *footers* hold information that you want printed at the bottom of every page. You can create two headers and two footers on every page, although usually one header/footer is for odd pages and the other header/footer is for even pages. Headers and footers can contain graphics, page numbers, titles, the filename, revision dates, or any other information about the document.

You create the header or footer on the page where you want it to start. For ease of editing, this is usually the top of the document. For pages where you don't want the headers and footers to print (such as title pages or the first page of a letter), you can suppress the header and footer. You can also use Delay Codes to postpone the effect of a formatting code. See the section "Suppressing and Delaying Codes" later in this chapter.

Formatting codes, such as margin changes and fonts, that you want to affect headers and footers as well as the body text, should be inserted in the DocumentStyle, rather than in the document itself. To edit the DocumentStyle, choose File, Document, Current Document Style.

To insert a header or footer, follow these steps:

1. Click Insert, Header/Footer to open the Headers/Footers dialog box (see Figure 8.17).

**Figure 8.17**
In the Headers/
Footers dialog box,
Header A is selected
by default.

If necessary, select Header B, Footer A, or Footer B.

**NOTE**

> Here's a new feature for you. If you have set specific margins in the document and you want the header/footer margins to match the document margins, place a check mark in the Align with Document Margins check box of the Headers/Footers dialog box. This is a shortcut to setting the margins for both the document text and the header/footer text in the Document Initial Style.

Click Create. What happens next depends on which view mode you're using. Either way, the property bar now has some handy buttons you can use:

- In Page mode, the insertion point moves up to the top of the page, within the header guidelines (see Figure 8.18).
- In Draft mode, the insertion point moves to a header/footer-editing window. You won't be able to see the document text, only the text of the header.

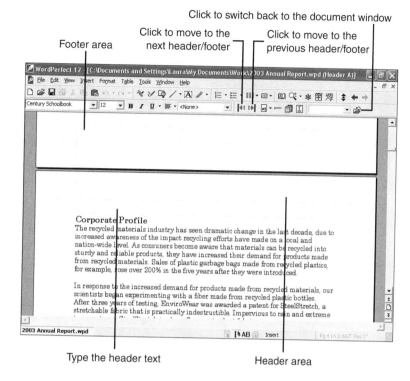

**Figure 8.18**
In Page View mode, you create and edit the header or footer onscreen, not in a separate window, as with Draft mode. In either mode, you have some new buttons on the property bar.

Click to switch back to the document window

Click to move to the next header/footer

Click to move to the previous header/footer

Footer area

Type the header text

Header area

4. Type the text of the header or footer. Using the menus, add the necessary graphics, tables, and other formatting elements. (Features that can't be used in a header or footer are grayed out on the menus.)

5. Click the Close button, or press Ctrl+F4, to switch back to the document window.

**CAUTION**

WordPerfect automatically inserts a blank line between the document text and the header or footer. Don't insert a blank line in the header or footer unless you want to increase the distance to two lines.

**TIP FROM**

*Laura Acklen*

Header and footer text in the same font size as the document text is distracting at its best, and downright ugly at its worst. If you're using a 12-point font for the body text, step down at least 2 points, preferably 4 points, for the header or footer text. If you're using a sans-serif font (such as Arial) for your headings and a serif font (such as Times New Roman) for your text, you might also consider using the sans-serif font for the header and footer text to further set it apart from the body text.

8

**TIP FROM**

*Laura Acklen*

In another lifetime, I installed local area networks in law offices and trained the staff in WordPerfect. One of the first standards we recommended was inserting the path and file-name (in a tiny 6- or 8-point font) in a footer that printed on every page but the first page. Anyone who read the document knew exactly where to find the file on the net-work. (Whether they had rights to the file was up to a system administrator.) To insert the filename in a header or footer, choose Insert, Other. Choose Filename or Path and Filename.

If you're in Page mode, you'll see the header or footer text onscreen with the rest of the document text. If you're working in Draft mode, you won't see header or footer text unless you edit the header or footer. To edit a header or footer, choose Insert, Header/Footer. Select the appropriate header or footer, and then click Edit.

 Because headers and footers are printed within the text area of a page, you should probably decrease the margins to allow more space for the body text. It's more attractive to pull the header or footer into the margin space. Remember to change the margins in the DocumentStyle (choose File, Document, Current Document Style), or enable the Align with Document Margins check box in the Headers/Footers dialog box (this is a new feature introduced in WordPerfect 11). Otherwise, the margin changes won't affect the placement of the headers and footers.

**NOTE**

Changing the top or bottom margins will always cause an automatic adjustment to the header and footer placement, even if you don't enable the Align with Document Margins option. Furthermore, enabling the check box only performs the action once. If you later make adjustments to the left or right margins, the header and footer will not automati-cally adjust to the new margins. To readjust the header and footer margins, choose Insert, Header/Footer, select the header or footer, enable the Align with Document Margins check box, and then choose Edit. You can immediately click the Close button because all you are doing is adjusting the margins, not the header/footer text.

 *If your header or footer prints on top of the page numbers, see "Headers/Footers Versus Page Numbers" in the Troubleshooting section at the end of this chapter.*

*If you have headers and footers popping up in places where they shouldn't, see "I Have Gremlins Formatting My Document" in the Troubleshooting section at the end of this chapter.*

That's how you create a header or footer. The following are some of the other options you can take advantage of:

 ■ You can insert page numbers by clicking the Page Numbering button on the property bar. A drop-down list of options appears (see Figure 8.19). Select the type of page num-ber you want to insert.

Select a page number type from the list

**Figure 8.19**
Click the Page Numbering button to insert any of the five types of page numbers in a header or footer.

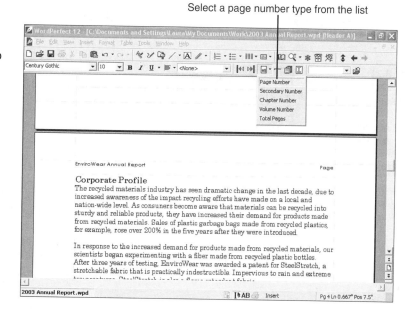

■ Click the Horizontal Line button to insert a graphic line in the header or footer.

**CAUTION**

> Make sure the insertion point is on a blank line when you click the Horizontal Line button. Otherwise, the graphics line plops down right on top of the text.

■ Click the Header/Footer Placement button to open the Header or Footer Placement dialog box (see Figure 8.20). The default is to print the header or footer on every page.

**Figure 8.20**
Specify on which pages you want the header or footer to print in the Placement dialog box.

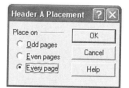

**NOTE**

> Although I usually create one separate header for odd pages and another for even pages, occasionally I use two headers on the same page. One usually contains something standard, such as the title of the document. The other contains something that changes periodically in the document, such as chapter numbers and names. To keep the two headers from overlapping, I keep the first header's text at the left margin and the second header's text flush against the right margin. I make sure to use short titles and chapter names so that they don't run into each other in the middle of the page!

■ Click the Header/Footer Distance button, and then type the distance that you want between the header or footer and the body text in the Distance dialog box (see Figure 8.21).

**Figure 8.21**
You can adjust the space between the header (or footer) and the text in the Distance dialog box.

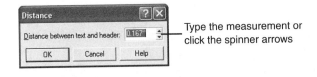

Type the measurement or click the spinner arrows

**TIP FROM**

*Laura Acklen*

When you're working in a header or footer, the Numbering option on the Format, Page menu is gray and there is no option for Value/Adjust under Insert Page Number. So, how are you supposed to adjust the page number in a header or footer? First, insert the page number in the header or footer. Switch back to the document window and choose Format, Page, Numbering. Change Position to No Page Numbering, and then click Set Value and change the page number there. Click OK twice to get back to the document.

## SUPPRESSING AND DELAYING CODES

The Suppress feature prevents headers, footers, watermarks, and page numbers from printing on a particular page. It's frequently used to keep these elements from printing on the title page. You have to place a Suppress code at the top of every page on which you don't want a header, footer, page number, or watermark to print.

Click on the page where you want to suppress a header, footer, page number, or watermark, and then choose Format, Page, Suppress. The Suppress dialog box opens (see Figure 8.22). Place a check mark next to the elements that you want to suppress, or choose All to select all the elements at one time. Click OK.

**Figure 8.22**
In the Suppress dialog box, choose the page elements you do not want to print on the current page.

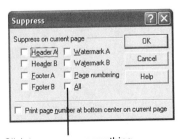

Click to suppress everything

The Delay Codes feature postpones the effect of formatting changes for a specified number of pages. A delay code is used in situations where you want to skip more than one page (for example, if you want to skip past the table of contents, preface, or other introductory material before printing headers, footers, or page numbers).

With delay codes, you can insert all your formatting at the top of the document, and then selectively apply the formatting after a certain number of pages. To go one better, you can put all the delay codes in the DocumentStyle, where they can't accidentally be deleted during editing.

To create a delay code, follow these steps:

1. Choose Format, Page, Delay Codes. The Delay Codes dialog box appears (see Figure 8.23).

**Figure 8.23**
Type the number of pages that you want to skip in the Delay Codes dialog box.

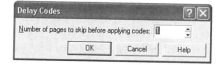

2. Type the number of pages in the Number of Pages to Skip Before Applying Codes text box (or click the spinner arrows to select the number). Click OK to switch to the Define Delayed Codes editing window (see Figure 8.24).

Click to insert a graphic image
Click to create a header or footer          The title bar identifies the window

**Figure 8.24**
You can postpone the action of many formatting codes by placing them in delay codes. Delay codes can be inserted in the document or in the DocumentStyle.

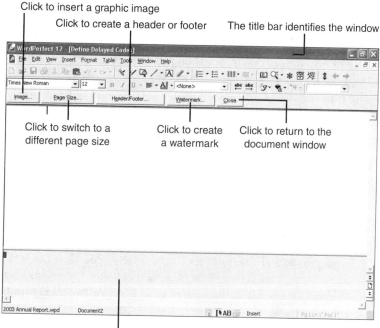

Click to switch to a different page size          Click to create a watermark          Click to return to the document window

Reveal Codes is on so you can see the codes as you insert them

3. Use the menus or the buttons on the feature bar to insert the necessary formatting codes.

4. Click the Close button to return to the document window.

8

No matter where you are on the page, WordPerfect automatically inserts this delay code at the top of the page: [Delay: #]. The # represents the number of pages you want to skip. (WordPerfect calculates the number of pages to skip based on physical pages, not page numbers.) If your insertion point is on page 5 and you set a delay code to skip 3 pages, the code [Delay: 3] is inserted at the top of page 5. On the page where the formatting takes effect, a [Delay Codes] code that contains the actual codes is inserted at the top of that page. If you move the red cursor to the left of this code, it expands to show you the codes within.

**NOTE**

The trick to the Delay Codes feature is to realize that you are actually inserting formatting codes into a code—a delay code. If you create Header A in a delay code, you can't edit that code from the document window; you can only create another Header A. The two headers are independent of each other. The header/footer that you create in a delay code overrides the header/footer that you create in the document. To modify a formatting code in a delay code, you have to edit the delay code by turning on Reveal Codes and double-clicking the [Delay: #] code to edit the contents.

 *If you're struggling with bizarre formatting in a document, see "I've Got Delay Codes Popping Up All Over the Place" in the Troubleshooting section at the end of this chapter.*

# SETTING UP COLUMNS

Columns help to break up information and make it easier to read. Take a look at your daily newspaper—it's much easier to read across a short section of text than it is to read across an entire page (especially with small fonts). There are four types of columns in WordPerfect:

- Newspaper—Text flows down the first column until the bottom of the page is reached, and then wraps up to the top of the next column. Newspaper columns are used in newsletters, magazine articles, and newspapers.

- Balanced Newspaper—Text flows across from column to column so that the columns stay (roughly) the same length, no matter how much text you type in. Because the text is constantly readjusting, typing in balanced columns is awkward. It's best to type the text and then turn on the columns.

- Parallel—Text flows down the first column until you push it over to the next column. Typing in parallel columns isn't bad because you decide when you want to move to the next column. However, editing in parallel columns is about as much fun as working on your income taxes. For this reason, most WordPerfect users turn to the Tables feature when they need side-by-side columns.

  → To learn how to create and edit tables, **see** "Creating Tables," **p. 294.**

- Parallel with Block Protect—These columns operate in the same fashion as regular parallel columns except that each row of columns is kept together. If one column in the row becomes so long that it moves down to the next page, the entire row is moved.

## DEFINING COLUMNS

Columns can be defined before or after you type text. During a heavy revision, you might find it easier to work outside columns. When you're finished revising, you can turn columns on and have WordPerfect reformat the text.

To define columns, position the insertion point where you want the columns to start. You can also select a portion of text to be formatted into columns so the rest of the text isn't affected.

**TIP FROM**

*Laura Acklen*

It's common to have a title or heading that spreads across the top of the columns, so you might want to leave a blank line or two at the top of the document, and then define the columns underneath, right at the beginning of the text.

The fastest way to define columns is to click the Columns button and then choose the number of columns (see Figure 8.25). These columns are created with a half-inch gutter (that is, space between columns), which is considered a standard setting.

Click to turn on columns

**Figure 8.25**
You can click the
Columns button to
turn on columns.

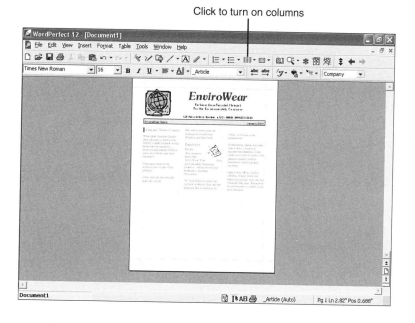

You can easily adjust the column and gutter widths (the space between columns) by clicking and dragging the column guidelines (choose View, Guidelines, Columns) or the markers on the Ruler (choose View, Ruler). If you want to define balanced columns, or if you want a little more control (and who doesn't?), you can use the Columns dialog box to define the columns.

To define columns with the Columns dialog box, follow these steps:

1. Choose Format, Columns to display the Columns dialog box (see Figure 8.26).

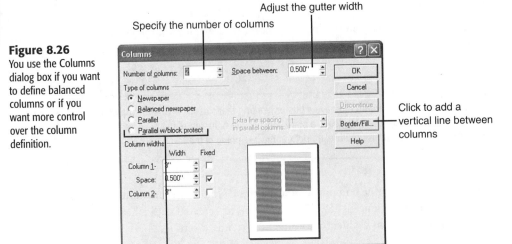

**Figure 8.26**
You use the Columns dialog box if you want to define balanced columns or if you want more control over the column definition.

Specify the number of columns

Adjust the gutter width

Click to add a vertical line between columns

Choose the column type

2. If you want more than two columns, type the number of columns in the Number of Columns text box.

3. Choose a column type in the Type of Columns section.

4. If necessary, increase or decrease the gutter width in the Space Between text box.

5. If necessary, adjust the individual column widths and space between the columns in the Column Widths section.

6. If you want a vertical line to appear between the columns, click the Border/Fill button. Scroll down through the Available Border Styles list box until you see the Column Between style (see Figure 8.27). Click OK.

→ If you're curious about graphic lines and how to customize the line styles, **see** "Inserting Horizontal and Vertical Lines," **p. 378.**

→ For more information on adding borders, shading, and drop shadows, **see** "Adding Borders, Drop Shadows, and Fills," **p. 217.**

**N O T E** | Don't worry if you don't see the vertical line between the columns on the sample document in the Columns dialog box. Because you applied the line in the Column Border/Fill dialog box, you'll see the line on the sample document there, not in the Columns dialog box.

**Figure 8.27**
The Column Between border style applies a thin vertical line between each set of columns.

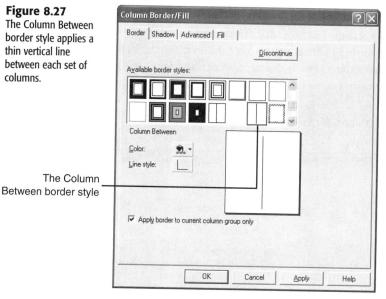

The Column Between border style

**7.** Click OK to close the Column Border/Fill dialog box and turn on the columns (see Figure 8.28).

 If your balanced columns are not balanced, see "My Balanced Newspaper Columns Are Uneven" in the Troubleshooting section at the end of this chapter.

**Figure 8.28**
In this document, three balanced newspaper columns have been defined. The gutter space has been reduced to .3 inch.

Balanced newspaper columns

You can turn columns on and off as often as you like. To turn off columns, click the Columns button, and choose Discontinue (or choose Format, Columns, and then click Discontinue). When you're ready to turn columns on again, either click the Columns button and choose the number of columns (to define the default newspaper columns with 1/2 inch gutter), or choose Format, Columns to define columns with settings other than the defaults.

8

## TYPING AND EDITING IN COLUMNS

Typing and editing in columns can be a little tricky. You can save yourself some frustration if you finish typing and editing the text before you turn on columns. If, for some reason, you need to work in columns, the mouse is the quickest method for moving the insertion point—just click where you want to go. Table 8.1 lists some keyboard shortcuts you can use.

**TABLE 8.1  SHORTCUTS FOR MOVING AROUND IN COLUMNS**

| Press This | To Do This |
| --- | --- |
| Ctrl+Enter | Start a new column (insert a column break) |
| Alt+right arrow | One column to the right |
| Alt+left arrow | One column to the left |
| Alt+End | Last line in the column |
| Alt+Home | First line in the column |

## HYPHENATING WORDS

When you're formatting text into columns, hyphenating words becomes an important issue. If you hyphenate too much, you frustrate the reader; if you don't hyphenate enough, you get gaps in the text. You can let WordPerfect decide where words should be hyphenated with the Hyphenation feature. WordPerfect uses the installed Oxford Dictionary to determine the correct place to hyphenate a word. Choose Tools, Language, Hyphenation to open the Line Hyphenation dialog box (see Figure 8.29).

Turn on automatic hyphenation

**Figure 8.29**
The Hyphenation feature will automatically hyphenate words if they extend past a specified hyphenation zone.

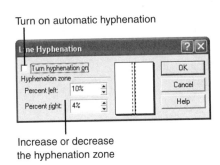

Increase or decrease
the hyphenation zone

To turn on automatic hyphenation, choose Turn Hyphenation On. The hyphenation zone is a narrow area that surrounds the right margin. If you decrease the hyphenation zone values, more words will be hyphenated; if you increase the hyphenation zone values, fewer words will be hyphenated.

If you prefer to specify where words should be hyphenated (if they extend into the hyphenation zone), there are several other methods that can be used. Choose Format, Line, Other Codes to display the Other Codes dialog box (see Figure 8.30).

**Figure 8.30**
The Other Codes dialog box contains a series of hyphenation codes that can be assigned, one word at a time.

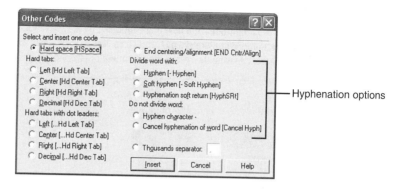

Hyphenation options

Choose from the following options:

- Choose Hyphen if you want to insert a hyphen in a word. The word will be hyphenated regardless of where it falls on a line.

- Choose Soft Hyphen if you want the word to be hyphenated only if it spans the hyphenation zone. The hyphen remains invisible until the word moves close to the end of the line. You can also press Ctrl+Shift+hyphen to insert a soft hyphen.

- Choose Hyphenation Soft Return to divide a word without using a hyphen, but only if the word spans the hyphenation zone. Use this option for words that are divided by slashes, an en dash, or an em dash.

- Choose Hyphen Character if you want to keep text together on either side of a hyphen.

- Choose Cancel Hyphenation of Word if you want to exclude a certain word from automatic hyphenation. The word will be wrapped to the next line if it happens to span the hyphenation zone.

# USING MAKE IT FIT

Didn't your mother tell you there would be days like this? Your letter's signature block spills over to the second page...or your newsletter doesn't have quite enough text to fill the page. It happens to the best of us. Before you run screaming from the room at the prospect of spending an hour adjusting font sizes and margins, take a deep breath and let WordPerfect do all the dirty work.

Make It Fit does just that—it makes text fit however many pages you specify. Now, you can't make one page of text stretch out into three pages, and you can't take three pages of text and expect to squeeze it into one page. The number of pages that you specify must be at least 50% of the current size.

You can use Make It Fit on selected text or on the entire document, so if you want to work on only a section of text, select it first. Choose Format, Make It Fit to open the Make It Fit dialog box (see Figure 8.31). (If you selected text, the Top Margin and Bottom Margin options are not available.)

**8**

Type the desired number of pages

**Figure 8.31**
Make It Fit adjusts margins, font size, and line spacing to expand or contract text so that it fits within a specified number of pages.

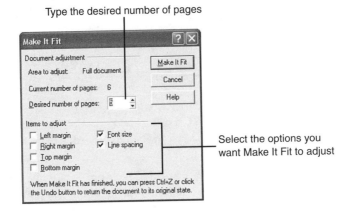

Select the options you want Make It Fit to adjust

Take a look at the current number of pages and then type the number of pages that you want to fill in the Desired Number of Pages text box. Select the options that you want Make It Fit to use to reformat the text and then click Make It Fit. It may not be obvious, but if you don't want Make It Fit to alter one of the settings (the top/bottom margins, for example), make sure you remove the check mark next to the setting.

# ADDING BORDERS AROUND PAGES

Adding page borders is so similar to adding borders around paragraphs that I'm only going to cover the difference between the two here.

→ For more information on adding borders, drop shadows, and fills, **see** "Adding Borders, Drop Shadows, and Fills," **p. 217.**

There are 35 additional borders available for pages in the Page Border/Fill dialog box—they are called fancy borders. To see them, choose Format, Page, Border/Fill to open the Page Border/Fill dialog box. Click the Border Type drop-down list arrow and choose Fancy. When you choose Fancy borders, a Change button appears in the dialog box (see Figure 8.32). Click the Change button to open the Change Folder dialog box, where you can choose another borders folder.

Click to switch between Line and Fancy borders

**Figure 8.32**
The fancy borders are available only in the Page Border/Fill dialog box.

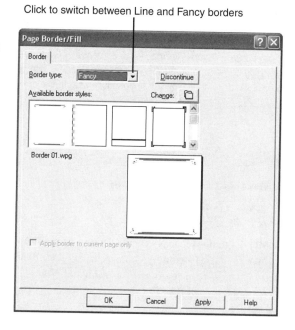

**CAUTION**

When you create a border using the line styles, WordPerfect automatically allows space between the text and the border, which is positioned on the margins. A fancy border can overwrite the text, so you might have to make some adjustments to the margins.

To apply a line page border to the current page only, choose Apply Border to Current Page Only. In most cases, you apply a page border to all the pages in the document to maintain consistency. However, you can turn the border off on certain pages if you want. Click on the page where you want the border to stop, and then choose Format, Page, Border/Fill, Discontinue.

**TIP FROM**

*Laura Acklen*

The Page Border/Fill dialog box offers a list of fancy borders. You can customize these borders in Presentations and then save them with the same name or a different name. The fancy borders are located in the folder specified in the Files Settings dialog box. Choose Tools, Settings (or press Alt+F12), Files, click the Graphic tab, and look in the Default Fancy Borders Folder text box for the location.

TIP FROM

*Laura Acklen*

> Round-cornered borders add an interesting effect. You can change the border corners for the line borders to anything from slightly rounded to almost circular. To round off the corners on a border, choose Format, Page, Border/Fill. Click the Advanced tab, and then click Rounded Corners. To adjust the amount of roundness, type a value in the Corner Radius text box. Keep an eye on the sample document to see how the roundness looks.

# TROUBLESHOOTING

## CAN'T FIND THE RIGHT MARGINS TO CENTER THE PAGE

*I've been trying unsuccessfully to adjust the top and bottom margins so that I can center titles on the title page. There must be an easier way!*

There is—it's called Center Page, and it takes only a second to set it up. Choose Format, Page, Center. Choose Current Page to center the current page. Choose Current and Subsequent Pages to center pages from the insertion point on. Choose No Centering to stop centering pages (after you've used the Current and Subsequent Pages option).

## EDITING A CUSTOM PAGE NUMBER

*I decided to go back and add some text to a plain page number. After I made the change, I noticed that part of my document has the revised page number, but the rest has only the original page number. What's going on here?*

When you edit a custom page number, you have to be sure you go back to the page where you created the custom page number. This might be at the top of the document or the beginning of a new section or chapter. Going back to the original page gives you the opportunity to edit the original code, rather than create another code (with your changes) later on in the document that conflicts with the original code.

## MANUAL FEED IS ON ALL THE TIME

*I made a few changes to one of the paper size definitions, and now whenever I print something, I have to insert every piece of paper into the manual feed tray.*

You've accidentally changed the paper source to manual, so the printer thinks that you want to insert the paper by hand. This is a great feature when you want to manually feed the letterhead and allow the printer to grab second sheets from the tray, but it's a real pain when it gets turned on by accident. Select the paper size in the Page Setup dialog box and click the Edit button. Click the Source drop-down list arrow and choose Default.

## HEADERS/FOOTERS VERSUS PAGE NUMBERS

*I have my page numbers positioned in the bottom center of every page, but they are printing on top of the footer text. Isn't there some way to print the footer text in one place on the line and the page number somewhere else?*

As you've already surmised, page numbers, headers, and footers all use the same area of the page. Most of the time they all get along. When a conflict occurs, the page number doesn't replace the header or footer (or vice versa); they are both printed, one on top of the other.

You have two choices: You can either choose another position for the page number (such as the bottom right), or you can insert the page number as part of the footer. A third choice might be to place a hard return or two at the end of the footer so it pushes the footer text slightly up on the page. This might cause the footer to display above the page number, so if you aren't happy with the results, try one of the other fixes.

### I Have Gremlins Formatting My Document

*I don't know what I did to deserve this, but I'm working on a document for a friend, and all sorts of crazy things are happening. Headers and footers are popping up in places where they don't belong, page numbers are starting midway through the document, and margin changes are coming out of nowhere. When I print, the document comes out on two different types of paper. The worst part about the whole thing is that I can't find a code to delete or edit and I've even used Find and Replace to try to locate it.*

It is rather unsettling to see formatting changes that can't be traced back to a code. One of two things can cause this type of situation: styles and delay codes. There could be styles in the document that contain the offending formatting codes, or the formatting codes might be inside a delay code. Either way, you can't remove or edit the formatting codes until you've located the style or delay code that contains the codes. Start at the top of the document and look for a [Delay:#] code (you might consider using Find to locate it). Double-click the code to edit the contents.

A style code could be anywhere. Use Find to locate the style code, and then double-click it to edit the contents.

### I've Got Delay Codes Popping Up All Over the Place

*I'm working on a document that someone sent me via e-mail and I can't figure out where all of the delay codes are coming from. What can I do to clean up this document?*

The person who sent you the document might not be intentionally entering delay codes, but they are undoubtedly doing something which WordPerfect interprets as a request or need for a delay code.

For example, if you change the margin in the middle of a paragraph, a delay code will be placed at the top of the page (instead of a margin code). If the page began with hard returns or at the beginning of a paragraph, a margin code is placed at the top of the page instead of a delay code.

Repeated adjustments to the margins is one thing that often causes extra delay codes, but it really depends on what else is going on in the document, where the cursor is when margins are changed, and so on. Another thing that can result in lots of delay codes is importing documents from Word format—there are several Word formatting arrangements that are converted to delay codes when the document is imported to WP. Keep in mind that version 12 does a much better job of converting Word documents than previous versions.

### MY BALANCED NEWSPAPER COLUMNS ARE UNEVEN

*I've defined balanced columns and typed in text, but the columns aren't all the same length.*

You probably have some blank lines in there throwing things off. Turn on Reveal Codes and delete any extra [HRt] codes. You might also have some formatting options that conflict with columnar formatting. Click in the paragraph that isn't balanced, and then choose Format, Keep Text Together and deselect all the options.

### ROUNDED CORNERS DON'T DISPLAY CORRECTLY

*I've rounded the corners on a page border, but the corners still look square on the screen.*

Rest assured, the rounded corners will print correctly even though they aren't displayed onscreen. To display rounded corners, WordPerfect would have to redraw the screen every time you type a character, which would result in serious performance degradation.

# PROJECT

Just as you saw in Chapter 7, "Formatting Lines and Paragraphs," a few small changes can make all the difference in the world. Take pity on the annual report that you see in Figure 8.33. The information is no doubt comprehensive and exhaustively researched. The only problem is that it's dull and boring. Figure 8.34 shows the same annual report with a few improvements. The information that you need to make these changes is included in this chapter, so I won't duplicate the steps here.

A decorative page border has been added to the title page. This border was discontinued on the second page so that it affects only the first page. Headers and footers were created at the top of the first page, but they are suppressed on the title page. The header contains document identification text. The footer has a "page x of y" page number centered on the line. Finally, the top and bottom margins have been reduced to .667 to reclaim the space taken up by the header and footer.

**Figure 8.33**
This annual report contains everything you need to know about the company, but it doesn't look interesting to read.

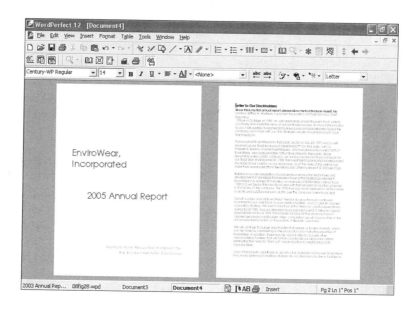

Document information in the header

**Figure 8.34**
This annual report looks more inviting and gives the impression that the person who prepared it paid close attention to details.

Fancy page border

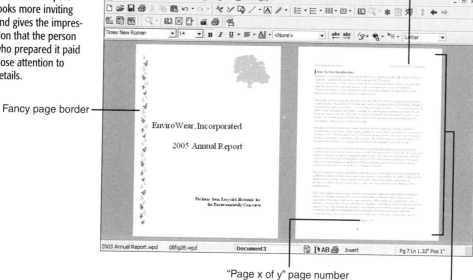

"Page x of y" page number

Margins reduced to reclaim the space lost by theheader and footer

# FORMATTING WITH STYLES

## In this chapter

*by Read Gilgen*

# A QUICK OVERVIEW OF STYLES

You like doing things in style. But you also like to be quick about it. WordPerfect has just the answer for you: styles.

Most of us begin making our documents look good by using the "brute force" method. If the document needs to be fixed, we just add a formatting code here or there until it approximates what we're looking for. Unfortunately, if you have to create that kind of document again, you'll spend lots of time trying to duplicate the steps you took, and often you don't really end up with the same results.

Suppose, for example, you want each section heading in your document in a certain font and size, and you want them all bold and italic, with a horizontal line underneath that extends the width of the page. Instead of applying each of those elements to each heading, one by one, you can apply a style to each heading that already includes all those elements.

*Styles* are named collections of formatting procedures, such as fonts, margins, tabs, and so on. When you apply a style in your document, you apply one or more formatting options. Thus, everything with a particular style has the same look.

In addition, any change you make to a style automatically changes any text where you already applied that style. For example, if you decide you don't want your headings in italic, you can remove the italic format from your style, and WordPerfect removes it from each place the style was used. The other formats of the heads, such as font, size, and so on, remain intact.

Like many of WordPerfect's features, styles can be both easy to use and complex. More often than not, you'll find yourself using styles occasionally to make your work easier and more professional looking. But when you need the full power that styles have to offer, you won't be disappointed because WordPerfect will be there to help.

# STYLES VERSUS MACROS VERSUS QUICKWORDS

Just what is the difference between styles and macros? Couldn't you just create a macro to accomplish the formatting you want?

Indeed, macros are powerful and can perform many formatting tasks. However, after you run a macro, you end up with formatting codes in your document as if you had placed them there yourself. *Macros* automate the process of inserting format codes, but otherwise there is nothing in the document to distinguish the fact that you used a macro instead of formatting the text one step at a time.

Styles, on the other hand, remain in the document and format the text they are applied to. If you remove the style, you remove all the formatting it provides, not only in one location, but everywhere it appears in the document. If you change a style, the change takes place automatically throughout the document. Thus, styles offer much more flexibility and control for formatting than do macros.

*QuickWords*, words that expand when you type them and which can include formatting, is another powerful formatting tool. But like macros, the end result is simply text and format codes as if you had created each code yourself.

→ For information on using QuickWords, **see** "Setting Up QuickWords," **p. 160.**

→ For more information on macros, **see** "Using Macros to Automate Repetitive Tasks," **p. 816**.

# USING QUICKFORMAT TO CREATE STYLES ON-THE-FLY

WordPerfect's QuickFormat feature enables you to make and use styles on-the-fly. You begin by formatting text, and then copying and applying the results at other locations in the document. Consider, for example, the document shown in Figure 9.1. Suppose you want to make each header stand out by changing its font and making it both bold and italic. Follow these simple steps:

**Figure 9.1**
The use of styles makes it easy to apply consistent formatting throughout a document—for example, in section headings.

Section heading

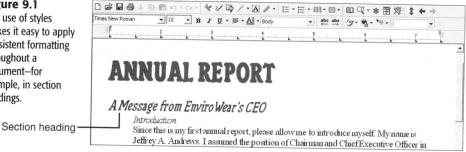

1. Begin by applying the formatting you want to the first section heading. For example, if you change the font, and add bold and italic, you get the result you see in Figure 9.1.

2. Position the insertion point anywhere on the formatted heading, and choose Format, QuickFormat, or click QuickFormat on the toolbar. WordPerfect displays the QuickFormat dialog box (see Figure 9.2).

**Figure 9.2**
The QuickFormat dialog box enables you to capture a formatting style and apply it to selected text or to heading paragraphs.

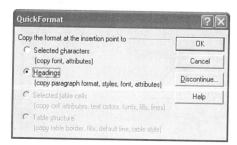

3. Because you want to produce consistent-looking headings, choose the Headings option.

4. Click OK, and WordPerfect returns you to the document, but now the mouse pointer is shaped like a paint roller with a trailing swath of paint (see Figure 9.3).

**Figure 9.3**
The mouse pointer changes to indicate that you will apply a heading style when you click the mouse.

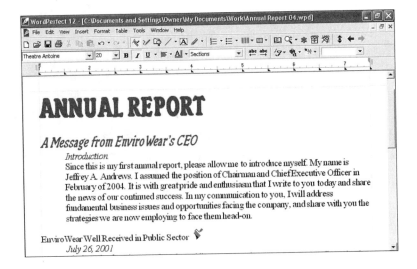

5. Move to the next section heading, point the tip of the paint swath at the heading, and click. WordPerfect applies the styles from the first heading to the heading you click.

6. Continue through the document, clicking each heading to apply the QuickFormat style.

7. To turn off the QuickFormat process, choose Format, QuickFormat; or simply click the QuickFormat button on the toolbar.

Each time you create a QuickFormat style, WordPerfect adds the style to your style list and numbers it (for example, QuickFormat1, QuickFormat2, and so on). If you want to use the style again, you can follow the same procedures listed previously or you can apply the style from the style list, following these steps:

1. Position the cursor on the heading you want to format.

2. Choose Format, Styles. WordPerfect displays the Styles dialog box (see Figure 9.4).

**Figure 9.4**
You can use the Styles dialog box to select and apply a style to your document.

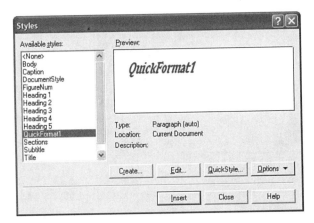

3. Click the QuickFormat style you created for the headings (for example, QuickFormat1).

4. Click Insert. WordPerfect applies the style to the heading.

Heading format styles apply to entire paragraphs. If you want to copy only fonts and attributes and apply them to selected text, the procedure is a bit different:

1. Begin by applying the formatting you want to your text. For example, you can add fancy underlining to bold, italic text, as shown in Figure 9.5.

**Figure 9.5**
You can use QuickFormat to pick up special formatting and apply it to selected text.

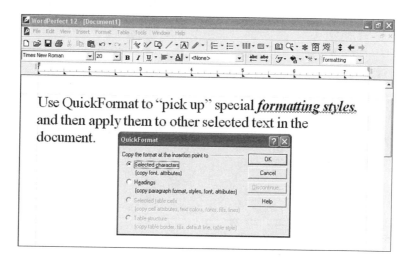

2. Position the insertion point anywhere on the formatted text, and choose Format, QuickFormat, or click QuickFormat on the toolbar. WordPerfect displays the QuickFormat dialog box (refer to Figure 9.2).

3. Because you now want to copy fonts and attributes, choose Selected Characters.

4. Click OK. WordPerfect returns you to the document and the mouse pointer is shaped like a paint roller with a trailing swath of paint.

5. Move to the text you want to format and use the mouse to select it (see Figure 9.6). When you release the mouse button, WordPerfect applies the styles from the original text to the text you just selected.

**Figure 9.6**
QuickFormat by characters applies a formatting style to selected text instead of to whole paragraphs.

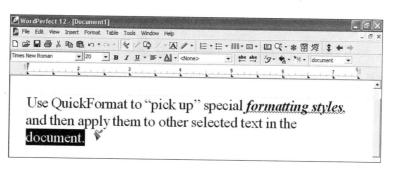

6. Continue through the document, selecting text to which you want to apply the QuickFormat style.

7. Turn off QuickFormat by choosing Format, QuickFormat, or by clicking the QuickFormat button on the toolbar.

**NOTE** QuickFormats are saved with the current document, but are not available to other documents you create. For more information on renaming, editing, and saving styles for use in all your documents, see the section "Creating Custom Styles," later in this chapter.

# UNDERSTANDING STYLES

Styles are primarily formatting tools. A style consists of various format elements that you apply collectively to all or part of a document. If all you ever need is a quick and easy way to apply basic formatting, QuickStyles will probably do the trick. But if you need to explore the full power of WordPerfect's styles, you also need to understand how and where they work.

## TYPES OF STYLES

Although styles are relatively easy to create and use, you can become confused when you first encounter paragraph styles, template styles, or system styles. It helps to think about styles as different types, depending on their function or location.

First, there are three basic *types* of styles, each with its own purpose, and named according to the portion of the document it affects:

- Document (or open) styles
- Paragraph styles
- Character styles

Second, there are three *locations* for styles:

- Document styles (styles saved with a document)
- Template styles (styles saved in templates)
- System styles (WordPerfect's default styles)

Finally, there are *feature* styles that apply to specific types of text, such as the following:

- Specialized text styles, such as hyperlinks and headings
- Outline styles for bullets, numbered paragraphs, and outlines
- Graphics styles for graphics boxes, text boxes, equation and figure numbers, and so on
- Footnote and endnote styles
- Header, footer, and watermark styles

→ For information on bullet, list, and outline styles, **see** "Organizing Information with Lists and Outlines," **p. 333.**

→ For information on styles for graphics boxes, **see** Chapter 13, "Customizing Graphic Shapes and Images."

→ For details on footnote, endnote, and other specialized heading styles, **see** "Formatting Footnotes," **p. 571**.

Styles can be a combination of any of these categories. For example, a numbered outline style is also a paragraph style, and can be stored in the current document or in a template for use in all your documents.

### DOCUMENT, PARAGRAPH, AND CHARACTER TYPES OF STYLES

Document styles are found at the beginning of the document because they establish certain features such as paper size, margins, tab stops, line spacing, and fonts for the entire document. These are *open* styles, as opposed to *paired* styles, because they are turned on and left open throughout the document. In earlier versions of WordPerfect the DocumentStyle style is called Document Initial Styles.

If you insert formatting codes in your document but don't get the results you expect (for example, page numbers are in the wrong font), you probably need to look at the DocumentStyle (see the section "Editing Styles" later in this chapter).

Paragraph styles, as the name indicates, affect entire paragraphs. You typically use paragraph styles for such things as headings, headlines, titles, and bibliographic entries.

A paragraph style overrides DocumentStyle settings, or other settings created by the insertion of formatting codes. To apply a paragraph style, simply place the insertion point anywhere in the paragraph, and then choose Format, Styles. WordPerfect displays the Styles dialog box (refer to Figure 9.4). Select the style you want and click Insert to apply that style. Note, in Figure 9.7, that the style affects the entire paragraph, but does not affect paragraphs before or after the style.

**Figure 9.7**
A paragraph style formats the entire paragraph to which it is applied, but does not change the formatting before or after the paragraph. Note the pair of style codes in Reveal Codes.

Style codes ⎯

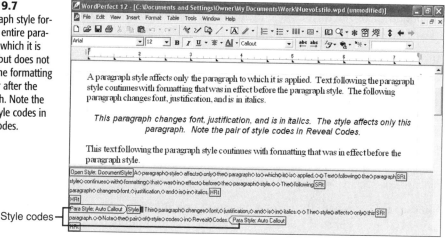

Character styles affect sections of text, but not whole paragraphs or documents, and are usually limited to text attributes such as font, font size, bold, and italic. They also override paragraph or document styles.

Although character styles seem similar to pairs of WordPerfect attribute codes (such as bold), they are much more easily changed. For example, you can use a style called Citation to apply underlining to books you reference. If you later decide to put citations in italic instead of underlining them, you simply change the style, and WordPerfect automatically updates all citations.

### THE LOCATION OF STYLES

WordPerfect always stores styles you create or import in the document itself (see Figure 9.8, which illustrates the location of styles and where they can be stored). You can edit such styles, but they affect only the current document. However, if you save custom styles to a template, you can apply them to other documents as well.

**Figure 9.8**
WordPerfect styles that come from the WordPerfect system and from templates can be modified or created by the user within a document. Modified styles can be saved with the document or to other templates.

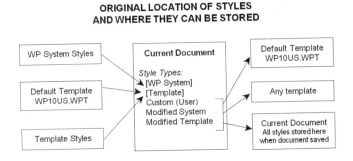

Certain default styles are part of the WordPerfect system, and as such are always available to restore settings that you might have changed. You cannot change these styles, but you can import them and then change them for the current document. Further, you can save system style changes to a template.

All WordPerfect documents are based on templates that contain styles, macros, toolbars, keyboard definitions, and so on. By default, regular documents start by using the wp12us.wpt template (us varies, depending on the language and country version of WordPerfect you use). Other specialized documents, such as calendars, newsletters, and fax cover sheets, are based on templates that contain their own special styles.

Thus, the current document contains styles that came from a template (either the default template or a specialized template) or from the WordPerfect system. The current document can also contain styles you create or edit.

You can save styles with the current document only, or you can save them to one of the specialized templates or to the default template for use with future documents. You cannot change the system settings because these are used to restore styles to their default settings.

The following sections describe how to use styles, and how to create, edit, save, and retrieve them.

### FEATURE-SPECIFIC STYLES

This chapter explores how to create and edit styles in general. These principles and procedures also apply to feature-specific styles such as footnotes or graphics. However, you might have to approach them differently. For example, the Styles list does not include a footnote style. However, suppose you modify how that style is used by choosing Insert, Footnote/Endnote; and then in the Footnote/Endnote dialog box choosing Options, Advanced; and in the Advanced Footnote Options dialog box, editing the numbering style. Doing so edits the style and WordPerfect adds the edited style to the current document's style list (see Figure 9.9).

**Figure 9.9**
If you modify WordPerfect system styles, the modified style appears in the list of available styles in that document. Otherwise, unless you import them, WordPerfect system styles do not appear in the list.

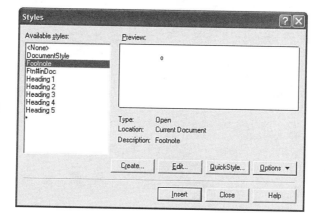

You can also edit a WordPerfect system style (those that come with WordPerfect, such as footnotes) directly from the document's styles list (see "Editing Styles," later in this chapter). By default, WordPerfect displays only the heading system styles. To display all system styles, from the Styles dialog box, choose Options, Settings, and then in the Styles Settings dialog box, make sure WordPerfect System Styles is checked and choose WordPerfect Heading Styles and All Other System Styles (Header/Footers, Numbering, and so on). Click OK to return to the Styles dialog box where WordPerfect now displays all System styles along with any document-specific styles you might have created.

# USING WORDPERFECT'S STYLES

Whether your document contains few or many styles, and whether these styles come from a template, from the WordPerfect system, or from your own creation, using styles is simple.

Determine exactly where you want to apply a style. You can apply styles to

- The entire document—This requires editing the DocumentStyle (see the section "Editing Styles," later in this chapter) or positioning the cursor at the beginning of the document to apply an open style.

- A paragraph—Simply position the cursor anywhere in the paragraph you want to format.

- A selection of text—Use the mouse or the keyboard to select the specific text you want to format.

**TIP FROM**

> To apply a character style, you must first select the text you want. WordPerfect normally selects entire words at a time, but you can select the specific characters you want by holding down the Alt key while dragging the mouse. You also can select text one character at a time by holding down the Shift key while moving the cursor with the keyboard.

To apply a style, follow these steps:

1. Click the Styles drop-down list on the property bar (see Figure 9.10).

**Figure 9.10**
The fastest way to select a style is to choose one from the Styles list on the property bar.

```
<None>          ▼
<None>
Footnote
Ftn#inDoc
Heading 1
Heading 2
Heading 3
Heading 4
Heading 5
•
QuickStyle...
```

2. Click the style you want to use.

If you want a bit more control over which style you use, follow these steps instead:

1. Choose Format, Styles or press Alt+F8. WordPerfect displays the Styles dialog box (see Figure 9.11).

2. In the Available styles list, click the style you want to use. WordPerfect displays an approximation of the effect of the style in the Preview box.

3. To apply the style to the document, click Insert.

4. To close without applying the style, click Close, or press Esc.

**NOTE**

> The list of styles you see varies depending on the template you start with, the styles you import, changes you make to feature styles (such as footnote numbering), and custom styles you create, including QuickFormat or QuickStyle styles.

**Figure 9.11**
The Styles dialog box enables you to select, create, edit, or save styles. You can also preview the effect of a style before you insert it.

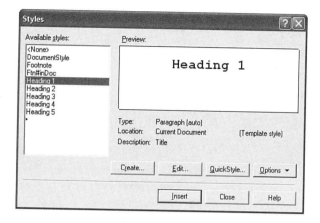

9

# CREATING CUSTOM STYLES

Predefined styles might be of some use to you, but you'll notice the real value of styles only after you create and use your own. Fortunately, styles are easy to create and edit.

## CREATING QUICKSTYLES

One of the easiest ways to create a basic formatting style is to first format some text as you want the style to look and then use the QuickStyle feature to create a style based on that formatting.

To use QuickStyle, follow these steps:

1. Format the text selection or paragraph with the features you want to include in the style. For example, in Figure 9.12, the paragraph is 10-point Arial italic, and is right justified.

**Figure 9.12**
You can format text first, and then use QuickStyle to create a style based on the format you used.

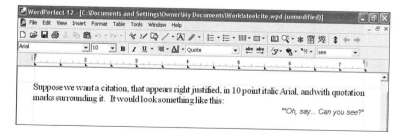

2. Position the cursor anywhere in the selection or paragraph. You need not select the text.

3. Choose Format, Styles (or press Alt+F8) to access the Styles dialog box.

4. Click QuickStyle to display the QuickStyle dialog box (see Figure 9.13).

**Figure 9.13**
In the QuickStyle dialog box, you name the style and designate the type of style you want it to be. You can also add an optional description that helps you remember what the style is used for.

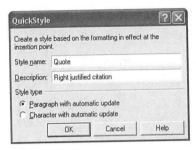

**TIP FROM**

*Read Gilgen*

You can also select the QuickStyle feature by clicking the drop-down Styles list on the property bar and selecting QuickStyle.

5. In the Style Name text box, type the name of the style, using 20 or fewer characters.

6. You can also type a longer description in the Description text box. This can be useful later if you want to use the style, but can't remember what it does by the name alone.

7. Choose Paragraph if you want the style to apply to entire paragraphs, or Character if you want to format only selected text.

**NOTE**

QuickStyle does not always convert formatting settings to a style. For example, if you change the margins for a single paragraph, or use a tab to indent the first line, QuickStyle does not save these formatting changes. However, QuickStyle does recognize paragraph formatting that you change using the Paragraph Format dialog box (which you reach by choosing Format, Paragraph, Format).

8. Click OK to add the style to your current document and to return to the Styles dialog box. Your new style appears in the Available Styles list (see Figure 9.14).

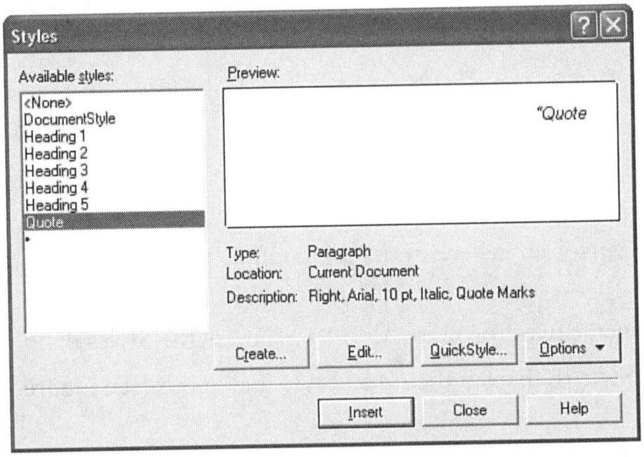

**Figure 9.14**
The Preview box in the Styles dialog box enables you to preview the effect of a selected style.

When you click a style, note that WordPerfect displays the effect of the style in the Preview box, and also displays the longer description that you provided.

## CREATING STYLES

If you know what you want in your style, you can often create the style more quickly and with more control by accessing the Styles Editor dialog box and adding style information directly into the style. In addition, you can add specific text or special characters, along with formatting information.

For example, to create the Quote style, first set up the style by following these steps:

1. Open the Styles dialog box by choosing Format, Styles or by pressing Alt+F8.
2. Click Create to open the Styles Editor dialog box. Figure 9.15 shows the Styles Editor dialog box, with Show 'Off Codes' already selected and codes added to the editing screen.

**Figure 9.15**
The Styles Editor dialog box, shown here with both on and off codes, gives you control over the content and effect of a style.

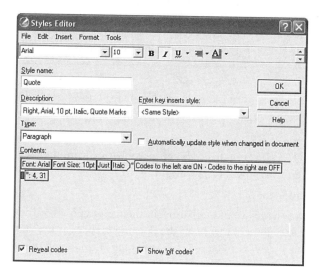

3. Provide a style name (for example, Quote).
4. Provide a description (for example, right-justified, italic Arial text).
5. By default, when you press Enter at the end of a paragraph that uses a style, the next paragraph continues using the same style. If you want to turn off the paragraph style when you press Enter, replace <Same Style> with <None> in the Enter Key Inserts Style box.
6. Because you want to apply the style to an entire paragraph, be sure Paragraph appears in the Type box.

7. If you want changes to one Quote-style paragraph to appear automatically in all other Quote-style paragraphs, check the Automatically Update Style When Changed in Document check box.

8. Do *not* click OK yet; you want to stay in this dialog box.

You're now ready to add the style's formatting codes to the Contents box. This box displays the style in a Reveal Codes format, where you can add text, special characters, and format codes. Suppose, for example, you want your Quote paragraph to add a quotation mark at the beginning of the paragraph, and another at the end, along with other formatting codes (refer to Figure 9.15). Follow these steps:

1. Choose the font style from the Font list on the property bar or from the Font dialog box (which you access by choosing Format, Font).

> **NOTE**
> The menus and property bar in the Styles Editor are similar to those in the regular WordPerfect screen, but features that cannot be added to styles are not included in the menus. For those features that are available, you access and insert format codes with the same menu choices or keystrokes that you do in a regular WordPerfect document.

2. Choose the font size from the property bar or from the Font dialog box.

3. Choose Italic from the property bar or from the Font dialog box.

4. Choose Right Justification from the property bar or from the menu (which you access by choosing Format, Justification, Right).

5. Type a quotation mark (").

All the codes you see are those that begin the paragraph. WordPerfect automatically turns off these codes and reverts to the document codes at the end of the paragraph. However, you also want to close your paragraph with a quotation mark. Continue with the following steps.

6. Click Show 'Off Codes'. WordPerfect displays a separator button. Codes to the left of the button are those that begin the paragraph, and those to the right of the button are those that end the paragraph.

7. Position the cursor to the right of the separator button.

8. Type another quotation mark (").

> **TIP FROM**
>
> *Read Gilgen*
>
> If you're using WordPerfect's SmartQuotes, the Styles Editor inserts another opening quotation mark where you should have a closing quotation mark. Simply type any character, such as a space, before typing the quotation mark to get the proper closing quotation mark. Then delete the character, leaving only the closing quotation mark to close the paragraph.

**9.** Check your style settings one more time and then choose OK to save your style in your current document.

## EDITING STYLES

To edit a paragraph or character style, access the Styles dialog box, select the style you want to edit, and click Edit. WordPerfect displays the Styles Editor dialog box, where you can make changes just as you do when you create a new style (see the preceding section, "Creating Styles").

**TIP FROM**

*Read Gilgen*

Instead of creating new styles from scratch, you can often save time by editing an existing style that's similar to the one you want to create. Simply give the style a new name and make any changes you want.

Editing DocumentStyle follows a similar approach, but has a more far-reaching impact on your document. You can access the Styles Editor and view the DocumentStyle style in three ways:

- Choose File, Document, Current Document Style.

- Choose Format, Styles, and from the Available Styles list, select DocumentStyle and click Edit.

- Access Reveal Codes (by choosing View, Reveal Codes, or pressing Alt+F3). In the Reveal Codes window, double-click the Open Style: DocumentStyle button at the beginning of the document.

WordPerfect displays the Styles Editor dialog box (see Figure 9.16).

**Figure 9.16**
You can also use the Styles Editor to edit an open style, one that affects an entire document.

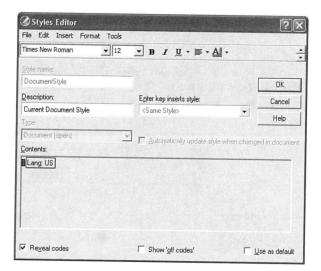

Out of the box, WordPerfect comes with certain preset styles. For example, by default, documents are in portrait orientation, have 1-inch margins on all sides, are singled-spaced, and have tab stops at every 1/2 inch.

Note that none of these settings appear in the DocumentStyle. However, if you want to change the default settings, this is the place to do it.

To change the document styles for just the current document, edit the DocumentStyle style just as you do other styles. If you also want to make these changes the default for all your new documents, click Use As Default. WordPerfect then saves the Document Style information to your default template so that any new documents you create use these changed styles.

**NOTE**

Changes to the default template do *not* change the styles in documents that you have already created. Such changes apply only to new documents that you create after making the changes.

**TIP FROM**

*Read Gilgen*

A common problem WordPerfect users encounter is that they insert a formatting code, but find that it doesn't format everything they expect it to. For example, if you insert a margins code at the beginning of the document, that code affects the body of the text, but headers, footers, and footnotes all retain the original default margins.

To ensure that a formatting code affects the entire document, change the settings in the DocumentStyle style.

## SAVING STYLES

When you create or edit a style, that style is automatically saved in your current document. If you later open the document, the style is still there, available for your use. Unfortunately, custom styles are not automatically available to you in other documents or templates.

However, you can save your custom styles to WordPerfect's default template for use in all documents you create. You can also save a style to a custom template, one that you use only for a specific type of document (for example, a news release).

**NOTE**

When you save a style to another template, you actually *copy* the style from the current document to that template.

To save a style to the default WordPerfect template, follow these steps:

1. Open the document that contains the style you want to save.
2. Access the Styles dialog box by choosing Format, Styles or by pressing Alt+F8.

3. Select the style you want to save to the default template and choose Options, Copy. WordPerfect displays the Styles Copy dialog box (see Figure 9.17).

**Figure 9.17**
To save a style, copy the style to another document or template.

4. Choose Default template and then click OK.

WordPerfect now displays the style in the Available Styles list, with the notation that it's located both in the current document and also in a template as a template style.

Now, if you open a new blank document, your style appears in the style list. You can use the style as you do any other style.

The procedure for copying a style from your current document to another template is a bit more complicated, but only because there are more steps to follow:

1. Copy the style from your current document to the default template, as described in the preceding steps.

**TIP FROM**

*Read Gilgen*

If you want a custom style available to you in all your documents, including templates, you need not copy it to individual templates. By copying it to the default template, it is accessible from all your documents.

2. Choose File, New from Project; or press Ctrl+Shift+N to display the PerfectExpert dialog box (see Figure 9.18).

**Figure 9.18**
You can use the PerfectExpert dialog box to open a template file and then import styles to be used with the template.

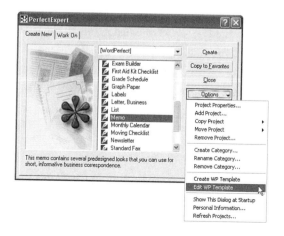

3. From the Create New tab, select the template to which you want to copy your custom style.

4. Click Options, and select Edit WP Template. WordPerfect displays the WordPerfect editing screen, along with the template you are editing, and the Template toolbar (see Figure 9.19).

**Figure 9.19**
You can use the Template toolbar to copy styles and to save them with the current template document.

Template feature toolbar

5. Click the Copy/Remove Object button on the Template toolbar. WordPerfect displays the Copy/Remove Template Objects dialog box, as shown in Figure 9.20.

**Figure 9.20**
You can use the Copy/Remove Template Objects to copy styles from another document or template to the current document.

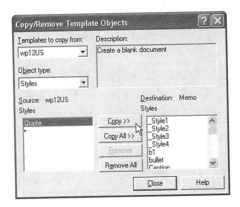

6. From the Templates to Copy From list, choose the default WordPerfect template, wp12us.wpt (wp11us.wpt if you're using WordPerfect 11), if it isn't already chosen.

7. Select Styles from the Object Type drop-down list. WordPerfect displays your custom styles in the Styles list on the left side of the dialog box.

8. Click the style you want to copy, even if there's only one style listed, and click the Copy>> button to add it to the list of styles in the current template.

9. Click Close to return to the template.

10. Click the Close button on the Template toolbar and answer Yes when asked whether you want to save changes to the template.

Now, whenever you create a new document based on your edited template, your custom style is available to you, even if the style is later removed from your default template.

→ If you need help working with WordPerfect templates, **see** Chapter 23, "Building Documents with Templates."

## DELETING STYLES

If you create a style, it stays in the document unless you delete it. Sometimes you simply want to clean up your document and remove any unnecessary custom styles.

To remove a custom style from your current document or from the default template, follow these steps:

1. Access the Styles dialog box by choosing Format, Styles or by pressing Alt+F8.

2. Select the style you want to remove. Note the type of style it is, and whether it is a template style or in the current document only.

3. Click Options, and select Delete. WordPerfect displays the Delete Styles dialog box (see Figure 9.21), which includes all custom styles that can be deleted, whether from the current document or from the default template.

**Figure 9.21**
You can remove styles from the current document by using the Delete Styles dialog box.

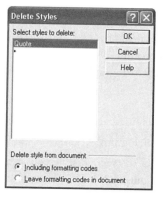

> **NOTE**
>
> You can remove only custom styles; you cannot delete system styles. If you choose a system style, the Delete option is grayed out and you cannot delete it.

4. Select the style or styles you want to delete.

5. Choose how you want to delete the style. You can delete the style by choosing one of these options:

   • Including Formatting Codes—This removes the style and the formatting it produces.

   • Leave Formatting Codes in Document—This removes the style, but replaces it with formatting codes that become part of the text, but that you must remove or format one by one, as you do with normal text.

6. Click OK to delete the style.

## USING STYLES TOGETHER

You can increase the power of styles by linking them in the same document. For example, if you have a style that defines your company logo, you can nest that style in other styles used in newsletter headings, company letterhead, fax cover sheets, and so on. Then, if you change the logo style, it automatically updates other styles in which it is embedded.

To insert one style inside another, access the Styles dialog box, select the style in which you want to embed another style, and choose Edit. Then, in the Contents box of the Style Editor, choose Format, Styles and select a style to insert, and then click Insert.

**NOTE**

Generally, styles that contain other styles should be document (open) styles because paragraph styles can be difficult to use. In any case, you cannot embed one paragraph style within another.

Styles that usually follow one another can be made to *chain*, or link, from one style to the next. For example, after you type a section heading, WordPerfect could automatically switch to the next style, such as a subtitle or a paragraph that begins with a drop cap.

To link two styles, follow these steps:

1.  Access the Styles dialog box and select the first style you want to use.
2.  Click Edit to display the Styles Editor dialog box.
3.  In the Enter Key Inserts Style box, select the second style you want to use from the drop-down list of available styles (see Figure 9.22). Only custom styles appear; template and system styles do not.

**Figure 9.22**
In the Styles Editor dialog box, you can choose to chain, or link, a style to another style.

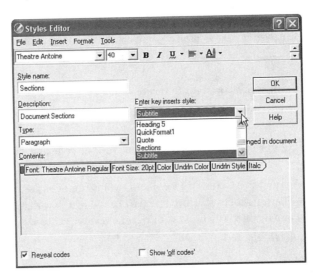

4. Click OK to return to the Styles dialog box.

5. If you want to link the second style to a third style, repeat steps 1–4. Otherwise, click Close to save the linked styles in the current document.

**NOTE**

> You cannot link from document (open) styles or from system styles.

**TIP FROM**

*Read Gilgen*

> Don't forget that the default for all paragraph styles is to continue with the same style when you press Enter. If you want to turn off the style when you press Enter, you can choose <None> from the Enter Key Inserts Style box.

9

# WORKING WITH STYLES FROM OTHER FILES

If you, or someone else, creates a document that contains styles you want to use, you might have to import those styles to your current document. For example, if you want to use a style that you know exists, but that doesn't show up on the Styles list, find the file or template, and then import the style and make it part of the current document.

To import styles from one file or template into a current document that doesn't have the styles, follow these steps:

1. Open the document that does not currently have the styles you want.

2. Access the Styles dialog box, click Options, and choose Retrieve. WordPerfect displays the Retrieve Styles From dialog box (see Figure 9.23).

**Figure 9.23**
To import styles from the WordPerfect system or from another template, use the Retrieve Styles From dialog box.

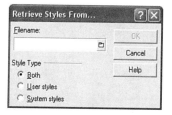

3. Use the Browse button to locate the file or template that contains the styles you want to retrieve and click Select.

4. You can choose to retrieve only user styles, only system files, or both. Click OK.

5. When asked whether you want to overwrite current style, answer Yes.

WordPerfect imports the style types you requested and adds them to the styles you already have in your current document. Save your current document to save the styles with that document.

TIP FROM

*Read Gilgen*

> If you aren't sure about the styles you imported, you should check them out *before* you save your document. Also, you can always close the document without saving, which discards the imported styles.

TIP FROM

*Read Gilgen*

> Another easy way to move a single style from one document to another is to open both documents and use Reveal Codes to copy the style code from the first document and paste the code into the second document. Note that if you're copying paragraph styles, you'll have to copy both the beginning and ending codes along with the text in between.

# TROUBLESHOOTING

### TOO MUCH UNINTENDED QUICKSTYLE

*I tried to apply a QuickStyle to a heading, but applied it to a whole paragraph instead.*

This can happen when you're trying to apply formatting by using the mouse. Simply click Undo on the toolbar or press Ctrl+Z. Then try it again.

### CREATING A GLOBAL STYLE

*I created a style, but now it doesn't appear on the list of available styles.*

When you create a style, you save it in your current document only. If you want to make the style available for all your documents, you must copy the style to the default template. In the document that contains the style you want to copy, choose Format, Styles, and then select the style you want to copy. Click Options, and select Copy. Choose Default Template and click OK.

### MISSING CUSTOM STYLES

*I saved my custom style to the default template, but when I open my documents, that style doesn't seem to be available.*

Styles saved to the default template are available only for newly created documents. You must import custom styles from your default template to the current document.

### TOO MANY CHANGES

*I wanted to change a bold, italic paragraph back to normal text, but when I did, other paragraphs changed, also.*

You tried to change a paragraph style that automatically updates when you change the text. Instead, access the Styles drop-down menu on the property bar and select <None>, or delete the style codes in Reveal Codes.

# PROJECT

Nearly any repetitive formatting task can be accomplished more easily and with more consistency by using styles. One simple example is a product list, such as the one shown in Figure 9.24. Each item in the list has a name, a part number, and a description. Suppose you want to set off each element with a different font, style, size, and color. You also want to make it easy to type the entries, chaining one style to the next.

**Figure 9.24**
A product list is a perfect candidate for styles because it needs repetitive yet consistent formatting of the name, part number, and description.

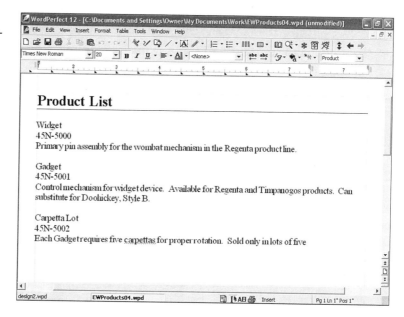

Follow these steps to create three chained styles: PartName, PartNumber, and Description:

1. Create at least one set of entries for each type of text, such as Widget, 45N-5000, and Primary pin assembly for the wombat mechanism in the Regenta product line, as shown in Figure 9.24.

2. Apply formatting to each element:

   - PartName—Choose a sans-serif font (for example, Arial), make it 14 point, and change the color to blue.

   - PartNumber—Add italic.

   - Description—No change to the body of the text.

3. Click the PartName heading and choose QuickStyle from the Styles list on the property bar.

4. Supply the name of the style to be used (for example, PartName).

5. Choose Paragraph with Automatic Update, and click OK.

6. Repeat steps 3–5 for the other two styles (PartNumber and Description).

Having created the basic style for each element, you now must modify two of the styles to add an indent code and also to chain the styles together. Follow these steps:

1. Access the Styles dialog box by choosing Format, Styles or by pressing Alt+F8.

2. Select the PartName style and click Edit.

3. Click the drop-down menu for Enter Key Inserts Style, and choose the style you want to chain to (for example, PartNumber).

4. Unless you need to make other changes, click OK.

5. Select the PartNumber style and click Edit.

6. Click the drop-down menu for Enter Key Inserts Style, and choose the Description style.

7. Position the cursor at the beginning of the codes in the Contents box and choose Format, Paragraph, Indent to insert a hard-left indent code.

8. Make other changes as needed and click OK.

9. Select the Description style and click Edit.

10. Click the drop-down menu for Enter Key Inserts Style, and choose the PartName style.

**NOTE** If you want to end the sequence after the description style, choose <None> from the Enter Key Inserts Style menu.

11. Position the cursor at the beginning of the codes in the Contents box and choose Format, Paragraph, Indent to insert a hard-left indent code.

12. Make any other desired changes and click OK.

13. If you want to add these styles to your default template, choose Options, Copy, Default Template and click OK.

Finally, to use the styles, simply apply them to preexisting text or on a new line, by following these steps:

1. Choose the PartName style either from the Styles dialog box or from the Styles drop-down list on the Property bar, type the part name heading, and press Enter.

2. Type the part number and press Enter.

3. Type the description and press Enter.

4. Repeat steps 1–3 until you complete your product list.

The completed list, with styles applied, appears in Figure 9.25. If you decide to change the style of any of these three elements, change the format of the text where the style is applied to change it in all locations of that style (for example, change Arial to Lucida in the PartName heading).

**Figure 9.25**
The product list, with consistent styles, is more appealing, easier to read, and better organized. Making formatting changes in any paragraph results in the same changes being made to all paragraphs with the same style.

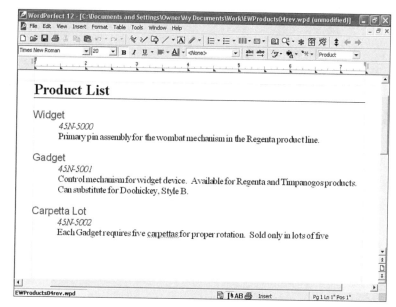

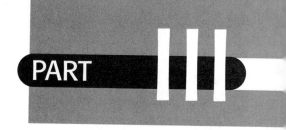

# ORGANIZING INFORMATION

# WORKING WITH TABLES

# UNDERSTANDING TABLES

Of all WordPerfect's special features, the Table feature offers perhaps more practical uses and enables you to enhance the effectiveness and attractiveness of your documents more than any other.

A *table* consists of rows and columns of data arranged and formatted to make the data easy to read or understand. For example, consider the WordPerfect table shown in Figure 10.1.

**Figure 10.1**
Even simple data lists look better and are easier to read in a WordPerfect table.

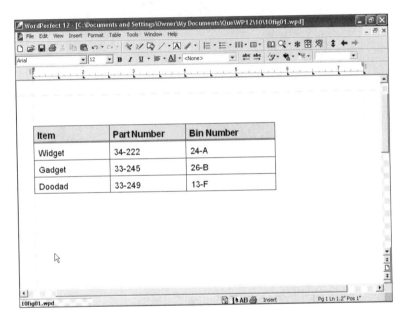

The structure of a table is very much like the structure of a spreadsheet, and in fact, you can even use WordPerfect tables for spreadsheet functions. In a table, WordPerfect labels the rows with numbers (1, 2, 3, ...) and the columns with letters (A, B, C, ...). The intersection of a column and a row is a cell. You identify each cell according to the row and column in which it resides (A1, B3, C14, and so on). In Figure 10.1, for example, the word Widget is in the first column (A) and the second row (2); therefore, Widget is in cell A2.

→ For information on WordPerfect's table spreadsheet capabilities, **see** "Using Spreadsheet Formulas in Tables," **p. xxx.** [Chapter 15]

All other table features are options. For example, you can change the appearance of the lines that WordPerfect uses to separate table cells, or you can omit them altogether. You can change text justification, rotate or skew text, and add text attributes. You can adjust the width and height of any column or row. You can even create formulas to calculate numeric information.

Using WordPerfect's table formatting options, you can create any kind of table—from simple lists to complex invoices, from schedules to calendars, from programs to scripts, and more (see Figure 10.2).

Designing, creating, and modifying a table is a visual and artistic venture. Don't be afraid to experiment, and don't be upset if the results are not quite what you expected. Simply try again.

**Figure 10.2**
With WordPerfect's Table feature, you can even create complex forms, such as invoices.

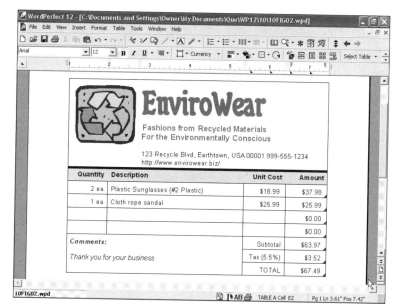

## PLANNING TABLES

Before you actually create a table, you can save a great deal of time by doing some preliminary planning. First, ask yourself what you want to accomplish with your table. Do you merely want to present straightforward information more clearly, or do you want to design a more complex, heavily formatted form?

Next, determine the approximate number of rows and columns you want. You can have up to 64 columns and 32,767 rows (or 2,097,088 cells), although it's unlikely you'll ever use that many. You do not need to know the exact number of rows or columns because you can add or insert them while you work with your table. Knowing this information in advance, however—especially the number of columns—can make creating, modifying, and using your table much easier.

You can also benefit from determining and selecting the font style and size you want to use before you begin. Again, this is not critical because you can change fonts as you work with your table.

Finally, consider the number and placement of tables. You might need to place two tables of dissimilar structure one after the other, rather than try to create just one table. Also, you might need to place two tables beside each other, in which case you might want to use columns or graphics boxes.

# CREATING TABLES

After you determine the number of rows and columns you want, you create WordPerfect tables with one of two easy methods: using the menus or using the toolbar.

To use the menus to create a table, follow these steps:

1. Position the insertion point in your document where you want to insert a table.

2. Choose Table, Create, or press F12. WordPerfect displays the Create Table dialog box (see Figure 10.3).

**Figure 10.3**
The Create Table dialog box lets you specify the number of columns and rows you want in your table.

3. Type the number of columns and the number of rows you want.

4. Click Create to create the table (see Figure 10.4).

**Figure 10.4**
A simple table with four columns and five rows: Notice that the columns are evenly spaced and extend from margin to margin, and the property bar shows table-specific functions.

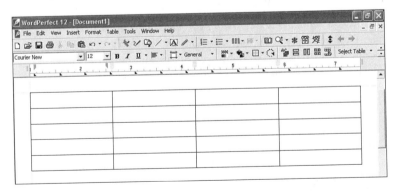

**NOTE**

The Drag to Create a New Table option in the Create Table dialog box enables you to create a table inside a text box. You drag the area where you want the text box, and then WordPerfect inserts the table you specify in the dialog box. After the table is created, you can work with it as described in this chapter. Choosing this option makes it the default until you deselect it.

→ For more information on creating and manipulating text boxes, **see** "Adding Text Boxes As Graphic Objects," **p. 409.**

**TIP FROM**

*Read Gilgen*

The Drag to Create a New Table option is particularly useful if you need to place two tables side by side. Simply create each table separately, positioning them next to each other.

**10**

To create the same table by using the toolbar, follow these steps:

1. Position the insertion point in your document where you want to insert a table.

2. Click the Table QuickCreate button, and hold the mouse button down to display a grid.

3. Drag the mouse down and to the right until the pop-up grid highlights the number of columns and rows you want (see Figure 10.5). If you need more columns or rows than are displayed on the grid, keep dragging the mouse; WordPerfect expands the grid until it is up to 32 columns by 45 rows. At the top of the grid, WordPerfect specifies the number of columns and rows, in that order, that you have selected.

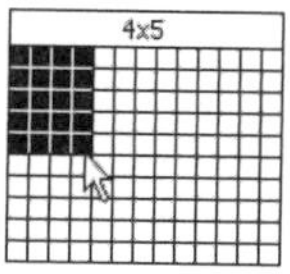

**Figure 10.5**
Using the Table QuickCreate button on the toolbar, you click and drag the mouse to select the number of rows and columns you want in a table.

4. After you have displayed the number of columns and rows you want, release the mouse button. WordPerfect creates the table with the number of columns and rows you indicated.

**TIP FROM**

*Read Gilgen*

If you decide you don't want to create a table, simply drag the mouse pointer to the top of the grid and when No Table appears, release the mouse button.

**NOTE**

> If you selected Drag to Create a New Table in the Create Table dialog box, you can also drag to create using the QuickCreate button. After you choose the number of rows and columns, you click and drag the area where you want to place your table. To turn off this option, choose Table, Create and uncheck Drag to Create a New Table.

## TOOLS FOR WORKING WITH TABLES

The most obvious tool for working with tables is the menu. Additional help is also available on the QuickMenus and on the property bar.

With the insertion point located inside a table, choose Table from the menu to find most of the table-related options you're likely to need (see Figure 10.6).

**Figure 10.6**
Table-related menu items can be found on the Table menu.

You can also quickly access a menu of options by right-clicking on a table. The Table QuickMenu is nearly identical to the regular Table menu (see Figure 10.7).

**NOTE**

> If the insertion point is located anywhere outside the table, the property bar does not display table-related options. Likewise, most options on the Table menu are not available. If you right-click outside the table area you will not get the table-related QuickMenu.

## USING SPEEDFORMAT

By default, all the cells in a WordPerfect table are surrounded by single lines, and the table has no border. You can customize the lines and borders of a table, and WordPerfect's SpeedFormat feature makes it easy to modify the look of your table.

**Figure 10.7**
The Table QuickMenu is nearly identical to the one you find on the Table menu.

**TIP FROM**

*Read Gilgen*

Although you can change the design and format of a table at any time, SpeedFormat usually works best if applied before making other format changes. Therefore, if you know what kind of look you want, use SpeedFormat immediately after creating your table.

If you create the table using the menus, you can choose the SpeedFormat feature from the Create Table dialog box (refer to Figure 10.3). If you have already created a table, you can position the cursor anywhere inside the table and choose SpeedFormat from the Table drop-down menu on the property bar, or from the Table QuickMenu. WordPerfect then displays the Table SpeedFormat dialog box (see Figure 10.8, which shows a style already selected).

**Figure 10.8**
When you select a SpeedFormat style such as Fancy Fills, you apply a predefined set of formats, lines, and fills to your table.

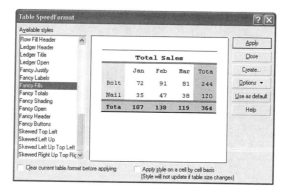

The Available Styles list box lists several predefined table formats. When you click a style, WordPerfect displays a sample table in the preview box. For example, if you select the Fancy Fills style, WordPerfect formats your table with a centered title bar and with shading and line changes to set off the data (refer to Figure 10.8).

**TIP FROM**

*Read Gilgen*

> Not all designs match the function of the table you are creating. For example, the Single Bold Title style actually changes the structure of your table. If you don't like the format you select, you can simply select other styles until you find the one that works best for your table.

## CONVERTING TABULAR COLUMNS TO TABLES

You might have existing text that you want to place in a table, but you don't want to retype that text. Fortunately, WordPerfect provides a simple method for creating a table from text that is formatted in tabular columns. In fact, this capability might be the easiest yet most practical use for tables.

Suppose that you have a list of company employees that includes names, offices, and telephone numbers. The three columns of data are separated by single tabs, as follows:

| | | |
|---|---|---|
| Prochniak, Mary | VH279 | 7-1408 |
| Pflug, Martin | VH246 | 7-4965 |
| Murphy, Dianna | VH299 | 7-6543 |

To convert data in tabular columns to a table, follow these steps:

1. With the mouse or keyboard, select all the text to the end of the last line of data. Don't include the final hard return, or you'll end up with an extra row in your table.

2. Choose Table, Convert, or press F12. WordPerfect displays the Convert: Text to Table dialog box (see Figure 10.9). Alternatively, you can click the Tables QuickCreate button on the toolbar and choose Tabular Columns from the drop-down list.

**Figure 10.9**
The Convert: Text to Table dialog box is used for converting preexisting data to a table.

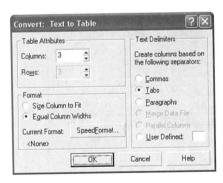

3. Choose Tabs Column (the default) and any other options you want, and click OK. WordPerfect converts your tabular columns of data into a table (see Figure 10.10).

**Figure 10.10**
After converting data from tabular columns into a table, you might need to use column width and other formatting to adjust the layout of the data.

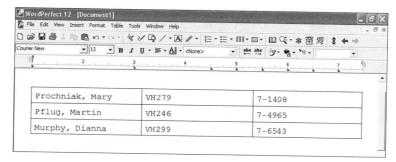

| Prochniak, Mary | VH279 | 7-1408 |
| Pflug, Martin | VH246 | 7-4965 |
| Murphy, Dianna | VH299 | 7-6543 |

Although this procedure is easy, the key to successfully converting tabular columns to a table lies in the format of the original text. You should use tab settings for each column so that only one tab separates each column of data. If, for example, you use WordPerfect's default 1/2-inch tab settings and use more than one tab to separate some of the entries, WordPerfect adds extra cells in the table for the extra tabs. The result can be quite messy.

## CONVERTING TABLES TO OTHER FORMATS

Sometimes you don't want your table data in table format. For example, you need to export the information to a format that can be used in a non-WordPerfect database.

To convert table data to another format, position the insertion point in the table and choose Table, Convert. WordPerfect displays the Convert: Table to Text dialog box, shown in Figure 10.11.

**Figure 10.11**
The Convert: Table to Text dialog box enables you to convert table data into other formats.

You can convert the data in two ways:

- You can separate the data from each cell in a row with commas, hard returns, tabs, or with any other character you specify. Note that rows of data are separated by hard returns.

- You can change the data into a WordPerfect merge file format, where each cell is separated by an ENDFIELD code and each row is separated by an ENDRECORD code.

  → For information on working with WordPerfect data in other programs, **see** Chapter 15, "Importing Data and Working with Other Programs."

# WORKING WITH TABLES

If you thought it was easy to create a table, you'll find it even easier to work with the information you place in tables.

Consider each table cell a miniature document with its own margins and formatting. As you enter text, WordPerfect wraps the words within the cell, vertically expanding the row to accommodate what you type (see Figure 10.12). You can enter and edit text in a cell just as you do in a document.

**Figure 10.12**
A table can contain more than one line of text in a cell. Notice that the row automatically expands vertically to accommodate the text you enter.

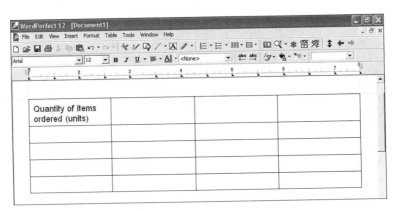

## MOVING AROUND IN A TABLE

When you first create a table, WordPerfect positions the cursor at the upper-left corner of the table, in cell A1. Notice that the General Status indicator, on the application bar at the bottom of the screen, displays the name of the current table (Table A in this case) and the cell location of the cursor, Cell A1 (see Figure 10.13). When you move the cursor to a new cell, WordPerfect indicates on the status bar the location of the new cell.

**Figure 10.13**
When the cursor is located within a table, WordPerfect displays the current cell location on the application bar.

Table cell indicated in general status area of the application bar

To move the cursor one cell to the right, press the Tab key. To move the cursor one cell to the left, press Shift+Tab.

Note that if the cursor is in the last cell of a row, pressing Tab moves the cursor to the first cell of the next row. Pressing Shift+Tab while the cursor is in the first cell of a row moves the cursor to the last cell of the previous row.

When you reach the last cell of the last row of your table and press Tab, WordPerfect adds a row and advances the cursor to the first cell of the next row.

→ For more information on how to insert or delete rows and columns in a table, **see** "Changing Table Size," **p. 309.**

Of course, you can also use the mouse or the arrow keys to move the cursor in your table (see Table 10.1). However, if you're using the keyboard, it is usually quickest and most efficient to use the Tab and Shift+Tab keys.

| TABLE 10.1 | MOVING THE INSERTION POINT IN A TABLE |
|---|---|
| **Action** | **Result** |
| Tab | Advances one cell to right |
| Shift+Tab | Moves one cell to the left |
| Arrow keys | Moves any direction (must travel through text) |
| Home, Home | Moves to left column in row |
| End, End | Moves to right column in row |
| Mouse click | Click directly in the target cell |

## USING QUICKFILL

The idea behind WordPerfect's QuickFill feature is that WordPerfect can examine the first few entries in a series and automatically determine the pattern that is being used. WordPerfect then fills in the remaining blank cells in the series based on that pattern.

WordPerfect can automatically insert such things as numbers, days, months, and so on. To use QuickFill to automatically fill in table cells, follow these steps:

1. Type the data you want in the first three cells of a series of cells. For example, type Mon, Tue, and Wed at the top of the first three columns.

2. Select the cells you want filled, including the first three you already typed (see Figure 10.14).

**Figure 10.14**
You can select a sequence of cells and several blank cells, and use QuickFill to fill in the missing data.

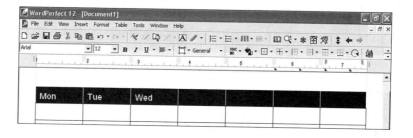

**3.** Choose QuickFill from the Table menu or from the Table QuickMenu. WordPerfect automatically supplies the remaining information (see Figure 10.15).

**Figure 10.15**
QuickFill knows how to fill in the remaining cells in a series.

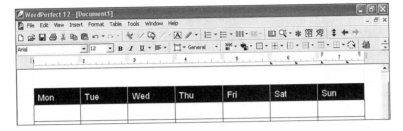

Some of the series that QuickFill can complete for you include the following:

- Numbers—For example, 1, 2, 3, ... or 5, 10, 15, ...
- Days—For example, Monday, Tuesday, Wednesday, ... or Mon, Tue, Wed, ...
- Months—For example, Jan, Feb, Mar, ...

**N O T E**

If you supply information that WordPerfect cannot extrapolate, it simply repeats the cells that contain information across the remaining selected cells.

## SELECTING TEXT AND CELLS

Within a single cell, you select text the same way you do in a document—by using the mouse or the keyboard.

If you cross a cell boundary while selecting, WordPerfect begins selecting entire cells. For example, if you click the mouse in the middle of the text in cell A1 and begin dragging the mouse toward cell B1, WordPerfect highlights just the text until the mouse pointer crosses over into cell B1. At that point, the entire cells (A1 and B1) are highlighted and the mouse pointer changes to an arrow (see Figure 10.16). As you continue to drag the mouse to other cells, these cells also become part of a selected block.

**Figure 10.16**
You can select entire cells by dragging the mouse pointer across the edge of the cell until the pointer turns into an arrow. Continue dragging the pointer across cells to select multiple cells at once.

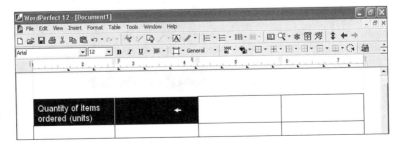

**TIP FROM**

*Read Gilgen*

> To select only part of the text from more than one cell, without selecting an entire cell, press the Select key (F8) and then use the arrow keys to precisely select the text you want.

You can use this method to select rows of cells, columns of cells, and entire tables of cells. However, to select a single cell, you position the mouse pointer within the cell you want to select and move the pointer slowly toward the left line of the cell until the pointer changes to a single arrow. This arrow indicates that you are about to select cells rather than just contents. Click once to select the cell. Click twice to select the entire row of cells. Click three times to select the entire table. To select a column, move the pointer toward the top line of any cell in the column until the pointer turns into a single upward-pointing arrow. Click once to select the cell, twice to select the column, and three times to select the entire table.

**NOTE**

Select Table ▾

> If your screen's resolution is set high enough, you will see the Select Table button on the property bar. Click the button's drop-down menu to select an entire table, column, or row.

 *If you've been having trouble with selected cell text moving where you don't want it, see "But I Didn't Want That There!" in the Troubleshooting section at the end of this chapter.*

**TIP FROM**

*Read Gilgen*

> If you choose Table, Row/Col Indicators to display the row and column indicators at the edge of the screen, you can click the number of a row or the letter of a column to select an entire row or column.

## DELETING TEXT FROM CELLS

To remove text from within a single cell, you use the Delete and Backspace keys as you do with any other text.

A quicker and easier method for deleting the contents of entire cells, especially if the cell contains a large amount of text, is to select an entire cell using the method described in the preceding section. Then press Backspace or Delete, and WordPerfect removes the entire contents of the cell.

**TIP FROM**

*Read Gilgen*

> Don't forget to use Undo if you accidentally delete the contents of a cell.

You can use the same method for deleting the contents of an entire row, column, or table. However, because this can be a bit more destructive, WordPerfect displays a dialog box asking exactly what you want to delete. For example, if you select all of Row 1 and press Delete or Backspace, the Delete Structure/Contents dialog box appears, with Rows selected (see Figure 10.17). If you click OK, you actually remove the entire row from the table. If you choose Cell Contents Only, and then click OK, only the contents of that row are removed; the row itself remains.

**Figure 10.17**
The Delete Structure/Contents dialog box enables you to delete the contents of cells or entire rows or columns.

If you select and attempt to delete all the cells in the table, WordPerfect offers several options in the Delete Table dialog box (see Figure 10.18).

**Figure 10.18**
The Delete Table dialog box enables you to delete the entire table, remove all the data from the table, remove formulas only, or convert the table to another format.

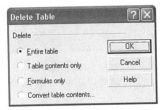

## CUTTING, COPYING, AND PASTING TEXT IN TABLES

You can cut, copy, and paste text to and from table cells the same way you do in text documents.

By selecting entire cells, you can quickly and easily cut or copy all the text along with its formatting to a new location. For example, suppose that you want to copy all of Row 1 to Row 2. Select the entire row and then choose Cut or Copy, and the Cut or Copy Table dialog box appears (see Figure 10.19).

Now you can choose to move the current selection (the contents, but not the table structure), the entire row (the contents and the structure), or the entire column. To cut the entire row, select Row, and then click OK. Position the cursor where you want to paste the row, and choose Paste to insert the row at the insertion point.

**Figure 10.19**
You can use the Cut or Copy Table dialog box to cut and paste entire rows, columns, or groups of cells.

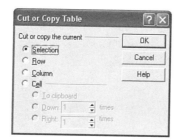

**TIP FROM**

*Read Gilgen*

One of the best uses for the drag-and-drop method of cutting and pasting is when you need to move table cells, rows, and columns from one location to another. After selecting the cells you want to move, simply use the mouse to drag the selection to the new table location and release the mouse button.

## DELETING, CUTTING, AND COPYING TABLES

To delete, cut, or copy an entire table, including its structure, select the table from before the table to beyond the end of the table; then delete, cut, or copy the table.

To restore a deleted table, you can use Undo (Ctrl+Z). If you cut or copied the table, you can paste it in the new location.

## SAVING AND PRINTING TABLES

A table is always part of a document, even when the table is the only element in the document. The procedure for saving tables, therefore, is exactly the same as the method for saving documents.

If you want to save a table alone, or just part of your table, first select the table or the cells you want to save, and then choose File, Save As (or press F3). WordPerfect asks whether you want to save the entire file or just the selected text. If you choose Selected Text and provide a filename, WordPerfect saves just the selected cells, along with their format and contents, in a new, separate file.

Also, you print tables the same way you print other kinds of text. If you print using a dot-matrix printer (does anyone use these anymore?), you might want to turn off table lines to speed printing (dotted or dashed lines actually increase printing time). However, table lines do not significantly affect printing speed on inkjet or laser printers.

→ For more information on saving a WordPerfect document, **see** "Saving Documents," **p. 25.**

→ For information on printing, **see** Chapter 6, "Printing, Faxing, and E-Mailing."

# EDITING TABLE STRUCTURE

When you create a WordPerfect table, certain default settings apply:

- Evenly spaced columns and rows
- No special formatting of the contents of the cells
- Single lines that separate the cells of the table
- No special border around the table
- Full-justified tables (the tables themselves extend from margin to margin)

The real beauty of the Table feature is that you can easily make all kinds of adjustments to these default settings. When you make changes to the shape and size of table cells, columns, and rows, you are editing the layout of the table, or the table structure.

WordPerfect offers several methods for changing the layout of tables: the Table menu, the property bar, the Table QuickMenu, the mouse, and the ruler bar.

→ For details on table editing tools, **see** "Tools for Working with Tables," **p. 296.**

**TIP FROM**

*Read Gilgen*

> Don't forget that in order to use table-editing tools, you first need to position the cursor somewhere inside the table.

## CHANGING COLUMN WIDTHS

Often, instead of evenly spaced columns, you need a table with columns of unequal width. To quickly change the width of a column, position the mouse pointer directly on the line separating two columns until the pointer changes into a double-headed arrow (see Figure 10.20). When you click and hold down the mouse button, WordPerfect displays a dotted guide that helps you position the new column margin. Notice that a QuickTip box also appears, displaying the exact widths of the column to the left and the column to the right. Simply drag the column divider right or left until you have the desired width.

**TIP FROM**

*Read Gilgen*

> Don't forget that Undo can be very useful as you experiment with table adjustments.

You can perform the same task by dragging the column markers on the ruler bar (see Figure 10.21). Notice that the status bar also displays the exact position of the column separator line: Position: 4.25.

**Figure 10.20**
You can change column widths by dragging the column divider with the mouse.

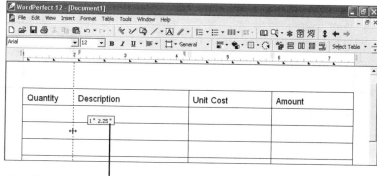

QuickTip shows table column measurement

Column separator position indicator

**Figure 10.21**
You can use the mouse to drag the inverted triangles on the ruler bar to size your table columns.

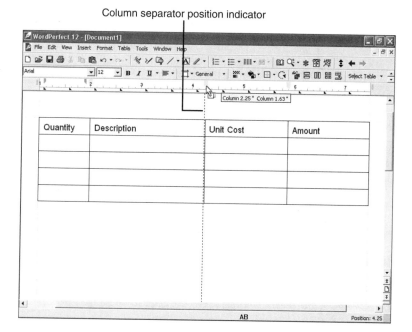

**TIP FROM**

Read Gilgen

To change column widths proportionally, hold down the Shift key while moving the column separators. For example, in a four-column table, hold down Shift and drag the line between Columns A and B to the right until the last three columns are 1 inch wide (refer to the number on the right side of the QuickTip box). Release the mouse button, and you now have evenly spaced columns at the right side of the table.

Adjusting column width in this manner is not very precise, but if you already have text in the columns and can see that the columns are wide enough, or if the measurements don't really matter, this method is quick and easy.

Sometimes you simply want to be sure that the columns are wide enough to display each cell's information on one line (for example, a list). To adjust a column's width to fit the text in its cells, position the cursor in the column you want to adjust, and from the Table menu or the QuickMenu choose Size Column to Fit. Columns adjusted in this manner expand to the right, thus reducing the width of columns to the right.

If you want exact column measurements, position the cursor in any cell of the column you want to adjust and from the Table menu or the QuickMenu choose Format. WordPerfect displays the Properties for Table Format dialog box (from here on, we'll call this simply the Table Format dialog box). Click the Column tab (see Figure 10.22).

**Figure 10.22**
The Table Format dialog box is used for formatting table columns, as well as tables, table rows, and table cells.

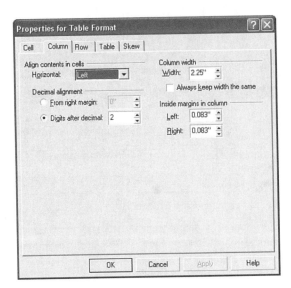

In the upper-right corner of the dialog box, type the measurement you want in the Width box. Also, choose Always Keep Width the Same to prevent proportional sizing of columns from affecting this particular column.

## CHANGING TABLE SIZE

After you create a table, you often discover that it has too many or too few columns or rows. You learned earlier how to add rows at the end of a table by pressing Tab while in the last cell of the table. You can also insert or delete rows or columns at any location in the table.

To add rows to your table, position the cursor where you want the new row or rows and from the Table menu or the QuickMenu choose Insert. WordPerfect displays the Insert Columns/Rows dialog box (see Figure 10.23).

**Figure 10.23**
The Insert Columns/Rows dialog box enables you to add rows or columns to your table.

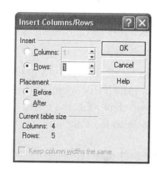

By default, WordPerfect assumes that you want to insert a single row preceding the current cursor position.

**TIP FROM**

Read Gilgen

The easiest and quickest way to insert a single row before the current cursor position is to press Alt+Insert. You can also click the Insert Row icon on the property bar.

Choosing Before inserts the specified number of rows or columns at the location of the cursor, pushing the rows down or columns to the right to make room for the new rows or columns. Choosing After adds another row or column following the location of the cursor. This option is particularly useful when adding columns at the right of the table.

**NOTE**

Keep in mind that columns or rows you add or insert assume the special formatting attributes—such as lines and text formats—of the column or row that is selected when you choose Insert.

To decrease the size of a table, you can delete rows or columns. Position the cursor in the first row or column you want to delete, and from the property bar Table menu (or from the QuickMenu) choose Delete. From the Delete Structure/Contents dialog box, which is similar to the Insert Column/Rows dialog box (refer to figure 10.23), specify the number of columns or rows you want to delete and click OK. The Delete dialog box also enables you to delete the contents of only specified rows or columns.

The easiest and quickest way to delete a single row at the current cursor position is simply to press Alt+Delete.

## JOINING AND SPLITTING CELLS

If you use a table for complex purposes, such as a form, you often need cells of varying sizes. You can join and split cells to create such cells.

To join two or more contiguous cells (for example, all the cells along the top row of a table), simply select the cells you want to join and from the Table menu and choose Join, Cell; or from the QuickMenu, choose Join Cells. WordPerfect joins the cells, which now appear as one large cell. Figure 10.24 shows an invoice title added after joining the cells.

**Figure 10.24**
You can join several table cells—for example, all the cells in the first row—making them one large cell across the top.

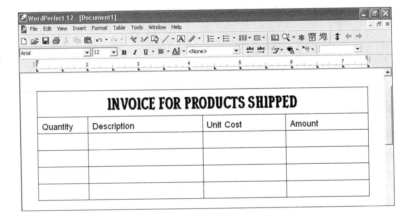

You can use this method to join any number of cells in rows, columns, or blocks. Joined cells become one cell, occupying the space formerly occupied by the individual cells.

You can use the QuickJoin button on the property bar to simply drag and join cells.

WordPerfect also enables you to split a cell into two or more cells. To split a cell, follow these steps:

1. Position the cursor in the cell you want to split.

2. From the Table menu choose Split, Cell; or from the QuickMenu choose Split Cell. WordPerfect displays the Split Cell dialog box (see Figure 10.25).

**Figure 10.25**
The Split Cell dialog box enables you to split a cell into two or more rows or columns.

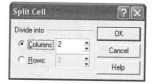

Indicate the number of columns or rows you want to divide the cell into, and click OK. You can further divide split cells as much as you need to. However, splitting a cell into additional rows also expands the other cells in the same row to accommodate the size of the split cell.

You can split and join cells even more quickly by using the QuickSplit and QuickJoin features, which enable you to use the mouse to visually split and join cells. To use QuickSplit to split cell columns, follow these steps:

1. From the Table menu, choose Split, QuickSplit Column, or more easily, click the QuickSplit Column button on the Properties toolbar. WordPerfect changes the mouse pointer as shown in Figure 10.26, and also displays a dashed line and QuickTip measurements that indicate where the split will occur.

**Figure 10.26**
You can use QuickSplit to quickly split cells into columns or rows.

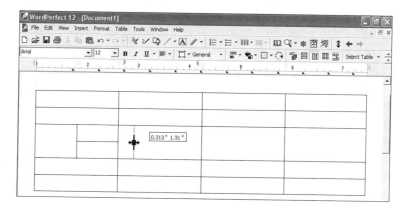

2. Position the mouse where you want the split to occur and click the mouse.

3. Split the same cell or other cells as needed.

4. Turn off QuickSplit by clicking the QuickSplit Column button once again.

You can also use QuickSplit to split cells by rows. Choose Table, Split, QuickSplit Row, or more easily click the QuickSplit Row button on the Properties toolbar and follow the same procedures just described. Be sure to click the button again to turn it off.

If you want to split both rows and columns at once (that is, two rows, two columns), choose Table, Split, QuickSplit Row/Column, or click the QuickSplit Row/Column button on the Properties bar. Click it again to turn off this option. Note that although you can vary the width of the split columns, WordPerfect automatically splits a row into two rows of equal height.

**TIP FROM**

*Read Gilgen*

If you need to join cells (for example, you accidentally split a cell, or need to join several cells so you can split them differently), hold down the Shift key and drag across the cells to be joined.

## CHANGING ROW STRUCTURE

WordPerfect automatically determines the amount of vertical space in a row based on the amount of text in its cells. The cell requiring the most vertical space sets the height for the entire row.

**TIP FROM**

*Read Gilgen*

If the cell row seems too high, check to see whether you have an extra hard return in any of the cells in that row. Delete the hard return and the row will return to its normal height.

You can easily and quickly change a row's height by dragging the bottom line of the row up or down. WordPerfect displays a QuickTip showing the size the row will become when you release the mouse button.

Sometimes you need to set a specific row height, either to limit the amount of text you can enter into the row's cells or to make sure that a row contains a minimum amount of space, regardless of whether the cells contain data. A good example of the latter situation is a calendar in which you might want a fixed row height, regardless of the number of events on any given day. To fix row height, follow these steps:

1. Access the Table Format dialog box (by choosing Format from the QuickMenu or from the Table menu).

2. Click the Row tab. WordPerfect displays options for formatting a row (see Figure 10.27).

3. In this dialog box you set the row height and the number of lines of text per row. Although the options don't appear related in the dialog box, you can combine row height and lines of text per row in these ways:

    • Automatic and Multiple Lines—This combination, the default, automatically adjusts the row height to accommodate as many lines as necessary.

**Figure 10.27**
To format an entire row of cells, click the Row tab in the Table Format dialog box.

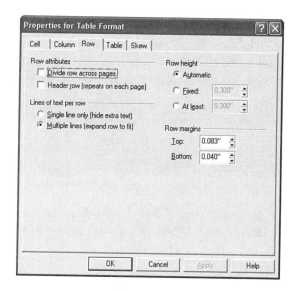

- Fixed and Multiple Lines—This combination uses a fixed height and enables you to enter multiple lines, but only up to the specified height. You use this combination when you create a calendar, for example.

  Make sure that any fixed height you select is high enough to accommodate at least one line of text. Otherwise, text that might appear onscreen will not print.

- Automatic and Single Line Only—This combination automatically adjusts the row height to accommodate a single line of text, regardless of the text's height (font size). If you choose these options and press Enter while entering text in your table, the cursor automatically advances to the next cell.

- Fixed and Single Line Only—This combination maintains a fixed height but enables you to enter only one line of text. The font size for that line of text must be small enough to fit into the specified row height.

- At Least—This, along with Multiple or Single line options, guarantees that the row will be a minimum height, but can expand if necessary to accommodate extra text.

4. Type the amount of space you want (for example, 1-inch fixed height for a calendar row), and click OK.

By default, WordPerfect does not allow rows that contain multiple lines to span printed page breaks. This can create problems if you have rows with an unusually large number of lines, because you end up with large blank spaces at the bottom of the page. Some tables even contain so much text that a row exceeds the height of the entire page! To avoid these problems, simply choose Divide Row Across Pages.

## CREATING HEADER ROWS

Because a table can consist of up to 32,767 rows, it might span several pages. If you create a long table, you might want certain information (such as column headings) to repeat at the top of each page. Such rows are called header rows. To create a header row, follow these steps:

1. Position the cursor in the row you want to designate as a header row.

2. Access the Table Format dialog box, and click the Row tab (refer to Figure 10.27).

3. Choose Header Row (Repeats on Each Page).

4. Click OK.

WordPerfect displays an asterisk (*) next to the cell reference in the general status area of the application bar (for example, Cell A1*) to indicate that the row is a header row.

**NOTE**

Header rows don't have to begin with the first row, but if you want more than one header row, the rows you specify must follow one another.

## CREATING SKEWED ROWS AND COLUMNS

Tables often require header rows where text doesn't quite fit horizontally. Although you can rotate text (see the section "Formatting Cells," later in this chapter), you can enhance the readability of your table by using skewed, or angled, cells and text.

The table shown in Figure 10.28 includes both a skewed row and a skewed column. To skew table rows or columns, follow these steps:

**Figure 10.28**
You can skew the cells in the top row, or in the left or right columns, along with the text they contain. You can also join skewed corners for a cleaner look.

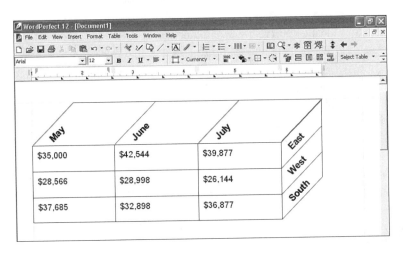

1. Access the Table Format dialog box and click the Skew tab (see Figure 10.29).

**Figure 10.29**
You can use the Skew tab of the Table Format dialog box to skew rows or columns.

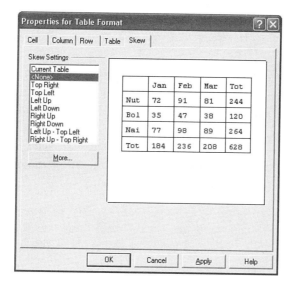

2. Click any of the available Skew settings. The preview box displays the effect of the skew style.

3. To customize the skew settings, click More. WordPerfect displays the Edit Skew dialog box (see Figure 10.30).

**Figure 10.30**
To customize how rows or columns are skewed, use the Edit Skew dialog box.

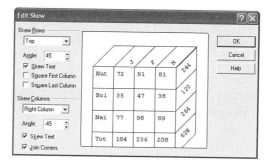

4. Choose from among these options (use the preview box to see what each option will do):

- Skew Rows—You can choose to skew the top row or none at all. You cannot skew a bottom row or a row in the middle of the table.

- Angle—By default, WordPerfect skews at a –45 degree angle, but you can increase or decrease the angle from –70 degrees (leaning far to the left), to +70 degrees (leaning far to the right).

- Skew Text—Choose this option to make the text align with the skewed cell.

- First Column—If the skewed row leans to the right, you might want to square the first column. If it leans to the left, this option could clip some of the cell's contents.

- Square Last Column—Square the last column if the skewed row leans to the left.

- Skew Columns—You can choose to skew the left or right columns, or none at all. You cannot skew both right and left columns in the same table.

- Join Corners—If you skew both a top row and a column, and if they lean toward each other, you can choose to have them join corners. This means that the total of their angles does not exceed 90 degrees, and the outermost corners of their row and column join in a square (refer to Figure 10.28).

**TIP FROM**

*Read Gilgen*

10

> Don't forget that you can repeat header rows, including skewed rows, at the top of each page. Simply access the Table Format dialog box and from the Rows tab, select Header Row.

# FORMATTING TABLE TEXT

The preceding section focuses primarily on features that help you create the layout, or structure, of a table. It is also important that you make sure that the text itself contributes to the effectiveness of your presentation. Therefore, you need to understand how text attributes and text alignment apply to table cells.

## UNDERSTANDING FORMATTING PRECEDENCE

Each time you choose a text formatting option, you have to consider whether that attribute should apply to the entire table, to a column, or to a cell or group of cells. Whether a change you make affects a cell depends on formatting priority. Changes you make to a specific cell or group of cells have precedence, or priority, over changes you make to columns. Changes made to cells or to columns have precedence over changes made to the entire table.

Suppose, for example, that you specify that the data in a single cell should be centered (the heading of a column, for example) and then specify that the data for the entire column should be decimal-aligned. The change made to the column has no effect on the center-alignment change you make to the individual cell.

Keep this in mind, especially as you format columns. Any changes to a cell you might have made (and forgotten about) are not changed when you specify something different with column or table formatting.

## FORMATTING TEXT IN COLUMNS

To modify the text formatting of all the cells in a column, position the cursor in the column you want to format, access the Table Format dialog box, and click the Column tab. WordPerfect displays the dialog box controls for formatting columns (see Figure 10.31).

**Figure 10.31**
To format columns, use the Column tab in the Table Format dialog box.

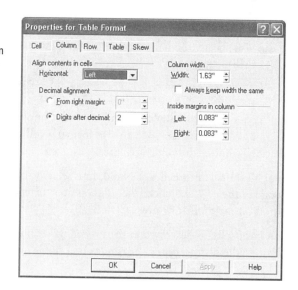

**TIP FROM**

*Read Gilgen*

To format several adjoining columns simultaneously, select cells on the same row from all the columns you want to include. Then access the Table Format dialog box and click the Column tab.

Perhaps one of the most commonly needed column formats is the horizontal alignment of text, which you change in the Align Contents in Cells area of the Table Format dialog box. Choose from the following options:

■ Horizontal—Use the drop-down menu to choose Left, Right, Center, Full, or All alignment.

→ For a complete description of text alignment types, **see** "Justifying Text," **p. 80.**

■ From Right Margin—Enables you to align numbers at the decimal point, and the decimal point aligns at the distance you specify from the right margin of the cell.

■ Digits After Decimal—Enables you to align numbers at the decimal point, and the decimal point aligns with enough space to accommodate *n* number of digits. The actual distance varies depending on the font size.

**TIP FROM**

*Read Gilgen*

If you want to decimal-align a column of numbers, but want them to appear farther from the right edge of the table column, choose From Right Margin in the Column tab of the Table Format dialog box.

In addition to column width, explained earlier in this chapter in the section "Changing Column Widths," you can also specify the left and right text margins for your columns. The default is 0.083 inch (1/12 inch).

## FORMATTING CELLS

Within cells, you format text as you normally do in a document. Simply select the text and add whatever attributes you want. However, you can also format a cell so that any text you add to the cell automatically acquires the cell's attributes.

For example, if you want all the text in a cell to be bold, first select the cell (move the mouse pointer to the edge of the cell, and click when the pointer turns to an arrow), and then click the Bold button on the toolbar or press Ctrl+B.

After you format a column of cells, as described in the preceding section, you might find that you also need to change the justification or attributes of a single cell or group of cells within that column.

To change the format of a single cell, other than for text attributes, position the cursor in the cell you want to change, access the Table Format dialog box, and click the Cell tab. WordPerfect displays the controls for formatting cells (see Figure 10.32).

**Figure 10.32**
To format cells in a table, use the Cell tab in the Table Format dialog box.

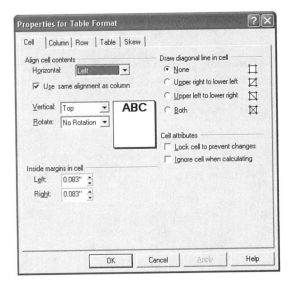

To change the format of a group of cells, select the cells you want to change and access the Table Format dialog box. The changes you choose from the Cell tab then apply to each of the selected cells.

**N O T E**

Although it might seem logical to click the Row tab to format all the cells in a row, you must select all the cells first and then click the Cell tab from the Table Format dialog box to format the row of cells.

Many of the options for formatting cells are identical to those used for formatting columns, such as the alignment or inside margins options. Other options used only for formatting cells include

- Use Same Alignment As Column—By default, each cell assumes the attributes that are in effect for the column in which it resides. Thus, when you first choose the Table Format dialog box Cell tab, the Use Same Alignment as Column check box is selected. If you select a justification that differs from the column type, WordPerfect deselects this box. To reassign the column defaults, click Use Column Justification. WordPerfect automatically turns off any cell attributes that conflict with the default column formats.

- Vertical—By default, WordPerfect vertically aligns all text in a cell at the top of the cell. Choose Bottom or Center to change the vertical alignment of the text in a cell. In addition, you can rotate the text within a cell by choosing 90 Degrees, 180 Degrees, or 270 Degrees.

**N O T E**

When WordPerfect rotates text, it actually takes text you type and places it in graphics text boxes. To edit the information in rotated cells, you must click the text in the cell, make your changes in the Text edit screen, and click Close.

➔ For more information on working with text graphics boxes, **see** "Adding Text Boxes As Graphic Objects," **p. 409.**

- Lock Cell to Prevent Changes—This option protects a cell from being altered. For example, if you want to prevent a user from entering data in certain cells in a form, you can lock them.

- Ignore Cell When Calculating—If the cell contains numbers that you don't want calculated during a math operation, you can specify that WordPerfect ignore the numbers.

➔ For information on using formulas and calculations in WordPerfect tables, **see** "Using Spreadsheet Formulas in Tables," **p. 489.**

- Draw Diagonal Line in Cell—You can add diagonal lines to cells by choosing one of these options: None, Upper Right to Lower Left, Upper Left to Lower Right, or Both.

## FORMATTING AN ENTIRE TABLE

Most of the changes you make to tables are to columns and cells. Sometimes, however, you might want to use a certain format as a default for an entire table. When you click the Table tab in the Table Format dialog box, WordPerfect presents the same controls used for columns and cells (see Figure 10.33).

**Figure 10.33**
For changes that affect the entire table, use the Table tab in the Table Format dialog box.

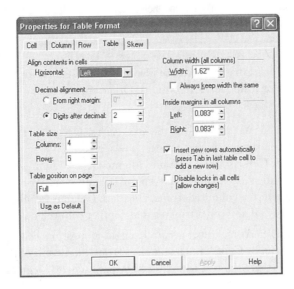

The options you select apply to the entire table, *except* to columns or cells you already modified.

Three options apply only to tables:

- Table Position on Page—By default, tables are full-justified in your document, which means the table stretches from left margin to right margin. This option lets you change the justification of the table itself, not the text in the cells of the table.

- Insert New Rows Automatically—Deselect this check box to prevent WordPerfect from adding a new row to the table when you press Tab in the last cell of the table.

- Disable Locks in All Cells—This option lets you quickly disable any cell locks you might have set. After you finish modifying the locked cells, uncheck this box again to reset the locks.

# CHANGING TABLE LINES, BORDERS, AND FILLS

One part of a table's effectiveness is lines, which help the reader better understand the information. For tables in which a user needs to fill in information, lines also help show where to enter appropriate data. By default, WordPerfect surrounds each cell with a single line, giving the appearance that the table also is surrounded by a single line. In fact, there is no border at all around a WordPerfect table. In addition to lines, you can fill the entire table or individual cells with varying patterns or colors of shading.

## UNDERSTANDING DEFAULT LINE STYLES

The default style for table lines is a single line. Although it might seem that a single line appears on all four sides of a cell, only two sides typically make up a cell: the left and the top. If you were to "explode" a typical table of three rows and three columns, the cells would resemble the cells shown in Figure 10.34. (Notice that lines appear on the right and bottom sides of cells on the right and bottom of the table.)

**Figure 10.34**
An exploded WordPerfect table illustrates default line segments.

| A1 | B1 | C1 |
| A2 | B2 | C2 |
| A3 | B3 | C3 |

When you specify a line style other than the default, you force WordPerfect to display that style at the location you specify. But you must be careful: If you specify a single line for the right side of a cell, even though its adjoining single cell line does not print, the line does not align with the other single lines in that column. In Figure 10.35, for example, notice that the single line between cells A2 and B2 does not align with the other lines between columns A and B. To avoid this situation, make changes only to the top and left sides of cells whenever possible.

**Figure 10.35**
If you change lines other than the default left and top lines, your table lines might not align properly.

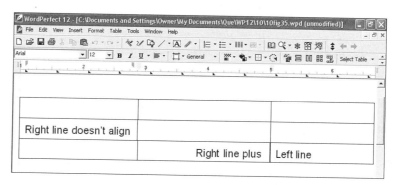

If you change both adjoining cell sides, you can create interesting effects because both lines print (refer to Figure 10.35, where two adjoining single lines appear to create a single thick line).

## CHANGING CELL LINES

Changing the default single line between cells is simple. You can change to another line style or decide to use no line at all. To change a table cell line style, follow these steps:

1. Position your cursor in the cell.

2. Choose Table, Borders/Fill. Alternatively, you can press Shift+F12, or you can choose Borders/Fill from the QuickMenu. WordPerfect displays the Properties for Table Borders/Fill dialog box (see Figure 10.36).

   This dialog box defaults to controls for the outside of the current selection and lists the current style for each of the line segments included in the selected cells. Unless you change them, each line uses the default (single line).

**Figure 10.36**
The Table Borders/Fill dialog box is used to change line styles for cells, groups of cells, the entire table, or the table border.

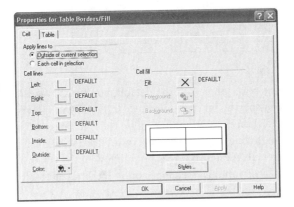

3. Click the palette button of the cell's line segment you want to change (for example, Bottom). WordPerfect displays a palette of line style choices (see Figure 10.37).

**Figure 10.37**
You can choose a table line style from a palette of choices.

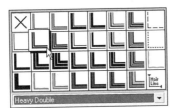

4. Move the mouse pointer to the style you want to use. The name of the style appears in a drop-down list at the bottom of the palette. If you want to see more styles, click the drop-down list.

5. From the palette or the drop-down list, select the style you want. The preview box shows the result of the selection.

6. After choosing each line style you want, click OK or press Enter. WordPerfect makes the change to your table.

**NOTE**

Depending on the resolution of your computer's monitor or the scale of your document display, single lines might not appear at all, or double lines might appear as a thicker single line. To be sure you have the correct line, you can increase the zoom percentage of your document.

If you select more than one cell, the Borders/Fill dialog box changes, and the default choice considers the group of cells as one large cell, with additional inside lines. Options you can choose include

- Left, Right, Top, or Bottom—Changes in these line styles affect only one side of the group of cells. For example, if you choose Left, only the left line of the left column of cells changes.

- Inside—Only those lines that separate cells change with this option.

- Outside—All the lines on the outer edges of the groups of cells change. Changing this option automatically changes the styles of the left, right, top, and bottom styles. If you then change an individual side, the word Mixed appears beside this button.

**10**

**TIP FROM**

*Read Gilgen*

If you want to change most of the lines to a certain style, change the Outside line style first, and then make changes to individual sides.

## TURNING OFF CELL LINES

To turn off the line between two cells, position the cursor in one of the cells, choose Borders/Fill from the QuickMenu, and change the appropriate line segment to <None> (click the large X on the palette).

To turn off all the cells in a table, select all the cells, select Borders/Fill from the QuickMenu, and change all the Inside and Outside lines to <None>.

Whenever you choose <None> as the line style, WordPerfect displays instead a light-gray gridline. The gridline does not print, but it does help you know where the cell lines are located. Figure 10.38 shows table gridlines for a table that contains no cell lines.

**NOTE**

You might be able to use SpeedFormat to turn off lines. Choose SpeedFormat from the QuickMenu, select the No Lines No Border style, and click Apply. If you previously made changes to any cell line, SpeedFormat will not affect that change.

**Figure 10.38**
If you select <None> as your line style, WordPerfect still displays a grid to help you see where your cells are located.

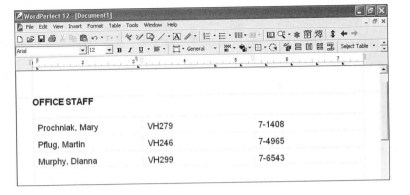

You can also change the default line style to <None> by choosing Borders/Fill from the QuickMenu, and then clicking the Table tab. Then in the Default Cell Lines area, click the Line button and choose <None>. Note, however, that any changes you made to individual line segments still print.

**TIP FROM**

*Read Gilgen*

If you're a long-time WordPerfect user and are used to using parallel columns to format your text, consider using tables without lines instead. The effect is the same, but working with tables is much easier than working with parallel columns.

## CREATING CUSTOM LINES

In addition to using predefined line styles, you can create your own custom line styles and effects. Furthermore, you can save your custom lines in style templates or in SpeedFormat table styles and use them over and over.

To create a custom line (for example, a colored single and dashed line), follow these steps:

1. Choose Format, Graphics Styles. WordPerfect displays the Graphics Styles dialog box (see Figure 10.39).

**NOTE**

Note that in the Graphics Styles dialog box you can create or edit box, line, border, or fill styles. The procedures for each type are similar.

2. Choose Line to display existing line styles, and to prepare for creating a new line style.
3. Click Create. WordPerfect presents the Create Line Style dialog box (see Figure 10.40).

**Figure 10.39**
You can use the Graphics Styles dialog box to create a new graphics line style.

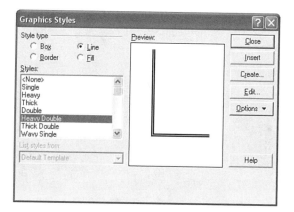

**Figure 10.40**
The Create Line Style dialog box, as it appears after following the steps to create a custom line, is used to customize your line styles.

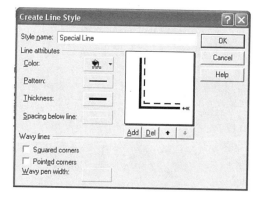

4. In the Style Name text box, type a unique name (for example, Special Line).

5. Change the color, pattern, and thickness of the first line by using the corresponding palette buttons.

6. Click Add to add another line to the style. Note that the arrow in the preview box points at the currently selected line. You can use the up and down arrows beneath the preview box to select lines in the style.

7. Change the Color, Pattern, and Thickness of the second, or any other, line, using the corresponding palette buttons.

8. If you want spacing between the lines, select a spacing width from the Spacing Below Line palette.

9. Click OK to return to the Graphics Styles dialog box. The name of the newly created style appears on the list of available styles.

10. Click Close to return to your document. You can now use the new line style when you access the Borders/Fill dialog box.

If you want to keep your new line style only in the current document, simply use the line style wherever you want and save the document. However, if you think you want to use this line style in other documents, you can save it in a template.

→ For details on working with customized styles, **see** "Creating Custom Styles," **p. 273.**

## CHANGING BORDERS

The border around a WordPerfect table is separate from the lines that surround each of the cells in the table. By default, a WordPerfect table border has no border style. To change a border style, follow these steps:

1. From the Table menu or from the QuickMenu, choose Borders/Fill.

2. From the resulting Table Borders/Fill dialog box, click the Table tab to display table-related lines and fill options (see Figure 10.41, shown with several options chosen).

**Figure 10.41**
You can use the Table tab of the Table Borders/Fill dialog box to change your table border.

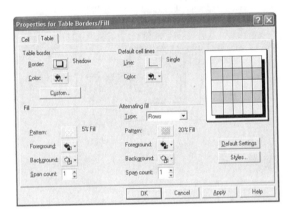

3. In the Table Border area, choose a border style from the Border palette. Note the resulting effect in the preview box.

4. Click Apply to apply the changes but to remain in the dialog box, or click OK to apply the changes and return to your table.

**NOTE**
If you choose specific styles for both the border and the outside table cell lines, both styles print.

In addition to the standard list of border styles, you can customize your border to include special combinations of lines, shading, and even drop shadow border effects.

To customize a table border, follow these steps:

1. Access the Table Borders/Fill dialog box and click the Table tab (refer to Figure 10.41).

2. Select any border style that approximates what you want. (Unless a border style is selected, you can't customize the border!)

3. Click Custom to display the Customize Border dialog box (see Figure 10.42).

**Figure 10.42**
You can use the Customize Border dialog box to change the border style—for example, by adding a drop shadow to the table.

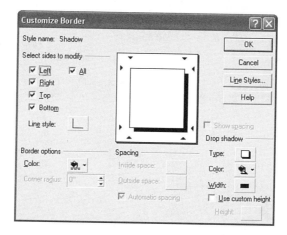

4. Change the Line Style for any of the sides selected. If All is checked then all sides are changed at the same time.

5. Click Color to choose a line style color (see Figure 10.43). If you click Use Line Style Color, the customize screen reverts to the color of the line style you originally selected.

**Figure 10.43**
You can choose a new line color from the palette or choose Use Line Style Color to force your line to use the default color of the selected line style.

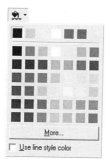

6. To add a drop shadow, choose the Type, Color, and the Width you want.

7. When you are satisfied with your changes as shown in the preview box, click OK.

8. Click OK again to apply the custom border to your table.

As with line styles, you can also save custom border styles.

→ For more information on how to save styles for future use, **see** "Creating Custom Styles," **p. 273.**

## CHANGING FILLS

WordPerfect enables you to fill individual cells, groups of cells, or the entire table with black, colors, or shades of gray or color. Unless you have a color printer, however, the most practical use for this feature is to shade cells you want to set apart from the rest of the table. Suppose, for example, that you want to set off the column headings from the rest of a table. To shade a cell or group of cells, follow these steps:

1. Position your cursor in the cell (or select the group of cells) you want to change.

2. From the Table menu or the QuickMenu, choose Borders/Fill. WordPerfect displays the Table Borders/Fill dialog box (refer to Figure 10.36).

 3. From the Cell Fill area, click the Fill Palette button. WordPerfect displays a palette of fill patterns (see Figure 10.44).

**Figure 10.44**
The fill cell palette offers an array of fill patterns, including gradient fills.

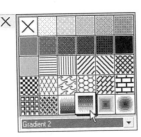

4. Click the fill pattern you want.

 5. Change the foreground color or the background color, as desired. Usually the foreground color is the pattern.

6. If what you see in the preview box is what you want, click OK to apply the fill style and to return to the table.

**TIP FROM**

*Read Gilgen*

If you plan to print text in a cell, even when using a non-color printer, use a light color such as yellow, or if you are filling with a dark color, choose 20% fill or less. Higher percentages of shading with darker colors usually make reading text contained in that cell difficult.

You can select different shading or fill styles for any number of cells in your table. You can even create your own custom fills, including gradient shading and special patterns.

**TIP FROM**

*Read Gilgen*

You can create white text on black background cells by using the reverse.wcm macro that comes with WordPerfect. Simply select the cells you want to change, and then choose Tools, Macro, Play, and play the reverse.wcm macro. The macro lets you choose the background color, the text color, and whether the cells should be a table header.

→ For more information on how to use WordPerfect macros, **see** Chapter 26, "Using Experts and Macros."

# TROUBLESHOOTING

### MOUSE PRACTICE MAKES PERFECT

*I'm not too steady with the mouse. When I try to use the table grid to create a table, I sometimes get the wrong number of rows or columns.*

As you practice, you'll get better at choosing just the right size. If you make a mistake, just click the Undo button on the toolbar (or choose Edit, Undo). The table goes away, and you can try again.

### BUT I DIDN'T WANT THAT THERE!

*Sometimes when I try to select cells in a table, the content of those cells ends up in some other part of the table.*

You're probably inadvertently using WordPerfect's drag-and-drop feature. After selecting part of the cells you want, you're letting the mouse button go, and then clicking the already selected cells again and dragging to what should have been the last cell in your selection. When you release the mouse button, the first selection of cells is moved (dropped) into the new location. If this happens, just click the Undo button on the toolbar (or choose Edit, Undo) and try again.

### TABLE COLUMN ALIGNMENT

*I changed the format of my table column to decimal-aligned, but the text still appears left-aligned.*

This is an easy mistake to make. When you used the Table Format dialog box, you probably forgot to click the Column tab, so all you formatted was a single cell.

To correct the problem, position the cursor in that column again, and then choose Format from the QuickMenu. This time, click the Column tab and make the desired changes.

### EDITING ROTATED TEXT

*I rotated text in some table cells, but I now need to change the text, and I can't figure out how to edit it.*

When WordPerfect rotates text, it actually takes text you type and places it in graphics text boxes. To edit the information in the rotated cells, you click the text in the cell, make your changes in the Text edit screen, and click Close.

→ For more information on working with text graphics boxes, **see** "Adding Text Boxes As Graphic Objects," **p. 409.**

### JUSTIFICATION CHANGES AREN'T ACCEPTED

*After making a justification change to a column, one of the cells doesn't seem to accept the new change.*

This is usually because you formatted a single cell at some point. To make the cell match the rest of the column, position the cursor in that cell, choose Format from the QuickMenu, and with the Cell tab selected, make sure the Use Column Justification check box is selected.

### PLACING GRAPHIC IMAGES

*I can't seem to position my graphic image properly in a table cell.*

Graphics images require enough room to display properly. You might have to reduce the size of the graphic image or increase the width or height of the table cell. There is no exact rule for accomplishing this task, so keep trying (and using Undo) until you get it the way you want it.

# PROJECT

So many potential uses for tables exist that an entire book could be written describing samples and exploring table options. Here's just one possible use.

Suppose you need to create a telephone message form for your business. Follow these steps:

1. Create a table, with four columns and eight rows. Figure 10.45 shows the simple table that you will transform into a complex form.

**Figure 10.45**
To create a complex form, begin with the basic table structure.

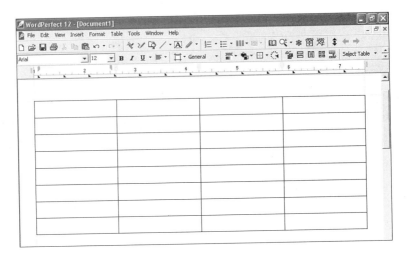

2. Select cells B1 through D1 and use the QuickMenu to join the cells.
3. Use Borders/Fill to change the left line of cell B1 to <None>.
4. Join cells A2 and B2, and join cells C2 and D2.
5. Join cells A3 and B3, and join cells C3 and D3.
6. Select cells A4 through B6 and choose Borders/Fill to change the inside lines to none.
7. Join cells C4 and D4.
8. Join cells C5 through D6.

9. Join cells A7 through D7, and drag the bottom line of row 7 to allow for about two inches of message space.

10. Select cells A8 through C8, and use Borders/Fill to turn off the inside and top lines.

The structure of the message form is shown in Figure 10.46.

**Figure 10.46**
After you modify the table structure to fit your needs, you can add text and graphic data.

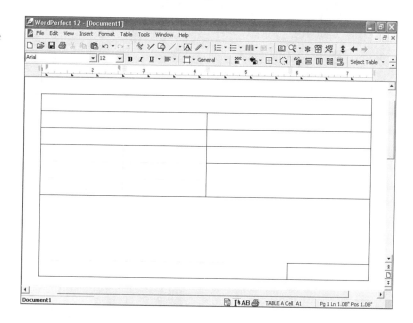

Now add the text content of the message form, using Figure 10.47 as a reference. Insert your company graphic in cell A1, and type your company name and address in cell B1 (if necessary, adjust the height of the row by dragging the bottom line). Instead of using bullets for the "please call" options, simply choose a character from Insert, Symbol (or Ctrl+W), followed by a space.

**Figure 10.47**
A complete phone message form, created from a WordPerfect table.

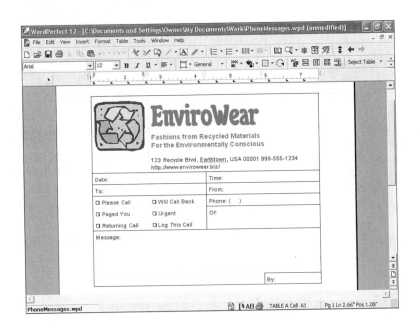

# CHAPTER 11

# ORGANIZING INFORMATION WITH LISTS AND OUTLINES

# UNDERSTANDING OUTLINES

Not all text is narrative prose. Sometimes you use WordPerfect to create structured lists, such as the following, that summarize and organize information:

- Agendas
- Notes for a speech
- A summary of points covered in a class or workshop
- Overhead transparency lists
- To-do lists
- Structured reports with executive summaries
- Legal documents that require structured headings

Any time you need to organize information in lists, WordPerfect can help with numbered, bulleted, and text lists and outlines. Figure 11.1 shows examples of four types of WordPerfect lists.

11

**Figure 11.1**
WordPerfect enables you to create numbered and bulleted lists, as well as outlines to help you organize information.

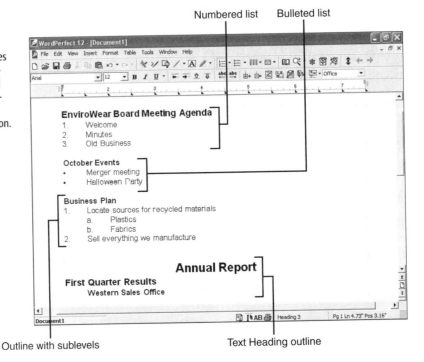

Numbered list   Bulleted list

Outline with sublevels   Text Heading outline

# WORKING WITH BULLETED AND NUMBERED LISTS

Bulleted and numbered lists help draw attention to important bits of information. For example, you might use bullets to list product features or highlights of an upcoming event. You might prefer to use numbers for a "to do" list, or an agenda, where sequence of the various items is important.

Lists with bullets or numbers are nothing more than paragraphs with special styles added. Typically, the style includes a bullet or number character followed by an indent code to set off the text of the paragraph (refer to Figure 1.1).

## USING QUICKBULLETS

The old "brute force" way to add bullets was to type an asterisk (*) followed by the bulleted information. WordPerfect offers QuickBullets, a quicker and easier method to automate the process. To use QuickBullets, first turn on the feature by following these steps:

1. Choose Tools, QuickCorrect.
2. In the QuickCorrect dialog box, click the Format-As-You-Go tab.
3. Make sure the QuickBullets option is checked in the Format-As-You-Go options list.
4. Click OK.

To use QuickBullets, start at the left margin, type an asterisk (*) and press the Tab key. WordPerfect automatically inserts a bullet, followed by an indented paragraph. If you look behind the scenes in WordPerfect's Reveal Codes (by choosing View, Reveal Codes or pressing Alt+F3), you see that WordPerfect applies a paragraph style to each bulleted item (see Figure 11.2). If this feature seems to get in your way and you end up with bullets when you really wanted asterisks, follow the previous set of steps to turn the feature off again.

→ To learn more about the Styles feature, **see** Chapter 9, "Formatting with Styles."

Creating bullets to help accentuate items in a list is quick and easy using QuickBullets, but you also can control exactly which bullet you want to use. You can even decide later, if you want, to use numbers instead of bullets.

## CREATING BULLETED LISTS

To create a bulleted list, follow these easy steps:

1. Choose Insert, Outline/Bullets & Numbering (a daunting menu entry). WordPerfect displays the Bullets & Numbering dialog box.
2. Click the Bullets tab to display a list of predefined bullet list styles (see Figure 11.3).

**11**

**Figure 11.2**
Bulleted or numbered paragraphs are controlled by paragraph styles.

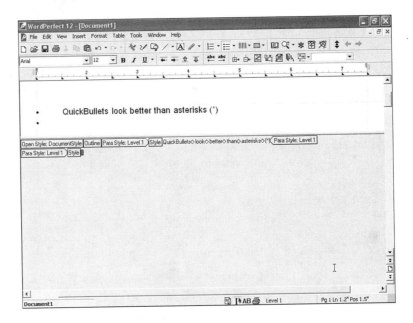

**11**

**Figure 11.3**
You can use the Bullets tab of the Bullets & Numbering dialog box to choose a bullet style for your list.

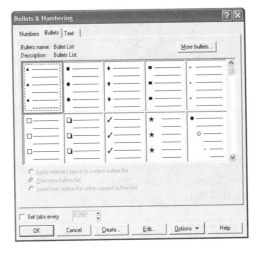

3. Click the style you want to use and click OK. WordPerfect inserts the chosen bullet style, which includes the bullet character and an indented paragraph.

4. Type the text of the first bullet.

5. Press Enter, and WordPerfect inserts the next bullet (see Figure 11.4).

6. Repeat steps 4 and 5 until you finish the list, and then press Enter one last time.

7. Press Backspace or click the Bullet button to erase the last bullet and turn off the bullet paragraph style.

**Figure 11.4**
When you use a bullet style, pressing Enter automatically adds a new, bulleted line.

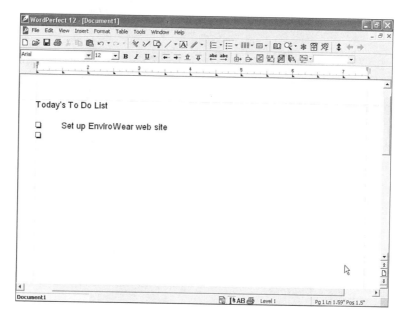

**NOTE**

You can also create a bulleted list by clicking the Bullet button on the toolbar, which places the currently selected bullet style in your document. To turn off the bullet style, simply click the Bullet button again.

11

**TIP FROM**

Click the drop-down arrow on the Bullet button to see a palette of available bullet styles. Then hover over a bullet style with the mouse pointer to see the effect in WordPerfect's real-time preview, or click More to go to the Bullets & Numbering dialog box.

## CREATING NUMBERED LISTS

Most people forget that computers are very good at keeping track of and calculating numbers. This includes numbered lists, and WordPerfect is excellent at making sure your numbered list is correct.

You create numbered lists very much the same way you create bulleted lists:

1. Choose Insert, Outline/Bullets & Numbering.

2. Click the Numbers tab and choose a number style (see Figure 11.5). Use the scrollbar to see all the styles.

3. Click OK, and WordPerfect places a number style in your document that includes a number, typically followed by a period and an indent code.

**Figure 11.5**
WordPerfect provides
several predefined
numbered list styles.

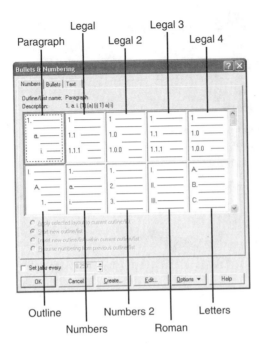

Legal
Paragraph    Legal 2    Legal 3    Legal 4

Outline    Numbers 2    Letters
Numbers    Roman

---

**TIP FROM**

*Read Gilgen*

You can start a numbered list quickly by clicking the Numbering button on the toolbar.
Choose different styles by clicking the drop-down arrow on the Numbering button.

---

4. Type some text, and when you press Enter, WordPerfect automatically increments the
   number for you.

5. Press Backspace or click the Numbering button on the toolbar to turn off the numbered list.

## EDITING LISTS

Before long you'll want to know how to vary or edit the list. For example, you might want
an extra blank line between each outline item, or you might need to add a new numbered
line. The following are some of the ways to modify a bulleted or numbered list:

- Add an extra blank line while creating the list—If you are creating a list for the first
  time, after you press Enter, simply press Enter again to move the bullet or number
  down one line.

- Add an extra blank line after creating the list—Position the cursor on the line you want
  to move. Press Home to move the insertion point to the left end of the text, and press
  Enter to move the line down.

- Insert a new line—Position the cursor at the end of the line preceding the location where you want to insert a new line and press Enter. WordPerfect inserts a new number or bullet. Type the text of the new bulleted paragraph.

**NOTE**

> Note that when you add or remove a numbered line, WordPerfect automatically assigns the correct number in sequence, and also increases or decreases the numbers of each line following the change. This powerful feature can save you lots of time because you don't have to retype the numbers each time you make a change.

**TIP FROM**

*Read Gilgen*

> Because numbered lists are so easy to create and edit, you should get in the habit of using them even for short lists. Simply click the Numbering button on the toolbar, or press Ctrl+H to begin a numbered list.

*If pressing Ctrl+H turned off outline numbering in your paragraph, see "How Did I Turn Off Outline Numbering?" in the Troubleshooting section at the end of this chapter.*

- Remove a line—Delete the text and bullet or number, as you do any text you want to remove. If you're using numbers, WordPerfect automatically renumbers your list.

- Change a normal text paragraph to a bullet or number—If you have already typed the text of the bullet (for example, a paragraph you want to highlight with a bullet), click the Bullet button or the Numbering button on the toolbar. WordPerfect adds the bullet or number style to the paragraph.

- Change a bulleted or numbered paragraph to normal text—If you decide you don't want a bullet paragraph, position the cursor anywhere on the paragraph and click the Bullet button on the toolbar. To convert a numbered paragraph to normal text, click the Numbering button on the toolbar.

**TIP FROM**

*Read Gilgen*

> To toggle between bulleted or numbered paragraphs and normal text, you can click the Bullet button on the toolbar, or you can simply press Ctrl+H.

## CHANGING THE BULLET OR NUMBERING STYLE

Changing the numbering or bullet style can be as easy as selecting a different predefined style or as complex as creating an entirely new bullet or numbering style.

Suppose, for example, you want to change a numbered list to one that uses capital letters. Follow these steps:

1. Access the Bullets & Numbering dialog box by choosing Insert, Outline/Bullets & Numbering.

**TIP FROM**

*Read Gilgen*

You can bypass the menus to access the Bullets & Numbering box by clicking the drop-down menu on the Numbering button or the Bullet button on the toolbar, and then choosing More from the palette of choices.

2. Click the Numbers or Bullets tab, depending on the style you want to change to.

**NOTE**

You can change any list from one style type to another. For example, you can change a numbered list to a bulleted list, and vice versa.

3. Click the style you want, for example, the Letters style (refer to Figure 11.5).

4. Choose one of the listed options:

   - Apply Selected Layout to Current Outline/List—This option appears when the insertion point is located within a WordPerfect list of any kind. Selecting the option applies the selected style to the entire list (see Figure 11.6).

A new style within a list

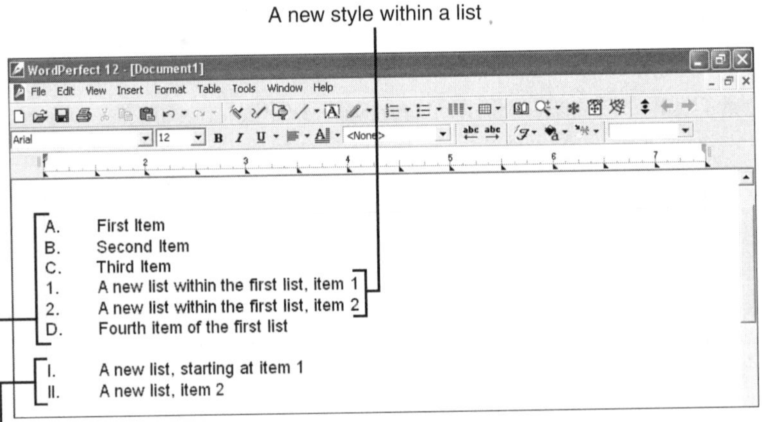

**Figure 11.6**
You can use number-ing/outline options to create new lists or to modify the sequence in an existing list.

An entirely new list style, using letters

| A. | First Item |
| B. | Second Item |
| C. | Third Item |
| 1. | A new list within the first list, item 1 |
| 2. | A new list within the first list, item 2 |
| D. | Fourth item of the first list |
| I. | A new list, starting at item 1 |
| II. | A new list, item 2 |

A new style following a list

   - Start New Outline/List—This option starts a new style at the insertion point. If you are in the middle of a list, the new style does not affect items before the insertion point—only those after it. If you are at the end of a list, it simply starts a new list, beginning at number 1 if you are using numbers. This option is the default when you click the Numbering button on the toolbar.

- Insert New Outline/List Within Current Outline/List—If the insertion point is resting on a list paragraph, that paragraph becomes the first item in a new list. Items added after it are also part of the same list style. Items in the original list, however, are not changed (refer to Figure 11.6).

**TIP FROM**

Numbers or letters nested within another outline that uses numbers or letters can be quite confusing. Instead, consider using numbers for main topics and bullets for the subtopics.

- Resume Numbering from Previous Outline/List—If you turned off the list style, and inserted other normal text (including hard returns), you have the option of picking up where you left off, both in style and numbering sequence. If you choose another style, this option is not available (it is grayed out) and you must start a new list.

5. You also can choose a different tab setting for your numbered lists. For example, if the default 1/2 inch is too wide, click Set Tabs Every and enter the amount in the counter box (for example, 1/3).

**TIP FROM**

Read Gilgen

Reducing the amount of tab space between the bullet or number and the text can give your list a tighter, cleaner look. However, don't make the amount too small because wider, two- or three-digit numbers in numbered lists can cause the text to look uneven.

6. Click OK to apply the new style and options to your list.

# WORKING WITH OUTLINES

WordPerfect was one of the first programs to offer fully functional outlining capabilities. Unfortunately, the feature was somewhat difficult to master, and as a result it is still one of WordPerfect's best-kept secrets. WordPerfect 12 changes all that with its easy-to-use, yet powerful, outlining feature.

*Outlines* work very much like lists, but add another dimension. For example, a typical list includes items that all have the same relative importance. Outlines items, on the other hand, are arranged hierarchically to show their relative importance. Consider the two lists shown in Figure 11.7.

In Figure 11.7, the list presents only one level of relatively equal information, numbered 1, 2, 3, and so on. The outline, however, presents multiple levels. Each level is identified by its indentation and by its numbering style. For example, the first proposed solution, item a under point 3, contains two sublevels that explain the reason for the proposal. WordPerfect enables you to use up to nine levels.

**Figure 11.7**
Outlines are like lists, but add sublevels for greater depth in organizing information.

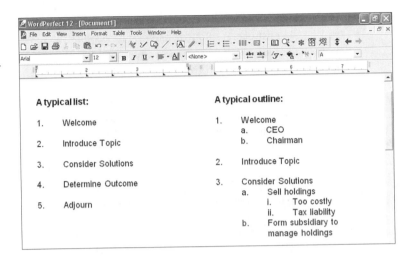

The advantages of working with outlines become evident after you begin working with them. They are easy to create, they are even easier to edit, and they make the task of organizing information a snap. You'll soon wonder how you ever got along without this feature.

## CREATING AN OUTLINE

Although WordPerfect offers several outline styles, the numbered paragraphs style is the default. To create a simple numbered paragraph outline, position the insertion point at the left margin, and then follow these steps:

> **NOTE**
>
> Although WordPerfect offers a myriad options, you'll first step through the basics to see just how easy it is to create a multilevel outline. You'll return to the details after that.

1. Choose Insert, Outlines/Bullets & Numbering. WordPerfect displays the Bullets & Numbering dialog box, with the Numbers tab and Paragraph style selected (refer to Figure 11.5).

> **NOTE**
>
> If you've recently used another number or bullet outline style, you might have to click the Numbers tab and select the Paragraph outline style.

2. Click OK, and WordPerfect places a number, followed by a period and an indent in your document (for example, 1.).

3. Type the content of the first paragraph—for example, Welcome (refer to the outline in Figure 11.7 for sample text you can type).

**TIP FROM**

*Read Gilgen*

You can also begin a numbered paragraph outline by clicking the Numbering button on the toolbar, or by pressing Ctrl+H.

**CAUTION**

Make sure the insertion point is positioned horizontally where you want the outline to begin (usually at the left margin of the document), and also on a blank line. If the insertion point is located inside an existing paragraph, WordPerfect converts the paragraph to a numbered outline paragraph when you turn on outlining. If you accidentally number a text paragraph, simply use Undo or press Ctrl+H.

4. To insert the next number, press Enter. If you want to move the number down another line before you type, press Enter again.

5. To create the next line at the second level, press Tab. WordPerfect moves to the next tab stop and changes the number to a letter (for example, a).

6. Type the content of the first subtopic.

7. Press Enter, and WordPerfect inserts the next number at the same level as the preceding paragraph (for example, b).

8. Type the second subtopic, and press Enter.

9. Before typing, press Shift+Tab to move the letter to the left and change it to a number (for example, 2).

10. Continue typing and inserting numbers until you finish the outline. Remember to use the following keys:

   • Press Enter to add a new numbered line.

   • Press Tab to move to the next level to the right.

   • Press Shift+Tab to return to a previous level to the left.

11. Press Enter one last time and then press Backspace to delete the unneeded outline number and to turn off outlining.

**TIP FROM**

*Read Gilgen*

You can also end a numbered paragraph outline by clicking the Numbering button on the toolbar, or by pressing Ctrl+H.

**NOTE**

You can only use up to nine outline levels. WordPerfect does not allow you to tab past the ninth level.

## UNDERSTANDING OUTLINES

Now that you understand how easy it is to create an outline, you can explore other options and features.

### OUTLINE TERMINOLOGY

If you understand outline terminology, it's easier to understand the feature. The following are some of the terms used to describe WordPerfect's outline features:

- Outline item—A paragraph of an outline, identified by a single number or bullet.

- Body text—Any nonoutline text. Such paragraphs might appear between outline items in an outline, and also include blank lines (for example, a hard return).

- Level—Outline level refers to the horizontal position of the outline item, relative to other outline items. For example, items at the left margin are at the first level. Outline items that appear at the first tab stop are at the second level, and so on.

- Family—A group of outline items that belong together. For example, in Figure 11.7, items 1.a and 1.b are all part of the item 1 family of outline items, and items 3.a.i and 3.a.ii are part of the 3.a family.

- Promote—To give an outline item more importance, by moving the paragraph to the left. The item is also said to have been moved up a level.

- Demote—To give an outline item less importance, by moving it to the right. The item is also said to have been moved down a level.

### USING THE OUTLINE PROPERTY BAR

When the insertion point is located within an outline, WordPerfect displays several Outline tools on the property bar (see Figure 11.8).

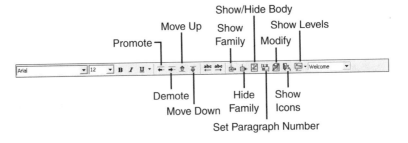

**Figure 11.8**
You can use Outline buttons on the property bar to work with your outlines.

The options represented by these buttons include the following:

- Promote—Changes the current outline level to the previous, higher level. The cursor can appear anywhere in the text of the current outline level. This action has the same effect as pressing Shift+Tab when the insertion tab immediately follows the outline number.

■ Demote—Changes the current outline level to the next, lower level. This is the same as pressing Tab when the insertion point immediately follows the outline number.

**TIP FROM**

Although you can demote and promote outline items using the property bar, you'll find it much faster and more natural to stick to the keyboard when creating outlines, using Tab and Shift+Tab respectively.

■ Move Up—Moves an outline item, or selected family, up one line, while preserving the outline level. You can click several times to keep moving the item up in the outline.

■ Move Down—Moves an outline item, or selected family, down one line, while preserving the outline level.

■ Show Family—If you have hidden the sublevels of the current outline item, this option enables you to show all the sublevels again.

■ Hide Family—Hides all the sublevels of the currently selected outline item. If the item has no sublevels, this option has no effect.

■ Show/Hide Body—This option hides all nonoutline text, such as titles, narrative paragraphs, and even blank lines (hard returns). Click the button again to show the body text along with the outline. This is particularly useful when you're using text outline headings, and you want to collapse the narrative into an outline format (see the section "Creating Text Outline Headings," later in this chapter).

■ Set Paragraph Number—Click this button to display the Set Paragraph Number dialog box (see Figure 11.9). Although you can select only numbers, the value of the current outline item changes accordingly; for example, a. changes to c. if you change the value from 1 to 3. This is particularly useful if you want to begin a new outline or numbering sequence later within the same document.

■ Modify—Use this option to modify the current paragraph style (see the section "Creating and Editing Outline Styles," later in this chapter).

**Figure 11.9**
You can use the Set Paragraph Number dialog box to set the current number of an outline item.

■ Show Icons—This option displays outline icons to the left of the outline itself (see Figure 11.10). T represents body text, and 1, 2, and so on indicate the levels of the outline items. You can click a number to select the item and its family.

■ Show Levels—Use this option to collapse or expand an outline. For example, if you want to display only first-level outline items, click this option and select One. All other levels remain hidden until you select Nine to show all levels again.

**Figure 11.10**
The Show Icons option displays outline level indicators in the left margin.

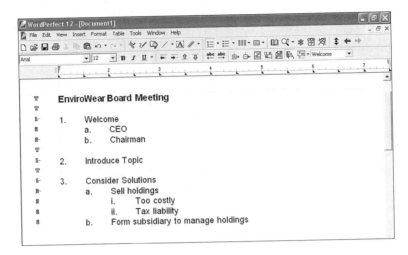

## EDITING OUTLINE TEXT

Editing the text in an outline is as easy as editing any other text. However, you might also find that you accidentally add or remove outline numbers as you edit your text.

If you accidentally add a paragraph number (for example, you press Enter and add the number), simply press Backspace to remove the number, and press Backspace again to remove the blank line.

If you accidentally remove a paragraph number (for example, you press Backspace when you didn't intend to), just click the Numbering button on the toolbar, or press Ctrl+H. Alternatively, you can press Backspace again to position the cursor at the end of the previous line, and press Enter to add the paragraph number.

## HIDING AND SHOWING OUTLINE FAMILIES

If your outline is fairly extensive, with lots of text and sublevels, you can hide some of the text by hiding families or showing only certain levels.

To hide all the sublevels of a specific outline family, follow these steps:

1. Position the cursor anywhere on the first line of the top level of the family you want to hide.

2. Click the Hide Family button on the property bar. WordPerfect collapses the outline for that family, showing only the top outline level and hiding all the others (see Figure 11.11).

---

**TIP FROM**

If you select Show Icons, and the outline level numbers appear in the left margin, you can double-click an outline level number to hide (or show) its family.

**Figure 11.11**
You can collapse the sublevels in an outline family by using the Hide Family button.

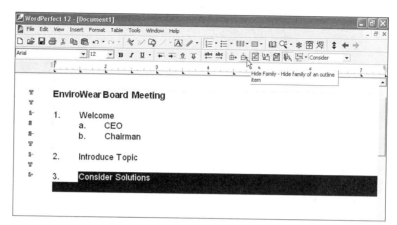

 To show all outline levels in a family, click the Show Family button on the property bar.

You can also display only the top levels of an outline, hiding all the rest. This is sometimes referred to as collapsing an outline. For example, you could have an agenda that displays two levels for all the participants, but hides the third level, where you list details that you don't want them to see.

 To collapse an outline, showing only the top levels, click the Show Levels button on the property bar, and choose the number of levels you want to display (for example, Two). To expand an outline to show all levels, click the Show Levels button, and choose Nine.

**CAUTION**

If you choose <None> from the Show Levels menu, you hide the entire outline, and the Show Levels button disappears from the property bar. The only way you can redisplay your outline is to choose View, Toolbars, and select the Outline toolbar. You can then click the Show Levels button on the toolbar and select the number of levels you want to display.

**NOTE**

When you collapse an outline or hide a family of outline text, a bug in WordPerfect also hides body text that follows hidden sublevels. If you intend to print your collapsed outline, you might need to insert blank lines (hard returns) to restore the spacing you want. If you then expand the outline, you will have to remove the extra blank lines.

## MOVING AND COPYING IN AN OUTLINE

Selecting outline items or families and moving or copying them is a bit trickier than simply cutting and pasting, as you are used to doing.

To select an outline family—for example, just a single outline item—you can use any of the following methods:

■ Using the mouse, select the line beginning at the left of the outline number, and continue to the end of the text for the outline item, including the hard return.

**CAUTION**

> To fully select an outline item, you must also include the hard return at the end of the line. Positioning the cursor exactly to the left of an outline number is difficult. Therefore, you should use one of the other methods for selecting an outline item or family.

■ Using the mouse, position the pointer in the left margin, opposite the outline item you want to select. When the pointer turns to an arrow, double-click to select the outline item. This selects the outline number, the text of the outline item, and also the hard return at the end of the line.

■ Using the keyboard, position the cursor on the first line of the outline item, and press Home twice. Then press and hold down Shift while moving the cursor to the next line of the outline. Continue holding the Shift key, and press Home twice to move to the left of the next item's outline number.

These methods also work when selecting an outline item along with its sublevels (the entire family). In addition, consider these procedures:

■ To select an entire family, first click the Show Icons button on the property bar to display outline level numbers in the left margin. Then click the level number that corresponds to the family you want to select, and WordPerfect selects the entire family (the outline item and its sublevels), along with the hard return at the end of the last item.

■ You can also hide all the sublevels of the family, and then simply select what appears to be a single outline item. WordPerfect selects the sublevels along with the family's "parent" outline item.

After you select the portion of the outline you want to cut, copy, or delete, choose the appropriate action from the Edit menu, from the toolbar, or by using the keyboard, or use the mouse to drag and drop the selected outline text.

To paste an outline item or family, position the cursor at the left margin (to the left of the outline number), and choose Paste from the Edit menu, from the toolbar, or by using the keyboard.

**TIP FROM**

*Read Gilgen*

> Although the Windows graphical interface begs you to use the mouse, when working with outlines, the keyboard can be much quicker and more precise. You can press the Home key twice to move to the left of an outline number, and use the Shift key along with cursor movement to select text.

Instead of cutting and pasting an outline family, you can select a family by clicking the corresponding outline icon and then use the Move Up or Move Down buttons to move the parent along with the family to a new location.

## ADJUSTING OUTLINE LEVELS

The real power of a WordPerfect outline is the capability to add or remove outline entries and to adjust the levels of those entries. As you do, WordPerfect automatically renumbers your entries.

To add an outline item, position the cursor following the preceding item and press Enter. WordPerfect inserts a new outline number at the same level as the preceding outline item. Before typing, press Tab to demote the item, or press Shift+Tab to promote the item.

Adjusting outline levels after you type the entries is just as easy. Position the cursor on the first line of the outline item you want to adjust, press Home to move the cursor to the beginning of the line (but following the outline number), and press Tab to demote the item, or press Shift+Tab to promote the item.

## RENUMBERING AN OUTLINE

Normally, you do not have to worry about outline numbering because WordPerfect takes care of it automatically for you. When you add or remove lines, or adjust the level of an outline item, WordPerfect also adjusts the numbering so you don't have to.

However, if you want to set the numbering differently from what WordPerfect displays, you can do that, too. For example, if you begin a second outline in your document, WordPerfect tries to continue with the numbering sequence from the first outline. Instead, to have the numbering start over for the second outline, follow these steps:

1. Position the cursor where you want to change the outline number. Normally, you do this before beginning the new outline, but you can also place the cursor on an existing outline item.

 2. Click the Set Paragraph Number button on the property bar. WordPerfect displays the Set Paragraph Number dialog box (see Figure 11.12).

**Figure 11.12**
You can set a new outline number value with the Set Paragraph Number dialog box.

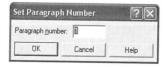

3. Set the number you want to use and click OK.

**NOTE**

Although you can select only numbers, the value of the current outline item changes accordingly. For example, a. changes to c. if you change the value from 1 to 3.

WordPerfect changes the outline number to the one you selected. Figure 11.13 shows the new numbering, along with a heading for the new outline section. If you change the number in an existing outline, WordPerfect also automatically adjusts the numbers at the same level within the same family.

**Figure 11.13**
Changing the value of an outline number causes WordPerfect to renumber the numbers that follow it.

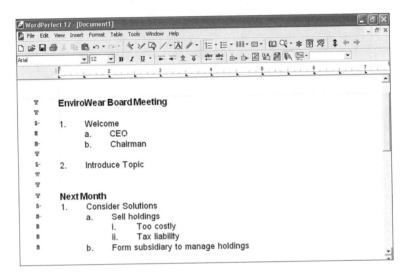

## CREATING AND EDITING OUTLINE STYLES

WordPerfect offers a good selection of number and bullet styles. However, if the style you really need isn't available, you can create your own. For example, you might want to use numbers for first-level items, combined with bullets for the second and third levels. Or, you might just want to change the punctuation or other formatting of one or more levels. Sometimes creating a new outline style might involve simply editing an existing style to make it more like what you want.

To create a new outline style, follow these steps:

1. Choose Insert, Outline/Bullets & Numbering to access the Bullets & Numbering dialog box.

2. If you can, find a style that's already close to what you want, and select it.

You can save time and effort by creating an outline style based on an existing outline style.

3. Click Create. WordPerfect displays the Create Format dialog box (see Figure 11.14).

**Figure 11.14**
You can use the Create Format dialog box to create or edit an outline style.

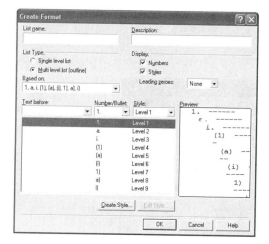

4. Type a name for your new style in the Outline/List Name box, and add an optional Description.

5. Choose the type of outline you want: Single Level List, or Multi Level List.

6. You can choose a Number Set (see Figure 11.15), although this isn't entirely necessary.

**Figure 11.15**
You can use predefined number sets or create your own in a custom outline style.

7. The dialog box lists all the levels used in this outline style, and at the top of the list are the following controls:

- Text Before—If you want text to appear before each outline number (for example, "Section"), select an option from the drop-down list or type your own text in this box.

- Number/Bullet—You can click the drop-down list and choose a number or bullet, or scroll down the drop-down list and click More (see Figure 11.16), which takes you to the Symbols dialog box, where you can choose from dozens of bullet icons (see Figure 11.17). After you choose the number or bullet you want, you can also add punctuation in the Number/Bullet text box, such as a period, a colon, or parentheses.

**Figure 11.16**
A drop-down menu offers several bullet and number styles, or you can choose More.

**Figure 11.17**
The Symbols dialog box offers dozens of possible bullet icons that you can use in a custom outline style.

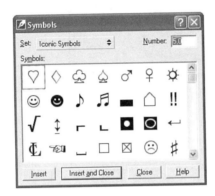

11

- Style—This applies predefined styles to the text and number or bullet you select. For example, the Level 1 style adds an indent code. You can further create and use formatting styles by choosing Create Style, creating the style, and then selecting it from the Style drop-down list. See Chapter 9, "Formatting with Styles," for more information on creating and editing styles.

8. Preview the results of your choices in the Preview area.

9. After you create or edit the style to your satisfaction, click OK to return to the Bullets & Numbering dialog box. Your new style now appears among the other styles (see Figure 11.18).

10. To use the style, click OK.

**TIP FROM**

One of the options in the Create Format dialog box is to use leading zeroes. This, along with text prefixes, can be handy for creating sequential parts lists, tickets, invoices, work orders, and the like, where you want to maintain a fixed number of digits. For example, you could have PN-001, PN-002, PN-003, and so on, up to PN-999, simply by creating the style, and using a numbered list with that style.

**Figure 11.18**
Custom outline styles appear in the palette of styles available in the Bullets & Numbering dialog box.

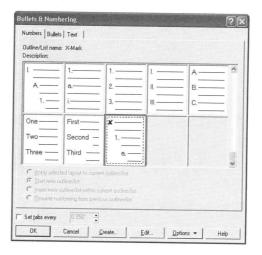

If you save your document, you also save the outline style with the document. However, if you want to save your style for use with other documents, you must access the Bullets & Numbering dialog box, and choose Options. Then save the style as described in Chapter 9.

→ For more information on saving styles that can be used in other documents, **see** "Saving Styles," **p. 278.**

# CREATING TEXT OUTLINE HEADINGS

WordPerfect also helps you create structured documents by using outline headings. Consider the document shown in Figure 11.19. Each section heading is a text outline style, and the corresponding level number appears in the left margin. In fact, you work with text heading outlines much more like you work with styles than you do with outlines.

## CREATING OUTLINE HEADINGS FROM A NUMBERED OUTLINE

One method for creating text outline headings is to create a regular numbered outline first. Make all major section headings outline level one, secondary section headings outline level two, and so on. However, do not apply outline headings to the narrative paragraphs included in the sections. These should be body text. When you complete the outline (see Figure 11.20), follow these steps:

1. Choose Insert, Outline/Bullets & Numbering. When WordPerfect displays the Bullets & Numbering dialog box, click the Text tab (see Figure 11.21).

2. Click the text style you want to use, typically the Headings style, and click OK.

WordPerfect now changes the numbered outline to a heading outline (refer to Figure 11.19).

Subtopics (Heading 2)     Major sections (Heading 1)

**Figure 11.19**
You can create structured text documents using the text-headings outline format.

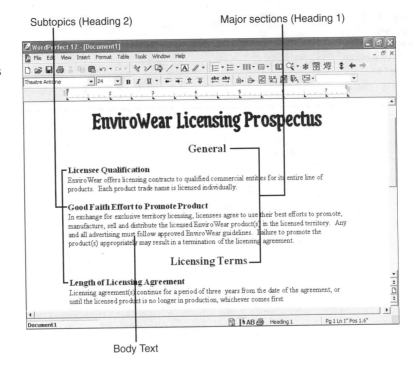

Body Text

**Figure 11.20**
One method for creating text outline headings is to create a regular numbered outline first.

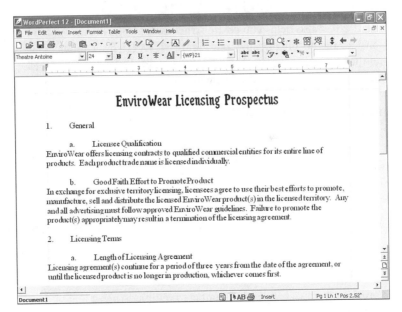

**Figure 11.21**
You can choose a text heading outline style from the Text tab of the Bullets & Numbering dialog box.

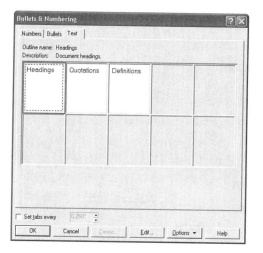

**CAUTION**

After you convert a numbered outline to a text-heading outline, you cannot change it back to a numbered outline without a great deal of effort. If you think you might want to use the numbered outline again, you should save the numbered outline before converting it to a text-heading outline.

11

## ADDING OUTLINE HEADINGS TO NEW OR EXISTING TEXT

A second method for creating a text-heading outline is to add heading styles to section and topic headings. You can also use this method to convert regular text to a structured text-heading outline.

To add heading styles to new or existing text, follow these steps:

1. Position the cursor on the line you want to make a heading (either a new line or existing text).

2. Choose Format, Styles. WordPerfect displays the Styles dialog box (see Figure 11.22).

3. Select the heading style you want. The heading number (for example, Heading 1) should correspond to the outline level you want. WordPerfect also displays the effect of that style in the preview box.

4. Click Insert to apply the heading style to the current paragraph.

5. Repeat steps 1–4 for all other headings in the document.

→ To learn how using headings can make it easier to define and generate a table of contents, see "Using Heading Styles to Mark Text," **p. 595**.

After you create the text-heading outline, you can use most of the tools on the property bar to work with the document. For example, you can use the following:

**Figure 11.22**
The Styles dialog box includes default text-heading outline styles.

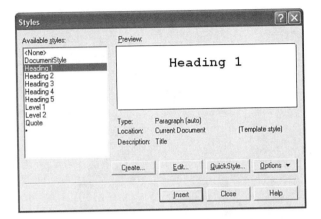

 ■ Show Icons—If you click this button, WordPerfect displays outline level numbers and text body icons in the left margin (refer to Figure 11.10). You can double-click outline level numbers in the margin to show or hide outline families.

 ■ Show Levels—Use this to display only certain levels, such as major section headings. All sublevels and their associated body text are hidden.

 ■ Promote/Demote—You can adjust the text heading outline levels by clicking the Promote or Demote buttons. For example, if you want to make a topic level heading a section heading, you could simply promote the topic.

 ■ Move Up/Down—Use these buttons to rearrange headings.

 ■ Hide Body—This works only on a single family at a time.

> **NOTE**  The Set Paragraph Number option does not work in text heading outlines.

# TROUBLESHOOTING

### HOW DID I TURN OFF OUTLINE NUMBERING?

*I pressed Ctrl+H as you suggested, but it turned off the outline number of my paragraph.*

Indeed, Ctrl+H (or clicking the Numbering button on the toolbar) turns off outline numbering for the current paragraph. You must first press Enter and then turn off outline numbering for the blank numbered line you just created. If you accidentally turn off numbering for a paragraph, simply position the cursor anywhere in the paragraph and click the Numbering button on the toolbar, or press Ctrl+H.

### Skipping Cursor

*I can't seem to move the cursor to the left of my paragraph number. Instead, when I press the left-arrow key, it skips up a line.*

Press Home once to move to the left of text of the numbered line. Then press Home again to move to the left of the paragraph number.

# Project

One of the easiest, yet most functional, uses for the outline feature is to create an agenda. When you use the default paragraph numbering style, not only can you create a numbered list, but you can also use other outline features to customize the agenda.

The following steps help you prepare an agenda that you can customize, using one version for yourself, and one for those attending your meeting:

1. Turn on the default paragraph numbering by clicking the Numbering button on the toolbar, or press Ctrl+H.

2. Create a fully defined agenda, using Tab to create sublevel information. As shown in Figure 11.23, make sure to add notes to yourself in the outline's sublevels, because the audience will see only what you place in level one.

**Figure 11.23**
You can create a detailed agenda for yourself using the default paragraph numbering style.

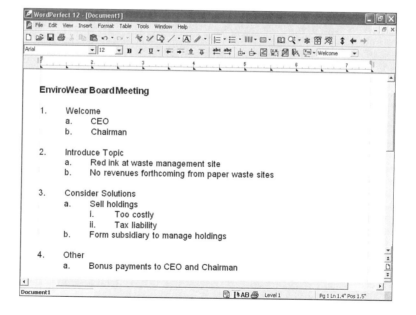

3. Print a copy for you.

4. Click the Show Levels button on the property bar, and choose One to hide all levels except level one (see Figure 11.24).

**Figure 11.24**
You can use the Show Levels option to show only the levels of the agenda you want everyone to see.

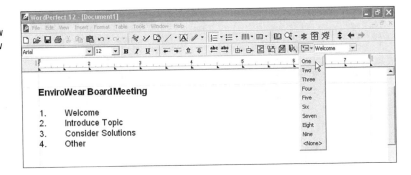

5. Sometimes hiding levels also removes extra blank lines between outline items. If necessary, add hard returns to add the needed blank lines.

6. Print a copy for those attending the meeting.

7. If you need to revise the agenda, show all levels again (click the Show Levels button on the property bar and choose Nine). Then repeat steps 2–6.

# WORKING WITH GRAPHICS

CHAPTER **12**

# ADDING GRAPHICS TO DOCUMENTS

**I**n this chapter

*by Read Gilgen*

# INSERTING GRAPHIC IMAGES

Although WordPerfect can do wonders with your text alone, it also provides a dazzling array of graphic elements that can jazz up nearly any document. Graphic images are only one of the available elements; you can also use horizontal and vertical lines, text borders, graphic shapes such as arrows, and background graphics called watermarks.

**CAUTION**

Working with graphics is fun! You can spend lots of time fiddling with graphic elements and have a great time following your creative instincts. However, remember that the basic content of the document should be your first concern. Then you can apply a judicious amount of graphics to enhance or illustrate what you say in the document.

**NOTE**

All the examples of graphics used in this chapter can be found in the WordPerfect Scrapbook or on the WordPerfect CD-ROM (Disc 2), except as noted.

## INSERTING CLIP ART

When you think graphics, you think pictures. Indeed, graphic images not only are easy to use, but what you learn about working with images also applies to nearly every type of graphic element used in WordPerfect. Increasingly, WordPerfect users have access to Internet images, scanned pictures, or photos from digital cameras.

Perhaps the easiest of all graphic images to use is *clip art*, which is predesigned artwork that comes with WordPerfect. Although you might be more interested in using that picture of your new Gizmo 2005 product, what you learn about working with clip art images will apply to photos as well.

To insert a clip art image in your document, follow these easy steps:

1. Position the cursor at the location where you want to insert the graphic image.

2. Choose Insert, Graphics, Clipart, or click the Clipart button on the toolbar. WordPerfect displays the Scrapbook dialog box (see Figure 12.1), which includes clip art, along with photos, video, and audio clips.

3. Scroll through the list of images and click the one you want.

4. Click Insert to place the image in your document.

**TIP FROM**

Read Gilgen

You can also place a clipart image in your document by dragging it from the Scrapbook dialog box and dropping it in your document.

**Figure 12.1**
The WordPerfect Scrapbook provides more than 10,000 clip art images (on CD-ROM), as well as photos and audio and video clips.

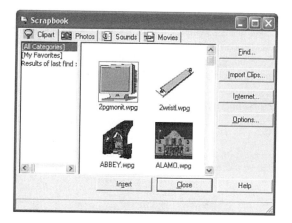

Note that the image pushes aside the text that surrounds it, in the shape of a rectangle (see Figure 12.2). Note also in the figure that a special Graphics property bar appears to help you manipulate and modify the image.

**Figure 12.2**
Graphic images are contained in graphics boxes that you can change by using sizing handles and the Graphics property bar options.

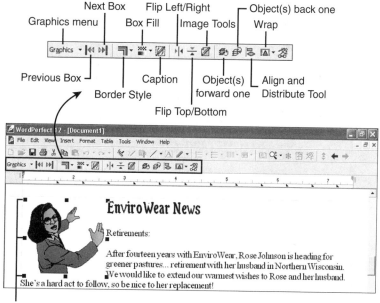

The rectangle that surrounds the image is called a graphics box, and when selected is surrounded by eight black boxes called sizing handles (refer to Figure 12.2). If you click elsewhere in the document, these handles disappear. If you click the image, you select the object, and the sizing handles appear again.

NOTE

> Images, and nearly all graphic or other inserted objects, are placed inside graphics boxes. As you work with graphics, you need to remember whether you're working with the graphics box (the container), or with the image (the content) itself. For example, you can change the border style or the size and shape of the box. Independent of any changes you make to the graphics box, you also can change the size and attributes such as brightness or contrast of the image within the box.

*If you are unable to delete an image you've inserted, see "Making It Go Away" in the Troubleshooting section at the end of this chapter.*

*If you are unable to make changes to a graphics box, see "Editing a Graphics Box" in the Troubleshooting section at the end of this chapter.*

*If you can't seem to select a graphics box, see "Difficulties Selecting a Graphics Box" in the Troubleshooting section at the end of this chapter.*

## RESIZING AND MOVING GRAPHICS

Now the fun begins. Unless you are very, very lucky, the graphic image probably isn't the right size or in exactly the right location. Fortunately, moving and sizing a graphics box is extremely easy.

To move a box, first select the box by clicking once on the image. Note that the mouse pointer changes to a four-way arrow (see Figure 12.3), which indicates that you are about to move the object. Drag the image to the precise location you want and release the mouse button to drop the image. You can do this over and over, until you place the image exactly at the right spot.

**Figure 12.3**
You can use the mouse to drag images and drop them where you want them.

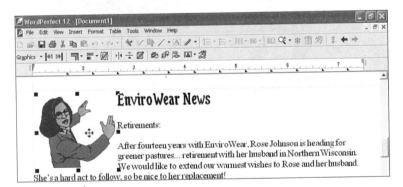

CAUTION

> Be careful not to double-click an image. Double-clicking any graphics box enables you to edit the contents of the box. If you double-click an image, you open WordPerfect's graphics editor. If this happens by mistake, simply click outside the graphics image area (for example, in the text) and start over.

To modify the size of the graphics box, use the sizing handles. Point at any of the corner sizing handles, and the mouse pointer turns into a two-way diagonal arrow (see Figure 12.4). Click and drag the sizing handle toward the center of the image to make it smaller, or away from the image to make it larger. Using the corner sizing handles also forces the image to grow or shrink proportionally.

**Figure 12.4**
Corner sizing handles enable you to enlarge or reduce the size of an image proportionally.

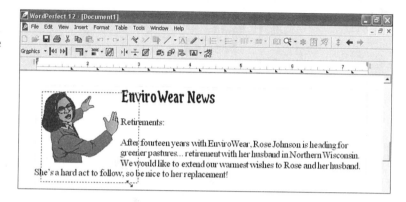

To change the size of the graphics box, and also distort the image it contains, point at any of the four sided handles so that the mouse pointer turns into a vertical or horizontal two-way arrow (see Figure 12.5). Click and drag the handle to change the shape of the box. You can create some very interesting effects by using the side handles, such as short, fat giraffes, or long, skinny pigs!

**Figure 12.5**
Dragging side handles distorts the image, sometimes in interesting ways!

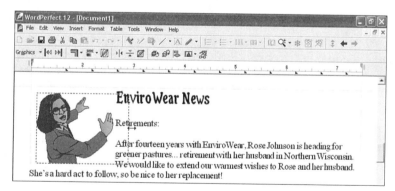

## SETTING BORDER, WRAP, AND FILL OPTIONS

Although the graphics box takes up rectangular space in your document, you might want to add a border to set it off more clearly from your text. To add a border to your graphics box, follow these steps:

1. Select the image by single-clicking it. The sizing handles indicate the box you selected.

**2.** Click the Border Style button on the property bar to display a palette of border styles (see Figure 12.6).

**Figure 12.6**
You can add a variety of border styles to graphics boxes.

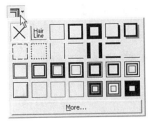

**3.** Click the border you want to use. WordPerfect adds the border to the graphics box (see Figure 12.7).

**Figure 12.7**
A border around your image helps set it off from the text.

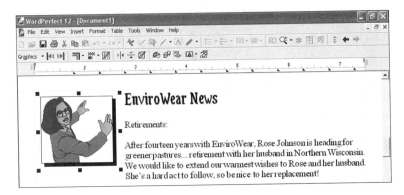

**TIP FROM**

Don't forget that simply hovering the mouse pointer over the style on the palette for a moment enables you to preview the style in the document before you actually select it.

In addition to borders, you can create a background for the box, which fills the box behind the image. WordPerfect calls this a fill pattern. With the graphics box selected, click the Box Fill button on the property bar and choose a fill pattern from the palette (see Figure 12.8).

Using predefined borders and fills is a good place to start. But as you become more experienced with what looks good, you can customize your graphics boxes to make them more distinctive.

**Figure 12.8**
You can fill in the background behind an image with a variety of fill patterns, including gradient shading.

Notice the More button in Figure 12.6 and Figure 12.8. This is just one way to access the Box Border/Fill dialog box (see Figure 12.9, which shows a border already selected). You can also access this dialog box by clicking the Graphics button on the property bar and choosing Border/Fill; or you can simply right-click the image and choose Border/Fill from the QuickMenu.

**Figure 12.9**
The Box Border/Fill dialog box gives you greater control over the properties of your graphics box.

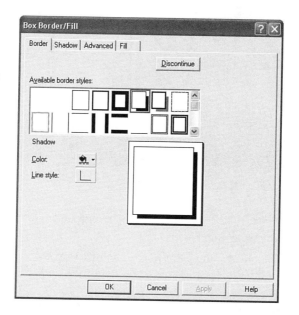

On the Border tab of the Box Border/Fill dialog box, you find the same palette of styles you find behind the Border Style button on the property bar. The default style is to include a bit of spacing between the image and the text, without any line. Here you can choose a different line style, and click Color to select a line color from a palette. Clicking the Discontinue button has the same effect as clicking the <None> style in the upper-left corner of the list.

The Fill tab offers the same palette of choices you find on the property bar, with the following additions (see Figure 12.10):

- If you choose a solid pattern, you can choose a color from the Foreground palette. Changing the Background color has no effect on solid colors.

**Figure 12.10**
The Fill tab of the Box Border/Fill dialog box enables you to add patterns, gradient shading, and even image backgrounds.

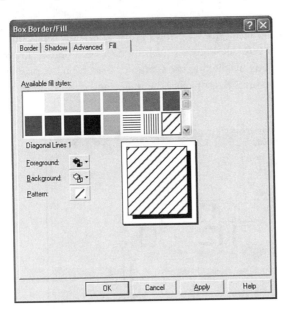

- If you choose a pattern, you can also specify the foreground and the background colors. Pattern lines use the foreground color.
- If you choose a gradient shading pattern, you choose a start color and an end color. WordPerfect blends the background from one color to the other.

The Advanced tab enables you to further customize your borders and fills (see Figure 12.11, which has several changes already made). Custom options include the following:

- You can change the amount of space between the border and the image by changing the inside spacing. Select a predefined spacing amount from the spacing palette, or specify an exact measurement in the spacing palette text box, as shown in Figure 12.12.
- You can choose rounded corners for the box, and you can even specify how round the corner radius should be.

**Figure 12.11**
You can fine-tune spacing, corners, and gradient shading in the Advanced tab of the Box Border/Fill dialog box.

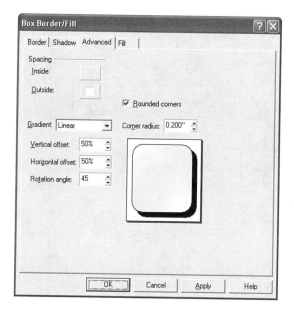

**Figure 12.12**
The Spacing palette helps you set just the right amount of space between your image, the text, and the surrounding box.

- You can modify the style and angle of your gradient shading. For example, if you want to create a linear reflective effect, you can adjust a light starting color to 50% vertical offset against the darker ending color. You can also change the rotation angle (for example, 45%), and then adjust the horizontal offset as needed.

The Shadow tab enables you to add an offset shadow to the graphics box in any direction (see Figure 12.13). Begin by choosing the general direction of shadow you want; then, use the scrollbars or the counter boxes to specify the exact shadow height and shadow width. You can also change the shadow color.

 By default, text wraps around both sides of a graphics box. If you want to change the way it wraps, click the Wrap button on the property bar (see Figure 12.14). Point at each menu option and observe the effect on the text surrounding the graphics box. Click an option to apply it to a graphics box.

→ To learn what all the text wrap options mean and how to use them, **see** "Making WordPerfect Text Work with Graphic Objects," **p. 396.**

→ To **see** how to use graphic objects, **see** "Customizing Graphic Images," **p. 413.**

**Figure 12.13**
The Shadow tab of the Box Border/Fill dialog box enables you to create attractive drop shadows.

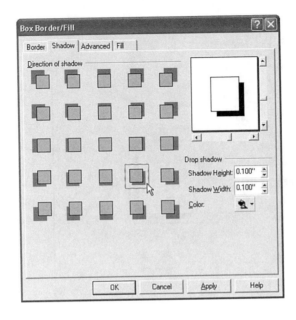

**Figure 12.14**
WordPerfect enables you to wrap text around your graphics nearly any way you want.

## USING THE SCRAPBOOK

 WordPerfect's Scrapbook is a power tool for organizing and finding just the right graphic image for your document. You access the Scrapbook by choosing Insert, Graphics, Clipart, or by clicking the Clipart button on the toolbar. WordPerfect displays the Scrapbook (see Figure 12.15).

**NOTE**

The Scrapbook itself does not contain graphic images, but instead is a catalog of images available for you to use.

**Figure 12.15**
The Scrapbook is WordPerfect's system for helping you manage and use graphics and other multimedia images.

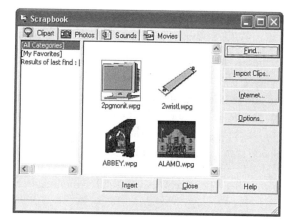

When searching for images, maximize the Scrapbook Screen before scrolling through the displayed images. WordPerfect has to open each image from its source location, which can cause delays in displaying the images. Also, when possible, go directly to a category instead of scrolling through [All Categories].

By default, the WordPerfect Scrapbook displays the basic collection of installed clip art images. The other tabs in the dialog box display installed photographs, sound files, and video clips.

Although you can scroll through the collection to find the image you want, you can also use the Find feature to search for images based on filenames or keywords. To find a Scrapbook item, click Find. WordPerfect displays the Find Scrapbook Item dialog box (see Figure 12.16).

**12**

**Figure 12.16**
The Find Scrapbook Item dialog box helps you search for images using keywords, filenames, and file types.

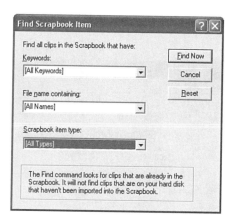

### SEARCHING FOR SCRAPBOOK IMAGES

You can search for images in the Scrapbook using one or more of the following options:

- Keywords—All images in the basic clip art collection have keywords assigned to them. Type a keyword to see which images might fit.

- File Name—If you know the name of the file, or even if you know only part of the file-name, you can type the name in the File Name Containing edit box.

- Scrapbook Item Type—There are many graphic image types, and each is identified by the filename extension. For example, WordPerfect's standard format typically ends in .wpg. Internet graphic images usually end in .jpg or .gif. If you have imported different graphic images to your Scrapbook, you can search for the images based on their image type.

> **NOTE**
>
> Non-WordPerfect images such as photos or Internet graphic images can be found on the Photo tab of the Scrapbook.

Suppose you want to find all the images that have rivers or lakes in them. To find an image using a keyword, follow these steps:

1. Click Find to open the Find Scrapbook Item dialog box (refer to Figure 12.16).
2. Type the keyword in the Keywords edit box (for example, *water*).
3. Click Find Now.

WordPerfect searches for all images that have matching keywords and displays the results, as shown in Figure 12.17. Note the new category on the left side of the dialog box: Results of Find. You can return to the complete list of images by clicking [All Categories]. You can then also return to the found images by clicking the Results of Find category. If you want to search for photos or other non-WordPerfect images, be sure to click the Photos tab before following the previous steps.

**Figure 12.17**
WordPerfect creates a separate Scrapbook category to display the results of a search for graphic images.

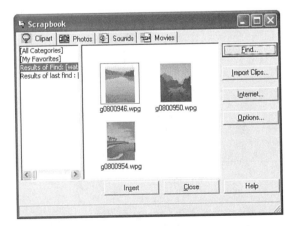

For more successful searches, try different keywords, but search for only one at a time. Also, try both the singular and plural forms of the keyword because WordPerfect does not find parts of words.

**NOTE**

If you close the Scrapbook, all Results of Find categories are lost, except the most recent one. When you open the Scrapbook again, the result of your last search is listed as Results of Last Find.

### ADDING KEYWORDS TO SCRAPBOOK IMAGES

WordPerfect's default keywords are quite limited, but you can add your own keywords to images in the Scrapbook. Simply select the image, click Options, and choose Item Properties. WordPerfect displays the Scrapbook Item Properties dialog box (see Figure 12.18). Add any new keywords in the Keywords edit box, separating each keyword with a space (do not use commas to separate keywords). If it might make a difference later when you're searching, include both the singular and plural forms of a keyword. Click OK to return to the Scrapbook.

**Figure 12.18**
Use the Scrapbook Item Properties box to add keywords or to assign an image to one or more categories.

Adding your own keywords in the Scrapbook can be quite handy when you later search for images. A little time spent adding keywords can pay off in the long run.

## USING SCRAPBOOK CATEGORIES

If you have an extensive collection of clip art, you can organize it into specialized categories. To create and use categories, follow these steps:

1. Choose Options, Create Category, and when prompted, type a category name and choose OK. WordPerfect then displays the category in the list at the left of the Scrapbook.

2. Select an image you want to include in the new category.

3. Choose Options, Item Properties to access the Scrapbook Item Properties dialog box (refer to Figure 12.18).

**NOTE**

Note that you can also add new categories from the Scrapbook Item Properties dialog box.

4. Click the category to which you want to add the image.

5. Click OK.

After you create a category, you can also use the Options button to rename or remove it.

**NOTE**

Removing a category, or even a single scrapbook image, does not delete it from your hard disk. It simply removes it from the Scrapbook.

## IMPORTING IMAGES TO THE SCRAPBOOK

You can import individual graphic images to your Scrapbook, as well as clip art collections from earlier versions of WordPerfect. You can also import non-WordPerfect clip art, including Internet images or digital photographs (see "Using Other Clip Art" later in this chapter).

**NOTE**

Importing images to the Scrapbook does not actually place the file for that image in the Scrapbook. Instead, WordPerfect merely inserts a cataloged reference back to the original file. If the file later becomes unavailable, the cataloged Scrapbook image remains, but a large red X on the graphics means that you cannot open the actual image from the Scrapbook.

To import individual graphic images, follow these steps:

1. From the Scrapbook, select the category to which you want to import the image.

2. Click Import Clips and then use the Insert File dialog box to browse to the graphic image you want to import.

3. Click Open to import the image.

4. WordPerfect displays the Scrapbook Item Properties dialog box (refer to Figure 12.18). Add keywords if you like, assign the image to one or more categories, or add a new category for the image. Click OK to add the image to your Scrapbook.

**NOTE**

If you select several images to import at one time, WordPerfect asks whether you want to set properties for each item. Unless you are importing relatively few images, answer No, and set image properties later. Otherwise, you are stuck either setting the properties or having to click Cancel for each and every imported image.

5. After you import images and add keywords, click Options and choose Update All Thumbnails. Although this might take several minutes, you can't use keywords to find your newly imported files until you do.

WordPerfect 7 and 8 also shipped with useful graphics that you can import into your WordPerfect Scrapbook. Such collections typically come in a single file that ends with the .scb filename extension.

To import such collections, follow these steps:

1. In the Scrapbook, create a new category to which you will import these graphic images.

2. Click Import Clips.

3. Browse to find the .scb file (for example, compact.scb, which is the name of the sample clip art used in WordPerfect 8). Click Open.

4. Although WordPerfect warns that this might take a few minutes, it usually takes only a few seconds to import the collection. When asked whether you want to delete the original file, answer No.

WordPerfect 9 did not package its clip art in .scb files. As a result, you must import individual files if you want to include them in your WordPerfect Scrapbook.

The clip art collections found in WordPerfect 10, 11, and 12 are identical, so there is no need to import images from these versions, for example, from 10 to 12.

### USING CD CLIP ART

When you install WordPerfect, by default, only a handful of images are actually copied to your computer (or to your network). The rest of WordPerfect's extensive collection, including some 10,000 clip art images, remains on your CD-ROM.

**NOTE**

> Prior to version 10, WordPerfect shipped with a printed catalog of available clip art images. Since WordPerfect 10, you can find a PDF-formatted electronic catalog on the second CD-ROM. You must use Adobe Acrobat Reader (also included) to view or print these pages.

To use the CD clip art, follow these easy steps:

1. Insert the CD-ROM that contains the graphic images (usually disc 2).

2. If the CD automatically displays an installation screen, close it.

3. Open the Scrapbook. WordPerfect automatically finds the graphics on the CD and adds several new categories to your scrapbook (see Figure 12.19).

**Figure 12.19**
When the Clip Art CD is inserted, the Scrapbook displays several new categories and thousands of new clip art images.

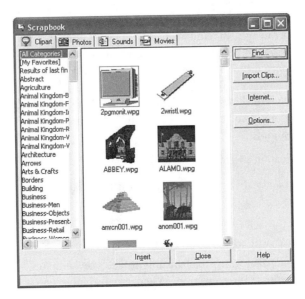

4. Click a category, and then select and insert a graphic image as you usually do.

**TIP FROM**

*Read Gilgen*

> If you'll be accessing the Scrapbook often, don't close it after inserting an image. Instead, minimize the Scrapbook and then click the Clip Art button on the toolbar to return to the Scrapbook. That way, any CD-based images you might have viewed remain active, along with their keywords.

You should be aware of the following when using CD clip art:

- When the CD is in the CD-ROM drive, all CD images are available. If the CD is removed, the categories and the images from the CD disappear.

- You cannot change the item properties for CD images. However, you can copy a CD image to one of your own categories where you can then change the properties.

- If you want to use the CD images from you hard drive or from a network drive in the Scrapbook, you must import the individual graphic images.

- If you're using a network version of WordPerfect, you should ask your system administrator to copy the clip art folders to a network drive that is accessible by everyone.

**NOTE**

You can copy the CD images to your hard drive and make them work automatically with the Scrapbook, but the process is tricky and involves modifying the Windows Registry. Go to the Corel Web site, and search the Corel KnowledgeBase for the word "Scrapbook" to find more information. At the time of this writing, Article 206652 covered this topic.

Unless you're comfortable editing the Windows Registry, you are better off just making sure the CD is available and inserted in your CD-ROM drive when you are working with the Scrapbook.

### USING OTHER CLIP ART

You can import nearly any kind of graphic images into your Scrapbook, including .jpg and .gif Internet images, or photographs that have been scanned or that come directly from a digital camera. By default, however, non-WordPerfect images such as these can be found on the Photo tab of the Scrapbook, not on the Clipart tab.

→ To learn more about inserting non–clip art images, such as digital photos, directly into your document without using the Scrapbook, **see** "Importing Graphics," **p. 417.**

**12**

For example, if you click the Internet button in the Scrapbook, WordPerfect connects you to the Corel Web site where you can download a variety of WordPerfect and other images. After you place these images on your hard drive, you can add them to your Scrapbook.

**NOTE**

The Internet button promises more than it delivers. This button links to Corel's OfficeCommunity.com Web site, which, although it is no longer updated, still provides some useful clip art images.

# USING LINES AND BORDERS

Although images are the most obvious graphic elements one adds to a document, other elements such as lines and borders also add visual impact and help organize the text in the mind of the reader. Horizontal lines can help identify divisions or sections of text—

for example, a horizontal line that separates the heading information of a memo (TO:, FROM:, and so on) from the message of the memo. Vertical lines help the reader follow the flow of text—for example, in the columns of a newsletter.

## INSERTING HORIZONTAL AND VERTICAL LINES

To insert a horizontal line that extends from one margin to the other, simply place the cursor where you want the line, and choose Insert, Line, Horizontal Line, or press Ctrl+F11. WordPerfect places a thin, single, black line in your document (see Figure 12.20). Because the line is a graphical line, not based on text characters, it fits perfectly between the margins even if you later change the margins or the font of the document.

**Figure 12.20**
Easy to add, horizontal lines help separate sections of text.

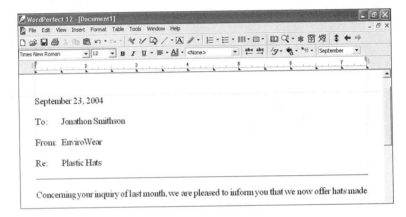

Inserting vertical lines works the same way. Simply position the cursor where you want the vertical line (for example, at the left margin), and choose Insert, Line, Vertical Line, or press Ctrl+Shift+F11. WordPerfect inserts a thin, single, black vertical line in your document that extends from the top to the bottom margins. Note, however, that because the vertical line sits nearly on top of the text, this default location is not terribly useful.

Fortunately, you can easily create custom lines that are any length, size, or color, and that you can place anywhere in the document. Because lines are graphic objects, you can also move and edit default horizontal or vertical lines.

To move a line (for example, you could move a vertical line just to the left of the left margin), follow these steps:

1. Move the mouse pointer toward the line until it changes to an arrow.
2. Click the line to select it. WordPerfect treats the line just like it does any graphics box. Sizing handles appear, and the mouse pointer changes to a four-way arrow (see Figure 12.21).

12

**Figure 12.21**
If you select a graphic line, you can move and size it the same way you do any graphic image.

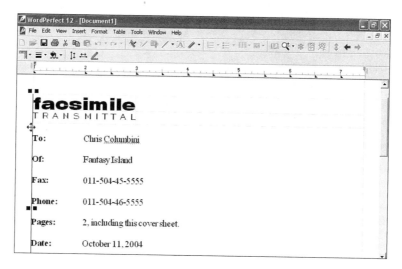

3. Drag the line to the new location (for example, about 1/10 inch to the left).

4. Click anywhere in the text to deselect the line.

Indeed, you treat graphic lines as you do any other graphic object. Here are some examples:

- To delete a line, simply select it and press Delete or Backspace.

- To change the size or shape of a line, drag the sizing handles. For example, to make a thicker line, drag any of the sizing handles from the center of the line until you see the size you want. By default, WordPerfect creates a solid black line.

- To edit a line, right-click it and choose Edit Horizontal (or Vertical) Line from the QuickMenu, or simply double-click the line. Alternatively, you can select the line and choose Edit, Edit Graphic Line from the menus.

Whether you choose to edit an existing line or to create a custom line, the dialog box and the options are the same. Choose Insert, Line, Custom Line, and WordPerfect displays the Create Graphics Line dialog box, which is identical to the Edit Graphics Line dialog box you get if you choose to edit an existing graphics line (see Figure 12.22).

In the Create Graphics Line dialog box you can create a vertical or horizontal line, and preview the results before inserting the line into your document. Options for creating or editing a horizontal graphic line include the following:

**TIP FROM**

*Read Gilgen*

If you edit a horizontal line and select Vertical Line, you remove the horizontal line and replace it with a vertical line.

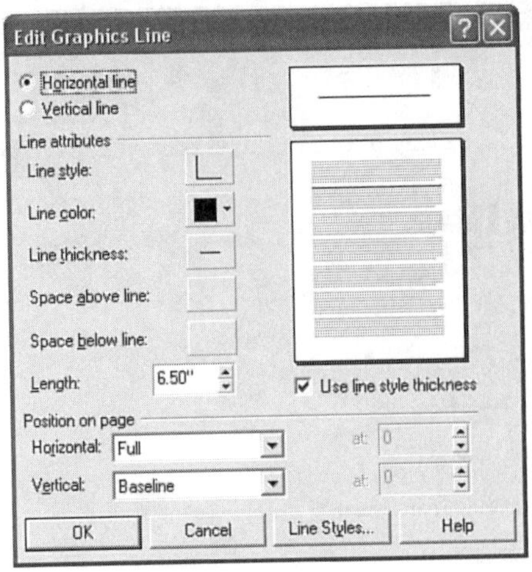

**Figure 12.22**
You can create a custom line length, thickness, or color by using the Create Graphics Line dialog box.

- Line Style—By default, WordPerfect inserts single, black lines. You can click the palette button to choose from other predefined line styles (see Figure 12.23). The drop-down list at the bottom of the palette gives you the same choices as clicking the Line Styles button at the bottom of the dialog box.

**Figure 12.23**
WordPerfect offers many predefined line styles to choose from when creating a custom line.

- Line Color—You can choose a different color from the palette. If you want to reset the color, choose Use Line Style Color from the palette.
- Line Thickness—You can choose a new line thickness from the palette, or specify an exact thickness in the counter box on the palette.
- Space Above Line/Space Below Line—These options appear only when creating or editing horizontal lines. To put distance between the line and its surrounding text, choose more space from the palette buttons.
- Length—The default length for horizontal lines is the distance between the left and right margins. If you want a longer or shorter line, specify the length here.
- Horizontal—This option refers to the location where the line begins or how it is aligned horizontally. The left, right, center, and full options are obvious. Set enables you then to specify a measurement in the At box that indicates the exact location where the lines begin, relative to the left edge of the paper. By default, when you choose Set, WordPerfect gives you the location of your cursor, and adjusts the line length to extend from that point to the right margin.

- Vertical—By default, WordPerfect places a horizontal line at the baseline (bottom of the characters) on the line of text your cursor is on. If you choose Set, you then specify the distance from the top edge of the paper to where the line begins.

When editing or creating a vertical line, the dialog box changes slightly, and some of the options work differently. The following are some examples:

- Border Offset—This appears only when you're creating or editing vertical lines and is used to specify the amount of space between the vertical line and the text to its right.

- Length—The default length for vertical lines is the distance between top and bottom margins. If you want a longer or shorter line, specify the length here.

- Horizontal—You can align a vertical line at the left, right, or center of the text, or set the exact horizontal location of a vertical line on the page. If you choose Column Aligned, the At box changes to After Col, and you indicate which column the line should follow.

- Vertical—Here you can align a vertical line at the top, bottom, or center, or from the top to bottom margin of the text (full). If you choose Set, you then specify the distance from the top edge of the paper to where the line begins.

→ To learn more about creating newspaper style columns, **see** "Setting Up Columns," **p. 250.**

**TIP FROM**

*Read Gilgen*

If you want to create different lines between each of the columns (for example, one thick line and one thin line) or otherwise customize the lines between columns, use this Custom Line feature. However, if all you want is single thin black lines between your columns that extend from the top to the bottom margins, choose Format, Columns, Border/Fill to access the Columns Border/Fill dialog box. Then choose the Column Between style. No fuss, no muss.

12

## ADDING BORDERS TO PARAGRAPHS AND PAGES

You can apply line styles to surround text paragraphs and document pages. These text borders are very similar to borders used for graphics boxes. Unlike lines you insert, borders are styles you apply to various WordPerfect elements such as text paragraphs and columns. The information on customizing borders in the section "Setting Border, Wrap, and Fill Options," earlier in this chapter, applies also to text and page borders.

→ For more information on adding line borders to paragraphs, **see** Chapter 7, "Formatting Lines and Paragraphs."

→ For more information on adding line borders to pages, **see** "Adding Borders Around Pages," **p. 256.**

# INSERTING SHAPES

If you think adding clip art and lines is fun, wait until you start adding shapes. Beginning with version 8, WordPerfect added the capability to draw graphic shapes directly on a document, a feature that has been dramatically enhanced in recent releases of WordPerfect.

WordPerfect's graphic shapes fall into three basic categories. Although each has similar characteristics, you create, edit, and manipulate each slightly differently:

- Lines—Each of the line types has a beginning and end, and you can even add arrow heads or tails to them.
- Closed shapes—These include boxes, circles, action buttons, and specialty shapes.
- Callout shapes—These are similar to closed shapes, but they also enable you to add text in them to make it easier to create callouts.

You can access shapes in one of the following ways:

- From the menus, choose Insert, Shapes to display the Draw Object Shapes dialog box (see Figure 12.24).

**Figure 12.24**
The Draw Object Shapes dialog box offers a complete array of graphic shapes, but it is a bit more clumsy to use than the toolbar buttons.

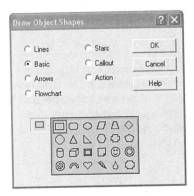

- From the Graphics toolbar, choose View, Toolbars, and then select the Graphics toolbar and click OK; or simply right-click the WordPerfect toolbar and choose Graphics. WordPerfect displays the Graphics toolbar, from which you can choose various shapes (see Figure 12.25).

**Figure 12.25**
The Graphics toolbar makes it quick and easy to add a graphic shape to your document.

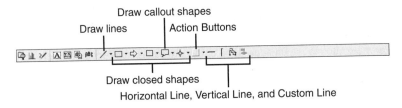

■ From the Draw Combined Shapes button on the WordPerfect toolbar. This button combines several of the most useful shapes into one easily accessible button.

**NOTE**

The Draw Combined Shapes initially looks the same as the line button on the Graphics toolbar. However, as you select a different shape—for example, a star—that shape appears on the button. Also, the Draw Combined Shapes button gives you access to all of WordPerfect's shapes, not just lines.

The following sections concentrate on the Draw Combined Shapes button. You'll probably want to use the menus and Graphics toolbar as well to explore the full range of graphic shapes.

## ADDING LINE SHAPES

 To examine the choices available on the Draw Combined Shapes button, click the drop-down arrow on the right side of the button. WordPerfect then displays a palette of choices (see Figure 12.26). These include several line styles, closed objects, and callout styles.

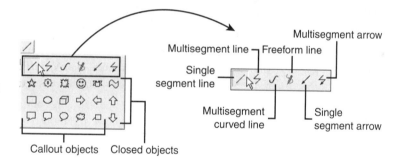

**Figure 12.26**
The most commonly used graphic shape types are included on the Draw Combined Shapes button on the toolbar.

12

To draw a line shape on your document, follow these steps:

1. Click the line style you want to use from the Draw Combined Shapes palette (refer to Figure 12.26). WordPerfect displays the icon for that style on the button, and the button appears to be selected.

2. Move the mouse pointer to the text area and note that it is a crosshairs shape.

3. Position the pointer where you want the line to begin.

**TIP FROM**

These procedures are used for creating both lines and arrows. You can save time by always starting lines at the tail of the imaginary arrow, and ending them at the arrowhead.

4. Click and drag to the opposite end of the line.

**TIP FROM**

*Read Gilgen*

You can draw a line from a center point by holding down the Ctrl key while you drag your line. As you drag away from the center point, the line extends an equal distance in the opposite direction.

**TIP FROM**

*Read Gilgen*

You can constrain your lines to 15-degree angles by holding down Alt+Shift while you drag the line. Thus, your lines can be perfectly aligned horizontally, vertically, or at 15, 30, or 45 degrees, and so on.

5. If you're creating a single-segment line or arrow, release the mouse button to add the line on top of your text.

For other line types, the procedures vary slightly:

- If you're creating a multisegment line, click to change directions. Drag to the next juncture and click. Continue until you reach the end; then, double-click the mouse to complete the line.

- If you're creating a multisegment curved line, click each time you want to start a new curve. As you drag the mouse in a new direction, note that WordPerfect rounds the line on both sides of the point that you click. To complete a curved line, double-click.

- Freeform drawing works just like drawing with a pencil. Click and drag in any direction, and WordPerfect draws a line to match. Release the mouse button to complete the line.

**TIP FROM**

*Read Gilgen*

You can draw freeform segments of multisegment lines or arrows by holding down the mouse button instead of releasing it before you change directions. When you want to resume straight lines again, release the mouse button.

After you complete your line shape, note that WordPerfect places the shape in a graphics box, complete with sizing handles (see Figure 12.27). The shape also covers any text or other objects that lie beneath it. You can adjust the size of the box or move the box as needed.

**CAUTION**

If you add several shapes or objects in the same area, it can become difficult to accurately select and move or modify some of the objects. If this happens, simply right-click where you think the object is, choose Select Other from the QuickMenu, and select the object you want.

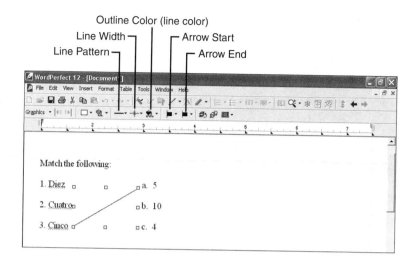

**Figure 12.27**
Graphic shapes are easy to use, and layered on your text, they add pizzazz and clarity to your document.

With the shape selected, WordPerfect displays the graphics line editing tools on the property bar (refer to Figure 12.27).

The following are some of the changes you can make to a shape:

- Shadow—From the palette of choices, you can create a drop shadow in any of four directions.

- Shadow Color—The shadow color is a solid color and not a lighter version of the shape's color. For example, if you want a gray shadow for a black object, you must choose gray as the shadow color.

- Line Pattern—Choose from solid and dashed or dotted lines. If you click the large X, you get no line.

**CAUTION**

If you choose no line for a line shape, you lose arrowhead options on the property bar. Simply double-click the line (guess where it is!) to display the Object Properties dialog box, where you can make all the changes you need.

- Line Width—Choose the width of your line.
- Outline Color (Line Color)—Choose the color you want the line to appear.
- Arrow Start—Change the look at the beginning of the line by using one of the arrow heads or tails from the palette (see Figure 12.28).
- Arrow End—You can change the look at the end of the line. Note that you can actually have two arrowheads, two tails, or any other combination you like.

**Figure 12.28**
You can create attractive and functional arrows by adding arrow tails and heads to graphic lines.

- Object(s) Forward One or Object(s) Back One—If you create more than one shape in the same area, the most recent object lies on top of the stack of objects. This option enables you to change the order of an object to be in front of or behind other objects.

- Wrap—By default, text does not wrap around the shapes, but instead the shapes appear in front of the text. You can change the way text wraps just as you do for any graphics box.

## ADDING CLOSED OBJECT SHAPES

The lines of closed object shapes come together, such as in a circle, and thus their inside area is closed. By default, such objects are drawn with thin single lines and are filled with an aquamarine-like green color (your results may vary).

You draw closed shapes differently from the way you draw open shapes. Let's use a five-point star to illustrate the procedure:

1. Click the drop-down palette on the Draw Combined Shapes button to display the list of available shapes (refer to Figure 12.26).

2. Click a closed object, such as the five-point star. WordPerfect displays the star on the button, and the pointer turns into crosshairs.

3. Position the pointer at one corner of the area you intend to fill with the shape (for example, the upper-left corner).

4. Click and drag the pointer to the opposite corner (for example, the lower-right corner).

5. Continue holding the mouse button while you move the pointer, until you have exactly the right size and proportions.

**TIP FROM**

*Read Gilgen*

If you hold the Shift key down while dragging the mouse, WordPerfect constrains the object to be symmetrical—for example, a circle instead of an oval or a square instead of a rectangle.

6. Release the mouse button to place the object on the document (see Figure 12.29).

Glyph

**Figure 12.29**
Closed object and callout shapes are filled with color. Note the glyph, which is used to change the style of a graphic shape.

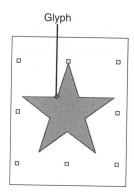

If the object has one or more glyphs, which are small pink-colored diamond handles, you can manipulate the shape or the perspective of the shape. For example, on the five-point star, you can drag the glyph toward the center of the object to create a skinny starfish look. You can drag it away from the center to create a fat sheriff's star look.

The glyphs on a circle (oval) enable you to create a partial circle, a pie shape (with a missing piece), or an open arc (see Figure 12.30). Drag the glyph around the edge of the circle. When you release the mouse button, a small gray square appears in the middle of the circle. Click it once to create a pie, click it again to create an arc, or click it again to close the partial circle.

**Figure 12.30**
You can drag the circle glyph and click the center box for three different partial-circle effects.

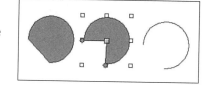

12

You can, of course, use the sizing handles to further change the shape or size of the object, and you can move the object to the exact location where you want it.

In addition, with the shape selected, WordPerfect also displays the graphics editing tools on the property bar (refer to Figure 12.27). The buttons are the same as those used for lines, except that the Arrow Start and End buttons are replaced by the Fill Style palette and buttons to change the foreground and background fill colors.

**TIP FROM**

*Read Gilgen*

If you want to create a contoured area around which text wraps—for example, to reserve space for something you must paste into the printed copy—you can create a closed object shape. Then, change the wrap option to contoured, both sides; change the line style to none, and change the fill color to white.

**NOTE**

Although you can make many changes to the properties of closed objects from the property bar, you have more precise control and more options by double-clicking the object and using the Object Properties dialog box.

## ADDING CALLOUT SHAPES

Callout shapes are similar to closed object shapes, and are created by following the same procedures. The difference is that after you create a callout, WordPerfect also creates a text box inside it, where you can type text to go along with the callout (see Figure 12.31).

Text box handles

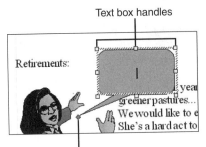

**Figure 12.31**
A callout is a closed object shape with a text box.

Glyph to move callout pointer

You can create a callout in several ways:

- Type text to fill in the callout text box. By default, such text is centered both horizontally and vertically, but you can change the text just as you do other text in your document. For example, you can change the alignment or change the font or color.
- Use the sizing handles to change the size of the callout area. If what you type exceeds the space of the callout area, WordPerfect does not automatically expand the box, so you need to use the sizing handles to resize the area.
- Reorient the callout pointer. Drag the glyph at the end of the callout pointer to any side of the callout, and stretch the pointer until it's directed at the callout source (see Figure 12.32).

**Figure 12.32**
You can move the callout pointer to any side of the callout by dragging the glyph.

**NOTE**

> You might have to deselect the callout and select it again to get the crosshairs pointer you need to move the callout glyph (refer to Figure 12.32).

■ Use other options on the property bar to modify the callout object. For example, you can change the fill pattern or color, position the callout behind text by changing the wrap option, and so on.

■ Right-click the object and use the QuickMenu for other tools, such as wrap, position, or size.

**TIP FROM**

> Instead of using new text in a callout text box, you can position the callout so that it encloses text already in the document. If you simply want to see through the callout to the text behind, turn off the fill pattern. If you want to keep the fill pattern and still see the document text, change the callout's wrap option so that it appears behind text.

# USING WATERMARKS

In expensive bond paper, a watermark in the paper itself lends a distinctive look. Hold a piece up to the light, and you see an image—perhaps along with words—that helps identify the paper brand or content. WordPerfect watermarks also add a distinctive look by adding a lightly shaded graphic image behind the text of your document.

Watermarks are extremely easy to create:

1. Position the cursor at the beginning of the document.

**NOTE**

> Watermarks function like headers in that they appear on every page, beginning at the page where you insert the watermark code, continuing until you turn off the watermark.

2. Choose Insert, Watermark. WordPerfect displays the Watermark dialog box (see Figure 12.33).

**Figure 12.33**
You can use the Watermark dialog box to create or edit background watermark graphics.

3. If this is a new watermark, and the first one you've created in this document, choose Watermark A, and click Create. WordPerfect next displays a blank, full page where you create or edit the watermark graphic. Figure 12.34 shows what the Watermark screen looks like after you have added a watermark.

**Figure 12.34**
A watermark image is text or a graphic image, displayed at 25% brightness.

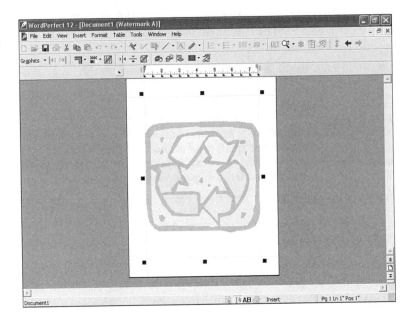

4. You can use graphics from any source that you would use in the document itself. For example, you can click the Clipart button to display the Scrapbook.

5. Scroll through the Scrapbook list until you find the graphic image you want.

6. Select the graphic and click Insert to place it on the Watermark screen (refer to Figure 12.34).

Note that the graphics box, complete with sizing handles, fills the entire page. The image itself is shaded lightly so as not to interfere with the text that will appear on top of it. You can size and position the graphic image just as you do any other graphic image, using the mouse and the sizing handles.

Click outside the graphics box area (in the margins, for example), and WordPerfect displays on the property bar the following options for modifying the watermark (see Figure 12.35):

**Figure 12.35**
The Watermark property bar helps you modify a watermark graphic.

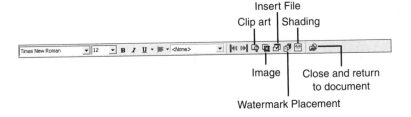

- You can add other images, and size and position them by clicking the Clipart, Image, or Insert File buttons.

- You can choose whether to place the watermark on odd pages, even pages, or both, by clicking the Watermark Placement button.

- You can change the shading of the watermark by clicking the Shading button. By default, both text and graphic watermarks are shaded only 25% of their full color (or darkness).

**CAUTION**

Rarely do you need or want to make a watermark darker. Doing so usually conflicts with document text in front of the watermark. More often, you need to lighten the watermark to make it less conspicuous.

 When you're satisfied with the look of the watermark, click the Close button on the property bar. If the watermark graphic is selected (that is, if you can see the sizing handles), you can close the Watermark editing screen by choosing File, Close. WordPerfect then returns you to the document-editing screen and displays the watermark in the background (see Figure 12.36).

**Figure 12.36**
Watermarks can add attractive, as well as useful, backgrounds to a text page.

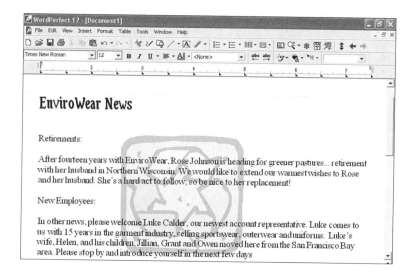

# USING KEYBOARD-MOUSE COMBINATIONS

When creating shapes, it's easy to think only of using the mouse. However, as noted in several tips throughout this section, you can also modify mouse actions by using the keyboard. Table 12.1 lists these shortcuts.

TABLE 12.1    KEYBOARD-MOUSE COMBINATIONS FOR DRAWING SHAPES

| Keystroke/Mouse Action | Effect |
| --- | --- |
| Shift+Drag | Symmetrical (Squares, Circles, Stars: all closed shapes) |
| Alt+Shift+Drag | Snap to angle in 15-degree increments |
| Ctrl+Drag | Shape starts from center and expands outward (lines, closed) |
| Shift+Ctrl+Drag | Symmetrical shapes starting from the center (closed shapes) |

# TROUBLESHOOTING

### MAKING IT GO AWAY

*I inserted the wrong image, but I can't seem to use Delete or Backspace to get rid of it.*

WordPerfect does not delete the box code when you backspace or delete unless Reveal Codes is on. You can, of course, turn on Reveal Codes to delete the graphics box code, but an easier way is to click the object to select it. Now, pressing Backspace or Delete does indeed remove the image.

### EDITING A GRAPHICS BOX

*I want to edit my graphics box, but can't find the tools I need.*

Don't forget that you must first select a graphic image, so that the sizing handles appear, before the Graphics menu and other graphics buttons appear on the property bar. You must deselect it to get back your normal text editing tools.

### DIFFICULTIES SELECTING A GRAPHICS BOX

*You tell me to select a graphics box, but for some reason I can't do so.*

If you add several shapes or objects in the same area, it can become difficult to accurately select and move or modify some of the objects. If this happens, simply right-click where you think the object is, choose Select Other from the QuickMenu, and select the object you want.

### WHERE DID ALL THIS COME FROM?

*I tried to select a graphic image, but now there's a funny-looking hashed line around the edge of the graphic and a toolbar down the left side.*

If you double-click a graphic image, WordPerfect opens the image in the draw program editor (actually, it opens the image in Corel Presentations). Click outside the graphics box (for example, in the text), and WordPerfect closes the editor. In the future, to select an image, just single-click it.

# PROJECT

Using WordPerfect's graphics features, your creative genius can kick into high gear. But adding attractive graphics doesn't have to be time-consuming or difficult. In this example, you'll add talking children to an article describing earth-friendly environmental policies.

Begin by creating your text. This is an extremely important first step because you don't want to add graphics until you've settled on how much text you have and where it should be located (see Figure 12.37).

**Figure 12.37**
Before adding graphics, you should create, edit, and format your text.

To add the children, follow these steps:

1. Position the cursor where you want the children to appear—for example, at the right side of the document.
2. Click the Clipart button on the toolbar (your Graphics CD, Disc 2, should be in your CD-ROM drive).
3. Scroll through the Scrapbook until you find the children (in the category People-Children), and click Insert.
4. Position and size the image exactly where you want it.
5. Right-click the image, choose Wrap, and change the wrap to contour on the left side of the image.
6. Click the Draw Combined Shapes button and choose a callout shape style.
7. Draw the callout shape to the upper left of the children.

8. Type the text of the callout in the text box; for example, `Please take care of our planet!`

9. Click outside the text box to deselect the callout and then click the callout.

10. Drag the glyph to reposition the callout pointer, so that it points at the children.

11. Use the QuickMenu or the property bar to change the callout's color (for example, to light yellow) and the callout's wrap (for example, contour on the left side).

The end result, as shown in Figure 12.38, looks great, and as you can see, it wasn't at all difficult to create.

**Figure 12.38**
You can insert graphics and callouts to add emphasis and pizzazz to your documents.

CHAPTER **13**

# CUSTOMIZING GRAPHIC SHAPES AND IMAGES

**In this chapter**

*by Read Gilgen*

# MAKING WORDPERFECT TEXT WORK WITH GRAPHIC OBJECTS

Graphic elements such as clip art, lines, or watermarks can do wonders to spice up an otherwise mundane document. However, the core of the document is still the text. Getting text and graphics to coexist in your document requires some skill and a lot of patience. Not only must you find room for your graphic images, but you have to make sure the text is readable and that the graphics support rather than overwhelm what you're trying to say. In addition to what you learn here, trial-and-error also will be your teacher.

**CAUTION**

Using graphics, especially on computers that have limited memory (that is, RAM), increases the chances of program crashes. Save your work frequently while working with graphics to avoid losing painstaking work.

**NOTE**

All graphic images used in this chapter can be found in the Scrapbook or on the WordPerfect Office CD-ROM, Disc 2, unless otherwise noted.

## WRAP OPTIONS

 When you insert a graphic image in your document, you insert a rectangular graphics box that contains the image. How the body of your text interacts with the graphics box, or with the image it contains, depends on the *wrap* method you choose.

By default, WordPerfect wraps text on both sides of a graphics box rectangle. To see other wrap options, right-click the graphics box and choose Wrap from the QuickMenu (see Figure 13.1).

**Figure 13.1**
You can choose wrap options from the Wrap Text dialog box.

WordPerfect offers five basic options for wrapping text around an image (see Figure 13.2 for examples of each):

**Figure 13.2**
Wrapping text means making room around a graphics box for the text that surrounds it. You can also wrap text in front of or behind images.

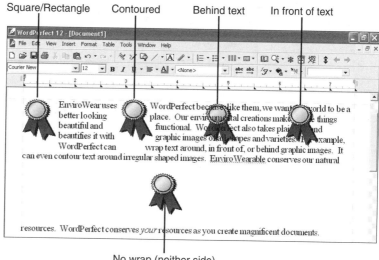

■ **Square**—This option leaves a small margin of white space between the outside of the graphics box rectangle and the text that surrounds it. The side the text appears on depends on the other options you choose. For example, you can choose to wrap text on both sides, on the left or the right sides, or only on the largest side (the side with the most text).

**CAUTION**

> If you use the option to wrap text around both sides, you should check the wrapped text to make sure the image has not split words and that the way the words wrap makes sense. Consider not only the visual result, but also the text flow; because wrapped images interrupt the text flow, you need to verify that the reader will be able to follow along.

■ **Contour**—Using the Contour option, you can wrap the text so that it contours to the image contained in the box, instead of to the box itself (refer to Figure 13.2). This can result in a very professional-looking document. You can also specify which sides the text appears on. Note, however, that if you add a border of any kind to a contoured graphics box, the wrap option reverts to Square.

■ **Neither Side**—This option means you do not wrap text around the box, but instead, leave blank spaces on each side of the graphic image. In effect, the text wraps only on the top and bottom of the graphic image. For example, equation graphics boxes, by default, do not wrap on either side.

■ **Behind Text**—When you place an image behind the text, or in front of the text, you effectively turn off wrapping altogether. This option is used whenever you need to position an image without disturbing the text around it, such as in a poster (see Figure 13.3).

**13**

**Figure 13.3**
By turning off the wrap option, placing a larger image in front of the text and a smaller image behind the text, you create a sense of three-dimensional depth in a sign or poster.

- In Front of Text—When you place an image in front of the text, you also effectively turn off wrapping altogether. You often use this option in documents such as posters where covering part of the image with text doesn't interfere with what's being presented (refer to Figure 13.3).

**NOTE**

If you select the Front of Text option but the graphic doesn't print in front of the text, try choosing the option from the Advanced tab in the Print dialog box to Print Text as Graphics.

**TIP FROM**

*Read Gilgen*

An even easier way to select a wrap style is to click the Wrap button from the property bar. As you hover the mouse pointer over each option, WordPerfect previews the effect in the document itself. You can click an option to apply it to the selected graphics box.

## WORKING WITH GRAPHIC LAYERS

If you add more than one graphic element at the same location, you create layers of graphics. The bottom layer is the image you inserted first, and the top layer is the graphic you inserted most recently. If you select an object and also move it, that object moves to the top layer. WordPerfect also helps you specify the order of the graphics layers.

By changing the size and order of the objects in the layers, you can combine graphics into rather interesting and effective images. For example, in Figure 13.4, four clip art images are shown in their original size. If you want to create a stack of dollar bills, make that and the stack of gold bullion proportional to Scrooge, and place a dollar bill floating behind him, you must change the order of the layers.

**Figure 13.4**
Four graphic images have been inserted in the document, layered one of top of another, at their original size.

 If you're having trouble selecting the graphics box you want, see "Selecting the Correct Graphics Box" in the Troubleshooting section at the end of this chapter.

If you accidentally double-click an image, see "Exiting the Graphics Editing Screen" in the Troubleshooting section at the end of this chapter.

To change the order of graphic object layers, follow these steps:

1. Click the object you want to change (for example, the flying dollar bill object).

**TIP FROM**

*Read Gilgen*

If you select an image, but the sizing handles don't seem to match the graphics box for that image, click again until you select the correct box. This works even if the box you want to select is hidden behind another image.

2. Click the Graphics menu on the property bar (see Figure 13.5), or right-click the object and choose Order from the QuickMenu.

**Figure 13.5**
You can access Graphics menu commands from the property bar or from the QuickMenu.

13

3. From the menu choose one of the following options:

- To Front—This moves the object all the way forward, to the top layer.
- To Back—This moves the object all the way backward, to the bottom layer.
- Forward One—This moves the object forward only one layer. Other objects may still remain on top of or in front of it.
- Back One—This moves the object back only one layer, so other objects may remain beneath or behind it.

4. Repeat steps 1–3 until all the objects are in the proper order.

Now, after you adjust the size (by dragging the sizing handles of the graphics box) and position (by dragging the graphics box) of the graphic objects, you create the effect of a composite graphic image, as shown in Figure 13.6. You may have to resize, relocate, and reorder images several times to get just the effect you want.

**Figure 13.6**
You can size, position, and change the layer order of multiple graphics to create the effect of one image.

> **NOTE**
>
> Setting some images to wrap in front of the text and others to wrap behind the text creates two separate groups of graphics layers, each separated by the text itself. If you try to make a graphic that is behind the text move to the front, it only moves to the top layer of all the images that reside behind the text. Likewise, moving an image that is in front of the text all the way to the back causes it to move only to the bottom layer of all the images that reside in front of the text.

## CHANGING SIZE AND CONTENT OPTIONS

Moving and sizing objects with the mouse is quick and easy, but not always perfectly accurate. If you're creating a complicated layout of text and graphics, you might find it easier to use dialog boxes to specify exact locations, sizes, and content of the graphics boxes.

To specify an exact size for a graphics box, follow these steps:

1. Select the graphics box.

2. Click the Graphics menu button on the property bar, or right-click the graphics box.

3. Choose Size from the menu. WordPerfect displays the Box Size dialog box (see Figure 13.7).

**Figure 13.7**
You can use the Box Size dialog box to specify an exact height or width of an image.

4. Set the width and height and click OK.

The options for width and height include the following:

- Full—This means that the graphic will extend from margin to margin.

- Set—Use this option to specify the exact measurement of the graphics box. This is particularly useful when you want several images to be exactly the same size, such as in a photo gallery.

- Maintain Proportions—Unless you intend to distort the image, you should set the exact size of one side, and then choose this option for the other.

## ANCHORING IMAGES

By default, WordPerfect images are anchored to a page. That is, if you move the text, the images remain at the same location on the page. You can also anchor images to paragraphs or to characters. In these cases, the images move as the text moves. To set the exact position of a graphic image, follow these steps:

1. Select the image.

2. Click the Graphics menu on the property bar, or right-click the image and select Position.

3. Choose one of the following methods from the Attach Box To drop-down list for anchoring the graphic, and specify the image's precise location:

- Page—This is the default anchor when you insert a graphic image. The position options change in the Box Position dialog box (see Figure 13.8) if you select a different anchor. You can adjust the horizontal position relative to the left edge of the paper, the margins, or text columns. You set the vertical position relative to

13

the top edge of the page, or to the top or bottom margins. Typically, the image moves with the text of the page it is anchored to, but if you check Box Stays on Page, the image remains on the current page (for example, page 1).

**Figure 13.8**
Options for anchoring an image to a page are found in the Box Position dialog box.

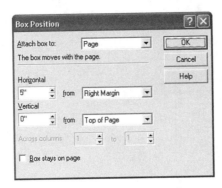

• Paragraph—If you choose to attach the box to a paragraph (see Figure 13.9) the box moves with the paragraph. You can specify the horizontal position relative to the left edge of the paper, to the margins, or the center of the paragraph. You set the vertical position relative to the top of the paragraph. With the box anchored to the paragraph, when you drag the box with the mouse, a pushpin appears to show you which paragraph the box is anchored to (see Figure 13.10).

**Figure 13.9**
You can choose Paragraph in the Box Position dialog box to display these options.

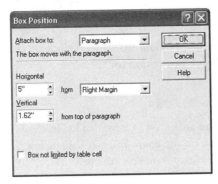

13

• Character—The image moves as the character it is anchored to moves. Note in Figure 13.11 the many options for positioning the image relative to the character. The preview box shows the effect of each option. Character anchoring is a more precise way to attach an image to your text, but it also can cause problems with the text that surrounds it because the line height of the text changes to accommodate the graphic image (see Figure 13.12).

A pushpin indicates the location of the paragraph anchor

**Figure 13.10**
When an image is anchored to a paragraph, a pushpin appears as you move the graphic to show you where it is anchored.

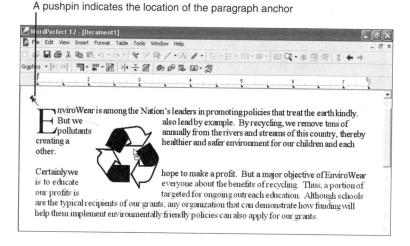

**Figure 13.11**
You can choose the character anchor type to display these options, which enabled you to preview the results.

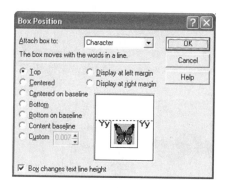

**Figure 13.12**
If you anchor an image to a character, you cause the text line height also to change to the height of the graphics box.

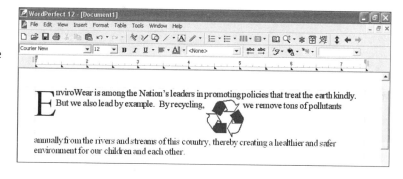

4. Click OK to apply the specified positioning to the image.

 *If you're having trouble with graphics not moving when you edit your text, see "Anchoring Images Correctly" in the Troubleshooting section at the end of this chapter.*

## USING ALIGN AND DISTRIBUTE

The Align and Distribute feature enables you to position objects on the screen more precisely than you can by merely dragging and dropping the objects. For example, if you want several graphic objects to appear evenly spaced across the top of the page, such as in a photo gallery of your real estate offerings, you can use the Align and Distribute feature to place each object in its proper place, quickly and easily.

The Align and Distribute tool involves two separate concepts and procedures. One is to align all the objects relative to a location on the page. The other is to distribute all the objects relative to one another.

To align five graphics across the top of the page, for example, follow these steps:

1. Select all five objects by holding down the Shift key while clicking on each separate object. Note that you can select graphic images, graphic shapes, or even text boxes (see the example in Figure 13.13).

**Figure 13.13**
You can align and evenly distribute several objects at once by selecting them and using the Align and Distribute tool.

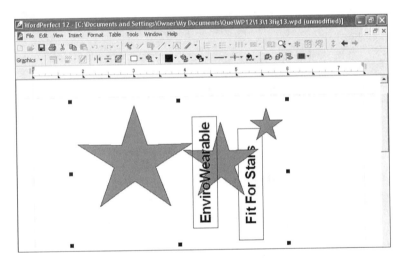

2. Click the Align and Distribute button on the property bar, or right-click the selected objects and choose Align and Distribute from the QuickMenu. WordPerfect displays the Align and Distribute dialog box (see Figure 13.14).

3. On the Align tab, choose the location on the page where you want to align the objects. For example, if you want all the objects aligned at the top edge of the document, select Top from the Vertical Alignment section, and Edge of Page from the Align in Relation to the Page section.

4. Click OK to align the objects at the top margin.

**Figure 13.14**
Use the Align options in the Align and Distribute dialog box to align objects relative to the page and to one another.

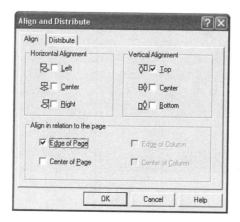

WordPerfect warns you that using this tool might change the anchor positions of the objects. Go ahead and click OK, because you can always use Undo if things don't work the way you expect them to. Note also that WordPerfect maintains the relative horizontal position of the selected objects.

**TIP FROM**

*Read Gilgen*

Don't forget that before you can use Undo, you must first click somewhere else in the document to deselect any graphic images you might have selected.

**NOTE**

You can use the Align option to align single objects. However, you must have at least two objects selected to use the Distribute option.

To spread the objects evenly across the page, follow these steps:

1. With the objects selected, click the Align and Distribute button on the property bar, or right-click the selected objects and choose Align and Distribute from the QuickMenu. WordPerfect displays the Align and Distribute dialog box.

2. Click the Distribute Tab to view the Distribute options (see Figure 13.15). If the options are grayed out, you have only one object selected and you'll have to go back and select at least two objects before you can use the Distribute option.

3. Select any horizontal option to spread the objects horizontally, or any vertical option to spread them vertically. The options refer to how the objects will line up relative to evenly spaced division points across the page. For example, choosing Center will align the center of the objects on those division points.

**13**

**Figure 13.15**
Use the Distribute options in the Align and Distribute dialog box to spread out objects relative to the page and to one another.

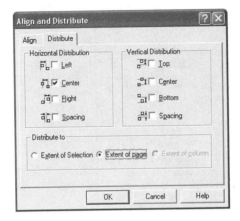

4. Click Extent of Selection if you want the objects to spread across the space currently occupied by the selected objects, or select Extent of Page if you want them to spread from margin to margin.

5. Click OK, and WordPerfect distributes the objects evenly across the page, as shown in Figure 13.16.

**Figure 13.16**
The Align and Distribute feature makes it easy to position multiple objects evenly across the page.

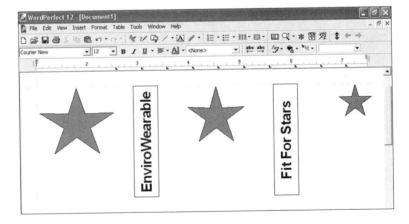

**NOTE**

Unless you have several objects selected, you might see little, if any, difference when choosing different distribution options. You might have to experiment to find which settings work best for you.

## ADDING CAPTIONS

Image captions are useful for identification. Not only can you add text description, but you also can add figure numbers that automatically sequence throughout the document.

To add a caption, follow these easy steps:

1. Select the graphic.

2. Click the Graphics menu on the property bar, or right-click the graphic and choose Caption. WordPerfect displays the Box Caption dialog box (see Figure 13.17).

**Figure 13.17**
The Box Caption dialog box enables you to create, edit, and position captions for a graphics box.

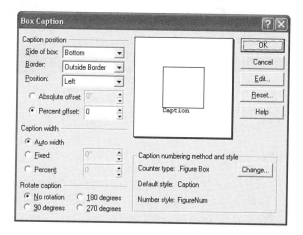

**NOTE**

You cannot add captions to graphic shapes such as lines or arrows, but you can add them to clip art and other images you place in a graphics box.

3. Click Edit to create the text of the caption. WordPerfect automatically places the figure numbering style along with the text *Figure n* (where *n* is the number of the box to which you're adding a caption). If you don't want that information, press Backspace once to delete it.

4. Type the caption information. Use the property bar to modify the font, size, and other attributes of the text.

**CAUTION**

The font of the caption is based on the document default font. If you change the font in the text, but don't change the default font, the caption font might not match your text.

5. Click the Close button on the property bar to return to your text, or just click in the text area. WordPerfect adds the caption to your graphics box, as shown in Figure 13.18.

**NOTE**

When you add a caption outside the graphics box border, the graphics box extends to include the caption, but a graphics box border surrounds only the image. Document text wraps around both the image and the caption.

13

**Figure 13.18**
Captions add information and are numbered sequentially to help you refer the reader to the images in your document.

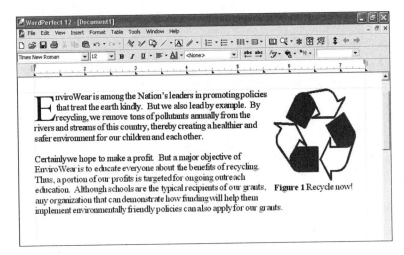

By default, WordPerfect creates captions that appear at the bottom left, outside the graphics box border. Using the Box Caption dialog box (refer to Figure 13.17), you can modify the caption to fit your needs. The options include the following:

- Side of Box—You can place the caption on the top, bottom, right, or left of the graphics box.

- Border—You can place the caption inside or outside the box border.

- Position—You can position the caption at the left or right, top or bottom, or center of the side you select. Or you can be even more precise by specifying an exact offset, by measurement or by a percentage of the available width.

- Caption Width—You can let WordPerfect do the calculating for you, or you can specify an exact measurement or percentage of available space for the width of your caption.

- Rotate Caption—If you place the caption on either side of the graphics box, you might want to rotate the caption 90 degrees (left side) or 270 degrees (right side). Rotating top or bottom captions doesn't make much sense, but you can do it.

- Caption Numbering Method and Style—By default, WordPerfect counts boxes according to the types of boxes they are. For example, each figure box is numbered sequentially, as are text boxes, equation boxes, and so on. You can change the box type, which also changes the box number. However, unless you are working with a long document where box numbers are important, you do not need to change the box type.

- Reset—Use this option if you want to delete a caption. This also sets options back to their original defaults.

# ADDING TEXT BOXES AS GRAPHIC OBJECTS

Text boxes are similar to graphics boxes except that their content is text instead of graphic images. Text boxes are useful for adding labels to your document—for example, on top of a graphic image.

## CREATING TEXT BOXES

To create a text box, follow these steps:

1. Position the cursor where you want to place the text box.
2. Click the Text Box button on the toolbar, or choose Insert, Text Box from the menu. WordPerfect places in your document a text box with a single-line border, aligned at the right margin (see Figure 13.19). The hash marks around the text box and the blinking cursor indicate that WordPerfect is waiting for you to add or edit text.

**Figure 13.19**
A text box is distinctive in that it is surrounded by hash marks, and the blinking cursor indicates where to type or edit text.

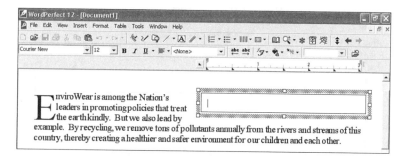

3. Type, edit, and format the text of the text box. If the text wraps, or if you press Enter, the box expands vertically.
4. Drag the right-center sizing handle far enough to the left that you don't have a lot of extra white space in the right side of the box.
5. Move the box itself by positioning the mouse pointer at the edge of the box (the pointer becomes a four-way arrow), and dragging the box to the desired location.
6. Click outside the box to deselect it.

**NOTE**

> To edit a text box, click the text area of the box. To move a box, however, you must move the mouse pointer to the edge of the box until you see the four-way arrow. To select a box to delete it, you must first click the edge of the box. Otherwise, you only delete text within the box.

You can apply all box formatting options to text boxes, the same way you do to graphics boxes. For example, you can change the way text wraps around the text box, the border, the background, and so on.

**13**

**TIP FROM**

*Read Gilgen*

If you want to add a text label to a graphic image, create a text box and wrap it in front of the text. You might have to change the order of the graphic image and the text box so that the text box appears in front of the image.

## ROTATING TEXT

Often you need labels that aren't horizontal. Fortunately, you can easily rotate the text within a text box. To rotate text in a text box, follow these steps:

1. Select the box. Remember that you must click at the edge of the box, not in the text area, so that the Graphics property bar appears.

2. Click the Graphics menu on the property bar and choose Content. WordPerfect displays the Box Content dialog box (see Figure 13.20).

**Figure 13.20**
You can use the Box Content dialog box to rotate text in a text box.

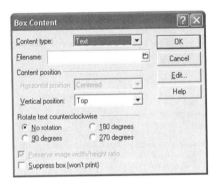

3. From the Rotate Text Counterclockwise section, choose 90, 180, or 270 degrees.

**NOTE**

You can rotate the contents of a text box only in 90-degree increments. If you need to rotate text at some other angle, you must create the text as a graphic drawing object.

→ For more information on adding custom text images, **see** Chapter 14, "Adding Drawings and TextArt."

4. Click OK to rotate the text in the text box.

If you rotate text, the editing process for that text changes. When you click the text box that contains rotated text, WordPerfect opens a Text Box Editor screen (see Figure 13.21). Although it appears that you have the whole screen to work with, WordPerfect limits the editing area to match the width of the text box itself. Make any changes you want and click the Close button on the property bar to return to the document.

**Figure 13.21**
When editing rotated text, you use the Text Box Editor screen. Note that text wraps at the text box margins, not at the margins of the editing screen.

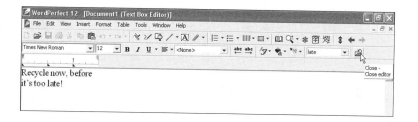

**TIP FROM**

If you intend to add a lot of text to a rotated text box, select the box first and drag the side sizing handles to give yourself more room. Then, click the center of the box to enter the Text Box Editor screen.

*If you want to move a rotated text box and can't do so without going into the special editing screen, see "Moving a Rotated Text Box" in the Troubleshooting section at the end of this chapter.*

## STICKY NOTE BOXES

One particularly useful text box style is the sticky note text box. This box is similar to other text boxes, but it contains a yellow background and it wraps in front of your document text, just like a sticky note! Unfortunately, this custom text box is a bit hard to find unless someone shows you where it is.

To add a sticky note to your document, follow these steps:

1. Position the cursor on the line where you want the sticky note.

2. Choose Insert, Graphics, Custom Box. WordPerfect displays the Custom Box dialog box (see Figure 13.22).

**Figure 13.22**
Among styles available in the Custom Box dialog box is the Sticky Note Text style.

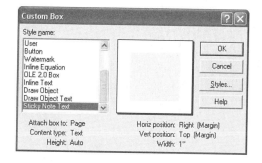

**13**

3. Scroll through the Style Name list box, and select Sticky Note Text.

4. Click OK to add a sticky note text box to your document.

You edit and manipulate the sticky note text box the same way you do any text box. Because the box covers text, you might want to have it wrap behind or beside the text, or simply remove it before printing.

→ For information on WordPerfect's document collaboration features such as Comments, Document Compare, and Document Review, **see** Chapter 17, "Collaborating on Documents."

## WATERMARK TEXT BOXES

Watermarks need not be only graphic images. You can also create your own text watermarks.

To create a text-based watermark, follow these steps:

1. Choose Insert, Watermark from the menu.
2. If you're creating a new Watermark A, click Create.
3. In the Watermark A editing screen, add text and format it. For example, you can change the font, the font size (72 points equals 1 inch high), center the text horizontally, or center the page vertically (by choosing Format, Page, Center).
4. Note in Figure 13.23 that WordPerfect automatically changes solid black text to 25% gray. However, you can also lighten or darken that shading by choosing Format, Font, and by changing the font's shading percentage.
5. If you want, you can also add graphic images along with your text.
6. Click the Close button to add the watermark to your document.

→ To learn more about using WordPerfect's watermark feature, **see** "Using Watermarks," **p. 389.**

**Figure 13.23**
Text used as a watermark appears at 25% black. You can use text along with images in a watermark.

# CUSTOMIZING GRAPHIC IMAGES

In Chapter 12, "Adding Graphics to Documents," and so far in this chapter, we have focused on modifying and manipulating the graphics box, or the container of the graphic image. Borders, sizing, backgrounds, and wrapping are all elements that apply largely to the box border. But graphics boxes are like windows through which you view the contents—you can also modify or customize what you see inside the graphics box.

## CHANGING BOX CONTENTS

You can change the contents of a graphics box, or the way the image is displayed, without affecting the size, border, or other changes you have made to the graphics box itself.

To change the contents of a box, first select the box, and then from the Graphics menu on the property bar, choose Content. WordPerfect displays the Box Content dialog box (see Figure 13.24), where you have the following options:

**Figure 13.24**
You can use the Box Content dialog box to change the image or to change the type of content used in a box.

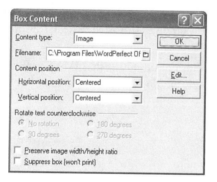

- Content Type—Typically, content is an image. However, you can also choose Empty (a box with nothing in it), Text, or Equation. A final choice, Image on Disk, is useful if you want to display and print the image with the document, but don't want to store a copy of the image in the document itself. For example, if you specify that the graphics used for a letterhead logo remain on disk, you don't store a separate copy of the image with each letter you produce.

**CAUTION**

> If you choose to use the Image on Disk option, the image does not print if someone else who does not have access to that image tries to print the document. In a network environment, be sure that images you want everyone to be able to use are accessible by everyone before using this option.

13

NOTE

If you edit the image (for example, you double-click the image and open it in the Draw program), the content type changes to OLE object and the filename changes to Presentations 12 Drawing.

→ For more information on using the Draw program, **see** "Adding Drawings by Using Presentations," **p. 428.**

- Filename—You can use the Browse button to find and insert a graphics file into the current box, replacing the one that's already there.
- Content Position—These settings affect where the content appears within the box. By default, images are centered both vertically and horizontally. However, if you change the box size, you might want to position the image at the left or right, or at the top or bottom of the box. If the content of the box is text, you can also rotate the text in 90-degree increments.
- Preserve Image Width/Height Ratio—If you drag the side sizing handles when reshaping a box, the graphic image also becomes distorted. Check this option to prevent image distortion.
- Suppress Box (Won't Print)—This option means that WordPerfect prints the document with space reserved for the image, but does not print the image or the box border or caption, if any.

## USING IMAGE TOOLS

WordPerfect's image tools enable you to customize a graphic image itself. You can move the image, rotate it, flip it, size it, or change its brightness and contrast.

To access the image tools, first select the graphics box of the image you want to edit and then click the Image Tools button on the property bar or right-click the graphics box and choose Image Tools from the QuickMenu. WordPerfect displays the Image Tools dialog box (see Figure 13.25).

Typically, you choose an option and use the mouse, or select from palettes of options to make changes to the image. The following are some of the options:

- Rotate—Click this option, and WordPerfect displays four diagonal sizing handles at the corners of the image, but inside the graphics box. Drag a handle to the right or left to rotate the image inside the box.

TIP FROM

Read Gilgen

When you rotate an image, often the edges of the image don't fit within the box without being trimmed. To avoid this, scale (zoom) the image to a smaller size, and then rotate it.

**Figure 13.25**
The Image Tools dialog box enables you to modify the image inside a graphics box.

- Move—After clicking this option, drag the image in any direction. Remember that the graphics box is like a window through which you view the graphic image. If you move part of an image beyond the border of the graphics box, you place it out of sight, and that part of the image does not display.

**TIP FROM**

You can move an image beyond the edge of a graphics box border if you want to crop or trim part of the image. For example, if the very bottom of an image isn't pertinent to your document, you can move the image down far enough that the edge of the box crops the bottom of the image.

- Flip—You can flip the image horizontally, flip the image vertically, or both.

**TIP FROM**

If all you want to do is flip the image, just click the Flip buttons on the property bar and bypass the Image Tools dialog box altogether.

- Zoom—Clicking this option gives you a palette of three choices (see Figure 13.26). The magnifying glass enables you to click and drag an area of the image. WordPerfect then zooms to that area. Clicking the up/down arrow displays a scrollbar that enables you to decrease (up) or increase (down) the size of the graphic image. The 1:1 option restores the image to its full, original size.

13

**Figure 13.26**
The three image zoom tools enable you to crop an image, scale it, or restore it to its original size.

CAUTION

If you size the image by cropping it, WordPerfect resizes the graphics box to match the cropped image. If you restore the image, it goes back to being the complete image, but it might not fit neatly inside the newly defined box. You might have to move the image inside the box, or drag the box sizing handles to restore the graphics box shape and size.

- BW Threshold—If you want to print the image in black and white (without shades of gray), choose one of the options on the BW Threshold palette. To turn color back on, click the large X button on the palette.

- Contrast—This palette, which is similar to the Brightness palette shown in Figure 13.27, enables you to adjust the dark/light contrasts in an image.

**Figure 13.27**
The Brightness palette enables you to choose a preset brightness. The Contrast palette looks similar and works the same way.

- Brightness—This palette (refer to Figure 13.27) helps you choose a shading for the colors of the image. Watermark images, for example, use buttons from the bottom row of the palette.

- Fill—These options generally aren't terribly useful. The blue butterfly is the default (as shown in the Brightness and Contrast palettes) when you're using all of the image's colors. The others display only those parts of the image that are black and white.

- Invert Colors—This option creates a negative of the image.

- Edit Contents—This option opens the image in the drawing editor.

  → For more information on the drawing editor, **see** "Adding Drawings by Using Presentations," **p. 428.**

- Edit Attributes—If you need to make precise settings to a variety of attributes, you can choose this option to display the Image Settings dialog box (see Figure 13.28), where you select the attributes you want to change, specify exact settings, preview the results in the preview box, and click OK to apply them to the image.

**Figure 13.28**
The Image Settings dialog box enables you to specify by exact numbers the changes you want and to preview them.

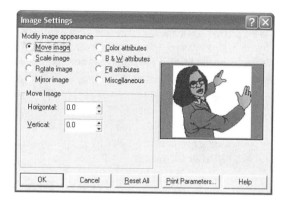

- Reset Attributes—If you want to restore all the original image settings, choose this option.

To close the Image Tools dialog box, click anywhere in the document, or click the Close button on the dialog box.

## EDITING IMAGES IN PRESENTATIONS

The preceding sections deal with modifying an entire image—for example, its brightness or rotation. However, if you install Corel Presentations as part of the Office 2000 suite (which is highly recommended), that program also serves as the drawing editor in WordPerfect. With it you have a full range of options for editing WordPerfect clip art and other graphic images. For example, you can remove or add parts of images and change coloring.

→ To learn more about using the drawing editor (Corel Presentations) to edit images, **see** "Editing WordPerfect Graphics in Presentations," **p. 440.**

# IMPORTING GRAPHICS

One of WordPerfect's strengths is its capability to import graphic images from a variety of sources. WordPerfect clip art is in the .wpg (WordPerfect Graphics) format, but there are many different graphic formats in use today. You can insert most types of graphic formats from other programs, as well as photographs from scanners or from digital cameras.

In Chapter 12 you learned how to insert images using WordPerfect's Scrapbook. In this section you learn how to insert image files directly into WordPerfect.

## INSERTING OTHER GRAPHIC TYPES

To insert a graphic image other than WordPerfect's clip art images, choose Insert, Graphic, From File. WordPerfect opens the Insert File dialog box, which is identical to the Open File dialog box. You can use this dialog box to browse to various graphic files.

13

**NOTE**

If you use the preview box in the Open File dialog box, you'll find that it does not display any file type other than WordPerfect graphics (.wpg). However WordPerfect does import a wide variety of graphic types. If you're not sure whether you can import a certain image type, just try it and see what happens.

When you identify the file you want, select it and click Insert. WordPerfect automatically converts and imports the following graphic file types (the graphic format is followed by the typical filename extension used by that format):

| Graphic File Type | Filename Extension |
| --- | --- |
| Adobe Photoshop | .psd |
| AutoCAD | .dxf |
| CALS compressed bitmap | .cal |
| CompuServe GIF | .gif |
| Computer Graphics Metafile | .cgm |
| Corel Compressed Presentation Exchange | .cdr |
| Corel Presentation Exchange | .cdx |
| Corel Draw (3/4/5/6/7/8/9/10/11) | .cdr, .pat |
| Corel Draw Template (4/5/6/7) | .cdt |
| Corel PhotoPaint (7/8/9/10/11) | .cpt |
| Encapsulated PostScript | .eps |
| Enhanced Windows Metafile | .emf |
| FAX/TIFF | .tif |
| GEM Paint bitmap | .img |
| Harvard Graphics | .ch3, .psr, .sh3, .sy3, .tp3 |
| Hewlett-Packard Graphics Language | .plt |
| JPEG bitmap | .jpg |
| Kodak Photo CD | .pcd |
| Lotus PIC | .pic |
| Macintosh PICT | .pct |
| MacPaint bitmap | .mac |
| MicroGrafix graphic | .drw |
| OS/2 bitmap | .bmp |
| PC Paintbrush graphic | .pcx |
| Portable network graphic (PNG) | .png, .gif |
| Scalable Vector Graphics | .svg |

| Graphic File Type | Filename Extension |
| --- | --- |
| Scitex CT bitmap | .sct |
| TIFF graphics | .tif |
| TrueVision Targa bitmap | .tga |
| Windows bitmap | .bmp, .dib |
| Windows icon | .ico |
| Windows metafile | .wmf |
| WordPerfect Graphics 5 | .wpg |
| WordPerfect Graphics 6/7/8/9/10/11/12 | .wpg |
| WordPerfect Works 2.0 Paint | .wpw |

Even if you don't use the WordPerfect graphics editor (Corel Presentations), it's likely that the graphics program you use can save its files in one of these formats.

**NOTE**

> WordPerfect graphics are vector graphics because they are created by drawing lines between reference points, or vectors. If you move the vectors, the lines change, but they also remain smooth because they're being drawn from one point to another. Other programs, notably paintbrush-type programs, create bitmap graphics by filling in areas with dots, or bits. If you change the size of a bitmap image (for example, to make it larger), you often see jagged edges because WordPerfect can't fill in the missing dots.
>
> Whenever possible, save and use graphics in a vector format because these give you the greatest flexibility as you size them for your document.

It's quite unlikely that you'll run across many of these graphic file types. Besides the .wpg format, some of the most common formats are those associated with the Internet (.gif, .jpg) or with digital cameras (.jpg, .tif). It's nice to know, however, that if you need to use one of these unusual formats, WordPerfect is up to the task.

## INSERTING GRAPHICS FROM A SCANNER

One great way to obtain images for documents is to use a scanner. For example, you can scan family photos directly into a WordPerfect document to put together a book of memories.

You first set up WordPerfect to interact directly with your scanner and then scan the picture. Follow these steps, which are typical for most scanners:

1. Choose Insert, Graphics, Select Image Source. WordPerfect displays the list of scanners in the Select Source dialog box, shown in Figure 13.29.

2. Choose the device that matches your scanner and click Select.

3. Make sure your scanner is connected to your computer and is turned on.

13

**Figure 13.29**
WordPerfect Office supports several types of scanners so that you can use WordPerfect to scan images directly into your documents.

4. Place the item to be scanned on the scanner.

5. Choose Insert, Graphics, Acquire Image. WordPerfect starts your scanning software.

6. Scan a preview image, make adjustments as necessary, and then make a final scan.

**NOTE**

The software for each scanner varies, and so do the specific procedures. Most, however, are relatively simple to understand and use.

7. WordPerfect deposits the scanned image directly in your WordPerfect document (see Figure 13.30 for an example of a scanned image). You can move or size the image, add borders, or modify the image by using image tools.

**Figure 13.30**
Scanned images, such as photos, fit nicely in WordPerfect documents.

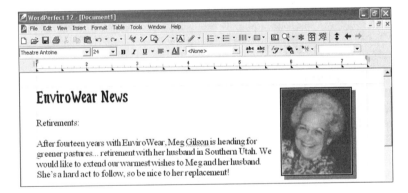

**TIP FROM**

The Contrast and Brightness controls in the Image Tools dialog box are particularly useful for lightening or darkening scanned photographs.

*If you're having trouble making scanned images look good in WordPerfect, see "Choosing the Right Size for Scanned Images" in the Troubleshooting section at the end of this chapter.*

## INSERTING GRAPHICS FROM THE INTERNET

Another great source for graphic images is the Internet. Web sites contain graphic images that might be just what you need. Some sites offer collections of free buttons, lines, and other kinds of clip art.

**CAUTION**

Just because images can be downloaded from the Internet does not mean they are free. Copyright laws and restrictions apply to Internet graphics as they do to print graphics. If you aren't sure whether you can use a graphic image, you should ask the owner of the Web site that contains the image.

To use an image from an Internet Web site, follow these steps:

1. In your Internet browser, right-click the image you want to download.
2. From the pop-up menu, in Netscape choose Save Image As, or in Internet Explorer choose Save Picture As.
3. Provide a name and local destination (for example, c:\My Documents\My Pictures\webimage.jpg). Use the same filename extension as used on the Web site—for example, .gif or .jpg.
4. Click OK to save the image.
5. Switch to WordPerfect and choose Insert, Graphics, From File.
6. Browse to the location where you saved the image, select the image, and choose Insert.

WordPerfect converts the image from the Internet format (.gif or .jpg) and places it in the document (see Figure 13.31 for an example of an Internet image, at both normal and enlarged sizes). You then can move or size the image, add borders, or modify the image by using image tools.

**NOTE**

Try to capture and use images that are close to the size you want. Small images, when enlarged in WordPerfect, tend to look jagged. Larger images, when made small, sometimes lose critical parts. This is the nature of bitmapped graphics, and beyond choosing the right size to begin with, there really is nothing you can do to improve the quality of the image.

13

→ For more information on editing bitmap images, such as scanned images or images from the Internet, in WordPerfect's Presentations program, **see** "Editing Bitmap Graphics in Presentations," **p. 443.**

**Figure 13.31**
Graphics captured from the Web also import nicely into WordPerfect. Note, however, that small Web graphics, when enlarged too much, begin to display jagged edges.

## TROUBLESHOOTING

### SELECTING THE CORRECT GRAPHICS BOX

*I have several graphics boxes, some sitting on top of others. How can I select just the one I want?*

Normally, to select a box you click it once. If there are several boxes, just click again (wait a moment between clicks), and note that the sizing handles change each time you do. When the sizing handles match the image you want, it's selected. You can also right-click on the stack of images, choose Select Other, and then select the image you want from the list of images displayed.

### EXITING THE GRAPHICS EDITING SCREEN

*I clicked a graphic, but my screen seemed to go all haywire, with a funny-looking line around the image and a toolbar on the left side of the screen. What happened?*

You probably double-clicked the image. Single-clicking selects the image, but double-clicking edits the image. In the case of a graphics box, WordPerfect takes you to the drawing editor, hence the different toolbars. To close the image editor, click in your text, outside the graphics box. Or, you can click the Close button on the toolbar.

### MOVING A ROTATED TEXT BOX

*I created a text box and rotated its text, but I can't seem to move the box. Every time I click it I go to the editing screen.*

Selecting a text box that contains rotated text is a bit difficult because in some cases, even when you click exactly on the box border, you enter directly into the Text Box Editor screen. To select such a text box without entering the Text Box Editor, hold down the Shift key and click the box, or right-click the box, and from the QuickMenu choose Select Box. Then make sure the mouse pointer is at the edge of the box and you see a four-way arrow before you try to drag the box to a new location.

### CHOOSING THE RIGHT SIZE FOR SCANNED IMAGES

*I scanned a picture of my family, but it doesn't look very sharp in my WordPerfect document.*

Scanned graphics are bitmapped graphics and aren't designed to be enlarged. When you enlarge them, they turn out the way you describe. To get the best picture quality possible, right-click the graphic, choose Size, and set both the Width and Height to maintain proportions. This might reduce the size of the image, but it will make the image look much better. If you need a larger image, you should rescan the image, setting the saved size to match the size you need.

### ANCHORING IMAGES CORRECTLY

*I just used the Make It Fit feature, but now my graphics are all over the place and they don't fit with the text anymore.*

This is one peril of using the Make It Fit feature. If your graphic images are anchored to the page, they remain in place even when the text moves (for example, when you use Make It Fit). You can reduce this problem by anchoring graphic images to paragraphs or characters, so that the images move as the text moves. If you have a page with a lot of graphics on it, you could select other contiguous pages and apply Make It Fit just to those pages, thus leaving the graphics page alone. In any case, anytime you use Make It Fit, you need to check your document and perhaps make adjustments to the position of your graphics boxes.

# PROJECT

A common, and very practical, use for text boxes is to use them as labels in combination with graphic images or shapes. Suppose you want to make a flyer for the EnviroWear Walkathon that's taking place next Saturday. You just happen to have a nifty graphic, and want to make the flyer look like a billboard sign.

Follow these steps to make the sign:

1. Open a new, blank document. Change the Page Setup from portrait to landscape, if that's more appropriate to the graphic image you'll be using.

2. Choose Insert, Graphics, Clipart, or click the Clipart button on the toolbar.

3. From the Scrapbook or from the clip art CD-ROM, choose the billboard graphic and click Insert.

4. With the image selected, click Graphics on the property bar, and choose Size.

5. In the Box Size dialog box, choose Full for the width, and Full for the height.

6. Click the Zoom button on the toolbar and choose Full Page so you can see the entire page (see Figure 13.32).

**Figure 13.32**
Set the horizontal and vertical size of the image to Full to fill the page.

7. Click the Wrap button on the property bar and select Behind Text. This enables the text box to coexist on the same page as the text.

8. Deselect the image. The easiest way is to click in the margin, but you can also right-click the image and choose Unselect Box from the QuickMenu.

9. Click the Text Box button on the toolbar, or choose Insert, Text Box from the menu. WordPerfect displays a one-line, relatively small text box.

10. Using the property bar, change the font size (for example to 50 points) and the font style if you want.

11. Type the text.

12. Drag the sides of the text box to move it, size it, and arrange the text so it fits properly within the memo note area.

13. Right-click the edge of the text box and choose Border/Fill from the QuickMenu.

14. Click Discontinue to turn off all borders.

15. Make any final minor adjustments, such as adding other text boxes or graphic images, and save the document, which could look somewhat like the example in Figure 13.33.

**Figure 13.33**
You can combine a text box with a graphic image to create an attention-getting flyer that communicates your message.

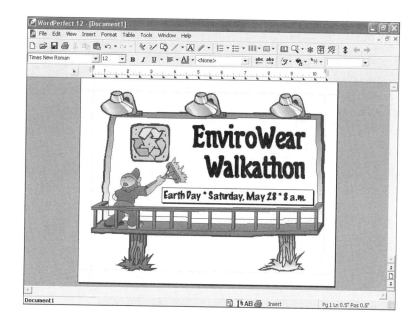

These steps are the basic procedures for adding a text box to an image. However, you will find that some experimentation is required to get just the right font, font size, and location. Fortunately, WordPerfect makes it quick and easy. Besides, isn't this more fun than typing that boring report?

# ADDING DRAWINGS AND TEXTART

*by Read Gilgen*

# ADDING DRAWINGS BY USING PRESENTATIONS

WordPerfect's Draw feature, a light version of Corel Presentations, is so powerful that it deserves special attention. Adding someone else's graphics and drawing cool shapes are fun and useful, but with the Draw program you can add your own custom graphics and even modify graphics from other sources. No longer must you limit yourself to someone else's artwork. For example, you can create a custom company logo, a graph using graphic images, or a simple clip art image extracted from a more complex image.

 When you choose Insert, Graphics, Draw Picture, or click the Draw Picture button on the toolbar, WordPerfect opens an editing window in which you can create and edit graphics using the tools found in the Corel Presentations drawing program (see Figure 14.1). In addition to the window, you also see somewhat different toolbars, and at the left side of the screen is a tool palette that looks a lot like some of the tools you use when working with graphic shapes and boxes. Further, if you click some of the menu items, you'll note that certain features you're used to seeing are gone, replaced by other features you've never heard of before.

**NOTE**

The Draw Picture feature is actually a window into the Corel Presentations program. If you are using a standalone version of WordPerfect, or if you did not install Presentations when you installed the WordPerfect Office suite, the Draw Picture feature will not be available to you. I highly recommend that you install Presentations if it is available.

**Figure 14.1**
The Draw program is actually the Corel Presentations program, and works right within WordPerfect.

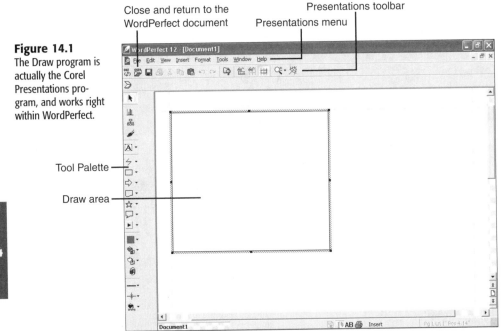

**NOTE**

> The Presentations program is a full-featured drawing and slide show presentation program. If you start Presentations by itself, typically it expects you to create a slide show. However, you can also use it as a drawing program. This chapter focuses only on the drawing features that are most useful to you as you work with Presentations inside WordPerfect.

## WORKING WITH DRAW

When you create a new Draw figure, WordPerfect limits you to a predetermined portion of the WordPerfect screen. You can stretch or shrink that editing window to fit your needs.

**NOTE**

> For the sake of brevity, we refer to the Draw Picture program simply as Draw (for example, "Use Draw to create a text line").

If you want to edit a graphic image, double-click the image to open an editing window the same size as the image's graphics box.

However, if you want to open a larger editing window, hold down the Alt key and double-click the image. WordPerfect opens a separate Corel Presentations drawing window (see Figure 14.2). This window can be sized as large as you'd like it to be. You can even maximize the window to a full screen. Using this separate window can make it easier to see and work with your drawing. When you close the window and return to your document, WordPerfect scales the drawing to fit the original image window in your document.

**Figure 14.2**
If you use the Alt key while double-clicking an image, you open a larger Presentations editing screen.

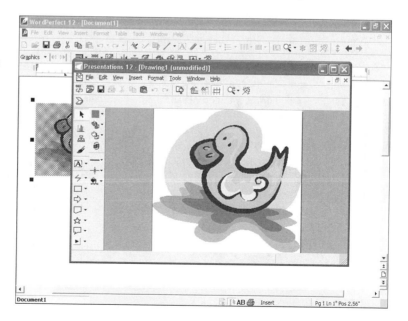

14

**TIP FROM**

When editing a graphic image in WordPerfect, hold down the Alt key and double-click to open a full Corel Presentations editing screen.

*If you're frustrated by the results you get as you experiment with the Draw program, see "Using Undo" in the Troubleshooting section at the end of this chapter.*

## USING SHAPES IN A DRAWING

The processes for creating shapes in WordPerfect and in Draw are almost identical. In fact, shapes may even be easier to use directly in WordPerfect because you don't have to enter and exit Draw. Nevertheless, what you know about WordPerfect shapes applies to creating and working with your own artwork in Draw.

There are, however, a few differences that can make using Draw worth your time:

- Draw has a greater number of shape drawing tools. These include the closed, multi-sided, curved, and straight-line objects, and lines drawn with Bezier curves.

- By default, when you create a shape in WordPerfect, the shape wraps in front of the text. When you create a shape in Draw, it becomes part of a WordPerfect graphics box, and text wraps around that box in a square.

- Because Draw shapes are in graphics boxes, you can also use captions and borders with them.

- You can blend shapes from one color to another, and even (partially) from one shape to another.

- You can add 3D effects to any shape.

- You can warp shapes into other predefined shapes.

> → For information on how to create and manipulate various shapes, such as lines, closed objects, and callouts, **see** "Inserting Shapes," **p. xxx.** [Chapter 12]

> → For information on how to add 3D and warp effects, **see** "Adding Special Effects to Text," **p. xxx.** [later in this chapter]

## ADDING TEXT TO A DRAWING

Although WordPerfect is the premiere program for creating, editing, and formatting text, when it comes to graphical presentation of text, Draw offers several advantages, including the following:

- Text rotated at any angle
- Gradient shaded text
- Text shaped to curved objects
- Three-dimensional text
- Text warped to fit predefined shapes

In WordPerfect, you can rotate text in text boxes only in 90-degree increments. However, if you want to angle text at 45 degrees, for example, you need to create the text in Draw and add the graphics box containing the text to your document.

To create text in Draw, follow these steps:

1. Choose Insert, Graphics, Draw Picture, or click the Draw Picture button on the toolbar. WordPerfect opens the Draw editing window (refer to Figure 14.1).

2. Click the drop-down menu or the Text Objects button on the Draw tool palette to display text options (see Figure 14.3), which include the following:

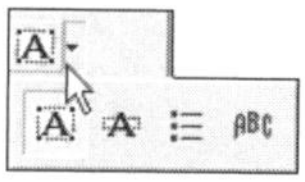

**Figure 14.3**
Draw offers a variety of ways to create text objects.

- Create a text box when you want to create more than one line of text.

- Create a text line when you want to limit the text to just one line.

- Create a bulleted list.

- Create text with special effects, such as that created by TextArt or QuickWarp.

**TIP FROM**

> Often, working with text lines, rather than text boxes, is more efficient in the long run because you can rotate and rearrange text more easily.

3. Click the tool you want (for example, text line) and move the mouse pointer to the area of the screen where you want to start the text line. Note that the mouse pointer becomes crosshairs.

4. Click to begin the text line.

5. Type the text.

6. Select the text where you want to change or add the formatting, such as font, size, and bold.

**NOTE**

> If you select the font, size, and color before creating text, what you select applies to all the text objects you create during the editing session. When you exit the Draw session, however, Draw reverts to the standard black, 36-point, Times New Roman font.

14

7. To close a text box, click anywhere else on the Draw screen. To close a single line of text, you can also just press Enter.

Although you already selected a font size, you may want to make some adjustments. You can drag the sizing handles of a text box in Draw to make the text larger or smaller. To size a text object, follow these steps:

1. Single-click the text box you want to size. Note that Draw displays only four sizing handles (see Figure 14.4).

**Figure 14.4**
Text objects in Draw have only four sizing handles. Pressing Shift while dragging a handle enables you to distort the text.

2. Drag any of the sizing handles to enlarge or reduce the text proportionally.

3. Hold down the Shift key while dragging a sizing handle to stretch the text horizontally or vertically.

To rotate a text object, follow these steps:

1. Single-click the text box you want to rotate to select it.

2. Click the Rotation Options button on the toolbar, and choose Manual Rotation, or right-click the object and choose Rotate from the QuickMenu. WordPerfect places rotation and skewing handles around the outside of the text box, and an axis in the center of the box (see Figure 14.5).

Rotation handles
Skew handles      Rotation axis

**Figure 14.5**
You can rotate text at unlimited angles in Draw.

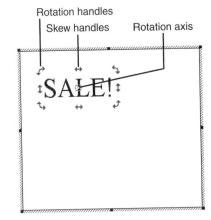

3. Drag a corner handle to rotate the text on its axis (see Figure 14.6).

**Figure 14.6**
When you drag a rotation handle, Draw displays an outline showing where the image will be when you release the mouse button.

4. Drag a side handle to skew the text (see Figure 14.7).

**Figure 14.7**
You can drag a side handle to skew the text, and Draw previews the location of the skewed object.

Finally, before returning to your document, you should make the Draw screen approximately the same size as the text box. The borders of the Draw screen become the borders of the graphics box that contains the special text, and you don't want too much empty space between the text and borders of the box. Simply move the text object to the upper left of the Draw screen, and then drag the sizing handles of the Draw screen to fit the text box (see Figure 14.8). Click in your document to close the Draw screen.

**Figure 14.8**
You should try to make the size of the WordPerfect graphics box match the size of the objects it contains.

If you tried to use the menus to return to your document and can't figure out how to make Draw work, see "How to Get Out of the Draw Screen" in the Troubleshooting section at the end of this chapter.

14

TIP FROM

*Read Gilgen*

You can add as many graphic elements as you want to a single draw screen, including clip art, shapes, and text, all of which become a single graphics box in WordPerfect.

## MODIFYING TEXT APPEARANCE

In WordPerfect you can change a font's style and color. In Draw you can make many other changes as well. To modify a text object in Draw, select the text object and choose Format, Font. Alternatively, you can press F9 or right-click the object and choose Font. WordPerfect displays the Font Properties dialog box, which offers a wide range of font options.

The Font tab (see Figure 14.9) enables you to choose font type (Face), size, color, and other basic attributes, and to preview the results.

**Figure 14.9**
You can use the Font tab of the Font Properties dialog box to modify text objects in Draw.

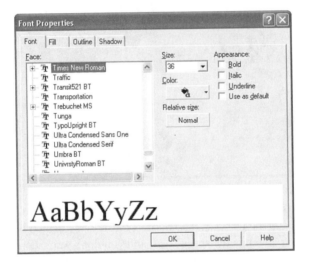

→ For information on using fonts, **see** "Choosing the Right Font," **p. xxx.** [Chapter 3]

The Fill tab (see Figure 14.10) offers three Fill Style options:

- None—Click this button (the button with the large X) to display only the outline of the text.
- Pattern—Click this button (the default, refer to Figure 14.10) to choose from a palette of pattern choices. Foreground color is the pattern color, and Background color is what shows through the pattern. You can reverse the colors for a negative effect.

**Figure 14.10**
With the Fill tab, you can use solid colors, patterns, or gradient shading.

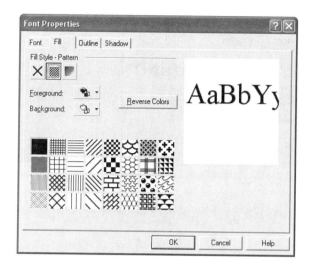

■ Gradient—Click this button to choose from a palette of gradient shaded fills (see Figure 14.11). You can also use Reverse Colors to switch the order of the gradient colors. To customize gradient settings, click Gradient Settings to display the Gradient Settings dialog box (see Figure 14.12), where you can change the angle (for example, 45 degrees to match rotated text), or the horizontal offset or vertical offset (where the foreground color is the stronger color). You can even specify the exact number of steps in the shading, although the default is the smoothest.

**Figure 14.11**
You can quickly select from among several preset gradient styles from the fill style gradient palette.

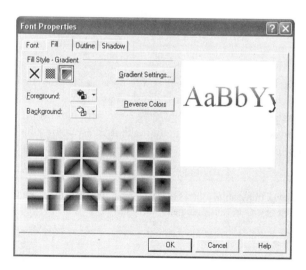

14

The Outline tab (see Figure 14.13, which shows the style palette selected) enables you to change the color, style (for example, solid or dashed), or thickness of the line that surrounds the text. You can also choose None (the large X) from the style palette to remove the font border line altogether.

**Figure 14.12**
You can customize
gradient shading in
text in the Gradient
Settings dialog box.

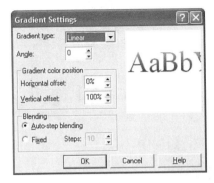

**Figure 14.13**
You can choose X
(None) or one of the
line styles from the
line style palette.

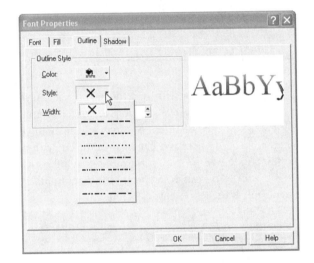

The Shadow tab (see Figure 14.14) enables you to create a shadow for the text in any direction you select. You then can further define the shadow side-to-side offset or up-and-down offset by dragging the scrollbars or by specifying a measurement in the counter boxes. Finally, you can change the shadow color and make it transparent (objects from behind the shadow can be seen) or not transparent (the shadow is a solid color).

**NOTE**

Shadow transparency works only with other objects in the Draw screen, not with text or other objects in your document.

When you finish your text modifications, click OK to return to the Draw screen. An example of text changes you can make in Draw is shown in Figure 14.15, where the text has gradient shading, no border line, and a transparent gray shadow.

14

**Figure 14.14**
It's easy to add or customize shadows on the Shadow tab of the Font Properties dialog box.

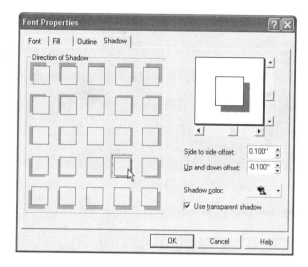

**Figure 14.15**
It's easy to customize text, as in this text that displays a different font, gradient shading, no border line, and a transparent gray shadow.

## ADDING SPECIAL EFFECTS TO TEXT

Draw includes two special-effects options that apply to text as well as to other graphics objects. Quick 3-D adds dimension and shading to text, and QuickWarp fits text into a pre-defined shape.

To access the Quick 3-D dialog box, select the text object and choose Tools, Quick 3-D (see Figure 14.16). The options you use depend on the look you're trying to achieve. Options include the following:

- Rotation—You can click a predefined rotation angle, or make your own adjustments to the X, Y, or Z axes of the letters.

- Color Adjustment—The percentage of color applies to the face of the letters. The 3-D shadow is automatically made proportionally darker.

- Perspective—On the Perspective tab (see Figure 14.17), you can choose Linear, Parallel, or Inverse, as shown by the samples.

- Depth—Also on the Perspective tab you can specify how deep the 3D effect should be.

14

**Figure 14.16**
You can add 3D effects to text from preset or customized styles in the Quick 3-D dialog box.

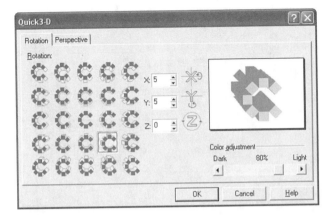

**Figure 14.17**
You can change the 3D perspective on the Perspective tab of the Quick 3-D dialog box.

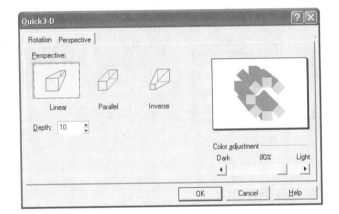

The QuickWarp feature is similar to TextArt (see the section "Creating TextArt" later in this chapter), but with only limited options. When you warp text, you make it change its shape to fit another predefined shape. Choose Tools, QuickWarp to display the QuickWarp dialog box (see Figure 14.18, which shows a shape selected). You can click a shape, preview it, and click OK to add the effect to your text.

**TIP FROM**

*Read Gilgen*

You can add both the QuickWarp and the Quick 3-D effects to a text or graphic object. For added effect, you can also apply either effect more than once to the same object.

14

**Figure 14.18**
You can warp text to fit a predefined shape in the QuickWarp dialog box.

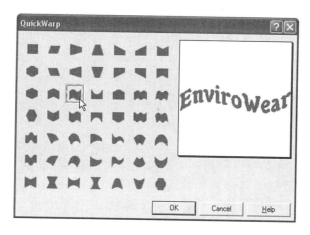

## CONTOURING TEXT TO SHAPES

You can contour text to other shapes, such as circles, half-circles, or even flat-sided objects. To contour text to the outside of a circle, for example, follow these steps:

1. Create the text line you want to contour.

2. Create the shape you want the text to contour to—for example, a circle, created from the Basic Shapes button on the tool palette.

3. Select both the text and the shape. If they are the only two objects on the Draw screen, you can choose Edit, Select All. If there are other objects on the screen, click the shape object, and then hold down the Ctrl or the Shift key and click the text object. You must pair one shape object with each text object you contour.

4. Choose Tools, Contour Text. WordPerfect displays the Contour Text dialog box (see Figure 14.19).

**Figure 14.19**
You can use the Contour Text dialog box to contour text to another Draw shape.

14

5. Choose the text position from the Position Text drop-down menu. Choices include Top Left, Top Center, Top Right, Bottom Left, Bottom Center, and Bottom Right.

6. If you want to display the contoured text without the graphic object, leave the Display Text Only box checked.

7. Click OK to contour the text (see Figure 14.20).

**Figure 14.20**
You can hide or leave visible the object to which text is contoured.

Some contoured text looks quite awful, but that's only because of the screen display. The printed result looks nice and clean.

**NOTE**

Certain software features work better in theory than in principle. Contouring text is one such feature. Single contoured objects seem to work quite well, but if you contour more than one text object (refer to Figure 14.20), you may encounter several problems. One is that one of the objects may not display properly. Another is that one of them may not print at all, even if it does display. Contouring to multi-sided shapes can also prove problematic.

Contouring text can be a cool, useful feature. But be aware that you may have to do a lot of experimenting to get what you really want, if you can get it at all.

## EDITING WORDPERFECT GRAPHICS IN PRESENTATIONS

WordPerfect ships with a collection of some 10,000 clip art images. Not enough, you say? Using the Draw program (Presentations), you can pull apart, modify, combine, or customize many of those clip art images to create just the image you need.

→ For information on using WordPerfect's clip art images, **see** "Inserting Graphic Images," **p. xxx.** [Chapter 12]

All this is possible in part because WordPerfect graphics are vector graphics. This means that clip art images are actually a combination of many images, each of which can be separated from the original clip art and modified.

**NOTE**

WordPerfect graphics are vector graphics because they are created by drawing lines between reference points, or vectors. If you move the vectors, the entire line changes. Other programs, notably paintbrush-type programs, create bitmap graphics by filling in areas with dots, or bits.

Modifying clip art images is an artistic endeavor, determined by your needs and by what you think looks good. Nevertheless, the basic procedures are the same no matter what you want to modify. For example, suppose you want to make a flyer with a chalkboard background for the announcement. You look through the clip art list and notice a chalkboard that just might do the trick; however, you don't want what's written on the chalkboard, and the chalk stick is in the wrong place. Furthermore, you're not sure that you want the chalkboard rotated.

To modify a WordPerfect clip art image in Draw, follow these steps (but don't be afraid to experiment along the way!):

1. Insert the clip art image in your document (for example, the chalkboard from the Scrapbook, Toys category).

2. Double-click the image to open it in Draw.

**TIP FROM**

*Read Gilgen*

Don't forget that you can open an image in a larger Presentations editing screen by holding down the Alt key and double-clicking the image. You can also drag the sides of the editing box to make it larger.

3. Click a part of the image you want to get rid of. If the sizing handles seem to indicate a larger selection than you anticipated, double-click the image again to begin separating the parts of the image. Eventually, you see sizing handles around that part of the image you want to work with—for example, a piece of the text (see Figure 14.21).

Sizing handles around
the letter "m"

**Figure 14.21**
You know which part of an image you are deleting by the location of the sizing handles.

14

**NOTE**

Double-clicking a combined image temporarily separates the parts of the objects that make up that image. You could also choose Edit, Arrange, Separate Objects, but that requires that you group the objects you want to keep later.

4. If there are many small objects you want to remove as a group, you can select several at a time by dragging the mouse to create a box that surrounds the multiple objects. For example, if you attempt to move the chalk stick and find that it's composed of two objects, you can use this step to select the whole chalk stick image and move it at once. You have to start where no object exists, so this can be tricky. Also, check to make sure you don't leave objects, or delete ones you want to keep. Use Undo and start over if you do.

5. You can make changes to any object or group of objects. Some changes you might make include the following:

   - Delete an object—For example, if you want to remove the text on the chalkboard, select it and press Delete.

   - Change colors—For example, you could change the chalk stick from white to yellow.

   - Change a shape—You can drag the sizing handles to skew or change the size of the object; for example, you could rotate the entire image.

   - Add other objects—For example, you could add a text line to the easel. You can even add other clip art images to the image.

6. When you finish modifying the clip art image (refer to Figure 14.21, which shows the modified clip art image), click outside the Draw window to return to your document, or click the Close Drawing button on the toolbar.

As you work with clip art images using Draw, you begin to understand how clip art designers do their work, which makes it easier for you to create your own images. You also discover certain limitations to editing existing clip art.

For example, clip art designers often use layers of solid colors as backgrounds to an entire image. When you remove the background from one part of an image, unfortunately you also remove it from other parts. Figure 14.22 shows how removing a solid black background can adversely affect an image. You want to keep the face, but not the neck on down, of the doctor clip art.

To remedy this sort of problem, you sometimes can add solid objects that cover just the part of the object you want to keep and then send that object to the back, or bottom layer. The black then shows through again as lines on the image (refer to Figure 14.22).

14

**Figure 14.22**
Clip art images are composed of layers. Removing a layer may remove more from an image than you expect. You can add a new background layer to the area you do keep.

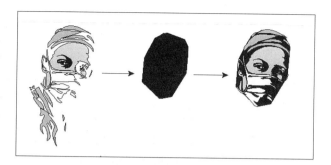

## EDITING BITMAP GRAPHICS IN PRESENTATIONS

You've searched high and low, and the very best graphic image you can find is a bitmap image from the Internet. But you still need to make a couple of minor changes. Fortunately, Presentations also includes a bitmap editor that you can use right from within WordPerfect.

**NOTE**

Bitmap images, created in paintbrush-type programs, are drawn by filling in areas with dots, or bits. Bitmaps are more difficult to modify because many bits must be changed. For example, just to change a line you must erase the bits of the old line, and draw all the bits of the new line.

*What do you do if features suddenly stop working? See "When Features Stop Working" in the Troubleshooting section at the end of this chapter.*

To edit a bitmap image in WordPerfect, follow these steps:

1. Insert the image in your document. Typically, you choose Insert, Graphics, From File. You then browse to find the file and click Insert.

2. Double-click the image to open the image in Draw. To give yourself more room to work, hold down the Alt key while double-clicking to open a larger editing area.

3. Double-click the image again to open it in the bitmap editor (see Figure 14.23).

4. You have a whole new set of tools available, including the paintbrush, flood fill, and air brush. Some of the ways you can modify the image include the following:

   - Erase—Use the eraser to remove parts of the bitmap image you don't want.

   - Zoom—Choose View, Zoom to zoom in on the bits, thus making it easier to modify bit by bit (see Figure 14.24).

   - Paintbrush—The paintbrush enables you to draw, freehand, in different colors and with different brush widths. You can use smaller brush widths for more detailed changes.

   - Flood Fill—Choose a color, and then click this tool in an area of color to replace that color with the new color. This requires a closed area to work; otherwise, the paint floods into other areas.

14

**Figure 14.23**
The bitmap editor is a paintbrush-type program within the Draw program.

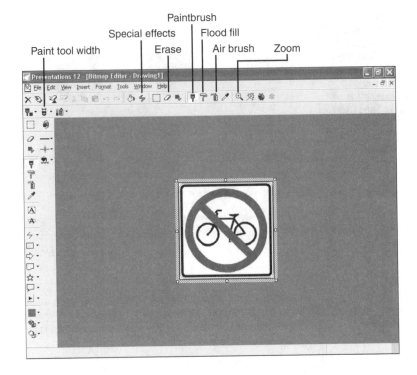

**Figure 14.24**
You can use Zoom in the bitmap editor to get in close to the individual picture bits.

- Air Brush—Using this tool is like using a can of spray paint. Try it!

- Special Effects—Click this button to open the Special Effects dialog box that enables you to blur, soften, sharpen, emboss, or add other special effects to the bitmap image.

**N O T E**

You can, and very well may, spend hours editing bitmap images. You'll discover almost immediately how difficult it is to make precise changes to an image. Just remember that you really don't have a choice if you want to edit a bitmap image, but that you do have special effects tools at your disposal to do things you can't do with vector graphics. Also, don't forget to use the Undo button when you make mistakes.

*Have you messed up the graphic image beyond hope? See "Aborting Bitmap Editing" in the Troubleshooting section at the end of this chapter.*

5. When you're done, click the Close button on the toolbar. On the other hand, if you've made a terrible mess of things, and would prefer to start over, click the Close Bitmap Editor button on the toolbar. Then, click Close to close the bitmap editor without saving the changes you made.

**C A U T I O N**

If you opened the Presentations window to edit your image, you can use the menu to close the editor. Choose File, Close Bitmap Editor, or File, Cancel Bitmap Editor. However, if you opened the regular Draw screen, choosing File, Close causes WordPerfect to close the entire document.

6. Click outside the Draw window to return to your document, or if you opened the larger Presentations window, choose File, Close and Return to update the image and return to your document (see Figure 14.25).

**Figure 14.25**
Even bitmap images can be modified with the bitmap editor to fit your needs.

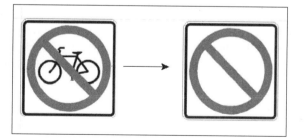

# CREATING TEXTART

TextArt is a text effects program that enables you to shape words and short phrases into pre-defined shapes and add shadows, textures, and dimensions to the text. In some ways it's like a super version of the Quick 3-D and QuickWarp features found in the Draw program (see the preceding section for information on Quick 3-D and QuickWarp).

TextArt is most often used for logos, banners, flyers, and the like. With a little effort, you can create stunning text effects.

## CREATING TEXTART TEXT

To create TextArt in a WordPerfect document, choose Insert, Graphics, TextArt. WordPerfect opens a large graphics box, along with the TextArt dialog box (see Figure 14.26).

**Figure 14.26**
You can use the TextArt dialog box to create and modify a TextArt image in a WordPerfect graphics box.

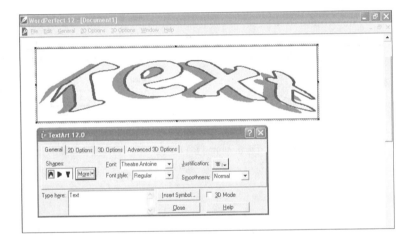

The Type Here box displays the word Text and the graphics box displays the TextArt effect on the word Text, using settings you selected the last time you used the TextArt feature. To add your own words, type them in the Type Here box. You can also add special characters by clicking the Insert Symbol button, or by pressing Ctrl+W. Note, however, that you can insert only a limited number of special characters, not the entire range of symbols normally available in the Insert Symbol dialog box.

**NOTE**

Although you can type a great deal of text in the Type Here box, generally your TextArt is more effective if you limit it to just a few short words.

Next apply several options to the text you typed, including:

- Shapes—WordPerfect displays only three shapes, but click the More button, and you have access to 57 different shapes (see Figure 14.27). Click the shape you want, and WordPerfect squeezes and warps the text into that shape (refer to Figure 14.26).

**Figure 14.27**
You can warp text to 57 predefined TextArt shapes.

NOTE

Depending on the speed of your computer and the amount of memory you have, TextArt can take up to several seconds to update changes you make. Be patient, and be sure to save your work often!

 *If you seem to have lost the TextArt dialog box, see "Getting the TextArt Program Back" in the Troubleshooting section at the end of this chapter.*

- Font—You can choose a font from a list of your installed Windows fonts.

TIP FROM

*Read Gilgen*

The amount of text, the font, and the shape you choose have, perhaps, more impact on what the TextArt shape will look like than any of the other options. Don't be afraid to try out several combinations until you find exactly what you're looking for.

- Justification—Normally, this option has little effect on your TextArt because the text fills the entire graphics box. However, if you change the size of the graphics box after creating the text, WordPerfect aligns the text according to your selection.
- Smoothness—The resolution of the TextArt drawing can affect display and printing times. Normally, you do not need to change this setting.
- 3D mode—This option adds another dimension to the object, but you might also want to make other changes on the 3D tabs.

## ADDING 2D TEXTART OPTIONS

After you create the text, font, and shape you want, you can adjust the pattern, color, shadows, and so on. Begin by clicking the 2D Options tab to find the following options:

- Pattern—You can choose None (you get a solid color), No Fill (you get only text outlines), or one of the patterns displayed on the palette (see Figure 14.28).

14

**Figure 14.28**
You can choose a solid color (None) or transparent text (No Fill), or use a pattern with your TextArt text.

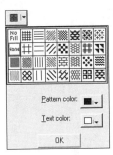

> **NOTE**
> If you click the 3D Mode check box, options on the 2D tab are grayed out. Likewise, if the box is not checked, options on the 3D tabs cannot be used.

- Shadow—You can click this button to display the shadow palette. You can select the direction and depth of the shadow, as well as the text color and the shadow color.

> **NOTE**
> Choosing the right color combination for the text and shadow should be one of your first tasks. Look for colors that complement each other, but that make the text readable. Also, if you plan to print to a black-and-white printer, such as a laser printer, choose colors whose grays complement each other. For example, yellow prints as a very light gray, whereas blue and red print nearly black.

- Outline—From the outline palette (see Figure 14.29), you can choose the thickness and color of the line that outlines the text. Again, you can change the text color to complement the line color.

**Figure 14.29**
You can use the outline palette to choose a line style to go along with your TextArt text.

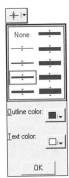

- Rotation—Unlike typical graphic objects that maintain their original shape while rotating, TextArt text skews as it rotates in order to stay within the graphics box and also to stay within the predefined TextArt shape you chose (see Figure 14.30). You can come up with some very interesting shapes using this option.

**Figure 14.30**
When you rotate TextArt text, it remains within the graphics box boundaries.

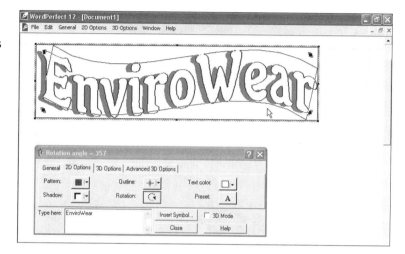

- Text Color—If you didn't already choose a color when choosing shadow or outline, you can do so here.

- Preset—If you're not feeling particularly creative, or you're in a hurry, you can choose from a limited number of predefined 2D effects.

**CAUTION**

If you choose any preset setting, you also lose all your carefully customized settings. Try these presets first, before spending time coming up with your own custom settings.

## ADDING 3D TEXTART OPTIONS

You can click the 3D Options tab to display the options available if you choose to display your TextArt in three dimensions (see Figure 14.31). These options, and some of the things you can do with them, include the following:

- Lighting—Lighting 1 and 2 function the same, but Lighting 1 is the text color and Lighting 2 is the shadow color. Click the color palette to change the color, and click the light source palette to choose a direction from where the light comes (see Figure 14.32).

14

**Figure 14.31**
The 3D Options tab enables you to add another dimension to your TextArt text.

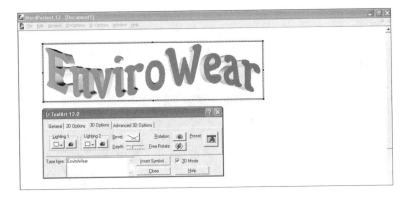

**Figure 14.32**
The light source palette helps you visualize the direction light comes from as it shines on your 3D text.

■ Bevel—This option enables you to shape the edge of the text, as if the letters were carved like wood molding. Choose a beveled shape from the palette (see Figure 14.33) to add this effect.

**Figure 14.33**
You can bevel the sides of 3D text with interesting effects.

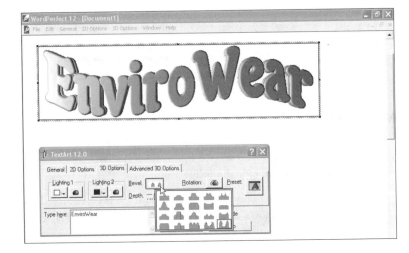

■ Depth—You can use the slider to increase or decrease the depth of the beveled edge.

■ Rotation—You can rotate the entire TextArt image left or right, up or down, by choosing from several preset rotations (see Figure 14.34).

**Figure 14.34**
Preset rotation angles make it easy to rotate 3D TextArt text.

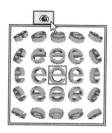

- Free Rotate—If you prefer to rotate the text yourself, click this option, and then use the mouse to drag the TextArt up, down, left, or right.

- Preset—Again, if you prefer to let TextArt do the work for you, you can choose from a palette of predefined 3D settings.

**CAUTION**

> Don't forget that choosing a preset 3D option cancels all other settings you may have painstakingly set up.

The Advanced 3D Options tab doesn't mean you have more complicated settings, but simply that you have more options (see Figure 14.35).

**Figure 14.35**
The Advanced 3D Options include textures.

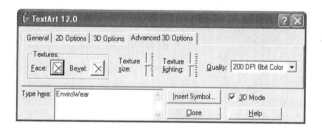

On this tab you can change the following settings, some of which are shown in Figure 14.36:

- Textures—WordPerfect provides a palette of interesting textures (nuts, tiles, fabrics, wood, and so on) that you can apply to the face of the text, to the beveled edge of the text, or both (see Figure 14.37).

- Texture Size—Use the slide control to increase (up) or decrease (down) the size of the texture pattern. If you want larger peanuts, for example, slide up. The size control applies to both the face and the bevel, if you use textures on both.

- Texture Lighting—This option controls the contrast between the Lighting 1 and Lighting 2 colors you selected on the 3D Options tab.

**14**

**Figure 14.36**
3D TextArt text is shown here with advanced options.

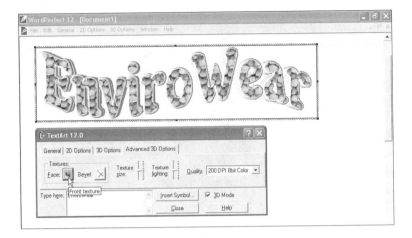

**Figure 14.37**
These textures can be applied to the face or the side of 3D TextArt text.

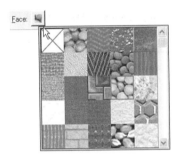

- Quality—Unfortunately, this option doesn't indicate how good your TextArt looks, but how well it will print on a color printer. DPI refers to the number of dots per inch that print, and bits refers to the richness of the colors you can use, especially for textures and gradient shadings.

## USING TEXTART IN DOCUMENTS

WordPerfect places TextArt images inside graphics boxes. As a result, they work like any other graphics box. You can add borders to the box, choose various wrap options, and size or move the box.

If you size the box using the side sizing handles, you also change the shape of the original TextArt.

If you choose to wrap the TextArt box in front of or behind your text, you can make it appear that the TextArt and text are designed to work together.

Figure 14.38 shows how a TextArt image combines with regular text to create a logo.

14

**Figure 14.38**
TextArt in a graphics box can interact with regular document text to create useful effects.

# TROUBLESHOOTING

### USING UNDO

*It seems like nothing I do turns out right. Pretty soon my graphic is a complete mess. Is there anything I can do besides delete it?*

Even artists have rags to wipe up their messes. Although it may seem absurdly elementary to mention this, you really must think Undo whenever you try something that you don't like. You should use Undo immediately because if you wait, you may not be able to restore whatever you messed up.

### HOW TO GET OUT OF THE DRAW SCREEN

*When I edit an image and choose File, Close, WordPerfect closes my entire document. I want to close just the Draw editor.*

If you click the Close button on the toolbar, WordPerfect closes just the editor. If you chose to use the larger Presentations screen (holding down Alt while double-clicking the image to be edited), the menu is different and you can indeed choose File, Close and return to the document.

### WHEN FEATURES STOP WORKING

*Sometimes when working with graphics, certain features suddenly stop working or disappear from the toolbar. What's wrong and how can I fix it?*

Sometimes, especially when working with memory-intensive features such as graphics, features that you've used before suddenly don't work. This is WordPerfect's quirky way of telling you it's getting forgetful. Often the only way to remedy this situation is to exit WordPerfect altogether, and even sometimes to reboot your computer, before starting WordPerfect again. Doing this usually causes the features magically to start working again. This generally is not a problem with more modern computers with 512MB of RAM or higher.

### ABORTING BITMAP EDITING

*I've messed up my bitmap editing so badly, and it seems I can only undo one action. I don't want to save the whole mess by returning to the Draw screen. What can I do?*

Fortunately, you can abort a bitmap editing session by clicking the Cancel Bitmap button on the Bitmap toolbar. This returns you to the Draw screen without keeping any changes you may have made. In the Draw screen, you have multiple levels of Undo, but you don't in the bitmap editor.

### GETTING THE TEXTART PROGRAM BACK

*When I'm working with TextArt, I seem to lose the TextArt dialog box.*

The TextArt program is separate from WordPerfect. When you accidentally switch back to WordPerfect, you hide the TextArt program. Simply double-click the TextArt image to restore the TextArt program dialog box.

## PROJECT

It's all the rage these days. Text with fuzzy shadow backgrounds that seem so real it appears the text is really floating off the page. Can you do that in WordPerfect? You bet. It's not a simple menu item, but it's easy to do using a combination of Draw text and bitmap editing. Figure 14.39 shows some text with the nifty shadow background.

**Figure 14.39**
Using both the Draw and bitmap editors, you can create this modern-looking shadow effect.

To create something like that, follow these steps:

1. Begin by choosing Insert, Graphics, Draw Picture; or click the Draw Picture button on the toolbar.
2. In the Draw screen, create the text. You can create shadows for anything, including shapes, but let's stick with the text shown in the example.

**NOTE**

It's important to make sure the basic object is complete before making a shadow copy. Otherwise, you'll just have to come back and do it all over again.

3. Select the text object (the sizing handles should be visible), and then hold down Ctrl while dragging a copy of the object to another part of the screen.

4. Click the font color palette and change the text copy to light gray.

5. Choose Tools, Convert to Bitmap to make the text copy a bitmap image. You'll get a warning about how irreversible this is. Laugh at the danger as you click Convert.

6. Double-click the new bitmap image to open the bitmap editor.

7. You're going to blur the image, so you need a little extra room at each side of the image. Move the pointer toward each side sizing handle, and when the pointer turns to a two-way arrow, click once. This creates the necessary room.

8. Choose Format, Set Transparent Color, check the No Transparent Color check box, and click OK. This makes the background white, which is the color that meshes with the blurred image.

9. Choose Tools, Special Effects, or click the Effect button on the toolbar. WordPerfect displays the Special Effects dialog box (see Figure 14.40).

**Figure 14.40**
The Special Effects dialog box enables you to blur bitmap images.

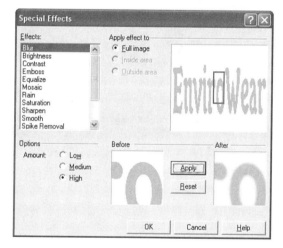

10. Click Blur, select High, and click OK. The blurred edge now mixes nicely with the white background.

11. Go back now, and choose Format, Set Transparent Color, and uncheck the No Transparent Color Box. Click OK. Note in Figure 14.41 how the white color blends with the edge of the blurred text; but, otherwise, the rest of the background is transparent.

12. Click the Close button on the toolbar to return the Draw editor with the blurred bitmap image.

13. Right-click the blurred image, and from the QuickMenu choose To Back.

14. Align the two text images so that the blurred image is a shadow to the regular text image.

**Figure 14.41**
Blurred images mix
the object's color with
the background color.

15. Choose Edit, Select All, and then right-click the objects and choose Group.

16. Size the graphics box to the size of the text object and click in your text to close the Draw editor.

That's it! Position the text wherever you want in your document. Although this might not be the quickest procedure you'll ever try, as you become more experienced at it, you'll find it takes only a minute or two, and that it's easy to add this effect to text or other graphics objects.

# INTEGRATING INFORMATION FROM OTHER SOURCES

# Importing Data and Working with Other Programs

*by Read Gilgen*

**I**n this chapter

15

# MOVING INFORMATION IN WINDOWS

In today's office, information is created in a variety of programs. The smartest workers learn how to move and reuse that information, instead of creating it over and over again. In most cases information can be moved easily from one place to another by cutting and pasting. Some information comes in specific, proprietary formats, and must be exported from one format, and imported into WordPerfect in a format that WordPerfect can understand.

## USING THE CLIPBOARD

The key to moving data in Windows is the Windows Clipboard. Despite the clever name, the Clipboard really is an area of your computer's memory that is reserved for temporarily holding information you place there. You can retrieve the information and use it wherever you want, as often as you want, until you replace the information with something else or until you turn off your computer.

In WordPerfect, you can cut or copy information in a variety of ways, including by using the Edit menu, the toolbar, the QuickMenu, and keystrokes such as Ctrl+X or Shift+Del to cut, and Ctrl+V or Shift+Ins to paste.

→ If you need a review of the many ways you can cut and paste in WordPerfect, **see** "Moving and Copying Text," **p. 53.**

Typically, each time you copy or cut information, Windows clears the Clipboard and adds what you've cut or copied. You can, however, add more than one selection to the Clipboard at a time. Choose Edit, Append to add more items to the Clipboard. Then when you paste, WordPerfect pastes all appended items at once.

**N O T E**

You can append only text selections to the Clipboard. You cannot append graphics.

When you move text in WordPerfect, you normally also move the formatting codes associated with that text. When you paste the text, you also paste its formatting codes. If the surrounding text happens to have the same formatting, the codes automatically disappear, but if it doesn't, WordPerfect inserts the formatting codes to preserve the original format of the source text, as shown in Figure 15.1.

You can, however, paste the text into your document in a variety of other ways. Choose Edit, Paste Special to access the Paste Special dialog box (see Figure 15.2). You then use this dialog box to paste using the following formats or options:

■ WordPerfect 12 Data—This option is equivalent to the normal Paste option; it inserts text as native WordPerfect 12 information.

**Figure 15.1**
Text imported by cutting and pasting often brings formatting codes along with it.

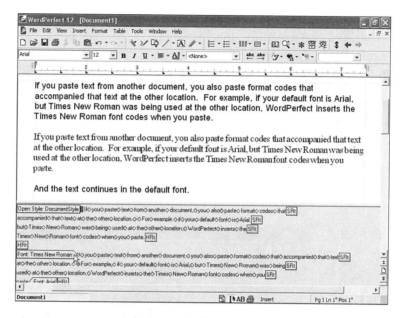

**Figure 15.2**
For greater control over how you import Clipboard data, use the Paste Special dialog box.

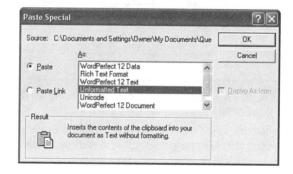

**NOTE**

Unless otherwise noted, references to WordPerfect 12 formats should read WordPerfect 11 for those using WordPerfect 11. Unlike Word formats, which frequently change from version to version, WordPerfect formats have remained essentially unchanged since version 6.

- Rich Text Format—Rich Text Format (RTF) is a quasi-standard method for translating some formatting between different programs. For example, although the Bold codes might be different for WordPerfect than they are for Word, RTF uses a Bold code that both can understand.

- WordPerfect 12 Text—This pastes only the text of the selection, not formatting or graphics.

15

- Unformatted Text—This option pastes only the most generic version of the selection in your document. All formatting, graphics, and so on are lost.

**TIP FROM**

*Read Gilgen*

A quick method for pasting unformatted text is to simply press Ctrl+Shift+V.

- Unicode—This is a relatively recent standard for text interchange; it tries to make sure that codes for foreign characters, among other things, are the same in all programs.
- Picture (Metafile)—This pastes the contents of the Clipboard into a graphics box. You can then size the box and position it as you do any graphics box (see Figure 15.3).

**Figure 15.3**

You can use the Picture option in the Paste Special dialog box to paste text into a graphics box, which you can then move and size. Note the graphic toolbar and the sizing handles around the text box.

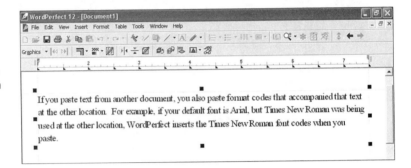

**NOTE**

The number and type of options in the Paste Special dialog box can change depending on the source of the information you copy.

For example, text copied from Web pages often contains a variety of style, font, line advance, and other formatting codes applied to every paragraph.

Although you have many options from which to choose, if all you really want to copy is the information itself, without formatting, simply choose the Unformatted Text option.

## DRAG AND DROP

One handy yet often overlooked method for cutting and pasting is drag and drop. The procedure is so simple that you often forget to use it. Follow these steps:

1. With the mouse, select the text you want to move.
2. Point the mouse pointer at the selected text so that the pointer turns to an arrow.

3. Click and hold down the mouse button and drag the pointer to the location where you want to paste the text. The mouse pointer appears with an arrow, a piece of paper, and an insertion point to indicate exactly where you will paste the text.

4. Release the mouse button to drop the text in its new location.

The text remains highlighted so you can move it again if you missed your mark. Of course, you can also use Undo. Also, although dragging and dropping has the same effect as cutting and pasting, WordPerfect does not paste a copy in the Windows Clipboard.

→ For details on cutting, copying, and pasting text, **see** "Moving and Copying Text," **p. 53.**

**NOTE**

Using drag and drop to move text is best suited for relatively short distances; dragging text from page 1 to page 8, for example, where lots of scrolling is required before you can drop the text, just isn't very practical. Sometimes regular cut and paste methods make more sense.

**TIP FROM**

*Read Gilgen*

One of the best uses for drag and drop is in tables, where you drag the contents of table cells along with cell formatting. You can even drag entire rows or columns within a table.

## COPYING AND PASTING BETWEEN WORDPERFECT DOCUMENTS

As you undoubtedly know, WordPerfect enables you to work with up to nine open documents at a time. Not only can you switch among documents to refer to information in them, but you can easily move information from one WordPerfect document to another. The most obvious method is simply to cut or copy text in one document, switch to another, and paste the text there. Easy. Done.

A not-so-obvious method, but one that is also easy to use, is drag and drop. Note in Figure 15.4 that two document tabs appear at the bottom of the WordPerfect screen. The current (active) document is highlighted (if you're not sure which is active, simply check the title bar for the name of the current document).

**Figure 15.4**
Document tabs at the bottom of the WordPerfect screen enable you to switch between documents, and also to drag and drop text from one document to another.

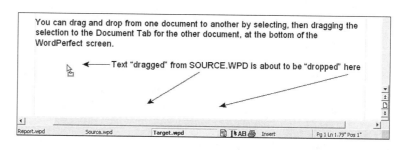

You can drag and drop from one document to another by selecting, then dragging the selection to the Document Tab for the other document, at the bottom of the WordPerfect screen.

Text "dragged" from SOURCE.WPD is about to be "dropped" here

Report.wpd    Source.wpd    Target.wpd    Insert    Pg 1 Ln 1.79" Pos 1"

To drag and drop from one WordPerfect document to another, follow these steps:

1. First, go to the target document and position the cursor where you want to paste text. When you return here with text you've dragged from the other document, you don't want to have to scroll to find your target before you can drop the text.

2. Switch to the source document (by clicking the document tab at the bottom of the screen).

3. Select the text (or graphics, or table, and so on) that you want to copy.

4. Click the selection and quickly drag it toward the document tab of the target document.

**TIP FROM**

> If you move too slowly toward the document tab, the document begins to scroll, and WordPerfect thinks you want to paste in the current document. If this happens, release the mouse button in the source document (which pastes the selection), choose Undo, and start over again.

5. Hold the pointer on the target document tab until WordPerfect switches to the target document.

6. Move the mouse pointer into the document area and release the mouse button to paste the document where you want it.

*Do you sometimes copy and paste something, only to find that the format of what you paste is completely different from where you're pasting it? See "Pasting Unformatted Text" in the Troubleshooting section at the end of this chapter.*

## COPYING AND PASTING BETWEEN PROGRAMS

The same principles you use when moving information within a program apply when moving information between programs. The Windows Clipboard serves as the great information storage tank, and text, graphics, and even other information can be retrieved and converted so that it can be used in the target program.

Suppose, for example, that you have a paragraph in a Word document that you'd like to use in a WordPerfect document. To move information from one program to another, follow these steps:

1. Open the source program (for example, Word).

2. Select the information you want to move.

3. Cut or copy the selection.

4. Switch to the target program (for example, WordPerfect).

5. Paste the information.

Information you copy from one program to another often carries styles and other attributes from the source program. If you open the Reveal Codes window, as shown in Figure 15.5, you see that WordPerfect inserts style codes, font codes, and other codes to preserve the original formatting of the text from the source document, in this case Word.

**Figure 15.5**
Pasting text from Word might also import Word's default format codes.

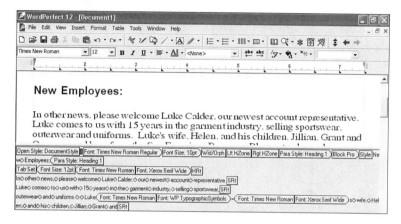

If you don't want all the formatting, but only the text, simply choose Edit, Paste Special, and then select Unformatted.

## USING THE CLIPBOOK PROGRAM

The Clipbook feature is a powerful tool included with WordPerfect beginning with Service Pack 2 of WordPerfect 10 (it was not included in the original release of WordPerfect 10). The Clipbook program, installed separately but automatically when you install WordPerfect, enables you to copy multiple text segments and graphics objects, creating customized collections, or clipboards, of clips from which you then can insert individual clips in any Windows document.

The Clipbook thus overcomes the limitation in the Windows Clipboard whereby cutting or copying replaces any previously cut or copied item.

For example, you can assign large chunks of text or graphics to individual keys, making it easy to compose documents by using a couple of keystrokes to retrieve stored components. When used on a corporate network, this enables central control and standardization of important phrases, paragraphs, terminology, letterhead logos, and more in place of individualized QuickWords or QuickCorrect shortcuts.

### USING THE CLIPBOOK

The Clipbook is a utility program that you start up by clicking the Windows Start menu and then choosing Programs, WordPerfect Office 12, Utilities, Clipbook. Nothing seems to happen, but a Clipbook icon appears in the System Tray, at the right side of the taskbar. If you double-click the Clipbook icon in the System Tray, the Clipbook appears (see Figure 15.6), with a list of keys and an otherwise completely blank screen, unless you have added items already to the Clipbook.

**Figure 15.6**
The Clipbook lists keys that cut or copied items can be assigned to.

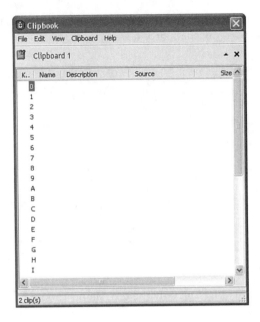

*Read Gilgen*

> The Clipbook program is independent of WordPerfect. It thus enhances the basic cut and copy procedures of Windows, and can be used with any Windows application.

By default, when the Clipbook program is loaded and the icon appears in the System Tray, using the conventional Windows keys for cutting (Ctrl+X) or copying (Ctrl+C) automatically pops up a Clipbook window that prompts you to select a key where the cut or copied items are to be stored. For example, if you want the item stored under the letter M, you simply press the M key and then press Enter. You can also right-click the key and select Paste. The Clipbook now displays the cut or copied item, along with information about the clip, such as its source, its size, and when it was created (see Figure 15.7).

To paste items from the Clipbook into any Windows application, simply press Ctrl+V. Then, press the key of the item to be pasted.

You can also use the mouse to move information to and from the Clipbook. With the Clipbook open, find the item you can use, click the key letter or number, and drag the item to your document.

Finally, you can also use various cut, copy, and paste methods to move information from one Clipbook key to another.

**Figure 15.7**

The Clipbook displays cut or copied items for the currently selected Clipboard, along with information about their source, size, and when they were created.

15

**CAUTION**

Dragging an item from the Clipbook is the same as cutting it from the Clipbook. To copy an item, hold down the Ctrl key while dragging it to your application.

You can also right-click any Clipbook key, and then choose Cut, Copy, or Paste to move the information.

If you want more information about the clip, for example, to see what kind of clip it is, or to give it a title or description, right-click the Clipbook key and choose Properties.

## SETTING UP THE CLIPBOOK

You can create a variety of custom Clipboards, and associate one of them as the default Clipboard when using the Clipbook. To create a new Clipboard and to set up a different default Clipboard, follow these steps:

1. From the Clipbook dialog box, choose Clipboard, Manage; or right-click the Clipbook icon in the System Tray and choose Manage. The Clipbook displays the Manage Clipboards dialog box, shown in Figure 15.8.

2. Click the Create button to create a new Clipboard, and provide a name for it, along with an optional description.

3. Click the name of a Clipboard to select it. If it's already the default Clipboard, the Default button on the toolbar is grayed out. If it's not the Default Clipboard, and you want it to be, click the Default button on the toolbar.

15

**Figure 15.8**
You can set up several Clipboards in the Clipbook, and you can choose any of them as the default Clipboard for transferring your cut or copied items.

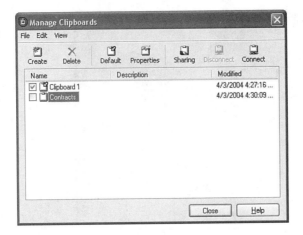

4. If you want to display a Clipboard in the Clipbook, check the check box to the left of the Clipboard and a green arrow appears to indicate that it will be displayed. You can display more than one Clipboard at a time in the Clipbook.

5. Click Close to return to the Clipbook. The Clipbook now displays your selected Clipboards, along with a list of keys (0–9, A–Z) for each to which you can assign clips that you copy or cut (refer to Figure 15.7).

**NOTE**

Because the Clipbook is actually a file, you can also set up the Clipbook on a network drive, and you can share Clipbook contents with other users.

### CHOOSING CLIPBOOK OPTIONS

The Clipbook operates with several default options that might not fit the way you work. You can change many of these options by opening the Clipbook (double-click the icon in the System Tray), and choosing File, Settings. Clipbook displays the Clipboard—Settings dialog box shown in Figure 15.9.

Options you find on the General tab include

- Popup Window Style—You can choose to have the Clipbook show your default Clipboard (the default), to display no Clipboard at all, or a minimized tip that reminds you which Clipboard is active, and which basic keys you need to press.

- Popup Window Location—If you don't like the Clipbook popping up in the middle of the screen you can change it.

**Figure 15.9**
You can change
Clipbook settings to
adapt it to the way
you work.

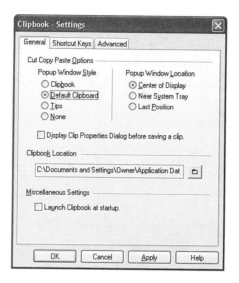

**TIP FROM**

*Read Gilgen*

You can resize the Clipbook Window and position it out of the way. If you choose Last
Position, the Clipbook remains rather unobtrusive.

- Clipbook Location—If you're using a shared network Clipbook, this enables you to
  specify the network location.

- Launch Clipbook at Startup—This makes using Clipbook automatic each time you
  start Windows.

On the Shortcut Keys tab (see Figure 15.10), you can change the default keystrokes used to
cut, copy, or paste. You can even set different shortcuts for specific applications.

The Advanced tab contains settings used for networked Clipbooks.

## USING OLE LINKING AND EMBEDDING OPTIONS

OLE means object linking and embedding. When you paste information from another program, WordPerfect can embed the information, and Windows can remember where the
information came from. When it comes time to edit the embedded information, simply
double-click it. Windows opens an editing window within WordPerfect, and switches you to
the source program so that you can edit in the original program, using that program's
menus, keystrokes, and other procedures. When you finish, you return to WordPerfect with
the updated information by clicking in the WordPerfect document.

**Figure 15.10**

You can customize which keystrokes you use to cut, copy, or paste to and from the Clipbook.

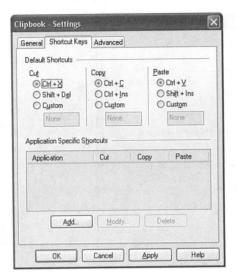

**TIP FROM**

Read Gilgen

If you use normal methods of copying and pasting information, WordPerfect inserts only the information you're copying and does not create an OLE link back to the original program. However, you can choose Edit, Paste Special and choose the format associated with the original program to paste the information and to establish the OLE link.

**TIP FROM**

Read Gilgen

If you drag and drop the information from the other program to WordPerfect, WordPerfect automatically establishes an OLE link. The procedure is similar to dragging and dropping text between WordPerfect documents: Find the target in WordPerfect, and then go to the source program and drag the selected information to the WordPerfect button on the Windows taskbar. When WordPerfect appears, drop the information in the WordPerfect document.

You can also create new OLE objects within WordPerfect. For example, you can create a Word document or even a PowerPoint slide inside a WordPerfect document. To create an OLE object that you embed in a WordPerfect document, follow these steps:

1. Choose Insert, Object to display the Insert Object dialog box (see Figure 15.11).

2. Select the object type from the list of options. Only the OLE-capable programs (called OLE servers) that are installed on your system appear on the list.

3. Click OK. The OLE server application starts and takes control of WordPerfect's menus and toolbars. It also opens an editing window in which you can use all the application's procedures to create the object (see Figure 15.12). This is called in-place editing.

4. Close the OLE editing window by clicking in the document. WordPerfect takes control of menus and toolbars again.

**Figure 15.11**
You can use the Insert Object dialog box to insert OLE objects.

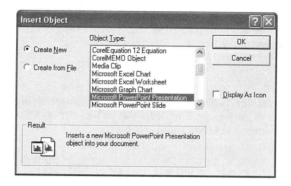

**Figure 15.12**
You can create or edit, in place, OLE objects such as PowerPoint slides or Word documents.

PowerPoint OLE Object

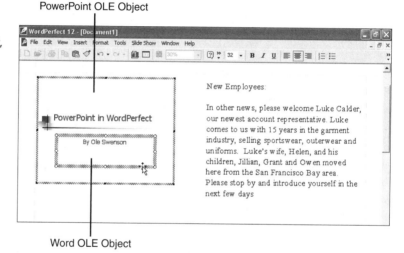

Word OLE Object

**NOTE**

> Some OLE server applications do not support in-place editing. Instead, they open a completely separate application window where you create or edit the object. You then exit the application to return to WordPerfect.

You can also embed or create a link to an existing OLE object created by another application. To create an OLE link, follow these steps:

1. Choose Insert, Object to open the Insert Object dialog box.
2. Click Create from File.
3. Browse to find the file you want to insert.
4. By default, WordPerfect inserts the file as an embedded object. However, if you choose Link, WordPerfect inserts the object and also creates a link to the original file so that changes made to that file are reflected in the WordPerfect document.
5. Click OK to insert the object in your document.

**TIP FROM**

Don't forget that many applications enable you to drag and drop objects from their programs into WordPerfect.

*Extremely large WordPerfect documents are unwieldy and take up a lot of disk space. If you're having trouble with such documents, it might have to do with OLE. See "Keeping Files Small" in the Troubleshooting section at the end of this chapter.*

# WORKING WITH WORD AND OTHER WORD PROCESSING DOCUMENTS

Let's face it. WordPerfect might be the best word processing program in town, but marketing muscle has helped Microsoft lay claim to a large portion of the Windows word processing turf. If you're lucky, your organization has standardized on WordPerfect alone. But more likely, you're faced with having to work on documents created initially in other word processing programs.

Fortunately, WordPerfect has kept pace with the need for interchangeability with other programs. In fact, Corel has placed a great deal of emphasis on providing up-to-date and accurate document conversions in each succeeding version of WordPerfect. Whether your other word processing program is WordPerfect 5.1 for DOS or Word 2003, you'll find it easier than ever to use WordPerfect to work with these documents.

## OPENING AND CONVERTING FILES FROM OTHER WORD PROCESSING PROGRAMS

The first step in working with a document from another word processing format is to open it in WordPerfect. Access the File Open dialog box, find the file, and click Open. WordPerfect briefly displays the conversion information box, and then opens the document in WordPerfect.

**NOTE**

In earlier versions of WordPerfect, a conversion dialog box indicated the format of the document and asked you to confirm the format before opening it. Perhaps because you might not even know the format of the document being converted, WordPerfect now takes charge and converts and opens the document without your intervention.

By default, WordPerfect installs all of its conversion filters, and thus you can be assured that if WordPerfect can convert a file, it will. WordPerfect supports and converts a number of common modern formats, including the following:

Ami Pro

ANSI/ASCII (Windows and DOS; Text, Delimited, C/R L/F to SRt)

DisplayWrite

HTML (Hypertext Markup Language)

IA5

Microsoft Word (many older versions for both DOS and Windows)

Microsoft Word 6.0/7.0 for Windows

Microsoft Word 97/2000/2002/2003 for Windows

MultiMate

OfficeWriter

RTF

RTF Japanese

SGML

Unicode

VolksWriter

WordPerfect (4.x, 5.x; Macintosh)

WordPerfect 5.1/5.2 (Far East)

WordPerfect 6.x, 7, 8, 9, 10, 11

WordPerfect Compound File

WordStar 2000

XyWrite

XML (Extensible Markup Language; UTF-8, UTF-16 Big Endian and Little Endian)

## USING DATA FROM UNSUPPORTED FORMATS

Despite WordPerfect's extensive support for automatic file conversions, you're bound to discover a document sometime that can't be opened in WordPerfect. When you try to open such a file, WordPerfect displays the Convert File Format dialog box (see Figure 15.13), and the Convert File Format From box shows Unsupported Format. There are a few methods for dealing with this problem:

**Figure 15.13**
If WordPerfect can't convert a file, it displays the Convert File Format dialog box, where you can choose an alternative conversion format.

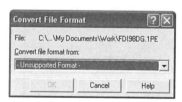

- If you know the source of the document (for example, WordPerfect 4.2), make sure you have installed the necessary conversion filters. If you think you know what program created the file, but aren't sure what version, try various options to see whether you can open the file.

15

- If you have the original program used to create the file, open the document in the other program and see whether you can save it to an intermediate format, such as RTF, that WordPerfect understands. You might lose some formatting in the translation, but you'll retain the content of the document.

- When all else fails, you can usually open the file as an ASCII file. Try the CR/LF to SRt option first because it converts the hard returns at the end of ASCII lines to soft returns, thus preserving text paragraphs.

**CAUTION**

> Always use the ASCII import as a last resort because you lose all document formatting with this option. ASCII imports also usually require extensive editing to clean up the resulting conversion.

## USING WORDPERFECT'S CONVERSION UTILITY

Although you can easily convert non-WordPerfect files one-by-one on-the-fly, you can also convert entire groups of files, and store the converted results in a folder you specify.

Suppose, for example, you have dozens of Word documents. Your company has come to its senses and is now switching to WordPerfect. You could create a special folder, for example "Conversion," and convert all your Word documents at once, saving them in that folder. To convert several documents at once, follow these steps:

1. Start the Conversion Utility by going to the Windows Start button, choosing All Programs, WordPerfect Office 12 (or WordPerfect Office 11), Utilities, and Conversion Utility (the exact location might differ on your computer).

2. In the WordPerfect Office Conversion Utility screen (see Figure 15.14), click the New Folder option, supply a name and location for the new folder, and click Create Folder.

**Figure 15.14**
You can convert non-WordPerfect documents to the WordPerfect format, en masse, by using the WordPerfect Office Conversion Utility.

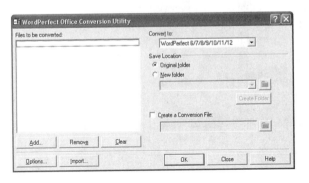

3. Click the Add button and browse to find and select the files you want to convert. Note that you can hold the Ctrl key and click to select more than one file at a time.

**TIP FROM**

*Read Gilgen*

If you want to select all files of a certain type, for example Word files with a .doc extension, in the Select Files to be Converted dialog box, click the View Menu button on the toolbar and choose Details. Then click the Type button at the top of the list to sort files by file type. You can then easily select all files of the same type.

4. Click Add to add the selected files to the conversion list. Repeat step 3 to add more files from other locations.

5. Click OK to convert the files.

Because it's easy to convert files only as you need them, you rarely need to use this utility. But if you do, it's nice to know it's there.

## EDITING A CONVERTED DOCUMENT

Although WordPerfect does a great job of converting a wide variety of document formats, inevitably you'll find that certain things don't convert cleanly.

The first reason is that WordPerfect tries to maintain the exact format of the original document. Because other word processing programs use different default layouts, this often causes WordPerfect to add margin, font, or style codes to the converted document that you wouldn't find in a typical WordPerfect document. For example, Figure 15.15 shows the Reveal Codes screen from a converted Word document, along with its opening styles in the Styles Editor dialog box.

**Figure 15.15**
You can use Reveal Codes to determine what codes, such as margins, tab sets, or styles, must be changed or deleted from an imported document.

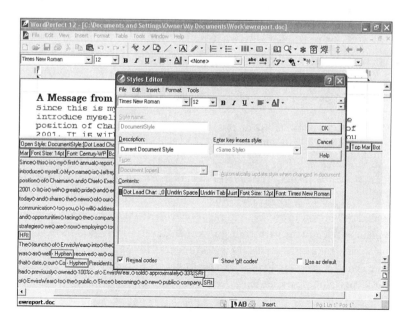

15

The second reason is that WordPerfect doesn't always know how to handle certain formatting. When WordPerfect guesses, it sometimes guesses wrong.

The resulting converted WordPerfect document must be cleaned up to become a truly useable document. The following are some strategies you can use to complete the conversion process:

■ Open Reveal Codes and see what kinds of codes you have to deal with. It might be that you can simply delete a few codes and be back to a standard WordPerfect layout.

**TIP FROM**

*Read Gilgen*

> Don't forget that you can delete codes by using the mouse to click and drag codes out of the Reveal Codes window.

■ In Reveal Codes, double-click the initial Open Style: Document Style button to display the document default codes (refer to Figure 15.15). Only codes that differ from WordPerfect's default codes appear in this dialog box. Remove any codes that shouldn't be there.

■ Use the Spell Checker, which often finds legitimate words combined with special characters.

■ Use Find and Replace to match codes or characters and to replace them with the appropriate codes or with nothing. For example, you might replace the typical Word margin setting of 1.25 inches with nothing, which returns the document to the default 1-inch WordPerfect margin. Although using Find and Replace can be a bit tedious, after you're familiar with what you need to replace, this can save you a lot of time.

■ Use macros if you have a lot of documents to clean up. You can use macros to set up, find, and replace various codes so you don't have to do these things manually.

→ To learn more about Find and Replace, **see** "Searching for Text by Using Find and Replace," **p. 148**

→ To learn how to use macros, **see** "Using Macros to Automate Repetitive Tasks" in Chapter 26, "Using Experts and Macros."

## SAVING AND EXPORTING TO OTHER WORD PROCESSING PROGRAMS

So, you're the only maverick in the office. They tell you you'll have to switch to Word someday, but you insist on keeping your trusted WordPerfect. Fortunately, you can also exchange documents with your co-workers, even if they don't use WordPerfect. You already know how to open and edit their documents. To send your documents to them in a format they can use, you simply use Save As to save the document. To save a document in a different format, follow these steps:

1. Choose File, Save As. WordPerfect displays the Save As dialog box.

2. Type the name of the file you want to use, unless you intend to use the same name.

3. Click the File Type drop-down menu and select the file format you want to convert to (for example, MS Word 97/2000/2002/2003 for Windows). In most cases, WordPerfect adds the appropriate filename extension (for example, .doc).

4. Click Save. WordPerfect converts the document into the selected format.

If you continue to work on the document and save it again, WordPerfect prompts you with the Save Format dialog box (see Figure 15.16). Unless you want to change back to the WordPerfect format, click the conversion format (for example, MS Word 97 for Windows) and click OK.

**Figure 15.16**
When you save a document whose original format is other than the current version of WordPerfect, WordPerfect asks which format you want to save it to.

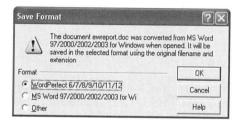

> **NOTE**
> When you convert and open a document from another format, you get the same Save Format dialog box the first time you save it. If you intend to keep the document in WordPerfect format, click OK, and WordPerfect does not prompt you again.

# IMPORTING AND USING DATABASE DATA

Data conversion typically centers on word processing information. But you can also convert and use data from other sources, such as databases and spreadsheets.

## CONVERTING TO WORDPERFECT FORMATS

WordPerfect's database format is the merge data file. Each record is separated by an end of record code, and each field is separated by an end of field code (see Figure 15.17). This structure is typical for any flat-file database—that is, individual records are divided into common fields.

Any database that uses a similar structure can be converted into a WordPerfect data file.

> **NOTE**
> Relational databases do not convert well to a typical merge data file format because they are too complex. Records with one set of fields relate to other records with a different set of fields. Each set of records, typically, is its own database. Because only information that can be extracted in a flat format (one type of record and set of fields) can be imported into a WordPerfect merge data file, you must import separately each table of a relational database.

**Figure 15.17**
Merge data files separate records and fields with merge codes.

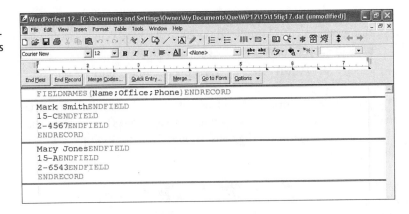

To import a database into a WordPerfect format, follow these steps:

1. Choose Insert, Spreadsheet/Database, Import. WordPerfect displays the Import Data dialog box (see Figure 15.18).

**Figure 15.18**
The Import Data dialog box enables you to import many database and spreadsheet formats.

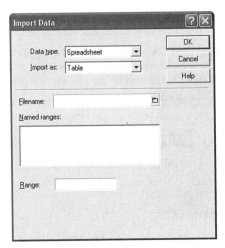

2. From the Data Type drop-down menu, select the format of the database you want to import. Database formats supported by WordPerfect include the following:

   - Clipper
   - dBASE
   - FoxPro
   - Paradox
   - ODBC (Microsoft's Open Database Connect) standard—for example, Microsoft Access and ODBC (SQL)
   - ASCII and ANSI delimited text

**NOTE**

Nearly any database program can create database files of ASCII-delimited text. ASCII is plain text, and delimiters separate the records and fields of such text. Typical delimiters include commas, spaces, quotation marks, and so on.

**TIP FROM**

*Read Gilgen*

If you convert a lot of the same type of ASCII delimited files, you can select Tools, Settings and use the Convert tab of the Convert Settings dialog box to set the ASCII delimiters you use most often.

3. From the Import As drop-down menu, select the target format in WordPerfect. Options include the following:

- Table—Each row is a database record, and each column is a field in a record.

- Text—Each line is a database record, and each field in the line is separated by a tab.

- Merge Data File—Records and fields import with merge codes (refer to Figure 15.17). This can be particularly useful if you want to manage or reuse the data—for example, in merge letters.

→ For more information on using merge data files, **see** "Merging a Form Document with a Data File" in Chapter 24, "Assembling Documents with Merge."

4. Browse to find a database filename of the same type as the data you selected.

5. The bottom portion of the screen changes depending on the type of database you import (see Figure 15.19). The ASCII delimited type, for example, asks you to specify just what the delimiters are. The example shows that fields are separated by commas, and records are separated by a combination line feed and carriage return. Change the delimiters, if necessary, to match those used in the database. Click the Delimiters or Characters drop-down menu to select nonkeyboard delimiters such as Tabs or Carriage Returns. Other databases enable you to choose which fields to import for each record. This can be particularly useful if the number of database fields is large.

6. Click OK to import the database into your WordPerfect document.

**TIP FROM**

*Read Gilgen*

With many database types, you can open the database directly through the Open File dialog box. When you do, WordPerfect recognizes the database format and automatically displays the Import Data dialog box with all the appropriate information already filled in.

If you import a database from a program such as Paradox, after clicking OK you might also see one or more of the options in the Import Data dialog box, shown in Figure 15.20.

15

**Figure 15.19**
In the Import Data dialog box, you can specify the delimiters to be used when importing an ASCII-delimited database.

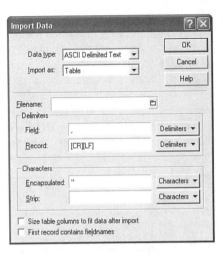

**Figure 15.20**
In the Import Data dialog box, import options are available when importing more complex data such as a database from Paradox.

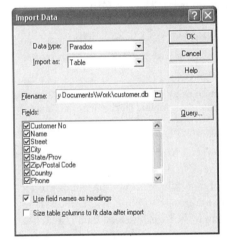

The options include

- Query—You can set criteria before importing data so that you get only the data you need (see Figure 15.21). For example, if you want only the records for customers from the United States, you could query the database and have it extract and import only those Country records that equal U.S.A.

**TIP FROM**

If you're not sure how to use the query criteria, click Example for hints and examples.

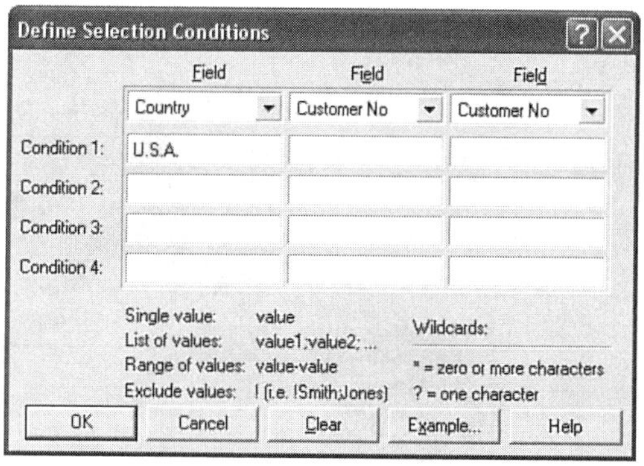

**Figure 15.21**
When importing a database, you can use the Define Selection Conditions dialog box to extract and import records that meet criteria you set.

- Fields—If the database contains a large number of fields, you might want to limit the number of fields that you import into the WordPerfect document. Select the ones you want to import, and deselect the ones you want to exclude.

- Table—If the file has multiple record types, each must be imported separately. Choose the record set you want from the Table list. The Paradox being imported in Figure 15.20 does not contain multiple record types, and therefore the Import Data dialog box does not show a Table list.

## LINKING DATABASE DATA

WordPerfect also enables you to link an imported database so that changes to the original database can be updated in WordPerfect. To link a database to a WordPerfect document, follow these steps:

1. Choose Insert, Spreadsheet/Database, Create Link. WordPerfect displays the Create Data Link dialog box (refer to Figure 15.20, which is identical to the Import Data dialog box).

2. Choose the data type, the target format (Link As), the name of the database, and other options.

3. Click OK to import the database, with links to the original database file.

You can also update the link and choose other link options from the Insert, Spreadsheet/Database menu:

- Edit Link—This option returns you to the Edit Data Link dialog box (refer to Figure 15.20, which, again, is the same as the Create Data Link dialog box), where you can change the name of the file, the target format, the fields to be imported, and so on.

- Update—This option displays the Update dialog box, which asks whether you want to update all links. If you answer Yes, WordPerfect goes back to the original database and refreshes the data in the WordPerfect document.

- Options—This displays the Link Options dialog box (see Figure 15.22). You can choose to automatically update linked data when the document opens. By default, WordPerfect

15

also displays link icons in the left margin of the document to let you know you have a linked database.

**Figure 15.22**
You can use the Link Options dialog box to specify how a linked database or spreadsheet should be updated. Note the link icon in the document margin.

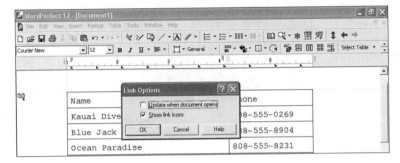

## SORTING DATABASE DATA IN TABLES

Sorting database information in WordPerfect tables is easy and practical. To sort table information, follow these steps:

1. Position the insertion point anywhere in the table.

2. Choose Tools, Sort, or press Alt+F9. WordPerfect displays the Sort dialog box (see Figure 15.23).

**Figure 15.23**
You can use the Sort feature to sort data in tables.

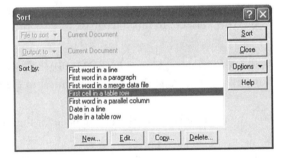

> **NOTE**
>
> WordPerfect enables you to sort information from a variety of formats, including tables, merge files, lines, and paragraphs. The procedures described here apply generally to other sorting as well.

3. Choose the type of sort you want. By default, the first time you sort a table, WordPerfect assumes that you want to sort by the first word in the first cell of each table row.

4. Click Sort to perform the sort.

**CAUTION**

Be sure to save your work before you perform any sort. By default, you cannot undo a sort, and you want to be able to return to a correct copy of the document if something goes wrong.

**NOTE**

Imported database tables already have header rows that do not get sorted with the rest of the data. In tables you create, you must use the Row tab of the Table Format dialog box to specify header rows before sorting. Otherwise, the header rows get sorted along with everything else.

If sorting by the first word of the first cell isn't what you had in mind, you can select a definition from the Sort By list and click Edit. You can also click New to create a new definition.

**NOTE**

It's usually best to leave original default sort definitions alone and to create new ones if you need different sort criteria. That way, you always have at least one unchanged example if you need to refer to it.

To create a new sort definition, follow these steps:

1. Access the Sort dialog box (refer to Figure 15.23).
2. Click New. WordPerfect displays the New Sort dialog box (see Figure 15.24).

**Figure 15.24**

You can use the New Sort dialog box to set up a new sort definition.

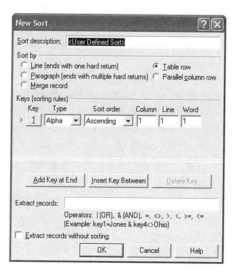

3. Edit the sort description (for example, USA Customer List Sorted by Phone Number).

4. Make sure Table Row is selected.

5. Edit the sorting rules, using these options:

- Key—The first sorting rule is also the first key. You can choose Add Key at End of the rules, Insert Key Between other rules, or Delete Key if there are two or more in the list.

- Type—You can choose Alpha or Numeric from the drop-down list. Alpha sorts in alphabetic order, and Numeric sorts by numeric value. In an Alpha sort, for example, 11 comes before 2.

- Sort Order—Choose Ascending (A–Z) or Descending (Z–A) from the drop-down list.

- Column—Specify the column of data to sort on.

- Line—Specify which line to sort on, if there is more than one line of text in the cells (for example, a multiline address).

- Word—Specify which word to sort on. 1 means the first word, 2 the second word, and so on. To count from the end of the line, specify –1 for the last word, –2 for the next-to-the-last word, and so on.

**TIP FROM**

*Read Gilgen*

When sorting by last name, specify –1. If you specify 2, you sort on the second name, even for people who have three names (for example, *Cynthia Lynn Lacayo*, sorts by *Lynn*).

- Extract Records—You can discard records that you don't want and sort the remaining records. Simply set up one key and specify what it should contain (for example, key1=U.S.A.).

6. Click OK to return to the Sort dialog box.

Setting up sort criteria takes some getting used to. Remember that the second key applies only *after* the first key has finished sorting. For example, you might make the first key sort by ZIP Code to group everyone by ZIP Code, and then make the second key sort by last name to alphabetize each ZIP Code group. See Figure 15.25, which shows the setup for sorting a customer list by phone number and extracts only records that contain U.S.A. in the second column.

Before sorting, you should consider at least one more option. Click Options in the Sort dialog box and choose Allow Undo after sorting if you want to be able to undo your sort. This setting remains in effect until you change it.

Finally, click Sort and see what happens. You will likely have the opportunity to use Undo and try it again.

**Figure 15.25**
The New Sort dialog box shows criteria for sorting a U.S.A.-only customer phone list.

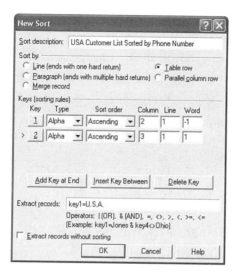

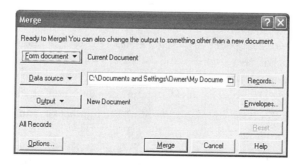

**TIP FROM**

*Read Gilgen*

> If you want to be able to undo a sort that doesn't work as you expected it to, choose Allow Undo from the Options in the Merge dialog box.

## USING DATABASE DATA WITH MERGE

Importing database information to a WordPerfect merge data file is faster and easier than typing all the data over again, but wouldn't it be even nicer if you could merge directly from the database file itself so you don't have two separate databases?

You can! To merge directly from a database file, follow these steps:

1. Create a merge form file.

   → For information on creating merge documents, **see** "Creating Form Files," **p. 758.**

2. Access the Merge dialog box (by selecting Tools, Merge, by pressing Shift+F9, or by clicking the Merge button on the Merge toolbar). WordPerfect displays the Merge dialog box (see Figure 15.26).

**Figure 15.26**
In the Merge dialog box, you can specify a database file in place of a standard merge data file.

**3.** Choose the type of database source file you'll use by clicking the Data Source drop-down menu, which includes the following options:

- File on Disk, for Paradox and WordPerfect merge data files
- Address Book, for address book files found on your computer
- ODBC, for Access, dBASE, or FoxPro files

**4.** Choose the options you want, such as Select Records to query the database, or Envelopes if you want to merge address information to envelopes along with the merge document.

**5.** Click Merge to perform the merge. WordPerfect merges the data directly from your database file with the merge form document.

## IMPORTING AND EXPORTING A DATABASE TO AND FROM TABLES

The Table Convert feature enables you to change ASCII-delimited text to table format, or to change table data into database or merge formats.

Suppose someone sends you a comma-delimited database file as a plain-text file. You can, of course, use the methods described earlier in this section to import the database file into a table. However, an easier method is to simply open the file and then convert it to a table. To convert onscreen data to a table, follow these steps:

**1.** Select all the data (that is, all the records of the database).

**2.** Choose Table, Convert. WordPerfect displays the Convert: Text to Table dialog box (see Figure 15.27).

**Figure 15.27**
The Convert: Text to Table dialog box helps you quickly convert a variety of data formats to a table.

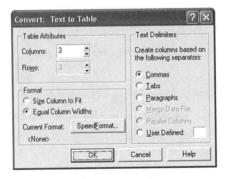

**3.** Choose the type of data being converted—that is, the type of delimiters being used to separate the fields of each record of the database. WordPerfect makes a guess (usually the correct one), but you can change that by choosing from among Comma, Tab, Paragraph, Merge Data file, Parallel Columns, or a delimiter of your own choosing.

**4.** Choose any other options you want, including the number of columns, column format, or table format using SpeedFormat.

**5.** Click OK to convert the text to a table.

Another handy use for this feature is to convert table data into delimited database format, or into a list or a merge file. For example, you might simply want a sequential list of addresses, without having to first create a merge form to extract the data from the table. Or, you might want to convert the table to a merge data file because you find that using a table isn't practical because you have too many fields.

To convert table data to a database or other format, follow these steps:

1. Position the insertion point anywhere in the table.

2. Choose Table, Convert. WordPerfect displays the Convert: Table to Text dialog box (see Figure 15.28).

**Figure 15.28**
The Convert: Table to Text dialog box helps you easily convert WordPerfect table data to other data formats.

3. Choose the format to which the data will be converted.

**NOTE**

When you convert data from a table to a text format, each field is separated by the delimiter you select, and each record is separated by an HRt code. The exception is the Paragraph format, where fields and records alike are separated by an HRt code.

**CAUTION**

You cannot convert the results of a Paragraph conversion back to a table. You can use Undo, but if you plan to reuse the data in a table format, you should save the converted table with a different filename.

4. Click OK to convert the table data.

**TIP FROM**

*Read Gilgen*

If you want to create an address list from your table, and want each address to be separated by a blank line, insert a column after the last column of your table before converting it to paragraph format.

**15**

# IMPORTING AND USING SPREADSHEET DATA

Another important type of data that you might need in a WordPerfect document comes from spreadsheets. Because spreadsheets are typically arranged in rows and columns, what better way to present spreadsheet data than in a WordPerfect table?

## CONVERTING SPREADSHEET DATA

WordPerfect can convert data from nearly any modern spreadsheet program, including Quattro Pro and Excel. To import a spreadsheet into WordPerfect, follow these steps:

1. Choose Insert, Spreadsheet/Database, Import.

**TIP FROM**

> If you simply open a spreadsheet, WordPerfect opens the Import Data dialog box and fills in most of the spreadsheet information for you.

2. From the Data Type drop-down menu, select Spreadsheet.
3. From the Import As drop-down menu, select the target format in WordPerfect. Options are the same as for databases, WordPerfect tables, plain tab-delimited text, and WordPerfect merge data files. Table is the default format.
4. Browse to find the filename of the spreadsheet you want to import.
5. Click in the Named Ranges box, or press Tab. WordPerfect displays any named ranges it finds in the spreadsheet, and shows the upper-left and lower-right cells of the range (for example, A1...F8).

**TIP FROM**

> Because spreadsheets can be much larger than a typical word processing page, it helps to create named ranges in the spreadsheet program to make it easier to extract only portions of a spreadsheet in WordPerfect.

6. If there are no named ranges, or you want to specify a different range, in the Range box type the upper-left and lower-right cells of the area of the spreadsheet you want to import.
7. Click OK to insert the selected portion of the spreadsheet in a WordPerfect table (see Figure 15.29).

## LINKING SPREADSHEET DATA

You can also link spreadsheet data to a WordPerfect table the same way you link database data (see the section "Linking Database Data," earlier in this chapter). The functions and options for each are identical.

**Figure 15.29**
An imported spreadsheet looks like any other WordPerfect table, except that it can also include table formulas, marked by a triangle in the lower-right corner of the cell.

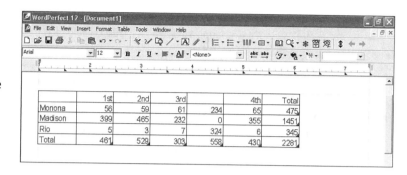

## USING SPREADSHEET FORMULAS IN TABLES

One huge difference between typical tables and tables that contain imported spreadsheets is that the latter also include formulas, and such tables function just like spreadsheets. In fact, even WordPerfect tables you create can also be made to function like spreadsheets by using formulas.

To work with formulas in WordPerfect tables, use the following options:

- The Formula toolbar—Position the insertion point in the table and choose Table, Formula Toolbar. Alternatively, you can right-click the table and choose Formula Toolbar from the QuickMenu. WordPerfect displays a formula bar and buttons to assist in working with table numeric data (see Figure 15.30, which also shows a formula in the Formula text box because the insertion point is in cell F5, which contains a formula).

**Figure 15.30**
A table can contain formulas that function like those in a spreadsheet.

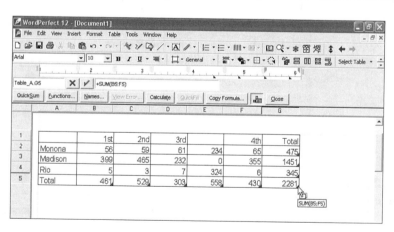

**15**

**TIP FROM**

*Read Gilgen*

Double-click a blue formula indicator in a table cell to display the Formula toolbar along with the formula for that cell.

- Row/column indicators—If the Formula toolbar is already displayed, click the Turn Row/Column Indicators On or Off button, or choose Table, Row/Col Indicators. WordPerfect displays spreadsheet-like row and column indicators (refer to Figure 15.30).

Working with formulas in WordPerfect tables is perhaps even easier than working with a spreadsheet program. Consider the price list table in Figure 15.31, which illustrates some of the following options you have in creating and working with table formulas:

**Figure 15.31**
This price list uses table formulas to calculate discount prices.

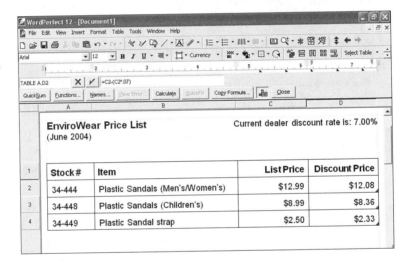

- The Formula text box—Here, you can type formulas. For example, to show a 7% discount price, in cell D2 you enter C2-(C2*.07).

**CAUTION**

Be sure your insertion point is in the cell where you want the formula before you click the Formula text box. Otherwise, you'll enter a formula where you didn't expect to.

- Accept Formula—Enters the formula into the table cell. You can also press Enter.

- Cancel Formula—Cancels the formula you might have been building. You can also press Esc.

15

- QuickSum—Click this button to quickly add all contiguous numeric cells above the cell that contains the insertion point. If the first cell above that point is blank, QuickSum adds contiguous cells to the left.

 *If you're having trouble making a column of text add properly, see "Ignoring Values in Text Cells" in the Troubleshooting section at the end of this chapter.*

- Functions—You can choose from a complete array of spreadsheet functions from the Table Functions dialog box (see Figure 15.32). Click a function to display a brief description of what it does and how to use it.

**Figure 15.32**
WordPerfect enables you to use a complete set of spreadsheet formula functions, such as the one used to calculate a periodic payment.

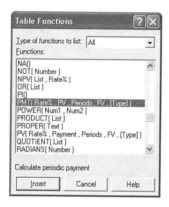

- Names—You can name cells and ranges of cells, and use those names in table formulas. You can even link the values of named cells in one table to formulas in other tables, or in floating cells.

- View Error—If you get an error message (if you build a formula incorrectly, for example), click this button to find out why you got the error and how to fix the problem.

- Calculate—You can force the table to recalculate. By default, tables automatically calculate when you make changes. If you have turned off this default (Table, Calculate), you'll need to recalculate your table after making any changes. Also, it's a good idea to recalculate everything one last time before printing.

- QuickFill—This option enables you to begin a series of numbers in a row or column, and then select the entire column and fill in the rest of the cells automatically.

- Copy Formula—The Copy Formula dialog box (see Figure 15.33) enables you to copy a formula to a specific cell, up or down, or to the left or right *n* number of cells.

**Figure 15.33**
You can use the Copy Formula dialog box to copy formulas to other parts of a table, just as you do in a spreadsheet.

15

**TIP FROM**

Read Gilgen

You can copy a formula by dragging its formula indicator to another cell.

**CAUTION**

When you copy a formula to another cell, the formula's cell references change to reflect their relative location. For example, if you copy the formula to add a column of numbers to a different column, the formula changes to add the numbers in the target column, not in the column from which it was copied. Although this is generally what you want to happen, be aware that you might have to check your copied formulas to make sure they are calculating what you expect them to calculate.

You can also use the row/column indicators to select entire rows or columns by simply clicking the row or column indicator. You can use drag and drop to move the selected row or column.

You can also access the Table menu or the QuickMenu and choose Format to change column alignments and other features. Choose Numeric Format from the same menus to apply formats such as currency and percentages (see Figure 15.34).

**Figure 15.34**
You can use the Properties for Table Numeric Format dialog box to set formatting for numbers, such as currency, percentage, and so on.

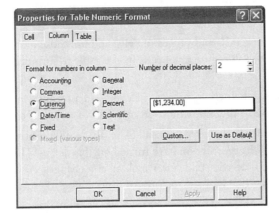

## USING FLOATING CELLS

Floating cells are another way of working with spreadsheet data, but in a somewhat unusual way. Floating cells are invisible cells that display their content as if they are part of the text that surrounds them. In Figure 15.35, for example, the discount percentage displayed in the floating cell is also referenced in the formulas in Column D that show the discounted price. If you change the value in the floating cell, the discounted price amounts also change.

**Figure 15.35**
A floating cell looks like other text, but the data is contained between two floating cell codes, shown here in Reveal Codes.

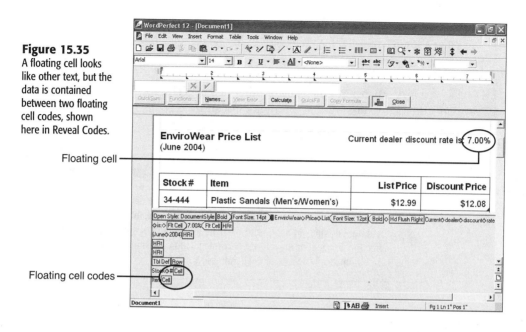

To create a floating cell, its formula, and numeric format, follow these steps:

1. Position the insertion point where you want the floating cell.

2. Choose Table, Create, or press F12. WordPerfect displays the Create Table dialog box (see Figure 15.36).

**Figure 15.36**
You can use the Create Table dialog box to create a floating cell.

3. Choose Floating Cell and click Create. WordPerfect inserts a pair of floating cell codes in your document and turns on the Formula toolbar (refer to Figure 15.35).

4. Click the Formula text box and then create the formula for the floating cell. Click the Accept Formula button to place the formula in the floating cell.

**TIP FROM**

You can point to table cells or other floating cells to build formulas in the Formula text box.

5. Click on the displayed text of the floating cell; then choose Table, Numeric Format, and select a numeric format for the floating cell (for example, Percent, to two decimal places).

That's it! As you make changes to the table or other floating cells, the results automatically recalculate. If you want to be sure, you can right-click any of these and choose Calculate from the QuickMenu.

**TIP FROM**

*Read Gilgen*

> One particularly good use for floating cells is a mortgage loan letter. If you've ever seen a form letter from the bank telling you what your mortgage rate will be, you know they don't sit down and type each of the loan figures in by hand. Indeed, you can create similar documents by using floating cells that contain the principal, interest rate, and number of payment periods, and yet another to calculate the amount of each payment. When you change the principal or the interest percentage and calculate the document, all the other cells automatically update quickly and easily.

# TROUBLESHOOTING

### PASTING UNFORMATTED TEXT

*Sometimes when I paste text, it's not the right font.*

When you copy text from another source, you also copy formatting codes. To paste unformatted text, choose Edit, Paste Special, and choose Unformatted.

### KEEPING FILES SMALL

*Some of my documents are getting huge and taking up a lot of disk space. All I've done is drag some data into them from Excel.*

This is a common problem with documents that contain OLE objects. For example, a WordPerfect document with a simple clip art object might be only 25KB in size, but if you edit the graphic in the Draw program, it becomes an OLE object and the document increases in size to more than 100KB. Instead, you might consider editing the clip art image outside of WordPerfect (for example, in Presentations), save the clip art image, and then insert the image into your WordPerfect document. The only other way to avoid this is to avoid using OLE, because this is a problem associated with the OLE technology, not with WordPerfect itself. You have to determine whether you want small files, or the convenience of editing objects in place in WordPerfect.

### KEEPING DATA UP TO DATE

*I imported information from a company database, but now someone updated the database and my document doesn't match.*

*Instead of importing a database that might change, choose Insert, Spreadsheet/Database, Link. That way, if the database changes, you need only update the link, not the whole database.*

### ADDING A FORMULA TO A FLOATING CELL

*I can't seem to add a formula to a floating cell.*

Open Reveal Codes and make sure the insertion point is positioned between the floating cell codes. Then, you can use the Formula toolbar to create a floating cell formula.

### IGNORING VALUES IN TEXT CELLS

*I created an invoice using a table, but when I calculate the total due, it's always wrong. I checked the formulas and they're all correct.*

Check to see whether your formula includes a text cell, and whether that text cell contains any numbers. WordPerfect ignores text and uses the numeric value of a cell that contains both text and numbers. For example, if you're adding an entire column, and the top cell contains an invoice number, the value of the invoice number is added to the total of the column.

To avoid this problem, right-click the cell, choose Format, and in the Cell tab of the Table Format dialog box, choose Ignore Cell When Calculating. Then recalculate the table, and the formula should now yield the correct result.

## PROJECT

WordPerfect's built-in spreadsheet capabilities, along with the ability to import database data, enable you to create wonderfully powerful documents. Suppose, for example, you want to build an invoice that links to a company price list. As the prices change in the database and are updated in the price list, so, too, do the numbers in the invoice change. Consider, for example, the invoice/price list shown in Figure 15.37, which is the result of a carefully set-up database table and table formulas.

> **NOTE**
>
> For details on how to perform some of the tasks in these procedures, refer to the appropriate sections of this chapter.

To create the invoice/price list document, begin by creating the price list:

1. Choose Insert, Spreadsheet/Database, Create Link. You want to link rather than import the data so that you can update the price list from the database as it changes.

2. In the Create Data Link dialog box, specify the database from which the information is drawn. Also, limit the fields you link to those you need for the price list (for example, Part Number, Description, and List Price). Click OK to create the linked database of prices.

**Figure 15.37**
You can combine a linked database of prices with a table and table math to create an automatically updated invoice.

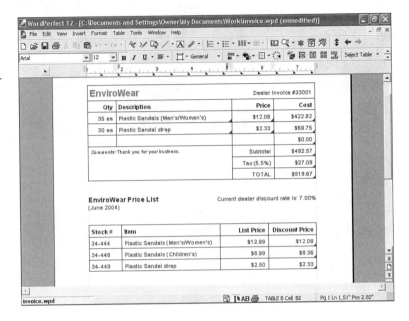

3. Insert a fourth column to the right of the table and adjust the column widths as necessary. Use Format to right-align the last two columns, and use Numeric Format to have them display for currency.

4. Above the table, create a floating cell that indicates the dealer discount: Current dealer discount rate is: Use Numeric Format to format the floating cell (7%) for percent.

**NOTE**

> You must turn on the Formula toolbar to create the percentage as a formula in the floating cell and to create other formulas used in these procedures.

5. In the first Discount Price cell of the price list, create a formula that multiplies the floating cell (above the table) by the list price (to the left of the cell). Check to make sure the formula works correctly (for example, +FLOATING_CELL_A*C2).

6. Copy the formula all the way down the price list.

Now you're ready to create the table for the invoice (refer to Figure 15.37). Position the cursor at the very top of the document and insert a table with the structure and labels shown in Figure 15.38.

→ For information on creating and editing a table structure, **see** Chapter 10, "Working with Tables."

**Figure 15.38**
You should create the structure, formatting, and labels of a table before adding the math formulas.

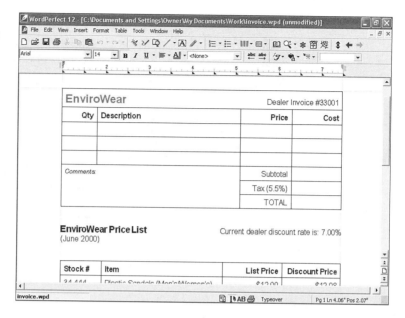

The table includes the following:

- Joined cells for the Invoice heading and for the comment box
- Right-aligned Columns A, C, and D
- Numeric formatting for currency in Columns C and D

Next, create the table formulas that link the price list values to the invoice and calculate the charges, by following these steps:

1. Create a formula in the first blank cell in Column D (for example, D3) that multiplies the quantity times the Price (for example, A3*C3). WordPerfect displays the value $0.00 in D3.

2. With the insertion point in cell D3, copy the formula down to match the number of rows that can contain an order item (for example, two times).

3. Click in the Subtotal cell of Column D and click QuickSum on the Formula toolbar. Again, WordPerfect displays $0.00.

4. Click the Tax cell of Column D and create a formula that multiples the subtotal times the tax in Column C (5.5%). Edit the formula to read D4*(−C5). Because WordPerfect interprets (5.5%) as minus 5.5%, you effectively change it to a positive value.

5. Finally, click the TOTAL cell of Column D, and create a formula to add the Subtotal and Tax cells from Column D.

Finally, you need to add information and prices from the price list. Follow these steps:

1. Copy product descriptions from the price list to the invoice (you can hold down Ctrl while dragging and dropping to copy, rather than move, the information).

2. Click in the cell in Column C, to the right of the description, and then click the Formula text box.

3. Click the cell in the price list that contains the discounted price. WordPerfect displays, for example, TABLE_A.D2 in the Formula text box.

4. Click the Accept button; or press Enter to place the formula/value in the invoice table.

**TIP FROM**

*Read Gilgen*

You could automate these steps by creating a macro that creates a new row in the Invoice table, copies the description to that row, and then creates a link from that row to the product list price. See Chapter 24, "Experts and Macros," for more information on recording and playing macros.

5. Repeat steps 1–4 for each product purchased.

6. Type the quantity ordered in Column A of the invoice (for example, 35 ea).

**NOTE**

WordPerfect ignores text in cells and uses the value of any numbers it finds.

7. Right-click the table and choose Calculate.

If all goes well, the correct values display in the appropriate cells (refer to Figure 15.37). If not, check your formulas to make sure they were created correctly.

Now, as you change the quantity ordered, the discount percentage, or the list price, and calculate again, the invoice updates automatically to give a correct total invoice.

**NOTE**

This chapter only begins to reveal the power of WordPerfect's table/spreadsheet capabilities. If you already know about spreadsheets, you'll quickly discover how to perform similar functions in WordPerfect. If you're new to spreadsheets, experiment with tables and formulas and you'll soon learn just what WordPerfect can do.

# CHAPTER 16

# INSERTING CHARTS

**I**n this chapter                                                         *by Read Gilgen*

# CREATING DATA CHARTS

WordPerfect communicates words effectively, and WordPerfect tables present numbers well. But numbers and words are often more effective when accompanied by charts that present information graphically.

WordPerfect's data chart feature can convert otherwise boring or unintelligible figures into bar charts, pie charts, and more. You can even link charts to tables of data right in WordPerfect.

To create a chart in WordPerfect, choose Insert, Chart. WordPerfect opens a chart editing window and a datasheet filled with sample data, along with the editing tools from the Presentations chart program (see Figure 16.1). A *datasheet* is a small spreadsheet.

**Figure 16.1**
When you create a chart, WordPerfect first displays a bar chart, complete with sample data.

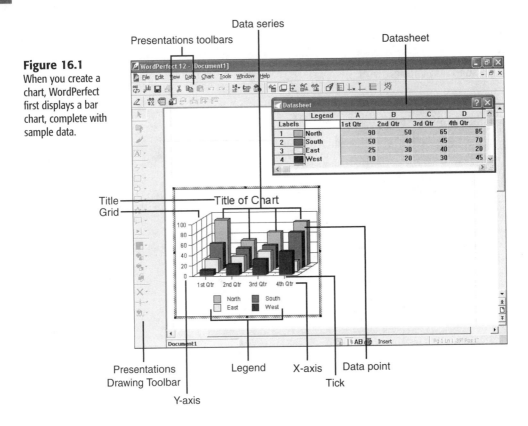

## ENTERING DATA IN DATASHEETS

The foundation for any chart is a series of numbers, and labels to identify those numbers (refer to the datasheet in Figure 16.1). Often, you create such numbers in a spreadsheet, and you can then import that data into the WordPerfect chart. You can also create the numbers in a WordPerfect table, and create the chart based on the table data. Finally, you can enter the numbers directly in the chart's datasheet.

If you use the datasheet for chart numbers, consider the following (see Figure 16.2):

- You can drag and size the datasheet to display a larger spreadsheet-like area.
- The legend identifies rows, or series of data—for example, the figures for the North, South, East, or West regions.
- Each series (that is, row) is represented by a color, along with the legend name.
- The labels refer to columns of data—for example, 1st Quarter, 2nd Quarter, and so on.
- Labels appear horizontally along the X-axis of the chart.
- The values of labels (sometimes broken down by series) are matched with numbers that appear vertically along the Y-axis of the chart.

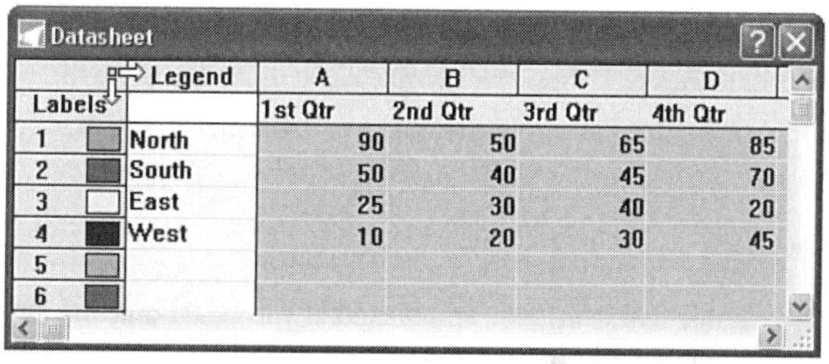

**16**

**Figure 16.2**
You can use the datasheet to prepare the underlying data for a chart.

| Datasheet | | | | | |
|---|---|---|---|---|---|
| ☞ Legend | A | B | C | D | |
| Labels | 1st Qtr | 2nd Qtr | 3rd Qtr | 4th Qtr | |
| 1 ☐ North | 90 | 50 | 65 | 85 | |
| 2 ☐ South | 50 | 40 | 45 | 70 | |
| 3 ☐ East | 25 | 30 | 40 | 20 | |
| 4 ☐ West | 10 | 20 | 30 | 45 | |
| 5 ☐ | | | | | |
| 6 ☐ | | | | | |

You edit labels and data the same way you do in a Quattro Pro spreadsheet. For example, you can click a cell and type replacement data. You can also select entire rows or columns by clicking the row or column indicator, and you can drag, size, copy, or delete the selected data. As you enter each number, WordPerfect automatically updates the chart to reflect the new number.

If you want to start from scratch, choose Edit, Clear All, and then click Yes when asked whether you want to clear all the data. You can also click the upper-left cell (refer to Figure 16.2, where the pointer displays both the row and column select arrows), and then press Delete. When prompted, you can choose to clear Data (the default), Format, or Both. Click OK to clear the data.

The chart editor in Presentations also enables you to use several menu options, along with corresponding toolbar buttons to assist in editing the datasheet. Choose Data to access the following options:

- Format—You can change the numeric formatting of selected cells (for example, to display currency or percent). These changes appear in the chart only if you use data labels.
- Column Width—You can change the width of columns in the datasheet.

- Formulas—You can create formulas in the datasheet, by using the Row/Column Formulas dialog box (see Figure 16.3), but you do not have nearly the power nor flexibility you have in a spreadsheet or even in a WordPerfect table. If you plan to use complex formulas, you should create the data in a spreadsheet or table, and then import the data (see the section "Importing Data into Datasheets," later in this chapter).

**Figure 16.3**
The Row/Column Formulas dialog box enables you to create simple formulas in the datasheet.

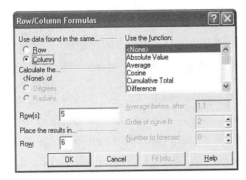

 ■ Recalculate—If you use formulas in the datasheet, and later change the data, you should recalculate the datasheet to make sure you have the correct results.

 ■ Sort—Select an area of data and sort it top to bottom, or left to right, in ascending or descending order.

**CAUTION**

You sort only that which you've selected. If you select only the legend text, for example, you sort only the text but not the data on the rows represented by the legend. You then have data that does not match the legends or labels.

To sort entire rows, including the legends and the data, click on the row indicators, and drag to select all the rows you want to sort. To sort entire columns, including data labels, click the column indicators and click and drag to select the columns you want.

*If you sort your data incorrectly, but now can't get the original, correct data back, see "Saving It Anytime" in the Troubleshooting section at the end of this chapter.*

 ■ Exclude Row/Column—If you don't want a certain row or column to appear in the chart, select the row or column and click this button. WordPerfect also partially hides the data in the datasheet (the numbers and text appear in light gray).

 ■ Include Row/Column—If you want to use a row or column that you've excluded, select that row or column and click this option. The data also reappears in the datasheet.

 ■ Range Highlighter—This option, on the View menu, lets you change the background colors in the rows and columns of the datasheet. It does not change the colors used to represent data in the chart itself.

To return to your WordPerfect document, click the document. The datasheet and Presentations tools disappear, leaving the data chart in a graphics box. Click the document again to deselect the data chart graphics box.

To edit the data chart, double-click it to return to the chart editor.

*If the chart doesn't look as good as it did while you were editing it, see "Don't Worry, Just Print It" in the Troubleshooting section at the end of this chapter.*

## IMPORTING DATA INTO DATASHEETS

Often the data you need for a chart already exists in a spreadsheet. You can import that data or link it to the chart. To import data from a spreadsheet, follow these steps:

1. Choose Data, Import, or click the Import button on the toolbar. WordPerfect displays the Import Data dialog box (see Figure 16.4).

**Figure 16.4**
You can use the Import Data dialog box to import chart information from a spreadsheet.

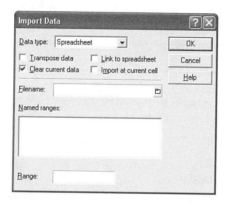

2. Choose the Data Type. Typically, you import data from a spreadsheet, but you can also import numbers from ASCII or ANSI delimited text.

3. Specify a filename. If you browse for a file, by default WordPerfect searches for Quattro Pro spreadsheets. You can, however, import from Lotus, PlanPerfect, or Excel, or from spreadsheet programs that can save data in those formats.

4. Select a range from the Named Ranges box. You can also type a specific range in the Range box, for example A3..D7.

**TIP FROM**

If you prepare a spreadsheet that is to be used in a WordPerfect document, it helps to name ranges, or small sections of the spreadsheet, to facilitate importing it into a chart or table.

5. Choose from the following options:

- Transpose Data—Typically, the heads of columns in a spreadsheet become the labels (the X-axis). To make the rows of a spreadsheet the X-axis, you transpose the data (that is, rows become columns, and columns become rows).

- Clear Current Data—You can merge spreadsheet data with what's already in the datasheet, but typically, you need to clear the data first.

- Link to Spreadsheet—Choose this option to link the spreadsheet and the chart so that the chart can be updated to reflect changes in the spreadsheet.

• Import at Current Cell—Unless you choose this option, WordPerfect imports the spreadsheet data to the upper-left cell of the datasheet.

**CAUTION**

Be sure to include the row and column headings in the range you import from the spreadsheet. Otherwise, spreadsheet numbers appear in place of labels and legends. If you don't have text labels in the spreadsheet, you can avoid this problem by positioning the cursor in cell A1 of the datasheet and using the Import at Current Cell option. You then must add the legend and labels by hand.

**TIP FROM**

*Read Gilgen*

When you import data from a spreadsheet, it often includes rows or columns that you really don't want to include in the chart. In the datasheet, select those rows or columns and choose Data, Exclude to hide them and to exclude them from the chart.

## CREATING A CHART BASED ON A TABLE

You can create a data chart using information you create in a WordPerfect table. This way, not only do you present the graphic illustration of the data, but you also present the data itself in case the reader wants to examine it more closely (see Figure 16.5). An added benefit is that the chart is automatically linked to the table, and changes you make to the table update quickly and easily in the data chart.

**Figure 16.5**
If you base a chart on a WordPerfect table, the reader can refer to both in the document.

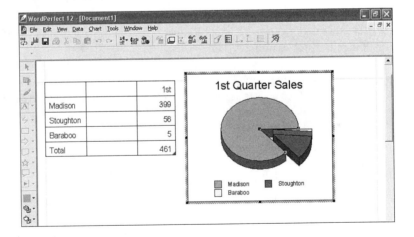

To create a data chart based on a WordPerfect table, follow these steps:

1. Create the table first. Make sure it includes the numeric information you want, and also text labels (column headings) and legend/series (row headings).

2. If you intend to include the entire table in the chart, go to the next step. Otherwise, select those cells you want to include, being sure to include labels.

3. Choose Insert, Chart.

WordPerfect opens the chart editing window and a chart that uses the table data (refer to Figure 16.5). No datasheet is necessary because the table serves that purpose.

To update a chart based on changes you make to its table, click the table, and choose Table, Calculate. WordPerfect recalculates any table formulas that need to be updated, and also updates the chart with the new data.

→ If you're not familiar with WordPerfect's table math capabilities and want to learn how to use this powerful feature, **see** "Using Spreadsheet Formulas in Tables," **p. 489.**

## CHOOSING CHART TYPES

The type of data you use and how you want to present it determine what kind of chart you use. By default, WordPerfect opens a three-dimensional bar chart. To see the wide variety of chart types available after opening a chart-editing window, choose Chart, Gallery. WordPerfect displays the Data Chart Gallery dialog box (see Figure 16.6), where you can choose from among 11 types of charts, and several styles for each:

**Figure 16.6**
The Data Chart Gallery dialog box displays several styles for 11 different chart types.

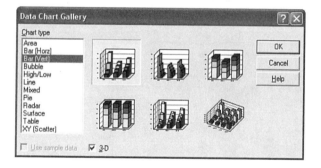

**NOTE**

If you click the Data Chart Gallery button on the toolbar, the palette presents only a limited number of gallery types.

■ Area—These are like line charts, but are filled in from the line down to the X-axis (see Figure 16.7).

**NOTE**

If you insert a new chart and change the chart type before adding data, WordPerfect changes the datasheet to show you, by example, what kind of data you need for each type of chart. You can also click Help in the Data Chart Gallery dialog box to access WordPerfect's online help, which shows examples of each chart type and describes in more detail how and when you typically use each type.

**Figure 16.7**
An area chart is like a line chart, with everything filled in between the X-axis and the data line.

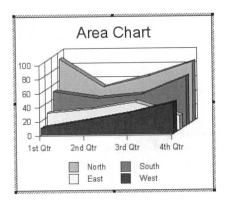

- Bar (Horizontal/Vertical)—Each data point is represented by a bar in this commonly used type of chart (refer to Figure 16.6). Vertical bar charts plot values against the Y-axis, and horizontal charts plot against the X-axis. Bar charts work best when they represent relatively small amounts of comparative data. Otherwise, they can be confusing to the reader.

- Bubble—This type of chart is used to plot three different values on two axes (see Figure 16.8). For example, you can plot units sold (X-axis), gross profit (Y-axis), and net profit (the size or radius of the bubble).

**Figure 16.8**
A bubble chart can plot three different values on two axes.

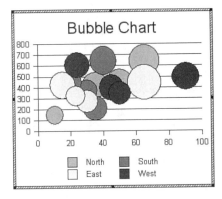

- High/Low—Often used to show stock market fluctuations, the high/low chart plots three values: the value at the beginning of a specified time period, the value at the end of the period, and the spread between the highest and lowest points at any time during the period (see Figure 16.9).

- Line—This type of chart is excellent for showing trends, even with large numbers of data points (see Figure 16.10). For example, attendance over a one-month period, with 30 data points, is easier to visualize with a line chart than with a bar chart.

- Pie—Pies, by definition, are whole (100%, 1.0, and so on). The pie slices represent fractions of the whole. You can use up to nine slices in a single chart (see Figure 16.11).

**Figure 16.9**
A high/low chart is often used to show stock market fluctuations.

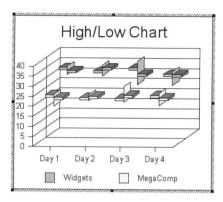

**Figure 16.10**
A line chart makes trends over a period of time easy to understand.

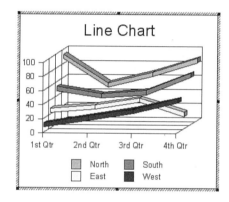

**Figure 16.11**
A pie chart represents parts of a whole (100%).

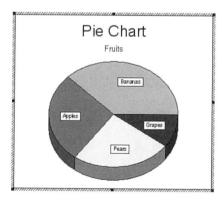

16

■ Radar—This type chart enables you to compare the relative strength of several data points. For example, you can plot team statistics in several categories (see Figure 16.12), and easily see how each team compares.

**Figure 16.12**
A radar chart compares the relative strength of several data points.

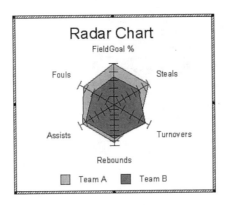

■ Surface—This type chart represents data values as a topography that bulges and dips like the contours of a landscape (see Figure 16.13). The color of the topography changes as the surface rises and falls. For example, you can use a surface chart to show business profits and losses as the peaks and valleys of a mountain range.

**Figure 16.13**
A surface chart shows peaks and valleys topographically.

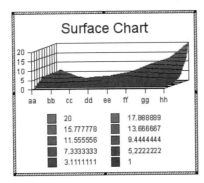

■ Table—Although this appears to be just a fancy table, cells of the table can also reflect the values they contain by their shading (see Figure 16.14).

**Figure 16.14**
A table chart shows table cells highlighted according to the values they contain.

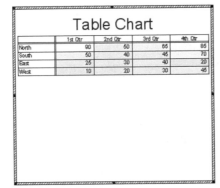

■ XY Scatter—This type of chart is unique in that the top row of the datasheet contains values, not text labels (see Figure 16.15). The data points in the chart represent the relationship between the data in the series and the data in the top row of the table that appears on the X-axis.

**Figure 16.15**
An XY scatter chart shows the relationship between the series data and the X-axis values.

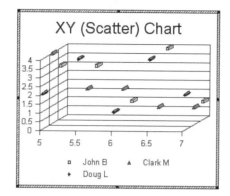

■ Mixed—Sometimes part of the data you want to show works best in a line chart, but another part is more understandable when represented by an area or bar chart (see Figure 16.16). You can use a mixed chart in this situation.

**Figure 16.16**
You can mix different chart types—such as bar, line, and area charts—within the same chart.

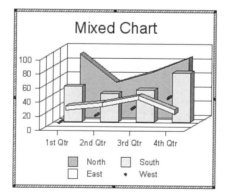

## CHANGING CHART LAYOUT

You can further modify chart types by changing their layout. For example, you can choose to display the chart in a flat two-dimensional layout, or give it some depth by adding a three-dimensional layout.

Each chart type can be modified, albeit some more than others. Consider, for example, the bar chart type, which is a typical example of available layout options. To modify a chart layout, choose Chart, Layout/Type, or click the Layout button on the toolbar. WordPerfect displays the Layout/Type Properties dialog box (see Figure 16.17).

**Figure 16.17**
Use the Layout/Type Properties dialog box to choose chart layout options.

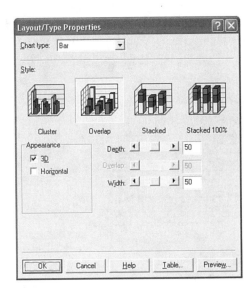

Among the layout choices for bar charts are the following:

- Cluster—Series bars are grouped beside each other.
- Overlap—Series bars are grouped, overlapping each other.
- Stacked—Series bars are stacked one on top of the other, with the height of the bar determined by the cumulative value of each bar.
- Stacked 100%—This option displays all the data points in a column as parts of the whole, just as a pie chart does. For example, 50 and 50 display at exactly the same height, as do 33 and 33.

Other options include 3D (including depth of the bar), No 3D (including amount of overlap), width of the bars, and horizontal orientation.

**TIP FROM**

*Read Gilgen*

Although 3D charts look nifty, a plain 2D chart can sometimes be more effective in communicating the information in the chart. Sometimes less is more.

The layout options for pie charts, another commonly used chart type, are shown in Figure 16.18.

**Figure 16.18**
Options for changing pie charts are quite different from typical bar chart options.

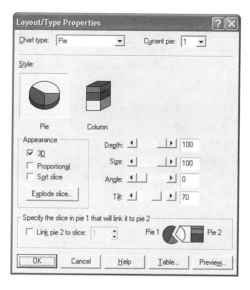

These include the following:

- Column—This is a stacked 100% bar chart.

- Proportional—If you have more than one pie chart (remember, you can have up to nine pie charts), this option enables each to be smaller or larger, depending on the total value of the parts of the pie.

- Sort Slice—Choosing this option arranges the slices of the pie in descending value, beginning at the 3 o'clock mark, and continuing counterclockwise around the pie.

- Explode Slice—If you want a slice to separate from the pie for emphasis, use this option. You can explode one or more slices from the pie (see Figure 16.19).

**Figure 16.19**
You can link a second pie to represent the details of a single slice in the first pie.

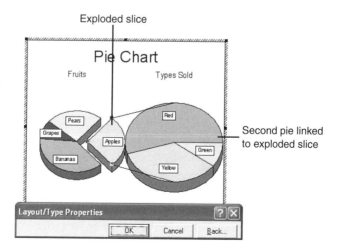

**TIP FROM**

_Read Gilgen_

> The easiest way to explode a slice from a pie chart is simply to click the pie slice in the chart editor and drag it away from the pie.

- Link Pie 2 to Slice—This option, illustrated in Figure 16.19, enables you to show how a second pie in the same datasheet represents a single slice in the first pie. For this option to be available, you have to add data for Pie 2 in the Datasheet, and also click somewhere on Pie 1 before choosing Chart, Layout/Type.

- Depth—This measures the thickness of the pie (like the thickness of a coin), with 100 being the thickest and 0 being the thinnest.

**NOTE**

> It may seem obvious, but you have to select the pie you want to change before you access the Layout/Type Properties dialog box.

- Size—This number is the percentage of the size of the other pie (for example, you can set Pie 2 at 50% the size of Pie 1).

- Angle—This refers to the location, clockwise, of the beginning of the first slice in the pie. By default, the first slice starts at the 3 o'clock position.

- Tilt—In addition to 3D depth, you can also modify the tilt of the pie. You can even tilt each pie differently.

Most of the other chart types include layout options similar to those described for bar and pie charts. If you're not sure what an option does, try it, and then click Preview to see the effect on the chart. WordPerfect then displays a minimized Layout/Type Properties dialog box (refer to Figure 16.19). Click OK to accept the changes, or Back to return to the full dialog box to make further changes.

**TIP FROM**

_Read Gilgen_

> Without actually changing the chart, you can click Preview to see the effect of your changes in the chart. WordPerfect reduces the size of the Layout/Type Properties dialog box. Click Back to return to the full dialog box.

## ADDING TITLES

After you complete the data in the datasheet and select a chart type and layout, you're ready to begin modifying the various chart elements that enhance the reader's comprehension of what the chart represents.

**Figure 16.19**
You can link a second pie to represent the details of a single slice in the first pie.

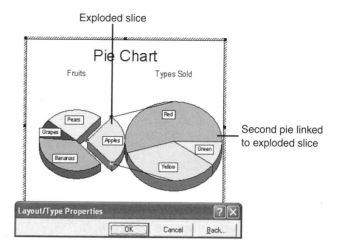

16

 You can probably focus better on the chart if you hide the datasheet. Choose View, Datasheet to toggle the datasheet off, or click the View Datasheet button on the toolbar.

To change the title of the chart, choose Chart, Title, or double-click the title. WordPerfect displays the Title Properties dialog box (see Figure 16.20).

**Figure 16.20**
You can create or edit the title in the Title Properties dialog box.

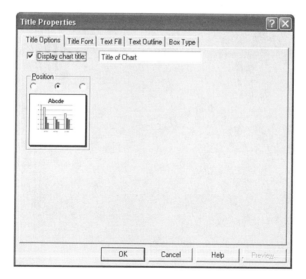

**TIP FROM**

*Read Gilgen*

The easiest way to access the dialog boxes and options for modifying chart elements is simply to double-click the element you want to change. When you get used to this, you'll rarely use menus or buttons to change chart elements.

The Title Options tab enables you to edit the title in the Display Chart Title text box. If you uncheck that option, the chart displays no title. Finally, you can also specify whether to display the title at the left, center, or right of the chart.

**TIP FROM**

*Read Gilgen*

You can drag the title box anywhere you want in the chart-editing screen. However, if you want to return the title to its original position, right-click the title and choose Reset Text.

To change the look of the title, use the Title Font, Text Fill, and Text Outline tabs, each of which enable you to modify the text in attractive and interesting ways. For example, you can change the font, size, and color, modify the type of fill pattern used (including gradient shading), and add a line around the outside edge of each character (an outline line).

→ For more information on modifying text using Presentations, **see** Chapter 14, "Adding Drawings and TextArt."

Finally, you can add a box border around the title by choosing a style from the Box Type tab (see Figure 16.21). If you choose a box style, WordPerfect gives you one more tab on the Title Properties dialog box for modifying the fill used with the title box.

**Figure 16.21**
You can add a border to a title on the Box Type tab of the Title Properties dialog box.

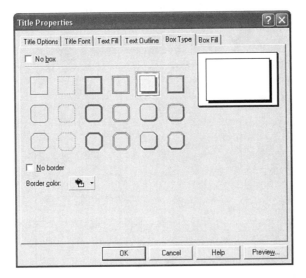

## ADDING AND MODIFYING LEGENDS

Legends help readers quickly identify what various elements on a chart represent. To add or modify a legend, choose Chart, Legend, or click the Legend button on the toolbar. WordPerfect displays the Legend Properties dialog box (see Figure 16.22).

**Figure 16.22**
You can modify the chart legend by using the Legend Properties dialog box.

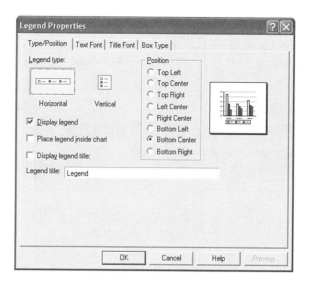

On the Type/Position tab of this dialog box you can use the following options:

- Legend Type—The elements of the legend can be arranged vertically or horizontally.

- Position—Click an option and use the preview box to see where the legend will appear.

- Display Legend—If you don't want a legend—for example, if you need more room for the chart itself—uncheck this option.

- Display Legend Title—Most people recognize a legend when they see one, but if you want to make sure, or if you want to call it something else, choose this option and change the legend title.

The other tabs in this dialog box enable you to change the font of the legend labels or the font of the legend title, or to add a box around the entire legend. Figure 16.23 shows a legend surrounded by a box, vertically arranged at the left of the data chart.

**Figure 16.23**
Legends, which you can place on any side of a chart, help readers identify the different series of data in a chart.

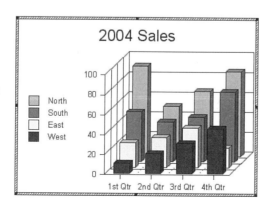

## MODIFYING X- AND Y-AXIS LABELS AND PROPERTIES

The X- and Y-axis options vary depending on whether they represent column headings (labels) or values. To discover the options for an X-axis that represents column headings, choose Chart, Axis, X. WordPerfect displays the X-Axis Properties dialog box (see Figure 16.24).

**Figure 16.24**
You can modify X-axis options with the X-Axis Properties dialog box.

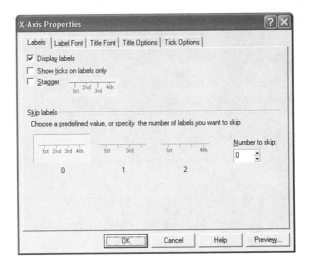

The Labels tab enables you to control how labels are displayed. Often labels contain more text than conveniently fits in the small amount of space available. The options on this tab include the following:

- Display Labels—You can, of course, choose not to display the labels at all. This isn't usually a real choice if you want your readers to know what the data relates to.

- Show Ticks on Labels Only—If you skip labels, you then can specify whether you still want to show the tick marks.

- Stagger—You can stagger the labels so odd labels appear at one vertical position, and even labels appear at another.

- Skip Labels—You can choose predefined values (for example, skip all even labels), or specify how many to skip (for example, skip 3 to display every fourth label).

You can use the Label Font tab to change the font of the labels (column headings) or the title of the X-axis.

**TIP FROM**

*Read Gilgen*

If your X-axis labels don't all fit, even after staggering the labels, try reducing the label font size.

The Title Options tab (see Figure 16.25) enables you to add a title to the Display Title box, and to display it. You can also display the title horizontally or vertically. Displaying the title vertically requires a brief title (for example, one word), and even then, this option takes up so much space that it forces the data chart to shrink dramatically.

**Figure 16.25**
You can use the Title Options tab of the X-Axis Properties dialog box to add a title to the X-axis.

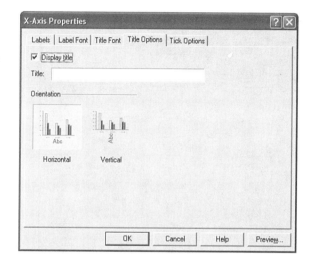

The Tick Options tab (see Figure 16.26) enables you to display major and minor tick marks, pointing away from the chart (out), or into the chart. Major tick marks correspond to the X-axis labels, and minor tick marks separate these major chart elements.

**Figure 16.26**
Tick marks help the reader associate labels or data values with the data in the chart.

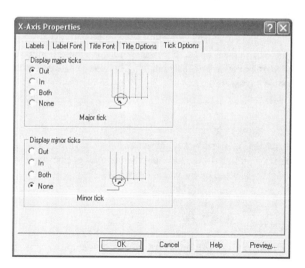

To discover the options for a Y-axis that represents numeric values, choose Chart, Axis, Primary Y. WordPerfect displays the Primary Y Axis Properties dialog box (see Figure 16.27). Font, title, and tick options are identical to those found on the X-Axis Properties dialog box.

**Figure 16.27**
You can use the Primary Y Axis Properties dialog box to establish how values display.

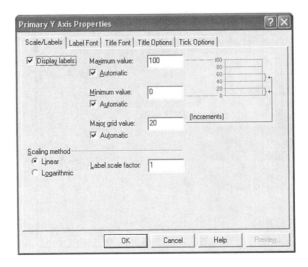

The Scale/Labels tab of this dialog box enables you to specify what values to display. Typically you use linear scaling, which enables you to set a maximum value, a minimum value, and the major grid value, which is the amount of increment between the numbers.

**TIP FROM**

If all the values are relatively high, you can distinguish the data points better by setting a higher minimum value. For example, showing the range from 80 to 100, instead of 0 to 100, makes it easier to tell the difference between a data point that represents 95 and one that represents 92.

**NOTE**

The options for X- and Y-axes are similar for all the data chart types except pie charts, which don't have a Y-axis, and table charts, which enable you to change the properties for table cells based on the values they contain.

## EDITING SERIES ELEMENTS

 A series represents all the data points in a row of the datasheet. Each series has its own color, shape, and style. To modify the properties of a series, choose Chart, Series or click the Series button on the toolbar. WordPerfect displays the Series Properties dialog box (see Figure 16.28). You can select the series you want to change by clicking the forward or back buttons at the left of the Series box.

**Figure 16.28**
You can modify how series of data are displayed in the Series Properties dialog box.

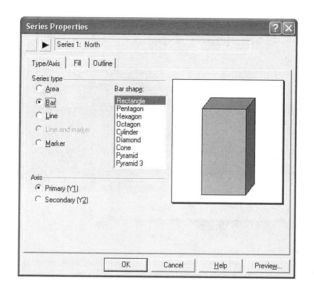

 *If you're having trouble printing your chart so you can distinguish the different series, see "Printing Contrasting Series in Charts" in the Troubleshooting section at the end of this chapter.*

Series types, found on the Type/Axis tab of the Series Properties dialog box, include the following:

- Area—The data is represented as an area chart, the data points connected, and the area filled in, down to the X-axis.

- Bar—Several bar shapes are available, including cylinders, cones, pyramids, and so on. Even in 2D layouts, many of these shapes use gradient shading to simulate dimension.

- Line—Only one option is available: a line that connects data points in a series. However, you can use the Line tab of this dialog box to change the thickness, style, and color of the line.

- Line and Marker—This option is not available if the chart is 3D. You use markers to highlight the data points in a line chart.

- Marker—When used with lines, markers of different shapes and sizes can effectively distinguish between series. For example, for one series you might use a star, and for another, a triangle. You can also specify the size of the marker.

You can also choose to plot a series against a secondary Y-axis. In some charts, one series might be so different in value from the rest of the series that the differences in its data points are barely discernible. To remedy that, you can plot the series against a second Y-axis, scaled for the values in the series, which appears at the right of the chart. Select the series, and choose Secondary (Y2). The chart shown in Figure 16.29 shows the result of applying different series types, with one series (the markers) plotted against a secondary Y-axis.

**Figure 16.29**
You can use a secondary Y-axis to set off series of two markedly different values.

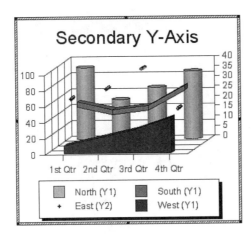

Finally, you can use the Fill and Outline tabs of the Series Properties dialog box to modify the color, fill style, and lines of any of the series shapes.

**TIP FROM**

*Read Gilgen*

> If you single-click a series on the chart or the legend, you can use the Presentations toolbar at the left of the screen to choose fill style, colors, and lines.

## MODIFYING OTHER CHART ELEMENTS

If you haven't already found enough options for modifying your chart, here are a few more (see Figure 16.30, which shows several of the following options).

**Figure 16.30**
You can modify the frame and grid that surround a chart. Be careful that things don't get too cluttered!

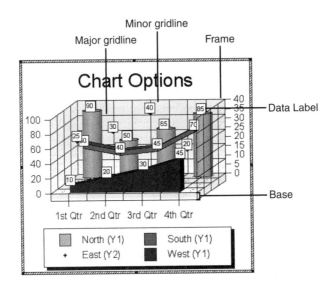

The following chart elements can easily be modified:

- Grids—Grids help the reader quickly associate values displayed on the Y-axis with data points in the chart. To modify a chart's grids, choose Chart, Grids, or click the Grids button on the toolbar to access the Grid Properties dialog box. You can choose whether you want to display horizontal or vertical grid lines, what style and color you want to use, and how many major and minor gridlines to use. Major gridlines usually have labels or values associated with them, and minor gridlines further subdivide the values of the major gridlines.

**TIP FROM**

*Read Gilgen*

> Don't forget that you can change the elements of a chart most quickly by double-clicking the element to display its properties dialog box.

- Frames—Gridlines are contained inside a chart frame, which is like a border to the chart. To modify the chart frame, choose Chart, Frame. You can choose which sides the grids should appear on (for example, left, back, front, bottom, and so on), what line style and color you want, and whether to include a base.

- Data labels—Typically you display labels only on the X- and Y-axes. However, you can also display the values of data points by using data labels. Choose Chart, Data Labels to display the Data Labels dialog box, where you can choose the position (outside or inside series element) and the font and box style used to display the labels. The toolbar icon displays *all* labels, or turns them all off.

- Perspective—In 3D charts only, you can change the horizontal and vertical angles of the chart to change the chart's perspective. This sometimes helps make data more visible. To change perspective, choose Chart, Perspective, and make changes in the Perspective dialog box.

- Base—The platform on which the 3D chart sits is called the base. You can change its height in the Frame Properties dialog box.

# CREATING ORGANIZATION CHARTS

Organization charts (usually called org charts) visually show relationships between various persons in an organization. The Draw program (based on Presentations) enables you to create and modify org charts, which then appear as graphics boxes within your WordPerfect document.

To create an org chart, choose Insert, Graphics, Draw Picture. This opens up the Presentations/Draw editing screen, complete with the Presentations toolbar.

Next choose Insert, Organization Chart. The mouse pointer turns to a hand. You can click and drag the area of the editor you want to use for the org chart, or simply single-click the editing screen to use the entire editing area.

**TIP FROM**

*Read Gilgen*

A quick and easy way to open an org chart in a WordPerfect document is to use a macro that comes with WordPerfect. Choose Tools, Macro, Play, and enter wp_org. The macro automatically opens a Draw window in Presentations and sets up a default org chart, ready for you to modify.

WordPerfect next displays the Layout dialog box (see Figure 16.31), where you choose an initial organization structure. Click the structure you want (the default is Single, Top Down) and click OK. If you're not sure which layout to use, select the default, which you can change later.

**Figure 16.31**
You must choose a layout for your org chart before you can proceed.

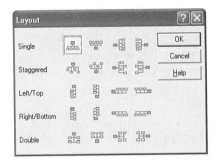

WordPerfect Draw places a basic org chart in the editing screen, and toolbar and Property Bar buttons appear to aid in modifying the chart (see Figure 16.32).

## CHOOSING AN ORG CHART LAYOUT

Layout refers to the relationship and orientation of the boxes that represent persons in the organization. If you decide to change the layout you selected when you created the chart, follow these steps:

1. Choose Edit, Select All to select the entire org chart.
2. Choose Format, Branch Structure to access the Branch Layout dialog box (see Figure 16.33).

**Figure 16.32**
You can use
Presentations tools to
create or modify an
org chart.

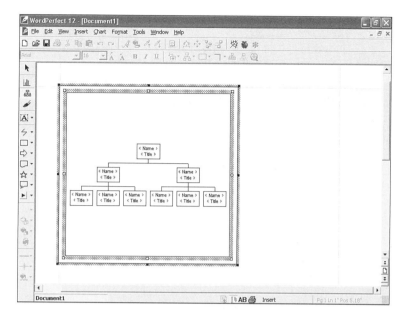

**Figure 16.33**
You can change the
layout or structure of
an org chart by using
the Branch Layout
dialog box.

3. Make changes as follows:

   • The Structure tab offers options that refer to how boxes at the same organizational level are laid out. The more boxes you have at the same level, the smaller they become. Staggering the boxes, or arranging them vertically instead of horizontally, might allow them to take up less space, and thereby become larger.

   • The Orientation tab of the Branch Layout dialog box enables you to make the org chart progress from left to right, right to left, top to bottom, or bottom to top.

 *If changes you make don't affect what you expect them to, see "Modifying an Entire Branch" in the Troubleshooting section at the end of this chapter.*

## ADDING AND REMOVING SUBORDINATES AND CO-WORKERS

The real work in developing the org chart comes in establishing relationships between various persons by adding, removing, and relocating boxes in the chart. Whether you organize the boxes first or fill in names and titles first doesn't really make much difference. Eventually you must do both.

To delete an individual, click the box and press Delete.

To add an individual, click a box near where you want to add the person. Then, depending of the type of box you want to add, choose one of these options:

- Manager—To insert a box above the currently selected box, choose Insert, Manager. WordPerfect inserts one box as the supervisor or manager.

- Coworker—To add a person at the same organizational level as the currently selected person, choose Insert, Coworkers. WordPerfect displays the Insert Coworkers dialog box (see Figure 16.34). You can choose how many co-workers to insert and whether they should go to the right or the left of the currently selected box.

**Figure 16.34**
You can use the Insert Coworkers dialog box to add persons at the same level.

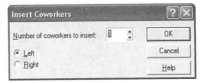

- Subordinate—To add a subordinate to the currently selected person, choose Insert, Subordinates. The Subordinates dialog box enables you to specify how many boxes to add.

- Staff—A staff person is not part of the line authority of an organization. Thus, the relationship is shown with a dotted line, and the staff person is shown off to the side and beneath his or her supervisor (see Figure 16.35). To add a staff person, click the supervisor's box, and then choose Insert, Staff. In the Insert Staff dialog box, indicate the number of staff members to insert and click OK.

You can also rearrange the boxes by clicking and dragging them to new locations, using these options:

- To move a person to a different manager, drag the box to the manager's box so that the box being dragged displays a downward-pointing arrow (see Figure 16.36). When you release the mouse button, the box is added at the end of the list of co-workers beneath that manager.

**Figure 16.35**
Staff boxes are connected with dotted lines, off to the side of the chart.

Staff box

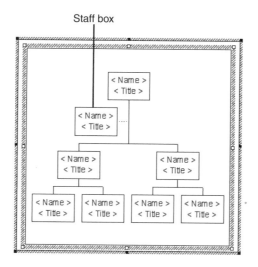

**Figure 16.36**
You can move a worker by dragging the person's box to a new manager's box.

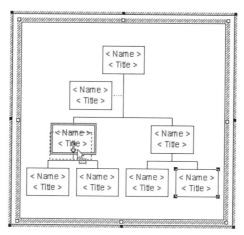

**CAUTION**

When you delete or move a box, you really are moving the position in the organization, not just the person. Thus, moving a box also moves the entire branch beneath the box. If you want to move just the person—for example, because he or she took a new job and his or her position will be filled by someone else—delete the person's name from the box and add it to another box at a new location.

**TIP FROM**

*Read Gilgen*

If you accidentally remove a box or a branch, don't forget you can use Undo to get it back.

■ To change the position of a co-worker, drag the box to another co-worker's box until a right- or left-pointing arrow is displayed (see Figure 16.37). Release the mouse button to place the person at the left or the right of the co-worker.

**Figure 16.37**
To rearrange the order of co-workers, drag a worker's box to another box until a horizontal arrow appears.

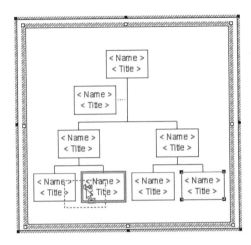

■ You can copy a box by holding down the Ctrl key while clicking and dragging the box to a new location. Too bad adding new employees in the workplace isn't this easy!

## ADDING AND MODIFYING ORG CHART BOX CONTENT

At some point, you have to enter names or titles in the boxes. But you also have several options when it comes to adding org chart information.

Org charts tend to be hierarchical, very much like the organization of a WordPerfect outline. You can create a WordPerfect outline of your organization, and then import the outline to create the org chart.

→ For information on creating WordPerfect outlines, **see** "Working with Outlines" in Chapter 11, "Organizing Information with Lists and Outlines."

To import a WordPerfect outline as an org chart, follow these steps:

1. Create and save a WordPerfect outline, making the organization correspond to outline levels (see Figure 16.38).

2. Create an org chart in WordPerfect, choosing any standard layout that is likely to match up well with your outline. At this point you should be in the Draw/Presentations screen, with the default sample layout in the editing window.

3. Choose Chart, Import Outline, and in the Insert Text dialog box, find the outline you created and saved in WordPerfect.

4. Click Insert, and WordPerfect imports the outline, replacing the sample org chart with one that matches your outline (see Figure 16.39).

**Figure 16.38**
You can create a WordPerfect outline of your organization, and then import the outline into an org chart.

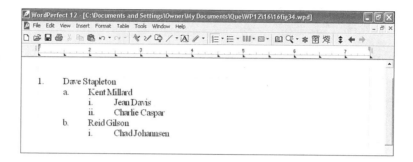

**Figure 16.39**
An imported outline quickly converts to an org chart.

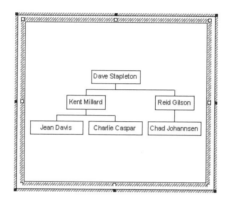

That's it! You now can edit the text in the boxes, or reorganize the boxes and relationships.

**TIP FROM**

*Read Gilgen*

After you edit an org chart, you can also export the data of the chart to a WordPerfect outline by choosing Chart, Export.

You can, of course, add text directly to org chart boxes. To do so, double-click a box, and WordPerfect enlarges the box and displays a cursor inside it (see Figure 16.40). Type the person's name, and then press Tab to advance to the next field (Title) in the box. You can also click elsewhere in the org chart to close this box.

**NOTE**

If you don't replace the field code (for example, `<Title>`), the final org chart displays nothing for that field.

If you don't need the additional title field, or if you want to add other fields for each box, follow these steps:

**Figure 16.40**
You can press Tab to move from field to field, and to add or edit org chart text.

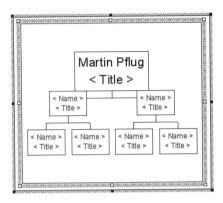

1. Select the box or branch of boxes you want to change. To select a branch, click the top box in the branch, and then choose Edit, Select, Branch. Alternatively you can right-click the top box in the branch and choose Edit Branch from the QuickMenu. To select all the boxes in the org chart, choose Edit, Select All.

2. Choose Format, Box Fields. WordPerfect displays the Box Fields dialog box (see Figure 16.41).

**Figure 16.41**
You can add or remove data entry fields for org chart boxes in the Box Fields dialog box.

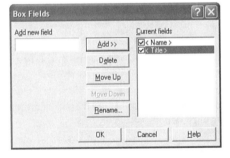

3. To remove a field for the selected boxes, uncheck the box next to it in the Current Fields box. If you don't need the field at all, you can Delete the field.

4. To add a different field, type a name for the field in the Add New Field box and click the Add>> button.

5. You can change a field by selecting it and clicking Rename, Move Up or Move Down (for example, to display the title above the name).

6. Click OK to accept your choices and to display the new fields in your org chart boxes.

## CHANGING ORG CHART STYLES

The structure and content of the org chart are your primary concern, just as the content of WordPerfect documents comes first. However, just as you do with a WordPerfect document, you can also make your org charts look good.

To modify an org chart box, follow these steps:

1. Select the box or boxes you want to modify.

2. Choose Format, Box Properties, or right-click the box and choose Box Properties from the QuickMenu. WordPerfect displays the Box Properties dialog box (see Figure 16.42).

**Figure 16.41**
You can add or remove data entry fields for org chart boxes in the Box Fields dialog box.

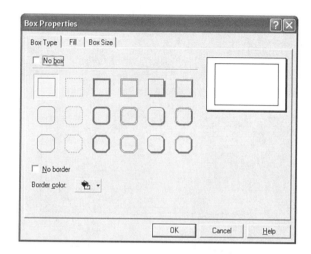

16

3. On the Box Type tab, click the style you want to use. You can also change the border color.

4. On the Fill tab, change the fill pattern (including gradient shading) and color.

5. The Box Size tab (see Figure 16.43) enables you to adjust the size of the org chart's boxes. By default, boxes automatically adjust so that they become smaller as more boxes and text are placed at the same level. You can specify that boxes adjust instead to the largest size in the branch or the entire org chart. You can also force text to adjust its size to fit the box. If you manually adjust the box size, you can make boxes that are larger than those sized automatically. Note that you can reset the size options and start over again without having to cancel all your Box Properties dialog box choices.

6. Click OK to apply the properties to the selected boxes.

One nifty formatting feature is the capability to pick up the attributes from one box and drop them onto another box.

 To pick up box attributes, click the box to select it, and then choose Format, Get Attributes or click the Get Attributes button on the toolbar.

 To drop box attributes on another box, select the box or boxes you want to modify and choose Format, Apply Attributes or click the Apply Attributes button on the toolbar.

 You can also modify connectors between boxes in the org chart. Select the branches you want to change (or select the whole org chart, if you want to change all connectors). Then

16

choose Format, Connectors. In the Connectors dialog box (see Figure 16.44), you can choose whether to show staff or subordinate connectors, whether to use right-angle or direct connectors, and the line style, color, or thickness of each type of line.

**Figure 16.43**
You can change the org chart's box sizes by using the Box Size tab of the Box Properties dialog box.

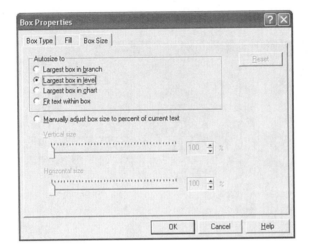

**Figure 16.44**
You can change the type or style of box connectors in the Connectors dialog box.

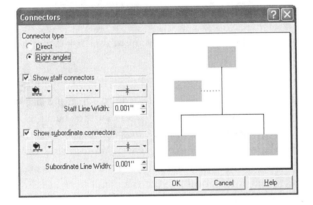

**TIP FROM**

*Read Gilgen*

If you don't like either of the connector choices, you can deselect the Show Connectors boxes and then use Draw/Presentations tools to add your own lines or arrows as objects on top of the org chart.

 You can also adjust vertical and horizontal spacing between boxes. This can be particularly useful if you want to make the org chart more proportional (as tall as it is wide, for example). Select the boxes or branches you want to adjust, and choose Format, Box Spacing. WordPerfect displays the Box Spacing dialog box (see Figure 16.45). Adjust vertical spacing by increasing or decreasing parent-to-child spacing. Change horizontal spacing by adjusting sibling-to-sibling spacing.

**Figure 16.45**
You can adjust the spacing between org chart boxes in the Box Spacing dialog box.

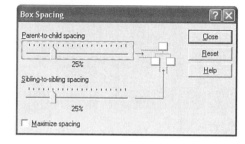

## COLLAPSING AND ZOOMING ORG CHART BRANCHES

If you create a large org chart to map the structure of your entire company, you can selectively display parts of that structure without having to delete sections you don't want to display.

 To collapse the subordinates of a selection, click a box, and then choose View, Collapse Subordinates or click the Collapse/Expand button on the toolbar. WordPerfect hides the subordinates, but displays a small downward-pointing arrow in the box to indicate that there's more that you can't see (see Figure 16.46). When you return to your WordPerfect document, this indicator does not display. To expand the subordinates, click the arrow, or click the Collapse/Expand toolbar button again, or choose View, Expand Subordinates.

Zoom to Chart

**Figure 16.46**
You can hide subordinates in the org chart, but an arrow indicates that they're still there.

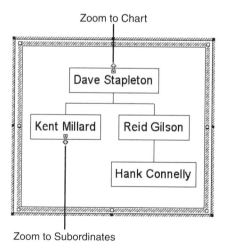

Zoom to Subordinates

 To display only one section of the org chart—for example, a department or group—click the head of that part of the org chart and choose View, Zoom to Branch, or click the Zoom Branch button on the toolbar. WordPerfect hides all other parts of the org chart, and also displays an upward-pointing arrow at the top box of the zoomed branch (refer to Figure 16.46). To return to the entire chart, click that arrow, or click the Zoom button on the toolbar, or choose View, Zoom to Chart.

# TROUBLESHOOTING

### DON'T WORRY, JUST PRINT IT

*When I'm editing my chart data, the chart looks great. But when I return to my WordPerfect document, the chart looks lousy.*

What you're seeing is only a display problem. Don't worry. When you print the chart, it will look just fine.

### SAVING IT ANYTIME

*I sorted data in my datasheet, but I did it wrong and can't remember what it looked like. There doesn't seem to be any undo.*

Unfortunately, Undo doesn't work while you're editing a chart. But you can save as often as you like. Simply click the Save button on the toolbar; or press Ctrl+S. That way, if you make a mistake, just exit the WordPerfect document, and open the last saved copy. You should always save your work before trying something new or complicated. Did you already lose your work? Sorry, but now you'll know for the next time.

### PRINTING CONTRASTING SERIES IN CHARTS

*In my document, the data charts look fine, but when I print them, I can hardly distinguish among the different chart series.*

This is common when you print to a black-and-white printer, such as a laser printer. You can try to change the series colors to use clearly different shades of gray, but if you have more than a few series, this might not be satisfactory. A more effective solution is to change the fill patterns of the series so they clearly contrast (for example, diagonal lines in different directions).

### MODIFYING AN ENTIRE BRANCH

*I changed the layout of my org chart, but only part of the chart changed.*

You must select all the branches you want to change. To select the whole chart, choose Edit, Select All.

# PROJECT

You're getting to the point where you can do some really fancy and also highly useful projects in WordPerfect. Let's suppose you've been keeping track of EnviroWear's annual sales in the major market, as well as in the smaller markets, and that you now need to present that information to the board of directors. Although they're highly intelligent people, they're also busy, so they want to know right now how you're doing. The other little twist is that the second-quarter report for the Stoughton store seems wrong, so you've put in a call to the Stoughton manager to check those figures.

On page 33 of the annual report, you want to insert the sales figures, and you'd also like to use an attractive chart to represent those figures. If the Stoughton numbers change, you want to reflect those changes as quickly as possible.

Begin by importing the data from the spreadsheet into a table. If you link, rather than import, the spreadsheet data, you can update the numbers when they arrive. Figure 16.47 shows the beginnings of the annual report with the table of data.

**Figure 16.47**
A linked spreadsheet, imported to a table, can be the beginnings of an impressive chart.

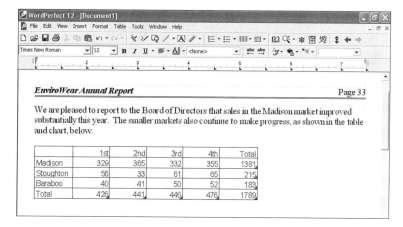

*EnviroWear Annual Report*                                                          Page 33

We are pleased to report to the Board of Directors that sales in the Madison market improved substantially this year. The smaller markets also continue to make progress, as shown in the table and chart, below.

| | 1st | 2nd | 3rd | 4th | Total |
|---|---|---|---|---|---|
| Madison | 329 | 365 | 332 | 355 | 1381 |
| Stoughton | 56 | 33 | 61 | 65 | 215 |
| Baraboo | 40 | 41 | 50 | 52 | 183 |
| Total | 426 | 441 | 446 | 476 | 1789 |

→ For details on how to link or import spreadsheet data to a WordPerfect table, **see** "Importing and Using Spreadsheet Data," **p. 488.**

The chart you want to create doesn't need the totals row and column, but it's important to show those in the table. To create a bar chart based on just the data, select the first four rows and the first five columns, which include labels and data, but exclude the totals. Right-click the selection and choose Chart. WordPerfect opens the chart editor, as shown in Figure 16.48.

Certainly the chart shows that Madison is doing well, but it's hard to see any progress in the smaller markets. To remedy that problem, you need to plot the two smaller markets against a secondary Y-axis. Take the following steps, but be creative along the way and choose any other options you want:

1. Modify the title. Double-click the title, and in the Title Properties dialog box, use the Title Options tab to change the title (for example, EnviroWear Sales). Make other changes to the font or appearance of the text.

**Figure 16.48**
The chart editor uses only the data you select in the table.

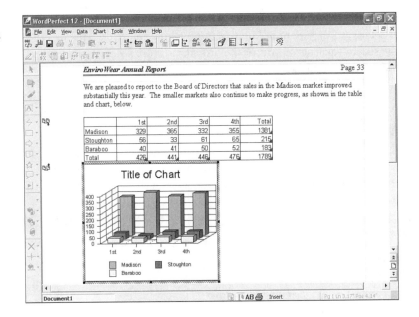

2. Change the smaller market series. Double-click a Stoughton data bar, and in the Series Properties dialog box, choose Secondary (Y2). Also change the series to a line type. Do the same for the Baraboo series. While you're there, you might also change the Madison series to something more interesting, such as a cylinder-shaped bar.

3. Add Y-axis titles. Charts aren't very useful if the reader doesn't know what the data points represent. Double-click a number on the primary Y-axis, and on the Title Options tab of the Primary Y-Axis Properties dialog box, add the title Large Market. Repeat this procedure for the secondary Y-axis, adding the title Smaller Markets.

4. Add a title to the labels. The reader doesn't have any idea what 1st, 2nd, 3rd, and 4th mean. Double-click a label, and on the Title Options tab of the X-Axis Properties dialog box, add 1999 Sales by Quarter.

5. Click in the WordPerfect document to close the chart editor. WordPerfect displays the chart, along with the table and text shown in Figure 16.49.

But wait…you were right. The Stoughton manager calls to tell you that the figures for the second quarter were indeed better than reported. Because it's only moments before the presentation to the board, you change the 33 in cell C3 to 53, right-click the table, and choose Calculate. WordPerfect updates the totals in the table, and also updates the chart, as shown in Figure 16.50. You print that page, insert it in the report, and hustle off to your meeting with the board.

**Figure 16.49**
Using a secondary Y-axis, and changing the chart types for the two small market series, you can better illustrate their progress over the year.

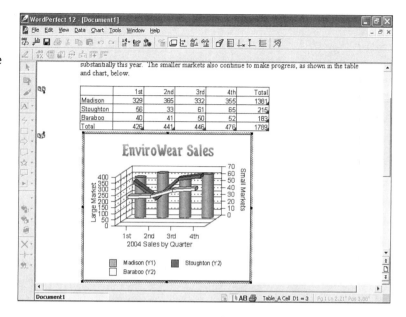

**Figure 16.50**
You can calculate a table, and the chart based on that table updates automatically.

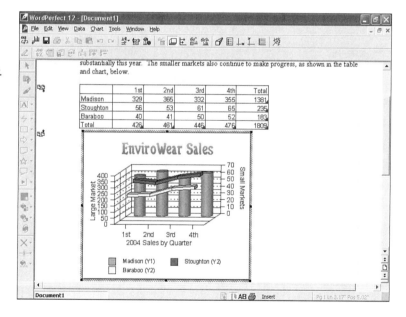

# PUBLISHING DOCUMENTS

# CHAPTER 17

# COLLABORATING ON DOCUMENTS

**In this chapter**

*by Laura Acklen*

# INSERTING DOCUMENT COMMENTS

Those sticky notes have really taken off, haven't they? They take up an entire aisle at the office supply store—along with all the desk accessories to hold them. I've got one on my monitor right now that reminds me of my submission dates!

WordPerfect offers an electronic equivalent to sticky notes—it's called a document comment. Comments can be inserted into a document, and they remain invisible until you open them. They aren't printed and they don't affect the formatting of the document. Consider the following uses:

- Store an idea as a comment, and then return to the comment later to develop the idea.
- Create a comment to remind yourself (or someone else) to come back and check the accuracy of a statement.
- Place instructions inside comments throughout onscreen forms to eliminate the need for printed instructions on how to fill out the form.

Comments are a valuable collaboration tool. Every member of a team that works on a document can insert his or her own comments, which can easily be differentiated from other comments. These comments might include suggestions for improving the document, changes to facts and figures, corrections, feedback, follow-up instructions, and other types of editing queries.

**NOTE**

> If you take a few seconds to fill in some information, your comments can be identified with your initials and a color. Choose Tools, Settings, Environment. Type your name and initials in the text boxes. Click the User Color button to choose a color from the palette. The color is used for the comment balloon icon that appears in the margin and for the comment bubble that displays the comment text.

## CREATING COMMENTS

When you're ready to create a comment, click in the section of text that you want to comment about. You don't have to be at the beginning of a line or at the top of a paragraph. You'll find that when you view the comment, an arrow points to the spot where you created the comment, so it's easy for the reviewer to see exactly what you are talking about.

**NOTE**

> Here's an enhancement that was introduced in WordPerfect 10—document comments aren't just for plain text anymore. You can now apply formatting to the text (such as add bold or italic, change the font) and you can insert graphics, tables, equations, charts, spreadsheets, and so on.

To create a comment, choose Insert, Comment, Create. The insertion point moves into the comment-editing window (see Figure 17.1). The property bar now has some helpful buttons for creating and editing comments. Hover over each button to display a QuickTip with the button name and a brief description.

**TIP FROM**

If you've already typed the text that you want to put in a comment, select the text, and then choose Insert, Comment, Create. The selected text is copied into the comment-editing window.

Insert the date

Insert your initials

Switch back to the document window

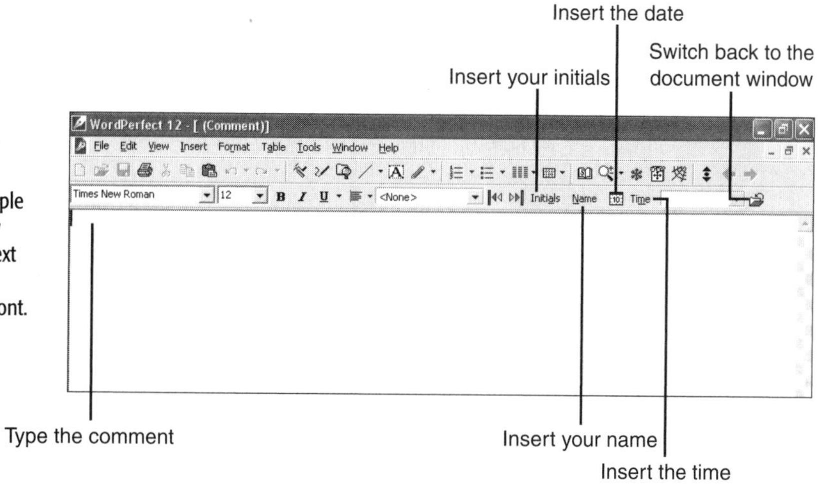

**Figure 17.1**
As you hover over fonts in the drop-down list, the sample text in the preview window and the text in the document morphs into that font.

**17**

Type the comment

Insert your name

Insert the time

 Type the text of the comment in the window. Using the buttons on the property bar, insert your initials, your name, the date, or the time. Click the Close button on the property bar when you're done.

In Page view, you can see the comment balloon icon (with the initials and the color you chose in Environment Settings) inside the left margin. If you don't specify initials or a user color in Environment Settings, the comment icon looks like a white bubble (see Figure 17.2).

**NOTE**

If you can't see these icons, click the Zoom button and choose Page Width, or click the left horizontal scroll arrow until the left margin space comes into view.

 *If you still can't see the margin icon after you've adjusted the zoom (or scrolled over to the left), see "Enabling Margin Icons" in the Troubleshooting section at the end of this chapter.*

Generic white comment balloon

**Figure 17.2**
Comment balloon icons are inserted in the left margin, so you might have to adjust the zoom setting or scroll over to the left to see them.

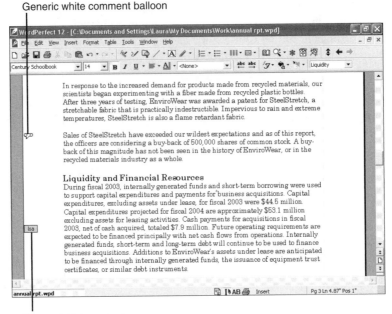

Comment balloon with user initials and color

In Draft view, comments appear in the text inside a gray box. If you created the comment in the middle of the line, the beginning of the line appears above the comment box; the end of the line appears below (see Figure 17.3). Most people find the gray comment boxes too distracting, so they switch to Page view, where the comments stay hidden.

**Figure 17.3**
In Draft view, comments are displayed in a shaded box, and if inserted in the middle of a paragraph, the paragraph will appear split apart at that point.

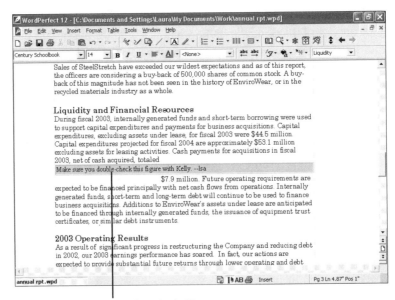

Comments are displayed in a shaded box

## VIEWING AND WORKING WITH COMMENTS

Page view is the preferred mode for working with comments because the comments stay hidden until you are ready to look at them. To view the contents of a comment, click the balloon icon in the left margin. The comment text appears in a balloon, with the arrow pointing down to the text where you created the comment (see Figure 17.4).

**NOTE**

In WordPerfect 10, the comment bubble was improved so it is less intrusive onscreen than it was in previous versions of WordPerfect. It is now sized to the length of the text only, so there isn't any empty space in the comment bubble.

**Figure 17.4**
The arrow at the bottom of the comment bubble points to the place in the text where the comment was created.

Comment balloon

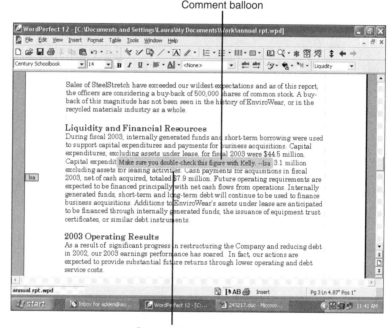

Comment arrow

You can do a few other things with comments:

- To edit a comment, right-click the comment icon or the comment text and choose Edit. You can also double-click the comment icon.
- While you're in the comment-editing window, choose File, Print to print the comment.
- To delete a comment, right-click the comment icon or comment text and choose Delete.

**TIP FROM**

*Laura Acklen*

Remember that you can delete a code by clicking and dragging it out of the Reveal Codes window. To strip out all the comment codes in one fell swoop, use Find and Replace to search for comment codes and replace them with nothing.

→ To learn more about the steps used to insert a code in the Find and Replace dialog box, **see** "Searching for Codes," **p. 150.**

- To convert a comment to text, right-click the comment text. Choose Convert to Text. The text of the comment is inserted right where you created the comment—it replaces the comment code.

- If the initials have been supplied in the User Information section (choose Tools, Settings, Environment), you can view information about when a comment was created, even if the date and time stamps weren't used. Right-click the comment balloon icon or the comment text bubble, and then choose Information. The Comment Information dialog box appears (see Figure 17.5).

- If you would prefer to hide the comment icons so they don't appear at all, you can deselect the Margin Icons option in Settings. Choose Tools, Settings, Display. Click the Document tab, and then remove the check mark next to Margin Icons.

**Figure 17.5**
The Comment Information dialog box lists the author, initials, user color, and the date/time the comment was created.

## USING THE HIGHLIGHT TOOL

Even the most stubborn opponents of automation can't deny the efficiency of working with information electronically. But hey, you go ahead—print the document and highlight the important passages with a highlighter pen. I'll stay right here and highlight the text onscreen with WordPerfect's Highlight tool and a few mouse clicks.

Just like a highlighter pen, the Highlight feature paints a bar of transparent color over the text. Just think about it—you can use different colors to color code certain types of information or you can ask fellow collaborators to choose different colors.

There are two ways to highlight text:

- To highlight existing text, select it, and then click the Highlight button. The currently selected color is used to highlight the text (see Figure 17.6).

- You can turn on the Highlight feature so that you can select text and apply highlighting in one step. Click the Highlight button, and the mouse pointer changes to a pen highlighter. Click and drag through the text you want to highlight. When you release the mouse button, WordPerfect applies the highlighting. When you're finished highlighting text, click the Highlight button again to turn highlighting off. Again, the currently selected color is used.

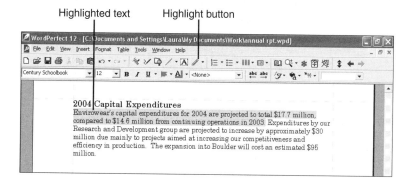

**Figure 17.6**
Just as you can use a highlighter pen to emphasize important information on a printed document, you can use WordPerfect's Highlight feature to highlight text onscreen.

## REMOVING HIGHLIGHTING

To remove highlighting from a section of text, click in the text, and then click the Highlight button. You can remove multiple instances of highlighting all at once by selecting the text that contains the highlighted sections and choosing Tools, Highlight, Remove.

## CHANGING THE HIGHLIGHT COLOR

The default highlight color is yellow, but you can choose any color you like from the palette. Click the arrow next to the Highlight button to open the color palette, where you can select another color. It's a good idea to choose a light color—the darker colors can make it difficult to read the highlighted text.

> **NOTE**
> When you select a different highlight color, the change is sticky, which means that the new color replaces the default color.

Highlighted text prints out in color on a color printer, and it prints as shaded text on a black-and-white printer. To print the document without the highlighting, you can temporarily hide the highlighting (but not the text on which the highlighting appears). Choose Tools, Highlight, Print/Show.

> **NOTE**
> If you're planning on sending this document to someone else to review onscreen, be nice and go easy on the highlighting. You don't want the reader to burn out his retinas trying to read the text.

# REVIEWING DOCUMENTS

The Internet is the world's virtual post office—these days it seems as though *everyone* has an e-mail address. Collaborating with people all over the world is as simple as attaching a file to an e-mail message and distributing it. But when you have a handful of people working on the same document, keeping track of the revisions can be a nightmare.

WordPerfect's Document Review feature can be used by both reviewers and the document's author. First, a reviewer uses Document Review to insert revisions (in a unique color). Then, you (the author) use the Document Review feature to find every revision (no matter how small). Each reviewer has a unique color, so each revision can be traced back to the person who made it. You can accept or reject each change, because you have the ultimate control over the document!

## MAKING REVISIONS

If someone has sent a document to you, you are considered the reviewer. You'll have your own color, so your changes can easily be distinguished from those of other reviewers.

To add revisions with Document Review, open the document, and then follow these steps:

1. Choose File, Document, Review. The Review Document dialog box appears (see Figure 17.7).

   **NOTE**

   If a document has already been saved with revision marks, the Review Document dialog box appears automatically when you open that document. Click Cancel if you don't want to use Document Review.

   **NOTE**

   The Document Review margin marker is a new feature that was introduced in WordPerfect 10. You can now add an indicator in the margin to show the author where changes have been made.

2. Click Reviewer. A Reviewer property bar appears at the top of the document. Your color is displayed in the Set Color button. Colors that have already been used are displayed, with the username, in the Other User Colors list box (see Figure 17.8).

3. If you want to change your color, click the Set Color button, and then choose a color from the color palette.

4. Make your revisions to the document. If you add text, it appears in your user color to indicate redline text. Deleted text appears in your user color, with a line running through it to indicate strikeout text.

5. When you're finished, click the Close button on the Reviewer property bar.

Enable the check box to turn
on the margin markers

**Figure 17.7**
You can use the
Review Document
feature as a reviewer
or as the author.

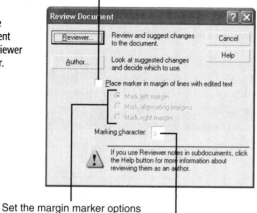

Set the margin marker options

If necessary, insert a new margin marker character

17

Click when you're done

Click the Set Color button to change your user color

**Figure 17.8**
The Reviewer prop-
erty bar displays a list
of reviewers and their
user colors.

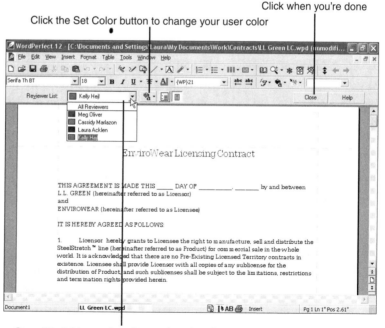

Open this list to see the other reviewer's colors

**NOTE**

You can edit revisions made by other reviewers, but you can't edit text that has been deleted by another reviewer. The only way to release that text is to review the document as the author and reject the deletion.

**CAUTION**

When you switch back to the document window, you won't be able to see the revision marks. Don't panic when you don't see your changes. They are there—they just aren't displayed in the user color.

When you're revising a document, you can do just about anything to it—you can change the margins, change the font, add headers and footers, add graphics, and so on. However, your user color is only tied to textual changes—that is, whatever you type in. For example, if you create a header, the header text appears in your user color.

→ For the steps to create a header, **see** "Adding Headers and Footers," **p. 243.**

**TIP FROM**

*Laura Acklen*

Each reviewer is identified by the username in the User Information section of Environment Settings. If you share a computer, you have to remember to type your name and initials each time you start WordPerfect, or your revisions will be identified with someone else's name. A macro that does that for you would be very handy.

→ For more information on creating macros, **see** "Creating Macros," **p. 824.**

## REVIEWING A MARKED-UP DOCUMENT

As the document's author, you have control over which revisions are actually made and which are discarded. As you review the document, each revision is selected. You can accept or reject each change individually, or you can accept or reject all changes at once. Inserted text displays in the user's color to represent redlined text; deleted text displays in the user color with a dash through to indicate strikeout text.

To review a document as an author, open the document, and then follow these steps:

1. Choose Author in the Review Document dialog box to display a Reviewer property bar at the top of the document (see Figure 17.9). This property bar is different from the property bar that you see as a reviewer. This one contains buttons for accepting and rejecting the revisions.

2. Click the Select the Next Annotation button to start reviewing the changes. WordPerfect selects the first revision and waits for you to accept or reject it.

3. Use the buttons on the Reviewer property bar to review the document:

   Click the Turn On or Off the Margin Markings That Have Been Made in the Document button to turn the display of the margin markers on and off.

   Click the Display Annotations in Normal Text Color button to turn off the redline and strikeout colors.

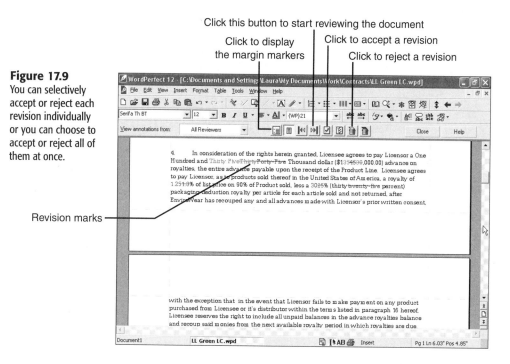

**Figure 17.9**
You can selectively accept or reject each revision individually or you can choose to accept or reject all of them at once.

Revision marks

Click this button to start reviewing the document
Click to display the margin markers
Click to accept a revision
Click to reject a revision

Click the Select the Previous Annotation button to move to the previous revision.

Click the Select the Next Annotation button to move to the next revision (or to start reviewing the document).

Click the Insert the Currently Selected Annotation into the Text of the Document button to accept the revision.

Click the Inserts All Annotations into the Document Text button to accept all the revisions at once.

Click the Deletes the Currently Selected Annotation button to reject a revision.

Click the Deletes All Annotations from the Document Text button to strip out all the revisions.

4. Click the Close button when you're finished, and then save the document.

**TIP FROM**

Change your mind about accepting or rejecting a revision? Click the Undo button to reverse the action.

CAUTION

Be careful when saving a document that contains redline and strikeout text to a different file format (such as Microsoft Word .doc format). The redline and strikeout text could be converted to plain text in the process, which would destroy your ability to accept or reject the changes.

*If your revisions show up as black text instead of appearing in the user color, see "My Review Color Is Broken" in the Troubleshooting section at the end of the chapter.*

*If you see the Review Document dialog box when you open certain documents, and you want to get rid of it, see "Getting Rid of the Review Document Dialog Box" in the Troubleshooting section at the end of the chapter.*

# ROUTING DOCUMENTS WITH OUTLOOK

WordPerfect has always had powerful tools for reviewing documents. In WordPerfect 11, a collaborative review feature was added. You can now route a document (as an e-mail attachment) to multiple reviewers, in a specific order. Each reviewer opens the attachment, makes her changes/comments, and closes the document. The document is then routed to the next person on the list. When the document has been reviewed by everyone on the list, it is sent back to you.

NOTE

In order to use the new routing feature, you must have Microsoft Outlook 2000 (or newer) on your system and have the Outlook address book designated as the default address book.

To route a document, you must first create a routing slip. The routing slip contains a list of recipients, in a specific order, and a message explaining what you want the reviewers to do.

To create a routing slip

1. Choose File, Document, Routing Slip. The Routing Slip dialog box appears (see Figure 17.10).

2. Type a subject in the Subject text box.

3. (Optional) Type a message in the Message text box. This is a great place to leave instructions for the reviewers.

4. Click Add to start creating a list of reviewers. The Add Reviewers dialog box appears (see Figure 17.11). Your Add Reviewers dialog box might look different, depending on which version of Outlook you have on your system.

5. Select the reviewer(s) in the list. Remember, you can click the first name, and then hold down the Ctrl key to select the others.

**Figure 17.10**
Build a list of review-
ers and give them
instructions in the
Routing Slip dialog
box.

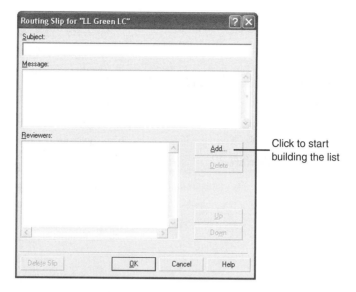

Click to start
building the list

**Figure 17.11**
The Add Reviewers
dialog box has a list of
Outlook address book
contacts from which
to choose.

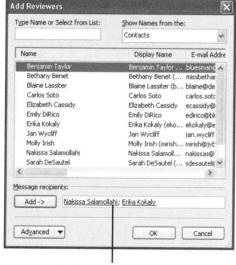

Build a list of recipients

6. Click the Add button to add the selected names to the Message Recipients list box.

7. Choose OK to return to the Routing Slip dialog box.

8. If you need to rearrange the reviewer names, select a reviewer name and then choose Up or Down. The document will be sent out to the reviewers in the order they appear on the Routing Slip so this is an important step.

9. Choose OK.

To give you an idea of what happens next, a reviewer will double-click the attached document in Microsoft Outlook. He will type his name and choose a color for his changes. After he is done making changes, he can either save the document and send it later, or he can send it on to the next reviewer. In addition, a reviewer can reassign a document to another reviewer on the routing slip. Presumably, this is so someone can send it back to a previous reviewer so that their comments can be reviewed.

Each reviewer can see the names of the other reviewers and their colors, so she can figure out who made what changes. A reviewer can edit additions made by other reviewers, but she will not be able to edit or undo previous deletions.

**NOTE**

This document routing feature is similar to the routing slip feature in Microsoft Word so you have the same functionality in both programs. However, you won't be able to import routing slips that were created in a Microsoft Word document.

**NOTE**

Remember, in WordPerfect 11/12, you can either use the Outlook Address Book or the WordPerfect Address Book, but not both at the same time. If you want access to the WordPerfect Address Book, you'll have to back into Settings and disable the Outlook integration. Choose Tools, Settings, Environment, and then remove the check mark next to Use Outlook Address Book/Contact List check box.

# COMPARING DOCUMENTS

Despite all the advantages electronic file transfers can bring, you might be reluctant to distribute your documents electronically because of the possibility of accidental (or intentional) changes being made to the text.

Only by comparing a reviewed document to the original can you be sure no unauthorized changes were made. The Document Compare feature compares two copies of a document and inserts revision marks for you. If text has been added, it's displayed in redline; if text has been deleted, it's copied back into the document as strikeout text. If so much as a space has been changed, you'll know about it.

**NOTE**

The Document Compare feature is designed to compare two documents in WordPerfect format. If you try to compare documents in different formats, you'll get unpredictable results.

## USING THE COMPARE DOCUMENTS FEATURE

To compare two documents, open the reviewed copy of the file first. Then, compare that document to the original. The differences between the two documents will be clearly marked.

To compare two documents, follow these steps:

1. Open the reviewed copy of the file.

2. Choose File, Document, Compare to display the Compare Documents dialog box (see Figure 17.12).

Click to browse for the file
Type the name of the file

**Figure 17.12**
Type the name of the file you want to compare to your own in the Compare Documents dialog box.

Click to create a new document with the revision marks
Click to place the revision marks in the open document

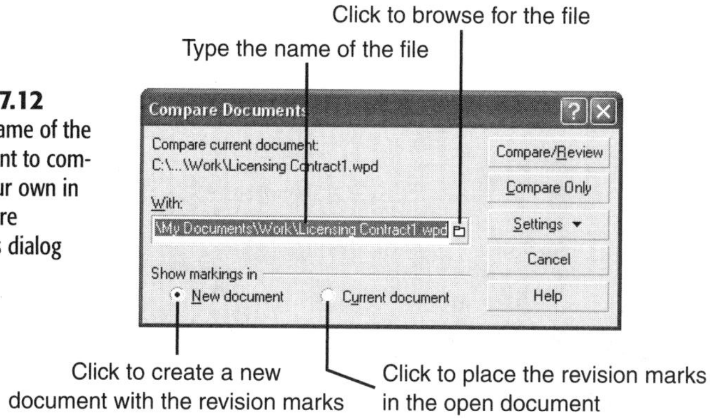

3. Type the filename for your copy of the document, or click the Files icon to browse for the file.

4. Choose one of the two options:

- Click Compare Only to compare the two documents and insert revision marks.

- Click Compare/Review if you want to compare the two documents, and then review the document as an author.

When the comparison is complete, a Document Compare Summary page is created at the top of the document (see Figure 17.13). Scroll down past this page to review the document. Text that has been inserted appears in red, and text that has been deleted appears as strikeout text.

If you choose Compare/Review after the compare is complete, WordPerfect sets you up to review the document as an author, with the Document Review feature (discussed earlier in this chapter, in the section "Reviewing a Marked-Up Document").

Because WordPerfect inserted all those revision marks in your document, it only seems fair that WordPerfect should take them back out. Choose File, Document, Remove Markings to display the Remove Markings dialog box (see Figure 17.14). Choose one of the options to remove the redline/strikeout text.

**Figure 17.13**
The Document Compare Summary page is a useful report to save as confirmation that two documents are identical.

Attributes for deleted text

Attributes for the inserted text

WordPerfect Document Compare Summary

Original document: C:\Documents and Settings\Laura\My Documents\Work\Licensing Contract.wpd
Revised document: @PFDesktop\:MyComputer\C:\Documents and Settings\Laura\My Documents\Work\Licensing Contract1.wpd
Deletions are shown with the following attributes and color:
    Strikeout, Blue RGB(0,0,255).
    Deleted text is shown as full text.
Insertions are shown with the following attributes and color:
    Double Underline, Redline, Red RGB(255,0,0).

The document was marked with 3 Deletions, 3 Insertions, 0 Moves.

Summary of changes

**Figure 17.14**
You can use the Remove Markings dialog box to strip out redline and strikeout text in any document, not just a compare document.

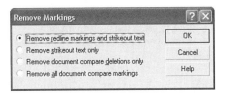

If you're not pleased with the way the redlined text looks and prints, you can change the way that text is formatted. Choose File, Document, Redline Method to open the Redline dialog box (see Figure 17.15). Choose a method for marking redlined text. If you choose one of the margin marking options, you can alter the redline character that appears inside the margin.

*If the redlined text prints only slightly lighter than the rest of the text, or if it appears no different from the rest of the text, see "The Redline Text Isn't Printing Correctly" in the Troubleshooting section at the end of the chapter.*

**Figure 17.15**
If you're not happy with the way your printer handles redline text, choose one of the margin-marking options.

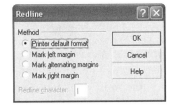

## CUSTOMIZING THE DOCUMENT COMPARE FEATURE

The magnet that attracts so many loyal WordPerfect users is the incomparable capability to customize features. The Document Compare feature is no exception, and users of previous versions of WordPerfect will be pleased with the depth of the new Document Compare Settings options that were introduced with WordPerfect 10.

There are separate customization options for the Compare Only option and the Compare/Review option. Both can be accessed in the Compare Documents dialog box, so choose File, Document, Compare to open this dialog box.

To customize the Compare Only option, click the Settings button; then, choose Compare Only to open the Document Compare Settings dialog box (see Figure 17.16).

Enter the enclosure character for text to skip

Click to turn off the summary report

**Figure 17.16**
The Options tab of the Document Compare Settings dialog box controls how the compare is carried out.

Select which elements to include in the comparison

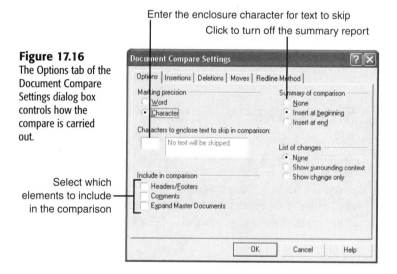

The Document Compare Settings dialog box has four other tabs:

- Insertions—Click the Insertions tab to select an attribute for marking new text. The default is for redline, double-underline. You can also choose a different color and an enclosure character for the new text.

- Deletions—Click the Deletions tab to choose an attribute for deleted text (besides strikeout). You can choose a different color, and you can select an enclosure character. You can also choose how you want deleted text shown.

- Moves—Click the Moves tab to choose where moved text appears. You can choose a color for moved text.

- Redline Method—Click the Redline Method tab to select a different type of redline marking and a different redline character. The options are identical to those in the Redline Method dialog box you open by choosing File, Document, Redline Method.

To customize the Compare/Review option, click the Settings button, and then choose Compare Then Review to open the Compare-Then-Review Settings dialog box (see Figure 17.17).

Type an enclosure character for text to skip

**Figure 17.17**
You can customize the Compare/Review option in the Compare-Then-Review Settings dialog box.

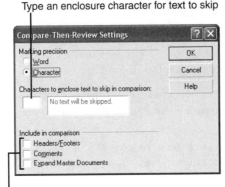

Select the elements to include in the compare

# ADDING A DIGITAL SIGNATURE

The Digital signature is another feature that was introduced in WordPerfect 10. You can add a digital signature to a document, which guarantees that it has not been altered since you signed it, and that you are actually the person who prepared the document. For example, if you collaborate on sensitive documents and use e-mail to send the file to others, it's particularly important that you be able to prove that you are the person who has sent it and that no one else has modified the document since you signed it. Think of it as an electronic driver's license or passport.

Digital signatures are used to authenticate the identity of individuals who are exchanging information across the Internet. Through the magic of asymmetric cryptography, two keys can be created—one is the public key and the other is the private key. The public key can be used to *verify* the private key, but it cannot be used to *identify* the private key. As long as the private key remains confidential, the identity cannot be forged.

**NOTE**

WordPerfect Office 11/12 support digital signatures from within WordPerfect, Quattro Pro, and Corel Presentations. For digital signatures to function properly, you must have Microsoft Internet Explorer (IE) 5.5 or later on your system (IE6 is required for WinXP or Win2K SP3 or higher). Even if you have another browser installed, such as Netscape or Opera, digital signatures will not work unless you have IE installed. WordPerfect Office 11 and 12 include Microsoft IE 6 (the browser component only). Visual Basic for Applications (VBA) 6.3 is also included, but it is not installed in a typical installation, so you need to do a custom install to get the VBA components. If you are using IE in a language other than English and you don't want to install IE 6, go to www.microsoft.com/downloads and download the most recent version.

If you choose not to install IE6 on your system (by deselecting the digital signatures component), and you do not have IE 5.5 installed (or IE 6 for WinXP and Win2K SP3 systems), you will not be able to use digital signature technology on your system.

*If you don't want to install Internet Explorer 6 and the digital signature updates, see "How Can I Avoid Installing Internet Explorer 6?" in the Troubleshooting section at the end of the chapter.*

## SIGNING A DOCUMENT WITH A DIGITAL SIGNATURE

Before you can add a digital signature to a document, you have to obtain a digital certificate and install it on your computer. After this is done, you can sign the document.

 Choose File, Signature, Sign Document, or click the No Signature button on the application bar to open the Sign Document dialog box (see Figure 17.18). Open the drop-down list, choose a signature from the list, and then choose OK.

**17**

**Figure 17.18**
The Sign Document dialog box shows if a signature is valid.

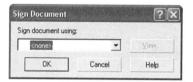

If the signature is valid, you'll see a Signature Valid button (green check mark) on the application bar. If the signature can't be verified, you'll see a Certificate Not Valid button (yellow exclamation point). And if the signature isn't valid, you'll see a Signature Invalid button (red X).

To view the certificate for a digital signature, choose File, Signature, Sign Document. Select the signature from the list and then choose View.

Detailed information about the digital certificate is displayed on the Information tab of the Certificate dialog box, including the name of the entity that issued the certificate, the dates the certificate is valid, and any intended uses of the certificate, as shown in Figure 17.19. You can also click the Signature Valid, Certificate Not Verified or Signature Invalid button on the application bar.

**Figure 17.19**
The Certificate dialog box offers information about the certificate.

Issuing authority

Certificate Information

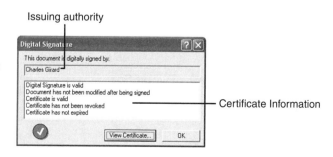

## SELECTING A VALIDATION METHOD

A digital signature remains valid as long as it hasn't expired and has been distributed by a valid authority. You can choose the method for validating digital signatures on your system. Choose File, Signature, Sign Document. Choose a signature from the drop-down list, and then choose View to open the Certificate dialog box. Click the Validation tab to display the validation methods. Choose from the following options:

- If you enable the Check Parent Certificates check box, WordPerfect checks the intermediate certificates of authority listed in your browser.

- With the Check Parent Certificates check box enabled, you can enable the Check Root Certificate, in which case WordPerfect checks the highest level of authority or trusted root certificates of the authority listed in your browser.

- If you enable the Check the Certificate Authority check box, WordPerfect accesses the Internet to determine whether a certificate authority is valid.

- Finally, if you disable the two check boxes, WordPerfect merely checks to see whether the file has been altered since it was signed.

# TROUBLESHOOTING

### ENABLING MARGIN ICONS

*I've just created a bunch of comments, and even though I changed the zoom setting to Page Width, I can't see the comment icons. What's up with that?*

There is a setting in the Display Settings dialog box that enables and disables the display of margin icons. Choose Tools, Settings, Display. Place a check mark next to Margin Icons to enable them. Use this option if you ever want to hide the comment balloon icons from view, in which case you would disable the check box.

### MY REVIEW COLOR IS BROKEN

*I'm reviewing a document with the Reviewer property bar displayed and a nice bright-blue user color all picked out. But my revisions aren't displaying in blue—they show up as black text like the rest of the document.*

Revisions to a document should appear in the user color, whether you are reviewing the document as a reviewer or as an author. If the revisions are displayed in black text, there might be a conflict with the Windows system colors on your system. Choose Tools, Settings, Display. In the Document tab, deselect Windows System Colors.

### GETTING RID OF THE REVIEW DOCUMENT DIALOG BOX

*Whenever I open certain documents, the Review Document dialog box is open. I know I can click Cancel to get rid of it, but I want to get rid of it permanently. Is there some way to keep it from displaying when I open these documents?*

Absolutely! All you have to do is accept all of the revisions, close the dialog box and save the document. From then on, it won't be considered a "review" document. Here's how: Open the document. Select Author. You should now see the document in the editing window with a toolbar on top of it. In the middle of the toolbar, there is a button that has three check marks on it. Hover over it with your mouse. You should see a QuickTip that says Inserts All the Annotations Into the Document Text. Click this button to accept all of the revisions at once. Now, click the Close button on the toolbar. Save the document.

### THE REDLINE TEXT ISN'T PRINTING CORRECTLY

*I'm trying to print a document with redline and strikeout text. The strikeout looks fine, but the redline doesn't look any different from the rest of the text. What am I doing wrong?*

By default, the redline method is controlled by the printer driver, not WordPerfect. Different types of printers can produce different forms of redline text. Open the document with the redline text. Choose File, Print, and then click the Advanced tab. Disable the Print in Color check box. Print the document—the redlined text should now print with a gray shaded background.

If this doesn't work for you, you can try the latest printer driver for your printer to see whether there is new functionality available. Otherwise, refer to the end of chapter project for information on how to alter the way redline text is printed.

### HOW CAN I AVOID INSTALLING INTERNET EXPLORER 6?

*I want to make sure that I don't install Internet Explorer (IE) 6 when I install WordPerfect. Is it possible to remove it if it's already been installed?*

To make sure you don't install IE 6, start the Setup program and choose a "modify" or "change" install. For WordPerfect Office 11, deselect the following components: WordPerfect, Entrust Security Integration; and Quattro Pro, OLAP. For WordPerfect Office 12, deselect the following components: WordPerfect, Entrust Security Integration.

And yes, you can uninstall Internet Explorer 6 later using the WordPerfect Office 11 or 12 Setup program to remove it.

# PROJECT

If you've ever had to read a hard copy with revision marks, you know it's difficult to read redlined text. Not only that, but some printers don't do such a great job printing redline. So, what can you do?

WordPerfect's Font Map feature gives you the flexibility of changing a font attribute (in this case, redline) to another font, font size, or font style. You can have the redline text appear in another font, so the redline text stands apart from the rest of the text. It's a good idea to pick a font that is stylistically different so it's easy to differentiate between the regular text and the redlined text. For example, if you use a serif font, such as Times New Roman, for the body text, choose a sans-serif font, such as Arial, for the redlined text.

When you edit the font mapping for an attribute, you are doing it for the current printer, not a specific document, so you don't need to open the document first.

Choose Format, Font, Settings, Edit Font Mapping to open the Edit Printer/Document Font Mapping dialog box (see Figure 17.20).

Select the font for the body text

**Figure 17.20**
You can assign a different font to the redline attribute so the redline text is easier to read on the printed copy.

Enable this check box for more options

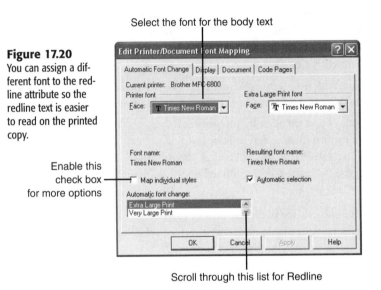

Scroll through this list for Redline

Select the font that you are using for the body text in the Printer Font Face list box (such as Times New Roman). Scroll through the Automatic Font Change list box and choose Redline. Choose a font in the Redline font Face list box (such as Arial). If you place a check mark in the Map Individual Styles check box, you can choose a different font size and style. For example, you might want to use italic or bold to further emphasize the redlined text.

Figure 17.21 shows how the redline text in the Arial font looks with the Times New Roman text.

**Figure 17.21**
If you don't like the way your printer handles redline, you can reassign the redline attribute to another font, size, or style.

Redline text is in Arial, bold, 12-point

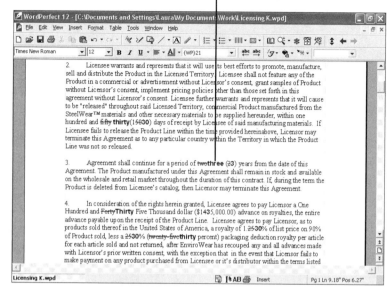

# CHAPTER 18

# WORKING WITH LARGE OR MULTIPART DOCUMENTS

**I**n this chapter                                                        *by Laura Acklen*

# INSERTING BOOKMARKS

Just as you can place a bookmark in a book, you can insert bookmarks into a long document, and then jump from section to section with just a few mouse clicks. In their simplest form, bookmarks help you to navigate through a long document. Raise the bar a little, and you'll use bookmarks to create hypertext links within a document. Raise the bar a little higher, and you'll use bookmarks to position the insertion point, or to move to the next prompt in a template. This section focuses on creating bookmarks to navigate through long documents.

→ If you are ready to create a link to another part of a document, **see** "Creating Hypertext Links," **p. 622.**

→ For more information on creating templates, **see** "Customizing WordPerfect's Templates," **p. 718.**

## INSERTING A BOOKMARK

A bookmark can be created to mark the beginning of a new chapter or section, a table or chart, the start of illustrative pages, or a section of text that is frequently revised—any position within a document. A bookmark can also be created to locate and select a portion of the text. The advantage of selecting text before you create the bookmark is that when you jump to that bookmark, the text is selected and you can then take action on the selection (such as moving or copying it).

Follow these steps to create a bookmark:

1. Click where you want to insert the bookmark, or select the text you want to use to create the bookmark.

2. Choose Tools, Bookmark to display the Bookmark dialog box (see Figure 18.1).

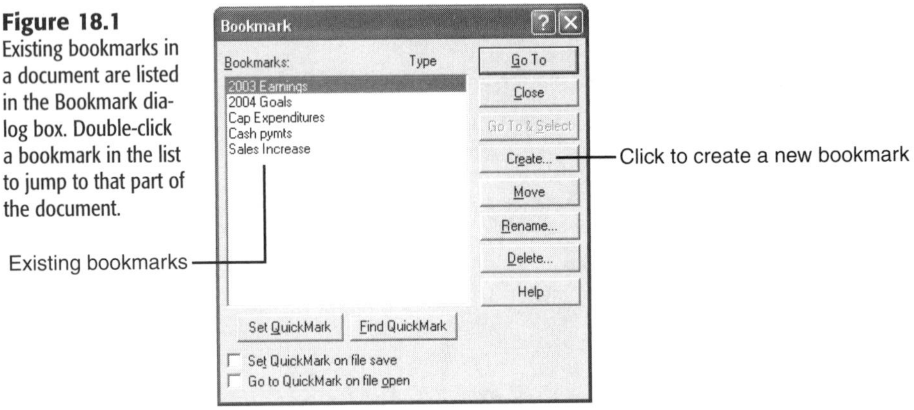

**Figure 18.1**
Existing bookmarks in a document are listed in the Bookmark dialog box. Double-click a bookmark in the list to jump to that part of the document.

Existing bookmarks —

Click to create a new bookmark

**CAUTION**

If you've selected a chart or graphics object, the Bookmark command won't be available. Click in the document window to deselect the object, and then select the text around the object if you want to include it in the selection.

3. Click Create. The Create Bookmark dialog box appears (see Figure 18.2). If you've clicked in the document, the text following the insertion point appears in the Bookmark Name text box. If you selected text, the selected text appears in the Bookmark Name text box, and there is a check mark in the Selected Bookmark check box.

**Figure 18.2**
Type a name for the bookmark in the Create Bookmark dialog box.

4. If necessary, type another name for the bookmark in the Bookmark Name text box. Click OK to return to the Bookmark dialog box.

**TIP FROM**

*Laura Acklen*

If you have Reveal Codes turned on, you can double-click the Bookmark code to open the Bookmark dialog box.

Now that you know how to create bookmarks, you're probably wondering how you're going to use them to move around. Bookmarks are integrated into the Go To feature, so you can use Go To when you want to jump to a bookmark. Or, you can open the Bookmark dialog box and choose one there. Here's how you use Go To to select a bookmark:

- Press Ctrl+G, or click the position information on the status bar, to open the Go To dialog box (see Figure 18.3). Click Bookmark in the Go to What list box, and then choose a bookmark from the Select Bookmark drop-down list (see Figure 18.4 in the next section).

**Figure 18.3**
You can use the Go To dialog box to move between certain elements in a document. Go To will also reselect the last selection.

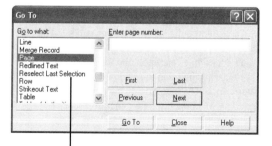

Click to reselect the last selection

18

NOTE

> If you skipped WordPerfect 10, you'll be pleasantly surprised with the enhanced Go To dialog box. In previous versions, there were only six different elements that you could jump to. Now, there are more than 30, including comments, footnotes, hyperlinks, redline/strikeout text, table of contents/authorities entries, and so on.

- Choose Tools, Bookmark. Select a bookmark, and then choose Go To. If you created the bookmark with selected text, and you want that text selected when you move to the bookmark, choose Go To & Select.
- Click the Browse By button and choose Bookmark. Now, click the Previous and Next buttons to move back and forth between bookmarks.

Bookmarks can be moved, renamed, and deleted in the Bookmark dialog box:

- To move a bookmark, click in the text where you want to place the bookmark. Choose Tools, Bookmark. Select the bookmark, and then choose Move.
- To rename a bookmark, choose Tools, Bookmark. Select the bookmark, and then click Rename. Type a new name for the bookmark in the Rename Bookmark dialog box, and then click OK.
- To delete a bookmark, choose Tools, Bookmark. Select the bookmark in the Bookmarks list box, and then click Delete. Click Yes to delete the bookmark, or click No if you change your mind.

CAUTION

> If you accidentally delete an important bookmark, close the Bookmark dialog box, and then click the Undo button to restore it. Be sure to click Undo immediately after you delete the bookmark, or you risk the possibility of undoing the wrong action.

TIP FROM

> Although you can't print out a list of your bookmarks, you can create a screen shot with the Bookmark dialog box open. You can then paste the screen shot into a blank document and print it for future reference. Choose Tools, Bookmark to open the Bookmark dialog box. Press Alt+PrintScreen to copy the screen to the Clipboard. In a document, press Ctrl+V or click the Paste button on the toolbar to paste in the screen shot. Finally, click the Print button to print the screen capture.

## INSERTING QUICKMARKS

A *QuickMark* is a one-time-use bookmark that you can use to save your place in a document. You can have WordPerfect create a QuickMark at the insertion point whenever you save a document. The next time you open the document, you can jump to the QuickMark with one keystroke, or you can have WordPerfect take you there automatically.

To create a QuickMark, click in the text where you want to set the QuickMark, and then choose Tools, Bookmark, Set QuickMark. Or you can press Ctrl+Shift+Q to create the QuickMark.

To find a QuickMark, press Ctrl+Q or choose Tools, Bookmark, Find QuickMark. You can also open the Go To dialog box, and then choose QuickMark from the Select Bookmark drop-down list (see Figure 18.4).

Click to view a list of bookmarks

Click to move to a bookmark

**Figure 18.4**
After you create a QuickMark in a document, QuickMark appears on the Select Bookmark drop-down list in the Go To dialog box.

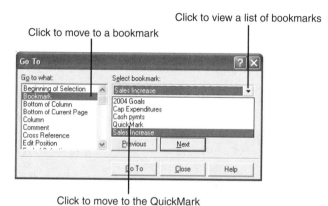

Click to move to the QuickMark

**TIP FROM**

If you want WordPerfect to take care of setting the QuickMark whenever you save a document, choose Tools, Bookmark. Place a check mark in the Set QuickMark on File Save check box. Put a check mark in the Go to QuickMark on File Open check box if you want to jump to the QuickMark when you open the document again.

# ADDING FOOTNOTES AND ENDNOTES

Footnotes and endnotes provide additional information about what is being said in the body of the text without interrupting the flow of that text. They might contain reference details, such as the name of the author, the title of the work, and the page number where the information can be found. They might also provide parenthetic or interpretive explanations of technical material.

**NOTE**

Footnotes and endnotes should not contain essential information because their very location indicates that the author does not consider them required reading.

The process of creating and editing footnotes and endnotes is virtually identical. Because footnotes are more popular, this chapter focuses on them. The differences are mostly self-explanatory, so you shouldn't have problems using the information here to create and edit endnotes.

## CREATING AND EDITING FOOTNOTES

A footnote has two parts: the footnote reference number and the footnote text. The footnote reference number is placed in the text when you create the footnote. The footnote text, along with a corresponding footnote number, is inserted at the bottom of the page. If the footnote is lengthy, WordPerfect splits the footnote and carries it over to the next page.

You can follow these steps to create a footnote:

1. Click in the text where you want the footnote reference number to appear.

2. Choose Insert, Footnote/Endnote to open the Footnote/Endnote dialog box (see Figure 18.5). WordPerfect suggests a footnote number, based on where you are in the document (before or after existing footnotes). If you want to create an endnote rather than a footnote, select Endnote Number.

**Figure 18.5**
You can choose to create a footnote or an endnote in the Footnote/Endnote dialog box.

3. Choose Create. What happens next depends on the view you're using. In Page view, the insertion point is placed at the bottom of the page in the footnote-editing area (see Figure 18.6). In Draft view, the insertion point is moved into a footnote/endnote-editing window. Either way, you have some new buttons on the property bar.

4. Type the text of the footnote.

**TIP FROM**

In Draft view, you can see the footnote numbers in the text, but you can't see the footnote text at the bottom of the page. Because they aren't displayed in the text, you have to create and edit footnotes in a separate footnote-editing window. I strongly recommend switching to Page view when you're working with footnotes and endnotes so you don't have to keep switching back and forth from the footnote-editing window to the document editing window.

Click to move to the next footnote/endnote

Click to move to the
previous footnote/endnote

Click to insert a
note number

**Figure 18.6**
The footnote area is
at the bottom of the
page, right on top of
the bottom margin, so
you can reduce the
bottom margin to
allow for more foot-
notes on a page.

Footnote reference
number

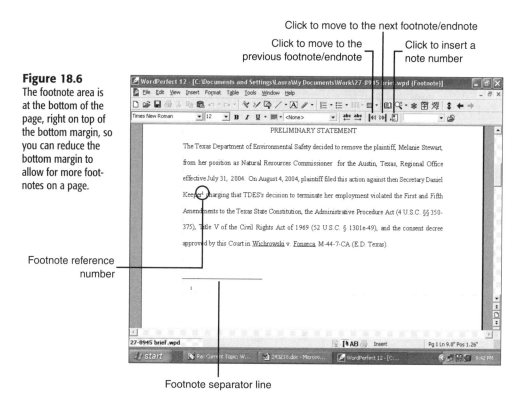

Footnote separator line

**TIP FROM**

If you accidentally delete the note number in the footnote text, click the Note Number
button to reinsert the number. Don't type the number yourself, or WordPerfect won't be
able to update the note numbers as you edit the document.

5. Click the Close button, press Ctrl+F4, or in Page view, click in the body text to move
the insertion point back into the text area. The footnote reference number appears in
the text (see Figure 18.7).

*If your footnote numbers reset to 1 at the beginning of each page (and you don't want them to),
see "My Footnote Numbers Keep Going Back to 1" in the Troubleshooting section at the end of
this chapter.*

## EDITING FOOTNOTES

Editing footnotes in Page View mode is simple—just click in the footnote area and make
your changes. To edit a footnote in Draft view, choose Insert, Footnote/Endnote, type the
number of the footnote you want to edit in the Footnote Number text box, and then choose
Edit. When you're done, click the Close button on the property bar.

**Figure 18.7**
The footnote reference number is tied to a footnote code so the footnote numbers are automatically updated as you edit the document.

Footnote reference number

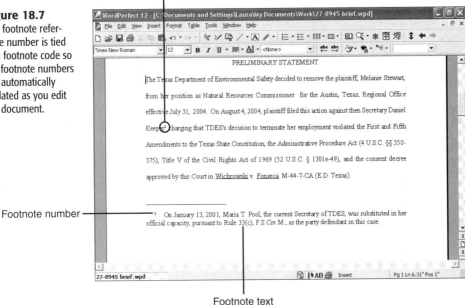

Footnote number

Footnote text

## DELETING FOOTNOTES

To delete a footnote, select the footnote reference number in the text, and then press Delete. You could also click and drag the Footnote code out of the Reveal Codes window. Because this deletes the footnote code, both the footnote reference number and the footnote text are removed.

 *If you are having trouble deleting a footnote, see "I Can't Get Rid of a Reference Number" in the Troubleshooting section at the end of this chapter.*

## MOVING FOOTNOTES

You might decide after you've typed in the text of the footnote that the footnote should appear elsewhere in the paragraph. Or, you might decide that you need to create a footnote that is almost identical to this one, so you want to copy the footnote, and then make the small changes. Moving and copying footnotes is easy—just cut or copy, and then paste the footnote reference number, just as you would any other piece of text. Because the footnote reference number represents the footnote code, you're actually copying and moving codes without having to work in Reveal Codes.

→ If you need a refresher on how to move and copy text, **see** "Moving and Copying Text," **p. 53.**

## ADDING ENDNOTES

By default, endnotes are grouped together at the end of the document, rather than printed at the bottom of a page. You can control where the endnotes are compiled with endnote placement codes. For example, a long document can be divided into smaller files, perhaps at major headings or sections, and then combined for final formatting. If you want the endnotes compiled at the end of each section, rather than at the end of the document, insert an endnote placement code at the bottom of each file.

To insert an endnote placement code, choose Insert, Footnote/Endnote, Endnote Number, Endnote Placement. Choose Insert Endnotes at Insertion Point if you're compiling all the endnotes together, or choose Insert Endnotes at Insertion Point and Restart Numbering if you're compiling endnotes at the end of each section and you want to restart numbering at one in each section.

→ For more information on breaking large documents into smaller pieces, **see** "Working with Master Documents and Subdocuments," **p. 580.**

**CAUTION**

> If the insertion point is inside the footnote area, the Footnote/Endnote option on the Insert menu isn't available. You have to click in the text and move the insertion point out of the footnote area to make the Footnote/Endnote option available.

**18**

## FORMATTING FOOTNOTES

WordPerfect makes some assumptions for you so that you can create and edit footnotes without having to worry about creating a separator line or making sure there is enough room between the body text and the footnote text. The footnote number is a superscripted Arabic numeral, and the first line of the footnote is indented. However, you might have a reason to change these settings, and it's easy enough to do.

Choose Insert, Footnote/Endnote, Options, Advanced to open the Advanced Footnote Options dialog box (see Figure 18.8), where you can tweak the footnote options.

Here are some of the changes you can make in the Advanced Footnote Options dialog box:

- Click the Method drop-down list arrow, and choose a different numbering method (lowercase/uppercase letters, lowercase/uppercase Roman, or characters).
- Click In Text to edit the style for the footnote reference number.
- Click In Note to edit the style for the footnote text.

**TIP FROM**

_Laura Acklen_

> It's fairly common to have footnote text in the same font as the document text, but in a smaller size. Click In Note to edit the footnote style, and then choose a smaller size from the Font Size drop-down list.

Type the amount of footnote to keep together

Choose a numbering method here

**Figure 18.8**
You can make adjustments to footnote formatting in the Advanced Footnote Options dialog box.

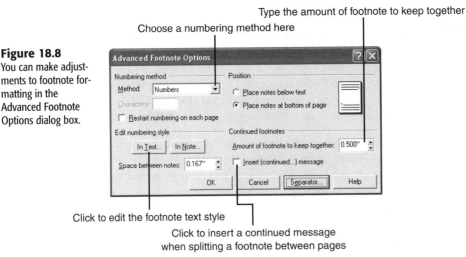

Click to edit the footnote text style

Click to insert a continued message
when splitting a footnote between pages

- Adjust the space between footnotes in the Space Between Notes text box.

- In the Amount of Footnote to Keep Together, specify how much footnote text you want kept together if the footnote is split across two pages.

- Put a check mark next to Insert (Continued) Message if you want WordPerfect to insert a continued message next to the separator line when a footnote is split across two pages.

**TIP FROM**

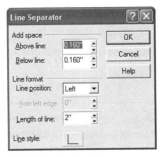

If a footnote is particularly long, you can force it to split between two pages. Press Ctrl+Enter to push the rest of the footnote text to the next page.

- Click Separator to open the Line Separator dialog box (see Figure 18.9). Make any necessary adjustments to the format of the separator line. You can also choose Options, Separator (in the Footnote/Endnote dialog box) to open the Line Separator dialog box.

**Figure 18.9**
You can set the spacing, positioning, length, and line style for the separator line in the Line Separator dialog box.

## FORMATTING ENDNOTES

Endnotes are grouped together on a page, so there are fewer options to set for them than there are for footnotes. In the Footnote/Endnote dialog box, choose Endnote Number, Options, Advanced to display the Endnote Options dialog box (see Figure 18.10), which is an abbreviated version of the Advanced Footnote Options dialog box.

**Figure 18.10**
Because endnotes are grouped together on a page, there is no need to position them, include a separator line, or print a continued message.

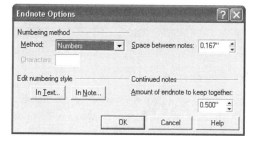

**NOTE**

Some aspects of the footnote/endnote features in WP12 have been adjusted so they could be matched up with Word's footnote/endnote features. For example, the footnote and endnote numbering styles have different names, but the names have been matched up so the conversion between formats is more accurate. These changes improve the results of the conversion when you save documents in Word format, and when you open Word documents in WordPerfect.

18

## ADJUSTING FOOTNOTE/ENDNOTE NUMBERS

If you ever need to make manual adjustments to the footnote numbers, in the Footnote/Endnote dialog box, select Options, Set Number to open the Footnote Number dialog box (see Figure 18.11). If you choose Endnote Number first, you get the Endnote Number dialog box, which looks the same as the Footnote Number dialog box.

**Figure 18.11**
You can use the Footnote Number dialog box to adjust footnote numbers.

**NOTE**

Footnotes and endnotes, like headers, footers, page numbers, and graphics box captions, are considered a part of the document's substructure. As such, they are formatted differently than the rest of the text. WordPerfect uses the settings in DocumentStyle to format these elements. So, even if you change the font at the top of the document, the

*continues*

*continued*

> footnotes/endnotes (and other elements) will appear in the font specified as the document default font, or the font selected in the DocumentStyle, which might not match the font you inserted.
>
> To make global changes to the document and the substructures, place all the formatting codes in the DocumentStyle. (The DocumentStyle code is always the first code in the document.) Choose File, Document, Current Document Style to edit the DocumentStyle.

## CONVERTING FOOTNOTES AND ENDNOTES

If you're really lucky, you have a boss or a professor who never changes the formatting guidelines for your reports. In the real world, however, that's not likely. One day you need footnotes, the next day, endnotes (and vice versa).

WordPerfect ships with two macros that completely automate the process of converting footnotes to endnotes and endnotes to footnotes. They are called *footend* and *endfoot* (original, huh?).

→ For a complete list and the steps to run the shipping macros, **see** "Running the Shipping Macros," **p. 818.**

There are two ways to run these macros:

- Choose Tools, Macro, Play. In the Play Macro dialog box, scroll through the list of macros, and then double-click Footend or Endfoot.

**CAUTION**

> If you don't see these two macros, choose Tools, Settings, Files, and then click the Merge/Macro tab. Make a note of the location shown next to the Default Macro Folder. Now, choose Tools, Macro, Play and browse to that folder. You might have to scroll down through the list to find them.

- You can turn on a Shipping Macros toolbar for quick access to the macros that come with WordPerfect. Right-click the toolbar, choose More, and then place a check mark next to the Shipping Macros toolbar (see Figure 18.12). (You have to scroll down to see this one.) Click Close to clear the Customize Settings dialog box. Now, click the Convert End to Foot button, or the Convert Foot to End button.

**CAUTION**

> You can't select a portion of the document, and then run the macro to convert only specific footnotes or endnotes. The footend macro converts every single footnote to an endnote and the endfoot macro converts every single endnote to a footnote.

**Figure 18.12**
The More option on the toolbar QuickMenu takes you to a complete list of available toolbars.

Place a check mark

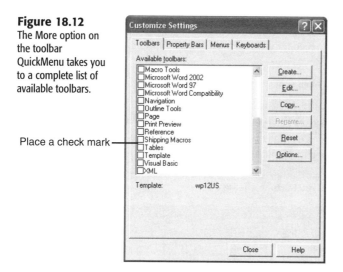

# SIMPLIFYING A COMPLEX DOCUMENT WITH CROSS-REFERENCES

Navigating a complex document can be made much easier with cross-references. References to other pages, figures, tables, and definitions show a reader how fragments of information are linked together. (You might have noticed that this book is liberally sprinkled with cross-references to guide you to other parts of the book that discuss related or complementary features.)

A cross-reference can point to a page, chapter, or volume number; a footnote or endnote number; a paragraph/outline number; a caption number; a counter; or any combination of these. It can be as simple as "see 'Contract Terms' on page 35," or as complex as "refer to footnote 5 on page 78 in Chapter 13."

When you create a cross-reference, you mark the place in the text where you want to insert the reference information. Then, you mark the target, or the item that you are referencing. The two marks share a common name—that's how they are matched up when you generate the cross-references.

## MARKING REFERENCES

References and targets don't have to be marked in any particular order, so you can mark the text as you type, or you can come back later and do it all at once. A reference in the text that refers to a nonexistent target displays a ? where the reference information should be. After you mark the target and generate the document, the question marks are replaced with the reference information.

Follow these steps to create a reference:

1. Type the descriptive text that precedes a reference. For example, type **see** `'Contract Terms' on page`.

2. Position the insertion point where you want the reference to appear. Make sure you leave a space between the descriptive text and the reference.

3. Choose Tools, Reference, Cross-Reference. The Cross-Reference tab of the Reference Tools dialog box appears (see Figure 18.13). The default reference type is page (for a page number), so if you're inserting a page number reference, you're all set to go.

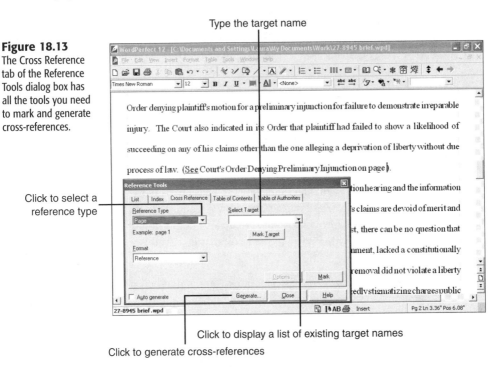

**Figure 18.13**
The Cross Reference tab of the Reference Tools dialog box has all the tools you need to mark and generate cross-references.

Type the target name

Click to select a reference type

Click to display a list of existing target names

Click to generate cross-references

4. If necessary, click the Reference Type drop-down arrow and choose a different reference type from the list (see Figure 18.14).

5. Click in the Select Target text box and type a target name for the reference (or if you've already marked the target, click the drop-down list arrow and choose the target name from the list).

**N O T E**

> The target name that you use to mark the reference must exactly match the target name that you use to mark the target. Target names are not case sensitive. If you're unsure of the target name, try marking the target first. When you mark the references to that

target, the target name will already be in the list. Highly complex documents can have similar target names, in which case you should mark targets (and their associated references) one at a time.

**Figure 18.14**
You can choose from nine different reference types in the Reference Type drop-down list.

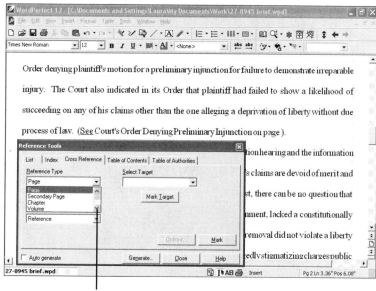

Click to scroll down through the list of reference types

6. Click Mark. WordPerfect inserts a reference code at the insertion point, and a question mark is used as a placeholder (see Figure 18.15).

7. If necessary, continue marking the references. When you are finished, click Close to clear the Reference Tools dialog box.

**NOTE**

Cross-references are a great way to point out related or complementary information in a long or multipart document. If the document will be reviewed onscreen, turn the reference text into a hypertext link that the reader can click to jump to the target. That way, readers can jump back to their places and continue reading.

## MARKING TARGETS

The target is the item that you want to refer to, so it might be a phrase, a footnote or endnote, a paragraph/outline item, or a graphics box. The trick to marking a target is to insert the code in the right place. Text references are easy—just click at the beginning of the phrase, paragraph, or section before you insert the code. To reference a footnote or endnote, you need to insert the code in the footnote or endnote text, not next to the footnote reference, as you might think. If you're referencing a graphics box, turn on Reveal Codes and position the red cursor right after the graphics box code.

**Figure 18.15**
If you haven't marked the target yet, a question mark serves as a placeholder.

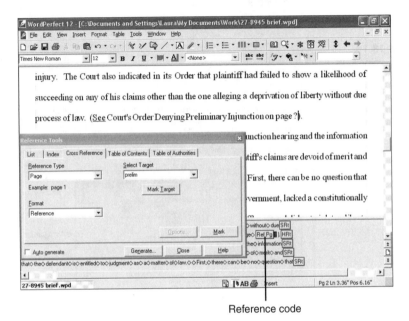

Reference code

**TIP FROM**

If you're worried that you might forget to include the target code should you ever have to move a graphic box, you can attach the target code to the graphic by placing the code inside a blank caption.

→ For more information on creating graphics box captions, **see** "Adding Captions," **p. 406.**

Follow these steps to mark a target:

1. Position the insertion point either by clicking in the text or turning on Reveal Codes and positioning the red cursor.
2. If the Reference Tools dialog box isn't onscreen, choose Tools, Reference, Cross-Reference. The Cross-Reference tab of the Reference Tools dialog box appears (refer to Figure 18.13).
3. Click in the Select Target text box and type the target name, or click the drop-down list arrow to choose a target from the list.
4. Click Mark Target. If you have Reveal Codes turned on, you'll see that WordPerfect inserts a [Target (target name)] code at the insertion point.

*If you made a few mistakes when you marked targets and references, see "I Typed the Wrong Target Name" in the Troubleshooting section at the end of this chapter.*

## GENERATING AUTOMATIC CROSS-REFERENCES

When you generate the cross-references in a document, WordPerfect matches the target names in the reference and target codes and inserts the reference information in the text. Depending on the complexity of the document and the references you've created, generating can put a strain on your computer's resources. For this reason, I highly recommend that you save the document beforehand.

To generate a document, click the Generate button in the Reference Tools dialog box, press Ctrl+F9, or choose Tools, Reference, Generate to display the Generate dialog box (see Figure 18.16). Click OK to generate the document.

**Figure 18.16**
The Generate option updates all the marked entries in a document at once.

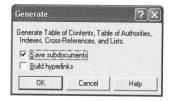

 *If the Generate button is grayed out, see "The Generate Button Isn't Available" in the Troubleshooting section at the end of this chapter.*

→ If you aren't sure whether you should select the Save Subdocuments option in the Generate dialog box, **see** "Generating Document References in Master Documents," **p. 585.**

**TIP FROM**

> If you're working on someone else's document, and the references are so messed up that you just don't know where to start, you might consider stripping out all the target and reference codes and starting over. In some cases, it's just easier to start with a clean slate. Use Find and Replace to search for both the target codes and the reference codes, replacing them with nothing.

→ To review the steps to use the Find and Replace feature to search for codes, **see** "Searching for Codes," **p. 150.**

## CREATING A CROSS-REFERENCE TO A GRAPHICS BOX COUNTER

Counters are used to number graphics boxes, usually within the caption. For example, I could use a counter to automatically number each figure in this chapter. Counters can be used to number all types of graphics boxes (figure, table, text, user, or equation). You can create a reference to any type of graphics box by referencing the counter.

Follow these steps to create a cross-reference to a graphics box counter:

1. If you haven't already do so, insert the graphic(s) or box(es).

   → For more information on creating graphics box captions, **see** "Adding Captions," **p. 406.**

2. Position the insertion point and type the descriptive text that precedes the reference. For example, type **See Figure**. Make sure you leave a space between the reference text and the reference.

3. If the Cross Reference tab of the Reference Tools dialog box isn't already displayed, choose Tools, Reference, Cross-Reference.

4. Open the Reference Type drop-down list, and choose Counter to display the Counter dialog box (see Figure 18.17).

**Figure 18.17**
You can select the type of graphics box that you want to reference in the Counter dialog box.

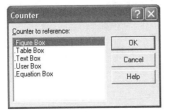

5. Click the graphics box counter type, and then click OK.

6. Type a target name in the Select Target text box or select the target name from the drop-down list.

7. Click Mark.

8. Click the graphics box you are referencing.

9. Type the target name in the Select Target text box or select the target name from the drop-down list.

10. Click Mark Target.

11. Click outside the graphics box (to deselect the box).

12. Click Generate, OK.

 *If you break a cross-reference when you move a graphics box, see "Discombobulated Graphics Box References" in the Troubleshooting section at the end of this chapter.*

# WORKING WITH MASTER DOCUMENTS AND SUBDOCUMENTS

The Master Document feature is ideally suited for any large project—an employee manual, a college dissertation, or a complex legal contract, for example. Writers often collaborate on a large project and then combine their work into one document. Without WordPerfect's Master Document feature, combining separate efforts is a time-consuming task that presents many challenges in numbering pages, creating a table of contents, setting up headers and footers, and generating cross-references.

Here's how it works: You create a document with links to other files. This is the master document. A subdocument is one of the linked files. When you expand the master document, each of the subdocuments is opened into the master document, which results in one huge document. Now you can work on all the text as a whole. You can search through the entire work, generate document references, make global formatting changes, and so forth. When you condense the master document, the subdocuments are saved and removed from the master document, leaving only the subdocument codes. For this reason, creating prefatory pages and introductory materials is easy because you don't have to scroll through all the text.

## BREAKING UP AN EXISTING DOCUMENT INTO SUBDOCUMENTS

Breaking up an existing document into subdocuments is simple—just select a section and save it to a file. You can divide the document into as many logical or manageable sections as you want. If necessary, you can create subdocuments within subdocuments. Subdocuments can be expanded independently, so you have complete control over how much of a document you work with at a time.

To create subdocuments from an existing document, select the section of text that you want to save in a subdocument. Keep in mind that you might someday use this subdocument in other master documents. With the text selected, click the Save button. In the Save dialog box (see Figure 18.18), choose Selected Text, and then click OK to display the Save File dialog box. Type a name for the new file, and then choose Save.

**18**

**Figure 18.18**
If you click the Save button with text selected, you can choose between saving the entire file or just the selected text.

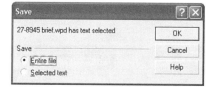

## CREATING A MASTER DOCUMENT

A master document is just a regular WordPerfect document, with text and formatting codes. What turns a regular document into a master document is the links to other documents—the subdocuments. There isn't anything special about a subdocument—it's a regular WordPerfect document, too, with text and formatting codes.

You might already have a master document shell, especially if you just finished saving sections of text into files (as described previously) so they can be subdocuments. If you haven't done this, go ahead and type whatever headings or introductory material you need before the text of the first subdocument. Click where you want to insert the subdocument text, and then choose File, Document, Subdocument. The Include Subdocument dialog box appears (see Figure 18.19). Select the subdocument file, and then click Include.

Select a file in the list

**Figure 18.19**
Include Subdocument
is one of the many
different file manage-
ment dialog boxes in
WordPerfect.

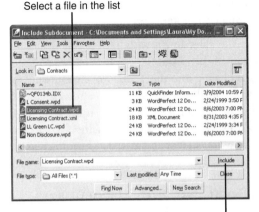

Click to insert the subdocument code

**TIP FROM**

The Reference toolbar includes three buttons for working with master and subdocuments: Subdocument, Expand Master, and Condense Master. Right-click the toolbar,
choose More, and then choose Reference. Choose Close to clear the Customize Settings
dialog box.

**18**

What happens next depends on your view mode. If you're in Page view, you have to scroll
over to the left to see the subdocument icon in the margin (see Figure 18.20). If you're in
Draft view, the name and path of the subdocument are displayed in a comment (see
Figure 18.21).

**Figure 18.20**
In Page view, the
position of a subdocu-
ment code is marked
by icons in the left
margin.

Subdocument icon

Subdocument code

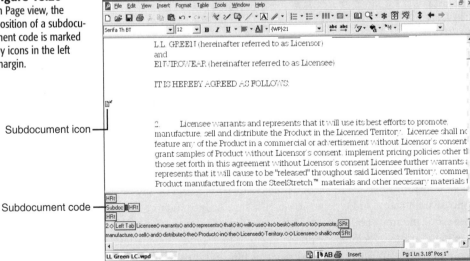

**Figure 18.21**
In Draft view, a subdocument is displayed as a comment.

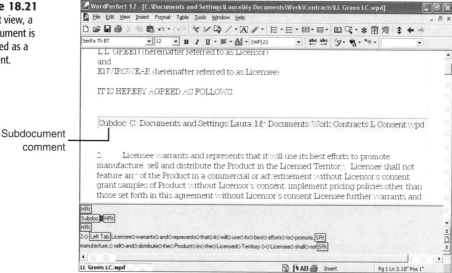

Subdocument comment

**NOTE**

Subdocuments can easily be rearranged in a condensed master document. Turn on Reveal Codes and select the [Subdoc] code. Press Ctrl+X to cut the code. Click where you want to insert the subdocument code, and then press Ctrl+V to paste the code.

It's a little more complicated to rearrange expanded subdocuments, but it can be done. Turn on Reveal Codes and make sure you include the [Subdoc Begin] and the [Subdoc End] codes when you select the text of the subdocument. Press Ctrl+X, click where you want to insert the subdocument text, and then press Ctrl+V.

 *If you can't see the filename in the Subdocument code, see "I Can't See the Filename in the Subdocument Code" in the Troubleshooting section at the end of this chapter.*

## EXPANDING AND CONDENSING MASTER DOCUMENTS

When you expand a master document, each subdocument is inserted into that master document. You can then work with all the text at once. You can do a global search and replace, mark the text for an index or a table of contents, apply styles, and proof for whitespace and consistent formatting; you can perform any task that involves working with the entire document.

To expand a master document, choose File, Document, Expand Master. The Expand Master Document dialog box opens, with a list of the subdocuments (see Figure 18.22).

A subdocument that has a check mark in its check box will be opened and inserted in the master document. If you remove a check mark, that subdocument won't be opened. So, you can expand only the subdocuments that you want to work with. Click OK to expand the subdocuments.

**Figure 18.22**
You can select the subdocuments you want to expand in the Expand Master Document dialog box.

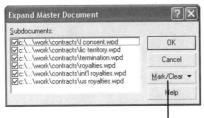

Click to mark all or clear all the check boxes

**TIP FROM**

If you have a long list of subdocuments and you want to expand only one or two of them, it's quicker to deselect them all, and then select the one or two that you want. To deselect all the subdocuments at once, choose Mark/Clear, Clear All. When you're ready to expand all the subdocuments, you can reselect them. Choose Mark/Clear, Mark All to mark them all at once.

**CAUTION**

If one of the subdocuments has been moved or deleted, you get an error message. You can either type a new path and filename or browse for the file. If you're not sure where the file is, choose Skip. Network users should make sure they are mapped to the drive where the subdocuments are stored.

**NOTE**

There are three different subdocument margin icons. The one with the down arrow is the [Subdoc Begin] code, the one with the up arrow is the [Subdoc End] code, and the one with the arrow tilting down to the left is a condensed subdocument [Subdoc path/ filename] code.

When you condense a master document, you get to select which subdocuments are condensed and which are saved. By selectively condensing certain subdocuments, you can work on related sections of a document without "wading through" the rest of the text. Even a huge 500-page legal brief can be easily revised by breaking it up into subdocuments, and then expanding and condensing only those sections that you want to work with.

To condense a master document, choose File, Document, Condense Master. The Condense/Save Subdocuments dialog box appears (see Figure 18.23).

Once again, the Mark/Clear button opens a drop-down menu of options that you can use to condense all or clear all and to save all or clear all. Otherwise, you can place a check mark next to the files that you want to condense and save.

This file will be condensed, but not saved

**Figure 18.23**
In the Condense/Save Subdocuments dialog box, you can place a check mark next to a file to save or condense it.

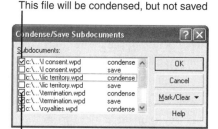

This file will be condensed and saved

**CAUTION**

Think carefully before you choose to save your changes to a subdocument, especially if the subdocument belongs to a colleague. To save your changes without overwriting the original file, move or copy the original file before you condense and save the subdocument. Currently, there is no provision for saving a subdocument under a different name.

**TIP FROM**

You should *always* condense a master document before you save it. Otherwise, you save the same information twice and consume twice the disk space. Remember, you've already saved the subdocuments, so you don't need to save that same information in the master document.

18

*If you have some stray subdocument text that won't disappear, or if the filename is missing in the Condense/Save Subdocuments dialog box, see "I Accidentally Deleted a Subdocument Code" in the Troubleshooting section at the end of this chapter.*

## GENERATING DOCUMENT REFERENCES IN MASTER DOCUMENTS

When you generate document references for a master document, WordPerfect automatically expands the master document, generates the document references, and then condenses the master document again. If this procedure modifies any subdocuments, by default WordPerfect saves the modified subdocuments over the originals. If you don't want changes saved to the subdocuments, you can deselect the option to save subdocuments in the Generate dialog box (refer to Figure 18.16).

➔ For information on creating a table of contents, **see** "Creating a Table of Contents," **p. 593**.

➔ For the steps to create an index, **see** "Creating Indexes," **p. 605**.

➔ To learn how to create a table of authorities, **see** "Creating a Table of Authorities or a Bibliography," **p. 598.**

➔ To learn how to create a list in a long document, **see** "Assembling Lists," **p. 611.**

## FORMATTING TRICKS

The key to working with master documents and subdocuments is learning how to create subdocuments that can function independently of the master document. The formatting codes that are necessary in a subdocument can cause problems in the master document, and vice versa.

Automatic Code Placement (the behind-the-scenes WordPerfect feature that positions certain codes for you) is a great timesaver. It eliminates a lot of frustration from not positioning the insertion point correctly when formatting (those of us who worked in versions of WordPerfect before the advent of Automatic Code Placement thought it was magical).

However, in the case of subdocuments, the Auto Line Formatter component of the Automatic Code Placement feature can strip out redundant codes, resulting in a subdocument that can no longer stand on its own. For example, let's say you have a double-spaced master document. When you expand a subdocument with a double-spacing code in it, the Auto Line Formatter strips out that code, because it's redundant. When you save the subdocument, it is saved without the double-spacing code so it is saved as a single-spaced document.

Now you're thinking, "Yeah yeah yeah, but what can I do about it?" You can place your formatting codes in an open style at the top of the subdocument...that's what. As long as the "redundant" codes are stored in the DocumentStyle of the subdocument, they can't be deleted by the Auto Line Formatter.

Here are some other things to consider as you format master documents and subdocuments:

- If you want each subdocument to start on a new page, you can either insert a hard page between each subdocument code in the master document, or you can insert a hard page at the top of each subdocument.

- Formatting codes in a subdocument can cause conflicts with codes in the master document. For example, if the master document has Header A defined, that header remains in effect only until another Header A code is reached. If the first subdocument has a Header A defined, that header replaces the header you defined in the master document. This can work to your advantage, however, if you want new header text at the beginning of each chapter or section.

- Styles in a master document override subdocument styles with the same name, so the subdocuments are reformatted according to the codes in the master document's styles. These same-name styles are saved with the subdocument, although styles with unique names are added to the master document's list of styles. Consider creating a template that contains the styles for your project, and then distributing the template among your colleagues so that they can use the styles when they create subdocuments.

- You can mark text for a table of contents, table of authorities, list, index, or cross-reference in both the master document and subdocument. You might find it easier to mark document references in an expanded master document. If you're marking headings for a table, list, or index, you might want to define a style for your headings with all the formatting plus the mark text codes.

- To number an expanded master document sequentially, place a page numbering code to start numbering pages with 1 immediately after the introductory pages (such as the table of contents).

- If you're working on a book, you probably want to increment the chapter numbers in each subdocument. Place a chapter number increment code at the beginning of each subdocument. At the beginning of the master document, insert a page number position code and a chapter number method code.

- If a document is to be printed on both sides of the paper, it's common practice to begin a new chapter or major section on the right side. You can accomplish this by placing a [Force: Odd] code in an open style at the top of each subdocument.

- Don't place footnote or endnote option codes in the subdocuments. These codes, which control spacing between footnotes, separator lines, and whether numbering should restart on each page, should only be placed in the master document.

- In most cases, footnotes should be numbered sequentially throughout a document. However, if you decide to restart the numbering in each subdocument, you need to place a footnote number set code in an open style at the top of each subdocument.

- You can opt to place all endnotes at the end of the document, or at the end of each sub-document. If you opt for the former, place an endnote placement code at the end of the master document and choose Insert Endnotes at Insertion Point in the Endnote Placement dialog box. For the latter, insert an endnote placement code at the end of the subdocument and choose Insert Endnotes at Insertion Point and Restart Numbering in the Endnote Placement dialog box.

- Marking text for cross-references in subdocuments is tricky because you have to remember the target names. Because expanding the master document compiles a list of all the marked targets, you might prefer to mark targets and references in an expanded master document.

# TROUBLESHOOTING

### MY FOOTNOTE NUMBERS KEEP GOING BACK TO 1

*When I insert a footnote on a new page, the numbering starts over at 1.*

The Restart Numbering on Each Page option is selected in the Advanced Footnote Options dialog box. To use continuously numbered footnotes for the entire document, choose Insert, Footnote/Endnote, Options, Advanced. In the Advanced Footnote Options dialog box, remove the check mark next to Restart Numbering on Each Page.

### I CAN'T GET RID OF A REFERENCE NUMBER

*I just deleted a footnote, but the footnote reference number is still in the paragraph.*

The footnote number in the footnote itself and the footnote number in the document are two separate entities. Deleting the text of a footnote and the number in the footnote area doesn't automatically remove the footnote reference number (you have to do it manually). On the other hand, deleting the footnote reference number deletes everything at once.

### I Typed the Wrong Target Name

*I made a few mistakes when I marked my targets and references. In one case, I've typed the wrong target name. On the next page, I need to move the reference. Can I correct these mistakes without starting over?*

If you make a mistake typing the target name, you need to delete the reference code and mark the reference again. If you just need to move the reference, select the explanatory text and the ? (or the reference information, if you've already generated the cross-references). You'll be selecting the text and the reference code, which can also be done in Reveal Codes if you prefer. Press Ctrl+X to cut the code, click where you want to insert the reference code, and then press Ctrl+V to paste the code.

### The Generate Button Isn't Available

*I've got the Cross-Reference bar displayed, but the Generate button is grayed out. The Generate option on the Reference menu is grayed out as well.*

If the insertion point is inside one of the substructure elements (such as a graphics box caption, a footnote, an endnote, a header, or a footer), the Generate option isn't available. Click in the document text. When you move out of the substructure's area, the Generate button becomes available.

### Discombobulated Graphics Box References

*I just moved a graphics box and now the reference information is incorrect. I've tried generating the document, but the reference is still wrong.*

When you click and drag a graphics box to move it somewhere else in the document, the target code doesn't go with it. The two become separated, so the reference information isn't accurate. There are a couple of ways to avoid this.

First, you can turn on Reveal Codes and carefully select both the box code and the target code, and then use Cut and Paste to move the selection.

Or, you can insert the target code in the graphics box caption. Right-click the graphics box, and then choose Caption. You can delete the default caption text, and then choose Tools, Reference, Cross-Reference. Select the target name from the list, and then choose Mark Target. Click in the document to get out of the caption, and then deselect the graphics box. No matter where you move this box, the target code stays with it.

### I Can't See the Filename in the Subdocument Code

*When I turn on Reveal Codes, I can see the folder path to the subdocuments but not the filename. Is there anything I can do to show the filenames in the codes?*

Unfortunately, there is a limitation to the number of characters that can be displayed in a code in Reveal Codes. If you have more than 55 characters, including the path and filename, you will only be able to see the first 55 characters. At this point, it isn't possible to increase the number of characters.

Thankfully, there is an easy workaround. If you change the default folder to the folder that your subdocuments are in, the subdocument codes will show only the filename (but not the path).

### I Accidentally Deleted a Subdocument Code

*I finished revising a master document, so I opened the Condense/Save Subdocuments dialog box to condense the subdocuments. I condensed all the subdocuments, but there is still some text that belongs to a subdocument in my master document. When I look again at the Condense/Save Subdocuments dialog box, I see that the filename for that subdocument is missing. What's happened?*

You've accidentally deleted one or both of the beginning or ending subdocument codes. When you do this, the subdocument text becomes a part of the master document. To rectify the situation, select the text and save it (using the original subdocument name). Then, reinsert the subdocument code.

If you are making heavy revisions to a document, you might want to turn on the option to get a confirmation message before deleting codes. Choose Tools, Settings, Environment. Click the Prompts tab, and then select Confirm Deletion of Codes and Stop Insertion Point at Hidden Codes.

# PROJECT

Cross-references make navigating through a long document much easier because they point out relationships between fragments of information. But even with the most detailed cross-reference, the reader must still go looking for the target information.

If the document is destined for a Web page or onscreen review, you can turn reference text into a hyperlink that takes you directly to the target.

First, create a bookmark for the target:

1. Click near the target.
2. Choose Tools, Bookmark, Create.
3. Type a name for this bookmark, and then click OK. You can use the same name as the target if you like.

Second, create a hyperlink to the bookmark:

1. Either type or select the reference text.
2. Choose Tools, Hyperlink to open the Hyperlink Properties dialog box.
3. Click the Bookmark drop-down arrow to display a list of bookmarks for the document.
4. Choose the bookmark that you want to link to.
5. Click OK to create the hyperlink.

The hyperlink text appears in a different color. To open the Hyperlink Properties dialog box so you can edit a hyperlink, right-click the hyperlink text and then choose Edit Hyperlink.

→ This is just the beginning of things you can do with hyperlinks. For more information, **see** "Creating Hypertext Links," **p. 622**, and "Creating Links to the Internet," **p. 628.**

CHAPTER **19**

# GENERATING TABLES, INDEXES, AND LISTS

## In this chapter

*by Laura Acklen*

# USING DOCUMENT MAP TO NAVIGATE LONG DOCUMENTS

Document Map, a new feature in WordPerfect 11, is the perfect companion to the table of contents, table of authorities, index, and list features. Though you might not create many tables of contents or indexes, you'll probably review some documents with these elements in them. If you do, you'll love this feature.

Document Map builds a roadmap of your document using table of contents, table of authorities, index, or list markers. You can quickly navigate through the document by clicking a reference marker in the document map.

To display the document map:

1. Open a document that contains markers for either a table of contents, table of authorities, or an index.

2. Choose View, Document Map (Alt+Shift+M) to display the document map. You can click a marker in the list to jump to that text in the document (see Figure 19.1).

Select the type of marker you want to use

**Figure 19.1**
The Document Map offers a convenient method to navigate through a lengthy document.

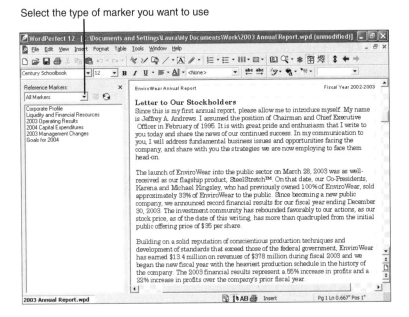

3. If necessary, choose a marker type from the Reference Markers list box to display only specific entries.

4. If you prefer a tree view, click the Turn On Tree View button. This view shows the reference markers in a hierarchal structure so it's easier to see headings and subheadings.

5. If you make any changes to the reference markers, click the Refresh the Document Map button to update the document map.

*If you get the error message "This document does not contain the necessary code to create a document map" when you try to open a file in WordPerfect, see "Document Map Error Message" in the Troubleshooting section at the end of this chapter.*

# CREATING A TABLE OF CONTENTS

Continuing in the fine tradition of providing powerful, yet easy-to-use large document tools, WordPerfect supports a five-level table of contents. Although any text that you mark in the document can be added to a table of contents, the most common entries are chapter names and section headings.

You can automate the process of marking headings for a table of contents by using WordPerfect's heading styles, or by adding the mark text codes to your own heading styles. (I'll get back to that later in this section.)

Creating a table of contents entry is simple: You select the text that you want to appear (in most cases, a heading), and then choose the appropriate table of contents level. WordPerfect surrounds the selected text with Mark Text codes. When you generate the table, WordPerfect grabs the text between the Mark Text codes, positions it in the correct table of contents level, and inserts a current page number next to it.

## MARKING TEXT

Selecting text for a table of contents can be a little tricky. You have to make sure that you don't include formatting codes, such as bold or italic, within the Mark Text codes. Otherwise, those codes affect the format of that entry and can potentially cause problems with other entries. If you do get some codes by accident, you'll know right away because, after you generate the table, you'll be able to see that certain entries are formatted differently.

To select text for a table of contents entry, follow these steps:

1. Choose Tools, Reference, Table of Contents to display the Table of Contents tab of the Reference Tools dialog box (see Figure 19.2).

2. Turn on Reveal Codes (press Alt+F3) and select the text that you want included in the table. Start selecting at the first letter of text and stop at the last letter so you don't accidentally include a formatting code.

3. Click one of the Mark buttons (refer to Figure 19.2) to mark this selection for a particular level in the table. For example, click Mark 1 to mark this entry for the first level in the table. Each table of contents level is indented by one more tab stop, so the second, third, fourth, and fifth levels are really sublevels of Level 1.

19

**Figure 19.2**
The Table of Contents tab of the Reference Tools dialog box has buttons for each level in a table of contents, so marking a selection can be done with one click.

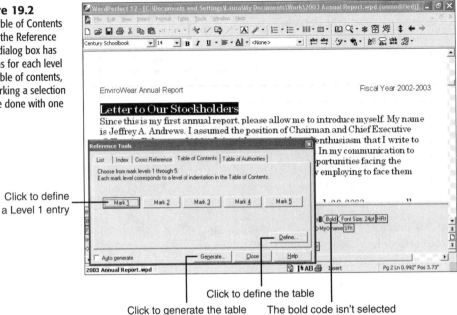

Click to define a Level 1 entry

Click to define the table

Click to generate the table    The bold code isn't selected

---

**TIP FROM**

*Laura Acklen*

If you want an automatic paragraph number to be included with a table of contents entry, make sure you include paragraph numbering codes when you select the text. If you don't want the paragraph numbers to appear in the table, start selecting right after the paragraph number (but don't include the tab or indent code that follows the paragraph number).

---

**TIP FROM**

*Laura Acklen*

The Define Table of Contents dialog box is actually a floating palette that can be docked at the top or the bottom of the screen, making it easier to see and work with the text you're marking. Drag the title bar of the dialog box toward the top or bottom of the screen until you see a thick line that stretches from the left to the right side of your screen. Release the mouse button to dock it. To undock it, click at the top of the dialog box and drag it towards the center of the screen.

---

WordPerfect inserts a mark text code [Mrk Txt T.O.C.] on each side of the selection. To expand the code so you can see the level for the entry, click the code in Reveal Codes. When you're finished marking text, you're ready to define where the table should be placed and how the entries should appear.

## USING HEADING STYLES TO MARK TEXT

WordPerfect's heading styles (Heading 1, Heading 2, Heading 3, and so on) include codes that mark the text for a table of contents. There are five heading styles, just as there are five levels in a table of contents. If you use these heading styles for your headings, you don't have to mark the text for the table of contents. All you have to do is define the table and generate it.

In many cases, the outline styles are used to create headings. You can create custom outline styles with table of contents codes so that headings created with the styles are automatically marked for a table of contents.

Relax—it isn't as hard as it sounds. When you create the new style, it contains all the codes of the existing style so you don't have to worry about getting the right codes in place.

To create a customized outline style:

1. Choose Insert, Outline/Bullets & Numbering.
2. Select the outline style that you used in the document, and then choose Edit.
3. Choose Yes to delete this style from the list or No to leave it alone.
4. Select the level that you want to edit in the list, and then click Create Style.
5. Type a name for this new style you are creating in the Style Name text box.
6. If necessary, place a check mark in the Show 'Off Codes' check box.
7. Click right before the Codes to the Left Are ON—Codes to the Right Are OFF code. Hold down the Shift key, and then press the right arrow to move past the Off code.
8. From the Styles Editor menu choose Tools, Reference, Table of Contents to display the Table of Contents tab of the Reference Tools dialog.
9. Click a Mark button to mark the heading text for a particular level in the table.
10. Click OK. One [Mrk Txt T.O.C.] code is inserted in the On side and another on the Off side.
11. If necessary, repeat steps 3–9 for other outline levels.

→ For more information on editing styles, **see** "Editing Styles," **p. 277.**

## DEFINING TABLES

You can define a table of contents whenever you like—before or after you've marked the entries. Defining the table is a two-part process. First, you create a page for the table, which in most cases is at the top of the document. Second, you define how you want the table of contents to look. You choose the number of levels and the position and format of the page number that goes along with each entry. You can also make global changes to the way table of contents entries are formatted by editing the five table of contents styles (one for each level).

Follow these steps to define a table of contents:

1. If necessary, create a new page and type a title for the table of contents.

2. Click on the line where you want the first entry to appear (usually 2–3 lines down from the title).

3. If the Table of Contents tab of the Reference Tools dialog box is displayed, click Define. Otherwise, choose Tools, Reference, Table of Contents to display the dialog box, and then click Define. The Define Table of Contents dialog box appears (see Figure 19.3).

Set the number of levels

**Figure 19.3**
In the Define Table of Contents dialog box, you can choose the number of levels for the table, and then select how you want the page numbers to appear.

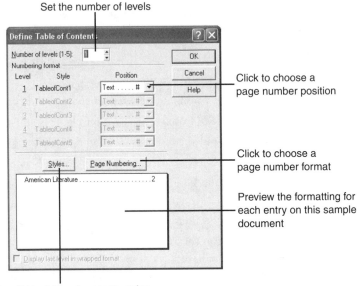

Click to choose a page number position

Click to choose a page number format

Preview the formatting for each entry on this sample document

Click to edit the table of contents styles

4. Type the number, or click the spinner arrows to set the Number of Levels (1–5).

5. Click the drop-down arrow for each available level and choose a page number position. (Depending on what you choose in step 4, some of the levels might not be available.)

6. Click Page Numbering to open the Page Number Format dialog box (see Figure 19.4). Select the document's page number format, or create a custom page number format, and then click OK.

→ For a complete discussion of creating customized page number formats, **see** "Switching to a Different Page Numbering Scheme," **p. 234.**

7. To edit the table of contents styles, click Styles. Select one of the TableofCont styles, and then click Edit. Click OK to return to the Define Table of Contents dialog box when you are finished making your changes.

→ For more information on editing styles, **see** "Editing Styles," **p. 277.**

8. Click OK. WordPerfect inserts the text <<Table of Contents will generate here>>.

**Figure 19.4**
In the Page Number Format dialog box, you can create a custom page number with page, chapter, and volume numbers.

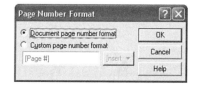

Now, you've defined the table of contents so that when you generate the table, the table of contents entries have a place to go. You're almost done. Now you need to do two more things:

- So that the first page of text following the table of contents starts on a new page, it might be necessary to insert a hard page at the end of the table of contents.

- Reset page numbering to 1 if you don't want the table of contents pages included in the page count. Also, if you've formatted the table of contents page numbers in Roman numerals, you might want to switch to Arabic numerals for the body text.

## GENERATING TABLES

When you generate a document, WordPerfect compiles all the document references and creates tables, lists, and indexes. Generating a document takes a lot of processing power, so before you begin, save the document. Better safe than sorry, I always say.

When you generate a document, all the document references (that is, the table of contents, the table of authorities, the index, lists, and cross-references) are generated at once. When you regenerate a document, the old tables, lists, and indexes are deleted from the document and rebuilt. This way, any entries that you've deleted are removed.

To generate a document, click the Generate button in the Reference Tools dialog box, or choose Tools, Reference, Generate. Or, you can press Ctrl+F9. The Generate dialog box appears (see Figure 19.5).

**Figure 19.5**
When you generate a document, all the document references are updated at once.

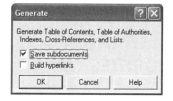

**NOTE**

If the Save Subdocuments check box is enabled, the Generate feature updates the document references in subdocuments. This can be extremely time-consuming because WordPerfect must open each subdocument, generate the references, and then save the subdocument. If you have links to subdocuments in this document, and you don't want to generate them, deselect Save Subdocuments in the Generate dialog box.

Click OK to generate the table of contents. Figure 19.6 shows a sample table of contents.

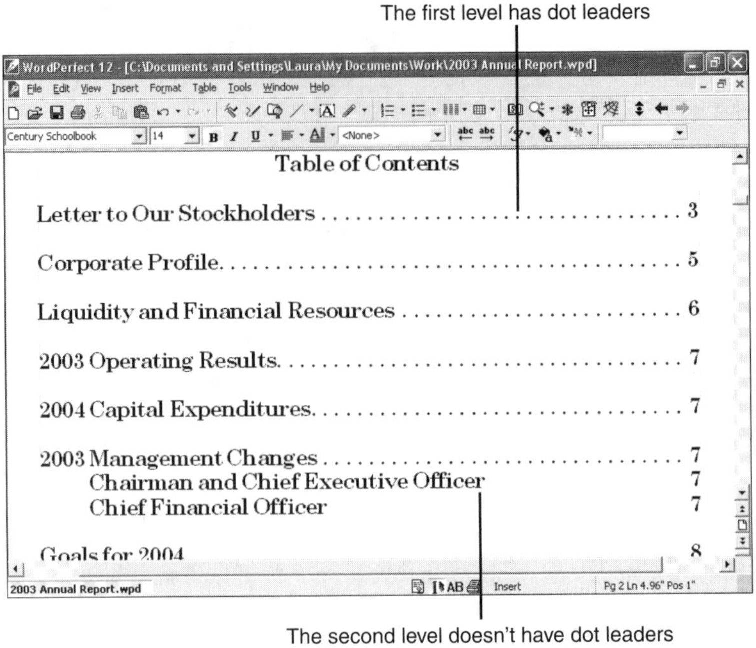

The first level has dot leaders

**Figure 19.6**
This table of contents has two levels, with no dot leaders for the second level.

The second level doesn't have dot leaders

**TIP FROM**

*Laura Acklen*

You can edit table of contents entries after you've marked them. Simply revise the text between the two [Mrk Txt T.O.C.] codes and then regenerate the table. Just make sure you don't accidentally delete one of the [Mrk Txt T.O.C.] codes.

*If some of your table of contents headings didn't make it into the table of contents, see "The Table of Contents Is Missing Entries" in the Troubleshooting section at the end of this chapter.*

*If some of the entries in the table of contents are bold or italic and others are not, see "Several Table of Contents Entries Are Bold" in the Troubleshooting section at the end of this chapter.*

# CREATING A TABLE OF AUTHORITIES OR A BIBLIOGRAPHY

A table of authorities is like a table of contents for a legal document. It lists the authorities, which are the legal references to other cases, statutes, rules, citations, regulations, amendments, and so on, that appear in the brief. You can also use the Table of Authorities feature to create a bibliography for any document that requires the identification of sources so this feature can be used in many other areas, not just the legal field.

A table of authorities (or bibliography) can be divided into sections to separate the different sources. For example, a typical table of authorities might be divided into sections for cases, statutes, and regulations. A bibliography might have sections for newspaper articles, journal articles, and books.

Before you start marking text in a document, sketch out a rough draft of the table of authorities (or bibliography) so you have an idea of how many sections you need and what they will be called. You'll need to specify a section when you mark an entry. (This is similar to marking a table of contents entry for a particular level.)

## Marking the First Authority

The first time you mark an entry for inclusion in a table of authorities, you define the actual text to be included in the table, so it's called marking the "full form." As usual, when you're ready to mark the entries, you should turn on Reveal Codes (press Alt+F3) so you can see exactly what you are selecting.

Follow these steps to mark an entry as a full form:

1. With Reveal Codes on, select the text that you want to appear in the table of authorities. Take note of nearby formatting codes—you may or may not want to include them in the selection.

**NOTE**

You can mark text for a table of authorities in the body text, as well as in footnotes, endnotes, and graphics box captions.

2. Choose Tools, Reference, Table of Authorities to display the Table of Authorities tab of the Reference Tools dialog box (see Figure 19.7).

3. Type the name of the section in the Type text box, or click the Type drop-down list arrow and choose an existing name from the list.

4. Click in the Short Form text box and edit the portion of the selected text or just type a one- or two-word abbreviation. The short form is the unique identifier that ties together the first authority and the following occurrences.

**NOTE**

The short form name must be unique, but it should also be descriptive enough so that you can easily associate the short form name with the full form.

5. Click Create. The Table of Authorities Full Form editing window appears, with the text that you selected at the top of the window (see Figure 19.8).

19

Type a section name

**Figure 19.7**
The Table of Authorities feature bar has buttons that really speed up the tedious process of marking entries.

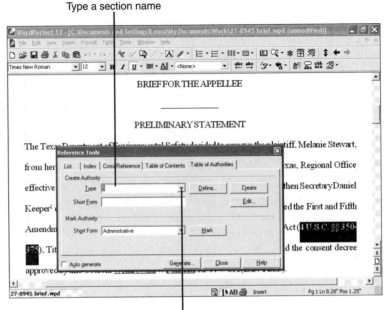

Click here to select a section name from the list

Click to change to a different section

**Figure 19.8**
You can freely edit an entry so that it appears exactly as you want it to in the table.

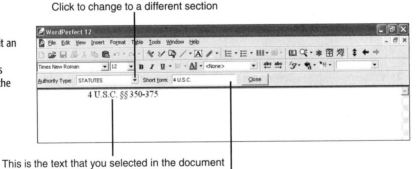

This is the text that you selected in the document
Click to type a different short form

**NOTE**

One of the advantages that the Table of Authorities feature has over the Table of Contents feature is the ability to edit the table entry separately from the text entry. In fact, the table entry can look completely different from the text entry because you can freely add font attributes, indentation, and blank lines—whatever you think is necessary to make the entry in the table of authorities easier to read.

6. Edit the text so that it looks exactly the way you want it to appear in the finished table. You can add or remove font attributes, indent text, add hard returns, and so on.

→ If you need a quick peek at the steps for indenting text, **see** "Indenting Text," **p. 209.**

→ If you want to use font attributes, **see** "Emphasizing Important Text," **p. 75.**

7. When you are finished, click Close. WordPerfect inserts a [ToA] code in the document.

**TIP FROM**

*Laura Achlen*

> If you move the insertion point to the left of the code, the code expands to show you the full details: [ToA: section name; short form text; Full Form]. The Full Form part of the code identifies it as a full form code (as opposed to a short form code, which is explained in the next section).

If you later edit a table of authorities entry, the text in the full form won't be modified. You must edit the full form to update the entry for the table. To edit a full form, choose Tools, Reference, Table of Authorities, select the related short form in the "Mark Authorities" section, and then choose Edit. You can also turn on Reveal Codes and double-click Table of Authorities code (either the full form or short form).

When the Edit Full Form dialog box appears (see Figure 19.9), select the full form in the list, and then click OK. This is a little confusing, so stick with me here—the full form is identified by its short form name in the Edit Full Form dialog box.

Select the full form from this list

**Figure 19.9**
If you revise the text of a table of authorities entry in the document, you need to make those same revisions to the full form.

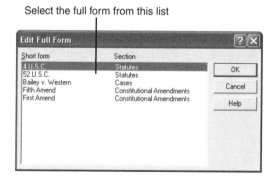

When you're in the table of authorities full form editing window (refer to Figure 19.8), you can revise the text, choose another section, or assign a different short form name.

## MARKING SUBSEQUENT AUTHORITIES

After you've finished marking the full form, you can go through the document and mark subsequent occurrences with the short form. This step is the quickest because you don't have to select the text—you simply click in the text and choose the short form from a list.

Follow these steps to mark an authority by using the short form:

1. Click in the authority/text.

2. Click the Short form drop-down list arrow and then select the short form in the list. If the short form is already displayed, you can skip this step.

3. Click Mark. WordPerfect inserts an abbreviated code in the document: [ToA:,short form text;].

**TIP FROM**

The last short form name you used is displayed in the Short form list box, so it's easy to continue marking subsequent occurrences of an authority. Simply click in the authority, and then click Mark. You might also consider using the Find feature in tandem with the Table of Authorities feature bar to quickly search for and mark all subsequent occurrences of each authority. You can have both dialog boxes open at the same time and it's a great way to navigate through a lengthy brief.

→ To get more information on searching for text, **see** "Searching for Text by Using Find and Replace," **p. 148.**

*If the list of short forms is getting cluttered with short forms that you don't use anymore, see "Obsolete Short Forms" in the Troubleshooting section at the end of this chapter.*

## DEFINING AND GENERATING TABLES

Just as you did for a table of contents, you have to create a page for the table of authorities (or bibliography) entries. You probably want the entries on a page by themselves, with headings for each section. You can create this page before or after you mark the authorities. When you have defined each section, you're ready to generate the table.

Follow these steps to define a table of authorities:

1. If necessary, press Ctrl+Enter to create a new page for the table.

2. If you want to set a page number format for the table of authorities pages, choose Format, Page, Numbering.

   → If you really want to get fancy with the page numbers, **see** "Adding Page Numbers," **p. 231.**

3. Click where you want a section of the table to appear.

4. Type a heading for the section, and then press Enter a few times to insert some space between the heading and the entries.

5. Click the Define button on the Table of Authorities feature bar. (If the feature bar isn't displayed right now, choose Tools, Reference, Table of Authorities.) The Define Table of Authorities dialog box appears (see Figure 19.10). The section names that have been used in this document, along with the three default sections, are listed next to the default numbering scheme, which is dot leaders trailing out to the page number at the right margin.

The default numbering style is shown

Click to edit the selected section

**Figure 19.10**
In the Define Table of
Authorities dialog box,
choose the section of
authorities that you
want to insert.

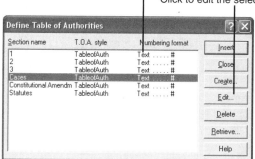

6. Click the section name, and then click Insert. WordPerfect inserts the following text at the insertion point: <<Table of Authorities will generate here>>.

7. Repeat steps 3–6 to define the location of each remaining section.

If the next page is the beginning of the body text, make sure you reset the page numbers back to 1 at the top of that page so that the table of authorities pages don't throw off the document page numbers.

**TIP FROM**

Consistency across documents is important. When you have figured out how you want to do something, such as defining a table of authorities, you can save time by retrieving that information from another document. To retrieve a table of authorities definition from another file, click the Retrieve button in the Define Table of Authorities dialog box to open the Retrieve ToA Definitions dialog box. Type the name of the file in the Filename text box, or click the Files icon to browse for it. When you've selected the file, the definitions for that document are displayed in the Name list box. Choose the definition, and then click OK to add them into the Define Table of Authorities dialog box.

19

By now you're hooked on the capability to customize virtually every aspect of the WordPerfect program, and you wouldn't even consider using another product that offered less flexibility. So, when you define a table of authorities, you expect to have the capability to customize the format of each of its sections. And you do—you can even edit the table of authorities style and then change the defaults for all future tables.

To customize the format of a particular section, select the section in the Define Table of Authorities dialog box (refer to Figure 19.10). Click Edit to open the Edit Table of Authorities dialog box (see Figure 19.11).

**Figure 19.11**
You can edit each section's entries and the table of authorities style in the Edit Table of Authorities dialog box.

Click to choose a page number position

Click to choose a page number format

Deselect this option to strip out underline codes

Select this option to show dashes between consecutive page numbers

Click to edit the table of authorities style

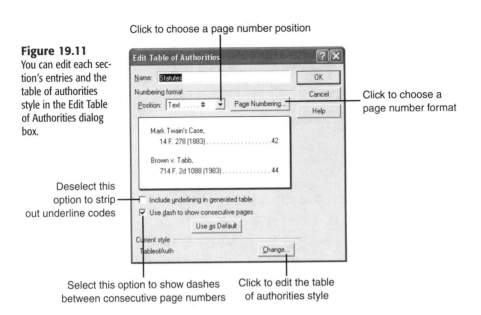

After you've marked all the entries, defined the location for each section's entries, and made the necessary adjustments in the Edit Table of Authorities dialog box, you're ready to generate the table. If the Table of Authorities tab of the Reference Tools dialog box is displayed, click the Generate button. Otherwise, choose Tools, Reference, Generate (or press Ctrl+F9). Choose to save changes to subdocuments or to build hyperlinks, and then click OK to build the table.

**CAUTION**

If you've accidentally typed a short form name incorrectly, or if you have short forms that don't have corresponding full forms, you'll get an error message when you generate the table. The problem entry will be preceded by an asterisk in the first section of the table so you can see which entries need repair. If the incorrect short form name has been used, simply delete the short form code and reinsert it. If the full form is missing, find the first occurrence of the authority, delete the full form, and then create a new full form.

WordPerfect searches through the document for each entry and inserts the page number(s) where the entry is found (see Figure 19.12).

**Figure 19.12**
This is an example of a table of authorities in a legal brief.

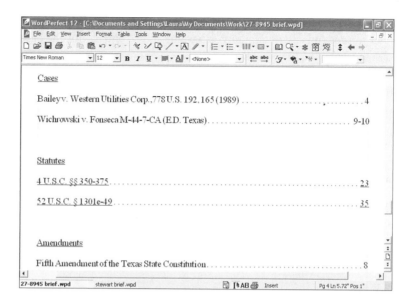

**NOTE**

The Law Office editions of WordPerfect 8 and 9 included a copy of CiteLink, a table of authorities generator. CiteLink can cut the time it takes to generate a table of authorities from hours to minutes. CiteLink is not included in WordPerfect Office 11 or 12, but it's available for a free download so all you need to do is get the latest release. Now called WestCiteLink, version 3.04 is available at http://west.thomson.com/store/product.asp?product_id=WestCiteLink. Version 3.04 is compatible with WordPerfect 11 build 11.0.0.305 (updated with Service Pack 1 and Hot Patch 2). A future version will include compatibility with WordPerfect 12.

# CREATING INDEXES

Take a look at the index at the back of this book and ask yourself, "Would I want to create one of these by hand?" Probably not, unless you're a wonderfully patient individual who can tolerate a very tedious task. I'm not, so I use WordPerfect's Index feature to help me create indexes for my lengthy documents.

Some say a good index can make or break a reference book. I hope the index for this book has already saved you some time (and frustration). The key to a good index is anticipating the needs of the reader. You need to try to think of all the ways readers might try to look something up and then point them in the right direction.

There are two methods to create an index; the one you use depends on how much time you have, and how much control you want over the process. If you mark the entries by hand, you have maximum control, but you might need to spend a lot of time doing it. Or, you can create a concordance file with a list of index information and let WordPerfect compile the index for you; this is fastest, but you have minimal control. For the best of both worlds, you can use a combination of both methods.

## CREATING CONCORDANCE FILES

A *concordance file* is a list of words or phrases that you want included in the index. When you generate the index, WordPerfect compares the entries in the concordance file with the text and, if a match is found, inserts the index entry with a page number. The advantage of creating a concordance file is that it's much faster than selecting and marking every index entry manually. The disadvantage is that you lose some flexibility.

 To create a concordance file, start with a blank document, and then type the index entries. Type only one entry per line, and make sure you press Enter at the end of the last line. Click the Save button, and then give the concordance file a name. You'll be prompted for the name and location later, when you generate the index.

**CAUTION**

> Concordance file entries are not case-sensitive, so if you type `Recycling`, the words recycling and RECYCLING are considered matches. However, when the index is created, WordPerfect uses the capitalization in the concordance file, not the capitalization in the document. This is important because when you create the concordance file, you need to make sure that you use the capitalization that you want to see in the index.

**TIP FROM**

> You have a pretty good memory if you can remember all the entries you want in the index! Even with gingko, my memory isn't that good, so I add entries to the concordance file while I'm working on a document. I keep both documents open and switch back and forth between the two.

**TIP FROM**

> It is usually easiest to work with the concordance file if it's in alphabetical order. In just a few seconds, you can sort the entries alphabetically. At the top of the file, choose Tools, Sort. Select First Word in the Line, and then choose Sort. As you add entries, you can repeat this process to keep the list in alphabetical order.

In WordPerfect 11 and 12, there is a brand new macro that helps you create a concordance file. In the Define Index dialog box, you'll see a Create button. When you click this button, the Concord macro plays. You'll see a Concordance File dialog box where you can choose what you want included or excluded in the concordance file. After you make your selections, the macro will create an alphabetized list of *every* unique word in the document. Think about that for a minute—every single word that you used in the document will appear in the list. Unless you want every word you used in the document included in the finished index, you'll need to edit the concordance list. When the macro is finished, you'll be able to open the concordance list and remove the words that you don't want to appear in the index. Save the concordance list so you can specify the filename (or browse for it) in the Define Index dialog box.

 *If the Concord macro seems to go into an endless loop, or if only a few of your entries are showing in the index, see "Cannot Create a Concordance File with the Concord Macro" in the Troubleshooting section at the end of this chapter.*

WordPerfect automatically marks each entry in the concordance file as a heading—you don't have to do a thing. However, if you want an entry to be listed as a subheading in the index, you have to mark that entry manually. See the next section for the steps to mark an index entry.

## MARKING INDEX ENTRIES BY HAND

Tedious? Yes. Precise? Absolutely. Marking every index entry in a document is a definite investment of your time and energy. The investment pays off when the reader can easily locate the information that you've painstakingly compiled together.

Marking index entries is simple—you select the text, and then click one of the buttons in the Reference Tools dialog box to mark the text for the index. Indexes have two levels, so you can mark an entry as a heading or as a subheading (underneath a heading).

Every instance of an index entry has to be marked. Otherwise, the list of page numbers next to the entry won't be complete. After you mark the first occurrence, use the Find feature to locate the other occurrences in the document, and then move on to the next index entry.

To mark text for an index, follow these steps:

1. Choose Tools, Reference, Index. The Index tab of the Reference Tools dialog box appears over the text (see Figure 19.13).

2. Select the text for the entry. (You can be a little sloppy selecting text here because if you accidentally grab an underline or bold code, WordPerfect won't apply the attribute codes to index text.)

3. Click in the Heading text box to mark this entry as a heading; click in the Subheading text box to mark this entry as a subheading. WordPerfect inserts the selected text in the text box.

4. If you are marking this entry as a subheading, type the heading that you want it to fall under in the Heading text box (or select an existing heading from the drop-down list).

**TIP FROM**

*Laura Acklen*

> The heading and subheading text don't have to match the text that you selected in the document. You can type exactly what you want to appear in the index heading (and subheading). This is helpful when the text in the document doesn't fit well in the index.

5. Click the Mark button to insert the index code.

**Figure 19.13**
The Index tab has buttons to speed up the process of marking the entries and creating the index.

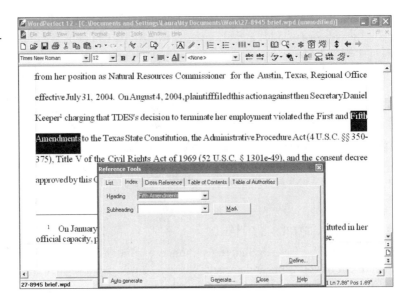

The next time you have to mark this entry, you can either select the text and then click in the Heading text box (to insert the selection), or you can select an entry off the Heading and Subheading drop-down lists.

**CAUTION**

When you revise a document, you're likely to make some changes to index entries. Because these changes aren't automatically reflected in the index codes, you need to delete the old code, and then insert a new one for the revised entry. In Reveal Codes, click and drag the index code out of the Reveal Codes window to delete it. Select the entry, and then mark it as a heading or subheading. The next time you generate the index, the entries will be updated.

## DEFINING AND GENERATING INDEXES

Defining an index is similar to defining a table of contents or a table of authorities, except an index is assembled at the end of a document. To set up and create an index page, follow these steps:

1. Move to the end of the document and press Ctrl+Enter to create a new page.

2. At the top of the new page, type a heading for the index.

3. If necessary, choose Tools, Reference, Index to display the Index tab of the Reference Tools dialog box.

4. Click the Define button on the Index tab of the Reference Tools dialog box to display the Define Index dialog box (see Figure 19.14).

Click to select a page number position

**Figure 19.14**
You can use the Define Index dialog box to select a page number format and position. You can also edit the heading and subheading styles and specify a concordance file.

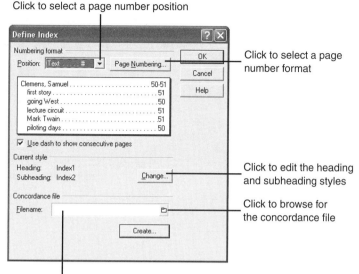

Click to select a page number format

Click to edit the heading and subheading styles

Click to browse for the concordance file

Type the name of the concordance file

5. If you want to use the default settings, you can skip to step 6. Otherwise, make the necessary changes to the following:

- Click the Position drop-down list arrow and choose a position for the page numbers in the list.
- Click Page Numbering to use a custom page number format.
- Click Change if you want to edit the two index styles.
- Type a filename in the Filename text box or click the File icon to browse for the concordance file.

6. Click OK. The following text is inserted at the insertion point: `<<Index will generate here>>`. An Index definition code is also inserted.

7. Click Generate. Choose to save changes to subdocuments or to build hyperlinks, and then click OK to build the index. Figure 19.15 shows a sample index.

**TIP FROM**

Flip back to the index in this book. Notice that the index is formatted into three columns. Have you *ever* seen an index not formatted in columns? To format your index in columns, see "Defining Newspaper Columns," in Chapter 8, "Formatting the Page."

*When you generated the index, if you received an error message that said one of the concordance file entries was too long, see "A Concordance Entry Is Too Long" in the Troubleshooting section at the end of this chapter.*

19

**Figure 19.15**
This is a sample of an index that might appear in the back of a WordPerfect reference book.

It's stylish to start each index section with a capital letter

You can easily insert a short graphics line under the capital letter

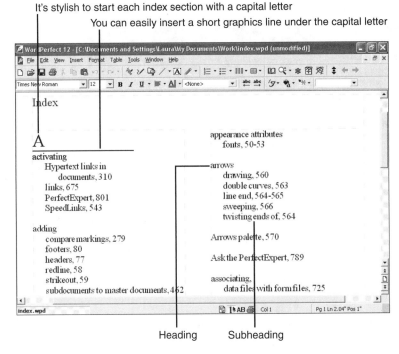

Heading    Subheading

An index has a lot more entries than a table of contents or table of authorities. The number of errors generally rises in proportion to the number of entries, so indexes tend to be more problematic than tables. After you generate the index, you might have some things to fix:

- Misspelled entries—Make a note of the page number for the misspelled entry, move to that page, and then turn on Reveal Codes (by pressing Alt+F3). When you locate the Index code for that entry, click on it or move to the left of it so the code expands and shows you the heading (and subheading) text. If the text is misspelled in the document, go ahead and correct it, but what you really need to focus on is the text in the heading or subheading because that's what shows up in the index. When you find the index code with the misspelled heading or subheading text, click and drag it out of the Reveal Codes window, and then re-create it.

- Entries with similar spellings—If you have multiple entries with similar spellings, you need to consolidate them into one entry. For example, if you have an entry for Recycling Initiative and another for Recycling Initiatives, you need to decide which entry you want to keep, and then delete and re-create the index codes for the other entry. Rather than use the Find feature to look for every index code, make a note of the page numbers so you can zero in on a page at a time.

- Remove outdated entries—Turn on Reveal Codes (by pressing Alt+F3), locate the index code, and then click and drag it out of the Reveal Codes window.

- Solitary headings—If you see a heading that needs a subheading, you can go back and add another index code for a subheading, or you can delete and re-create the original code with heading and subheading text.

- Scattered subheadings—If you see subheadings that would make more sense if they were combined into one subheading, you need to re-create the index codes for those subheadings. Make a note of the page numbers, move to the first page, and turn on Reveal Codes (by pressing Alt+F3). Delete the code, and then re-create it with the new subheading. Repeat for the other index entries with inadequate subheadings.

- Too many subheadings—A good rule of thumb is to have no more than a dozen subheadings under a heading. Of course, there are exceptions—check out the monster index at the end of this book! You can create a new heading and divide the subheadings between the original heading and the new heading. Of course, this means you have to delete and re-create codes. Decide which subheadings you want grouped under a new heading, and then delete the index codes for that subheading. When you re-create the index codes for those entries, use the new heading.

- Unexplained entries—If you have entries in the index that don't appear in your concordance file, there must be some index codes in the document. You can strip them out with the Find and Replace feature. Choose Edit, Find and Replace. In the Find and Replace dialog box, click in the Find text box, and then choose Match, Codes. Type i to jump to the Index code, and then choose Insert & Close. Leave the Replace With text box blank or with <Nothing> in it. Choose Replace All.

- Misplaced entries—When you generate an index, subheadings are automatically alphabetized under the heading. If you have subheadings that are out of order, there might be an extra space in front of the heading or subheading text. This can happen when you select text in the document, and then insert it into the Heading or Subheading text box. You know the drill by now—make a note of the page numbers, turn on Reveal Codes (by pressing Alt+F3), delete the code, and then re-create it.

**19**

# ASSEMBLING LISTS

A list is just what it sounds like—it's a list of items in a document. You might want to generate a list of all the figures or illustrations, with the numbers of the pages where they can be found in the document. If you have graphics boxes, you can have WordPerfect automatically place the caption text from each type of graphics box into a separate list. You can create multiple lists to handle all the different elements in your document (such as figures, tables, charts, and equations).

## MARKING ENTRIES

Assembling a list is just like creating a table or an index—you mark the entries, define the list, and then generate the list. To create a list, you have to mark the text that you want included in it. To mark a table, for example, select the table title or heading for the list (for example, Table 1.3, Continuing Education Classes), *not* the actual table definition code.

**CAUTION**

> If you mark a graphics box that doesn't include a caption, an entry is inserted in the list with a page number, but the entry is blank. In other words, you have a dot leader and a page number, but no text. Either create a caption for the figure or mark a title or heading instead.

Follow these steps to mark an entry for a list:

1. Choose Tools, Reference, List to display the List tab of the Reference Tools dialog box (see Figure 19.16).

Type the name of the list

**Figure 19.16**
Use the buttons on the List tab to speed up the process of marking entries, defining lists, and generating lists.

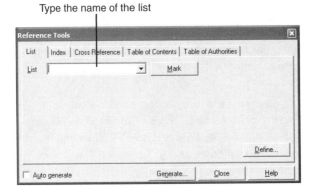

2. Turn on Reveal Codes (by pressing Alt+F3) and select the text that you want to appear in the list.

**19**

**CAUTION**

> You can't be sloppy when you're selecting text for a list—any formatting codes that fall between the marked text codes will affect that entry in the list (and possibly all the following entries).

3. If the name of the list is already displayed in the List text box, you can skip to step 4. If this is the first entry you've marked for a list, type the name of the list in the List text box. Otherwise, click the List drop-down list arrow and select the name of the list.

4. Click the Mark button. WordPerfect inserts [Mrk Txt List] codes on each side of the selection.

**NOTE**

> You can see which list an entry is assigned to if you expand the [Mrk Txt List] code. In Reveal Codes, move the red cursor before a code to expand it.

To revise a list entry, edit the text between the two [Mrk Txt List] codes. You can remove an entry completely by clicking and dragging one of the [Mrk Txt List] codes out of the Reveal Codes window (the mate is deleted automatically).

## DEFINING AND GENERATING LISTS

Long and multi-part documents tend to have more elements than the average document, and keeping track of them can be very time-consuming, both for the creator and for the reader. Creating a separate list for figures, tables, equations, and other elements can help you keep things organized.

**TIP FROM**

Generating a list of figure captions is a great way to check for consistency in figure numbering and to make sure the caption text is adequately descriptive.

You can define multiple lists in a document, each on its own page, or embedded in the body text. You can define lists before or after you mark up the document. Follow these steps to define a list:

1. Click in the document where you want a list to appear.

2. If you want the list on a page by itself, press Ctrl+Enter to insert a hard page.

3. Type a title for the list, and then press Enter a few times to create space between the title and the list entries.

4. If the List tab of the Reference Tools dialog box is displayed, click the Define button. Otherwise, choose Tools, Reference, List to display the feature bar, and then click Define. The Define List dialog box appears (see Figure 19.17). The names of lists that you've already used when marking entries appear.

**19**

Click to insert the list definition

**Figure 19.17**
In the Define List dialog box, you can choose the list that you want to insert.

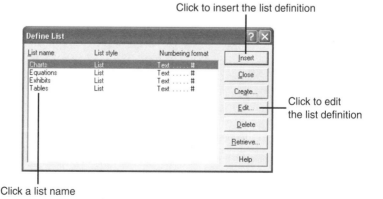

Click to edit
the list definition

Click a list name

5. Select a list name in the list box. By default, the entry has dot leaders out to the page number, which is positioned at the right margin. The page number format being used in the document is used on the list page numbers.

**NOTE**

If you're defining lists before marking entries in the text, you might not see any list names in the List Name list box. To create a new list, click Create, type a name for the list, and then click OK. Go ahead and create the list with the default settings; you can modify them from the Define List dialog box.

**TIP FROM**

*Laura Acklen*

Consistency across documents is important. When you've figured out how you want to do something, such as defining a list, for example, you can save time by retrieving that definition from another document. To retrieve list names from another file, click the Retrieve button in the Define List dialog box to open the Retrieve List Definitions dialog box. Type the name of the file in the Filename text box, or click the Files icon to browse for it. When you've selected the file, the list definitions for that document are displayed in the Name list box. Choose one or more list names, and then click OK to add them into the Define List dialog box.

6. To accept the default settings and insert a list definition code in the document, click Insert. WordPerfect inserts the following text in the document: `<<List will generate here>>`.

7. Repeat steps 1–6 to insert definition codes for all the list names. Click Close when you're done.

If the next page is the beginning of the body text, make sure you reset the page numbers back to 1 at the top of that page so that the List pages don't throw off the page numbers of the document.

If you want to modify the defaults, select a list name in the Define List dialog box, and then click Edit to display the Edit List dialog box (see Figure 19.18), where you have the following options:

- Click the Position drop-down list arrow and choose a position for the page numbers in the list.
- Click Page Numbering to use a custom page number format.
- Click Change if you want to edit the list style.
- If you want WordPerfect to insert the caption text in the list, click the List Box Captions Automatically drop-down list arrow and choose the type of box this list is intended for. For example, if this is a Figures list, choose Figure Box.

Click to choose a different
page number position

**Figure 19.18**
You can use the
options in the Edit List
dialog box to edit the
default page number
position and page
number format. You
can also select to
have WordPerfect
automatically insert
caption text in the list.

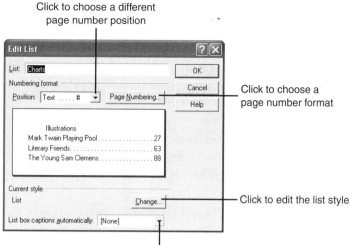

Click to choose a
page number format

Click to edit the list style

Click to choose the box type for the captions to be inserted in the list

When you're ready to generate the lists, click the Generate button. Choose to save changes
to subdocuments, or to build hyperlinks, and then click OK to assemble the lists. Figure
19.19 shows a sample list.

 If the captions are missing from a list of figures, see "Blank Entries in a Figure List" in the
Troubleshooting section at the end of this chapter.

List title

**Figure 19.19**
Lists make it easier for
the creator and the
reader to keep track
of where supportive
elements are located.

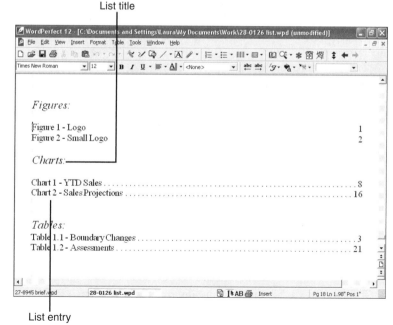

List entry

# TROUBLESHOOTING

## DOCUMENT MAP ERROR MESSAGE

*I turned on Document Map for one document and now, whenever I try to open another document, I get an error message that says the document does not contain the necessary code to create a document map. How do I get rid of this error message?*

The easy answer is to turn off the Document Map view. Document Map is "sticky," which means it stays on for all new documents. If the document that you are opening doesn't contain any index, table of contents, or table of authorities entries, WordPerfect won't be able to display a document map for that document. Hence, the error message. Choose View, Document Map, or press Alt+Shift+M to turn Document Map off.

If you still get the message, make sure your default printer is *not* set to a fax driver. This is known to cause this particular error. To change your default printer, choose Start, (Settings), Printers. Right-click the printer that you use the most and select Set as Default.

## THE TABLE OF CONTENTS IS MISSING ENTRIES

*I've just generated a table of contents, but not all the headings are showing up: I marked three levels of headings for the table, but only two appear.*

You have probably defined the table for only two levels, but have marked entries for three levels. Move to the top of the table of contents page. Turn on Reveal Codes (by pressing Alt+F3) and find the [Def Mark] code at the top of the page. Double-click the code to edit it. In the Define Table of Contents dialog box, click the up spinner arrow to increase the number of levels to three, and then click OK. Because you've edited the original code, there is no duplicate code to delete. Regenerate the table—the third-level headings should show up now.

## SEVERAL TABLE OF CONTENTS ENTRIES ARE BOLD

*After making some revisions and marking new entries for the table of contents, I regenerated the table. All the new entries are bold, but the rest of the table is not.*

When you select text to mark for a table of contents, you have to make sure that you don't include any formatting codes in the selection. If you do, those formatting codes are copied into the table of contents along with the selected text. You can turn on Reveal Codes (by pressing Alt+F3) and delete the [Bold] codes, but the next time you generate the table, they'll be back. A permanent solution is to go back to each new entry and delete the first [Mrk Txt ToC] code (which automatically deletes its mate). Then, position the insertion point on the first character and select only the text of the heading (plus any styles that are in place), but not the [Bold] codes. If necessary, choose Tools, Reference, Table of Contents to display the Table of Contents feature bar. Click a Mark button to reinsert the [Mrk Txt ToC] codes. Repeat for the other headings, and then regenerate the table.

## OBSOLETE SHORT FORMS

*While making heavy revisions, I removed some of the authorities that had been marked with a full form. Even though the full forms are gone, the short forms still show up in the list. Is there any way to strip out these obsolete short forms?*

Short form information is stored in the document prefix. If you haven't had any contact with the document prefix until now, it's invisible, you can't edit it, and it is the root of all document evil. Rebuilding the document prefix fixes all manner of problems. First, make sure the file isn't already open. Then open a blank document, type an **x**, and then press Enter. Click Insert, File. Select the file, and then click Insert. Delete the x and the blank line, and then resave the file. Save this document under the original filename so you don't have duplicate files lying around. When the document prefix is rebuilt, only the short forms that are used in the document appear in the list.

## A CONCORDANCE ENTRY IS TOO LONG

*I've just generated an index, and I get an error message that says "Unable to generate: concordance entry is too large," followed by the offending entry. What is the length limit on concordance file entries?*

A concordance file entry must not be longer than 63 characters. I tested this a bit and got flaky results between 55 and 60 characters, so your best bet is to keep the entries down to 50 characters or so.

## CANNOT CREATE A CONCORDANCE FILE WITH THE CONCORD MACRO

*I've tried to create a concordance file with the Create button in the Define Index dialog box, but it either goes into an endless loop, or only a few of my entries appear in the finished index. How can I fix this macro?*

If you have WordPerfect Office 11 and you have installed Service Pack 1, a glitch in the service pack has resulted in the need to recompile the shipping macros and any other macros that you have created. This includes the Concord macro, which is included with WordPerfect 11 and 12. The Concord macro is found in the \program files\wordperfect office 11\macros\wpwin folder. Choose Tools, Macro, Edit and browse to that folder. Select the concord.wcm file, and then choose Edit. Now, insert a space, delete the space, and then click the Save and Compile button. That's it!

## BLANK ENTRIES IN A FIGURE LIST

*I've just generated a list of figure captions, and some of the entries only have page numbers—there isn't any caption text, just dot leaders and page numbers. What did I do wrong?*

There is a setting in the Edit List dialog box where you can choose to have WordPerfect automatically copy the caption text into the list. If you haven't selected a box type, the captions won't be copied into the list.

Choose Tools, Reference, List. Click the Define button on the List tab. Select the list name for the figures, and then click Edit. Click the List Box Captions Automatically drop-down list arrow and then choose the type of box you have used.

# PROJECT

When you open a Microsoft Word document with a table of contents in WordPerfect, Word's table of contents styles are imported as well. The conversion process does its best to interpret Word's formatting, but the results are not always perfect. Rather than starting all over in WordPerfect, you can edit these styles to change the appearance of the table entries.

Follow these steps to edit the Microsoft Word table of contents styles:

1. Click at the top of the table of contents page.

2. Choose Tools, Reference, Table of Contents to display the Table of Contents tab of the Reference Tools dialog box.

3. Click Define to open the Define Table of Contents dialog box.

4. Click Styles to open the Table of Contents Styles dialog box (see Figure 19.20).

**Figure 19.20**
You can select a style in the Table of Contents Styles dialog box and edit it in the Styles Editor.

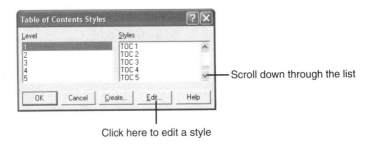

Scroll down through the list

Click here to edit a style

5. Scroll down through the Styles list box until you see the TOC 1 through TOC 9 styles. The numbers correspond to levels, so start with the TOC 1 style.

6. Click the TOC 1 style, and then click Edit. The Styles Editor opens (see Figure 19.21).

7. If you don't have Reveal Codes selected, select it now. Now you can see the codes in the TOC 1 style. To expand a code, click it or move the red cursor to the left of the code. To delete a style, click and drag it out of the Reveal Codes window. To edit a code, double-click it. (Don't ask me where the Small Caps code comes from—in Word, the table of contents didn't have any small caps text in it!)

8. Make the changes by using the menu in the Styles Editor rather than the WordPerfect menu.

9. Click OK when you're done.

10. Select the TOC 2 style, and then click Edit. Make your changes, and then click OK.

11. Continue selecting the TOC styles until you've edited the styles that are in use for this document. In other words, if there are four levels in the table of contents, you should edit TOC 1 through TOC 4.

**Figure 19.21**
You can use the menus in the Styles Editor to insert formatting codes in the style.

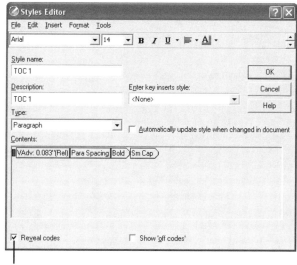

Click here to open a Reveal Codes window

# CHAPTER 20

# INTERACTIVE AND MULTIMEDIA DOCUMENTS

**In this chapter**                                              *by Read Gilgen*

# RETHINKING THE CONCEPT OF DOCUMENTS

Technological advances over the years have gradually increased the power of the written document to communicate more effectively. The typewriter made it easier to read the written word. Early word processors helped writers to organize their documents by offering the capability of cutting and pasting, and to proofread documents. Not too long ago, elements of desktop publishing, including complex layout and graphics, crept into the word processing arena.

Today we're on the verge of another leap forward, as technology enables us to get at information differently. No longer must we read a document on a printed page. Instead we can read it on a computer screen. No longer must we follow a document from beginning to end, but we can jump from one place to another, or even from one document to another. Further, because we're not tied to paper and print, we can add multimedia elements, including sound or video.

# CREATING HYPERTEXT LINKS

You're already used to using web page links, and you know that some web pages use links successfully in helping you navigate a document while others use links that seem to make little sense. The same concepts that pertain to creating links in web pages also apply to WordPerfect documents. In a nutshell, you want the reader to be able to jump from one place to another in your document, following logical links, and without getting lost.

The first step in creating a nonlinear document is to link sections so that the reader can jump from where they are to a target destination. You do this by creating *bookmarks*, which are like targets where you want to land, and then by creating hyperlinks, which enable you to jump from where you are to a target bookmark.

**NOTE**

> Before setting bookmarks in your document, you might want to visually sketch out how you view the organization of your document, including places readers will most likely want to go (bookmarks), and places from which you expect them to link. This makes it easier to systematically go through the document and add bookmarks and hyperlinks.

## CREATING LINKS WITHIN DOCUMENTS

To create a bookmark in a document, follow these steps:

1. Go to the spot in the document you want to bookmark.
2. Choose Tools, Bookmark. WordPerfect displays the Bookmark dialog box (see Figure 20.1, which shows a bookmark already displayed).
3. Click Create to display the Create Bookmark dialog box (see Figure 20.2).

**Figure 20.1**
You can use the Bookmark dialog box to create and manage your document's bookmarks.

**Figure 20.2**
The Create Bookmark dialog box suggests using adjacent document text, which you can edit or replace with something shorter or more descriptive.

**NOTE**

The Create Bookmark dialog box attempts to guess at the bookmark name, based on the text following the insertion point. Often these names are long, and not always descriptive. You should change them to shorter, recognizable, and descriptive bookmark names.

4. Type the name of the bookmark, and click OK to set the bookmark and to return to the document.

If you select text before setting the bookmark, WordPerfect uses the selected text for the bookmark name. WordPerfect also identifies the bookmark type as Selected (refer to Figure 20.1), which means that both the location and the selected text are part of the bookmark.

Bookmarks can be used any time—for example, to quickly go to a bookmark while editing. You can also set a QuickMark, which does not require a name, by choosing Set QuickMark (refer to Figure 20.1). You can access the QuickMark or other bookmarks by choosing Tools, Bookmark. You then click the bookmark you want to go to and click Go To.

You can also access your bookmarks by choosing Edit, Go To or pressing Ctrl+G. In the Go To dialog box, click Bookmarks and select a bookmark from the drop-down list (see Figure 20.3). Click Go To to jump to the selected bookmark.

20

**Figure 20.3**
The Go To dialog box is an easy way to jump to your document bookmarks.

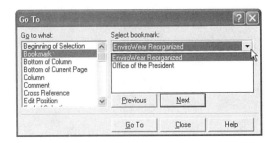

If you choose Set QuickMark on File Save, and also Go to QuickMark on File Open, the QuickMark is automatically set at the insertion point each time you save the document, and when you open it again, WordPerfect jumps directly to that bookmarked location. If the bookmark type is selected, you can also click Go To & Select, which causes WordPerfect to jump to the bookmark and select the bookmarked text.

After you have created bookmarks, you can create hyperlinks to those bookmarks. To create a hyperlink, follow these steps:

1. Create or find the text you want to link from. You should choose text that suggests to the readers that they can get more information by following the link.

    **NOTE**

    A common mistake in web page design is to create links using words like "click here" or "more," which aren't really descriptive of what the link relates to. Likewise, in your WordPerfect documents try using more descriptive links such as "text for Assembly Resolution AR1.33" or "2005 Prospectus."

    **TIP FROM**

    For very long documents, you can create a table of contents or menu at the beginning of the document and then use those entries to link to sections of the document.

2. Select the text or object to be linked.

    **NOTE**

    You cannot link from nothing. However, you can link from graphic objects as well as text. Whatever you link, you must select it first.

3. Choose Tools, Hyperlink. WordPerfect displays the Hyperlink Properties dialog box (see Figure 20.4).

**Figure 20.4**
The Hyperlink Properties dialog box enables you to create links to bookmarks, to other documents, and even to web or e-mail addresses.

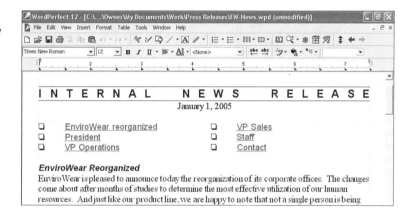

4. Click the Bookmark drop-down list, and select the bookmark you want to jump to.

5. Click OK to return to your document. WordPerfect displays the hyperlink using the current hyperlink style, which by default is blue, underlined text (see Figure 20.5).

**Figure 20.5**
Hyperlink text usually appears underlined and in blue.

After you create a link, assuming that hyperlinks are active (the mouse pointer appears as a hand), click the link to jump to the target bookmark.

**TIP FROM**

*Read Gilgen*

You can control the look of hyperlinked text by changing the Hypertext style. To do this, choose Format, Styles.

→ For more information on working with styles, **see** Chapter 9, "Formatting with Styles."

By default, hyperlinks you create are active, which means that if you click them, you jump to the targeted bookmark. If you don't want them active, choose Tools, Settings, Environment; then, on the General tab, deselect Activate Hyperlinks. The text continues to appear linked (underlined and blue), but if you click the link, nothing happens.

20

**TIP FROM**

*Read Gilgen*

If you want to edit many linked text locations by using the mouse, choose Tools, Settings, Environment, and on the General tab, deselect Activate Hyperlinks. You can then click on links and edit them without the fear of accidentally jumping to a bookmark. When you're through editing, choose Tools, Settings, Environment and select Activate Hyperlinks again to activate all links.

**CAUTION**

Because hyperlinked documents are not linear, it can become easy for a reader to get lost while following hyperlinks. You can help the reader by inserting links that jump back to the top of the document, or that return to a table of contents or menu.

**NOTE**

WordPerfect enables you to draw action shapes, such as forward, back, return, or home buttons, like those found in web browsers (choose Insert, Shapes, Action). You can link those shapes to bookmarks, thus helping the reader navigate your document.

→ For information on creating action shapes, **see** "Inserting Shapes," **p. 382.**

If you change your mind and need to edit or delete a bookmark or hyperlink, consider these options:

■ If you know where the code is located, move the insertion point to that location and open Reveal Codes (by choosing View, Reveal Codes or pressing Alt+F3). Then delete the bookmark or hyperlink code.

■ To remove a bookmark, which might be difficult to find in a document, choose Tools, Bookmark. In the Bookmark dialog box, select the bookmark you want to remove and choose Delete.

■ To rename a bookmark, access the Bookmark dialog box and choose Rename. This has the same effect as editing a bookmark, because there is nothing else to change.

■ To edit a hyperlink, whether text or a graphic image, right-click the link and choose Edit Hyperlink from the QuickMenu. WordPerfect displays the Hyperlink Properties dialog box (refer to Figure 20.4). Change the link and click OK. Note that you can edit hyperlinked text by choosing Tools, Hyperlink, but you must first use the keyboard to position the insertion point inside the hyperlink text area. Using QuickMenus is much quicker and easier.

## LINKING TO DOCUMENTS

You can also create hyperlinks from one document to another, and even to specific bookmarks within the target document. To create a hyperlink to another document, follow these steps:

1. Create the target document. If you intend to link to specific locations in the document, create bookmarks to identify those locations.

2. In the document from which you want to link, select the text or object you want to link and choose Tools, Hyperlink. WordPerfect displays the Hyperlink Properties dialog box (refer to Figure 20.4).

3. Type the full path and filename of the document you want to link to, or click the browse button at the right of the text box to browse for the file.

**CAUTION**

When linking to another document, be sure to include the full drive and path, along with the filename. Otherwise, WordPerfect might not be able to find the file when you try to link to it.

**TIP FROM**

*Read Gilgen*

If you're linking documents on a network drive for use by others, use UNC (universal naming convention) instead of drive letters. Others on the network might not have mapped their drives the same way you have. For example, instead of drive:\path\ filename, you should use \\server\volume:\path\filename.

4. If you're linking to a bookmark in the target document, type the name of the bookmark in the Bookmark edit box or select a bookmark from the Bookmark drop-down list.

**TIP FROM**

*Read Gilgen*

If you browse to choose the filename of the target document, WordPerfect also reads ahead and returns a list of valid bookmark names in the Bookmark drop-down list.

**CAUTION**

You should link to bookmarks by using the same upper- and lowercase characters found in the bookmark. Although WordPerfect ignores case, web pages don't. If you later publish your document as a web page, you might find that links don't work simply because the case in the bookmark and the link don't match.

20

5. Click OK to return to your WordPerfect document.

When you click a link to another document, WordPerfect opens that document. If you also specified a target bookmark, WordPerfect then jumps to that location.

If you intend for the reader to return to the original, or home, document, you should also place a link in the target document that jumps back to the home document. Remember that you can link text or graphic objects, such as action buttons.

## LINKING TO MACROS

You can also create a link to a macro, so that when you click the link, WordPerfect executes the macro. Macros could perform an action (such as sorting a table), or could even launch another program (such as the Windows Calculator).

To link to a macro, follow these steps:

1. Create the macro you want to execute.

   → For information on creating and using macros, **see** Chapter 26, "Using Experts and Macros."

2. In the document to which you want to link the macro, select the text or object from which you want to link.

3. Choose Tools, Hyperlink. WordPerfect displays the Hyperlink Properties dialog box (refer to Figure 20.4).

4. In the Document/Macro edit box, type (or browse for) the name of the macro you want to execute.

5. Click OK to save the link and return to your document.

Now you can simply click the link to execute the macro.

# CREATING LINKS TO THE INTERNET

The Internet has revolutionized the way we share information. The World Wide Web is a rich source of information. And many companies also use an intranet to store and share information via web pages. Either way, using external (Internet) or internal (intranet) web sites, you can create links so that with just a click of a button, the reader can jump from your WordPerfect documents to web documents.

**NOTE**

WordPerfect does not distinguish between Internet and intranet documents. Web documents are the same, and you access them the same, whether they're available to the whole world or just to your company site.

## USING AUTOMATIC HYPERLINKS

By default, WordPerfect automatically creates links to web site addresses and even to e-mail addresses. Type a Uniform Resource Locator (URL), followed by a space or hard return, and WordPerfect underlines the address, highlights it in blue, and creates a hyperlink to that address (see Figure 20.6).

**Figure 20.6**

If you type a space following a web or e-mail address, WordPerfect automatically creates a hyperlink.

**N O T E**

A *URL (Uniform Resource Locater)* is the standard method for describing a World Wide Web address. For example, in the following address you find three distinct components: http://www.mycompany.com/sales/june/report.html.

The first is the protocol being used to "serve" you the information (http://). The second is the name of the Internet computer, or web server, which consists of at least the domain name (mycompany.com) along with any other names that distinguish more than one server in that domain. The final component is the path to the specific document you want, ending in the actual filename (/sales/june/report.html).

**C A U T I O N**

Do not add a period or other end-of-sentence punctuation following a URL or e-mail address before typing the space or pressing Enter. Doing so adds that punctuation to the address, and as a result the link will not work.

WordPerfect also distinguishes between URLs and e-mail addresses, and creates an e-mail link when it finds an address that contains the @ symbol.

When you click an Internet link in a WordPerfect document, WordPerfect launches your default browser (for example, Netscape), and goes to the designated web site. If you click an e-mail address, WordPerfect launches your default mail program so you can create a mail message.

**N O T E**

What you believe to be your default mail program may not be what Windows thinks it is. If you click a mail link, and it opens a mail program that's not what you usually use (for example, Outlook), you have to change your system settings to recognize your mail program. Go to the Windows Control Panel, double-click the Internet Options icon, click the Programs tab, and from the Mail drop-down list, select your default e-mail program.

You might not like this automatic hyperlink feature, especially for printed documents, because links appear underlined and serve no useful linking purpose. To turn off the feature, follow these steps:

1. Choose Tools, QuickCorrect.

2. Click the SpeedLinks tab (see Figure 20.7).

**Figure 20.7**
You can turn off automatic hyperlink formatting in the SpeedLinks tab of the QuickCorrect dialog box.

3. Deselect Format Words As Hyperlinks When You Type Them.

4. Click OK to return to your document.

This setting remains until you change it again. Now by hand you must create hyperlinks to web and e-mail addresses. Note, however, that changing this setting does not remove links you have already created.

## USING SPEEDLINKS

SpeedLinks are like QuickCorrect words in that you type one word (for example, @EnviroWear), and WordPerfect automatically changes it to another (for example, EnviroWear without the @ symbol) and also adds a hyperlink to the corrected text (for example, http://www.envirowear.biz).

To create a SpeedLink, follow these steps:

1. Choose Tools, QuickCorrect.

2. Click the SpeedLinks tab (refer to Figure 20.7).

3. In the Link Word box, type the word you want to appear in your document.

4. In the Location to Link To box, type the complete URL you want to link to (for example, http://www.envirowear.biz). If you want to create a SpeedLink to an e-mail address, type **mailto:** followed by the e-mail address (for example, mailto:sales@envirowear.biz).

**NOTE**

You can use SpeedLinks to link to an Internet URL or e-mail address, or to another document. Use the browse button to find another document to link to.

5. Click Add Entry to add the SpeedLink to the list. WordPerfect adds the @ symbol to the beginning of the word.

6. Click OK to return to your document.

To use the SpeedLink, type the @ symbol followed by the SpeedLink word (for example, @EnviroWear). WordPerfect inserts the SpeedLink word as a hyperlink.

**CAUTION**

Do not use fully capitalized words or acronyms as SpeedLinks. When you do, WordPerfect also capitalizes the hyperlink, which then may not link properly because many web site addresses are case-sensitive.

## CREATING, EDITING, AND DELETING INTERNET LINKS

To create an Internet link without using the automatic hyperlink feature, follow these steps:

1. Select the text or object to which you want to attach a hyperlink.

2. Choose Tools, Hyperlink to access the Hyperlink Properties dialog box (see Figure 20.8, shown here with a URL).

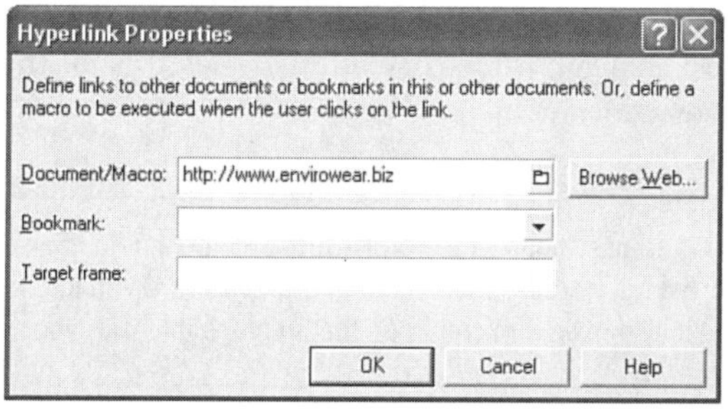

**Figure 20.8**
You can use the Hyperlink Properties dialog box to create links to web site URLs and e-mail addresses.

3. In the Document/Macro box, type the complete URL (for example, http://www.envirowear.biz). If you want to create a link to an e-mail address, type **mailto:** followed by the e-mail address (for example, mailto:sales@envirowear.biz).

4. If you are linking to a bookmark within a web page, type the name of the bookmark in the Bookmark box.

5. If you are creating a page that will be part of a web page frameset, you can specify the frame in which the linked web document or web site will appear. This option has no effect on hyperlinked WordPerfect documents.

→ For details on creating links for use with web documents, **see** "Using Hyperlinks," **p. 666.**

6. Click OK to add the hyperlink to the selected text or object.

To edit a hyperlink, right-click the link and choose Edit Hyperlink from the QuickMenu. Then, in the Hyperlink Properties dialog box, make any needed changes.

CAUTION

> When entering a URL by hand, be sure to carefully type the URL, including all special characters, such as the tilde (~). Generally, you should use lowercase characters. Some web servers distinguish between upper- and lowercase characters, and using an uppercase character in the URL might not work.

To remove a hyperlink, open the Reveal Codes window (by choosing View, Reveal Codes or pressing Alt+F3) and delete the hyperlink codes. There is no way to remove a hyperlink code using the menus or dialog boxes. However, you can use Find and Replace to search for the Hyperlink Begin codes and replace them with nothing. This removes the codes and the hyperlink style (for example, blue underlined text).

 *If you are having trouble making your Internet links work, see "Checking Links" in the Troubleshooting section at the end of this chapter.*

# EMBEDDING SOUNDS IN DOCUMENTS

You know documents have changed when they can talk back to you! Indeed, you can include recorded sound clips in your documents.

NOTE

> Before you can use sound in a WordPerfect document, you must have a sound-capable computer (with a working sound card and speakers). If you intend to record your own sounds, you also need a microphone that's compatible with your sound card.

## INSERTING SOUNDS

Assuming that your computer is wired for sound (that is, that your computer has a sound card, a microphone, speakers, and the appropriate sound software), follow these steps to add sound to a WordPerfect document:

1. Choose Insert, Sound. WordPerfect displays the Sound Clips dialog box (see Figure 20.9).

**Figure 20.9**
The Sound Clips dialog box lists clips already in the document, and also enables you to add or record clips.

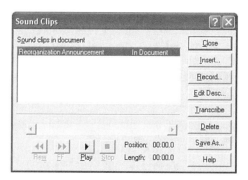

 *If you're not getting any sound from your system, see "Getting Wired" in the Troubleshooting section at the end of this chapter.*

2. Click Insert to select and insert a sound clip into the document. WordPerfect displays the Insert Sound Clip into Document dialog box (see Figure 20.10).

**Figure 20.10**
In the Insert Sound Clip into Document dialog box, you can specify the name of the sound file to insert.

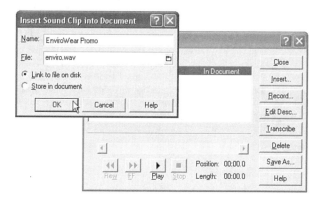

3. Browse to find the sound file you want. In this dialog box, you also have the following options:

- Name—You can change the name of the clip to something that describes it better than Clip #1, Clip #2, and so on.

- Link to File on Disk—This leaves the sound file on disk, either on your local hard drive or on a network drive. This also means the document will have a smaller file size, and that others might not have access to the sound file if they use the document.

- Store in Document—Selecting this option makes for a large file size, but it also means that regardless of where the document goes, the sound file travels with it.

**20**

**NOTE**

Typically, sounds used in Windows, especially voice recordings, are stored in .wav file format. However, you can also insert other types of sound files, such as music MIDI (.mid) files. The only requirement is that the proper sound drivers be installed in Windows to play these other sounds.

 *If you're having trouble playing MIDI files, see "Installing Sound and Video Drivers" in the Troubleshooting section at the end of this chapter.*

4. Click OK to close both the Insert Sound Clip into Document and Sound Clips dialog boxes and return to your document. WordPerfect displays a sound (speaker) icon in the left margin (see Figure 20.11, which also shows one other sound linking option).

A sound clip inserted as an object

**Figure 20.11**
The speaker icon in the left margin indicates that there is a sound clip inserted in the document. You can click the icon to play the sound.

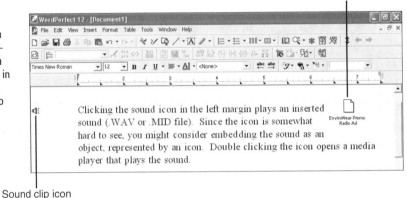

Sound clip icon

To play an inserted sound clip, click the speaker icon in the left margin.

**NOTE**

Depending on your view of the document, you might not see what's in the margins. You can decrease the zoom percentage, or scroll horizontally to the left to see the sound icon.

## LINKING SOUNDS

The biggest problem with inserting a sound as described in the preceding section is that the sound icon often is hidden from view in the left margin. The reader might have no idea that there's sound included with the document.

In earlier versions of WordPerfect (version 10 and before) you could create a more visible sound link by using the procedures described earlier in this chapter for linking a document to text or to a graphics object (for example, an action button). Unfortunately, a bug was introduced in version 11 that prevents linking a sound file to a graphic or text object. This bug still has not been resolved.

An alternative is to insert a sound object the same as you do a video object, and display the inserted object as an icon (refer to Figure 20.11). By double-clicking the icon, the reader activates a media player that plays the sound.

→ For information on inserting sounds as objects, **see** "Embedding Video in Documents" later in this chapter. The procedure for embedding sound and video clips is identical to that of embedding icons.

## RECORDING SOUNDS

You can also record your own sound file by using your computer's microphone. To do so, follow these steps before inserting the sound, as described previously:

1. Choose Insert, Sound to access the Sound Clips dialog box (refer to Figure 20.9).
2. Click Record. WordPerfect launches the Windows Sound Recorder program (see Figure 20.12).

**Figure 20.12**
With a microphone and the Windows Sound Recorder, you can record sounds to insert in your documents.

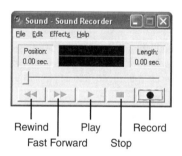

Rewind | Play | Record
Fast Forward | Stop

*If your microphone doesn't seem to work, see "Is the Right Switch On?" in the Troubleshooting section at the end of this chapter.*

3. Get your microphone and text ready, and click the Record button.
4. When you finish recording, click the Stop button.
5. Click the Play button to review the sound, and use other Sound Recorder tools to edit the selection (for example, clip it, amplify it, or even add an echo).
6. Choose File, Save (or Save As), and save the sound file; remember its name and location for future reference.

Now you need to follow the procedures for inserting a sound, using the file you just recorded.

## TRANSCRIBING RECORDINGS

One use for embedding a sound recording in a document is to later transcribe that recording (for example, a dictated memo). WordPerfect enables you to listen, and repeat as often as necessary, while typing the transcription. To transcribe a sound, follow these steps:

20

1. Choose Insert, Sound to access the Sound Clip dialog box (refer to Figure 20.9).
2. Select the sound clip you want to transcribe and click Transcribe. WordPerfect displays the Transcription feature bar (see Figure 20.13).

**Figure 20.13**
The Transcription feature bar helps you play segments of sound clips as you transcribe a recording.

**NOTE**

The transcription feature is a throwback to the days when one person would dictate a document into a tape recorder and another would write down the spoken word. However, recording long documents as computer sound files is not very practical, primarily because they take up a lot of computer disk space.

**TIP FROM**

*Read Gilgen*

One alternative to recording and transcribing text is to use a speech recognition program, such as Dragon NaturallySpeaking. WordPerfect is designed to work well with such programs, enabling you to convert your speech into commands and words on-the-fly, thus avoiding the creation of large sound files.

**TIP FROM**

*Read Gilgen*

You can activate the Transcription feature bar quickly by right-clicking the sound icon in the left margin of the document and choosing Transcribe.

3. Click the Play button to begin the sound.
4. Click the Pause button (which replaced the Play button when you began to play the sound).
5. Type the text you heard.
6. Click the Replay button to repeat just the most recent segment you listened to. You can repeat as often as you like.
7. Click Play again to continue. When you click Pause and Replay, WordPerfect repeats only the segment from which you stopped last to your current location.
8. Repeat steps 3–6 until you finish transcribing the document.
9. Click Close to close the Transcription feature bar.

**TIP FROM**

*Read Gilgen*

One interesting use for the Transcription feature bar might be for memorizing phrases or dialogs, or for working with foreign languages where being able to repeat segments is useful.

# EMBEDDING VIDEO IN DOCUMENTS

With the common availability of digital cameras that can also record short video clips, adding motion video to a WordPerfect document is finally a reality. Instead of merely describing a product, for example, you can use a video clip that shows the product in action, or from different angles.

Video clips are inserted and played as OLE objects, which means they are embedded in the WordPerfect document, but played by another program, a player that appears within WordPerfect.

→ For more information on OLE, **see** "Using OLE Linking and Embedding Options," **p. 469.**

**NOTE**

Typically, Windows video files use the .avi filename extension. Other types of video clips, such as those created by some digital cameras, or QuickTime (.mov) or MPEG (.mpg) files, also can also be embedded in WordPerfect documents.

To insert a Windows .avi video clip, follow these steps:

1. Choose Insert, Object. WordPerfect displays the Insert Object dialog box.
2. Click Create from File (see Figure 20.14).

**Figure 20.14**
You can insert OLE objects, such as video clips, using the Insert Object dialog box.

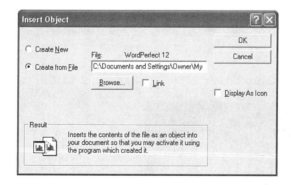

3. Browse or type the name of the video file you want to insert.
4. You can choose among these options:
   - Link—If you don't want the video clip to become part of your document, you can link to a copy on your computer or on the network by choosing this option.

- Display As Icon—You can display a still image (the first video frame) in your document, or you can choose this option to display an icon that lets the reader know a video image is available for viewing.
- Change Icon—If you select Display As Icon, this button appears; otherwise, you do not see it. Click the button to display the Change Icon dialog box (see Figure 20.15). Here you can select a new icon to represent the clip, and also provide your own custom label to identify the clip. Click OK to return to the Insert Object dialog box.

**Figure 20.15**
If you display the OLE clip as an icon, you can select a different icon than the one suggested by WordPerfect.

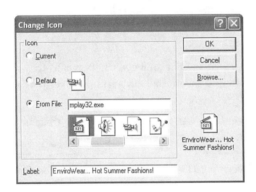

5. Click OK to insert the video clip.

Figure 20.16 shows two video clips—one of which is displayed as the first frame of the video clip, and the other of which is represented as an icon. Both are in graphics boxes, which you can move and resize as needed. Note, however, that if you increase the size of the video frame, you decrease the quality of the image.

**Figure 20.16**
Video clips can be displayed using the first frame of the clip, or can be represented by an icon. The Windows Media Player replaces WordPerfect menus and toolbars so you can start, stop, or rewind a video clip.

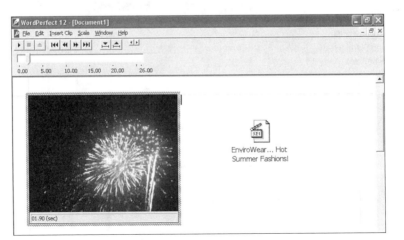

To play the clip, choose one of these options:

■ If you inserted the video frame without the link or icon options, you can double-click the frame, and then double-click it again to begin playing the clip in place in the document. You can also play the clip by clicking the Play button on the Windows Media Player controls, which appear in place of the WordPerfect menus and toolbars (refer to Figure 20.16).

**NOTE**

Windows has two media players, each named the same thing. The internal, built-in Windows Media Player is shown here, and it typically handles all native Windows video formats (.avi). Windows Media Player is a separate, full-featured program that can play all types of audio and video media, can work with playlists, and more. This program is just one of many standalone programs that can play video clips. If you have installed another such player as your default media player, such as WinAmp, or the RealPlayer, that program will launch in place of the Windows Media Player for non-.avi files.

■ If you linked the video clip, or if you used an icon to represent the video clip, you can double-click the object to launch the Media Player, which appears as a separate control program and viewing window (see Figure 20.17). You can use the player's controls to start, stop, rewind, and so on.

**Figure 20.17**
The Windows Media Player operates as a detached, separate program when associated with a linked or icon-represented video clip.

■ If you linked to a non-.avi type video file (such as .mpg or .mov), when you double-click the object you launch the default player for that type of video. For example, if you have WinAmp installed as your default .mpg player, WinAmp automatically plays .mpg files when you double-click them (see Figure 20.18).

The internal Windows Media Player, like other media players, offers a variety of options, including whether to include a caption, how to display lapsed time (time, frames, tracks), and so on. You can experiment with the player that appears on your system to discover some of the options available for presenting a video clip.

20

**Figure 20.18**
Linked or icon-represented non-.avi video clips play in the media player, such as WinAmp, that is associated with that particular media type.

# PUBLISHING INTERACTIVE AND MULTIMEDIA DOCUMENTS

Printing traditional documents requires a printer. It's quite simple, really. But publishing interactive and multimedia documents sometimes isn't quite so straightforward.

For readers to be able to read your documents, they must have computers that can do one or more of the following:

- Use WordPerfect—Although you can convert documents to Word, that doesn't necessarily mean that all links, sounds, video clips, and so on convert correctly. If the people who must read your documents don't use WordPerfect, they might not get the full picture.

- Connect to the Internet—If you have links that connect to web pages, you must be connected to the Internet via a local or dial-up connection if you want to view linked web sites. If some of your readers don't have Internet access, you need to make sure the document is still effective without its Internet links.

- Play sound files—Nearly every computer these days comes equipped with a sound card and speakers, but it's not a given that all needed sound drivers are installed. One person might be able to play .wav files, for example, but not MIDI files.

- Play video clips—Not every computer is set up to play even standard Windows .avi files. If you use other video formats, for example QuickTime files, the user might first have to install the QuickTime player.

As a publisher of electronic documents, you must make decisions about what's important, who your target audience is, and what percentage of your audience is likely to be able to read your document. Sometimes you can take steps to ensure that they can, such as convincing your computer support department that everyone needs sound cards and speakers, or that everyone should have QuickTime video players installed.

Finally, you also can, and should, design your documents so that they're still effective, communicating essential information, even without Internet links, sounds, or video clips.

# CREATING ACCESSIBLE DOCUMENTS

As noted at the beginning of this chapter, we can now interact with documents differently than we have in the past. This has a side benefit in that it can make documents even more accessible to the handicapped.

## UNDERSTANDING THE ISSUES

In 1991, the United States Congress passed the Americans with Disabilities Act, which has helped us understand the challenges that face persons who would like to have access to information, but who are physically challenged, or sight or hearing impaired.

In the past, the end result of a word processing document was the printed page alone, thus creating barriers to the flow of information—for example, for the blind. Further, with an emphasis on the graphical environment and the use of the mouse to accomplish basic tasks, many persons with physical limitations were also being edged out of the creative process.

However, recently we have seen an emphasis on providing access both to the word processing program as well as to the documents produced by the program.

## COREL'S COMMITMENT TO ACCESSIBILITY

Corel's commitment to provide accessible software is described in its Accessibility Initiative, which can be found at http://www.wordperfect.com/accessibility/. Besides adhering to government and industry accessibility guidelines, Corel is also concentrating on several specific issues, including the following:

- Keyboard Access—This objective is to make sure that users can access all program features and commands using only the keyboard, and documenting the method of access. For the first time in several versions of WordPerfect, for example, WordPerfect 10 ships with a keyboard template.

- Keyboard Focus—Focus is the button or menu item that is activated by pressing the Enter key. Navigating through a dialog box by pressing Tab to be able to arrive at desired functions is now more logical and easier. Further, screen readers can now determine the focus location so the user doesn't have to touch all the buttons to find what he or she needs.

20

- High Contrast—This emphasis is to allow for larger fonts so that characters are easier to distinguish. The implementation of the wheel mouse to zoom in or out on a document is a new feature in WordPerfect 10.

- Sound Alternatives—An error beep does no good if you can't hear it. This effort provides for alternative visual cues to complement sound-only cues.

- Speech Recognition—WordPerfect works well with speech recognition programs, such as Dragon NaturallySpeaking, which enables users to dictate content and to control the program using voice alone. The accuracy of these programs is very good, and it opens up a whole new world to those with severely restricted mobility.

## ADAPTING DOCUMENTS FOR ACCESSIBILITY

In addition to making the program easier to use, several of the document features discussed in this chapter can make information more accessible; for example

- Links—You can organize your information in sections, and provide links to help the visually impaired navigate better through your document. Imagine that you had to read a document through a straw, not being able to scan the page. You wouldn't know what to read and what not to read, and being afraid you'd miss something, you'd have to read the entire document. On the other hand, if you had a menu, you would have an overview, and could determine just what you needed to read. Links would take you quickly to the pertinent sections, and other links would return you to the menu.

- Alternate Text—Do you depend on communicating information by the graphic images you use? Will a blind person miss vital information because he or she cannot see an image? You can right-click an image and choose HTML Properties, and then on the Image tab add alternative text that describes what the image is all about. Screen readers can then read out loud the alternative text.

- Sounds—You can even insert sounds that the reader can listen to, thus enhancing his or her understanding of the printed information.

As you prepare your documents, consider the entire audience. What can you do to make your documents more accessible? With WordPerfect, it's relatively easy.

# TROUBLESHOOTING

### CHECKING LINKS

*I clicked a hyperlink to a web site and Netscape Navigator starts, but it won't display the web site.*

This could be one of several problems. Can you go to any site at all in Netscape Navigator? If so, check the URL in the WordPerfect hyperlink to make sure it's typed correctly, including upper- and lowercase. If you can't reach other sites in Netscape Navigator, make sure you're connected to the Internet (for example, that you've established a dial-up connection if you're not connected directly to the Internet).

Some companies set up firewalls to prevent others from accessing company networks. These firewalls also sometimes prevent employees from accessing anything beyond the company networks. If this seems to be the case, consult with your computer support department about possible solutions.

### INSTALLING SOUND AND VIDEO DRIVERS

*I've got a video file linked properly, but it won't play.*

Not everyone installs the necessary video players and drivers when they set up their Windows system. Further, some video formats require special players (for example, .mov files require the QuickTime player for Windows from Apple). Make sure all necessary drivers and players are installed.

### GETTING WIRED

*Why can't I hear any sound files on my computer?*

Although it is quite unusual these days, some computers do not have the necessary hardware installed to enable you to record sound files. You must have a sound card, a microphone, and speakers, in addition to the necessary software to make them work.

If you do have the necessary hardware and software, and assuming the wires are all connected properly, have you heard sounds before, but now you can't? It might seem obvious, but check to make sure the Windows volume control hasn't been turned down, or off. Click the Sound (speaker) icon on the taskbar and make sure Mute is unchecked and that the volume is not all the way down. You can also double-click the speaker icon to open the Master Volume dialog box.

Finally, some speaker systems use power from the computer, or from batteries. If you turn on the power without batteries installed, the speakers actually turn off the sound. Try turning off the power.

### IS THE RIGHT SWITCH ON?

*I have all the right hardware, but I still can't record sound files.*

Some microphones have switches you can use to turn them on and off. Some also have switches that adapt the microphone to different types of sound cards. Make sure your switch settings are correct for the type of microphone and sound card you are using.

You should also check Windows's microphone settings. Double-click the speaker icon on the Task Bar to open the Master Volume dialog box and make sure the Microphone is not muted or turned all the way down.

### WHICH VIDEO PLAYER?

*When I play .avi files, everything works as you describe it. But if I try to play video files from my digital camera, a different player comes up.*

The Windows Media Player typically works with .avi files because that is the standard Windows video format. Other formats, such as QuickTime (.mov) or MPEG (.mpg), use the standalone player that's associated with that file type. Players include Windows Media Player, WinAmp, Real Player, and others. As long as the video plays, be happy! Don't worry about which player is doing the work.

# PROJECT

Well-designed documents are easy for the reader to navigate. For example, in Chapter 18, "Working with Large or Multipart Documents," you learned how to create a table of contents to help the reader quickly find sections of a document. You can combine those tools with WordPerfect's linking capability to make it even easier for the reader.

For example, consider the EnviroWear Annual Report shown in Figure 20.19. You have no idea how long the document is, whether you must start at the beginning, or whether you might skip to more important sections later in the document.

**Figure 20.19**
Reading an entire annual report can be a daunting prospect. You can make the job easier by adding navigation aids.

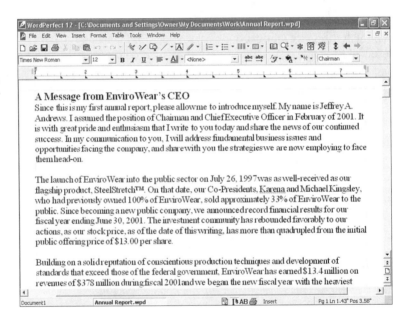

To begin, you can generate a table of contents that shows the location of various sections of the annual report. Further, you can link table of contents entries to their related section headings.

To create automatic table of contents hyperlinks, follow these steps:

1. Mark table of contents entries, and insert the table of contents definition at the beginning of the document.

   → For information on how to mark, define, and generate a table of contents, **see** "Creating a Table of Contents," **p. 593**.

2. Generate the table of contents. When WordPerfect displays the Generate dialog box (see Figure 20.20), choose Build Hyperlinks before clicking OK.

**Figure 20.20**
WordPerfect can automatically generate hyperlinks along with a table of contents.

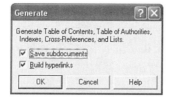

If you define the table of contents to display without page numbers, WordPerfect creates hyperlinks using the table of contents entries. Otherwise, hyperlinks appear only on the page numbers.

WordPerfect automatically generates a table of contents, complete with hyperlinked section entries (see Figure 20.21).

**Figure 20.21**
A hyperlinked table of contents makes it easy for readers to jump directly to different sections of the document.

Now you want to make it easy for a reader to return to the table of contents in case he or she doesn't want to read the entire report sequentially.

To create a linked action button that returns to the table of contents, follow these steps:

1. Go to the top of the document (or to the beginning of the table of contents), and choose Tools, Bookmark, Create. Provide the name of the bookmark (for example, Top of Report) and click OK.

2. Go to the end of the first section of the report (for example, the end of the CEO's message).

3. Choose Insert, Shapes, and click Action to display action button options (see Figure 20.22).

**Figure 20.22**
WordPerfect provides several action buttons that you can draw as shapes and hyperlink to other locations in the document.

4. Choose the one you want (for example, the Return or the Home icon) and click OK.

5. In the document, click and drag to create the action button. WordPerfect draws the button, and the sizing handles indicate that the button is selected. Move and size the button as needed, and also change button properties, such as color, from the Graphics property bar.

6. Choose Tools, Hyperlink to display the Hyperlink Properties dialog box.

7. Click the Bookmark drop-down list and choose the bookmark that takes you back to the top (for example, Top of Report).

8. Make sure Activate Hyperlinks is selected before choosing OK.

WordPerfect displays a hyperlinked action button (see Figure 20.23). If you click the button, you jump immediately to the bookmark at the top of the report. After you make sure the link works, you can copy the button and paste it, along with its links, to the end of each section in your document.

**Figure 20.23**
You can add hyperlinked text or other instructions along with a hyperlinked graphic image to help readers who might not know to click the link.

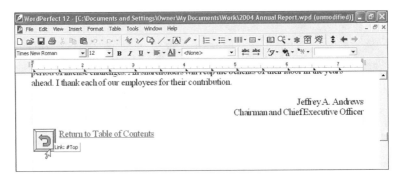

CHAPTER **21**

# PUBLISHING DOCUMENTS ON THE WORLD WIDE WEB

**I**n this chapter

*by Read Gilgen*

# UNDERSTANDING WEB DOCUMENTS

One of the most interesting phenomena in the past few years has been the development of the World Wide Web, usually referred to simply as the Web. Made possible by the development of the Internet over the past 20–30 years, the Web enables anyone—from large corporations to individuals—to create and publish information that is easily and readily available to anyone anywhere in the world. Today such phrases as "check out my web site" or "dot com" are part of our everyday vocabulary.

Part of the success of the Web lies in the basic nature of web documents. Unlike proprietary word processing formats that require specific word processors to be read, edited, or printed, web documents are standard ASCII (pronounced "ask-key") text documents that you can create with any common text editor.

At the heart of the web page is HTML (Hypertext Markup Language), which consists of tags that describe document formatting. This concept should be familiar to WordPerfect users, who are used to seeing formatting codes in the Reveal Codes window. Most HTML tags are used in pairs: one to turn on a formatting feature and another to turn it off. For example, the markup tags used to add boldface to a word look like this:

```
<strong>text in bold</strong>
```

A web document is placed on a web server, a computer that does nothing more than honor requests to "serve up," or send, documents to those who want to see them.

Finally, you use a web browser to view web pages. When you specify a web page address, or URL (Uniform Resource Locator), your browser contacts the designated web server over the Internet and requests a document. The server sends the HTML document to your computer, and then your browser translates it into the attractively functional web page you see on your screen (see Figure 21.1).

**Figure 21.1**
web servers send HTML text documents over the Internet to computers that use web browser software to view them.

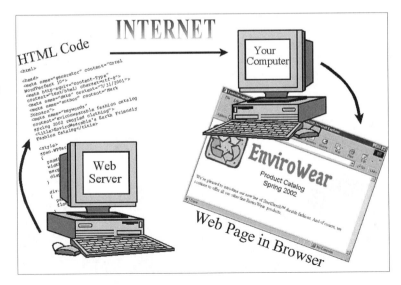

21

## WORDPERFECT AND WEB DOCUMENT LANGUAGES

Since version 7, WordPerfect has included the capability of creating HTML documents. WordPerfect's Internet Publisher Wizard enabled users to create documents using HTML-specific features, such as standard HTML Headings, document backgrounds, forms, and even customized HTML code. Further, one could open an HTML page and edit it in WordPerfect.

Unfortunately, standard HTML, although viewable by the largest number of browsers, severely limits the amount of formatting allowed in a document. Today's computer users demand more heavily formatted documents, which has led to changes in the complexity of HTML and the development of other markup languages and methods of publishing web documents. SGML (Standard Generalized Markup Language) and XML (eXtensible Markup Language) are two examples of specialized page languages that use standardized Document Type Definitions to far exceed the simple formatting capabilities of standard HTML. Finally, the use of Cascading Style Sheets (CSS) has emerged as a relatively easy but elegant method of defining the use of nonstandard HTML elements, thus permitting the publishing of documents that look much more like your original word processing documents.

WordPerfect no longer provides the capability to create and edit standard HTML documents. Instead, it enables you to publish your documents as web pages, converting your formatting using Cascading Style Sheets so that the document appears virtually the same on the Web as it does in WordPerfect. WordPerfect also includes the capability to develop web documents using SGML and XML.

In this chapter, we explore how you can use WordPerfect to create effective and attractive web documents.

**NOTE**

> WordPerfect isn't for designing web sites like you're used to seeing on the Web these days, with flashing graphics and JavaScript-based interactivity. Nevertheless, WordPerfect is quite good at taking standard content pages and converting them into pages that look good on the Web and that fit nicely within a web site of complex design.

→ For information on using XML in WordPerfect, **see** Chapter 22, "Working with XML Documents."

## PUBLISHING WORDPERFECT DOCUMENTS TO HTML

Publishing a WordPerfect document to HTML is really quite simple. Just follow these steps:

1. Save your file as a WordPerfect document.

2. Choose File, Publish to HTML. WordPerfect displays the Publish to HTML dialog box (see Figure 21.2).

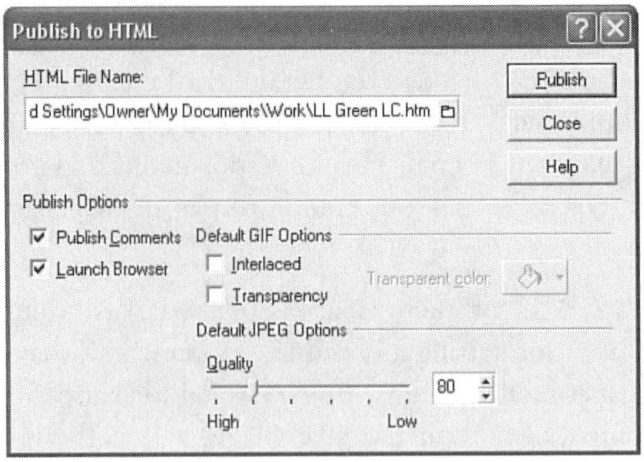

**Figure 21.2**
Use the Publish to HTML dialog box to choose options prior to publishing your document as a web document.

3. Click Publish. WordPerfect converts your document into HTML code and saves it as a web page document.

Figure 21.3 shows a WordPerfect document, and Figure 21.4 shows the same document as viewed in a web browser, having been first published to HTML.

**NOTE**

We'll save discussion of the Publish to HTML options until later, after we've had a chance to explore how to prepare documents for publication to the Web.

**Figure 21.3**
A WordPerfect document, ready for publishing to HTML.

**Figure 21.4**
A WordPerfect document, published to HTML, and viewed in a web browser.

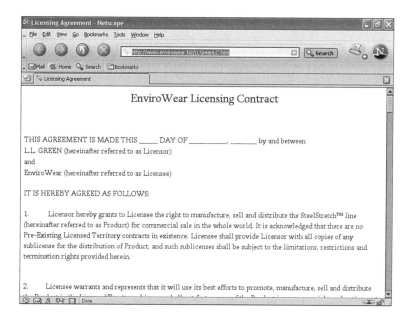

## CONSIDERATIONS IN PUBLISHING DOCUMENTS TO THE WEB

Although the process of publishing to HTML may be simple, there are several things you must consider before publishing a document to the Web:

- Web Page Format—WordPerfect provides two powerful, yet significantly different methods for publishing documents to the Web. One is HTML aided by the use of Cascading Style Sheets, the result of which is shown in Figure 21.4. The other is PDF, the Portable Document Format developed by Adobe Corporation. PDF can produce a more faithful representation of your original WordPerfect document than can HTML, but it does require the use of a special reader. Fortunately, nearly everyone has this free reader already installed.

- Browsers—Users must use web browser software to view web documents. The two most popular browsers are Netscape Navigator and Microsoft Internet Explorer. Other browsers include Mozilla, Firefox, Lynx, and Opera. Each has its own particular strengths and weaknesses, and preference for one browser over another is usually a matter of personal choice. However, browsers also come in different versions, which further complicates things. For example, older browsers might not support some features, such as Cascading Style Sheets, needed to view your published pages. Finally, browsers often interpret and implement HTML and other standards slightly differently. As you prepare your web pages, you'll have to consider whether your readers will have the appropriate version, or if they can easily obtain it. Fortunately, the latest versions of the two most commonly used browsers, Netscape and Internet Explorer, both display WordPerfect HTML pages very well.

21

**CAUTION**

> Internet Explorer 4.x and later, and Netscape Navigator 4.x and later are required to take advantage of WordPerfect's use of Cascading Style Sheets. Earlier versions offer little, if any, support for CSS specifications, which require that user-defined style sheets be able to merge with the document's style sheets.

- Platform—Part of the attractiveness of publishing to the HTML standard is that web documents can be viewed by browsers on a variety of computing platforms (for example, Windows, Macintosh, or Unix systems) and still look the same. Nevertheless there are some differences among these platforms, and you'll need to test your pages on those systems that your readers are likely to be using.

- Screen resolution—Most users these days view web documents at the SVGA (Super VGA, or 800×600) screen resolution. But some still have older systems and use a lower resolution of only 640×480. Some advanced users are already viewing web pages on their Personal Digital Assistants, or PDAs, such as a PalmPilot. You want to be sure that it's easy for readers to read the information on your web pages regardless of the screen resolution they're using.

- Fonts—Unless users have the same fonts on their computers as you do on yours, you might be limited to a few basic font styles. Consider whether a specific font is important to you.

- Accessibility—Some users come to your web site with visual disabilities and you need to consider whether your pages can be understood by the special readers they use. Some of the procedures discussed in this chapter address this issue specifically.

- Plug-ins—A plug-in is an addition to a web browser that adds functionality, such as the capability to display animations or video, play sound, or read certain non-HTML information. If your audience is not very computer literate, requiring viewers to download and install plug-ins might not be worth the trouble.

As you prepare your documents for publication to the Web, keep these considerations in mind.

# PREPARING DOCUMENTS FOR THE WEB

Many of the formatting features and procedures you use in a WordPerfect document can also be used as you create a web page. However, the more difficult task might be to learn what you *can't* use, and to create effective documents within the limitations imposed by HTML.

## PREVIEWING A WEB DOCUMENT

As you prepare your document, you can quickly preview how it will look in your favorite web browser. That way, you can easily make adjustments before taking the more formal step of publishing your document.

**21**

To preview how a WordPerfect document will look in a web browser, follow these steps:

1. Save your work.

2. Choose View, Preview in Browser. WordPerfect opens your default web browser (for example, Internet Explorer) and displays your document as if it were a web document (refer to Figure 21.4).

3. Switch back to WordPerfect and make any changes you want.

4. Repeat steps 1–2 to view the changes.

**NOTE**

> When you preview a document in your browser, WordPerfect makes a temporary copy of the html file named wpdoc.htm, usually located in your system's temporary folder (for example, c:\Documents and Settings\Owner\Local Settings\Temp).

**TIP FROM**

*Read Gilgen*

> You can quickly switch from your browser's preview back to your document by pressing Alt+Tab.

**TIP FROM**

*Read Gilgen*

> Because you need to preview your document in more than one browser, open your second browser (for example, Netscape) and choose File, Open (or Open Page) and type the location of the wpdoc.htm file (for example, c:\Documents and Settings\Owner\Local Settings\Temp\wpdoc.htm). Then use Alt+Tab to switch from one browser to another, or back to WordPerfect. Don't forget that while in WordPerfect you must choose View, Preview in Browser to update the page in your default browser, and that you need to click the Refresh, or Reload, button in any other browser you may be using.

## SETTING DOCUMENT PROPERTIES

When you open a web page in your browser, typically you see a descriptive title of the page in the title bar (for example, the blue bar at the top of the screen). This title helps you get a quick idea of what the page is all about, but it's particularly useful to those using screen readers because they can't otherwise scan the page. Further, the words in a web page title often become the keywords used to locate documents by Web search engines such as Yahoo!, Google, or AltaVista.

To set document properties for your web page, follow these steps:

1. Choose File, Properties. WordPerfect displays the Properties dialog box (see Figure 21.5).

**21**

**Figure 21.5**
Use the Properties dialog box to set the title and other key information for your web page.

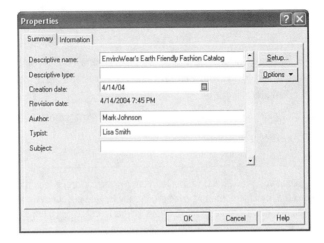

2. In the Descriptive Name text box, type the title you want to appear on the web browser's title bar. Make it relatively short, but as descriptive as possible. If you don't include anything here, the browser simply shows the page's URL. For example, "EnviroWear's Earth Friendly Fashion Catalog" will be much more helpful to the viewer than http://www.envirowear.biz/springcat05.html.

3. Click the scroll-down arrow to reveal the Keywords and Abstract text boxes. Add a few significant keywords, and if you want, a short abstract of the document.

4. Click OK to return to your document.

When you preview the document, the title now appears in the title bar (see Figure 21.6).

**Figure 21.6**
Descriptive names created in the Properties dialog box appear in the web browser's title bar.

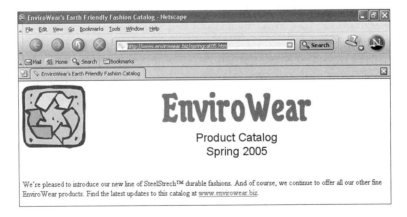

Although you don't see it, the HTML source code now includes keywords and descriptions used by search engines to make your document easier to find (see Figure 21.7).

Keywords

**Figure 21.7**
WordPerfect inserts keywords and abstracts into the web document's source code.

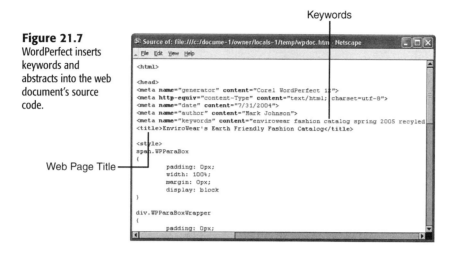

Web Page Title

**NOTE**

The source code for web documents is plain text, and as such can be viewed in any text editor.

## WORKING WITH TEXT

By default, WordPerfect web documents appear with a white background and black text, the same as what you see in WordPerfect itself. You can't change the background unless you go to another web page editor and add the necessary background color codes.

You can set a fill color (by choosing Format, Page, Border/Fill) but the results won't be what you expect. For example, a page filled with yellow in WordPerfect still shows a white border in the margins. You get the same results in Internet Explorer, but in Netscape, only the actual text shows a yellow background, whereas all other areas are white. WordPerfect also converts all fill patterns and gradient shading to solid colors.

**NOTE**

If you choose a textured or gradient fill, WordPerfect combines the foreground color with white, resulting in a solid pastel color.

→ To learn how to manipulate background fills and colors, **see** "Adding Borders, Drop Shadows, and Fills," **p. 217.**

21

Text alignment varies somewhat from what you're used to seeing in WordPerfect. For example, all tab types display properly in web browsers—even right or centered tabs, with or without dot leaders. However, HTML and WordPerfect permit only one space at a time—multiple spaces are reduced to just one space (see Figure 21.8).

**Figure 21.8**
WordPerfect's alignment features work well in web pages, except that you're limited to using one space at a time.

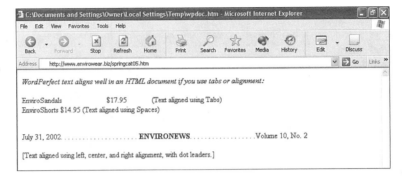

Paragraph formatting and alignment also reproduce well on the Web. For example, you can use First Line Indent (Tab), Indent (F7), Double Indent (Ctrl+Shift+F7), or Hanging Indent (Ctrl+F7).

You can also align text with Left, Right, and Center justification. However, Full and All do not work—the text remains left justified.

→ For information on text formatting, **see** Chapter 7, "Formatting Lines and Paragraphs."

## WORKING WITH FONTS

Standard HTML provides for the use of only three basic fonts: a sans-serif font such as Arial, a serif font such as Times Roman, and a monospaced font such as Courier.

→ For more information on using fonts, **see** "Choosing the Right Font," **p. 72.**

However, with the aid of Cascading Style Sheets, WordPerfect can use nearly any font and display it properly in the web browser (see Figure 21.9).

**Figure 21.9**
You can use nearly any font in your WordPerfect web page document and it will display in the web browser, so long as the browser's computer also has the same fonts.

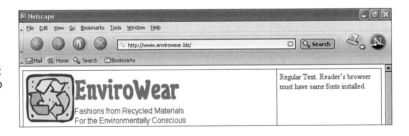

The only catch is a fairly significant one—the computer on which the web page is viewed must also have the same font(s) installed. If it doesn't, the web browser automatically chooses an alternative (usually Arial, Times, or Courier) to approximate the basic style of the web page font.

If you really need a specific font for a title or letterhead, for example, you can try these options:

21

- *Create the text in the Draw program*—Choose Insert, Graphics, Draw Picture, and then use the Draw tools to create a text image. Copy the image while in the draw program, return to WordPerfect, and then paste it into the document. If instead you just return from Draw, WordPerfect inserts the entire editing area into your document, including lots of white space. Text created this way is somewhat difficult to manage in terms of size and position, but fonts and colors are usually quite true to the original.

- *Create the text as a graphic image using TextArt*—If you want more options for the final look of the text, this feature works well. Note that colors don't always translate well from TextArt images to the Web. However, such images are easier to size and position than those created in Draw.

- *Create the text in any graphics program and save it in any file format (for example, JPG or PCX)*—Then, insert the image into your document just as you do any other graphic. This method is useful if you want to use the graphic over again, and depending on the graphics program you use, might give you more control over the final look of the text.

**NOTE**

> Although WordPerfect text boxes are positioned and otherwise act like graphics boxes, the contents are still text, and thus the use of fonts is still limited by what's available in the user's browser.

→ To learn how to create text as graphics, **see** "Creating TextArt," **p. 446.**

Standard HTML uses special heading styles to designate sections and subsections of a document. Such headings are distinguished by bold, larger text. Neophyte web page creators sometimes mistakenly use these headings to emphasize text, when they really should be used just to give structure to the document. Screen readers, in particular, key in on these structural elements to help blind readers navigate through documents.

WordPerfect has no equivalent structural style. The Heading styles in WordPerfect don't look anything like HTML Heading styles, nor do they lend structure to a web page (see Figure 21.10). Nevertheless, WordPerfect's Heading styles can be used to automatically generate a linked Table of Contents, as described in the "Using Hyperlinks" section later in this chapter.

You can create styles that simulate HTML Headings following the specifications in Table 21.1 (refer also to Figure 21.10).

**NOTE**

> When choosing a font size, whether in a style or in regular text, you should use Relative Size instead of a fixed-point size. Although the font sizes listed in Table 21.1 typically translate from 24 points for Extra Large to 8 points for Fine, browsers sometimes interpret fonts based on a base font that might be larger or smaller than the typical 12-point normal font size.

21

**Figure 21.10**
HTML Heading Styles aren't anything like WordPerfect's Heading Styles.

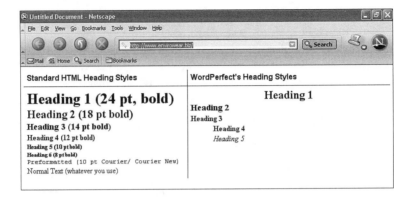

TABLE 21.1    HTML HEADING EQUIVALENTS IN WORDPERFECT

| HTML Style | WordPerfect Style |
| --- | --- |
| Heading One | Bold, Extra Large |
| Heading Two | Bold, Very Large |
| Heading Three | Bold, Large |
| Heading Four | Bold, Normal |
| Heading Five | Bold, Small |
| Heading Six | Bold, Fine |

→  To learn how to create styles and to use them in all of your Web, or other documents, **see** Chapter 9, "Formatting with Styles."

→  For information on using WordPerfect's Heading style to generate a linked Table of Contents, **see** "Using Hyperlinks," **p. 666.**

## USING OUTLINES AND BULLETS

Bullets and numbered lists are important tools for organizing information in any document. Since the inception of HTML, both bullets and outlines have been standard HTML features.

To create a bulleted list that looks very much like a typical web page bulleted list, follow these steps.

1. Choose Insert, Outline/Bullets & Numbering. WordPerfect displays the Bullets & Numbering dialog box.

2. Click the Bullets tab.

3. Click the Bullets style. There are several bullet styles shown, but only one that is named Bullets (see Figure 21.11).

4. Click OK to return to your document to begin using the Bullet style.

21

**Figure 21.11**
The Bullets style in WordPerfect's Bullets & Numbering dialog box is nearly equivalent to standard HTML bullets.

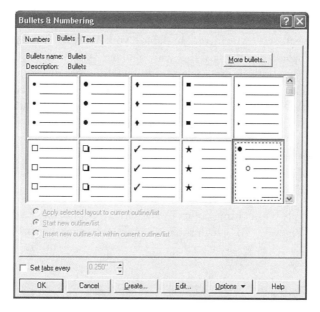

Use normal WordPerfect methods for creating outlines: Type text and press Enter to get a new bullet; before typing text press Tab to move to the right for a lower-level bullet; or press Shift+Tab to move to the left for a higher-level bullet.

→ To learn more about creating outlines using bullets or numbers, **see** Chapter 11, "Organizing Information with Lists and Outlines."

To create a numbered outline, follow the same procedures as previously described for a bulleted list, but instead choose an outline style. By default, HTML outlines use Arabic numerals, but the implementation of true outlining is impossible in standard HTML code. WordPerfect, on the other hand, can create correctly formatted numbered outlines (see Figure 21.12, which shows both standard HTML and WordPerfect outlines).

**Figure 21.12**
WordPerfect enables you to create real numbered outlines, unlike standard HTML, which can only create numbered lists.

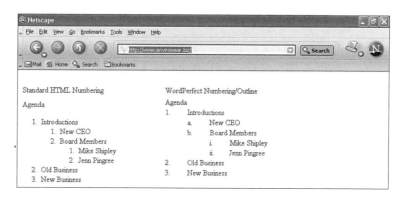

21

## USING COLLABORATION TOOLS

Considering the ease with which you can publish your WordPerfect documents to a company intranet, it would seem logical that you could use WordPerfect's collaboration tools to post documents for comment or review. Unfortunately, what you can do with collaborative markups is quite limited, and even then, those who view your web documents can't interactively revise them. Nevertheless, markups normally used for collaboration can be effective in highlighting and presenting supplementary information.

Some tools, which normally generate markup text automatically in WordPerfect, don't work when creating documents for the Web. For example, if you want to display strikeout text, you must select the text and apply the strikeout attribute in the Font Properties dialog box. For Redline text, you must select it, and change the font color to red. Likewise, you can select text and apply highlighting colors to give the effect of being marked with a colored highlighter (see Figure 21.13, which shows several types of markups).

**Figure 21.13**
Although you can manually mark up text in WordPerfect and display those marking in web documents, true automatic or collaborative markup is very limited.

Comment bubble

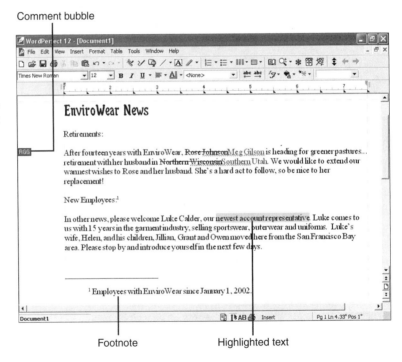

Footnote    Highlighted text

One collaborative tool that is quite nicely implemented, and which can be quite useful for presenting supplementary material, is the Comment feature. Simply position the insertion point where you want the comment, and then choose Insert, Comment, Create. Create the comment, including name, initials, date, or time, and then close the Comment editing screen. On your web document, a small comment bubble appears. When the reader clicks it, a tiny window appears to display the contents of the comment. In Internet Explorer, the font of the comment box matches that of the document (see Figure 21.14). In Netscape, the font is always in the default Times Roman font.

**Figure 21.14**
WordPerfect comments are used in HTML documents for comments as well as for footnotes or endnotes.

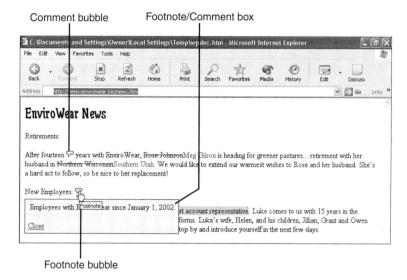

Comment bubble

Footnote/Comment box

Footnote bubble

Footnotes and endnotes also convert to Comments, instead of appearing as linked footnote/endnote numbers and jumping to a separate footnote/endnote area (refer to Figure 21.14). Comment bubbles are white, whereas Footnote/Endnote bubbles are yellow.

**NOTE**

When you publish your document, you have the option of publishing comments or not. The default is to include comments.

## WORKING WITH GRAPHICS

Early Internet information systems such as Gopher relied entirely on text. One of the features that helped vault the World Wide Web to its current preeminence is its capability to include visual images in web documents.

WordPerfect also has long been able to neatly integrate text and graphics to present information more powerfully than was possible with plain-text documents. To insert a graphic image in a WordPerfect web document, simply use whatever method you normally use to insert clip art or images from files.

However, the fine-tuned control one has over graphics in WordPerfect is largely lost in typical HTML documents. Graphic images can be left or right justified, but any other positioning is difficult to manage with any precision. The following are some of the options and considerations for positioning graphic images on your web page:

**21**

- By default, WordPerfect anchors graphic images to the page. However, both page-anchored and paragraph-anchored images behave the same in a WordPerfect web page.

- If you drag a page- or paragraph-anchored image to any position to the right of center, it will end up flush with the right margin. Anything positioned left of center will appear flush with the left margin (see Figure 21.15).

**Figure 21.15**
You're limited to left and right alignment of page- or paragraph-anchored graphic images. WordPerfect inserts blank space between text lines to accommodate character-anchored images.

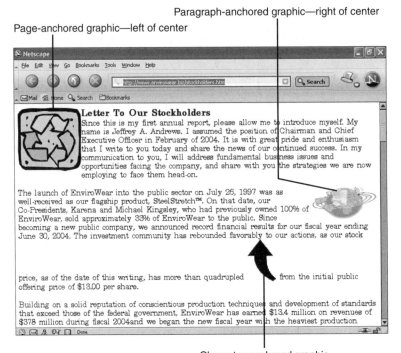

Paragraph-anchored graphic—right of center

Page-anchored graphic—left of center

Character-anchored graphic

- Vertically, the top of the image aligns with the top of the paragraph in which it's located in both page- and paragraph-anchored graphics.

- Text wraps around both page- and paragraph-anchored graphic images.

- Character-anchored images appear at the same horizontal location as the character to which they're attached.

- Text does not wrap around character-anchored images, unless you have vertically centered the image on the anchor character. Instead, WordPerfect inserts space between the lines of text to accommodate the image (refer to Figure 21.15).

- Most other options found in the Box Position dialog box have little or no effect on where the image will appear on the web page.

**CAUTION**

> Be sure to test pages that contain graphics in various browsers and platforms to make sure the results are what you want. For example, a lower-resolution screen will wrap the text to fit in the narrower screen margins, but the page-anchored images still appear at the right or left.

**TIP FROM**

*Read Gilgen*

> You might have some success in positioning an image by anchoring it to a character, and using Tab to move it to the right. Remember, however, that the real position can vary from browser to browser.

You can insert nearly any type of graphic image into your document, and when you publish your document to HTML, WordPerfect converts the images into one of two accepted formats, JPG or GIF. For example, although WPG (WordPerfect) graphics cannot be viewed in web browsers, you can choose to convert them to GIF images, which browsers can understand.

**NOTE**

> JPG stands for Joint Photographic Experts Group and is pronounced jay-peg. GIF stands for Graphics Interchange Format, developed by CompuServe, and is pronounced GIF (as in gift) or JIF (as in jiffy), depending on your preference.

WordPerfect also uses special styles to attach graphics box captions to images (see Figure 21.16). If you've ever considered creating captions in standard HTML, you can just sit back and be amazed that WordPerfect accomplishes this impossible task so elegantly.

→ To learn more about adding captions to graphics boxes, **see** "Making WordPerfect Text Work with Graphic Objects," **p. 396.**

The final step in preparing graphic images for the Web is to set their properties. Right-click an image and choose HTML Properties. WordPerfect then displays the HTML Properties dialog box (see Figure 21.17).

**NOTE**

> You can access the HTML Properties box *only* by right-clicking the image and selecting from the QuickMenu. The option does not appear on any other menu or toolbar.

In the HTML Properties dialog box you find these options:

- On the Image tab, you can add Alternate Text. This is the text that displays if users have graphics turned off in their browsers. Perhaps more importantly, it's the text used by screen readers to tell blind readers what the graphic image is all about. Don't simply say "Picture" or "Logo." Use more descriptive phrases such as "The EnviroWear Logo" or "John Smith receiving his retirement award."

**21**

**Figure 21.16**
WordPerfect even attaches graphics box captions to images when you publish them to HTML.

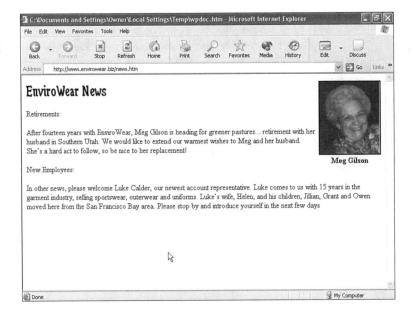

**Figure 21.17**
The HTML Properties dialog box lets you add Alternate Text and hyperlinks to an image, and specify its graphic format.

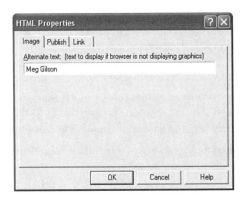

■ On the Publish tab, you can specify the format to which the graphic image is to be converted. By default, WordPerfect uses the GIF format, but you can also select the JPG format.

**NOTE**

Which graphic format is better for publishing to the Web? If your image consists mostly of line art, with mostly sharp edges and few colors, the GIF format usually is better. However, if the image has photo-like characteristics, with broad tonal ranges, the JPG format is preferred. However, either format generally will do the trick. JPG images sometimes are slightly smaller and thus download more quickly than GIF images.

21

- On the Link tab, you can specify a bookmark or another web document to which you can link the image. See the next section for a more complete description of how to link graphic images.

If you're like me, creating just the right graphic image for web pages really isn't an option because we just don't have the necessary artistic skills. Fortunately, there are plenty of resources for good graphic images, including the following:

- WordPerfect's clip art—WordPerfect ships with more than 10,000 clip art images.

  → For information on finding and adding these images to your web page, **see** Chapter 12, "Adding Graphics to Documents."

- Images you modify using Corel Presentations—Although you might not find exactly the image you want as a clip art image, you should look at each clip art image as a collection of images. For example, you want a pair of blue jeans. None of the images are of just blue jeans, but one of the images shows a teenager wearing blue jeans. You can use Presentations to edit the image, removing everything except what you want. You then save just the image as its own WPG graphics file.

  → For information on manipulating and customizing clip art images by using the Draw program, **see** "Editing WordPerfect Graphics in Presentations," **p. 440.**

- Images you create using Corel Presentations—If you have a specific layout of graphics and text that you can't seem to replicate in a WordPerfect web page, you can create the layout in Presentations, and then group the objects in the layout and save them as an image that you then can insert into your web page.

  You can save Presentations graphics in the standard WordPerfect (WPG) format, or use Save As to save them as GIF or JPG images. The key is to select the image first, and then save just the image, not the entire Presentations drawing screen.

**NOTE**

> Because of a bug in WordPerfect 11/12, text portions of drawings created in Presentations do not always convert properly when published to HTML. You should experiment but don't waste a lot of time trying to make text work when it simply will not do so.

- Images from other web sites—Often, while browsing the Web, you find just the image you'd like to use on your web page. Capturing and using graphic images from other web sites is quick and easy. Simply right-click the image in your browser, and from the QuickMenu, choose the option that enables you to save the image. Note where you save the image and its name, and then insert the image in your WordPerfect document.

**CAUTION**

> Just because you can capture an image from the Web doesn't mean that it's legal to do so. Copyright laws apply to published materials on the Web, just as they do to printed materials. If you have questions about whether you can use an image, you should contact the owner of the web page and ask permission.

21

**TIP FROM**

*Read Gilgen*

Many web sites provide collections of free clip art, including graphic lines, buttons, bullets, and more. Two places to look are at the Netscape and Microsoft web sites. You can also use any search engine, such as Google or Yahoo!, to find clip art sites.

Sizing web page graphics can affect the quality of the graphic when it's displayed in a web browser. In particular, bitmap graphics, such as GIF and JPG, distort badly unless they appear in their original size. WPG graphics can be sized any way you like because they don't convert to bitmap graphics until you publish the web page to HTML.

To ensure that a bitmap graphic remains at its proper size, follow these steps:

1. Select the graphic image.

2. Right-click the image and choose Size from the QuickMenu. WordPerfect displays the Box Size dialog box (see Figure 21.18).

**Figure 21.18**
You can use the Box Size dialog box to allow graphic images to display proportionally.

3. Choose Maintain Proportions for both the width and height, and click OK.

If you then find that the image is too large or too small, you really have no other option but to risk distortion by changing its size or re-creating the bitmap image in the proper size.

**TIP FROM**

*Read Gilgen*

If you save a Corel Presentations graphic image as a GIF or JPG file, try to specify the exact dimensions you will need so you won't have to distort the image after inserting it into your WordPerfect web page document.

## USING HYPERLINKS

The real power of the World Wide Web lies in the reader's capability to follow hyperlinks (usually referred to simply as links) to quickly jump from one location to another. Whether people who visit your site jump to another spot within the same web document, to another document at the same web site, or to an entirely different web site anywhere else in the world is all the same.

**21**

➔ For complete information on creating hyperlinks, **see** "Creating Hypertext Links," **p. 622**, and "Creating Links to the Internet," **p. 628.**

The methods for creating links in a web document are identical to those described in Chapter 20, "Interactive and Multimedia Documents." Consider the following:

- You can create links from text or graphics objects. The user jumps by clicking on the text or object.

- Internal links enable a reader to jump to another location in the same document. You first create bookmarks, and then create links to those bookmarks.

- External links enable a reader to jump to another web document, either one of yours or anywhere else on the Web.

  Typical external links include the following:

  - Links to a URL using the `http://` protocol (for example, `http://www.envirowear.biz`)

  - Links to an e-mail address using `mailto:` (for example, `mailto:sales@envirowear.biz`)

  - Links to an FTP site to download a file (for example, `ftp://supportfiles.envirowear.biz`)

To add a hyperlink to text, simply select the text, choose Tools, Hyperlink, and in the Hyperlink Properties dialog box specify the target document or bookmark.

**TIP FROM**

*Read Gilgen*

Don't forget that WordPerfect's QuickLink feature enables you to create a text link simply by typing a URL, an e-mail address, or an FTP site, followed by a space.

**NOTE**

The Target Frame option is designed to enable you to specify which frame of a web page frameset will display a link when clicked. The web document you create with WordPerfect must be one of the frames of the web page frameset. However, the actual frameset web page (for example, `index.htm`) must be created with a text editor such as Notepad, or a web page editor. WordPerfect cannot create frame-based web pages.

**TIP FROM**

*Read Gilgen*

Although intended to be used with frame-based web pages, the Target Frame option can be used to open a new instance of the browser, leaving the original copy of the browser open displaying the original WordPerfect page. Simply supply any name in the Target Frame text box.

21

You can also create links to graphic images. Suppose, for example, you want to display a gallery of your newest EnviroWear fashions, but you also want the reader to have complete information about each of the items in the gallery. Instead of presenting the pictures and descriptions all in one location, you can hyperlink the graphic image of the product to another location in the document that fully describes the product.

To link an image, follow these steps:

1. Create the target bookmark or determine the location of the target document.

2. Click the image to select it.

3. Choose Tools, Hyperlink. WordPerfect displays the Hyperlink Properties dialog box (see Figure 21.19).

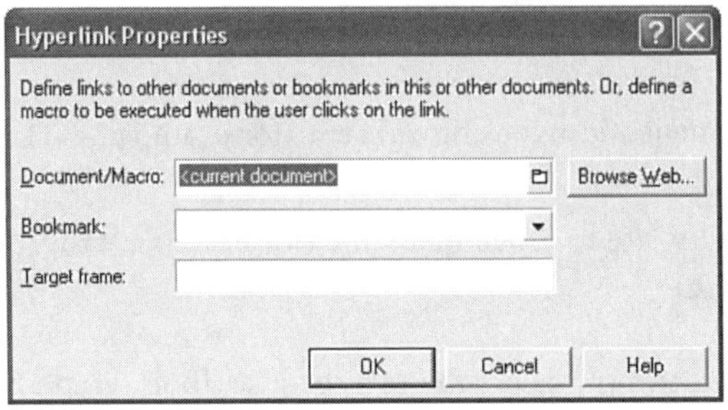

**Figure 21.19**
You can use the Hyperlink Properties dialog box to link not only text, but also graphic images.

Hyperlink Properties

Define links to other documents or bookmarks in this or other documents. Or, define a macro to be executed when the user clicks on the link.

Document/Macro: <current document>    Browse Web...

Bookmark:

Target frame:

OK    Cancel    Help

4. Specify the target bookmark or document and click OK.

Although the graphic image is now linked to a target, WordPerfect does not add any visual markers to the graphic to let you know it is linked. However, when viewed in a browser, the mouse pointer turns to a hand to indicate the image is linked.

**CAUTION**

After you add a hyperlink to an image, you can edit or change the link, but you cannot easily remove it. To remove a link, you must activate the Hyperlink Tools toolbar and click the Hyperlink Remove button. Otherwise, you must delete the graphic image and insert it again.

Although the procedure for creating links is relatively simple, remember that you must organize your document in such a way that the reader doesn't get lost after clicking a hyperlink. You need to include more navigational aids, such as a main menu or Table of Contents, and additional hyperlinks throughout the document that enable the reader to jump back to the main menu.

Although you can create a text menu and add hyperlinks that jump to various sections of your document, you can also use WordPerfect's Heading styles to help generate a Table of Contents. To create an automatically linked Table of Contents, follow these steps:

1. Mark each section with an appropriate Heading style (refer to Figure 21.10, which shows what each of WordPerfect's Heading styles looks like).

2. Position the cursor where you want the Table of Contents to appear, typically somewhere near the top of the document. You might even add "Table of Contents" and mark it as a major heading.

3. Choose Tools, Reference, Table of Contents. WordPerfect displays the Table of Contents dialog box (see Figure 21.20).

**Figure 21.20**
The Table of Contents dialog box displays buttons for defining and generating a Table of Contents.

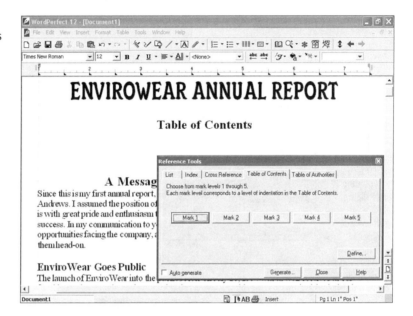

4. Click the Define button on the Table of Contents dialog box and WordPerfect displays the Define Table of Contents dialog box (see Figure 21.21).

5. Indicate the number of levels of Heading styles you have used (indicate "5" if you're not sure). The numbering style doesn't matter. Click OK.

6. Click the Generate button on the Table of Contents dialog box. WordPerfect displays the Generate dialog box (see Figure 21.22).

7. Be sure the Build Hyperlinks box is checked and then click OK.

WordPerfect automatically generates a table of contents as shown in Figure 21.23. However, when you publish the document to HTML, the Table of Contents appears as shown in Figure 21.24.

→ For more information on marking, defining, and generating a Table of Contents, **see** "Creating a Table of Contents," **p. 593.**

21

**Figure 21.21**
Use the Define Table of Contents dialog box to indicate how many Heading style levels you want to include in your Table of Contents. Choosing a particular style is not important.

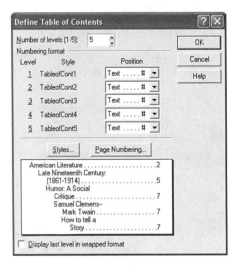

**Figure 21.22**
Select the Build Hyperlinks option in the Generate dialog box so that WordPerfect can automatically create a hyperlinked Table of Contents.

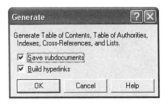

**Figure 21.23**
A WordPerfect Table of Contents uses the style you choose, and adds hyperlinks only to the page numbers.

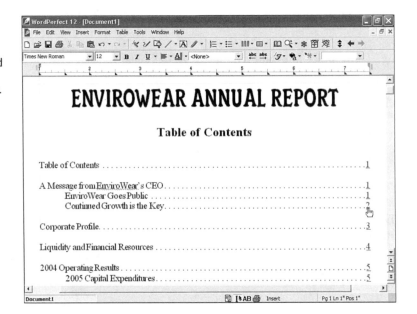

21

**Figure 21.24**
When published to HTML and viewed in a web browser, a WordPerfect Table of Contents appears as hyperlinked section headings, without page numbers.

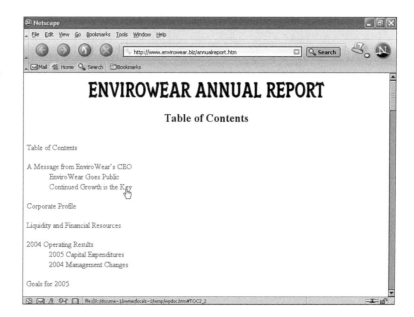

Getting from the Table of Contents to various sections of the document is one part of the navigation process. The other is getting back to the Table of Contents, or top of the document. One particularly useful tool for doing this is the Graphics Shapes option, which enables you to insert action buttons that serve as navigation tools for the reader. To create a hyperlinked action button, follow these steps:

1. Choose Insert, Shapes to display the Draw Object Shapes dialog box.
2. Click the Action Buttons radio button.
3. Click the shapes palette to see a selection of action button types (see Figure 21.25).
4. Choose the button type you want, and click OK.

**Figure 21.25**
Action button shapes can be quite useful for navigating a web document when used with hyperlinks.

5. In the location where you want the button, click and drag to create the size and shape button you want.

6. With the button still selected, choose Tools, Hyperlink, and select the target bookmark or document.

7. Click OK to add the hyperlink to the action button.

**TIP FROM**

*Read Gilgen*

Don't forget that you can easily change the color and other properties of an action button. Simply right-click the button and choose Properties.

Some readers like the visual cues that action buttons provide. But others prefer textual cues. Consider adding hyperlinked text—for example, "Return to the Main Menu." Then, with the action button selected, access the Graphics Position dialog box to anchor the action button to a character, and position the image so that the button aligns with the bottom of the text (see Figure 21.26).

**Figure 21.26**
Navigation links from inside a document back to the top or to a main menu help readers avoid having to read a document sequentially, from beginning to end.

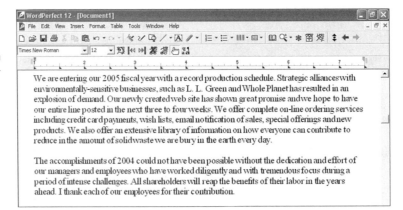

**NOTE**

Don't forget that blind readers need navigation assistance, too! For graphic images, be sure to add alternative text in the HTML Properties dialog box by right-clicking the button and choosing HTML Properties.

## WORKING WITH TABLES

Tables can help you organize and effectively present information on your web pages, just as they can in any document. Consider the table in Figure 21.27, which shows how several different table options appear in Netscape or in Microsoft Internet Explorer.

→ To learn more about using various table features, **see** Chapter 10, "Working with Tables."

**Figure 21.27**
A WordPerfect table as displayed in Netscape or in Internet Explorer.

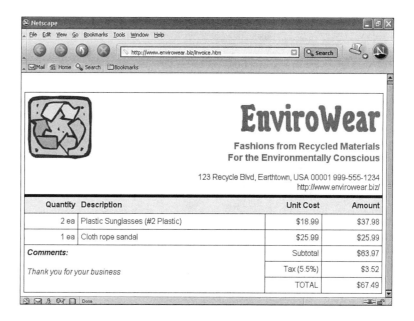

When using tables, consider the following as they apply to the most recent versions of Netscape or Internet Explorer. How tables display in other browsers, including older versions of Netscape and Internet Explorer, may vary.

- Table lines appear in as they do in WordPerfect, including lines of varying thickness.

- Changes in column width display properly in both browsers. Changes in Row Height display only in Internet Explorer, unless such changes are the result of expansion to accommodate text.

- By default, WordPerfect tables are fully justified. Thus, the Web version also extends from margin to margin, regardless of the size of the browser screen. Columns shrink or expand proportionally to fit the table into the screen. However, if you change the table format to left, center, or right justified, the table width remains fixed, extending beyond the edge of the browser screen if the table is too large to fit.

- Table borders don't always appear in browsers the way they do in WordPerfect, especially the fancier line styles. Some table borders replicate perfectly.

- Cell colors, or backgrounds, display in solid colors only. Gradient shading or patterns are converted to a solid color.

- Math formulas do not function in tables published to HTML, although the text of the numeric values does appear.

- Most other table features do not convert to HTML, such as skewed cells, rotated text, or diagonal lines.

**21**

**TIP FROM**

*Read Gilgen*

You can use a table to simulate text columns on a web page. For example, to create a two-column format, you create a table with only one row and two columns. You place all the text for the first column in cell A1, and the text for the second column in B1. You then format the table so that it does not display table borders.

**CAUTION**

Very old browsers often did not support viewing of tables, but most browsers today do. However, certain screen readers for the visually impaired read tables horizontally, row by row. If you use tables, consider whether the flow of information in them will make sense to all visitors to your web page.

# PUBLISHING TO HTML

The moment of truth has arrived. You've worked long and hard to get your web page ready, and now it's time to put it on a web server for the whole world to see.

The steps for publishing your document to HTML are quite simple, with relatively few options. Follow these steps:

1. Do a final check of your document for content (spelling, for example) and layout (are things where they're supposed to be?). Check links in your browser. Do they jump where they're supposed to?

2. Save your WordPerfect document one last time.

3. Choose File, Publish to HTML. WordPerfect displays the Publish to HTML dialog box (see Figure 21.28).

**Figure 21.28**
Publishing a document to HTML is quite simple, using the Publish to HTML dialog box.

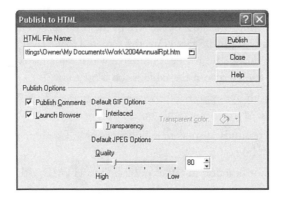

4. Type the name of the web page, ending it with .htm or .html, both of which are required filename extensions for web documents.

5. Choose from the following options:

- Publish Comments—If you want readers to be able to see document comments, leave this box checked. A small bubble icon appears on the web page for each comment and the reader clicks it to see the comment in a separate comment box or window.

- Launch Browser—If you want WordPerfect to open your saved document in your default browser to see how it looks, choose this option. If your document includes graphic images, choosing this option might be useful to make sure that the images exported and were saved correctly.

- Default GIF Options—If you're exporting any files as GIF images, these options will apply. Interlaced is a method whereby every other scan line of the image is displayed in the browser, followed by the remaining, or interlaced, lines. This option might be helpful for persons with very slow connections, but with today's speedier Web connections, this isn't too terribly important. Transparency means that a solid background color—such as the space in a photo around a person's head—appears transparent, thus allowing background text to show through that space. If you select this option, you also must choose the color that will be transparent. If you use a separate graphics program, you may have already set the image's transparency.

- Default JPG Options—You can reduce the size, and also the download time, of JPG graphics by reducing the image's quality. Extremely high quality—for example, 100%—doesn't usually make much difference on a computer screen, which already has limited resolution. However, although extremely low resolution might result in smaller files, the quality of such images will also suffer.

6. Click Publish and WordPerfect converts your document into HTML code, using styles.

WordPerfect also converts your graphic images to the format you have selected (JPG and/or GIF). To change the selected graphic output format, right-click the image, choose HTML Properties, click the Publish tab, and choose the desired format (see Figure 21.29).

**Figure 21.29**
When saving a document to HTML, you can specify the format of the document's graphic images in the HTML Properties dialog box.

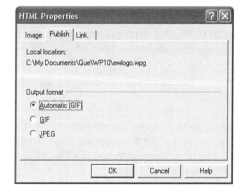

21

WordPerfect places converted images in a folder by the same name as the web page you just created. For example, if the document name is `myfile.htm`, graphic images are saved in the myfile folder, a subfolder of the one where `myfile.htm` is located. If the folder doesn't already exist, WordPerfect creates it.

**CAUTION**

When publishing to HTML a document that contains graphic images, the filename without an extension must not already be in use (for example, as the name of another document in the same folder). If it's already being used, WordPerfect doesn't report a problem, but images are not converted because the folder where they must be stored cannot be created. The result is that you won't be able to see the images when you view your document in a browser.

## MOVING FILES TO A WEB SERVER

You're now ready to transfer the published files to your web server. If you haven't done so already, you should contact your web server administrator and determine the exact procedures required for moving your web documents to the server. Two options are most common:

- If you're lucky, you might be able to publish your documents directly to a local or network drive. Many corporate intranets, for example, permit you to save documents directly on network drives that are accessible with a browser. Your Webmaster can tell you where to save your files and whether you need special access rights to such locations.

- If you transfer your files to a remote computer, you often do so using FTP, or File Transfer Protocol. This process involves establishing a connection over the network or by modem to the remote computer and then using FTP software to transfer the files. Your Webmaster can provide you with the necessary login and password information, as well as details as to where to save your files.

**NOTE**

Because all access to a remote server involves some security risk, Webmasters often establish security procedures that can complicate a simple FTP transfer. Consider this a necessary inconvenience that ensures the future integrity of your server and your documents.

**CAUTION**

When publishing a document that contains images, make sure that you transfer both the document *and* the images, and that the images are stored in a subfolder with the same name as the web document. Otherwise, the world will be able to see only the document, without the graphic images.

21

*If your web page has missing graphic images, see "Where, Oh Where, Is That Graphics File?" in the Troubleshooting section at the end of this chapter.*

**TIP FROM**

*Read Gilgen*

If you've already published your web page before and are merely updating it, and if the page's graphic images haven't changed, you need not transfer the images again to the web server.

## MODIFYING OR UPDATING PUBLISHED HTML DOCUMENTS

Instead of revising published HTML documents, WordPerfect's approach is to focus on the original WordPerfect document. Because you're working with the original, you have much greater control over the editing process. You then republish the document to HTML, replacing the earlier HTML version. For most of us, this is the easiest and most easily understood approach.

However, in some cases, you might need to tweak your published HTML document by inserting custom HTML code. For example, you might want to give the document a special background, or wallpaper, which you can't do from within WordPerfect.

To modify the code of an HTML document, open it in a plain-text editor, such as Windows Notepad, or in a specialized HTML editor such as DreamWeaver. Make the necessary changes and save the file.

**NOTE**

If you make changes to a published HTML document using another program, such changes will be lost if you then use WordPerfect to edit the original WordPerfect document and republish it.

In earlier versions of WordPerfect, you could open HTML documents and edit them in WordPerfect. The design of WordPerfect 11/12 makes this impractical, because the special formatting styles used in such documents sometimes do not translate well back to WordPerfect. For example, original automatic features, such as outline numbering or table formulas, are lost. Nevertheless, WordPerfect does do a pretty good job of converting primarily text-based documents, preserving most fonts and formatting.

# PUBLISHING TO PDF

HTML-based web pages are still the most common method of publishing and viewing web documents. However, other options do exist for getting your documents out to the world. WordPerfect includes two of these: publishing to PDF and using eXtensible Markup Language (XML) and Standard Graphics Markup Language (SGML). Publishing to PDF is becoming increasingly common and can be performed right from within WordPerfect.

→ For information on using XML in WordPerfect, **see** Chapter 22, "Working with XML Documents."

Adobe's PDF, or Portable Document Format, is the process by which you create documents that exactly match the original in terms of layout, fonts, and special effects. Readers can view these documents with the free Adobe Acrobat Reader, and thus they are not required to have WordPerfect installed on their system.

**NOTE**

Adobe Acrobat Reader is a free reader that understands PDF-formatted documents. Many web sites routinely publish documents in PDF format, and many users already have installed Acrobat Reader. They might see it only as an automatic plug-in to their web browser, but they can also start the program from the Start, All Programs menu. Also, just double-clicking a PDF document in the Windows Explorer automatically starts Acrobat Reader and views the PDF document.

## PREPARING DOCUMENTS FOR PDF

Nearly anything you create in a WordPerfect document is faithfully reproduced in a PDF document. If you're publishing a fairly long document to PDF, consider the following:

- Use heading styles, and create bookmarks throughout your document to provide a list of bookmarks for Adobe's Acrobat Reader.
- Create a Table of Contents, using hyperlinks to section headings. These will appear as clickable links in the PDF document.
- Create other hyperlinks to aid readers as they navigate the PDF document.

Before you publish your document, also make sure it's as complete and correct as you can. A PDF document is only as good as the content used to produce it.

To publish a WordPerfect document to PDF format, follow these steps:

1. Save the document one last time in WordPerfect format. You might need to come back to the original version later.
2. Choose File, Publish to PDF. WordPerfect displays the Publish to PDF dialog box (see Figure 21.30).
3. Specify the name of the PDF file in the Publish to File edit box. Typically, this is the name of the WordPerfect file, with a .pdf filename extension.
4. Click OK to publish the file to the PDF format.

## CHOOSING PDF OPTIONS

The Publish to PDF dialog box offers a wide variety of options, primarily designed to help you fine-tune the PDF document for its intended use. For example, you can choose from three predefined settings, which further change other settings in the PDF dialog box:

**Figure 21.30**
Use the Publish to PDF dialog box to create documents that anyone can read using the Adobe Acrobat Reader.

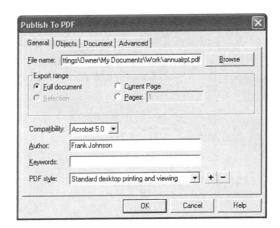

- Standard Desktop Printing and Viewing—This gives you a high-quality document, but options are chosen that help reduce the size of the file. For example, a 30K WordPerfect file with graphics and links might result in a 35K PDF file.

- Highest Quality—This style uses the most options, including embedding all of the fonts in the PDF document. The result can be a much larger file. For example, a 30K WordPerfect file might result in a 180K PDF file. Although such files take much longer to download from a web site, the recipient of the file has more options in terms of the quality and the interactivity of the file.

- Smallest File—This style uses the most aggressive optimizing options to result in a small file, which can be downloaded quickly. Such files also can be viewed in Acrobat Reader version 3, but many quality and navigation options are lost. Using this style, for example, a 30K WordPerfect file might result in a 28K PDF file.

Other options on the General tab of the Publish to PDF dialog box include the capability to publish all or part of a document, to make it compatible with older versions (3 or 4) of Acrobat Reader, and to add author and keyword information.

Unless you change the filename, WordPerfect saves the file with the same name as the original, but with the .pdf filename extension. WordPerfect publishes PDF documents so quickly that it's easy to think nothing has happened. You can verify the PDF format by starting Adobe Acrobat Reader and opening the PDF file you just created (see Figure 21.31).

**CAUTION**

Although WordPerfect's implementation of the Adobe Acrobat standards is very good at converting your WordPerfect documents to PDF format, not everything converts perfectly. For example, some spacing between characters isn't perfect. Before you distribute the PDF version of your documents, you should check it both onscreen and by printing a page or two to make sure you can live with these minor problems.

21

**Figure 21.31**
The Adobe Acrobat Reader enables anyone, even non-WordPerfect users, to see your documents exactly as you intend them to appear. Readers can easily zoom in or out, print, or even use hyperlinks or bookmarks if you include them.

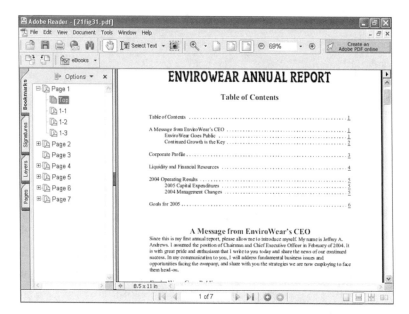

Although you can stay with the three default PDF styles, you can also choose various options to make your PDF document better meet your needs. Among the options found on the other three tabs of the Publish to PDF dialog box are

- Text and Fonts—You can embed fonts in the document if you want to be sure that all computers can view them properly. You can also have Adobe convert fonts to other types, such as Adobe's Type 1 fonts, and you can even specify that font characters are exported only for those characters actually used. Finally, you can specify that fonts should be treated as graphics (or *curves* as Adobe calls it), if for some reason the other options aren't satisfactory.

- Compression—You can specify whether to compress text and line art, and choose the type of bitmap compression from among LZW, ZIP, JPG, or none. The default is JPG compression, and with it you can further specify the resulting image quality.

- Document Options—You can specify whether to display hyperlinks or not, and how Acrobat Reader should start up when displaying the page: the page only, the page with a handy index of bookmarks, or a full screen with no Acrobat Reader menus. The default is Page Only.

- Advanced Options—You can specify whether the document should be optimized for the Web, whether to include embedded files, and what type of color output should be used: RGB, CMYK, Grayscale, or Native. The default is RGB, a basic color scheme.

You probably won't need to worry about these options because the standard PDF style combinations generally provide very satisfactory results.

21

## USING PDF DOCUMENTS ON THE WEB

Although PDF documents are useful in nearly any context, they are frequently used in place of web pages where formatting is of particular concern, such as with a company brochure or a newsletter.

You link to PDF documents just as you do with other HTML documents. Select the text or image you want viewers to click on, and create a hyperlink to the PDF document. Just make sure that the PDF document is transferred to the web server along with your HTML pages.

When users click a link to a PDF document, if Acrobat Reader is already installed on their computer, their web browser automatically starts Adobe Acrobat Reader and displays the document within the browser.

Users can also right-click the PDF link and download the PDF document to their own computer. They can then use Acrobat Reader to open and view the document.

**TIP FROM**

If you want to make sure all users can read PDF documents on your web site, consider placing a note along with a link to the Adobe web site where users can download and install the free Adobe Acrobat Reader.

# TROUBLESHOOTING

### RIGHT-SIZING GRAPHICS

*I'm using a graphic I created in Corel Presentations, but although it looks fine on my screen in WordPerfect, it looks lousy in my web browser.*

Bitmap graphics, such as GIF and JPG, cannot be enlarged without creating display problems. When you save a Corel Presentations image as a GIF or JPG file, specify the exact size you need on your web page so you don't have to change the size of the graphic in WordPerfect.

Further, a bug in WordPerfect 11/12 prevents most text created in Presentations from displaying properly in HTML pages. Consider publishing documents to PDF if such text is absolutely critical to your web page.

### SAVING AS HTML

*When I view my web page in a browser, I see lots of strange characters on the screen—they begin with WPC—but I don't understand anything after that.*

If you save your web page with the .htm or .html filename extension, but forget to publish it to the HTML format, that's what it will look like when viewed in a browser. Just open the file with WordPerfect and this time publish it to HTML.

### WHERE, OH WHERE, IS THAT GRAPHICS FILE?

*Everything looks good when I'm previewing my web page, but after I publish it, some of the graphics are missing.*

Several issues can affect your published web page. First, you must be sure that all elements of the page, including graphics, are published to the target location. If you manually copy or FTP files, you might miss a file. Second, when you publish the page, the web page references graphic images in a separate subfolder. If you place the images on the server in the same folder as the web page, the browser won't be able to find them. Finally, make sure the case of the filenames and locations is correct. Most Unix-based web servers distinguish between upper- and lowercase, whereas Windows does not. If your web page says to use Image.gif, and the name of the file on the server is image.gif, the server won't know what file to use.

### ALL BROWSERS ARE NOT CREATED EQUAL

*My web page looks good when I view it in my browser, but my friend says parts of it are messed up when she looks at it on the Web.*

Not all browsers view the same HTML code in the same way. For example, even different versions of Netscape or Internet Explorer can view a page differently. If users are viewing your page on a Macintosh, or if they're using Internet Explorer and you're using Netscape Navigator, they might get different results. As a web page creator, you should take the time to view your page in different browsers (usually Netscape Navigator and Internet Explorer) and on different platforms (PC and Mac), and then make adjustments to your page if possible so it looks good on all of them. If what you want to accomplish on your page just won't work in other browsers, you should note that on your page by including a link to the viewer download site that says something such as, "This page is best viewed using SuprBrowz. Click here to download the free viewer."

Finally, consider using Publish to PDF if an exact replica of your WordPerfect file is required.

# PROJECT

As noted several times in this chapter, one of your biggest challenges in creating web pages is to recognize the limitations of HTML in formatting things to look like what you're used to seeing in WordPerfect. Even features that seem to be available in WordPerfect might not work in all situations.

One example is the alignment of text in columns. Although you can format your document using newspaper style columns (by choosing Format, Columns), WordPerfect ignores column formatting when you publish your document to HTML.

Nevertheless, you still can create the effect of columns that both Netscape Navigator and Internet Explorer can display. You do this by creating a table with a single row, and as many columns as you want. Although this effect is most useful with columns of data, such as two columns of bulleted items, you can use it to simulate newspaper-style columns as well.

**CAUTION**

> Generally, tables should be used only for data, and then only when using proper table headings. Tables should not be used for text layout because screen readers don't know how to present such information to blind readers. The example here, however, works because screen readers read all of one cell and then move to the next cell to the right and read all of the text of that cell. Thus, the flow of text is exactly the same as if you were using newspaper-style columns.

Consider the list shown in Figure 21.32. Because it's a long list, the user has to scroll the web page to see it in its entirety. If you place this list inside a table, it spreads out horizontally for easier access.

**Figure 21.32**
A long list is difficult to use because the user has to scroll to see it all.

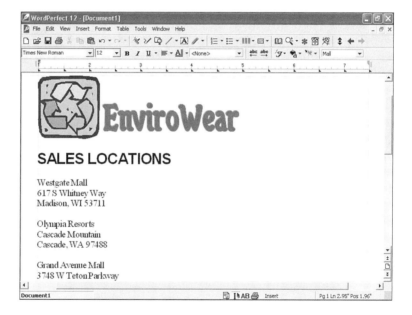

To create columns by using a table, simply create a table with just one row and the number of columns you need (for example, three). Also consider the following:

- Remove lines from the table so that the text appears to be in columns. Choose Table, Borders/Fill and on the Table tab, change Default Cell Lines to None.
- If you're placing text inside a table, you can cut and paste it into the cells. For newspaper-style columns, you have to determine how much text goes in each column because, unlike regular WordPerfect columns, WordPerfect can't calculate this for you.

- You can create irregular column widths by changing the table columns. However, because WordPerfect's default is to fully justify tables, the columns will automatically increase or decrease to fit your browser. If you want more precise column measurements, choose Table, Format, and on the Table tab, change Table Position to Left.

Using these tips, you can create a web page that looks like the one shown in Figure 21.33.

**Figure 21.33**
Tables can create the effect of columns in Netscape or Internet Explorer.

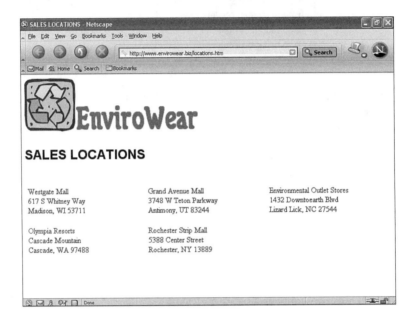

CHAPTER **22**

# WORKING WITH XML DOCUMENTS

**In this chapter**                                          *by Read Gilgen*

**22**

# UNDERSTANDING XML

XML. It seems to be all the rage these days. Nearly any up-to-date software product touts its XML capabilities as if you already knew what it is and why it's important to you. We can't promise that you'll understand XML completely by the time you finish this chapter, but we do hope you'll have a better idea as to what XML is, and how you can use it in practical ways.

In a nutshell, *XML is eXtensible Markup Language*, a method for defining document information and making it easy to transmit or reuse that information, without regard to proprietary software or operating systems.

## WHAT'S IN XML FOR YOU

Before jumping into definitions for XML, you probably want to know whether it's necessary or even worth the effort to learn about XML.

Honestly? For most individual work, using XML is of little intrinsic value or interest. If you work on your own, and creating really good-looking documents for printing is your primary use for WordPerfect, you really need not read much further, unless of course you'd like to know what the fuss is all about. If you're in an environment where sharing and reusing document information is important, you probably do need to know about XML. In any case, it's quite possible that someday XML will also be useful for the rest of us, so a quick tour of this chapter might be worth your time.

One of the great challenges in our information society is the proliferation, and repetition, of information. How many times have you created a document, only to find that someone needs the same information but they use a different word processor? Sometimes you have no common format other than the Web or a PDF version, both of which enable you to see the information, but offer virtually no capability to reuse that information directly.

Consider another example. You write the Great American Novel, and of course you publish it first in hard-bound form. It sells well, and the publisher now wants to make it available in paperback or even electronic formats. In the past, the publisher would have to spend a great deal of time reworking the document to adapt it to the new formats: with smaller type and different page layout for a paperback version, or with links and navigation tools for an electronic book or PDA version.

XML comes to the rescue by making it possible to reuse information without having to replicate or re-create it.

In XML, when you create your documents, you define the elements of the document in structured ways: book, chapters, sections, paragraphs, and so on. You then apply a definition document that interprets what those elements mean and how they should be used, and only then do you worry about how those elements are to be displayed.

Again, however, this probably isn't enough to drive you to use XML. More likely you've come to this chapter because your company is requiring you to create XML-compliant documents. In a multiuser environment, the reuse of information in a variety of contexts is probably the best argument for understanding and using XML.

Although XML can be quite complicated, how much you need to know about XML can vary widely from those who design the Document Type Definition files (a lot), to those who create the basic document information (not too much).

**NOTE**

> Working with XML involves new concepts and approaches to publishing a document. Before you try to learn how to use XML in WordPerfect, you should be thoroughly familiar with all WordPerfect basics. You should also be familiar with current Windows operating systems, including how to use Windows-based applications, how to browse for files, and so on.

## DEFINING XML

XML stands for eXtensible Markup Language, and it's a simpler, easier-to-use subset of SGML, or Standard Generalized Markup Language.

More likely you've heard of HTML, or Hypertext Markup Language. So how are these different? Consider the following snippet of code in HTML:

```
<html>
<body>
<h1>Working with XML</h1>
How are <i>HTML</i> and <i>XML</i> different?<p>
</body>
</html>
```

HTML uses *tags* to mark up the text, which then are translated by your Web browser to show such elements as heading styles (<h1>) and attributes such as italics (<i>). Anyone used to seeing WordPerfect's Reveal Codes recognizes the use of paired tags to turn on or off attributes or formatting features. HTML codes are standardized so that any web browser can read and interpret them. Their primary purpose is to help browsers *format* content. If you need to go beyond standard HTML definitions, you might be out of luck.

Now, consider the following snippet of XML code:

```
<fruitbasket>
<apples>Granny Smith</apples>
<pears>Bartlett</pears>
<grapes>Concord</grapes>
</fruitbasket>
```

None of these codes are anything you ever learned in an HTML class. Nevertheless, you'll note that this code is *well formed*. That is, each beginning tag has an ending tag, and each set of tags is properly nested within a hierarchical structure.

The problem, however, is that unless someone comes along to tell us what these tags mean, they aren't terribly useful. Fortunately, XML enables you to use or create definitions for its elements in separate files called *Document Type Definitions*, or *DTDs*. When an XML

**22**

document is paired with a DTD, and its elements match those of the DTD, it is said be valid. Proper XML must be both *well-formed* (without syntactic errors) and *valid* (elements in the right places as determined by the DTD).

> **NOTE**
>
> Several government and professional organizations have created their own standardized DTDs that facilitate the exchange of information in their particular arena. These include the DocBook DTDs designed for narrative and technical books, or the NITF for the newspaper industry.

## WORDPERFECT'S APPROACH TO XML

WordPerfect tries to make creating XML documents easier by offering the same familiar WordPerfect interface, along with a structured, yet simplified, XML editing environment.

In the XML domain, you typically must create a DTD, and then create an XML document using the elements defined in the DTD. You also have to validate your XML document, and then apply formatting layouts to it depending on how you want to use the document's information.

WordPerfect incorporates the same elements but a bit differently. Starting with a DTD, you compile the DTD, which becomes part of a WordPerfect template. You then create your document using a template. You can then use or create new layouts and quickly switch from one layout to another, all while using the same XML document.

# CREATING AN XML DOCUMENT

We're going to put the cart before the horse for a while. As noted previously, you need a DTD and a template before you can actually create an XML document. However, most of you won't ever need or want to worry about creating DTDs or templates. So we'll start with the assumption that someone else already has created these for you, and you're now ready to create a document.

## CHOOSING AN XML TEMPLATE

Fortunately, WordPerfect comes with a few sample templates. For example, to create a newsletter article from the XML template for news, follow these steps:

1. Choose File, New XML Document. WordPerfect displays the Select or Create an XML Project dialog box (see Figure 22.1).
2. Select a category/project from the left column, for example xmlnews.
3. In the XML Components column at the right, select the layout you want to work with. In this case, there are only two, so select xmlnews-n.
4. Click Select and WordPerfect displays a blank XML editing screen (see Figure 22.2).

**Figure 22.1**
You create an XML
document by selecting
an XML project based
on XML templates.

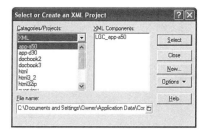

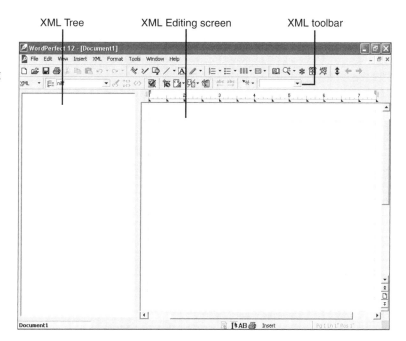

XML Tree          XML Editing screen          XML toolbar

**Figure 22.2**
Although you edit
XML documents using
familiar WordPerfect
procedures, the
screen layout, menus,
and toolbars change
to assist you in the
XML task at hand.

## CREATING XML DOCUMENT CONTENT

At this point you could certainly begin typing as you normally do in WordPerfect, but you would only create invalid XML content. Instead, you need to insert valid XML elements and then add content within those valid elements. For example, follow these steps for adding newsletter content:

1. Choose Insert, Elements, or click the XML button on the toolbar and choose Elements. WordPerfect displays the Elements dialog box (see Figure 22.3), which provides only those elements that are valid at this point in the creation of the document.

2. The only valid element is nitf (News Industry Text Format), so select it and click Insert. WordPerfect inserts a pair of nitf codes, offers to let you modify the nitf attributes, and also begins the XML tree structure in the left pane.

**Figure 22.3**
The Elements dialog box helps you select only valid XML elements.

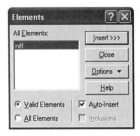

3. Unless you know that you want to change an attribute, you need not select anything. However, try selecting version from the Attribute Name list. Click Edit Value to select it. The information appears in the actual XML code, but you'll not see it in your document.

4. Click Close and WordPerfect automatically inserts the next sequence of required elements. If you want, you can type a title for the document, such as "Newsletter." Although this isn't really part of the displayed document information, it can be used as part of the structural identification of the document.

5. Click Close to close the Elements dialog box.

6. Position the cursor between the body tags.

7. Click the Valid Elements drop-down list on the toolbar to see what elements are v alid at this point of the document. This news article DTD allows for body.head, body.content, and body.end. Choose body.head.

**TIP FROM**

For some reason, the cursor tends to jump around after you select elements from the drop-down list. To avoid this, choose Insert, Elements and select elements from the Elements dialog box.

8. With the cursor between the body.head tags, you now see various valid elements, such as hedline (headline), byline, and so on. Click hedline to insert the hedline tags.

9. Between the hl1 (headline 1) tags type the title of your newsletter article, for example EnviroNews. Note that the font and font size are considerably larger than the regular text (see Figure 22.4). This is because a layout rule has been applied to the hl1 element as part of the XML template. You'll learn about layouts later in this chapter.

10. Position the cursor before the closing body.head tag. Note that the hedline element is no longer valid because you have already used it. You might want to try adding the byline tag, and also add your name.

11. Position the cursor before the closing body tag, and insert the body.content tag.

12. Position the cursor before the closing body tag, and insert the body.end tag.

**Figure 22.4**
Layout rules can be associated with specific XML elements.

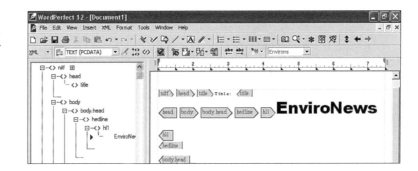

13. Choose File, Save, and supply a filename. WordPerfect automatically saves the document in XML (UTF-8) format, but if not, choose File, Save As, and choose the XML (UTF-8) format before saving.

**CAUTION**

> The WordPerfect XML editor is notorious for crashing at unpredictable moments. Even more so than usual, it's a good idea to save *early* and save *often*.

You can further experiment by inserting valid body.content and body.end elements, along with your own text.

## WORKING WITH THE XML EDITOR

You've already discovered that the XML Editor in WordPerfect is somewhat different from the standard WordPerfect interface. Let's take some time to explore the various components of the XML editor screen (refer to Figure 22.2).

The XML tree, at the left of the screen, shows the structure of the document and whether XML elements are valid. Although this screen can be helpful when you validate your document, it really doesn't offer much help while you're creating your document. If you want more editing space, you can turn off the tree by choosing XML, and deselecting Show XML Tree.

Another difference is that the Menu changes, adding XML options and removing Table options. In addition, the options under Insert and Format change dramatically to reflect XML-related tasks. Other XML Editor menu options are nearly the same as those found on standard WordPerfect menus.

Finally, the XML Editor displays the XML toolbar, which provides quick and easy access to the more important XML editing activities (see Figure 22.5).

22

**Figure 22.5**
The XML toolbar
helps you quickly
create valid XML
documents.

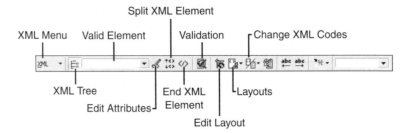

The buttons on the XML toolbar specific to editing XML documents include

- XML—Most of the elements found under the XML menu, or represented by XML toolbar buttons, can also be found under the XML drop-down menu. Clicking the XML button can be a handy way to remember what options are available, although using a toolbar button directly might be quicker and easier once you're familiar with its use.

- XML Tree—Click this button to turn the XML tree view on or off.

- Valid Elements—This drop-down list displays elements you can use at the current position of your cursor. You can also insert valid elements from this list by clicking the element from the drop-down list.

- Edit Attributes—This option is reserved for those elements that require further definition, such as the root (first) element of the document. It does not apply to most elements, and has nothing to do with formatting attributes.

- Split XML Element—Clicking this button splits the current element, in effect replicating the element. This can be particularly useful when creating a series of paragraphs. For example, with the cursor in a current paragraph, you click the button and a new pair of paragraph tags appears, without having to position the cursor outside the paragraph tags and then insert a new set of paragraph tags.

- End XML Element—Clicking this button usually moves the cursor past the closing tag. Because the WordPerfect XML editor automatically creates pairs for most elements, this option really isn't required to create closing element tags.

- Validation—At any time, but certainly before saving or publishing an XML document, you can check the validity of the elements you've used.

- Edit Layout—Clicking this button opens the WordPerfect XML Project Designer, where you can create or modify layouts for the current XML document.

- Layouts—If you have more than one layout assigned to the current XML document, clicking this button enables you to choose from among them.

- Change XML Codes—This button's name is somewhat misleading because it doesn't actually change XML Codes. It does change how tags are displayed in your XML document. By default, XML tags display fully (refer to Figure 22.4). However, you can also choose to display no tags at all, or to display markers (see Figure 22.6). As you begin working with XML documents, you'll probably want to display the full XML tags. As you gain more experience, or if you want to view how the document will look, choose one of the other options.

**Figure 22.6**
You can use markers to indicate XML elements instead of using descriptive tags or not using anything at all.

## VALIDATING AN XML DOCUMENT

The two requirements for an XML document are that it must be well-formed and that its elements must be valid. As you create the document, WordPerfect makes it difficult to use elements incorrectly. However, as you edit a document, you might inadvertently add or delete elements in such a way that they are no longer well-formed or valid.

At any time, but certainly before saving an XML document, you should validate your document. Otherwise you defeat the purpose of an XML document in that others won't be able to use or reuse your document because they won't understand its structure and elements.

WordPerfect makes it easy to quickly determine what does and doesn't meet these criteria, using either of two methods:

- The first is to use the XML Tree view. If you turned this view off, turn it back on by choosing XML, Show XML Tree, or click the XML Tree button on the toolbar. In the XML Tree problems are noted by an inverted yellow triangle. If you hover the mouse pointer over the triangle, WordPerfect displays a brief description of the problem.

- The second method is to validate the entire document by choosing XML, Validation, or by clicking the Validation button on the toolbar. WordPerfect displays the Validation dialog box (see Figure 22.7). By default WordPerfect tries to find all possible errors, starting at the beginning of the document. Click Start and WordPerfect quickly moves through all of the document's elements, pausing only to report problems it finds (see Figure 22.8).

Unfortunately, until you become more experienced creating valid XML code, some of the descriptions offered during validation might be difficult to interpret. For example, if the message tells you that an element is not allowed at this point, it could mean that the element should be nested within another element and that you've either moved the nested element, or accidentally deleted the element that should surround it.

**Figure 22.7**
Although you have many validation options, generally you stick to the defaults when validating an XML document.

**Figure 22.8**
Error messages can help you determine and fix XML coding problems.

For example, in Figure 22.8 you are told that element hl1 is not allowed at this point in body.head. If you position the cursor before or after the hl1 tags, you'll note in the valid elements list that you could have a hedline or byline at this point. You then realize that somehow the hedline codes are missing.

If you simply insert the hedline tags, the hl1 tags and accompanying text are still not where they should be, nested within the hedline tags, and thus the code is still invalid. If you select the hl1 tags and text and move them to within the hedline tags, you've fixed the problem. Better yet, before inserting the hedline tags, select the hl1 tags and text, and *then* insert the hedline tags that correctly wrap around the selected elements.

# FORMATTING AN XML DOCUMENT

The most important thing to remember about an XML document is that *data is data*! That is, the content of your document is of primary concern. If the structure and elements are well-formed and valid, you or anyone can use that data and display or present it in a variety of formats, or layouts.

## UNDERSTANDING XML LAYOUTS

In a typical XML process, the document itself and the DTD don't concern themselves at all with how the document is to be formatted. All they care about is making the document content useable.

For example, you can create an element such as `<model></model>` and valid content might include the various automobile models in your inventory. Such an element is concerned only with the content, and thus is very different from typical HTML codes (or even WordPerfect formatting codes) that define *how* something is to be displayed, such as bold, italic, large font, and so on.

Formatting of XML data can be accomplished in a variety of ways, using whatever tools are available. For example, one could create Cascading Style Sheets (CSS), or use other separate programs to describe how various XML entities should be displayed.

Fortunately, WordPerfect includes its own XML Project Designer that enables you to define how various elements are to be displayed. These definitions are collected in *layouts* and are stored in the same XML template that contains the DTD.

## CREATING AN XML LAYOUT

Some templates that ship with WordPerfect contain basic layout information. For example, the news article template displays normal text in a certain font (Garamond), while displaying the headline in a different, larger font (Arial Black, 32 pt).

At some point, however, you or someone else must determine exactly how you want to display the content of an XML document. You do this by using WordPerfect's XML Project Designer, where you can create entirely new layouts, or modify existing ones. Further, you can create up to 10 different layouts and store them in the same XML template.

Suppose, for example, you have created the content for your XML newsletter (refer to Figure 22.4). Click the Edit Layout button on the toolbar. WordPerfect displays the XML Project Designer (see Figure 22.9).

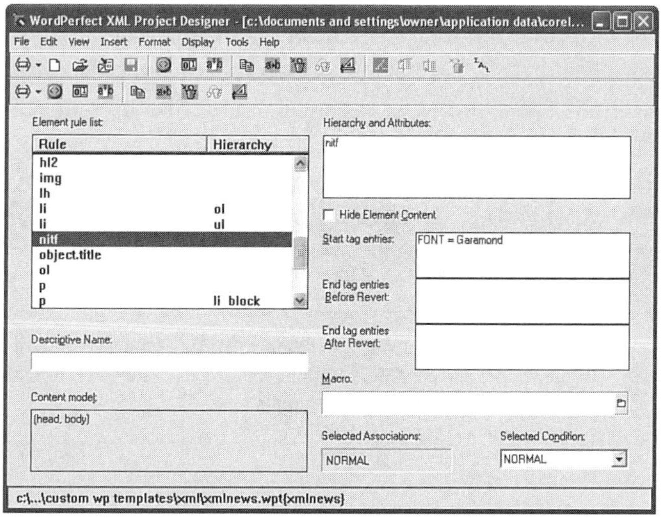

**Figure 22.9**
The WordPerfect XML Project Designer is a separate program that helps you modify rules for displaying XML elements.

**22**

You can edit the default xmlnews layout, but you're better off creating a new layout so you don't lose the original. To create a new layout, based on the original layout, follow these steps:

1. Choose File, New, Layout. WordPerfect clears the XML Project Designer lists.

2. Choose File, Retrieve. WordPerfect displays the Retrieve Layout dialog box (see Figure 22.10).

**Figure 22.10**
You retrieve an XML Layout (component) from an existing XML template (project).

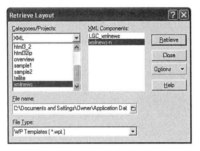

3. Choose the layout you want to insert by choosing a project (template), for example, xmlnews, and then choose the layout from the component list, for example, xmlnews-n.

4. Click retrieve and WordPerfect inserts the selected collection of elements into your new, about to be created, layout.

5. Before you proceed, choose File, Save to save your new layout. WordPerfect displays the Select Layout dialog box (see Figure 22.11). You can overwrite an existing layout (be careful!), or supply a new name in the Layout Name text box. Click Save.

**Figure 22.11**
Use a unique name to identify the type of layout you're creating for your XML template.

You now can begin to modify the rules for any of the document's elements, which include overall attributes, and what attributes or text to insert before or after the element appears. These rules are what determine how the document's content is displayed. For example, suppose you don't like the default Garamond font used in the original layout. To change an element, follow these steps:

1. Select the element you want to change in the Element rule list. For example, the default font is set in the nitf element, which is the root, or first element in the document.

2. Choose Edit, Edit Rule, or simply double-click the rule in the Element rule list, directly under the Rule column, not the Hierarchy column. WordPerfect displays the Element Rule dialog box (see Figure 22.12).

**Figure 22.12**
Elements define content. You create your own rules for displaying that content.

3. Note that the Start Tag rule specifies the Garamond font. Select that rule and click Delete to remove it. If you only want to change it, you could double-click the rule entry to go directly to the Font dialog box.

4. Click Format, Font, and from the Font dialog box choose the font, size, and other attributes you want to serve as your default document font. Click OK.

5. Click OK again to return to the XML Project Designer.

You can now select other items you want to change. To see some of the possibilities, try changing two of the headline elements by following these steps:

1. Click the hedline element. Notice that it doesn't include font information, although it does indicate that two lines will separate the headline from the next element in the document.

2. Click the hl1 element. This is the element that actually contains the headline content. Double-click it to open the Element Rule dialog box.

3. Double-click the Font rule, and change it from Arial Black to something more interesting. Click OK.

4. Choose Paragraph, Justification, Center to center the title, and then click OK.

5. In the Element rule list, double-click the byline element. WordPerfect displays the Element Rule dialog box.

6. Choose Display, Text. Because the content of the byline element contains only a person's name (for example yours), you need to add text that precedes that content. In the Text dialog box, type **By** followed by a space, and click OK. WordPerfect inserts the new rule following the Font rule (see Figure 22.13).

**Figure 22.13**
Not only can you add rules, but you can also change the order in which they're applied to an element.

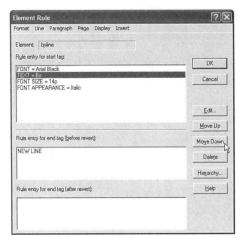

7. Unfortunately, in its current position, "By" will be in the right font, but won't be the right size or in italics. Change the order of the text rule by clicking Move Down until it follows the other rules, and then click OK.

You have a great deal of flexibility in defining the rules by which XML elements are to be displayed. You can even choose not to display elements by checking the Hide Element Content box. For example, select the Title element, and check the Hide Element Content box, so that the title element doesn't display in the document.

When you're finished editing the layout, choose File, Save. If you haven't named your new layout, WordPerfect displays the Select Layout dialog box (refer to Figure 22.11). You can overwrite an existing layout, or supply a new name in the Layout Name text box. Click Save. Having saved the layout in its associated WordPerfect XML template, you then close the Project Designer to return to WordPerfect's XML editor.

 You now can apply your new layout, or any other defined layout, by clicking the Layouts button on the toolbar and selecting the layout you want. If you select None, you'll see what your document content looks like without any formatting.

In the future, if you create a new XML document based on this modified XML template, you can still use the same saved layouts. This is a great tool for standardizing the look of your documents, which can be a real timesaver in a corporate environment. Most individuals, however, will find this process to be more work than is necessary for their personal documents.

# PUBLISHING AN XML DOCUMENT

Sharing your XML documents with other people can be as simple as providing them with your basic XML data, or providing them also with DTD and layout information. You can also print the document.

> **NOTE**
> WordPerfect offers a Publish to XML option (found under File, Publish To, XML), which is different from the process described in this section.

## SAVING AN XML DOCUMENT

By default, when you save a new XML document, WordPerfect assumes you want to save it in XML format. Choose File, Save (or Save As), and WordPerfect displays the Save File dialog box. Note that the file type is XML UTF-8. Supply a filename and click Save. WordPerfect saves the file with an .XML filename extension.

## PRINTING AN XML DOCUMENT

You print an XML document just as you do any WordPerfect document. However, consider the following:

■ Apply a layout that works well for a printed document. For example, no layout, or one designed for a Web page, might not look good on the printed page.

- What you see in the XML editing screen is what you print. Unless you want them there, first turn off the Display codes or markers. Click the Change XML Codes button on the toolbar, and select Hide Codes (see Figure 22.14). You can turn them back on again if you want them for further editing.

**Figure 22.14**
If you hide the XML codes, you get a better idea as to how your layout rules affect your XML document.

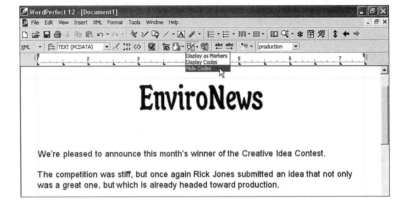

## DISTRIBUTING AN XML DOCUMENT

If you decide to share your XML document with someone else electronically, you also need to provide the XML template from which the document derived. Because the template contains the DTD and layout information, the XML document is nothing more than a collection of data and undefined (invalid) tags without the template.

In a corporate environment, typically such templates are accessible by everyone in a central network drive and folder. When you open an XML document from someone else, your networked version of WordPerfect automatically checks in the shared template folder and matches the DTD and layout information for that document.

If you don't all share the same template folder, you need to provide *both* the XML document and its template. The recipient then must save the template in his or her default template folder (for example, C:\Documents and Settings\Owner\Application Data\Corel\PerfectExpert\12\Custom WP Templates\XML). Then, when the recipient opens the XML document in WordPerfect, WordPerfect finds the associated template and knows just what to do with the XML document.

# UNDERSTANDING ADVANCED XML TASKS

As noted earlier, if you're an individual working alone, using XML is going to be of little importance to you. On the other hand, if you're working in a shared environment where standards are important, XML can be of great value.

Nevertheless, most individuals don't want or need to know about the inner workings of XML. Creating DTD files, compiling DTDs, or creating XML templates and corporate

XML layouts likely will be the responsibility of your company's Information Technology personnel. Such individuals are better equipped to deal with the somewhat arcane intricacies of the XML process.

Nevertheless, the following is designed to give you a sense of what these advanced tasks are all about, in case you want to know, or if you need to discuss these matters with an expert.

---

**Help for Advanced Uses of XML**

WordPerfect provides a couple of fairly useful aids to learning about its approach to creating XML documents. One is a tutorial that can be found in the WordPerfect XML Project Designer. In Windows, go to All Programs, WordPerfect Office 12 (or 11), Utilities, XML Project Designer, and then within that program choose Help, WordPerfect XML Tutorial. The tutorial doesn't begin with document creation, but rather with creating and compiling DTDs. Thus, it might be useful to survey this entire chapter first to get an overall sense of the process before tackling the tutorial.

The other aid is a comprehensive, 138-page XML Manual that WordPerfect published in PDF format and shipped with WordPerfect Office 2000 and WordPerfect 9. WordPerfect revamped its XML procedures with WordPerfect 9, but little has changed since then except minor modifications and bug fixes, and thus the manual is still applicable to XML and WordPerfect 11 and 12. If you can find a copy of WordPerfect Office 2000, you'll find the xml9en.pdf file on the distribution CD. You might also be able to find the file by searching for it on the Internet.

In addition, you can find other helpful resources on the Web. For example, I searched for WordPerfect XML and found two articles that talked about using XML for the U.S. Patent Office (http://www.uspto.gov/ebc/ efs/downloads/documents/efswp.pdf) and another for working in an academic law instruction environment (http://www.cali.org/conference/2001/postconf/2001C23d1/).

Many articles and books are written about XML, but you also need to find those that show how it is used in WordPerfect.

---

## UNDERSTANDING DTD FILES

A Document Type Definition (DTD) file provides definitions for tags you use in an XML document. XML is much more flexible than HTML because you can use literally any tag to define XML content, so long as you define it so others know what to do with it.

DTD files are nothing more than ASCII files. If you open the xmlnews.dtd file in Notepad, you find definitions for every element in the News Industry Text Format (nitf) document type. The following snippets are from that DTD:

```
<!-- Document header -->
<!ELEMENT head (title, base?)>
```

Note that the "head" tag refers to the document heading—a non-printing part of the document—and includes the required title and optional base tags (indicated by the question mark).

```
<!-- Story headline group -->
<!ELEMENT hedline (hl1, hl2*)>
```

In the hedline element of the document, authors can define one main headline (hl1), and one or more (*) sub-headlines (hl2).

22

```
<!-- Story headline -->
<!ELEMENT hl1 (#PCDATA | chron | copyrite | event | function | location | money
 | num | object.title | org | person | virtloc | a | br | em | lang | pronounce | q)*>
```

Finally the headline itself (hl1) can include optionally (indicated by |) one or more (indicated by *) elements, include text (#PCDATA) and other identifiable pieces of information (such as org, person, pronounce).

The language required to create a valid DTD is not terribly difficult. However, because they try to establish standards for certain types of documents, and because such standards usually come from committees, the actual creation of new DTDs usually is left up to the experts.

Several industry standard DTDs have emerged, including those from the government, the technical publishing industry, and the news industry. One of the most common DTDs is the docbook standard, which is currently in revision 4.2. This is the standard DTD by which WordPerfect documents are published to XML, unless otherwise designated. Industry standard DTDs also tend to develop slowly over time, with lots of feedback from users and discussion by committee members before new DTD versions are released. Thus some DTDs are more than a couple of years old, but on the other hand, that does provide for a certain degree of stability in an otherwise rapidly changing computing world.

## COMPILING DTD FILES

To use a DTD to create a new WordPerfect XML document, you must first compile the DTD and make it part of a WordPerfect template. You do so using WordPerfect's XML Project Designer, and the result is incorporated in a WordPerfect XML template.

The DTD itself must be properly created. WordPerfect provides virtually no help in troubleshooting compiling problems, other than to indicate there are problems. If the compiler encounters errors, it will not create a template. Thus, you have to resolve all errors before you can create a new template based on a DTD.

In addition, if any additional information is needed, such as reference to external files that describe how to deal with graphic images, these must be properly noted in a catalog file.

**NOTE**

> The requirements for creating a valid DTD are quite stringent. The possible combinations and problems that can arise are far beyond the scope of this book. This section is included in case you are provided with a DTD and need to compile it before using it.

To compile a DTD file and generate an XML template, follow these steps:

1. Open the WordPerfect XML Project Designer by going to the Windows Start menu and choosing All Programs, WordPerfect Office 12, Utilities, WordPerfect XML Project Designer. WordPerfect opens the XML Project Designer.

2. Choose File, DTD Compile. WordPerfect displays the WordPerfect DTD Compiler dialog box (see Figure 22.15).

**Figure 22.15**
When you compile a valid DTD file, it then becomes part of an XML template.

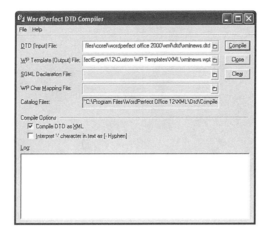

3. Specify the full path and filename for the DTD (input) file.

4. Specify the full path and filename for the new template (output) file. Typically this should be in the same location as your other XML template documents.

5. Make sure the Compile DTD as XML box is checked.

6. Click Compile. WordPerfect then compiles the DTD, and generates a WordPerfect XML template. If there are any errors, the template is not generated and WordPerfect displays error messages in the Log area of the DTD Compiler dialog box.

7. If the compilation is successful, click Close, and then exit the XML Project Designer.

Now, when you choose File, New XML Document, your recently compiled template appears as one of the available projects.

## PUBLISHING WORDPERFECT DOCUMENTS TO XML

In WordPerfect 11 a new option was added to the File menu: Publish to XML. The option sounds intriguing, but it's not all that it seems to be.

This option essentially enables you to take already created WordPerfect documents and convert them to raw XML, based roughly on the Docbook 4.2 specification. Unfortunately, the conversion is quite rough, and in addition, there is no way to open the converted XML documents and immediately create layout options. That's why this topic is included under Advanced XML Topics. If you want to create useable XML documents, you're better off doing so using XML templates.

Nevertheless, if you need to convert existing documents to XML so that someone else can work with the resulting raw XML content, these are the steps:

1. Open an existing .wpd file into WordPerfect.

2. Choose File, Publish To, XML. WordPerfect displays the Publish to XML dialog box (see Figure 22.16).

**Figure 22.16**
The Publish to XML feature enables you to quickly convert existing WordPerfect documents to raw XML, without any layout information.

3. By default, WordPerfect converts the document using the same filename, but with an .XML extension. Change the file name if you wish.

4. If the document contains graphic images, you can specify how these are to be converted.

5. Click Publish to convert the document to XML content.

# TROUBLESHOOTING

### CRASH

*While working with the XML Editor, it sometimes crashes for no apparent reason.*

Unfortunately that is the nature of WordPerfect's XML Editor beast. You'll often find that if something you're working with crashes, it will do so over and over again. You can try two things.

First, make sure you save your projects early and often. Press Ctrl+S regularly to save your work, so you won't lose it should the XML Editor crash.

Second, try exiting WordPerfect and Windows altogether and starting them again. Help the editor forget its crashes and perhaps it will work better for you.

### CAN'T VALIDATE

*When I try to save my XML project, I sometimes come up with validation errors. Should I save anyway?*

You can certainly save your documents with its errors. However, before you share the document with others, you should be sure to resolve any validation errors.

Remember that errors can be related to structure or syntax, and thus these are not well-formed. Errors can also involve undefined or misused elements or tags, in which case the code is not valid. Although it can be difficult to figure out why the document does not validate, take the time to make sure your document is valid.

# PROJECT

Creating new XML documents is one way to work with XML. But it's quite likely you also have many other documents you've already created. Can you convert them to XML? If so, can you work with them like you do with other XML documents you create?

The answer is a resounding "Sort of!" In this project, you'll convert a typical existing WordPerfect document into raw XML, and then generate a generic set of layout rules to make it easier to work with the resulting document.

To convert an existing document to XML, follow these steps:

1. Open the WordPerfect document.
2. Choose File, Publish To, XML. In the Publish to XML dialog box, click Publish.

WordPerfect converts and saves the document with the same file name, but with the .xml extension.

To begin working with the converted XML document, open the XML file. Although it was saved using the Docbook 4.2 specification, WordPerfect opens it using the Docbook 3 specification. This really is of little concern to you, unless someone who really needs to know asks you.

If this is the first time you open a published XML document, you will have to follow these steps:

1. In the Select WordPerfect Category/Project dialog box, select the XML category from the drop-down menu, and select docbook3 project from the list. Click Next.
2. In the Select WordPerfect Template dialog box, click Next.
3. In the Create Layout dialog box, check Create Generic Layout When Project Designer Is Invoked and click Next.
4. In the Select Catalog File dialog box, click Next.
5. Finally, in the Project Summary dialog box, click Finish. WordPerfect displays the opened document in the XML editor (see Figure 22.17).

If you have already followed these steps once, each time you open a document you have published to XML, WordPerfect automatically displays the opened document in the XML Editor (see Figure 22.17). However, note that even with a variety of element tags, the document layout is non-existent. To make it easier to work with the document, you'll create some generic layout rules, following these steps:

1. Click the Edit Layout button on the XML toolbar to open the WordPerfect XML Project Designer.
2. Choose Tools, Create Generic Rules. WordPerfect generates a rather lengthy list of elements and rules based on the current document (see Figure 22.18).

**Figure 22.17**
XML documents converted from WordPerfect files contain no layout information.

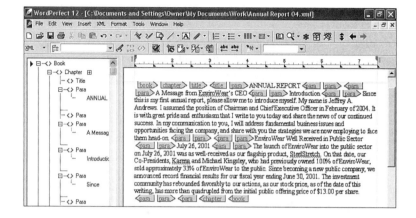

**Figure 22.18**
The list of Generic layout rules can be rather lengthy. Because WordPerfect has no idea which ones you need, it gives you all of them.

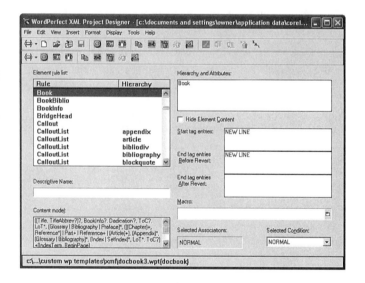

3. Choose File, Exit and WordPerfect asks if you want to save changes to the template. Click Yes, and then in the Select Layout dialog box provide a name for this generic layout, for example Generic, and click Save.

4. In the XML Editor, click the Layouts button on the XML toolbar and select the name of the layout you just saved to apply the generic layout rules (see Figure 22.19).

At this point you can edit the document itself, or return to the XML Project Designer and edit, add, or delete layout rules, as described in this chapter.

This approach is somewhat clumsy, but it's better than starting from scratch if you have existing WordPerfect documents that you want to work with in XML.

**Figure 22.19**
Applying generic layout rules, you can at least get a better idea as to what a converted document should look like.

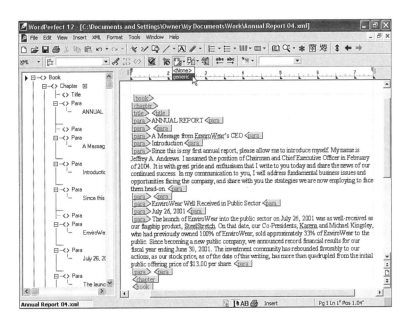

PART **VII**

# AUTOMATING EVERYDAY TASKS

# CHAPTER 23

# BUILDING DOCUMENTS WITH TEMPLATES

**In this chapter**

*by Laura Acklen*

**23**

# USING WORDPERFECT'S TEMPLATES

Whether you realize it or not, you use a template every time you create a new document. The wp11us.wpt/wp12us.wpt template (for the U.S. version of WordPerfect) is the default template, and it contains all the default settings for new documents. Although the default template is blank except for the initial settings, a typical template is like a fill-in-the-blanks document. It contains the formatting, layout, and standard blocks of text—all you have to do is provide the content. Voilà! A document is created, ready to print, fax, or e-mail. It takes about 30 seconds to create a fax cover sheet, not three to four minutes to edit another cover sheet, and certainly not 10 minutes to type it from scratch. Multiply that by the number of times you use a fax cover sheet, or invoice, or legal time sheet, and you've saved enough time to actually go *out* for lunch.

WordPerfect 11 (and 12) ship with over twenty templates and more are available for a free download. You might not have to create your own for quite a while, if ever. When you do venture out and create your own template, you'll be able to use any of the existing templates as a model, so all you have to do is make minor adjustments. In just a few minutes, you can even turn your own documents into templates.

**NOTE**

WordPerfect Office 12 includes a brand new product, called WordPerfect OfficeReady, designed to make it easier than ever to organize and access templates. It comes with 40 new templates that can be used in WordPerfect, Quattro Pro, and Presentations. It's called a "browser" because you can navigate through the template categories and display a high-resolution preview of the template in a nice big window.

It's a separate program, so you start it from an icon on the desktop (if you have one), or from the Start menu. To use the Start menu, choose Start, (All) Programs, WordPerfect Office Ready, Start WordPerfect OfficeReady. There is a user guide available (choose Help, Table of Contents) to get you started. Additional templates will be made available for a free download, or a small fee, as they are developed.

## CHOOSING A PROJECT TEMPLATE

WordPerfect templates are also referred to as "project templates" because PerfectExpert projects act as the front end for the templates. Each template has a corresponding PerfectExpert project that guides you through the process of filling in the template. Rather than open a template just as you would any other document, you select the project that you want to work on. The template is opened in the document window, and the PerfectExpert panel opens on the left side of the screen. You simply click the project buttons and choose from a list of options to alter the style, add other elements, and fill in the important text.

**TIP FROM**

The PerfectExpert is a powerful ally. When your users don't want to learn the ins and outs of WordPerfect just to create standard documents, it can be your best friend. The easiest way to include the PerfectExpert in custom templates is to base your custom template on an existing WordPerfect project.

To create a new document based on a WordPerfect template, choose File, New from Project (or press Ctrl+Shift+N). The PerfectExpert dialog box appears (see Figure 23.1). If necessary, click the Create New tab. Scroll through the list of projects, and then double-click the one you want to run.

The last four projects you used

**Figure 23.1**
In the PerfectExpert dialog box, you can choose the project template you want to use to create a document.

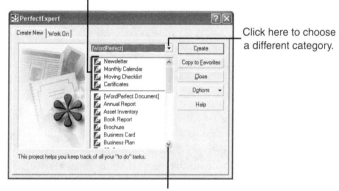

Click here to choose a different category.

Click here to scroll down through the list.

 *If you get an error message when you try to open a project template, see "Missing or Damaged Template Files" in the Troubleshooting section at the end of this chapter.*

If you don't see the project you want, click the category drop-down list arrow at the top of the project template list and choose another category. Select [WordPerfect] for a list of all the templates that are installed on your system. Keep in mind that the selection of templates that comes with WordPerfect 11 and 12 is much smaller than with previous versions. There are lots of theories as to why this was done, but the prevailing opinion is that Corel wanted to drive traffic to its web site so that as more templates are developed, they can be made available for free download.

**NOTE**

To those of you who have upgraded from a previous version of WordPerfect, the selection of templates in WordPerfect 11 and 12 may seem sorely lacking. Granted, you can download more, but what about the templates that you used in a previous version? Can you use those? See the section titled "Using Templates from Earlier Versions of WordPerfect" at the end of this chapter.

**CAUTION**

Some of WordPerfect's templates require personal information. If you haven't filled that in yet, you'll be prompted for it the first time you open a project template that uses the personal information. Skip down to the section "Filling In Personal Information," later in this chapter, and take care of that before you move on.

Before the project starts, you might see a PerfectScript macros message box (see Figure 23.2) that explains there are macros in the document and if you don't know the source of the document, you might want to disable the macros.

**Figure 23.2**
The PerfectExpert message box gives you an opportunity to disable the macros in an unfamiliar template.

If you're using one of the templates that shipped with WordPerfect, or a template from a trusted source, you can choose No, you don't want to disable the macros. However, if you are unsure of the source, it's best to choose Yes to disable the macros. Granted, the results won't be the same, but it's better safe than sorry. At all costs, resist the urge to enable the check box that turns off the PerfectScript macros message box. In the fight against computer viruses, the capability to disable macros in a document is a fundamental tool. Turning off this message box will remove your capability to choose to disable or enable the PerfectScript macros.

 *If you accidentally turn off this message and you want to get it back, see "Re-Enabling the PerfectScript Message" in the Troubleshooting section at the end of this chapter.*

When you open a template, the PerfectExpert panel opens next to the template (see Figure 23.3). The buttons in the PerfectExpert panel give you options for customizing the template by choosing from the available variations.

Now you can start building the document by clicking the buttons in the PerfectExpert panel. For example, in the Fax Cover Sheet project, click the Fill in Heading Info button to open the Fax Cover Sheet Heading dialog box, where you can type all the To and From information (see Figure 23.4). Remove the check mark next to any item that you don't want on the fax cover sheet. Click the drop-down list arrows to choose items that you've already used in these fields. Otherwise, type the information in the text boxes.

PerfectExpert panel

Click here to fill in the To and From information.

**Figure 23.3**
PerfectExpert projects incorporate templates and PerfectExpert ask-and-you-shall-receive formatting to auto-mate many aspects of document production.

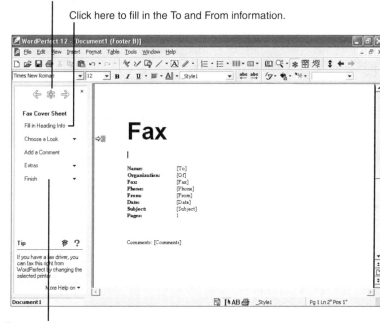

Click here to check spelling, print, fax, or save.

Remove the check mark if you don't want to use the element.

**Figure 23.4**
After you type the information in the Fax Cover Sheet Heading dialog box, WordPerfect inserts it in the appropriate places in the template.

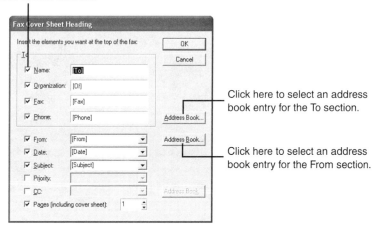

Click here to select an address book entry for the To section.

Click here to select an address book entry for the From section.

Click the top Address Book button to fill in information from an Address Book entry in the recipient's section. Click the bottom Address Book button to fill in information in the sender's section. Click OK when you're done. The information is inserted into the template, and you're ready to continue creating the document.

## FILLING IN PERSONAL INFORMATION

A good number of project templates require personal information (such as a name, company, address, and fax number), which you can type in once and have WordPerfect insert for you whenever it's necessary. If this information hasn't been created yet, you are prompted for it when you open a template that uses it (see Figure 23.5).

**Figure 23.5**
If you haven't filled in the personal information, you are prompted for it the first time you open a project template that uses it.

When you click OK, the Address Book dialog box opens with a list of available address books (see Figure 23.6). You need to select an address book entry that contains the personal information. Click the book with your personal information, select the entry in the list, and then click Insert. That's it—you're in.

**Figure 23.6**
The list of Address Books in the Address Book dialog box varies depending on how your system is set up.

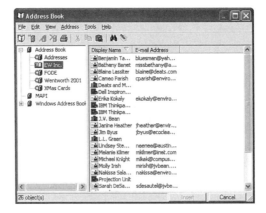

If you haven't created your own entry, click the Create a New Address Entry button on the toolbar. In the New Entry dialog box, select the kind of entry you want to create, and then click OK. The Properties dialog box for that kind of entry appears. Figure 23.7 shows the Person Properties dialog box.

When you finish, choose OK to get back to the template. Now you can start building the document. If you like, skip back to the text following Figure 23.3 for a quick review of how to use the fax cover sheet project template.

→ For more information on the Address Book feature, **see** "Working with Address Books," **p. 784.**

**Figure 23.7**
The Person Properties dialog box is the most comprehensive of the Properties dialog boxes, with six different tabs.

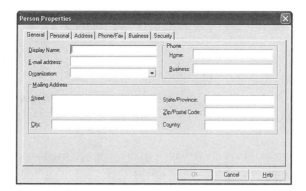

## EDITING PERSONAL INFORMATION

When you select a personal information entry in an Address Book, the entry becomes the default for all the templates. In many offices, computers are shared, so users need to select their own personal information entry in an address book.

To select a different personal information entry, open the PerfectExpert dialog box by clicking File, New from Project (or by pressing Ctrl+Shift+N), and then choose Options, Personal Information. A message box appears and identifies the current personal information entry (see Figure 23.8). Click OK to open the Address Book dialog box, where you can select another personal information entry.

**Figure 23.8**
The personal information can be changed each time a different user uses the computer.

---

### Get More Templates in a Free Download

Beginning with the release of WordPerfect 10, the number of templates that are included with the program was reduced. Corel announced that it would be making additional templates and projects available in a free download. These templates and projects can be downloaded from www.officecommunity.com in the Download Gallery section and from Corel's ftp site at ftp://ftp.corel.com/pub/WordPerfect/wpwin/10/english/templates. Although the templates were written for WordPerfect 10, they will work just fine in WordPerfect 11 and 12.

The files on the FTP site are in an uncompressed format, so you need to download both the WPT and AST files in each folder (category). There is a README file in each folder with instructions for installing. There is also a "thumbnail" folder in each category, containing a GIF file that will show you what each created project form might look like. To download the complete collection all at once, scroll down to the WP 10 Temp.zip file and download it to your computer.

---

# CUSTOMIZING WORDPERFECT'S TEMPLATES

Every new document you create is based on the default template, which contains all the default settings. Some of these settings are listed in Table 1.1 in Chapter 1, "Getting Comfortable with WordPerfect." This template can be customized to suit specific requirements. For example, if you want 1.5-inch margins, specific tab settings, and widow/orphan protection always on, you can make these changes to the default template so that they are in place for all new documents.

WordPerfect's project templates are designed so that you can use them right away. They are generic enough to work in most situations, especially when time is more important than personalization. However, when you're ready to customize the templates, you can revise a template as easily as you revise any other document. It is especially important that you back up the original template before you start revising so that if something goes wrong, you can always revert to the original.

## EDITING THE DEFAULT TEMPLATE

If you routinely use settings other than the defaults, you can place these settings in the default template. The next time you create a new document, the new default settings will be in place. The default template contains a lot more than initial settings. It contains the majority of your customization efforts (such as QuickWords, custom toolbars, menus, and keyboards), so it is particularly important that you make a backup copy of the file before you make changes.

Before you make a move, search for the file—`wp11us.wpt` or `wp12us.wpt`—for the US version. Change the US to the two-letter abbreviation for your language and you should be good to go. After you find the file, make a copy and name it to `wp11usold` (or `wp12usold`). If the changes that you make to the default template cause any problems, you can revert to the original default template by renaming or deleting the new template and renaming the old template to its original filename. In other words, rename `wp12us.wpt` to `wp12usbad.wpt`, and then `wp12usold.wpt` to `wp12us.wpt`.

Editing the default template is a little tricky. You don't click on the [WordPerfect Document] entry in the list of projects and choose Options, Edit WP Template, as you might think. You have to select the template file from the list of custom templates instead. I like to think that WordPerfect is designed this way to avoid accidental modifications—not just to confuse me.

Follow these steps to edit the default template:

1. Choose File, New from Project. If necessary, click the Create New tab.
2. Click the category drop-down list arrow and choose the Custom WP Templates category. By default, there are two files in this folder: the default template and the QuickWords file (see Figure 23.9).

QuickWords template

**Figure 23.9**
The Custom WP Templates category contains the default template, the QuickWords template, and any custom templates you create.

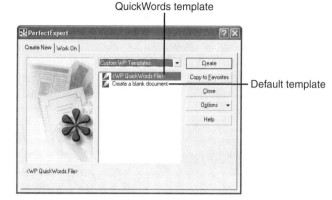

Default template

**NOTE**

You use the <WP QuickWords File> template when copying abbreviations or QuickWords from older templates so you can use them in WordPerfect 11 or 12. See the section "Copying Objects from Other Templates" later in this chapter for more information.

3. Select Create a Blank Document from the list.

4. Choose Options, Edit WP Template. The template opens in a document window, and the Template toolbar is displayed on top of the property bar (see Figure 23.10).

Click to close the template editor

**Figure 23.10**
When you edit a template, the Template toolbar is added to the top of your screen.

5. Revise the template as you would any other document. Bear in mind that your changes will be applied to every new document from here on out, so be careful about the type of formatting codes and text you include.

6. When you're finished, click the Close button to close the Template Editor, and then choose Yes to save the template.

**CAUTION**

Is the Edit WP Template option grayed out? If you select the [WordPerfect Document] entry in the list, and then click Options, the Edit WP Template option is grayed out because you can't edit the default template this way. Click the category drop-down list arrow and select Custom WP Templates. Select Create a Blank Document, and then choose Options, Edit WP Template.

TIP FROM

*Laura Acklen*

> There is a great shortcut for editing the default template. Turn on Reveal Codes and locate the Open Style: DocumentStyle code at the top of the document. Double-click the code to open the Styles Editor. Make the necessary changes and then place a check in the Use As Default check box. Choose OK; then, confirm whether or not you want to save your changes to the default template.

TIP FROM

*Laura Acklen*

> By default, any new styles you create are stored with the particular document. If you want to be able to use those styles with other documents, you need to save the new styles to the default template, which is available to all new documents. See the section "Saving a Style" in Chapter 9, "Formatting with Styles," for more information.

NOTE

> The default template folder (specified in File Settings) is where the default template is stored. Any custom templates that you create are also saved to this folder. The templates that ship with WordPerfect are stored in a different location. They are copied to the `\program files\wordperfect office 11\template` or `\program files\wordperfect office 12\template` folder.

## BACKING UP TEMPLATES BEFORE MAKING REVISIONS

You should always make backup copies of your templates before you edit them. If something goes wrong, you can revert to the original copy and start over.

In the PerfectExpert dialog box, right-click the template that you want to revise. Choose Project Properties to display the Modify a Project dialog box (see Figure 23.11). The Command Line list box has the name of the folder and the name of the template file. Click in the text box, and then press End to move to the end of the entry. Scribble down the name of the file.

**Figure 23.11**
The Modify a Project dialog box has the name of the template file and the name of the project file for a selected project template.

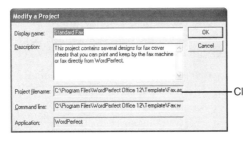

Click here and then press End.

In the Open File dialog box, move to the `\program files\wordperfect office 11\template` or `\program files\wordperfect office 12\template` folder. There are two types of files here. Template files are shown as WordPerfect 11 (or 12) Documents; project files are shown as AST files. Right-click the template file, choose Rename, and then type `<filename>-old` as the new filename. For example, the fax template filename would now be `fax-old`.

## REVISING WORDPERFECT TEMPLATES

Call me lazy, but adding my company logo was the full extent of my template customizing. If you're more ambitious, you might want to change the headings, select a different font, remove elements that you won't use, or modify the formulas used to calculate figures in tables.

Follow these steps to revise one of WordPerfect's templates:

1. Choose File, New from Project.
2. Select the template you want to revise.
3. Choose Options, Edit WP Template. The template is opened into the document window, and the Template toolbar is turned on (see Figure 23.12).

Click here when you're done.

Click here to change the description text.

Template feature bar

**Figure 23.12**
You can edit a template as easily as you edit a regular document.

4. Using the same techniques that you use on a regular WordPerfect document, revise the template.

→ For more information on adding template prompts that help you remember what you're supposed to be typing, **see** "Using Prompt Builder," **p. 729.**

You can change the name that appears in the list of project templates. While editing a template, click the Description button on the Template toolbar, and then type a new name in the Template Description dialog box. Keep it short, so that the name doesn't extend too far over in the list.

**5.** Click the Close button when you are through. When you are prompted to save your changes, click Yes.

It's better to add functionality to templates than to take it out. Your changes aren't written in stone, so if you decide later to pull something out of a template, it will take only a minute. If you remove functionality, however, it might take hours to re-create (and that's assuming that you have the expertise to do it).

**NOTE**

The modifications that you make in a template affect only new documents you create with the template; the documents based on the template that you've already created won't be affected at all.

# CREATING NEW TEMPLATES

Creating a template from scratch is definitely a last resort. Two other options are much faster. First, you can save an existing document as a template. You're bound to have at least a couple of "form" documents that you use over and over. Fax cover sheets come to mind, but so do supply requests, time sheets, network maintenance bulletins, expense reports, newsletters, equipment checkout sheets, and so on.

Second, you can revise an existing template, and then save your changes as a new template. You can use as your starting point one of your own templates or one of the templates that came with WordPerfect, and then just make the necessary adjustments. After all, a lot of effort goes into the development of a template—it would be a shame to let that go to waste.

## BASING A TEMPLATE ON AN EXISTING DOCUMENT

Basing a template on an existing document is the best option for building a library of templates that you can start using right away. Think of documents that you use often in which some of the information stays the same (such as memo headings and the sender's name) and some of the information changes (such as the recipient, date, subject, and content of the memo). Strip out the information that changes, leave the information that doesn't, and voilà—you've got yourself a template.

**NOTE**

> This might seem like a complicated way to achieve the same result that you get by revising an existing document and saving it under a new name. But hang on for a second—there's more to it than that! Filling in a blank template is just the tip of the iceberg. You can build on the template later, adding automation features such as the capability to select information from an address book. Furthermore, system administrators can deploy templates with standardized styles, macros, toolbars, menus, and keyboards (you'll learn more about this later).

Follow these steps to create a template from an existing document:

1. In a blank document, choose File, New from Project.
2. Choose Options, Create WP Template. A blank template opens in the document window, and the Template toolbar is displayed at the top of the screen.

3. Click the Insert File button (or choose Insert, File) to display the Insert File dialog box.
4. Select the filename for the existing document, and then choose Insert.
5. Strip out the variable text, and then make any other necessary revisions.

**TIP FROM**

*Laura Acklen*

> With a QuickMark, you can position the insertion point in a specific place when creating a new document based on a template. For example, you might want to jump to the fax number line in a fax cover sheet template so that the user can type the fax number as soon as the document opens. Before you save the template, click where you want the insertion point to be, and then press Ctrl+Shift+Q to set a QuickMark. To find the QuickMark later (as you fill in the template), press Ctrl+Q.

6. Click the Close button when you're finished.
7. Click Yes when you're asked whether you want to save the template. The Save Template dialog box appears (see Figure 23.13).

Type a descriptive name here.

**Figure 23.13**
In the Save Template dialog box, you can type a description for the template and a name for the file, and then choose a category to store the template in.

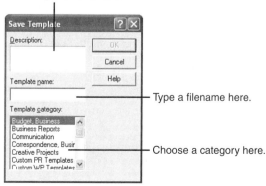

Type a filename here.

Choose a category here.

8. In the Description text box, type a descriptive name to appear in the template list.

9. Type a filename in the Template Name text box. Don't type an extension—WordPerfect assigns the .wpt extension to templates so that they can be recognized as templates and not as documents.

10. Choose the category where you want the template stored in the Template Category list box.

11. Click OK to save and close the template.

 *If you can't find a template that you've just created in the list, see "My New Template Isn't Showing Up" in the Troubleshooting section at the end of this chapter.*

After you've converted some of your documents to templates, you might want to consider how you can delegate document production by distributing the template. For example, attorneys aren't crazy about learning the ins and outs of WordPerfect just to create and revise their own documents. If a savvy legal secretary were to create a library of templates, and then copy them to an attorney's computer, that attorney could create some fairly sophisticated documents without ever taking a class or reading a book. As you'll see in later sections of this book, you can actually create an environment that shields the user from the intricacies of the software by providing customized styles, menus, keyboards, and toolbars.

**TIP FROM**

Templates cannot be password protected. If you need to password protect a template, you're better off saving it as a regular document and choosing Password Protect in the Save As dialog box.

## BASING A TEMPLATE ON ANOTHER TEMPLATE

One of the most basic concepts of document production is saving time by sharing work products. You revise an existing document (yours or someone else's), and then save it as a new file. Everyone benefits from the time and energy that goes into creating documents. This same concept carries over to templates. If the design you are looking for is similar to an existing template, by all means, edit that template, make the changes, and then save it as a new template.

To create a new template based on an existing template, follow these steps:

1. Choose File, New from Project.

2. Select the template you want to revise.

3. Choose Options, Edit WP Template. The template is opened into the document window, and the Template toolbar is turned on.

4. Choose File, Save As to open the Save Template dialog box (refer to Figure 23.13).

**TIP FROM**

*Laura Achlen*

I know you haven't made your changes yet, but I strongly recommend that you immediately save the template to a new name. If something terrible happens while you're editing the template, the original is unharmed, so you have the option of starting over.

5. In the Description text box of the Save Template dialog box, type a new descriptive name to appear in the template list.

6. Type a filename in the Template Name text box. Don't type an extension—WordPerfect assigns the .wpt extension to templates so they can be recognized as templates and not as documents.

7. In the Template Category list box, choose the category where you want the template stored.

8. Click OK to save the template. Now, you are free to make changes to this template without fear of harming the original file.

# WORKING WITH PROJECTS AND CATEGORIES

The same way files are organized into folders, templates are organized into categories. WordPerfect's projects are organized into predefined categories. You can create your own categories, and then move and copy templates into them. Let me give you an example: You might want to set up a category for a new or timid user's templates, and then point to that category so only a few templates show up in the list.

You have the following options for managing projects and categories:

- Add projects to a category—You can select the category in the drop-down list. Choose Options, Add Project, and then answer the questions. I'll come back to this later in the section that covers converting templates from older versions of WordPerfect.

- Copy a project to another category—You can select the project, and then choose Options, Copy Project. Choose the new category from the pop-up list.

- Move a project to another category—You can select the project, and then choose Options, Move Project. Choose a category from the pop-up list.

- Delete projects you no longer use—You can select a project, and then choose Options, Remove Project. Take a minute to review the Project Properties dialog box, and then click OK to confirm the removal (or bail out by clicking Cancel).

**NOTE**

The Remove Project command doesn't delete the template from the hard drive; it just removes the reference to that project from the `projects.usr` file, which is the "index" file for templates. If you want to remove the project entirely, you have to delete the file manually.

- Create new categories—You can create your own categories for projects and templates. Choose Options, Create Category, and then type the name of the category in the Display Name text box. Click OK.

- Rename categories—You can rename a category. Select the category in the drop-down list, and then choose Options, Rename Category. Type the new name in the Display Name text box, and then click OK.

- Delete categories that you no longer use—You can select the category in the drop-down list, and then choose Remove Category. Take a close look at the category name in the Display Name text box, and then confirm the deletion by clicking OK (or bail out by clicking Cancel).

**TIP FROM**

If you have temporary employees come in when things get busy, group together the templates that you want them to use and put them in their own category. Select that category in the drop-down list so only the templates that you want the temps to use are displayed in the list.

*If you accidentally delete the wrong category and need to rebuild the* `projects.usr` *index file, see "My New Template Isn't Showing Up" in the Troubleshooting section at the end of this chapter.*

## Copying Objects from Other Templates

*Template objects* are features that can be embedded into a template. They include property bars, toolbars, menu bars, styles, keyboards, macros, and XML components. When you customize WordPerfect by adding buttons to the toolbar or creating styles and macros, you are creating objects that are stored in the default template.

Think about the WordPerfect wizard at your firm. She created custom toolbars for the company's marketing materials. She created standard styles for formatting company correspondence. She customized the menus to remove unused features and to add features that are used often. She has customized WordPerfect in ways that you can only dream of.

Count yourself lucky if you have someone like this in your company, because you can take advantage of all her hard work by simply copying the objects into your default template.

Follow these steps to copy objects from another template:

1. Make a copy of the other template and give it a different name (such as `sarah` or `wpexpert`).

2. Copy the template to the default template folder specified in the File Settings dialog box (choose Tools, Settings, Files, and then click the Template tab).

3. Choose File, New from Project.

**NOTE**

> Keep in mind that while these steps describe how to copy objects into your default template, you can just as easily copy them into any other template.

4. Click the category drop-down list arrow and choose Custom WP Templates.

5. Select your default template <Create a blank document> in the list, and then choose Options, Edit WP Template.

6. Click the Copy/Remove Object button on the Template toolbar to display the Copy/Remove Template Objects dialog box (see Figure 23.14).

Click here to choose a template from which to copy.

**Figure 23.14**
In the Copy/Remove Template Objects dialog box, you can copy an object from one template to another.

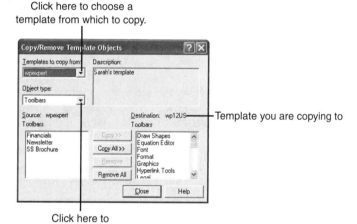

Template you are copying to

Click here to choose an object type.

7. Click the Templates to Copy From drop-down list arrow and select the template that has the objects that you want to copy (for example, sarah or wpexpert). (This is the WordPerfect genius' template.)

8. Click the Object Type drop-down list arrow and choose the object you want to copy. Depending on which object you choose to copy, the Source list displays a list of those objects. For example, if you choose Menu Bars in the Object Type drop-down list, a list of available menu bars appears in the Source list box (see Figure 23.15).

9. Select the item you want to copy in the Source list box and click Copy >>. Or, you can click Copy All >> to copy all the items at once.

10. If the object names are identical, you get a message asking you to confirm the replacement. Click Yes.

11. Repeat steps 4 and 5 until you've copied all the objects that you want.

12. Click Close.

**Figure 23.15**
When you choose an object type, a list of items appears in the Source list box, where you can select and copy them to the other template.

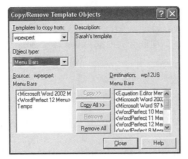

TIP FROM

*Laura Acklen*

You can remove objects from a template as easily as you can add them. Follow the preceding steps, except in step 9, click Remove to delete the selected item or click Remove All to strip out all the items at once. Note that objects associated with the main document window cannot be removed.

TIP FROM

*Laura Acklen*

Toolbars, menus, and custom keyboards can all be copied from one template to another in the Customize Settings dialog box (which you get by choosing Tools, Settings, Customize). Click the Toolbars, Menus, or Keyboards tab, and then click Copy. Click the Template to Copy From drop-down list arrow and choose the template you want to copy from. Choose the item that you want to copy from the list box. Click the Template to Copy To drop-down list arrow and choose the template you want to copy to. Click Copy.

Template objects can be stored in the default template or the additional objects template. The additional objects template is a secondary default template. The name and location of the additional objects template is found in the Template tab of the File Settings dialog box. You can use the objects in this template along with, or in place of, the objects in the default template.

In a networked environment, a system administrator can implement company standards by customizing an additional objects template and keeping it on a network drive. Each user has his or her own default template on the local drive, so each is free to customize WordPerfect. As an added precaution, the additional objects template can be set up as read-only to prevent accidental modification.

Furthermore, if a network administrator wanted to distribute a set of templates through a company, he could copy those templates into an additional template folder and then set that folder's location at each workstation. Folders can be created within that additional template folder to organize the templates into categories. The last step would be to refresh the list of projects at each station so the new templates show up in the list. Choose File, New from Project, click the Options button, and then choose Refresh Projects.

# USING PROMPT BUILDER

Let's say you're the WordPerfect wizard in the company and it's your job to develop templates for distribution to the rest of the staff. The experience level of your co-workers varies widely—some employees understand how to fill in the blanks, and others don't.

The solution? Use Prompt Builder to create messages that ask users for information, and then plug that information into the template. It's as close as you can get to sitting right next to the users, explaining what they are supposed to do.

Follow these steps to insert prompts in a template:

1. In the PerfectExpert dialog box, select the template you are developing, and then choose Options, Edit WP Template.

2. Click where you want to place the information that the user types.

3. Click the Build Prompts button on the Template toolbar to display the Prompt Builder dialog box (see Figure 23.16).

**Figure 23.16**
In the Prompt Builder dialog box, you can create messages that prompt the user for information.

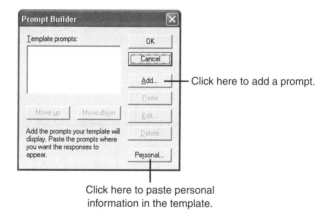

Click here to add a prompt.

Click here to paste personal information in the template.

4. Click Add to display the Add Template Prompt dialog box (see Figure 23.17).

**Figure 23.17**
In the Add Template Prompt dialog box, you can type the prompt text and select an address book field to link the prompt to.

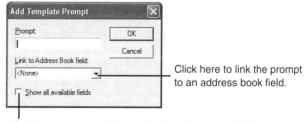

Click here to link the prompt to an address book field.

Click here to show all the available address book fields.

5. Type the message in the Prompt text box. You can type up to 160 characters, but you should try to keep it short (20 to 30 characters).

6. Click OK to add the prompt to the list in the Prompt Builder dialog box. Now that you've added the prompt to the list, you can paste it into the template.

7. Select the prompt in the Template Prompts list box, and then click Paste to insert it in the template. The prompt appears at the insertion point, with brackets around it (see Figure 23.18).

**Figure 23.18**
Using Prompt Builder, you can generate prompts that remind the user what to type.

New prompt

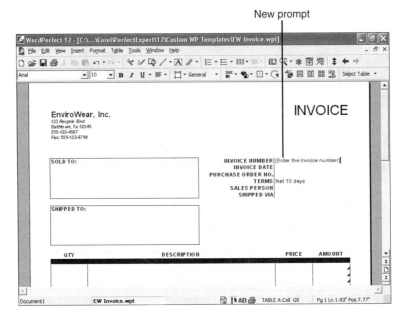

When you open a template with prompts, the Template Information dialog box appears with a list of the prompts in the template (see Figure 23.19).

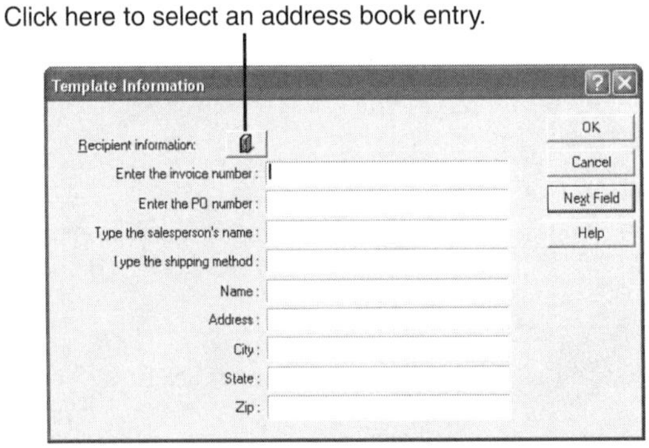

Click here to select an address book entry.

**Figure 23.19**
The Template Information dialog box contains text boxes for each of the prompts in a template.

## Working with Template Prompts

As you revise a template with prompts, you might have to move a few of them around. You might even decide to delete a section of the template, rendering some of the prompts obsolete. The key is to keep the template prompts and Prompt Builder prompts in sync. You can remove prompt text from a template, but you'll see that prompt displayed the next time you use the template if you don't remove the prompts from the Prompt Builder list.

Here are a few things to keep in mind as you work with the template prompts:

- Moving prompts—Make sure you select the brackets ([]) on each side of the prompt text, and then cut and paste the prompt.

- Rearranging prompts in Prompt Builder—When you run a template, you are prompted to fill in the information in the order in which the prompts appear in the Prompt Builder list. So, if you don't mind typing the ZIP Code before the name, leave them alone. Otherwise, arrange the prompts in the order that's easiest for you to fill them in. Select the prompt that you want to move, and then click Move Up or Move Down.

- Deleting prompts—After you've deleted the prompt text in the template, you have to delete the prompt in the Prompt Builder dialog box; otherwise, you'll still be prompted to type in the information, even though it isn't inserted anywhere. In the Prompt Builder dialog box, select the prompt, and then click Delete, Yes.

- Editing prompts—You can delete the old prompt text in the template. Select the prompt in Prompt Builder, and then choose Edit. Revise the prompt text and/or change the Link to Address Book field (you'll learn more about this in the next section). Reinsert the new prompt.

## Linking Prompts to Address Book Fields

Your company can have five employees or 5,000 employees—in either case, the client information is the most valuable asset. Maintaining a centralized list of names, addresses, and phone numbers is essential, and with the WordPerfect and Outlook address books, it's easy to do. Using one of the address books on your system, you can insert client information directly into a template.

You still have to create a prompt for the information, but WordPerfect fills it in for you when you select an entry from an address book. Follow these steps to link a prompt to an address book field:

1. Edit the template, and then click where you want the address book information to appear.

2. Click Build Prompts. In Prompt Builder, click Add.

3. Type the prompt text in the Prompt text box.

4. Click the Link to Address Book Field drop-down list, and then select a field from the list (see Figure 23.20).

CAUTION

> If you don't see the field you want, click the drop-down list arrow again (to close the list). Place a check mark next to Show All Available Fields, and then click the Link to Address Book Field drop-down list arrow again.

5. Click OK, and then paste the prompt into the template.

**Figure 23.20**
In the Add Template Prompt dialog box, you can link the prompt to an address book field.

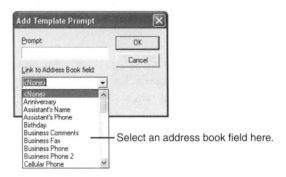

Select an address book field here.

When you run the template, the prompts appear in the Template Information dialog box (refer to Figure 23.19). Click the Address Book button to display the Address Book (or Outlook Address Book) dialog box, with a list of the Address Books on your system (refer back to Figure 23.6).

When you select an address book entry and choose Insert, WordPerfect displays a Format Address dialog box (see Figure 23.21).

**Figure 23.21**
You can choose from one of the predefined address formats in the Format Address dialog box.

Select the address format that you want to use, and then click OK twice to plug the information into the prompts that you linked to address book fields (see Figure 23.22).

 *If you're having trouble using fields from your Outlook address book in template prompts, see "My Outlook Address Book Fields Are Missing" in the Troubleshooting section at the end of this chapter.*

Information from the address book

**Figure 23.22**
After you select an entry from an address book, WordPerfect plugs that information into the template, replacing the prompts.

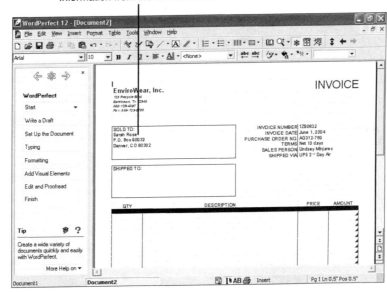

## INSERTING PERSONAL INFORMATION IN A TEMPLATE

Remember when you first used the Template feature and you had to select a personal information entry in the address book? Well, guess what? You can insert information from that entry into a template, too. For example, if you want a user's name to appear in a Salesperson or an Author prompt, you can insert a personal field for the person's name in the template.

To insert data from the personal information entry in the address book, click in the template where you want the information to appear. Open the Prompt Builder dialog box, and then click Personal. The Personal Fields dialog box appears (see Figure 23.23). Select a field, and then choose Paste.

**Figure 23.23**
By using the Personal Fields dialog box, you can paste one of the personal information fields into the template.

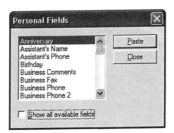

The personal information prompt appears in angle brackets (<>), so it looks different from the other prompts, which appear in square brackets ([]). When you run the template, the information is inserted from the Address Book (see Figure 23.24).

**NOTE**

You won't see the prompts you create for personal information in the Template Prompts list box of the Prompt Builder dialog box.

Personal information prompt

Regular prompt

**Figure 23.24**
Personal information prompts are surrounded with angle brackets, and regular prompts are surrounded by square brackets.

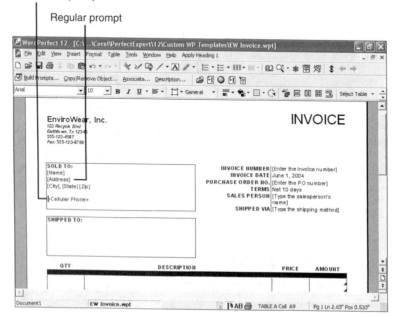

# CUSTOMIZING THE WORKING ENVIRONMENT

The toughest part of supporting computer users is catering to different levels of expertise. A manufacturing company, for example, might have a technician on the plant floor who needs to fill out production logs. Upstairs in the administrative offices, there is a temporary worker who has never worked with your company's documents before. Down the hall is the management team, which generates reams of reports, but doesn't seem too interested in learning the program.

If this is a typical day in your office, you've just found the perfect reason to implement templates. By using the Template feature and the PerfectExpert panel as your front end to WordPerfect, users can crank out documents without ever learning how to use a menu.

## ASSOCIATING MENUS AND KEYBOARDS

As you saw in an earlier section, you can attach objects to templates so that they are available only when you are using that template. Rather than create a monster list of menus or keyboards, you can embed them into various templates. The same goes for macros—you can create macros and attach them to a template. From that point forward, they are template macros, so they don't even show up in the macros folder.

→ If you are intrigued by the idea of embedding macros in templates to reduce macro clutter, **see** "Creating Template Macros," **p. 825.**

Now let's take this one step further. You can create an association to menus and keyboards so that they show up only in certain editing modes. As you change modes, the menu or keyboard layout changes dynamically and automatically.

The different editing modes in WordPerfect are

| | |
|---|---|
| Main (normal document window) | Graphics |
| Comments | Headers |
| Endnotes | Outline |
| Equation Editor | Tables |
| Footers | Watermark |
| Footnote | |

23

Follow these steps to create an associate to a feature:

1. Edit the template to open it in the editing window and display the Template feature bar.

2. Click Associate on the Template feature bar to display the Associate dialog box (see Figure 23.25).

Click here to display the features.

Click here to display the macro triggers.

**Figure 23.25**
In the Associate dialog box, you can associate a menu or a keyboard to a particular feature's editing mode.

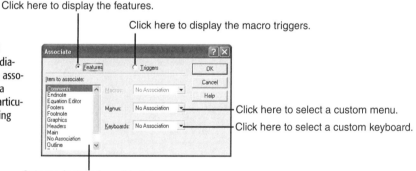

Click here to select a custom menu.
Click here to select a custom keyboard.

Select a feature from this list.

3. If necessary, choose Features.

4. Choose the editing mode you want to associate (Headers, Tables, Graphics, and so on).

5. Click the Menus or Keyboards drop-down list arrow and choose the menu (or keyboard) that you want to associate with this editing mode. Alternatively, choose No Association in the Menus or Keyboard drop-down lists to remove the association.

6. Repeat steps 4 and 5 to define other associations.

7. Click OK when you're finished.

**CAUTION**

If the menu or keyboard that you want to use doesn't appear in the list, you haven't attached it to this template yet. Cancel out of the Associate dialog box, and then either create the menu or keyboard or copy it from another template. See the section "Copying Objects from Other Templates," earlier in this chapter, for more information.

## ASSOCIATING MACROS TO TRIGGERS

Macros work a little differently. You don't associate them with an editing mode, but with an event, or trigger. Table 23.1 lists the macro triggers and what they do.

For example, say you have set up a shared workstation for paralegals to use. These systems have templates to generate standard legal documents. In each template, you associate a macro with printing, so when the user sends a document to the printer, this macro runs and prompts for the client number. After this information is typed in (and plugged into a resource usage log so you can bill the printing costs back to the client), the document is printed.

You could also associate a macro with opening a template. This macro would prompt for the paralegal's name and the client number, so the paralegal's time spent creating and printing the document could be billed back to the client.

### TABLE 23.1 MACRO TRIGGERS

| Macro Trigger | What Does It Do |
|---|---|
| Post Close | Runs in the active window after you close a window. |
| Post New | Runs after you open a new document by using File, New. |
| Post Open | Runs after you open a document by using File, Open. |
| Post Print | Runs after you send a job to the printer. |
| Post Startup | Runs when you start WordPerfect. This macro must be associated with the default template to work. |
| Post Switch Doc | Runs in the active window after you switch from another window. |
| Post Tables | Runs after you create a table definition, but before you type anything. |
| Pre Close | Runs before you close the window by choosing File, Close. |
| Pre New | Runs before you open a new document by using File, New. |
| Pre Open | Runs before you open another document by using File, Open. |
| Pre Print | Runs after you choose File, Print, but before the document is sent to the printer. |
| Pre Switch Doc | Runs in the active window before you switch to another window. |
| Pre Tables | Runs after you create a table (by using Insert, Table), but before the table definition is created in the document. |

Follow these steps to associate a macro with one of these triggers:

1. Edit the template to open it in the editing window and display the Template feature bar.

2. Click Associate on the Template feature bar to display the Associate dialog box (refer back to Figure 23.25).

3. Click the Triggers option.

4. In the Item to Associate list box, select the trigger you want to use (see Figure 23.26).

Choose a trigger from this list.

**Figure 23.26**
In the Associate dialog box, you can assign a template macro to an event or a trigger.

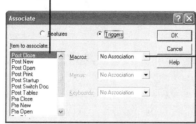

Choose a template macro from this drop-down list.

5. Click the Macros drop-down list arrow and choose the macro you want to associate with this trigger. Alternatively, choose No Association to remove a trigger association.

6. Repeat steps 4 and 5 to define the other trigger associations.

7. Click OK when you're done.

**CAUTION**

The macro you want to associate to a trigger must already be a part of the template, or it won't appear in the Macros list. If you don't see the macro you want, cancel out of the Associate dialog box, and then create the macro and copy it to the template. See the section "Copying Objects from Other Templates" earlier in this chapter for more information.

**TIP FROM**

*Laura Acklen*

Template macros increase the size of the file, so try to avoid embedding large macros in your templates. The larger the template, the slower it runs.

**NOTE**

If you've created a template from scratch and you've added prompts to it, you're probably wondering how to display the Template Information dialog box, where users can fill in the prompts and have WordPerfect insert the information into the template. (You might want to refer to Figure 23.19 to refresh your memory.)

*continues*

*continued*

> The answer is the `TemplateFill()` macro command, which starts the DoFiller feature. You can create a simple macro with just this command, and then associate it with the Post New trigger. If you already have a template macro associated with the Post New trigger, you can edit that macro and add the command to the macro. Choose Tools, Template Macro, Edit to edit the template macro.

# USING TEMPLATES FROM EARLIER VERSIONS OF WORDPERFECT

Heavy-duty template users don't want to hear that they can't use their existing templates in the newest release of WordPerfect. And they don't have to. The templates that you created in previous versions can be used in WordPerfect 11 and 12. Some might have to be converted, and those using address book fields might need some fine-tuning, but for the most part, your hard work won't go down the drain.

First, you need to copy the templates to the template folder where the WordPerfect 11 (or 12) templates are stored (\program files\wordperfect office 11\template or \program files\wordperfect office 12\template), or the Custom WP Template folder that is specified in the File Settings dialog box (choose Tools, Settings, File, and then click the Template tab). You can create subfolders in either of the template folders to organize the templates. These folder names appear as categories in the drop-down list (see Figure 23.27). This naming system helps keep the older templates separate from the templates that shipped with WordPerfect 11 and 12.

Drop-down list of category names.

**Figure 23.27**
Subfolders of the Templates folder appear as categories in the list.

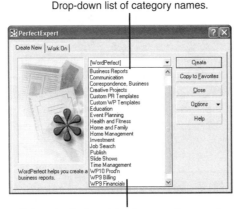

Categories for templates from previous versions

After you've copied the templates over, follow these steps to prepare templates for use in WordPerfect 11 (or 12):

1. Choose File, New from Project.

2. Select Options, Add Project. This launches an expert to guide you through the proc of adding a new project template (see Figure 23.28).

**Figure 23.28**
There is an Add Projects Expert to guide you through the process of adding a new project template to the list.

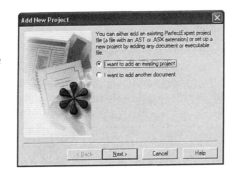

23

3. The default selection is to add an existing project, so choose Next.

4. Browse for the AST file that corresponds to the desired project template. The filename will be the same as the template—only the extension is different. WordPerfect 7 or earlier templates might not have an associated AST file. If this is the case, choose Back, choose Add Another Document, and then choose Next to proceed.

5. After you select the AST file, you might be able to choose Finish to add the project. Otherwise, you will be prompted to select the corresponding template (WPT) file. Now, you can choose Finish.

At this point, you've associated the template to the PerfectExpert, but you still need to debug, recompile, and save, if necessary, any existing macro commands within the template.

Follow these steps to recompile the macro commands in a template:

1. Choose File, New from Project.

2. Select the newly associated template.

3. Choose Options, Edit WP Template. Click Yes to convert the template. Click Yes to overwrite the original template.

4. Choose Tools, Template Macro Edit. You can now make your changes, save, and recompile the macro commands within the template.

→ For more information on debugging, saving, and recompiling macros, **see** "Using Macros from Previous Versions of WordPerfect," **p. 839.**

**NOTE**

The older the version of a macro, the more difficult it may be to debug the macros due to changes in the macro language from one version to another. When converting from WP8 macros, there can be a significant amount of syntax errors; with WP9, you will have fewer issues; and WP10 should be fine.

As you have seen, you can convert a template by editing it and then saving your changes. Even if you haven't made any changes, this triggers the tconvert.wcm macro that converts the template. You can also run the tconvert.wcm macro manually by choosing Tools, Macro, Play. Scroll down, and then double-click tconvert. When the Convert Template dialog box appears, type the name of the template or click the Files icon to browse for the file. Click OK to convert the template, and then save the template.

→ To learn more about the macros that come with WordPerfect, **see** "Running the Shipping Macros," **p. 818**.

 *If you try to convert an old template and get the error message* tconvert.wcm not found, *see "tconvert.wcm Not Found" in the Troubleshooting section at the end of this chapter.*

**TIP FROM**

*Laura Acklen*

> You will run into problems using templates with links to address book fields that no longer exist. If the older version of WordPerfect is still available, edit the template in that version and remove all the links to address book fields. Next, edit the template in WordPerfect 11 (or 12) and reselect the address book fields. Otherwise, edit the template in WordPerfect 11 (or 12), delete the prompts, and then re-create them.

# TROUBLESHOOTING

## MISSING OR DAMAGED TEMPLATE FILES

*When I choose File, New from Project and double-click a project, the following error message appears:* <filename>.wpt cannot be opened or retrieved: the file cannot be found.

The template file associated with this project is missing or damaged. You can get a fresh copy of this template file from the WordPerfect Office CD. Keep in mind that when you reinstall the PerfectExpert Projects, any changes that you made to the those templates will be lost (unless, of course, you saved your changes with a new template name).

In previous versions, you were able to restore an individual template file by copying it over from the WordPerfect Office CD. Sadly, the installation program had to be redesigned in order to run on the newer Windows operating systems, and so files are now stored in "cabinets." To get a fresh copy of a template file, you'll have to do a repair install, which fixes missing or corrupt files, shortcuts, and Registry entries.

It only takes a few minutes, so locate and insert the WordPerfect Office 11 (or 12) CD. If the Install Wizard doesn't start automatically, choose Start, Run, and then browse to the CD drive. Double-click on intro.exe to start the install.

Choose Repair Installation Errors in the Program, and then choose Next. Choose Detect and Repair Errors in the Program, and then choose Begin. Click Finish when the repair is complete.

After you've repaired the templates, use the Refresh command to update the project list. In the PerfectExpert dialog box, choose Options, Refresh Projects, and then click OK.

If you continue to get the message, it could be that the template list doesn't accurately reflect what is actually installed on your system. This can sometimes happen when you upgrade from a previous version. You can rebuild the projects list by renaming and re-creating the `projects.usr` file. Exit WordPerfect and then click Start, Search, All files and Folders in Windows XP/2000; click Start, Find, Files or Folders in Windows 98. Type **projects.usr** in the Filename text box. If necessary, scroll down and choose a drive to search in the Look In list box. Click Search or Find Now. When the file appears in the list, right-click it and then choose Rename. Type **projects.old** and then press Enter. Start WordPerfect, and choose File, New from Project. There will be a short pause while the `projects.usr` file is re-created. The new list should now reflect the projects that are actually installed.

**NOTE**

> If a project file is missing or damaged, you might still get the PerfectExpert panel when you open the template, but the buttons in the panel are for creating a generic document. They are not the buttons that control the template. You'll need to do a quick repair install to repair (or replace) the template files.

### RE-ENABLING THE PERFECTSCRIPT MESSAGE

*I didn't mean to, but I accidentally checked the box to turn off the PerfectScript message box that asks if you want to disable macros in the document or not. Is there any way to turn that message back on?*

Absolutely! It involves editing the Registry though, so if you aren't comfortable doing this, you should find someone who is. Offer to buy them lunch if they will make this change for you.

Before you get started, make sure you back up the Registry. That way, if something goes awry, you have a backup copy to fall back on.

Using Regedit, go to the HKEY_CURRENT_USER\Software\Corel\WordPerfect\ 11\HideDialogs\Contains Script and HKEY_CURRENT_USER\Software\ Corel\WordPerfect\12\HideDialogs\Contains Script key. Change the value from 2 to 0 (zero).

### MY NEW TEMPLATE ISN'T SHOWING UP

*I just created and saved a new template, but now I can't find it in the list. Where did the template get saved?*

When you save a template, you type a description that appears in the project list and a template filename. The last step is to select a category where the template is saved. Because you don't have to type anything (you select a category from a drop-down list), it's easy to overlook that last step.

If you don't choose a category, WordPerfect stores the new template in the first category in the list: Business Reports. In the PerfectExpert dialog box, click the category drop-down list arrow and then choose Business Reports. Select the new template from this list, choose Options, Move Project, and select the proper category from the pop-up list.

If the new template doesn't appear in the Business Reports category (or in the other categories), you need to rebuild the project index, which contains a list of all the templates and categories. Click Start, Search, All Files and Folders in Windows XP/2000; click Start, Find, Files or Folders in Windows 98. Type **projects.usr** in the Filename text box. If necessary, scroll down and choose a drive to search in the Look In list box. Click Search or Find Now. When the file appears in the list, right-click it; then, choose Rename. Type **projects.old** and then press Enter. Choose File, New from Project. WordPerfect should hesitate for a moment while the index is rebuilt; then, the list of projects should appear. Look in the Business Reports category first.

### MY OUTLOOK ADDRESS BOOK FIELDS ARE MISSING

*When I try to create prompts that are linked to my address book fields, the fields from my Outlook address books don't show up. What do I need to do to make these appear in the list?*

You must activate the Outlook integration before you can use information from your Outlook address book. Choose Tools, Settings, Environment. Enable the Use Outlook Address Book/Contact List check box. Click OK, and then Close. Your Outlook address book fields should now appear in the Edit Template Prompt dialog box.

### TCONVERT.WCM NOT FOUND

*I'm trying to convert an old WordPerfect template, and I've tried editing the template and running the tconvert macro. Either way, I'm getting the error message "tconvert.wcm Not Found." Where is this file?*

This is a shipping macro that is installed with the program, so either the macro wasn't installed, or WP is looking in the wrong place. Choose Tools, Settings, Files, and then click the Merge/Macro tab. Make a note of the path listed in the Default Macro Folder text box. Now, choose Tools, Macro, Play. Verify that this is the same folder as the one listed in Settings. If it isn't, browse to the folder that was listed in Settings and look for the macro there.

If you still can't find it, go ahead and get a fresh copy from the CD. A repair install only takes a few minutes. Locate and insert the WordPerfect Office 11 (or 12) CD. If the install wizard doesn't start automatically, choose Start, Run, and then browse to the CD drive. Double-click on intro.exe to start the install.

Choose Repair Installation Errors in the Program, and then choose Next. Choose Detect and Repair Errors in the Program, and then choose Begin. Click Finish when the repair is complete.

You should now be able to locate the tconvert.wcm macro in the folder that is listed in Settings.

# PROJECT

You probably have users who are fighting the upgrade because they are afraid they'll lose all their hard work in customizing the program. Not so. You can transfer almost everything—addresses, macros, QuickWords, toolbars, keyboards, menus, templates, custom dictionaries, styles, labels, and, of course, documents. WordPerfect uses the same file format in version 6.1, 7, 8, 9, 10, and 11, so you won't have any problems opening and editing documents created in previous versions.

**TIP FROM**

*Laura Acklen*

> WordPerfect Universe has an excellent FAQ that explains what files you need to backup for an uninstall, reinstall, or an upgrade. You can search through the forum posts and read all you want for free. You need to register in order to post a question, but that can wait until later. Visit www.wpuniverse.com. On the left side, the top pane has a list of links to the forums. Click FAQ. Scroll down and click the thread titled "What files do I need to backup if I need to uninstall/reinstall/upgrade?"

A good bit of the customization that you do in WordPerfect is saved to the default template as objects. All you have to do is copy these objects from the default template for the previous version to the default template for WordPerfect 11 or 12.

Here are the steps for transferring over the custom templates, toolbars, property bars, styles, menus, keyboards, and template macros. These steps assume installation on a local hard drive:

1. Copy the templates that you created in the previous version to the WP Custom Templates folder for WordPerfect 11 (or 12). The location of the WP Custom Templates folder is shown in the File Settings dialog box. Choose Tools, Settings, Files, and then click the Template tab. If you have created subfolders for your templates, copy the entire folder structure into the WP Custom Templates folder. (The subfolders will appear as categories in the list.)

2. Follow the steps shown in the "Using Templates from Earlier Versions of WordPerfect" section for each of the templates (you don't have to do them all right now), and then save them (even if you didn't make any changes). Editing a template triggers a conversion if one is necessary to make the template useable in WordPerfect 11 (or 12).

3. The next step is to copy the objects from the old default template into the default template for WordPerfect 11 (or 12). If you didn't copy the default template for the previous version of WordPerfect in steps 1 and 2, you need to do that now. The default template for the previous version needs to be copied into the Custom WP Templates folder for WordPerfect 11 (or 12):

- For version 11 on Windows 98/ME, copy the `wp11us.wpt` file from the `\windows\application data\corel\perfectexpert\11\custom wp templates` folder. On Windows NT 4, copy the `wp11us.wpt` file from the `\WinNT\profiles\<username>\application data\corel\perfectexpert\11\custom wp templates` folder. On Windows 2000/XP with SP4, copy the `wp11us.wpt` file from the `\documents and settings\<username>\application data\corel\perfectexpert\11\custom wp templates` folder.

**NOTE**

> In Windows 2000/XP, the Application Data folder is a hidden folder. To show hidden files and folders in Windows, open Explorer. Choose Tools, Folder Options, the click the View tab. Select the Show Hidden Files and Folders option. Choose OK.

- For version 10 on Windows 98/ME, copy the `wp10us.wpt` file from the `\windows\application data\corel\perfectexpert\10\custom wp templates` folder. On Windows NT 4, copy the `wp10us.wpt` file from the `\WinNT\profiles\`*`<username>`*`\application data\corel\perfectexpert\10\custom wp templates` folder. On Windows 2000/XP with SP4, copy the `wp10us.wpt` file from the `\documents and settings\<username>\application data\corel\perfectexpert\10\custom wp templates` folder.

- For version 9 on Windows 98/ME, copy the `wp9us.wpt` file from the `\windows\application data\corel\perfectexpert\9\custom wp templates` folder. On Windows NT 4, copy the `wp9us.wpt` file from the `\WinNT\profiles\`*`<username>`*`\application data\corel\perfectexpert\9\custom wp templates` folder. On Windows 2000/XP with SP4, copy the `wp9us.wpt` file from the `\documents and settings\`*`<username>`*`\application data\corel\perfectexpert\9\custom wp templates` folder.

- For version 8, copy the `wp8us.wpt` file from the `\corel\suite8\template\custom wp templates` folder.

- For version 7, copy the `wp7us.wpt` file from the `\corel\office7\template` folder.

- For version 6.1, copy the `standard.wpt` file from the `\office\wpwin\template` folder.

4. Now, edit the WordPerfect 11 (or 12) default template. Choose File, New from Project. Click the category drop-down list arrow and choose WP Custom Templates. Select Create a Blank Document from the list.

**CAUTION**

> This step is a little tricky because now you have two "Create a Blank Document" entries (one for WordPerfect 11 or 12 and one for the default template from the previous version of WordPerfect). In my experience, the first one is the WordPerfect 11 (or 12) default template and the second one is the default template for the previous version. Just to be on the safe side, right-click the first one, and choose Project Properties. In the Project

> Template Properties dialog box, click in the Project Filename text box. Press End to move to the end of the line so you can see the filename—now you know which default template it is!

5. Choose Options, Edit WP Template to edit the WordPerfect 11 (or 12) default template.

6. Click the Copy/Remove Objects button on the Template toolbar.

7. Click the Templates to Copy From drop-down list arrow, and then select the previous version's default template (i.e. WpxxUS.wpt, where *xx* is the version number for the U.S. edition).

8. Click the Object Type drop-down list arrow and choose the type of object you want to copy. For example, choose toolbars to copy the toolbars.

9. Select the items you want to copy, and then click Copy >>.

10. Click Close when you're done.

11. Save the changes to the template. You should now make a backup copy of the template because you've just made some changes.

Styles won't show up in the template unless you specifically save them to the default template. If you still have the previous version of WordPerfect, copy the styles to the default template for that version, and then copy that revised template back over to the WordPerfect 11 (or 12) Custom WP Templates folder, and try again. If you don't have the previous version on your system anymore, open a document that contains those styles in WordPerfect 11 (or 12). Select the styles that you want, and then save them to the WordPerfect 11 (or 12) default template.

Transferring over your QuickWords is fairly simple—you just copy the QuickWord file from the previous version so you can replace the blank QuickWord file in WordPerfect 11 (or 12). You can either search your system for QW8EN.WPT, QW9EN.WPT, QW10EN.WPT, or QW11EN.WPT (for the English version of WordPerfect), or look for the file in the folders mentioned in step 3. The QuickWords template is stored in the same folder as the default folder. When you've found the file, copy it to the WP Custom Templates folder for WordPerfect 11 (or 12), also mentioned previously. Switch to that folder and rename the QuickWords template that came with your new version (WordPerfect 11 or 12) to QWxxENOLD.WPT. Now, rename the template file from the previous version to QW11EN.WPT or QW12EN.WPT, depending on your new version number. Let me restate what you are doing, just to make sure I'm clear. You are taking your old QuickWords file and replacing the new, blank QuickWords file, bringing all of your QuickWords from the previous version into the new version.

If you've added words to the QuickCorrect list, or otherwise customized your user word list, you can bring that into the new version. The concept is the same as for QuickWords— you are replacing the default user word list with the customized user word list by copying and renaming the user word list file, called WTxxUS.UWL. The default location for the user word list in WordPerfect 8/9/10/11 on Windows 98/ME is \my documents\corel user files; in Windows 2000/XP it is \documents and settings\<*username*>\my documents\corel user files; in Windows NT 4 it is \winnt\profiles\<*username*>\my documents\corel user files. Make a copy of the user word list file and paste it into the folder for the new version. Rename the new version to WTxxUSOLD.UWL, and then rename the user word list for the old version so it can be used in the new version: WT11US.UWL or WT12US.UWL, depending on the new version number.

To transfer over your address books, you'll need to export them from the previous version. Export each book to .abx or .txt format. In WordPerfect 11 (or 12), make sure you have des-elected Outlook Integration (choose Tools, Settings, Environment, remove the check mark next to Use Outlook Address Book/Contact List). Next, open the address book and create a new address book for each address book that you want to import. So, if you have four address books to import, create four new address books in WordPerfect 11 (or 12). In the Address Book dialog box, choose File, Import/Export. Select Import, Next. In the Import From list, select the TXT file that you created when you exported your address book from the previous version. In the Import To list, select the blank address book that you created. Click Next, and then click Next again to move past the Field Mapping screen. Click Finish. You'll see a brief message box during the import. Repeat the steps for each address book until you have all of your address books in the new version of WordPerfect.

→ For more information on copying styles to the default template, **see** "Saving Styles," **p. 278**.

→ For more information on transferring macros from a previous version, **see** "Using Macros from Previous Versions of WordPerfect," **p. 839.**

→ For more information on migrating address books, **see** "Importing and Exporting Address Book Entries," **p. 797.**

# ASSEMBLING DOCUMENTS WITH MERGE

# GETTING FAMILIAR WITH MERGE TERMINOLOGY

Everyone calls it a *mail merge*, but you can really pull together *any* type of information to produce *any* type of document. So, although you hear more about using the Merge feature to produce personalized letters, envelopes, and labels, it's also a very powerful tool for organizing key pieces of information.

As the term suggests, a merge is a combination of information from two different sources. Typically, you have a form file, which is the document, and one data file, which contains the information you want to insert. The form file is just a regular document with merge codes in it. The merge codes act as markers for the information from the data file.

A data file is organized into records, which contain fields for every piece of information. Using the mail merge example, the data file is a list of names and addresses, and the form file is the letter. Each person, client, or event has a *record* that is divided into *fields*, such as name, company, address, and phone.

# WORKING WITH DATA FILES

It's easiest to build a data file first, so you can use the field names that you create in the form document. Field names are used to identify the merge field codes that you create to organize the data file. For example, a typical data file might contain these fields: Name, Company, Address, City, State, Zip, Phone, Fax, and E-mail. Field names are optional, though—you can use Field1, Field2, Field3, and so on, if you prefer.

The main thing to keep in mind when you're creating the data file is that more fields mean more flexibility. For example, if you have three separate fields for the city, state, and ZIP Code, you can arrange the list by ZIP Code. The same goes for the name—if you use one field for first name and one field for last name, you can arrange the records by the last name and you can break out the first name for a personalized salutation. Each field can be acted upon individually. This is how the Publisher's Clearinghouse folks make those letters seem so personal. The last letter I received had my city and county broken out and used in the letter, as well as my name, address, and state. And these letters are extremely effective!

# CREATING DATA FILES

It's easy to create a data file from scratch, but before you do, make sure you don't already have the information stored somewhere else. There are several ways to convert information from other sources into a merge data file. You might have a little cleanup to do, but at least you aren't entering the information all over again. If you already have a file to work with, you can skip down to the next several sections, which contain information on converting tables and importing data into merge data files.

Follow these steps to create a data file from scratch:

1. Choose Tools, Merge or press Shift+F9 to display the Merge dialog box (see Figure 24.1).

Click to create
a data file                                Click to browse for a file

**Figure 24.1**
Use the Merge dialog box to set up a data file and a form document, and then merge them.

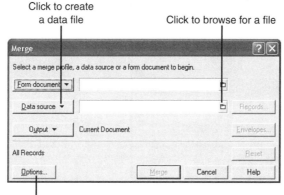

Click to set the merge options

→ For more information on pulling records directly from the Address Book during a merge, **see** "Merging with the Address Book," **p. 765.**

2. Choose Data Source to open the list of data sources that can be used in a merge.

3. Choose Create Data File to display the Create Data File dialog box (see Figure 24.2). This is where you create the field names.

Type the name of the field

**Figure 24.2**
In the Create Data File dialog box, you can create and edit the field names for the data file.

4. Type the name of the first field name in the Name a Field text box.

5. Press Enter or choose Add to insert the field name in the Fields Used in Merge list box.

6. Repeat steps 3 and 4 until you've entered all the field names. If you misspell a field name, or change your mind, select the field, and then choose Delete. Figure 24.3 shows a typical list of field names.

**Figure 24.3**
Here is a list of field names that you might use for a merge data file.

Click to format the data in a table

*If you can't enter all of the information you need in a field, see "I Can't Enter More Than 250 Characters in a Field" in the Troubleshooting section at the end of this chapter.*

**TIP FROM**

The order of the field names is important because this is the order in which you'll type the information. If you need to rearrange the field names, select a name and then choose Move Up or Move Down.

7. If you want the records formatted into a table, place a check mark in the Format Records in a Table check box.

**TIP FROM**

Formatting a data file in a table has many advantages. In a table, each field has its own column, and each row is one record. Data files that aren't formatted as a table have merge codes that separate fields and records. You have to be especially careful when editing this type of data file so you don't accidentally delete one of the merge codes. The main disadvantage is that if you have a lot of fields, you'll get a table with lots of columns, so it's harder to navigate around and you won't be able to see all of the information on one screen.

8. Click OK when you're finished. The Quick Data Entry dialog box appears (see Figure 24.4). You can use this dialog box to enter and edit records in the data file.

9. Type the data for the first field and then press Enter or Tab (or choose Next Field) to move down to the next field. Press Shift+Tab or choose Previous Field to move back up a field.

10. Continue entering the information in each field. When you press Enter in the last field, a new record is created. You can also choose New Record from any field to create a blank record.

**TIP FROM**

Don't include extra spaces or punctuation marks when you enter the data. For example, don't type a comma after the city. All formatting and punctuation marks should be in the form document.

**Figure 24.4**
Most people prefer using the Quick Data Entry dialog box for creating and editing records in the data file.

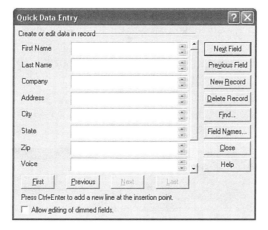

**TIP FROM**

You can move back and forth between records by clicking the Previous and Next buttons at the bottom of the Quick Data Entry dialog box. Click the First button to move to the first record; click the Last button to move to the last record.

11. Choose Close when you're finished.

12. Choose Yes to save the data file to disk. The Save File dialog box appears (see Figure 24.5).

13. Type a name for the data file in the File Name text box and then click Save.

**NOTE**

WordPerfect suggests a .dat extension for data files. If you follow this suggestion, you can choose WP Merge Data (*.dat) from the File Type drop-down list and display only merge data files in the file list, which makes it easier to locate your data files.

**Figure 24.5**
You can type a name for the data file in the Save File dialog box.

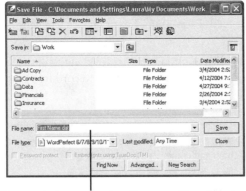

The Auto-suggest filename feature suggests a filename with a .dat extension

When the Save File dialog box closes, you can see the data that you've entered so far. Figure 24.6 shows the data in table format. Notice that the Merge feature bar has been added to the top of the screen. The generic property bar has also morphed into the Tables property bar with lots of buttons for working with tables.

Each field name is a column

Merge feature bar

Tables property bar

**Figure 24.6**
Formatting the records in a table has many advantages. Not only is it easier to read the information in table format, but you can easily manipulate the data by using the buttons on the Table property bar.

Each record is a row

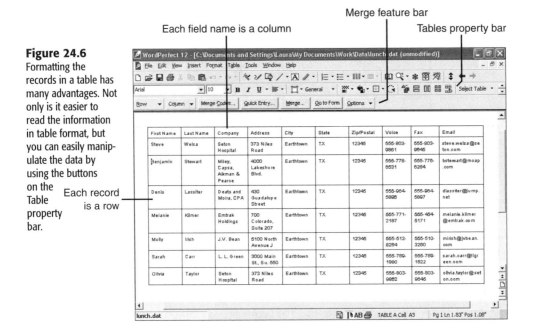

After you've finished entering the information, you can always go back and edit it later. You can add and edit records directly (in the table or in the text file), or you can click the Quick Entry button on the Merge feature bar to open the Quick Data Entry dialog box.

24

**TIP FROM**

If you're doing heavy-duty data entry in a text data file, it slows you down to take your hand off the keyboard to click a button. Instead of clicking the buttons on the Merge feature bar, press Alt+Shift+F (or Alt+Enter) to insert an End Field code. Press Alt+Shift+Enter to insert an End Record code.

## EDITING FIELD NAMES

If you need to edit the field names, you can choose from several methods. First, if the data is in a table, you can simply edit the column headings. If the data is formatted as text (not a table), you can make your changes to the field names at the top of the data file (the field names are separated by semicolons).

Finally, you can do so from the Quick Data Entry dialog box (refer to Figure 24.4). Click the Field Names button to open the Edit Field Names dialog box, where you can add, rename, and delete field names (see Figure 24.7).

Type a new field name

**Figure 24.7**
From the Edit Field Names dialog box, you can add new fields, rename fields, and remove fields from the data file.

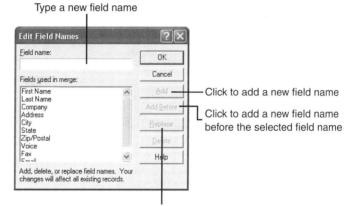

Click to add a new field name

Click to add a new field name before the selected field name

Click to replace the selected field name with the new field name

**NOTE**

If the Field Names button is grayed out in the Quick Data Entry dialog box, field names weren't created in this data file. See the section "Adding Field Names to a Data File" later in this chapter for the steps to add the field names.

**CAUTION**

Beware! Renaming and deleting field names deletes the contents of that field in every record. When you use Delete, you at least get a warning message, so you have a chance to bail out; you don't get a warning when you rename a field name. It's better to be safe than sorry—save the data file before you edit the field names.

**TIP FROM**

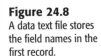

In large data files, you can use the Find feature to locate records quickly. In the Quick Data Entry dialog box, click the Find button to open the Find Text dialog box. Otherwise, press F2, press Ctrl+F, or choose Edit, Find and Replace to open the Find and Replace dialog box. In either dialog box, type the text you want to search for in the Find text box and then choose Find Next.

## CONVERTING TEXT DATA FILES TO TABLES AND VICE VERSA

When you create a data file, you have a choice. You can create the data file as a table or as a text file. You can see what the table looks like in Figure 24.6. Figure 24.8 shows what a data text file looks like. If you've inherited a text data file from someone else, and you prefer to work with tables, you can convert the text data file into a data file table.

Click to insert an End Field code

Click to insert an End Record code

The Field names record is at the top of the file

**Figure 24.8**
A data text file stores the field names in the first record.

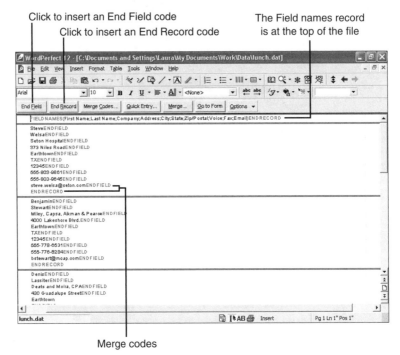

Merge codes

The following are the steps to convert a text data file into a table:

1. Position the insertion point at the beginning of the first data record (not the field name record).

2. Press Shift+Ctrl+End to select from the first data record down to the end of the file.

3. Choose Table, Create (or press F12). The Convert: Text to Table dialog box appears (see Figure 24.9).

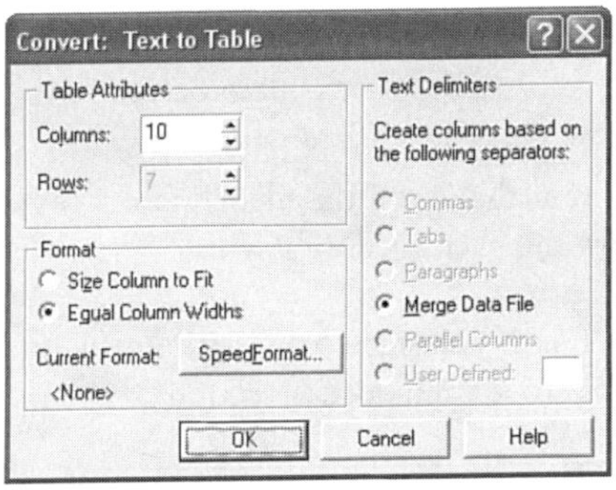

**Figure 24.9**
In the Convert: Text to Table dialog box, you can choose the type of text you want to convert to a table.

4. Choose Merge Data File and click OK. WordPerfect creates a column for each field and a row for each record and reads the field name record to assign the column headings.

You can also go the other way and convert a data file table to a text data file. Interestingly, you can even create a text data file from an ordinary table (without the field names). The following are the steps to convert a table into a text data file:

1. Move to the top of the document and turn on Reveal Codes (by pressing Alt+F3).
2. Move the red cursor to the left of the [Tbl Def] code (the table definition code).
3. Press Delete. The Delete Table dialog box appears (see Figure 24.10).

**Figure 24.10**
Depending on the type of table, you can choose to create the text data file with or without field names in the Delete Table dialog box.

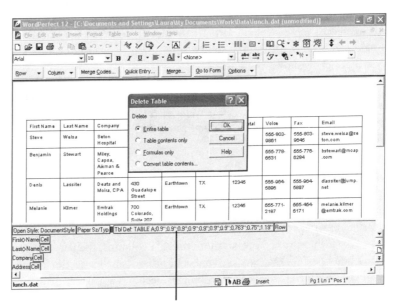

Table definition code

4. Choose Convert Table Contents to open the Convert: Table to Text dialog box.

5. Choose Convert Contents to Merge Data File (*.dat). Selecting this option also enables the option to use the text in the first row as field names.

6. If you have a field name record at the top of the file, choose Use Text In First Row As Field Names. Otherwise, leave the check box disabled.

WordPerfect creates the text data file. If you started out with a table that didn't have field names, you can add those now (the steps are in a later section).

---

**Navigating Through Long Data Files**

In a lengthy text data file, it's easy to lose your place. If you turn on line numbering, you have a number next to each field, which not only helps you keep your place, but also makes it easier to spot records with missing fields. Line numbers restart numbering at the top of every page, so every record has the same line numbers. At the top of the data file, choose Format, Line, Numbering. Place a check mark next to Turn Line Numbering On, and then click OK.

Also, the application bar has a General Status button (on the right, next to the Combined Position group) that displays the field name where the insertion point is currently located. The General Status button can be enlarged so that the entire field name shows (right-click the button, choose Settings, and then click and drag the left or right border of the button).

---

## IMPORTING DATA INTO MERGE DATA FILES

You can use files from other applications as data files, and in some cases, you need not convert them prior to the merge. In addition to files from other word processing programs, WordPerfect supports the import of data files created in spreadsheet and database programs. If field names were used in the source application, they are recognized and used by WordPerfect, as shown in Figure 24.11.

**TIP FROM**

*Laura Acklen*

If you're upgrading to WordPerfect 11/12 from a previous version of WordPerfect, you can use secondary merge files as data files.

Files from popular spreadsheet programs can be imported into WordPerfect and then used as merge data files. However, because spreadsheets are converted into tables, they are restricted by the same limitations as tables. For example, there is a 64-column limit on tables, so if the spreadsheet has more than 64 columns, the data in the remaining columns won't be imported. One workaround is to import smaller sections of the spreadsheet—this is where the convenience of named ranges becomes apparent. Another workaround is to save the spreadsheet as a database, and then import it into WordPerfect. For example, you can save a Quattro Pro spreadsheet as a Paradox database file, and then import the Paradox database into WordPerfect.

Each field ends with an End Field code

Field name record

Records are separated by a hard page

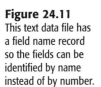

**Figure 24.11**
This text data file has a field name record so the fields can be identified by name instead of by number.

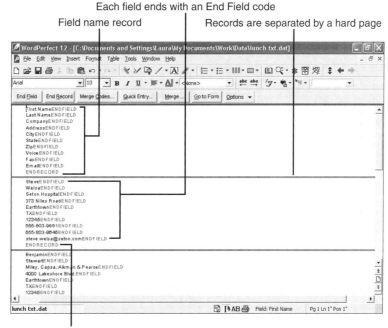

Each record ends with an End Record code

→ If you want to convert a spreadsheet file into a data file table, **see** "Converting Spreadsheet Data," **p. 488.**

→ If you want to create a link to a spreadsheet file, **see** "Linking Spreadsheet Data," **p. 488.**

The database format in WordPerfect is the same as a merge data file, so you can either convert the database file to a merge data file, or you can use it "as is." You might also consider creating links to a database file so that when you update the database, the data file information is updated as well.

→ If you want to convert the database file to a merge data file, **see** "Conversion to WordPerfect Formats," **p. 477.**

→ If you want to use the database file without first converting it to a data file, **see** "Using Database Data with Merge," **p. 485.**

→ If you want to create a link to a database file, **see** "Linking Database Data," **p. 481.**

## ADDING FIELD NAMES TO A DATA FILE

Often you inherit files from other users, who may or may not understand how to use the program. Such is the case with merge data files. Not everyone takes the time to create field names. Granted, you don't have to do it. As long as you don't mind referring to the fields by number, it's fine to leave the file that way. However, in files with lots of fields, field names are necessary to preserve your sanity.

Follow these steps to add field names to a text data file:

1. Press Ctrl+Home to move to the top of the document.
2. Click the Merge Codes button.
3. Scroll through the list, and then select the FIELDNAMES code.
4. Choose Insert, and then choose Close.
5. In the Create Data File dialog box (refer back to Figure 23.2), type the field names, pressing Enter between each field name.
6. When you are finished, choose OK to insert a field names records to the top of the data file.

At the end of the line, notice the End Record code, followed by a hard page (refer to Figure 24.8). Each record in a text data file is separated by a hard page break. This ensures that when you merge the data file with a form document, the resulting documents are on separate pages.

**TIP FROM**

*Laura Acklen*

> Field names can be added later by typing them into the Fieldnames code—just make sure you include the semicolons between them (but no spaces).

Follow these steps to add field names to data in a table:

1. Right-click in the first cell of the top row.
2. Choose Insert. The Insert Rows/Columns dialog box appears.
3. Choose Rows, choose Before in the Placement section, and then click OK.
4. Type a field name in each column.

When you're working in a table, you don't need to insert End Field and End Record codes because WordPerfect knows that each row is a record and each column is a field.

# CREATING FORM FILES

Relax—this is the easy part, and if you've already typed the document, you're almost done! An existing document can be turned into a form file in just seconds. You just insert the merge codes and save the document. Voilà! It's ready for a merge.

If you're creating the form file from scratch, make sure that you insert all the formatting codes you want in the finished documents. You definitely don't want to put formatting codes (or anything besides text) in the data file; otherwise, it is duplicated over and over again.

24

**TIP FROM**

*Laura Achlen*

> If you're upgrading from a previous version of WordPerfect, you might be more familiar
> with the terms *form file* or *primary merge file* that describe the form document.

If you want to use an existing document, open it now. In a new document, type any text that you need to precede the information that you want to insert during the merge. Then, follow these steps:

1. Choose Tools, Merge (or press Shift+F9) to open the Merge dialog box (seen in Figure 24.1).
2. Choose Form Document to open a drop-down list of options (see Figure 24.12).

**Figure 24.12**
Select how you want to create the form document: You can convert the current document into a form document or you can create a form document from scratch.

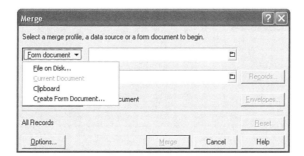

3. Choose Create Form Document. The Associate Form and Data dialog box appears (see Figure 24.13).

Type the name of the data file

**Figure 24.13**
In the Associate Form and Data dialog box, you can identify a data file or other data source for use with this form document.

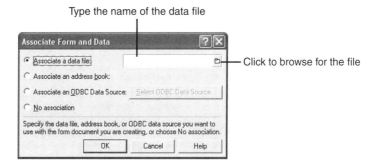

Click to browse for the file

4. Type the name of the data file in the Associate a Data File text box or click the Files icon to search for the file. If you haven't created the data file yet, or you don't know where it is, choose No Association.

   → For more information on associating an Address Book with a form document, **see** "Merging with the Address Book" later in this chapter.

5. Click OK. WordPerfect adds the Merge feature bar at the top of the document (see Figure 24.14). This document is now marked as a form document.

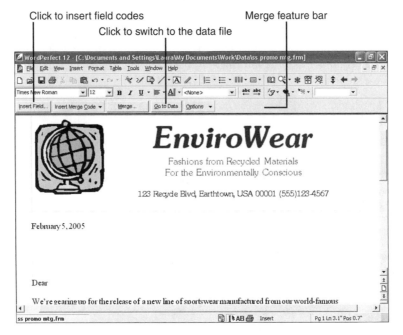

**Figure 24.14**
The Merge feature bar is included in every form document and data file that you create.

Click to insert field codes

Click to switch to the data file

Merge feature bar

NOTE

If you associated a data file in step 4, that file is now tied to this one. Whenever you need to edit the data, just click the Go to Data button on the Merge feature bar. WordPerfect opens the data file in another window and switches you to that window. To go back to the form document, click the Go to Form button in the data file window.

6. Position the insertion point where you want to insert the first piece of information. For example, in a typical mail merge, you insert the name and address information at the top of the letter.

7. Click the Insert Field button on the Merge feature bar. The Insert Field Name or Number dialog box appears (see Figure 24.15). The field names (or numbers) in the associated data file appear in the Field Names list box.

CAUTION

If you haven't associated a data file yet, the Insert Field dialog box won't have a list box full of field names. Instead, you can type in a field name or number and insert it in the data file.

**Figure 24.15**
In the Insert Field Name or Number dialog box, you can select a field name to insert in the form document.

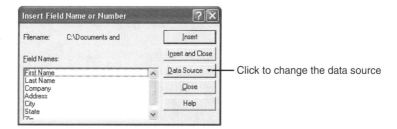

Click to change the data source

**TIP FROM**

When you associate a data file with a form document, it isn't written in stone. You can click the Data Source button in the Insert Field Name or Number dialog box and choose a different source. When you do, the field names from that source appear in the list.

24

8. Double-click a field name to insert it in the document. WordPerfect inserts the field name (or number) in parentheses, preceded by FIELD (see Figure 24.16).

**Figure 24.16**
Merge codes are displayed in a different color so you can pick them out from the rest of the text.

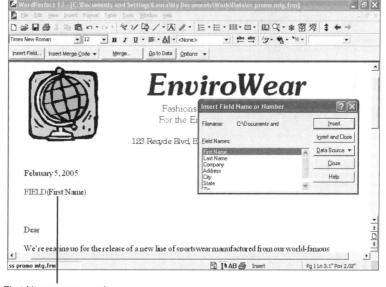

First Name merge code

9. Continue inserting field names as necessary to complete the form document. Click Close to close the Insert Field Name or Number dialog box. Figure 24.17 shows a sample letter with the mailing address and salutation field codes.

NOTE

Make sure you include any necessary spaces, commas, or other punctuation between the field names.

Space between the first and last names

**Figure 24.17**
A mailing address block and salutation have been constructed using field names from the data file.

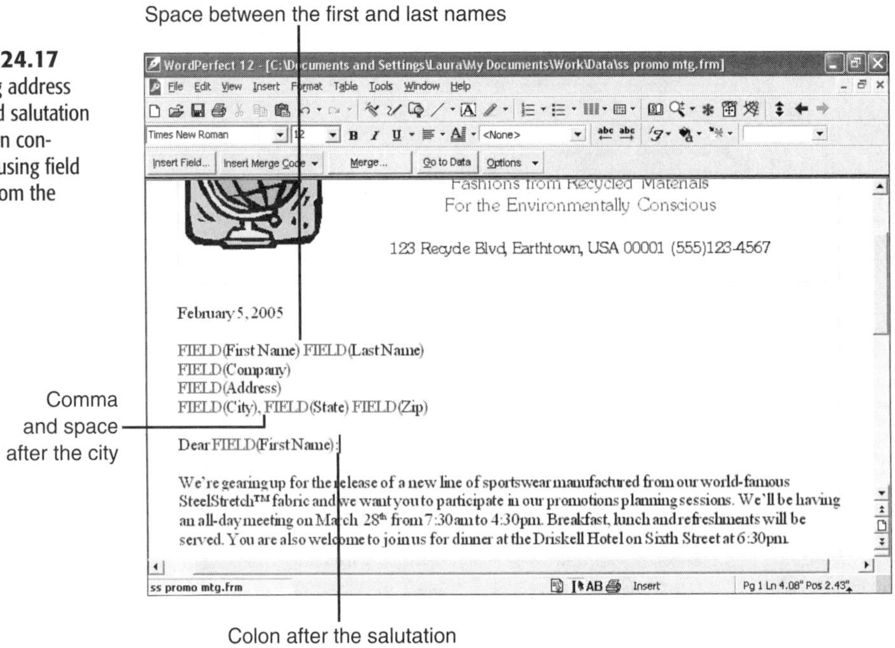

Comma and space after the city

Colon after the salutation

TIP FROM

*Laura Acklen*

Instead of typing in the date, you can insert a merge code that inserts the date for you when you run the merge. Click the Merge Codes button to open the Insert Merge Codes dialog box. Select Date in the Merge Codes list box, and then click Insert.

The most readily understood use of the Merge feature is in a mail merge, where you are merging a letter with a list of addresses. It's important to point out that Merge can be used for much more. A form document might be an invoice or billing statement with a database file as the data source. Or, how about a loan document, where the same information is plugged into a million different places? (You could import spreadsheet data into a loan application form document.) Or, someday you might need to create 250 "Hello...My Name Is" labels for an awards dinner, in which case the form document would be a labels form. Law offices often prepare multiple documents with the same information so they might put together a series of forms with one data file. Because each form need not use every field in the data file, there could be a collection of data in the data file that would serve multiple forms. These are just a few examples—the possibilities are endless.

**NOTE**

You can always turn a merge file (data file or form document) back into a normal document. In a form document, strip out all the merge codes by selecting and deleting them. Click the Options button on the Merge feature bar. Choose Remove Merge Bar. You'll see a message that tells you the file will not be recognized as a merge file. Click OK to continue or Cancel to bail out.

# MERGING A FORM DOCUMENT WITH A DATA FILE

Now you've got a form document and a data file, so you're ready to go. If you've got the form document or data file open, you can click the Merge button on the Merge feature bar. Otherwise, choose Tools, Merge, Merge to open the Merge dialog box (see Figure 24.18).

**Figure 24.18**
You can identify the form document, the data file, and the output location in the Merge dialog box.

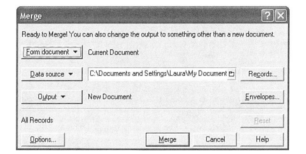

What you see in this dialog box varies depending on what files you have open (or if you have any files open at all). If you click the Merge button from the form document, Form Document is set to Current Document. If you've associated the form document with a data file, the name of that file appears next to Data Source.

If you've clicked the Merge button from the data file, the name of the file appears next to Data Source. If this data file is already associated with a form document, the name of that document appears next to Form Document. Otherwise, you'll need to type the filename next to Form Document or click the Files icon to search for the file.

Finally, if you aren't running the merge from either document, you see a blank text box next to Form Document and Data Source.

In any case, you need to fill in the blanks by typing the names of the files or clicking the Files icon to search for them. By default, Output is set to New Document. You can also set the merge to Current Document. Click the Output drop-down list arrow to see the other three options:

- Printer—Sends the output directly to the printer.
- File on Disk—Creates a file and places the output in the file.
- Email—Sends the output via electronic mail. See the section "Merging to E-mail," later in this chapter, for more information.

When you have everything filled in, click Merge. WordPerfect matches up the field names (or numbers) in the form file and the field names (or numbers) in the data file and inserts the information into the form. The results are displayed in the current document or a new document, unless you chose to merge directly to the printer, a file, or e-mail. Figure 24.19 shows the results of a mail merge.

**Figure 24.19**
WordPerfect combines the information from the data file with the text in the form document and creates a new document.

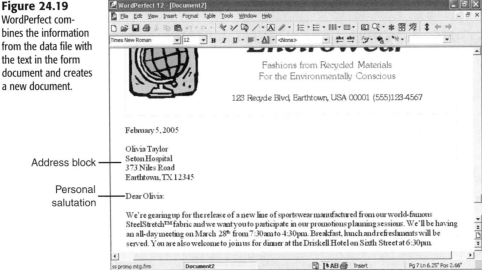

Address block

Personal salutation

If you got unexpected results when you merged the two files, see "This Isn't What I Expected" in the Troubleshooting section at the end of this chapter.

If you've noticed that QuickCorrect no longer works after you open a merge form or data file, see "Why Does Merge Cancel Out QuickCorrect?" in the Troubleshooting section at the end of this chapter.

**TIP FROM**

If you start a merge and then suddenly realize that you've done something wrong, press Esc to stop the merge.

**NOTE**

Unless you're merging to a file on disk so you can work with the results later, you don't need to save the results of a merge. If you do, you're duplicating the information that you have in the form document and data file. In most cases, you print the documents and then close the file without saving. Remember, it takes only a few seconds to run the merge again.

## MERGING WITH THE ADDRESS BOOK

WordPerfect's Address Book is integrated into all the suite applications, and it's well-suited for tracking all sorts of contact information. If you maintain a comprehensive address book, you might not ever create a data file again. During a merge, you can select records directly from an address book.

When you create a form document, you can associate the form with an address book instead of a data file (refer to Figure 24.13). If you need to switch to another address book, or if you created the form document with a different association, you can edit the association.

There are several ways to do this, but the most direct is to click the Insert Field button on the Merge feature bar, and then click the Data Source drop-down arrow. Choose one of the address books from the list. One of the advantages of this method is that you can see an updated list of field names right away.

After you insert the field codes from the address book, click the Merge button to open the Merge dialog box, and then click Merge.

➔ For the scoop on the Address Book, **see** Chapter 25, "Working with Address Books."

## CREATING ENVELOPES DURING A MERGE

If you are producing letters, you probably need envelopes or labels for them. You can create an envelope form when you merge so it's all done together. If you need labels, you need to create a labels form document and insert the field codes, and then merge that form with the data file. See the section "Merging to Labels," later in this chapter, for more information.

Follow these steps to generate envelopes during the merge:

1. In the Merge dialog box, click the Envelopes button. WordPerfect opens an envelope form document. If necessary, type the return address (or leave it out if your envelopes are preprinted).

**CAUTION**

> If the Envelopes button is grayed out, you'll need to specify the form document, data file, and output location. After you fill these in, the Envelope button will become available.

2. Press Ctrl+End to move down to the mailing address block. If necessary, delete the text in the mailing address block.

3. Click the Insert Field button to open the Insert Field Name or Number dialog box.

4. Double-click a field name (or number) to insert the field code. Include all the necessary spacing and punctuation between the fields (see Figure 24.20).

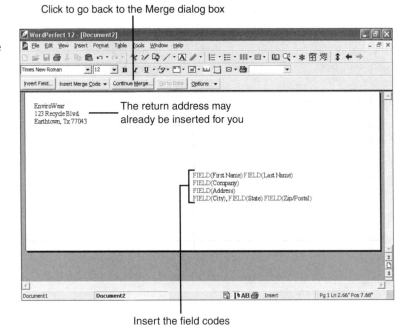

**Figure 24.20**
Creating the envelope during a merge has an advantage: WordPerfect creates the envelope form document and integrates it into the merge process.

Click to go back to the Merge dialog box

The return address may already be inserted for you

Insert the field codes

5. Click Continue Merge when you're finished. The Merge dialog box appears (refer to Figure 24.18).

6. Click Merge.

When a merge is complete, the insertion point is always on the last line of the last page, so don't panic if you don't see the letters right away. The envelopes are created at the end of the document, and you can either page up through the envelopes and proof them for accuracy, or you can press Ctrl+Home to move to the top of the document.

## MERGING TO LABELS

Creating labels isn't integrated in the merge process, but it takes only a minute to create a labels form, associate it with the data file, and merge.

Follow these steps to merge to labels:

1. If you've already defined the labels, you can skip down to step 4. Otherwise, in a blank document, choose Format, Labels to open the Labels dialog box (see Figure 24.21).

2. Choose Laser Printed or Tractor-Fed to narrow down the list, and then select the label definition that matches your labels.

**NOTE**

> Just because your label isn't listed in the Labels box doesn't mean the definition doesn't exist. Check the layout (such as 3 columns by 10 rows) or the dimensions, and compare them to the definitions in the list. You'll probably find an exact match (or at least a close approximation).

Click to insert the definition into the current document

**Figure 24.21**
You can choose label definitions for both laser-printed and tractor-fed printers in the Labels dialog box.

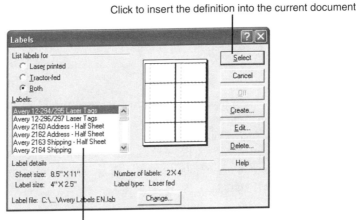

Select a label definition

3. Choose Select to insert the definition in the document.

4. Choose Tools, Merge, Form Document, Create Form Document, Use File in Active Window to display the Associate Form and Data dialog box (refer to Figure 24.13).

5. Specify a data source, and then click OK. The Merge feature bar appears in the label document.

6. Click the Insert Field button to open the Insert Field Name or Number dialog box (refer to Figure 24.16).

7. Double-click a field name to insert it in the label. Make sure you include all the spacing and punctuation between the fields.

8. When you're finished inserting field codes, click Close to close the Insert Field Name or Number dialog box. Figure 24.22 shows a completed label form.

9. Click the Merge button on the feature bar. Verify the data source and output location, and then choose Merge to create the labels.

**TIP FROM**

*Laura Acklen*

> You can take a shortcut when creating labels with the WordPerfect address book. Insert the label definition in a blank document, and then choose Tools, Address Book. Select the records, and then click Insert. Select a format in the Format Address dialog box, and then choose OK. WordPerfect creates a label for each record. For more information, see Chapter 25.

**Figure 24.22**
This form document is actually a sheet of labels, which will be filled in during the merge.

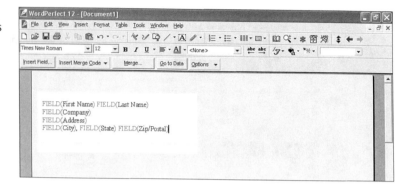

You can create a sheet of identical labels with the Merge feature. Create the label form and type the text of the label. Choose Tools, Merge. Choose Form Document, Create Form Document, Use File in Active Window, No Association, OK. Then, in the Merge dialog box, set the Data Source to None. Click Options to open the Merge Options dialog box (see Figure 24.23). Type the number of labels on the page in the Number of Copies for Each Record text box. Choose Merge.

**Figure 24.23**
You can enter the number of copies (labels) in the Merge Options dialog box.

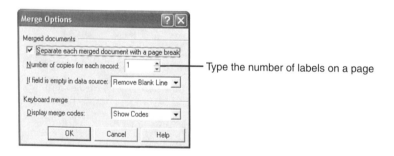

Type the number of labels on a page

**NOTE**

The maximum number of copies per record is 255, so that's the maximum number of identical labels you can create.

Figure 24.24 shows a page of identical labels. This is a notable exception to the "Don't save merge results" rule—you might want to save this label page for future printing.

**TIP FROM**

*Laura Acklen*

If every other label is blank, you need to remove the page break at the end of the original label. Close this document without saving and switch back to the label form document. Position the insertion point at the end of the address and press Delete until only one label is displayed. Try the merge again.

**Figure 24.24**
Using the Merge feature, you can create a sheet of identical labels.

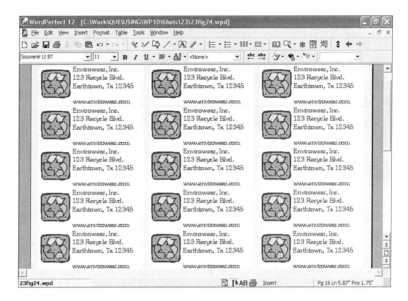

CAUTION

You might be tempted to send a partially used sheet of labels through your laser printer once again to print on the unused labels. However, the heat process from printing the sheet the first time can loosen unused labels, causing them to come off in the printer the second time around. Cleaning stuck labels from inside a laser printer is both time-consuming and costly.

## MERGING TO E-MAIL

Here's another intriguing possibility. You can create personalized messages and send them out via electronic mail. Think about it—you could send out meeting notices, press releases, billing statements, order confirmations, shareholder information, invoices, class schedules, responses to requests for information from your company's Web site—the list goes on and on.

Follow these steps to merge to e-mail addresses:

1. From either the data file or form document, click the Merge button on the Merge feature bar. Otherwise, choose Tools, Merge.

2. Set the form document and the data source.

3. Click the Output drop-down arrow and choose E-mail. The Merge to E-mail dialog box appears (see Figure 24.25).

Select the e-mail address field

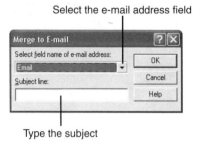

**Figure 24.25**
You can select the field that contains the e-mail address and type a subject for the messages in the Merge to E-mail dialog box.

Type the subject

NOTE

Changes to the Output settings in the Merge dialog box are sticky, which means they stay in effect until you change the dialog box settings again. Keep this in mind because the next time you merge, your output will be sent via e-mail.

**24**

4. Click the Select Field Name of E-Mail Address drop-down list arrow and choose the field that contains the e-mail address.

5. Type a subject in the Subject Line text box, and then click OK to return to the Merge dialog box.

6. Choose Merge.

7. If the Choose Profile dialog box appears, select a profile from the Profile Name drop-down list, and then click OK to start the merge.

## MERGING TO TABLES

Tables make popular form documents because they are incredibly flexible and easy to work with. You can merge a data file into a table form document, so that each record has its own row, with the insertion of the Repeat Row merge code.

Follow these steps to create a table form document:

1. Create a table with one row and as many columns as you need for the fields.
   → For the steps to create a table, **see** "Creating Tables," **p. 294.**

2. Click in the first cell (upper-left corner).

3. Choose Tools, Merge, Form Document, Create Form Document, Use File in Active Window. The Associate Form and Data dialog box is displayed (refer to Figure 24.13).

4. Select a data file, an Address Book, or an ODBC data source to associate with this form document, and then click OK.

5. Click the Insert Field button to open the Insert Field Name or Number dialog box.

6. Double-click a field name to insert it in the table. Make sure you include all the necessary spacing and punctuation between the field codes. Press Tab to move to the next cell or just click in the cell.

7. When you're finished inserting field codes, click Close to close the Insert Field Name or Number dialog box.

8. Click in the last cell of the last row, after any field codes or text.

9. Click the Merge Codes button on the Merge feature bar and then choose More to o₁ the Insert Merge Codes dialog box (see Figure 24.26).

**Figure 24.26**
The Insert Merge Codes dialog box includes a list of merge commands.

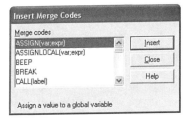

> **NOTE**
>
> The REPEATROW command is but one command in a long list of merge commands. The Merge feature has its own programming language for creating "intelligent" merge documents. Unfortunately, covering the merge commands is beyond the scope of this book. But don't despair—you still have the help topics. On the Index tab of the Help Topics dialog box, type `merge commands`, and then double-click the matching help topic in the list box.

10. Scroll down through the list, and then select the REPEATROW command.

11. Choose Insert, and then choose Close to insert the command, and close the Insert Merge Codes dialog box. The REPEATROW command is inserted in the last cell (see Figure 24.27). This command automatically creates a new row for each record in the data file.

**Figure 24.27**
You need the REPEATROW command in the last cell of the table, after the field name, if you want the merge to create a new row for every record.

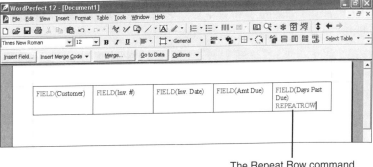

The Repeat Row command

12. Choose Merge to open the Merge dialog box.

13. Specify a data source and verify the output location.

14. Choose Merge.

CAUTION

> If you have empty cells in the table, those fields were empty in the data source. If that's the case, print this table so you can see which gaps you need to fill, and then close the table without saving. Open the data source and enter the missing data. Save your changes, and try the merge again.

# SORTING AND SELECTING RECORDS

Managing the data in your data source, whatever it might be, is an important part of your office automation system. You'll save hours if you can keep the information in a single source up to date. If you've been creating small data files for every project, stop right now. The more data files you have, the less likely you are to keep up with them.

It's easier to create larger data files where you can update everything at once. You can sort the records and then select only the records that you want to work with. For example, if you want to send a notice only to people living in a certain city, you can sort the records by the City field and then select the records that contain that city.

## SORTING DATA FILES

With the Sort feature, you can group common records, making it easier to select them for a merge or to update the information in the records. Bulk mail, for example, must be bundled according to certain postal standards. You could arrange the data file in ZIP/Postal Code order before you merge, for example.

The default sort is to arrange the records by the first column of the table or the first word in a merge data file. You can create your own sort if you want to sort by something else. There is a trick to doing this—instead of using field names, you specify the column number or the field number. Right now, you can't choose from a list of field names in the Sort dialog box, so you have to remember to count the columns or count the fields so that you know the number of the field.

→ The steps for sorting merge data files are almost identical to those for sorting a table, so for more information, **see** "Sorting Database Data in Tables," **p. 482.**

## SELECTING RECORDS

Nine times out of ten, you work with a larger set of data than you need for the merge. I mean, how often do you send a letter or e-mail to everyone in your Address Book? If the records have something in common, you can select them by specifying certain conditions. Or, you can simply choose which records you want from the list.

Follow these steps to select records from a data file:

1. In the Merge dialog box, make sure the data source is properly identified.

2. Choose Records to open the Select Records dialog box (see Figure 24.28).

**Figure 24.28**
In the Select Records dialog box, you can define the selection criteria to select records in a data file.

Click if you want to mark records manually

Click to specify a range of records

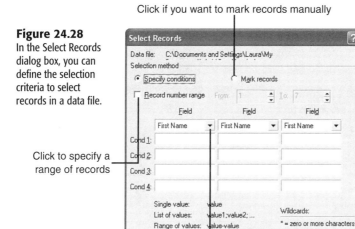

Click a drop-down list arrow to choose a field

Click to look at some examples

3. If you want to specify a range of records, put a check mark next to Record Number Range, and then type the beginning number in the From text box and the ending number in the To text box.

4. In the first column, click the Field drop-down list and select a field from the list.

5. Type the condition that you want to set in the Cond 1 text box.

> **NOTE**
>
> Each condition line defines a set of records that are to be selected (or excluded) from the merge. Each column defines the field for which you want to set the condition(s). You can define more than one condition for a single row, so more than one field can be involved. Only records that meet all the conditions in the row are selected. Specifying more than one row of conditions selects records that meet any row of conditions.

6. If necessary, select a field from the Field drop-down list and type the condition in the second column.

7. If necessary, select a field from the Field drop-down list and type the condition in the third column.

8. Repeat these steps to set any other conditions you want to use.

24

**TIP FROM**

If you've made a mess of things and you just want to start over, click Clear All to reset the fields and clear all the conditions.

9. Click OK when you're done to return to the Merge dialog box.

*If you're missing records that match your conditions, see "Not All the Records Are Being Selected" in the Troubleshooting section at the end of this chapter.*

When you aren't sure how to set a condition, WordPerfect gives you some excellent examples. Click the Example button at the bottom of the dialog box to display the Examples of Selecting Records dialog box (see Figure 24.29). There is even a second page that you can look at. Choose More to display the second page.

**Figure 24.29**
The Examples of Selecting Records dialog box has a series of examples to help you understand how to set conditions.

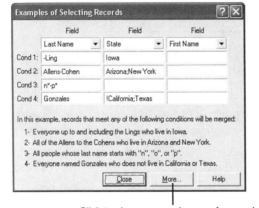

Click to view a second page of examples

In some cases, it's easier to mark the records manually, especially in cases where there is no common element. In this situation, choose Mark Records. The dialog box options change to those for selecting records directly from the data file (see Figure 24.30).

You can change which field appears first in the list. For example, you might need to see the cities, not the first and last names. Click the First Field to Display drop-down list arrow and choose a field from the list. Choose Update Record List to update the list with the new first field.

To select records, click the check box next to the record. If the records are one right after the other, click the first record, and then hold down the Shift key and click the last record. Otherwise, click the first record, and then hold down the Ctrl key while you click the other records. After you've selected the records, click the check box for a selected record to place check marks in all of the selected records check boxes. You can also select records with the keyboard by pressing the spacebar to place a check mark in the check box. Use the arrow keys to move up and down the list and the spacebar to select the records. Click OK when you're done to return to the Merge dialog box.

**Figure 24.30**
Selecting Mark Records enables you to manually select records from the data file.

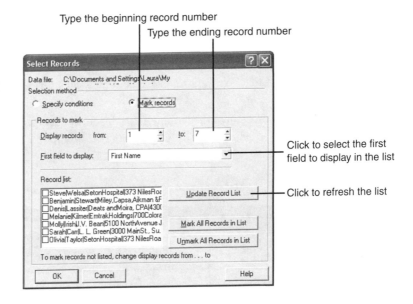

## CREATING FILL-IN-THE-BLANKS FORMS

You might have a project that seems ideal for a merge, except that some of the information is variable, so it isn't well-suited for a data file. Well, guess what—you don't have to have a data file to perform a merge. You can merge with the keyboard—in a manner of speaking.

A form document can be created with Keyboard merge codes that stop and wait for the user to type in the information, rather than pulling it from a data file. You can create a detailed message that explains what the user should be typing at this point. After the information has been entered, the merge will move on to the next Keyboard code.

Follow these steps to create a fill-in-the-blanks form:

1. If you've already created the document, open it now.
2. Choose Tools, Merge, Form Document, Create Form Document, Use File in Active Window.
3. In the Associate Form and Data dialog box, choose No Association.
4. Click in the document where you want to insert the Keyboard merge code.
5. Click the Insert Merge Code button and then choose Keyboard to open the Insert Merge Code dialog box (see Figure 24.31).

**Figure 24.31**
Type the message that you want to appear in the Insert Merge Code dialog box.

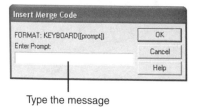

Type the message

6. Type the prompt text that you want to appear, and then click OK to insert the Keyboard code in the form.

7. Repeat steps 4–6 to insert any other prompts for this form document. Figure 24.32 shows a form document with four Keyboard codes that prompt for the heading information.

**Figure 24.32**
The keyboard code includes the message text in parentheses.

Keyboard code    Message text

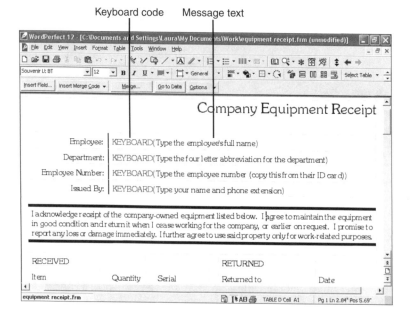

8. When you're ready to fill in the form, choose Tools, Merge, Merge or click the Merge button on the Merge feature bar. Verify the location of the data file (if there is one), the form document, and the output, and then choose Merge. When a keyboard command is encountered, the merge pauses and displays the prompt message (see Figure 24.33).

9. Type the requested information, and then press Alt+Enter or Alt+Shift+C (or click the Continue button on the Merge feature bar) to continue the merge.

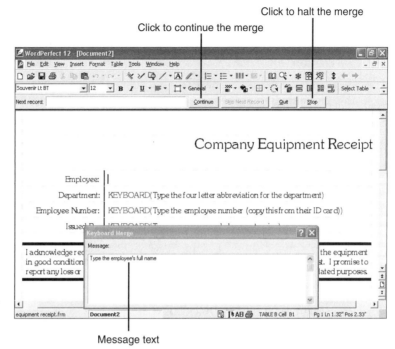

**Figure 24.33**
The prompt message that you type is displayed in a window at the bottom of the screen.

Click to continue the merge

Click to halt the merge

Message text

You can get the best of both worlds by combining a typical merge of a data file and form document with the flexibility of a fill-in-the-blanks form. Just include keyboard codes in the form document where you want the user to type the information. The rest of the fields can be filled in from the data file.

# TROUBLESHOOTING

### THIS ISN'T WHAT I EXPECTED

*I just did a merge, but I'm not getting the results I need. There are blank spaces where there should be data. I've also got blank lines in the middle of a few addresses.*

First, take a good look at the results. Can you detect a pattern? Is the state where the city should be? Are all the last names missing, or just one or two? When you're ready to proceed, close the merge results document without saving.

If you're having the same problem over and over, start with the form document. Make sure you have the right field codes in the right places. If you need to change a field code, select and delete the code, and then reinsert it. Save your changes and try the merge again.

If the problem occurs just in one or two entries, go straight to the data file and take a look at the records that are giving you trouble. Make sure the right information is in the right field. You might have actually typed the state in the city field by accident. Save your changes and try the merge again.

If the source file is a spreadsheet or database, you might have to do your proofing in the originating program. If this is inconvenient, consider converting the file to a merge data file so you can edit it in WordPerfect.

### I CAN'T ENTER MORE THAN 250 CHARACTERS IN A FIELD

*When I use the Quick Data Entry dialog box to enter information into merge fields, I can't enter more than 250 characters. Is there some way I can exceed this limitation?*

Actually, it's 255 characters, which is the limit for data entry into fields in the Quick Data Entry dialog box. As a workaround, you can edit the data directly and enter more information. Close the Quick Data Entry dialog box. On the Merge feature bar, click the Go to Data button. If you edit the data file directly, you can exceed the length beyond 255 characters.

### WHY DOES MERGE CANCEL OUT QUICKCORRECT

*I've noticed that after I work with the Merge feature, QuickCorrect no longer works. Why is it getting turned off?*

QuickCorrect is turned off when certain features are used in WordPerfect 11 (or 12). This is a "by-design" behavior (I haven't been able to find out why). All you can do is simply turn QuickCorrect back on after you work with merge files. The quickest way to do this is to record a macro that restores the QuickCorrect settings and then attach that macro to a toolbar button.

→ For more information on recording macros, **see** "Creating Macros," **p. 824.**

→ For more information on attaching macros to toolbars, **see** "Assigning Macros to Keystrokes, Toolbars, and Menus," **p. 828.**

### NOT ALL THE RECORDS ARE BEING SELECTED

*I've set up conditions to select a group of files, but not all the records that contain this information are selected. What's going on?*

When you set conditions, you have to make sure that you aren't pairing contradictory conditions that in effect cancel each other out. For example, if you search for records that contain a certain city *and* a company name, you won't find any of the records that contain that company name but are in a different city. Because every situation is different, it's a good idea to take a look at the examples. In the Select Records dialog box, click Examples. You can get to a second page of examples by clicking More in the Examples of Selecting Records dialog box.

# PROJECT

Someone just handed you a disk with a long list of names and addresses. She wants it used in a mass mailing that has to go out by this afternoon's mail run. You open the file and discover to your dismay that it's a list of names and addresses without any merge codes. Short of retyping the list, you're wondering, "How in the world can I turn this into a merge data file in just an hour?"

The answer? Stand back and let the Find and Replace feature work its magic. If you can figure out how the fields and records are divided, you can replace these elements with End Field and End Record codes. Here's how:

1. Open the file, and then immediately save it with a new name. This way, if your efforts backfire, you can always get back to the original list.

2. Turn on Reveal Codes so you can figure out what divides the fields and records. If there is a blank line between each record, the separator is two hard returns. If the list is in a label format, there is probably a hard page between each record. See the note at the bottom of these steps for more information on different kinds of separators.

3. From the top of the document, press Ctrl+F to open the Find and Replace dialog box. Choose Match, Codes to open the Codes dialog box (see Figure 24.34).

Click to display only the merge codes

**Figure 24.34**
The same Codes dialog box is used to select codes that you want to search for and codes that you want to insert in place of the search codes.

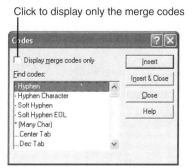

4. Scroll down the list and select the code that separates the records. For example, if there is a blank line between the records, select HRt and click Insert twice to insert two hard return codes. If there isn't a blank line between the records, insert one hard return code. You should now see [HRt][HRt] (or [HRt]) in the Find text box.

5. Click in the Replace With text box, and then select the HRt code and click Insert.

6. Click the check box next to Display Merge Codes Only so that the list of codes now shows only the merge codes. Select the End Record code, and then click Insert.

7. Remove the check mark next to Display Merge Codes Only to reveal the other codes. Select the HPg code, and then click Insert. The Find and Replace dialog box should now look like the one shown in Figure 24.35.

Search for two hard returns

**Figure 24.35**
The Find and Replace feature is set to look for two hard returns that separate the records and replace them with the codes that separate records in a merge data file.

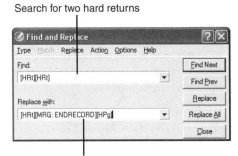

Replace with a hard return, an End Record code, and a hard page

8. Choose Replace All. Now it's time to insert the End Field codes after each field in the record. You've figured out that each field is on a line by itself, so the separator is a hard return.

9. Click in the Find text box and delete the contents. Choose Match, Codes to open the Codes dialog box again. Select HRt, and then click Insert.

10. Click in the Replace With text box and delete the contents. In the Codes dialog box, click the check box next to Display Merge Codes Only. Select the End Field code and then click Insert. Remove the check mark next to Display Merge Codes Only. Select HRt; then, click Insert and Close. The Find and Replace dialog box should now look like the one shown in Figure 24.36.

Search for one hard return

**Figure 24.36**
The Find and Replace feature is set to look for the hard return that separates the fields and replace it with the codes that separate fields in a merge data file.

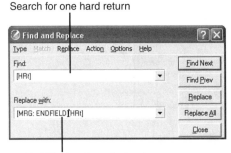

Replace with an End Field code and a hard return

11. Choose Replace All; then, close the Find and Replace dialog box. The next step is to identify the file as a merge data file and to name the fields.

12. Choose Tools, Merge, Data Source, Create Data File, Use File in Active Window, and then click OK. In the Create Data File dialog box, type a field name for every field in the file (even if you aren't planning on using them all in the form document). Click OK when you're finished and then save the file to disk.

13. Now that you have the Merge feature bar displayed, go through the file and make sure that there is an End Field code at the end of every field and an End Record code at the

end of every record. (This includes the field name record at the top of the document.) Make sure that every field is on a line by itself and that there is a hard page between each record. Every record must have the same number of fields, so even if a field is blank, you still need an End Field code for it (it just sits on the line by itself). If there are missing field codes, click the End Field or End Record buttons on the Merge feature bar to insert them.

14. Save your changes. Continue on with creating the form document and merging the two.

If you're converting a labels form into a merge data file, use the following Find and Replace operations:

| Find | Replace With |
| --- | --- |
| [HPg] | [HRt][MRG:ENDRECORD][HPg] |
| [HRt] | [MRG:ENDFIELD][HRt] |

Also, make sure that you delete the Paper Size/Type and the Labels Form codes at the top of the document. If you decide to use more than one field for the city, state, and ZIP, you can use the following search operation to break up the city and the state:

| Find | Replace With |
| --- | --- |
| ,<space> | [MRG:ENDFIELD][HRt] |

If you used two spaces between the state and ZIP, you can use the following search operation:

| Find | Replace With |
| --- | --- |
| <space><space> | [MRG:ENDFIELD][HRt] |

The last record can be problematic, so make sure you check it before you save the file and merge.

If you're converting a file where each record is on a line by itself and the fields have a comma between them, use the following Find and Replace operations:

| Find | Replace With |
| --- | --- |
| [HRt] | [MRG:ENDRECORD][HPg] |
| ,<space> | [MRG:ENDFIELD][HRt] |
| " | <nothing> |

The last operation removes any quotation marks that might be around text in one of the fields.

# CHAPTER 25

# WORKING WITH ADDRESS BOOKS

**In this chapter**

*by Laura Acklen*

# WORKING WITH ADDRESS BOOKS

The Address Book is tightly integrated with WordPerfect. You can keep track of any type of information: phone and fax numbers, addresses, e-mail addresses, birthdays, personal greetings, job titles, assistant and supervisor names, and so on. You can then use this information with the Merge feature to broadcast documents and e-mail messages.

If you have other address books on your system, you can use that contact information in WordPerfect. Corel has substantially expanded the range of integration with other mail system address books. The Address Book feature integrates with most MAPI services, LDAP servers, the Windows Address Book, and prior versions of CorelCENTRAL and WordPerfect address books.

 One of the exciting new features in WordPerfect 11 (and 12) is the capability to use the Microsoft Outlook address book. If you've been using Outlook as your contact information manager, you will be pleased to know that you can use that information in a mass mailing, to print labels and envelopes, and to route documents for review.

**NOTE**

> The Address Book is included with the Standard, Professional, Academic, and most OEM versions of WordPerfect Office 11 (or 12). You will also have it if you purchased WordPerfect Family Pack 5 (or 6) or if you received the WordPerfect Productivity Pack with your new computer.
>
> If you received a copy of WordPerfect with a new computer, you might not have access to the Address Book, which is actually a separate program (formerly known as CorelCENTRAL). Not all OEM versions include it because it's the manufacturer's choice to include it on their OEM CDs. If you are interested in using the Address Book, or using the Outlook address book with WordPerfect, you can upgrade to the Standard or Professional version of WordPerfect Office. Contact Corel at 1-800-77COREL for more information.

# CHOOSING BETWEEN WORDPERFECT AND OUTLOOK ADDRESS BOOKS

In WordPerfect 11 and 12, you have a choice. You can either use WordPerfect address books, or you can use your Outlook address book. This means that if you already have Outlook on your system and you've been adding information to the Contacts list, you can use that in WordPerfect.

On the other hand, if you don't have Outlook on your system, the WordPerfect address books are a great place to keep your contact information. If you will take the time to enter the information, you will find that you can manipulate it in many different ways. The next several sections discuss creating and editing entries in the WordPerfect Address Book. Outlook integration is discussed in the final section of this chapter, so if you prefer to work with Outlook, you can skip down to that section of this chapter.

## STARTING THE WORDPERFECT ADDRESS BOOK

Let's begin with the WordPerfect Address Book and cover the Outlook integration later. It will be easier to follow along if your system acts and looks like the system used in the figures. For this reason, I'm going to ask that you turn off the Outlook integration so that when you open the address book, you will see the WordPerfect Address Book.

To turn off Outlook integration, choose Tools, Settings, Environment. If necessary, remove the check mark next to Use Outlook Address Book/Contact List.

Now, let's start the WordPerfect address book and get familiar with it. Choose Tools, Address Book to open the Address Book dialog box (see Figure 25.1).

Blank address book

**Figure 25.1**
An empty address book called Addresses has been created, so you can start adding entries right away.

25

TIP FROM

If you use the Address Book often, you can add a button to your toolbar that opens the Address Book. Right-click the toolbar to which you want to add the button, and then choose Edit. Choose Tools from the Feature Categories drop-down list, and then select Address Book. Choose Add Button, and click OK.

*If you can't see your address books after installing SP1 on WordPerfect 11, see "Cannot Access Address Books After SP1" in the Troubleshooting section at the end of this chapter.*

## ADDING ADDRESS BOOK ENTRIES

The Address Book has been redesigned to store more information and to give you equal access to other address books on your system. If you're upgrading from a previous version of WordPerfect, you will be able to export those books from the previous version and import them directly into a WordPerfect address book. See the section "Importing and Exporting Address Book Entries," later in this chapter, for more information.

To open the Address Book and add some entries, follow these steps:

1. Choose Tools, Address Book. The Address Book dialog box opens (see Figure 25.2). By default, the first address book in the Address Book tree is open. You can open another one by clicking the plus sign next to the category, and then clicking the name of the address book.

Click to create a new address book entry

Address book group

**Figure 25.2**
The CorelCENTRAL Address Book dialog box gives you access to Corel's Address Book and other address books on your system.

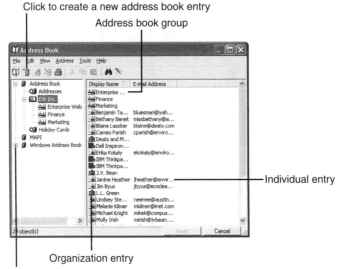

Individual entry

Organization entry

Click to view the Windows address books

**NOTE**

If you're upgrading from WordPerfect 7 or 8, you'll notice right away that the Address Book dialog box was redesigned for WordPerfect 11/12. The left pane of the Address Book dialog box has a list of all the address books on your system; the right side displays a list of records in the selected address book. There is a new toolbar with buttons for common tasks. The My Addresses and Frequent Contacts address books are rolled into one address book called Addresses. If you used the automatic dialer, brace yourself—it's gone. They have added Net2Phone functionality instead. Otherwise, the buttons you're used to seeing along the bottom of the dialog box have been moved to the menus and the toolbar.

2. Click the Create a New Address Entry button on the toolbar in the CorelCENTRAL Address Book dialog box. The New dialog box appears (see Figure 25.3).

**TIP FROM**

If you are creating records for members of the same organization, create the organizations first. As you create the records for the members, you can choose the organization from a drop-down list so you don't have to type it in each time.

**Figure 25.3**
You can choose the type of address book entry you're creating in the New dialog box.

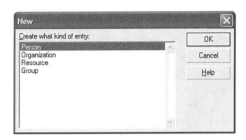

3. Choose one of the following options:

- Person—This is the most comprehensive entry you can create. There are six tabs where you can organize the information: General, Personal, Address, Phone/Fax, Business, and Security.

- Organization—This is a subset of the Person record, with three tabs: Address, Phone/Fax, and Security.

- Resource—You can maintain records on your company resources by identifying the name and type of the resource, the owner, the main phone number, and comments. A resource might be a conference room, projection unit, video-conferencing equipment, or laptop.

- Group—You can create a group of address book records to make it easier to broadcast messages and general correspondence.

Depending on the type of entry you choose, you get a blank record to fill in. Figure 25.4 shows an entry for a person. Type the information into the fields, pressing Tab to move to the next field and Shift+Tab to move back a field. Click the other tabs to enter data in additional fields.

 *If you're getting the wrong information from the address book plugged into your templates (via prompts), see "Scrambled Information from the Address Book" in the Troubleshooting section at the end of this chapter.*

Click to select an organization

**Figure 25.4**
The Person Properties dialog box has six tabs to help you organize data for an individual.

## CREATING NEW ADDRESS BOOKS

Address Books are designed to store a wide variety of information on individuals, organizations, resources, and groups. You can create books with contact names for each project you are involved in. An address book might be created for your holiday greeting card list, and yet another for the names of the children in your child's classroom. The possibilities are as varied as the people who use it.

To create new address books in the WordPerfect Address Book:

1. Choose File, New, press Ctrl+N, or click the Create a New Address Book button on the Address Book toolbar. The New Address Book dialog box opens (see Figure 25.5).

**Figure 25.5**
You can select the type of address book you want to create in the New Address Book dialog box.

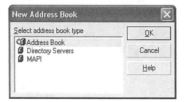

2. Select the type of address book that you want to create:
   - Address Book —Create a new WordPerfect address book.
   - Directory Servers—The WordPerfect address book lets you connect to and open directory server address books using Lightweight Direct Access Protocol (LDAP).
   - MAPI—You can access MAPI-compliant (Messaging Application Programming Interface) address books on your computer. For example, if you've created an address book in a MAPI-compliant application, such as Microsoft Outlook or Novell GroupWise, you can open and edit it in the WordPerfect address book.

Depending on the type of address book you select, you will see other dialog boxes in which you can specify a name and other properties for the new address book. When you are finished, the new address book is created, and the name appears in the left pane.

**NOTE**

You won't be able to create a MAPI-compliant address book unless your Windows messaging profile is set up for MAPI. For more information about setting up the Windows messaging profile, see your Windows documentation.

# USING ADDRESS BOOK INFORMATION IN WORDPERFECT

The beauty of keeping your information in an address book is that you can use it in a document, envelope, or label, whenever you want. A single entry or a series of entries can be inserted in just a few steps. You'll start to see the advantages of maintaining your contact information electronically when you see how easily it can be inserted into your documents.

Keep in mind that you can store all kinds of information in an address book entry, not just name/address/city/state/ZIP. There are almost 50 different fields that can be filled in, including birthday, anniversary, business comments, resource type, and owner to name just a few.

## INSERTING INFORMATION INTO A DOCUMENT

When you insert address book entries, you have a chance to choose a format for the information. You can opt for the US Standard, US Standard with Country, Name and Company, or Name, Title, Company.

When you want to insert more than just the basic address information, you can build a customized address format by selecting from a list of more than 50 fields.

Follow these steps to insert an entry (or entries) into a document:

1. Position the insertion point where you want to insert the information.
2. Choose Tools, Address Book.
3. Open the address book that contains the entry you want.
4. Select the entry (or multiple entries).
5. Click Insert in the lower-right corner. The Format Address Book dialog box appears (see Figure 25.6).

**Figure 25.6**
In the Format Address Book dialog box, select a predefined format from the list to see a preview.

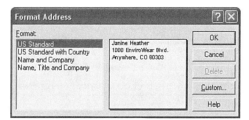

6. Select a format in the left pane and you'll see a preview in the right pane.
7. When you find the format you want, select it and choose OK to insert the entry (or entries).

## INSERTING ADDRESS BOOK ENTRIES ONTO ENVELOPES

The steps for inserting address book information onto an envelope are essentially the same as those for inserting the information into a document. The primary difference is that you start by creating an envelope. Another difference is that you cannot insert multiple entries from the Envelope dialog box. You can only insert one entry into the envelope. If you need to do a stack of envelopes, you should use the Merge feature instead.

Follow these steps to insert an address entry into an envelope:

1. Choose Format, Envelope to open the Envelope dialog box.
2. Click the Address Book icon in the Return Address section (to insert a return address) or the Mailing Address section (to insert a mailing address).
3. Open the address book that contains the entry you want.
4. Select the entry.
5. Click Insert in the lower-right corner. The Format Address Book dialog box appears (refer to Figure 25.6).
6. Select a format for the address book entry.
7. Choose OK to insert the entry.

At this point, you can either print the envelope or append it to the document, whichever you like.

## INSERTING INFORMATION INTO A LABEL FORM

Here again, the steps for inserting address book information onto a label form are essentially the same as those for inserting the information into a document. The primary difference is that you start by selecting a label form. Unlike envelopes, you *can* insert multiple entries onto labels. In fact, it's much quicker just to go straight to the address book for a sheet of labels, instead of setting up a merge.

Follow these steps to insert address book information onto a label:

1. Choose Format, Labels to open the Labels dialog box.
2. Select a label form from the list, and then choose Select to insert it into the document.
3. Choose Tools, Address book.
4. Open the address book that contains the entry you want.
5. Select the entry (or entries).
6. Click Insert in the lower-right corner. The Format Address Book dialog box appears (refer back to Figure 25.6).
7. Select a format for the address book entry (or entries).
8. Choose OK to insert the entry (or entries).

If you select more than one address book entry, WordPerfect automatically places each entry on a separate label. It's a favorite feature for ease-of-use and simplicity.

### CREATING A CUSTOM FORMAT

As previously mentioned, you can build a custom format to insert those pieces of information that don't appear in the four predefined formats (in the Format Address Book dialog box). After you create the new format, you give it a name and from then on, it appears in the list of formats in the Format Address Book dialog box.

Follow these steps to create a custom format:

1. In the Format Address Book dialog box, choose Custom. The Custom Address Format dialog box appears (see Figure 25.7).

2. Click in the Format box and move the insertion point to the location where you want to insert the field.

3. Select a field from the Fields list.

4. Click the Insert button.

5. When you are satisfied with the results, choose OK.

6. Type a name for the custom format and choose OK. The new format is added to the list in the Format Address Book dialog box.

25

Insert the field into the format

Select a field

**Figure 25.7**
Create your own custom format to insert additional address book information.

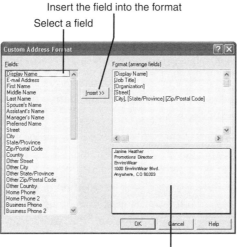

Preview the format here

# WORKING WITH ADDRESS BOOK ENTRIES

Creating an address book and typing in the entries is only half the battle. Someone has to maintain the information, right? Your contacts keep changing their cell phone numbers and e-mail addresses, so you have to stay on top of things to keep your information current.

Thankfully, working with address book entries is a breeze in WordPerfect. You have many options for editing, deleting (be careful here), moving and copying records between books, printing entries, and searching for information.

After you enter some records, you can do the following:

- Edit an entry—You can double-click the person, organization, or resource entries in the list to edit the information. You can also select the entry and then click the Edit an Address Entry button, or you can right-click and choose Edit. Make your changes, and then click OK to save the changes or Cancel to discard the changes.

- Delete an entry—You can select one or more entries, and then press Delete. You can also click the Delete an Address Entry button. Or, you can right-click the selection and choose Delete.

**CAUTION**

You're working without a safety net when you delete records in the address book because there is no way to restore an entry that you've deleted in error. The same holds true for deleting an entire address book. The only way to recover an accidentally deleted address book is if you can restore the files from a backup. One more reason to back up regularly—so a recent copy of your address book is secure.

**25**

- Move entries to another address book—You can select the entries in the list, and then click and drag them over to another address book (in the list in the left pane).

- Copy entries to another address book—Select the entries, and then choose Edit, Copy, or right-click the selection and choose Copy. Open the other address book, and then choose Edit, Paste, or right-click in the right pane and choose Paste.

- Print entries—You can print the current record, selected records, or all the records. Select one or more records, and then click the Print button on the toolbar or press Ctrl+P to open the Print dialog box.

- Search for text in the Display Name—This search tool will locate information in the display name field. Select an address book, and then click the Search for Specified Text button, or choose Edit, Find to open the Find dialog box. Type the text you want to search for, and then click OK. To search for information in the first name, simply type the name. If you want to search for last names (or anything beyond the first name), type an asterisk (*) before the search text. Records that contain the search text will be shown in an expanded dialog box (see Figure 25.8).

- Send e-mail—You can select an address book entry, and then choose Tools, Send Mail to start composing a mail message. If there is an e-mail address in the selected record, it's automatically inserted into the message. You can finish creating the message, and then send it as you normally would.

Text you searched for

**Figure 25.8**
In the Find dialog box, you can type the text you want to search for in the address book records.

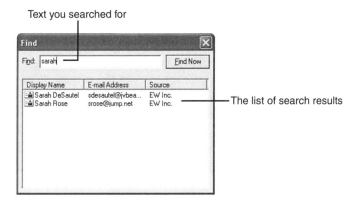

The list of search results

**NOTE**

When you send e-mail from the Address Book, you are using the default MAPI-compliant e-mail program set up in the Windows messaging profile. For more information on MAPI, see the help topic titled "Reference: Using the Address Book." For more information on installing Windows messaging and creating Windows messaging profiles, consult the Microsoft Windows documentation.

■ Publish an address book to HTML—You can publish your address books to HTML for publishing on the Web, or on a company intranet. Select a book, and then choose File, Publish to HTML to display the Publish to HTML dialog box (see Figure 25.9). Make your selections in the Layout and Range sections. Place a check mark next to the fields that you want included in the Columns to Publish list. If you want to include contact information at the bottom of the HTML file, click the Banner/Signature tab. Enable the Send Comments To check box, and then type your name in the text box. Enable the E-mail Address check box, and then type your e-mail address in the text box. In the Location tab, choose the drive and folder where you want the file saved. Type a filename in the Filename Prefix text box, and then choose OK.

**25**

**Figure 25.9**
Make your selections to build the HTML file in the Publish to HTML dialog box.

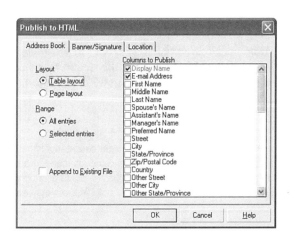

■ Open existing address books—You can open another address book in the list by clicking the plus sign next to the category. For example, to access the Outlook Express address book, click the plus sign next to Windows Address Book, and then click the Contacts book. You can add your other address books to the list by opening them in the Address Book. Choose File, Open to display the Open Address Book dialog box (see Figure 25.10), which shows a list of previously opened books. Click the CorelCENTRAL button to open other CorelCENTRAL books (you'll have the capability to browse for the files). Click the Other button to open address books that have not been opened previously and that are not CorelCENTRAL books.

*If you can't open a MAPI address book, or if you are getting the error message,* `MAPI address books will not be available. Please check the information services setup in the active user profile and your installation of Windows messaging,` *see "I Can't Open a MAPI Address Book" in the Troubleshooting section at the end of this chapter.*

*If you don't see all of your address books in the list, see "Some of the Address Books Are Missing" in the Troubleshooting section at the end of this chapter.*

**Figure 25.10**
Choose which address book you want to open in the Open Address Book dialog box.

■ Set access rights to an address book—You can set the access rights to an address book so that others have limited access. You can set an address book as hidden, so it cannot be seen by others, or read-only, so it can be viewed by others, but not modified. Select an address book, and then choose File, Rename. In the Security tab, enable the Hidden and/or the Read-only check boxes.

■ Set access rights to an address book entry—You can set the access rights to a specific address entry so that others have limited access. You can set an entry as hidden, so it cannot be seen by others, or read-only, so it can be viewed by others, but not modified. Select an address book entry, and then choose Address, Edit. In the Security tab, enable the Hidden and/or the Read-only check boxes.

**TIP FROM**

*Laura Acklen*

Your contact information is an invaluable resource and should be protected. It's extremely important that you make backup copies of your address books. A good time to do this is right after you make changes to the entries. To back up your address books, use the Import/Export Expert to export the books. You can only export one book at a time, so plan on repeating the steps for each address book. You might need these files if you decide to move your address books to another machine, or if you are uninstalling and reinstalling WordPerfect.

# CUSTOMIZING THE ADDRESS BOOK WINDOW

The default display settings in the Address Book window won't always show you what you need to see, so you might want to alter the display to make it easier to find information. You can do this in several ways: You can change the column headings and display different fields, or you can sort the records to group certain records together. You can also set a filter and specify what criteria must be met for a record to be displayed.

## SELECTING WHICH COLUMNS TO DISPLAY

By default, the address book window shows you the Display Name and Email Address fields for the entries. This information is helpful, but not very comprehensive. You can add columns to the address book window so you can see more information from the entries.

Note that you won't be able to remove the Display Name field from the address book window. The Display Name field is mandatory and as you saw earlier, the only one that can be searched to quickly locate records.

To change the fields (columns) displayed in the records list:

1. Right-click a column heading to display the Columns dialog box. A list of all the fields appears (see Figure 25.11). These settings can vary among address books.

2. Place a check mark next to each of the fields that you want to see listed. These settings "stick" with the address book, so you can customize the display of fields for each address book.

**Figure 25.11**
You can mark the fields that you want displayed in an Address Book list in the Columns dialog box. These settings can vary among address books.

## SORTING ADDRESS BOOK ENTRIES

Sorting address book entries is one way to group related records together. After they are grouped together, you can quickly select them and work with the entries as a group. For example, you might want to work with only those records in a certain state. Sorting in ZIP/Postal Code order can help you organize your entries for a bulk mailing.

Follow these steps to sort the address book entries:

1. Click the column heading for the field by which you want to sort. You can now select the sorted records for printing, e-mail, or merging. For example, you can print labels in ZIP Code order if you sort the records by ZIP Code before selecting them.

2. Click the column heading again to reverse the sort (ascending to descending and vice versa). The arrow on the column heading shows you which direction the sort is done.

**CAUTION**

> If you sort the address book entries, and then exit the Address Book and try to use the sorted entries in a merge, the sort won't stick. If you want to use sorted entries in a merge, you need to convert the address book to a merge data file and then sort it. See the section "Importing and Exporting Address Book Entries" later in this chapter for more information.

## FILTERING ADDRESS BOOK ENTRIES

If you have an especially large address book and you want to be able to view only a certain group of entries, such as everyone at Acme, Inc., you need to filter the entries. *Filtering* means that you tell the address book to show only the entries that include specific criteria, such as a company name such as Acme, Inc.

The rest of the entries in your address book seem to "disappear" when the entries are filtered; however, they are all still in the address book. They are just not being displayed. After you finish viewing the specific entries for Acme, Inc., you can remove the filter, and all your entries will be visible again.

To set a filter for address book entries:

1. Choose View, Filter to display the Filter dialog box (see Figure 25.12).

Click to select an operator

**Figure 25.12**
In the Filter dialog box, you can specify the criteria that must be met for the record to be displayed in the list.

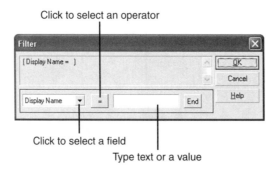

Click to select a field

Type text or a value

2. Click the first drop-down list arrow and choose a field. These fields are the column heading names, and you are choosing the one that you want the entries to be filtered by.

3. Click the operator button between the list box and the text box. Until you change it, the button has an equal sign on it.

4. Select an operator from the list. The operators are used to narrow down the list. For example, you can filter out all the records with a `Zip/Postal Code` of `Greater Than` `80300`.

5. Type the text or value that you want to use as a filter in the text box, and then click OK. To continue the example in step 4, you would enter `80300` as the Zip/Postal Code value. The program refreshes the list and displays only those records that meet the criteria.

**CAUTION**

The Filter and/or Remove Filter commands might not be available (they are grayed out). Choose View, Refresh if that happens and they should become available. Also, after you apply a filter, it stays there until you remove it. If you apply a filter and then close the Address Book, when you reopen it, the filter is still in place. You won't see a full list of records until you remove the filter. To switch back to the full list, choose View, Remove Filter.

## IMPORTING AND EXPORTING ADDRESS BOOK ENTRIES

Now that you know you can keep all of your contact information in one place, the question becomes "How can I get everything into the WordPerfect Address Book?" or "How can I transfer my address book information into other applications?"

The answers are as varied as the different programs that you can use to create and maintain contact information. You have a lot of options, so you're sure to find a way to get the information in (import) or copy the information out (export).

Unfortunately, space considerations don't permit detailed steps for every type of import or export operation. The following list of general concepts for importing and exporting should get you moving in the right direction:

- Using the Import/Export Expert—Corel designed this expert to walk you through the process of importing and exporting information. You can import address books from Corel Address Book 8 (`.abx`), text file format (`.csv`, `.txt`), and Outlook 97/98/2000/XP. You can export to text file format (`.csv`, `.txt`) and Outlook 97/98/2000/XP.

**CAUTION**

Group records cannot be imported or exported, so you'll have to manually re-create them. Also, if you import the Outlook Contacts, you'll only be able to get the name and e-mail address.

25

- Importing a merge data file—If you want to add names and addresses that you have stored in a merge data file to an address book, you can convert the merge data file into a text file and import the text file into an address book. If the records are in a list (not a table), you need to delete the FIELDNAMES code, and then replace the semicolon after each field name with an ENDFIELD code, and a hard return. You can do this with Find and Replace if you like. If the records are in a table, you can open and save the file as text without making any changes. In the Save As dialog box, choose ASCII (DOS) Delimited Text from the File Type drop-down list and then save the file. Now, you can import this .txt file directly into the address book.

- Importing spreadsheet and database files—Use the steps in the "Converting to WordPerfect Formats" section of Chapter 15, "Importing Data and Working with Other Programs," to save a spreadsheet or database file as an ASCII text file, which you can import directly into the Address Book. During the import process, you'll be able to "map," or match up, the field names from the ASCII text file with the Address Book field names, so you can be sure that the information from the text file is inserted in the right places.

 *If you get the error message "Invalid Field Name" when trying to import a data file into the Address Book, see "Invalid Field Name Error Message" in the Troubleshooting section at the end of this chapter.*

- Importing other address books—In most cases, you will be able to export addresses from another address book (such as Outlook Express) into an ASCII (or comma-delimited) text file, which can be imported directly into a WordPerfect Address Book. During the import process, the field names used in the other address book will be listed next to the fields in the WordPerfect Address Book. After you've matched up the field names, you can import the data.

- Importing Netscape address books—Netscape's address books can be brought into the WordPerfect Address Book by exporting from Netscape as a CSV or TXT file. Unfortunately, Netscape fails to insert the field names at the top of the file. You'll have to open the file in a text editor and add the field names manually before you can import it into a WordPerfect address book.

- Exporting to an ASCII text file—If you want to use WordPerfect address book data in another program, the universally accepted format is ASCII. After you've exported an address book to Text file (*.csv, *.txt), you can open, or import, the .txt file in another application.

- Exporting to a merge data file—The adrs2mrg macro that ships with WordPerfect converts an address book into a merge data file. The merge data file is not in table format, but it will have a field name record at the top.

**CAUTION**

There is an issue with the All Records option in WordPerfect 12. As a workaround, choose Select Records instead. You'll be able to choose your address book and then select records. If you click on a record, and then press Ctrl+A, you'll select all the records

> at once. Click the Insert button on the bottom-right corner, and then choose a format to perform the export.

→ To find out where the `adrs2mrg` macro is and how to run it, **see** "Running the Shipping Macros," **p. 818.**

→ For the steps to insert a code in the Find and Replace dialog box, **see** "Searching for Codes," **p. 150.**

**NOTE**

> The location of the address books has been changing with the different versions of WordPerfect, so the general rule is that you should export your books before an upgrade. After you have installed the newer version, you can import the address books from the previous version. This isn't always necessary, but it's almost foolproof.

- Using WordPerfect 10 Address Books—In some cases, the address books will not show up in the WordPerfect Address Book after an upgrade. If you didn't make backup copies of your address books before the upgrade, you'll need to reinstall WordPerfect 10 so you can use the Import/Export Expert to export the books. The best method is to export the books in CSV format. When you've exported all your books, you can uninstall WordPerfect 10, and then start WordPerfect 11 (or 12) and use the Import/Export Expert to import the books.

- Using WordPerfect 9 Address Books—You should be able to open the address books directly and use them just as you would any other address book. The WordPerfect 9 address books are found under the CorelCENTRAL button in the Open Address Book dialog box (refer back to Figure 25.10).

- Using WordPerfect 8 Address Books—If CorelCENTRAL8 is still installed on the system, address books can be opened under the MAPI tree. Choose File, Open, Other; then, select one of the CC8 books (such as My Addresses or Frequent Contacts). If you have already removed CorelCENTRAL8, but you have exported the files to ABX format, you can import them into a WordPerfect address book using the Import/Export Expert. Keep in mind that you must create a blank address book to import the addresses into. Note that you might not be able to import the custom field data into the WordPerfect address book.

- Importing WordPerfect 7 Address Books—Before you uninstall WordPerfect 7, you should export the addresses in WordPerfect 7 to an ABX file and then import the ABX file into a WordPerfect address book with the Import/Export Expert. If you have trouble importing an ABX file from WordPerfect 7, try changing the extension of the ABX file to CSV in Explorer or My Computer and then try the import again.

*If you cannot import previous address books into WordPerfect Productivity Pack, see "Cannot Import in the Productivity Pack Version" in the Troubleshooting section at the end of this chapter.*

**25**

# INTEGRATING WITH MICROSOFT OUTLOOK

 WordPerfect 11 introduced the capability to integrate with Microsoft Outlook address books. WordPerfect 12 includes some improvements. You can use entries in the Outlook address book for document routing and review, printing labels and envelopes, and merge operations. As mentioned earlier, you have to make a choice. You can either work with the entries in the WordPerfect address books, or the Outlook address book, but not both at the same time.

From the names, you would think that Outlook and Outlook Express were the same type of application. They are not. Outlook is a Personal Information Manager and Outlook Express is an e-mail/news reader. They both have address books, but they are completely separate from each other. You can work with both address books in WordPerfect, using two different methods.

You will be able to open the Outlook Express address book in the WordPerfect Address Book. The entries will appear in the Contacts folder under Windows Address Book. The Outlook address book is opened when you activate Outlook integration.

## OPENING THE OUTLOOK ADDRESS BOOK

When you're ready to work with the Outlook address book, you will need to "turn on" Outlook integration. To switch back to the WordPerfect address books, you have to turn Outlook integration back off.

Follow these steps to enable Outlook integration:

1. In WordPerfect, choose Tools, Settings, or press Alt+F12.
2. Click Environment.
3. Click the Use Outlook Address Book/Contact List check box to activate this feature.
4. Choose OK, and then Close to return to the document.

When you enable the Outlook integration, Outlook "takes over" the address book. When you open the address book, you will get the Outlook Address Book dialog box. The WordPerfect address books are not available at this point.

Follow these steps to open the Outlook address book/contact list:

1. Choose Tools, Address Book. The first time you use the Outlook address book, you will have to specify a profile in the Choose Profile dialog box (see Figure 25.13).

**Figure 25.13**
After you identify your profile, the Outlook Address Book will open when you choose Tools, Address Book.

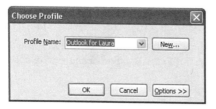

**2.** Either select a profile from the drop-down list or choose OK to use the default profile. The Outlook Address Book dialog box appears (see Figure 25.14).

**Figure 25.14**
The Outlook Address Book dialog box shows the entries in alphabetical order by name.

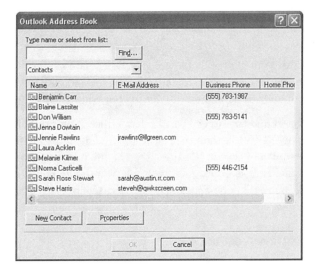

**CAUTION**

To integrate with the Outlook address book, WordPerfect has to be able to interface with that application. The Microsoft Windows standard for electronic messaging is called MAPI. Microsoft limits the contacts available under MAPI to those that contain an e-mail address or fax number. For this reason, only the entries that have an e-mail address or fax number will appear in the Outlook Address Book dialog box. If you don't have a fax number, enter a space or "dummy" character in the fax field. Incidentally, Microsoft also controls what is placed in the Display Name field.

**TIP FROM**

Your contact information is an invaluable resource and should be protected. It's extremely important that you make backup copies of your address books. A good time to do this is right after you make changes to the entries. For more information on how to back up your Outlook address books, see the Microsoft Knowledge Base article #287070. Go to http://support.microsoft.com and enter the article number.

 *If you get an error message when you try to set Outlook as your default e-mail client, see "Error When Setting Outlook as the Default Mail Client" in the Troubleshooting section at the end of this chapter.*

# TROUBLESHOOTING

## CANNOT ACCESS ADDRESS BOOKS AFTER SP1

*I just downloaded and installed SP1 for WordPerfect 11. When I try to access my address books, the Address Book dialog box is empty. Where are my address books?*

The good news is that your address books are safe. They have *not* been removed. The bad news is that a change was made in the folder name for the address books in SP1, so you'll have to rename your address book folder to get to your address books.

First, exit WordPerfect and any other WordPerfect Office application. In Explorer, open the My Documents folder. Right-click on the ccwin folder and choose Delete. Now, right-click the folder called ccwin9 and choose Rename. Rename the folder to ccwin. Close Explorer. Start WordPerfect and choose Tools, Address Book. You should now see your address books. If, for some reason, they still don't appear, choose File, Open, CorelCENTRAL, and browse to your address books.

## SCRAMBLED INFORMATION FROM THE ADDRESS BOOK

*I want to use my customized WordPerfect templates in a new version of WordPerfect. Most of them work just fine, but when a prompt is linked to an address book field, the wrong information is being inserted into the template.*

Some of the field names were changed in the WordPerfect address books, so you probably need to rebuild your prompts and link them to the proper fields. In WordPerfect 11 (or 12), open the template for editing. Delete the prompts that are linked to address book fields, and then reinsert them. Click Build Prompts, and then choose Add. In the Add Template Prompt dialog box, select Show All Available Fields. Type the prompt, and then choose the correct field from the list. Make sure that you save these changes.

## I CAN'T OPEN A MAPI ADDRESS BOOK

*I'm trying to open an existing address book, but I don't see MAPI in the list. Sometimes I also get a MAPI error message when I try to open an address book or work with the Merge feature.*

First of all, try opening the address book using File, Open, MAPI, and then selecting the address book from the list. If this doesn't work, you need to look at the type of MAPI mail client you have installed on your system.

For the WordPerfect Address Book to access MAPI-compliant address books, you must have an extended MAPI mail client installed and the extended MAPI version of MAPI32.DLL must be active. Extended MAPI mail clients include Outlook 97/98/2000/2003 (in CW mode), Groupwise, the basic messaging client installed with Windows NT 4, and some configurations of Notes, and many other e-mail clients. If you have Outlook Express, Netscape, or Eudora installed on your system, the simple MAPI version of MAPI32.DLL may be active, and you won't be able to access the MAPI-integrated address books from WordPerfect.

**TIP FROM**

*[signature: Laura Acklen]*

> You can right-click your `mapi32.dll` file and check the Version tab to determine whether your file is extended or simple MAPI—if it's extended MAPI, it will say so in the description.

In Netscape, you can usually disable the simple MAPI by changing your preferences. Choose Edit, Preferences, click Mail and Newsgroups, and then deselect the Use Netscape Messenger from MAPI-based Applications check box. As long as you have a version of extended MAPI on your system, when you reboot, the simple MAPI file will be replaced.

In Outlook Express, choose Tools, Options. Click the General tab, and then deselect the Make Outlook Express My Default Simple MAPI Client check box. Choose OK twice, and then reboot your computer.

**NOTE**

> You can also go into Control Panel, Internet (or Internet Options), Programs and select Microsoft Outlook (or any other application that supports Extended MAPI) from the E-mail drop-down list. This sets Outlook as the default mail client, which might be necessary for you to be able to see your MAPI address books. Make sure you choose Apply before you choose OK.

Extended MAPI/Messaging will be installed with the following operating system configurations: Windows NT 4.0, Windows 98, or Windows 2000 only if those were installed as updates to a system running Windows 95 or Windows NT (in which case the functionality will be retained from the prior 95/NT installation), Windows with Outlook in CW mode (if installed in Internet Mail Only mode you get only simple MAPI), Windows with Exchange Administrator (Exchange 5.5) or Exchange System Manager (Exchange 2000) installed, and Windows with MS Exchange Server. Windows XP/2000 users will not have extended MAPI or messaging as part of the operating system; they will have to download or order a messaging update from Microsoft, or install a third-party mail client.

### SOME OF THE ADDRESS BOOKS ARE MISSING

*Not all the address books are listed in the WordPerfect Address Book dialog box. Where did they go?*

The address books may very well be present on your system—they just haven't been opened in WordPerfect yet. In the WordPerfect dialog box, choose File, Open. Either select one of the previously opened address books, or click the CorelCENTRAL button to choose another WordPerfect address book, or click Other to browse your system for other address books. After you open an address book in WordPerfect, it will appear in the list of address books.

Also, new address books can be marked as Hidden (or Read-Only) as a security measure to protect against unauthorized access. If an address book is marked as Hidden, it won't appear to users who log on to that machine. If it's marked Read-Only, users won't be able to modify the records.

### INVALID FIELD NAME ERROR MESSAGE

*I'm trying to import a data file in the Address Book, but I get an error message that says there is an invalid field name. What does this mean?*

You probably have some punctuation in one of the field names. Open the data file and remove any punctuation marks from the field names. For example, if one of your field names is "City, State ZIP," the Address Book sees the comma as a field separator so the City field is assumed to be one field and the State ZIP field to be another. Save the file and try the import again.

### CANNOT IMPORT IN THE PRODUCTIVITY PACK VERSION

*When I bought my new computer, it came with WordPerfect Productivity Pack. I am trying to import an address book from a previous version of WordPerfect, but the Import/Export Expert option on the File menu is unavailable. Is there any way to get this address book into WordPerfect?*

WordPerfect Productivity Pack doesn't support importing and exporting address books. Because it is included free with new computer systems, some of the functionality has been disabled to encourage you to upgrade to the full version. After all, if none of us purchase the full version, WordPerfect will cease to exist.

That said, there is a workaround. If you have Outlook Express on your system, you can use it to import your book so it will be available under the Windows Address Book tree. Start Outlook Express, and then click on Tools, Address Book. Choose File, Import, Other Address Book. Select the format for the import file, and then choose Import. Browse to your address book and select it. Check to make sure the fields are mapped correctly, and then click Finish. Close the address book, close Outlook Express, and start WordPerfect. Choose Tools, Address Book to start the WordPerfect Address Book (if you haven't already, disable Outlook integration for this). In the left pane, open the Windows Address Book tree. Select Contacts to see your imported entries.

### ERROR WHEN SETTING OUTLOOK AS THE DEFAULT MAIL CLIENT

*When I open the WordPerfect Address Book, I am prompted to set Outlook as the default mail client. The problem is that after I click Yes, I get the following error message:* `Microsoft Outlook: Either there is no default mail client or the current mail client cannot fulfill the messaging request. Please run Microsoft Outlook and set it as the default mail client.` *Now what do I do?*

This can happen if the Outlook files are damaged, or if another mail program is running (such as Outlook Express or Mozilla), and you set Outlook as the default client. There are several steps you can try to resolve the issue.

- One—Close all open applications, including WordPerfect. Open WordPerfect and try setting Outlook as the default mail client again within WordPerfect. In other words, repeat your steps and see if it works this time.

- Two—Close all open applications, including WordPerfect. Open Microsoft Outlook and set it as the default mail client. Refer to the Outlook documentation for the steps to do this for your specific version of Outlook. Open WordPerfect and try to open the Address Book again.

- Three—Refer to the Microsoft Knowledge Base article #813745 for steps to repair Microsoft Outlook. Go to http://support.microsoft.com and enter the article number.

- Four—Disable Outlook integration from within WordPerfect and use the WordPerfect Address Book instead. Choose Tools, Settings, Environment, and then uncheck the Use Outlook Address Book/Contact List option.

**NOTE**

I would like to express my sincere appreciation to Debra Earle, volunteer C-Tech on the Corel newsgroups, for her assistance in testing and perfecting the "Importing and Exporting Address Book Entries" section and for her exhaustive research on the MAPI items when we did the WordPerfect 10 book. I was lucky enough to have Cyndy Zook do the technical edit on this chapter. She did an outstanding job researching the material and helping me update the information for WordPerfect 11 and 12. Thank you kindly ladies!

# PROJECT

Contact information is so important. It doesn't matter if you are a high-powered executive, a freelance reporter, a full-time student, or a stay-at-home mom, everyone has to figure out how to keep track of names, phone numbers, and e-mail addresses. I made the jump from pencil and paper when I got too busy to hand address my holiday cards. I distinctly remember spending a few days trying to decide the best place to store the information. I settled on creating address books in WordPerfect. Because I can export them to other formats, I could use the information in other applications. Add that to the fact that I could create my mailing labels and personalize the holiday letters in one step.

If you've already spent time putting your contact information into WordPerfect address books, you'll want to bring that information into WordPerfect 11 (or 12) when you upgrade. It's simple—you export the address books in the previous version, and then import them into the new version.

Here are the steps to bring your address books from version 8, 9, or 10 into WordPerfect 11 (with small modifications for WordPerfect 12).

### For WordPerfect 8:

1. In WordPerfect 8, open the address book.
2. Choose Book, Export, and then click on Entire Address Book.
3. Type in a filename for the exported file and select which folder you want to save it to.
4. Click OK.
5. Repeat steps 1–4 for each address book on your system.
6. In WordPerfect 11 (or 12), choose Tools, Settings, Environment, and then remove the check next to Use Outlook Address Book/Contact List. Click OK, and then Close. This turns off Outlook integration so you can get to the WordPerfect Address Book.
7. Choose Tools, Address Book.
8. Choose File, New, Address Book.
9. Type a name for the address book, and then choose OK. This creates a blank address book for your exported addresses.
10. Choose File, Import/Export Expert.
11. Select Import, and then if necessary, select Corel Address Book 8 (.abx) from the Import From drop down list. Choose Next.
12. In the Import From list box, choose the ABX file that you created in WordPerfect 8.
13. In the Import To list box, choose the blank address book you created in WordPerfect 11 (or 12). Choose Next.
14. Choose Next, and then Next again, and then Finish.
15. Repeat steps 8–14 for each of the ABX files that you want to import.

### In WordPerfect 9 and 10:

1. In WordPerfect 9 or 10, open the address book.
2. Choose File, Import/Export Expert.
3. Choose Export, and then if necessary, choose Text file (*.csv, *.txt) from the Export To drop-down list. Choose Next.
4. In the Export From list, choose the address book that you want to export.
5. In the Export To list, select the location where you want to save the file.
6. Type a filename in the File Name text box, and then click Next.
7. Choose Next, and then continuously click the Add button until all of the address book fields show up in the mapped section. Choose Next.
8. Choose Finish.
9. Repeat steps 1–8 for each address book on your system.
10. In WordPerfect 11 (or 12), choose Tools, Settings, Environment, and then remove the check next to Use Outlook Address Book/Contact List. Click OK, and then Close. This turns off Outlook integration so you can get to the WordPerfect Address Book.

11. Choose Tools, Address Book.

12. Choose File, New, Address Book.

13. Type a name for the address book, and then choose OK. This creates a blank address book for your exported addresses.

14. Choose File, Import/Export Expert.

15. Select Import, and then if necessary, select Text file (`*.csv`, `*.txt`) from the Import From drop down list. Choose Next.

16. In the Import From list box, choose the `.txt` file that you created in WordPerfect 9 or 10.

17. In the Import To list box, choose the blank address book you created in WordPerfect 11 (or 12). Choose Next.

18. Choose Next, and then Next again. The next step is to map the fields.

19. Select an imported field from the list on the left.

20. Click the drop-down list button in the Address Book Fields list, select the matching field, and then choose Add.

21. Repeat steps 19 and 20 for each field in the Imported Fields list (on the left).

22. Choose Next, and then choose Finish.

23. Repeat steps 10–22 for each of the `.txt` files that you want to import.

# CHAPTER 26

# USING EXPERTS AND MACROS

**I**n this chapter                                                                                  *by Laura Acklen*

# USING THE PERFECTEXPERT

In Chapter 23, "Building Documents with Templates," you learned how to use the PerfectExpert project templates to build specific types of documents. In this chapter, you'll learn how to use the "generic" PerfectExpert, which can guide you through the creation of all sorts of different documents. You can create documents with tables, columns, bulleted and numbered lists, graphics, shapes, borders, charts, outlines, headers, footers, page numbers, and so on. All the common formatting options, such as changing the margins, choosing fonts, setting tabs, using Make It Fit, adjusting line spacing, inserting symbols, and marking text, are available at the click of a button. You can even get to the document collaboration and proofing tools. In short, "It's in there."

 To start the PerfectExpert, click the PerfectExpert button or choose Help, PerfectExpert. The PerfectExpert panel appears on the left side of the screen (see Figure 26.1). You might recall from Chapter 23 that you click the panel buttons to choose additional options. The buttons with a down-facing arrow display pop-up menus.

This button opens a pop-up menu.

Down-facing arrow    This button opens another page of options.

**Figure 26.1**
The PerfectExpert panel has buttons that open pop-up menus and other pages with additional options.

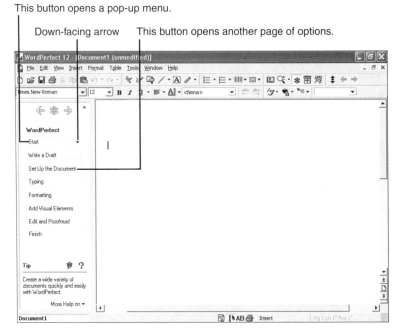

26

Clicking a panel button opens another page with more options (see Figure 26.2). If you want to move back to the previous page, click the Go Back button. As you continue to work in the PerfectExpert panel, the Go Forward button will become available.

 Clicking the mortarboard button launches your Internet browser (if available) and takes you to Corel's Learning Center on the Web. As of this writing, the link takes you to the

`OfficeCommunity.com` site, but that may change as more resources for WordPerfect 12 become available.

 Clicking the question mark button opens the Index tab of the Help Topics dialog box, where you can search for information on a particular feature.

Go Back button ⌐  ⌐ Go Forward button

**Figure 26.2**
A Set Up the Document page has buttons for frequently used formatting commands.

⌐Click here to display the Help Topics dialog box.
⌐Click here to go to the Learning Center on the Web.

By default, you are set to create the new document in a blank document window. You can, however, use the PerfectExpert to edit an existing document or project template. To do so, click the Start button in the PerfectExpert panel and choose New Project/Existing Document. In the PerfectExpert dialog box (see Figure 26.3), you can choose from the list of project templates or you can click the Work On tab and choose from a list of previously edited documents (work in progress).

→ To learn more about using project templates, **see** "Using WordPerfect's Templates" in Chapter 23.

I've kind of saved the best for last, but you *have* to see what happens when you open the PerfectExpert panel in an existing document. Let me give you a quick example. With the PerfectExpert panel displayed, I opened a newsletter. When I click in various parts of the newsletter, the PerfectExpert panel pages change to display options that are relevant for the feature used for that section of the newsletter. When I click on a table, I get the Table page; when I click on a title, I get the Title Look page; when I click in the newsletter text, I get the Newsletter page. And so on and so forth.

Click here to choose a document
that you've recently edited.

Click here to switch to a different
category of project templates.

**Figure 26.3**
You can open a
project template, or
a recently edited
document, in the
PerfectExpert dialog
box.

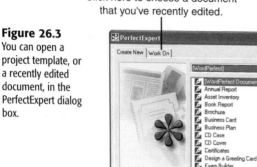

> **NOTE**
>
> This feature is perfect for the new (or timid) users because it is literally point-and-click document generation. All users have to do is click the PerfectExpert button to open the PerfectExpert panel where they can click buttons to get menus and dialog boxes that they might not have been able to find on their own.

# USING THE PLEADING EXPERTS

New in WordPerfect 11 (and included in WordPerfect 12), the pleading experts help you put together pleading documents quickly and easily. In general terms, a pleading is every legal document filed in a lawsuit, petition, motion, or hearing. They set out the facts and legal arguments that support that party's position. Pleadings are required by state or federal statutes and court rules to be in a particular form and format: typed, signed, and dated with the name of the court, title, and number of the case, and contact information for the attorney or person acting for him/herself included. In other words, pleading documents are created for virtually every type of case and must follow a strict set of formatting rules.

> **NOTE**
>
> The Legal Tools are not installed during a typical installation. If you don't have a Legal Tools option on your Tools menu, they haven't been installed yet. Choose Start, Control Panel, Add/Remove Programs. Select WordPerfect Office 11 (or 12), and then click the Change button. Choose Change Which Program Features Are Installed, and then click Next. If necessary, click the plus sign next to WordPerfect Office 11 (or 12) to open the tree. Click the plus sign next to WordPerfect. Click the button next to Legal Tools and choose This Feature Will Be Installed on Local Hard Drive. Choose Next, and then Begin. Choose Finish to close the Install Wizard.

Over the years, WordPerfect's pleading tools have evolved from a simple macro to create pleading papers to a full set of pleading creation experts that guide you through the entire process. First, you use the Pleading Expert Filler to enter the case information. Then, you use the Pleading Expert Designer to customize the pleading styles so your pleading documents conform to the filing requirements for your region.

**TIP FROM**

> If you just need to whip up a quick pleading document, you can do this with a pleading macro. Either click the Pleading button on the Legal toolbar, or choose Tools, Macro, Play (Alt+F10), and double-click `pleading.wcm` in the list. Make your selections in the Pleading Paper dialog box, and then choose OK to create the blank pleading paper.

## USING THE PLEADING EXPERT FILLER TO CREATE CASES

The first step to produce pleading documents is to set up the cases. New cases can be created from scratch, or you can create new cases based on existing cases. The case information is easily updated when it changes, so go ahead and get started with your cases by running the Pleading Expert Filler.

To create a new case with the Pleading Expert Filler

1. Choose Tools, Legal Tools, Pleading Expert Filler, or click the Pleading Expert Filler button on the Legal toolbar. The Pleading Expert Filler appears (see Figure 26.4).

**Figure 26.4**
The Pleading Expert Filler walks you through the process of creating and editing cases.

2. Choose Next to move to the Case Selection section (see Figure 26.5).
3. Enable the New Case option and type a name for the case in the New Case Name text box.
4. Choose Next to move to the Select Court section.
5. Select the pleading style that you want to use and type the judge's information.

**Figure 26.5**
In the Case Selection section, you can create new cases and edit existing cases.

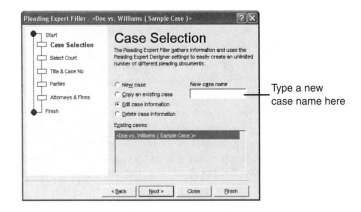

Type a new case name here

6. Choose Next to move to the Title & Case No. section.

7. Enter the relevant information here, and then choose Next to move to the Parties section.

8. Select which parties are involved and enter the name(s) of the parties.

9. Choose Next to move to the Attorneys & Firms section.

10. Enter the contact information for the attorney(s).

11. Choose Next, and then Finish. WordPerfect generates the pleading document (see Figure 26.6).

**Figure 26.6**
The completed pleading document has all the information you typed in, in the correct place and in the correct format.

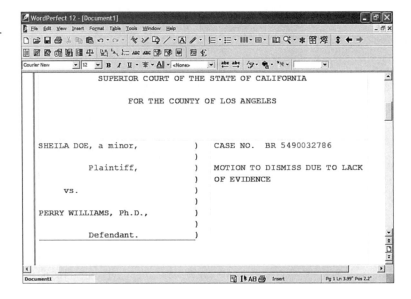

When you need to edit a case, you do so through the Pleading Expert Filler. Keep in mind that you can create new cases based on existing cases. You will save yourself some time entering the contact information.

To edit an existing case with the Pleading Expert Filler:

1. Choose Tools, Legal Tools, Pleading Expert Filler, or click the Pleading Expert Filler button on the Legal toolbar. The Pleading Expert Filler appears (refer back to Figure 26.4).

2. Choose Next, and then select the case you want to edit from the Existing Cases list.

3. Choose Next to start working through the different sections, making your changes as necessary.

All the steps necessary to complete a pleading are listed on the left side of the Pleading Expert Filler. You can click any of the items in the list to jump to that particular section.

## CREATING AND EDITING PLEADING STYLES

The preceding steps illustrate the creation of a pleading document using one of the two built-in styles. Specifically, Style 1 was used, with some modifications, to create the document shown in Figure 26.6. You can create your own pleading styles and select them from the list.

Creating your own custom pleading styles is a key piece of the puzzle, and it has been completely automated to save you time. The Pleading Expert Designer walks you through the entire process.

To create a new pleading style with the Pleading Expert Designer

1. Choose Tools, Legal Tools, Pleading Expert Designer, or click the Pleading Expert Designer button on the Legal toolbar. The Pleading Expert Designer appears (see Figure 26.7).

26

**Figure 26.7**
The Pleading Expert Designer walks you through the process of creating your own pleading styles.

2. Choose Next to move to the Create/Edit Pleading section (see Figure 26.8).

**Figure 26.8**
Select a style to edit, or type a new style name to create a new style in the Create/Edit Pleading section.

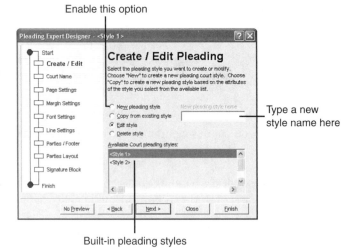

Enable this option

Type a new style name here

Built-in pleading styles

3. Enable the New pleading style option button, and then type a name for the style in the New Pleading Style Name text box.

4. Choose Next to move to the Court Name section.

5. Follow the prompts in the Pleading Expert Designer to complete the pleading style. Notice that as you work, the preview window is updated to show you how your pleading documents will look.

The new pleading styles that you create with the Pleading Expert Designer show up in the Select Court section of the Pleading Expert Filler so that you can select them when you create or edit cases.

**NOTE**

The steps to create a pleading style are listed on the left side of the Pleading Expert Designer. If you are only making a few changes, click any step to go directly to it.

# USING MACROS TO AUTOMATE REPETITIVE TASKS

Think about your day-to-day activities and ask yourself how much of what you do is repetitive. You may be spending valuable time repeating the same steps over and over, not realizing that you can speed things up considerably with a macro. Hmmmm. What is a macro?

Let me use a popular analogy to try to explain. A camcorder records video and sound on a videotape (or memory card). You can turn the recorder on, record the video, and then turn the recorder off. The video that you recorded is there for you to access when you play the tape back. The same is true for creating a macro, except instead of recording video, you record actions taken in a document window. You turn on the Macro Recorder, record your actions, and then turn off the Macro Recorder. Whatever you do between turning the Macro Recorder on and turning it back off is recorded in a macro. The next time you need to perform that series of steps, you play the macro and it does the work, at lightning speed. And, it does the same thing, without fail, every single time you run it.

Now, before you skip this section because you think that macros are only for tech-heads, think again. They can be extremely simple, such as typing out your standard letter closing, setting up a landscape page with 10-point Arial, or inserting a page number. Or they can be very complex, such as asking a series of questions and generating a customized document with standard sections of text (such as legal documents, loan forms, and insurance policies).

**NOTE**

> Previous users of WordPerfect will be pleased to find that the same keystrokes that have been in use since the early DOS WordPerfect days still work in WordPerfect 11 and 12. You can still press Alt+F10 to play a macro and Ctrl+F10 to record a macro.

If you're lucky, your firm has distributed a standard set of macros for everyone's use. If this is the case, all you need to know is how to run them, so let's start there. Later on, I'll explain how to create your own macros.

## PLAYING MACROS

The trick to playing macros that someone else has provided for you is knowing where they are stored. If you need to look around a bit, you can browse for them. Choose Tools, Macro, Play (or press Alt+F10) to open the Play Macro dialog box (see Figure 26.9). The location of the shipping macros varies depending on your operating system. If you don't see them in the list, look for a PerfectScript folder and go from there. To play a macro, double-click it, or select it and choose Play.

**26**

Double-click a macro file to play it.

**Figure 26.9**
The shipping macros are stored in a WordPerfect subfolder of the PerfectScript folder. The exact location varies depending on your operating system.

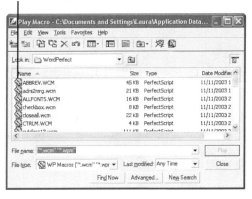

TIP FROM

*Laura Acklen*

The last nine macros that you played are listed at the bottom of the Macro menu. Choose Tools, Macro, and then select one from the list to play it.

CAUTION

If a macro "hangs," you'll have to cancel it manually. Press the Esc key, which will cancel the macro. A message box will appear stating that the macro was cancelled by the user. If the Esc key doesn't work, you can right-click the PerfectScript icon (little cassette tape) that sits in the system tray while a macro is running, and choose Stop. Choose Quit when you get the message that the macro is being cancelled at the request of PerfectScript. This method can be used to stop a macro mid-flow (even it isn't "hung").

## RUNNING THE SHIPPING MACROS

WordPerfect ships with a collection of macros that are helpful both to use and to examine if you want to become familiar with the PerfectScript macro language. Many of these macros were available in previous versions of WordPerfect, so you're likely to see that your old favorites are still around.

- `Abbrev.wcm`—Opens a QuickWords dialog box, where you can select a QuickWord and expand it in a document. The dialog box stays open so you can expand multiple QuickWords without opening the dialog box each time.

- `adrs2mrg.wcm`—Opens an Address Book to Merge dialog box, where you can choose an Address Book and then create a merge data file from the entire Address Book or just from selected records. This macro creates a text data file with a field name record at the top of the file.

CAUTION

There is an issue with the All Records option in the adrs2mrg.wcm macro in WordPerfect 12. As a workaround, choose Select Records instead. You'll be able to choose your address book and then select records. If you click on a record, and then press Ctrl+A, you'll select all of the records at once. Click the Insert button on the bottom right corner, and then choose a format to perform the export.

- `Allfonts.wcm`—This macro searches for all the fonts that are installed for the current printer and generates a list of the fonts along with a short sample of text (see Figure 26.10). Depending on the number of fonts you have installed, it might take a few minutes to generate the list. Also, your printer might not have enough memory to print the entire list in a single job. You can get around this limitation by printing only a few pages at a time.

Total number of fonts

**Figure 26.10**
The allfonts macro
compiles a list of fonts
that are installed for
the active printer.

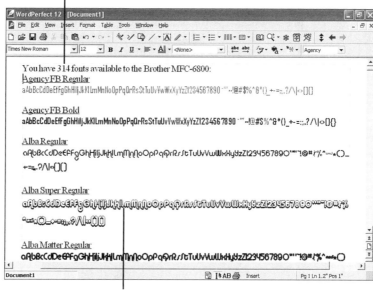

Sample text

 *If you don't see all these files in the macro list, see "Where Are the Rest of the Shipping Macros?" in the Troubleshooting section at the end of this chapter.*

- checkbox.wcm—This macro creates a check box that you can click to insert an x in the box and click again to remove the x. The check box is created as hypertext, so it will show up underlined and blue.

 *If you don't like blue, underlined check boxes, see "Changing the Hypertext Style" in the Troubleshooting section at the end of this chapter.*

- closeall.wcm—This macro displays a Close All Documents dialog box, where you can selectively save open documents before they are closed (see Figure 26.11). If documents are unnamed, you can specify a name for the documents in the dialog box. A Save check box lets you decide which documents should be saved before they are closed.

- ctrlm.wcm—This macro displays the PerfectScript Command dialog box, where you can select, edit, and insert macro commands in a macro. You don't have to open the Play Macro dialog box to select this macro. Just press Ctrl+M in the document window.

- cvtdocs11.wcm or cvtdocs12.wcm—These macros open the WordPerfect Conversion Expert dialog box, where you can choose to convert a single file, a folder, or a folder and its subfolders to several different WordPerfect formats. You can choose from WordPerfect 11, 10, 9, 8, 7, 6, 5.1, and HTML.

- DCConvert.wcm—This macro converts WordPerfect drop cap characters (for example, the first whole word is a drop cap) to a drop cap character that is Microsoft Word compatible (that is, a number of characters drop cap).

26

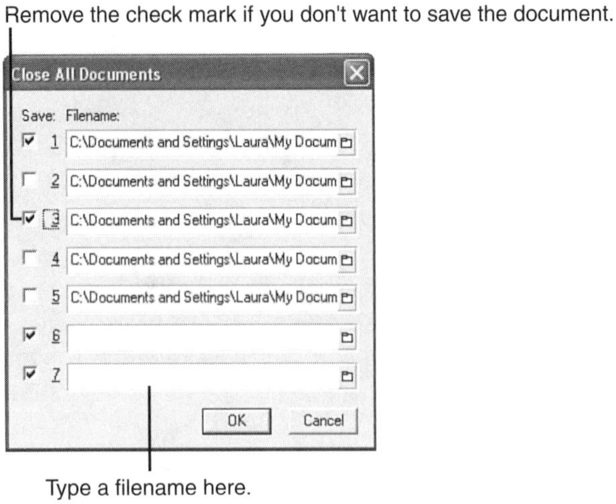

Remove the check mark if you don't want to save the document.

**Figure 26.11**
In the Close All Documents dialog box, you can select which documents you want to save before you close them.

Type a filename here.

- `endfoot.wcm`—This macro converts all the endnotes in a document (or just those in selected text) to footnotes. You must be outside the footnote/endnote area to run this macro.

- `Expndall.wcm`—This macro expands all the QuickWords in the document. You might use this if you work with documents with complex QuickWords. You might decide to turn off Expand QuickWords as you type them and then expand them all at once with this macro.

- `Filestmp.wcm`—This macro opens the File Stamp Options dialog box (see Figure 26.12), where you can choose to insert the filename or the filename and path into a header or footer. If the document has not been named when you run this macro, a filename code is placed in the header or footer. When you save and name the file, the filename (and the path) shows up in the header or footer. If you select Change Font, a Font Properties dialog box appears so that you can select the font (or font size) that you want to use for the file stamp.

**Figure 26.12**
You can select the type of file stamp and a location for it in the File Stamp Options dialog box.

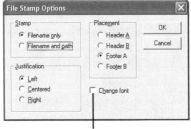

Click here if you want to use a different font.

- **flipenv.wcm**—This macro displays an Envelope Addresses dialog box, where you can type in the return address (unless you've already selected a personal information entry in the Address Book) and a mailing address. You can also select a mailing address from the Address Book. After you fill in the address information, you can choose an envelope size. The macro creates the envelope, only it flips it 180 degrees so that it is upside-down. This macro was created because some printers have trouble printing text within 1/4 inch of the top-left corner of an envelope, but they don't have a problem printing it within 1/4 inch of the lower-right corner. If you have one of these printers, this macro enables you to print the return address closer to the edge of the envelope.

- **Fontdn.wcm**—This macro reduces the font size by 2 points. If you select text before running the macro, only the selected text is affected. Otherwise, the change takes place at the insertion point and remains in effect until you change the size again.

- **Fontup.wcm**—This macro increases the font size by 2 points. If you select text before running the macro, only the selected text is affected. Otherwise, the change takes place at the insertion point and remains in effect until you change the size again.

- **footend.wcm**—This macro converts the footnotes in the entire document (or just in selected text) to endnotes. You must be outside the footnote/endnote area to run this macro.

- **Longname.wcm**—This macro is for everyone who used descriptive names in document summaries as a workaround for the restrictive DOS file naming conventions. This macro converts the descriptive filenames into long filenames, which can have up to 255 characters. When you run this macro, a Convert to Long Filenames dialog box appears (see Figure 26.13). You can either type the name of the drive and folder where the files are stored, or you can click the Files icon to open the Select Folder dialog box. Select the file(s) that you want to convert in the Select Files to Rename list, and then click OK. When the macro is finished, a record of the changes is created.

**26**

Click here to select a folder.

**Figure 26.13**
You can select the file(s) that you want to convert in the Convert to Long Filenames dialog box.

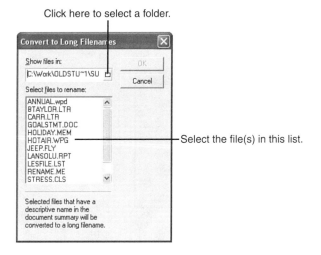

Select the file(s) in this list.

■ Parabrk.wcm—This macro displays a Paragraph Break dialog box, where you can choose a symbol or graphic to display at the next paragraph break. The symbol or graphic is centered on the blank line between paragraphs.

■ pleading.wcm—This macro displays the Pleading Paper dialog box (see Figure 26.14), where you can choose from a variety of options to generate a legal pleading paper.

**Figure 26.14**
In the Pleading Paper dialog box, you can set up line numbers, vertical lines, margins, fonts, page numbers, line spacing, and justification for a legal pleading paper.

■ prompts.wcm—This macro opens Prompt Builder, which helps you create prompts for your templates. You can create messages that help guide the user along in using the template. You must be editing a template (other than your default template) before you can run this macro.

→ If the capability to create prompts in your templates sounds appealing to you, **see** "Using Prompt Builder," **p. 729.**

■ reverse.wcm—This macro displays the Reverse Text Options dialog box (see Figure 26.15), where you can choose a color for the text and a color for the fill (or background). If you've selected text, you can place the reverse text in a text box. If you've selected table cells, the dialog box is a little different. You choose from three table-oriented options: Center Text, Lock Cell, and Header Row.

Click here to select a text color.

**Figure 26.15**
You can create white text on a black background, or many other combinations, in the Reverse Text Options dialog box.

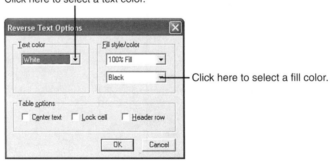

Click here to select a fill color.

**CAUTION**

> You can run this macro in a table cell that does not have text in it, but if you start to type the text and the color isn't right, you need to turn on Reveal Codes and make sure your cursor is between the two "color" codes before you type the entry.

- saveall.wcm—This macro displays the Save Open Documents dialog box, which is similar to the Close All Documents dialog box shown in Figure 26.11. It works the same way: If you want to save a document, place a check mark next to the filename. If necessary, you can change the filename and path before saving the file.

- Savetoa.wcm—This macro saves the current document, and then copies the file to a disk in drive A:. If you haven't named the document yet, you will get the opportunity to do so. When you name the file, don't worry about switching to drive A: or typing a: in the path. All you need to do is name the file—the macro saves it to drive A:.

- tconvert.wcm—This macro displays the Convert Template dialog box, where you can type in the name of a template that you want to convert for use in WordPerfect 11 (or 12). If you can't remember the name (or the location) of the template file, click the Files icon to search for it.

- uawp11en.wcm or uawp12en.wcm—According to the documentation, this macro is used by the PerfectExpert. You should not delete this file from the macros folder, so don't even think about getting rid of it!

- wp_org.wcm—This macro creates a basic organization chart that you can start filling in immediately. You get the same results that you would if you chose Insert, Graphics, Draw Picture to open the Presentations/Draw editing screen and then chose Insert, Organization Chart, and selected the first Single option in the Layout dialog box.

- wp_pr.wcm—This macro opens an outline from a WordPerfect document in Presentations as a slide show. You can run the macro whether you have an outline in the document or not, but Presentations has a hard time figuring out what to put on the slides with a regular document. The document is saved as pr_outln.wpd.

**26**

**TIP FROM**

*Laura Acklen*

> WordPerfect designed a toolbar with buttons for the most frequently used shipping macros. Right-click the toolbar, choose More, and then scroll down and place a check mark next to Shipping Macros.

*If you click one of the buttons on the Shipping Macros toolbar and you get an error message that the file can't be found, see "Where Are the Rest of the Shipping Macros?" in the Troubleshooting section at the end of this chapter.*

## CREATING MACROS

Now that you've played around with a couple of the shipping macros and you've gotten the general idea, you're ready to create a few of your own. Keep in mind that the first several attempts don't have to be perfect; you can keep recording the macro over and over again until you get it right.

**TIP FROM**

For all but the simplest macros, it's a good idea to jot down the sequence of events, so you do everything in the right order and don't forget anything.

Follow these steps to record your own macro:

1. You can record a macro in a blank document or in an existing document. In fact, it's most practical to create the macro the next time you need to perform a certain series of steps because you can create the macro and accomplish your task at the same time.

2. Choose Tools, Macro, Record or press Ctrl+F10.

3. Type a name for the macro in the File Name text box. A macro is automatically saved with the .wcm extension, which identifies it as a macro file.

4. If necessary, choose a location for your macro from the Save In drop-down list.

**NOTE**

By default, new macros are created in the macros folder, which varies according to the operating system on your computer. The locations of the default macro folder and the supplemental macro folder are specified in Settings. Choose Tools, Settings (or press Alt+F12). Click Files and then click the Merge/Macro tab. If you need to change the location, click the Files icon at the end of the text box to browse for the folder. It's a common practice to use the supplemental macro folder as a way to gain access to macros stored on a network.

5. Click Record. The Macro toolbar is displayed underneath the property bar (see Figure 26.16). The recorder is now on, so you're ready to start recording your actions.

Click here to stop recording.                    Macro feature bar

**Figure 26.16**
The Macro toolbar has buttons to help you record and edit macros.

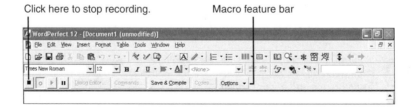

6. Type the text, work with the features, and do whatever you want to record for future use. The macro records all your actions, whether you use the keyboard or the mouse. There is one caveat—you have to use the keyboard to position the insertion point in the document window.

**TIP FROM**

You can insert a pause in a macro so a user can type something in. When you are ready for user input, click the Pause While Recording/Executing a Macro button (on the Macro toolbar). At this point, you can either type something and click the button again, or just click the button again to move past the pause. When you run the macro, the macro will pause and wait for input. When you press Enter, the macro resumes. See the project at the end of this chapter for more information.

7. When you're finished, click the Stop Macro Play or Record button (or press Ctrl+F10) to stop recording. The Macro toolbar disappears, and you are returned to a normal document window. The actions that you took while you created the macro have been performed on the document, so you've essentially killed two birds with one stone.

To run the macro, follow the steps detailed previously in the "Playing Macros" section.

*If you turn on the Macro Recorder and your fingers rebel against you and you make simple mistakes, see "I Made a Mistake While Recording a Macro" in the Troubleshooting section at the end of this chapter.*

*If you sometimes get an error message when you run a macro, see "I Get an Intermittent Error Message When I Run My Macro" in the Troubleshooting section at the end of this chapter.*

Now that you've created the macro, all sorts of possibilities open up. The first thing you'll probably notice is how tedious it is to play macros by choosing them from a File Open dialog box. Granted, the last nine macros that you played are listed at the bottom of the Macros menu, so you can get to those in a couple of mouse clicks. But what about the others? Changing to different folders and scrolling down through long lists of macros sort of defeat the purpose of running macros, doesn't it?

Thankfully, you have lots of options for putting macros in easy reach. You can assign macros to keystrokes, toolbar buttons, menu commands, and property bars. I'll cover assigning macros later in the chapter, in the "Assigning Macros to Keystrokes, Toolbars, and Menus" section. The next section explains how you assign and create macros in templates so that they are available only in a specific template.

## CREATING TEMPLATE MACROS

You can create macros specifically for use with a particular template. Because these macros are saved with a template, they do not appear in the list with the other macros, so they don't clutter up the macros folder. By definition, template macros must be created in a template.

26

You can do a lot of the same things with template macros that you do with regular macros. You can assign a template macro to a keystroke, toolbar, menu, or property bar. See the section "Assigning Macros to Keystrokes, Toolbars, and Menus," later in this chapter, for the steps to assign a macro.

There are several ways to add a macro to a template:

■ You can copy the macro from another template.

■ You can copy the macro from a macro file.

■ You can record the macro from scratch.

### COPYING FROM ANOTHER TEMPLATE

Don't reinvent the wheel! If someone else has developed template macros that you can use, by all means, use them! All you have to do is copy them over from their template and they are all yours.

Follow these steps to copy a macro over from another template:

1. Edit the template that you want to add the macro to.

2. Click the Copy/Remove Object button on the template toolbar to open the Copy/Remove Template Objects dialog box.

   → If you need a refresher on the steps to edit a project template, **see** "Revising WordPerfect Templates," **p. 721.**

   → For more detailed information on copying objects between templates, **see** "Copying Objects from Other Templates," **p. 726.**

3. Click the Templates to Copy From drop-down list arrow and select the template that has the macros you want to copy.

4. Click the Object Type drop-down list arrow and choose Macros. A list of available macros appears in the Macros list box (see Figure 26.17).

**Figure 26.17**
A list of macros in the selected template appears in the Macros list box, where you can select them for copying into the current template.

5. Select the macro you want to copy in the Macros list box and click Copy >>. Or, you can click Copy All >> to copy all the macros at once.

6. Click Close, and then save your changes to the template.

### TRANSFERRING A MACRO FILE

If someone has already created a macro that you want to include with a template, you can copy it directly from the file. Use this method when the macro that you want is a regular macro, not a *template* macro.

Follow these steps to copy a macro from a file:

1. Edit the template to which you want to add the macro.
2. Click the Copy/Remove Object button on the Template toolbar to open the Copy/Remove Template Objects dialog box.
3. Click the Object Type drop-down list arrow and choose Macros on Disk.
4. In the Source text box, either type the path for the macro that you want to copy or click the File icon to search for the macro file. When you locate the macro file, select it, and then click Select.
5. The path and name of the macro file are inserted in the Source text box.
6. Click the Copy >> button.
7. Repeat steps 4–6 to copy other macro files to the template.
8. Click Close when you're done.

### CREATING A TEMPLATE MACRO FROM SCRATCH

The last method is to create the macro from scratch. The steps are slightly different from the ones you used earlier in the chapter. First, edit the template to which you want to add macros; then, follow these steps to create a template macro from scratch:

1. Choose Tools, Template Macro, Record. The Record Template Macro dialog box appears (see Figure 26.18).

Type the name of the macro here.

**Figure 26.18**
You can verify the name of the template, and then type the name of the macro in the Record Template Macro dialog box.

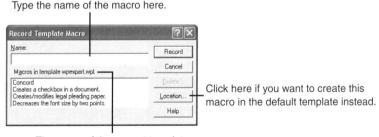

Click here if you want to create this macro in the default template instead.

The name of the current template

2. Type a name for the macro in the Name text box and then click Record.

 *If nothing happens after you enter the macro name and click Record, see "I'm Stuck in the Record Template Macro Dialog Box" in the Troubleshooting section at the end of this chapter.*

3. Get busy recording whatever it is that you want to do in this macro.

4. Click the Stop Macro Play or Record button (or choose Tools, Template Macro, Record) to stop recording. The Macro toolbar disappears, and you are returned to a normal document window.

**NOTE**

> For a macro to be associated with a trigger, it must have been created as a template macro. For example, you could set up a "preprint" trigger to run a macro that accepts client identification information so the printer resources can be billed back to the client.

→ To get the scoop on macro triggers, **see** "Associating Macros to Triggers," **p. 736**.

## CREATING QUICKMACROS

Ever have one of those days when you are forced into typing a long and complex phrase over and over again? And you don't want to create a macro because it's not likely that you'll have to type that same information again. Wouldn't it be nice if you could create a temporary macro just for that day? You can—it's called a QuickMacro.

QuickMacros are created as template macros—the only difference is that you don't name a QuickMacro. The QuickMacro is assigned to a temporary file for this session, and when you exit WordPerfect, the file is erased. You can have only one QuickMacro at a time. To replace a QuickMacro, simply create a new one. Follow these steps to create a QuickMacro:

1. Choose Tools, Template Macro, Record to display the Record Template Macro dialog box (refer to Figure 26.18).

2. Don't type a name—just press Enter or click the Record Button.

3. When you see the Macro toolbar, you can start recording the macro.

4. Click the Stop Macro Play or Record button (or choose Tools, Template Macro, Record) to stop recording. The Macro toolbar disappears, and you are returned to a normal document window.

The QuickMacro won't appear in the template macro list, but don't be fooled. It's in there. When you're ready to play the QuickMacro, choose Tools, Template Macro, Play. Press Enter, or just click Play.

## ASSIGNING MACROS TO KEYSTROKES, TOOLBARS, AND MENUS

There are a variety of different ways to put the macros you use the most right at your fingertips. You can assign a macro or a template macro to a keystroke (such as Alt+8), to a toolbar button, or to a menu. Macros (but not template macros) can also be assigned to the property bar. Let's start with the steps to assign a macro to a keystroke first, and then move on to the others.

### ASSIGNING MACROS TO KEYSTROKES

Because you spend most of your time with your hands on the keyboard, macros that are activated by a keystroke are immensely popular. The only problem is that many other features are already assigned to shortcut keys. You can either choose one that isn't currently assigned or you can replace the current assignment.

→ For the steps to edit a project template, **see** "Basing a Template on Another Template," **p. 724.**

The steps to assign a macro or a template macro to a keystroke are similar, so rather than repeat steps, I'll point out the differences as we go along. In every case, when you want to assign a template macro, you need to edit the template that contains the macro first. Then follow these steps to assign a macro to a keystroke:

1. Choose Tools, Settings (or press Alt+F12), and then click Customize. This opens the Customize Settings dialog box.

2. Click the Keyboards tab to display the available keyboards (see Figure 26.19).

The default keyboard

**Figure 26.19**
You can select the keyboard that you want to edit in the Keyboards tab of the Customize Settings dialog box.

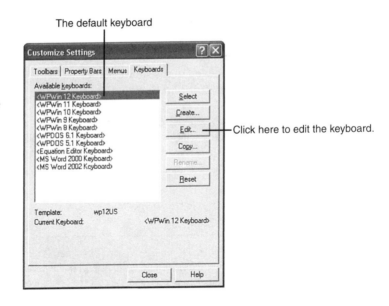

Click here to edit the keyboard.

3. If you want to edit the default keyboard, leave <WPWin 11 Keyboard> or <WPWin 12 Keyboard> selected. Otherwise, select another keyboard.

4. Choose Edit to display the Keyboard Shortcuts dialog box. This is where you choose the keystroke and select a macro.

5. Select the shortcut key that you want to use from the Choose a Shortcut Key list box.

6. Click the Macros tab to display the macro options (see Figure 26.20).

7. Click Assign Macro to Key to assign a regular macro to a keystroke; click Assign Template Macro to Key to assign a template macro to a keystroke.

Select a shortcut key in the list.

**Figure 26.20**
You can assign a macro to any keystroke that you see in the list, even if the keystroke already has something assigned to it.

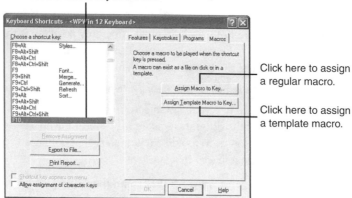

Click here to assign a regular macro.

Click here to assign a template macro.

8. Depending on which button you clicked in step 7, you see the Select Macro dialog box or the Select Template Macro dialog box. Either way, select the macro that you want to assign and then choose Select.

9. If you're assigning a template macro, skip this step. In the message box, choose Yes if you want the entire path to show up in the shortcut keys list; choose No if you want only the name of the macro displayed in the list.

**CAUTION**

If the macro is not stored in the default macro folder or the supplemental macro folder specified in File Settings, make sure that you save the macro with the full path.

10. Repeat steps 5–9 to assign other macros to shortcut keys.

**TIP FROM**

*Laura Acklen*

If you skipped WordPerfect 10, you haven't seen a cool new feature: printing lists of keyboard shortcuts. Choose Tools, Settings, Customize. Click the Keyboards tab. Select the keyboard that you want to print from, and then choose Edit. Choose Print Report to print a list of shortcut keys, or choose Export to File to save the list as a comma-delimited file (.csv).

## ASSIGNING MACROS TO TOOLBARS

Now that you understand the general concept, assigning macros to toolbar buttons is a snap. Again, the steps to assigning a regular macro and a template macro are similar, so I'll point out the differences as we go along. Remember that if you want to assign a template macro to a toolbar button, edit the template first. Then, follow these steps to assign a macro to a toolbar button:

1. Choose Tools, Settings (or press Alt+F12), and then click Customize. If necessary, click the Toolbars tab. A list of available toolbars is displayed in the Customize Settings dialog box (see Figure 26.21).

The default toolbar

**Figure 26.21**
You can select the toolbar that you want to edit in the Toolbars tab of the Customize Settings dialog box.

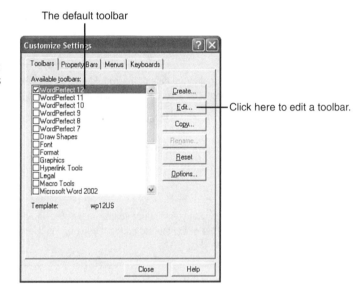

Click here to edit a toolbar.

→ For the steps to edit a project template, **see** "Basing a Template on Another Template," **p. 724.**

2. Select a toolbar, and then choose Edit to open the Toolbar Editor dialog box. This is where you choose a macro to assign to a toolbar button.

3. Click the Macros tab to display the buttons to add a regular macro or a template macro (see Figure 26.22).

**26**

**Figure 26.22**
You can add a macro or a template macro to a toolbar button in the Macros tab of the Toolbar Editor dialog box.

4. Click Add Macro to add a macro to a toolbar button, or click Add Template Macro to add a template macro to a toolbar button.

5. Depending on your choice, you see the Select Macro dialog box or the Select Template Macro dialog box. In either case, select the macro, and then choose Select. If you've assigned a macro, you are prompted to save the macro with a full pathname (Yes or No).

CAUTION

> If the macro is not stored in the default macro folder or the supplemental macro folder specified in File Settings, make sure that you save the macro with the full path.

6. Repeat steps 3–5 to assign other macros to toolbar buttons.

7. Click OK when you're finished making your changes.

CAUTION

> When you are finished with your toolbar editing, make sure you don't click the X button in the upper-right corner of the toolbar editor. If you do, you'll lose all of your changes. Choose OK instead.

A new button has been added to the selected toolbar. All macros have the same button picture of a cassette tape (see Figure 26.23). Click and drag the new button to position it on the toolbar.

New macro button

**Figure 26.23**
Macro buttons all use the same picture, that of a cassette tape. Pause over a macro button to display a QuickTip.

Because the buttons are all the same, you need help differentiating the macro buttons. While you're editing a toolbar, you can modify the properties for a macro button. Double-click the button to display the Customize Button dialog box (see Figure 26.24), where you can type text to appear on the button and the message for the QuickTip. Button text doesn't appear by default, so the second part of the process is to change the button option settings to show text in a button. On the Toolbars tab of the Customize Settings dialog box (refer to Figure 26.22), choose Options to open the Toolbar Options dialog box. Choose Text to display only the text, or Picture and Text to display both the picture and the text message.

Type the button text here.

**Figure 26.24**
You can type button text and the message text that you want to assign to a macro button in the Customize Button dialog box.

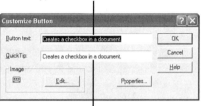

Type the QuickTip text here.

**TIP FROM**

If you would rather save space and not use text, you can change the graphic on the button. There is an option that enables you to edit the button, but it doesn't really produce good results because you are editing the actual pixels of the image. A better solution is to copy a graphic from another button. First, find a button whose graphic you like—scroll through the list of available features, trying various categories if necessary, watching the button graphic area below the feature list. When you find a button you like, click the Add button to add it to the toolbar, and then double-click it. Click the Edit button in the Image area, click Copy, click OK or Cancel, again OK or Cancel, double-click your macro button, click Edit, and then Paste, and then OK twice. (Then you can drag off the toolbar the button you had added just to be able to copy its picture.) This sounds complicated, but it's not. Give it a try just once and see if this will work for you.

**NOTE**

The steps to add a macro to a property bar are very similar to the steps to add a macro to a toolbar. The only difference is that you click the Property Bars tab, and then select the property bar that you want to edit. The Text property bar is the default, or the one that you see in a blank document. From here, you can repeat the preceding steps, starting at step 3.

**26**

### ASSIGNING MACROS TO MENUS

If you aren't concerned about the clutter, you can put your macros right on the menu bar. The name of the macro (or whatever else you want to appear) shows up on the menu bar right next to the other menu items. To play the macro, you just click the name on the menu bar.

As usual, if you want to assign a template macro, you need to edit the template first. Then, follow these steps to assign macros to the menu bar:

1. Choose Tools, Settings, and then click Customize.
2. Click the Menus tab to display a list of available menus (see Figure 26.25).
3. Select a menu, and then choose Edit to open the Menu Editor dialog box. This dialog box is almost identical to the Toolbar Editor dialog box shown in Figure 26.19.
4. Click the Macros tab.

**Figure 26.25**
You can create customized menus or edit the existing menus in the Menus tab of the Customize Settings dialog box.

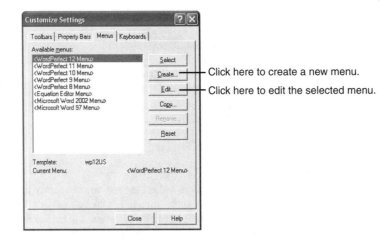

Click here to create a new menu.
Click here to edit the selected menu.

5. Click Add Macro to assign a macro, or click Add Template Macro to assign a template macro. Depending on your choice, you see the Select Macro dialog box or the Select Template Macro dialog box.

6. In either dialog box, select the macro, and then click Select.

7. Choose Yes if you want to save the macro with the entire path, or choose No if you don't want to. The name of the macro is added to the menu bar (see Figure 26.26).

Macro name on the menu

**Figure 26.26**
After you've added a macro to the menu bar, you can give it a friendlier name.

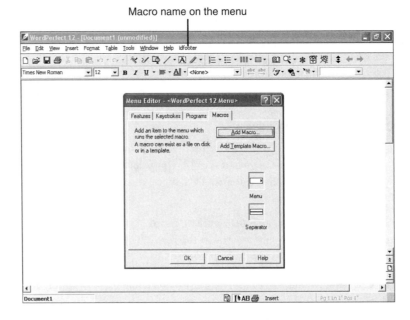

**CAUTION**

> If the macro is not stored in the default macro folder or the supplemental macro folder specified in File Settings, make sure that you save the macro with the full path.

**8.** Repeat steps 5–7 to assign other macros to shortcut keys.

If you save the macro with the path (so that you don't have to put it in the default macro folder), you'll see that the macro path takes up a lot of space on the menu bar. You can give the macro a friendlier name and a description that appears in the QuickTip. With the Menu Editor dialog box displayed, double-click the macro name on the menu bar to open the Edit Menu Text dialog box, which looks similar to the Customize Button dialog box shown in Figure 26.24. Type a friendlier name for the macro in the Menu Item text box and then type a description in the QuickTip text box.

To take this idea one step further, consider creating a Macros menu with your frequently used macro names on that menu. In the menu editor, drag the Menu button up and drop it on the toolbar, and then double-click it and type a name in the Menu Item box. If you want an underlined letter (like the other menus have), type an ampersand (**&**) just prior to the letter that is to be underlined—just make sure you don't pick a letter that is being used by one of the other menus. The letter "M" is available, so type **&Macros** to name the new menu "Macros" with an underlined M. Then, as you add macros to the toolbar, drag them down into the new Macros menu. You can add submenus within the menu and separators between groups of macros or submenus, and you can edit the macro name labels also to include an ampersand before a (carefully selected) letter if you want the macros to be accessible via the keyboard. Just make sure that none of the macros or submenus under the Macros menu have the same letter underlined. (Each submenu keeps its own list of underlined letter triggers, so if you have lots of macros to add, using submenus can help both make the list manageable and keep letters available.)

**26**

**TIP FROM**

*Laura Achlen*

> How many times have you opened WordPerfect just to address an envelope? Did you know that you can create a macro that opens the Envelope dialog box and then create a shortcut to that macro on your desktop? Here's how: Choose Tools, Macro, Macro Toolbar. Type the following information into the macro document and save it as env-dialog. Now, create a shortcut on your desktop that points to this macro. Right-click the desktop, choose New, Shortcut, browse to the Documents and Settings\<username>\Application Data\Corel\PerfectScript\12\WordPerfect\ folder, and select the env-dialog file. Give the shortcut a name and add it to the desktop. Here is the macro code:
>
> ```
>     Application (A1; "WordPerfect"; Default; "EN")
>     AppMinimize ()
>     EnvelopeDlg ()
> ```
>
> This macro idea was posted by Gary Mosier on WordPerfect Universe (www.wpuniverse.com).

## EDITING MACROS

Let's say that someone in your company is in charge of developing and distributing macros for everyone else's use. If so, count yourself lucky and make sure you say thank you once in a while because if you ever want some changes made, that is the person you'll have to go to.

However, if all you want to do is change a name, address, or other minor detail, you can save yourself some groveling by making the minor changes yourself. Furthermore, you might have an occasion to edit the macros that you created.

When you open a macro, you'll see that rather than record your exact keystrokes (as earlier versions of the macro language did), the Macro Recorder actually records the results of your actions. For example, if you use the menus to change the margins, you can't see the actual menu commands that you selected. Instead, you see the margin change itself.

You can edit macros and template macros with essentially the same steps. However, if you want to edit a template macro, you have to edit the template first. Then, follow these steps to edit a macro:

1. Choose Tools, Macro (or Template Macro), Edit. Depending on which type of macro you chose, you'll see the Edit Macro dialog box or the Edit Template Macro dialog box.

2. In either case, select the macro you want to edit, and then choose Edit. The macro appears in the document window (see Figure 26.27).

**CAUTION**

> Here's where things get a little tricky—you must use extreme care so that you don't accidentally delete (or modify) the macro commands. If you do, make sure you don't save your changes when you close the macro. Take a deep breath and start over.

3. Make the necessary corrections to the text portions of the macro. Unless you're comfortable with macro commands, it's a very good idea to leave them alone.

4. Click the Save and Compile button to save the macro before you close it. If there are any problems, you'll see an error message so you'll know right away if you need to fix something.

5. When you're finished, click the Close button on the menu bar to close the document window.

6. Choose Yes to save your changes to the macro.

---

**Recompiling Macros After SP1 for WordPerfect 11**

Due to an issue with Service Pack 1 for WordPerfect 11, you need to recompile the shipping macros and any macros that you have created after you install the service pack. To recompile the macros, choose Alt+F10 to display the list of macros in the Play Macro dialog box. Right-click each macro file, and then choose Compile. When you are finished, you can close the PerfectScript Editor. Also, because the WordPerfect templates depend on macros to run, you'll need to recompile the template files as well. There is a discussion on WordPerfect

Universe (go to www.wpuniverse.com and search the forums for "SP1+macros") that gives more information and has recompiled template files that you can download. You can also visit the WordPerfect FAQ newsgroup at news://cnews.corel.com/corel.wpoffice.wordperfect-faq for a zip file that contains recompiled templates and macros, plus two popular term paper templates: the American Psychological Association (APA) and the Chicago Manual of Style (Turabian).

This command selects the font.

This command changes the top margin.

Don't change this information.

**Figure 26.27**
This macro sets up a letterhead page, a new margin setting, a font change, today's date, a salutation, and a closing.

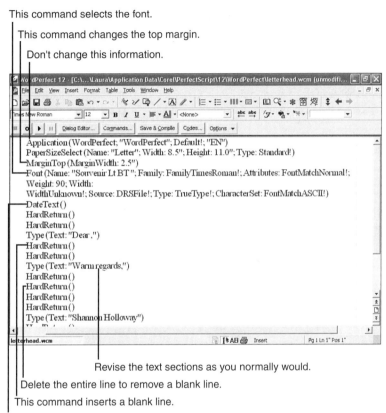

Revise the text sections as you normally would.

Delete the entire line to remove a blank line.

This command inserts a blank line.

This command inserts the current date.

## LEARNING MORE ABOUT PERFECTSCRIPT

If you're editing a macro that someone else has written, it's likely to be more complicated than the macro shown in Figure 26.26. You'll see lots of programming commands and you might be wondering where they come from.

WordPerfect's macro language is called *PerfectScript*. It is a command-based language that can be used to write macros in WordPerfect, Presentations, and Quattro Pro. You can do a lot more with PerfectScript than just play back recorded commands. Macros can stop and prompt for input, and then, based on that input, go to a different section of the macro and execute the commands there. Macros can be structured to display messages and customized dialog boxes. Information from other WordPerfect Office applications can be combined.

26

In fact, you can actually build complete document-building applications (or wizards) for those users with limited WordPerfect experience.

---

**Downloading the SDK for WordPerfect 11 and 12**

The Software Developer's Kit (SDK) is a set of tools that lets you customize WordPerfect Office applications for commercial or business use. The SDK contains reference materials, OLE automation samples, and PerfectScript tools, as well as code generation wizards, tools, and utilities for third-party add-ons to WordPerfect. One of the utilities, `wplook.exe`, is used to repair corrupt files. Corel recommends that you repair the file several times to make sure everything has been fixed.

The SDK can be downloaded from Corel's site. You'll need to first register as a partner at `www.corel.com/partners`. The base level is free so don't let the registration scare you off. You'll get access to the SDK, but also other resources that are available on CorelConnected. Depending on the level of membership, a partner can gain access to more information about the products that Corel offers.

---

Unfortunately, covering the PerfectScript macro language is beyond the scope of this book. Here are some places where you can go for help:

- Consult the help topics. Specifically, read the information under the heading "Recordings, Macros, and Automation Features" in the Contents tab of the Help Topics dialog box. Also, use the Index to browse through the list of topics under "macros."

- If you're inserting commands in the PerfectScript Commands dialog box, you can select a command in the list to view a brief description. (Remember the keyboard shortcut to open that dialog box is Ctrl+M.)

- You can view the User Guide for more information on Macros & PerfectScript. For WordPerfect 11, choose Start, (All) Programs, WordPerfect Office 11, Help Files, User Guide. For WordPerfect 12, choose Start, (All) Programs, WordPerfect Office 12, Support, User Guide.

**CAUTION**

> You must have the Adobe Acrobat Reader installed to view the Reference Center materials, so if you don't already have it installed, you'll be prompted to install it. Insert CD #2 and run the Install Wizard to install Adobe Acrobat Reader. You can also go to `www.adobe.com` and download the latest version of Adobe Reader.

- Buy a book that specifically covers macro programming with PerfectScript. Ask your local bookstore to do a search for you, or visit one of the online bookstores and search for `wordperfect macros`.

- Run through the excellent macro tutorial by Seth Katz. The tutorial assumes no previous macro experience and covers a lot of ground. Go to `http://www.shkatz.com/macrotut/index.html`.

**NOTE**

> You might recognize the name Gordon McComb, from other *Special Edition Using WordPerfect* books, or possibly from the "Macros" column that he wrote for *WordPerfect for Windows* magazine, or from the articles he has written for www.officecommunity.com. Gordon is widely recognized as a leading authority on WordPerfect macros. Rumor has it that, over the years, some of his applications have actually been incorporated into the program. Go to his site at www.gmccomb.com to check out his selection of macro books. (And no, I'm not getting paid to say this. )

## USING MACROS FROM PREVIOUS VERSIONS OF WORDPERFECT

The basic structure of the programming language hasn't changed since WordPerfect 6. New commands have been added to take advantage of new features and to use existing features more efficiently. The majority of the old commands have been retained to ensure backward compatibility.

A new warning system has been put into place that will warn you if a command is obsolete and might potentially be removed in future versions. This system works for macros developed with WordPerfect version 5 and beyond. The messages are only warnings—you can still use the command and you can ignore the warning. The macro will work just fine after it has been saved and compiled. You won't have to go through the warning messages again, unless you edit and recompile the macro. Compiling a macro is a dry run where the macro is checked for accuracy but isn't actually executed.

To convert macros from previous versions of WordPerfect, you have to open the macro and save it, which forces the macro to be compiled in WordPerfect. Follow these steps to convert macros:

1. Choose Tools, Macro (or Template Macro), Edit. Depending on which type of macro you choose, you'll see the Edit Macro dialog box or the Edit Template Macro dialog box.

2. In either case, select the macro you want to edit, and then choose Edit.

3. If you need to make some changes, do that now.

4. Click the Save & Compile button on the Macro toolbar.

5. Correct any errors listed by the macro compiler, and then click the Save & Compile button again. When you don't get any more errors, close the macro and save your changes.

 *If you are getting a bunch of warning messages when you run some of your macros, see "Warning Messages When Running Macros" in the Troubleshooting section at the end of this chapter.*

26

# VISUAL BASIC—DO YOU NEED IT?

WordPerfect Office includes support for Microsoft Visual Basic for Applications (VBA) programming language, which can be used as an alternative to the PerfectScript programming language. WordPerfect gets a gold star for being the only mainstream word processor to offer two powerful programming languages that can be used separately or in combination.

So, do you need it? It depends on whether you need to accomplish something that you can't do with PerfectScript. VBA is harder to learn and requires a much higher level of understanding of how WordPerfect operates. Prior experience with an object-oriented programming language is a definite plus.

**NOTE**

VBA support isn't installed by default, so if you want to use it, you have to install it from CD #2. Make sure you disable your antivirus program before you install any part of WordPerfect Office.

Unless you've been living under a rock, you've heard about all the macro viruses and the havoc they have wreaked on companies such as Microsoft, Intel, and Dell. These viruses are easy to spread because of the way Microsoft Word handles macros in a document. You might have heard that by installing VBA support with WordPerfect, you are leaving yourself open to macro viruses. Well, you're right to be concerned. If you've installed VBA support and you open a document that contains VBA macros (also called projects), the VBA macros are automatically triggered.

Thankfully, WordPerfect is designed in such a way that the risk is minimal and easy to avoid with a good antivirus program. There are also extra security measures built in to the version of VBA that ships with WordPerfect. Just make sure that you impress upon anyone who will listen that they should never, ever, ever, disable their macro virus security just because it's a pain to bypass the warning messages every time they open a file with VBA macros embedded in it.

**26**

**TIP FROM**

*Laura Acklen*

For more information on what VBA means to you, check out Gordon McComb's frequently asked questions (FAQ) document on VBA. Go to `www.gmccomb.com/vbafaq.html`. This piece was written when WordPerfect 9 was released, but the majority of it applies to WordPerfect 11 and 12. Also, read over the VBA section of the Release Notes document (`readme.txt` or `readme.html`), which is located on CD #1.

After all the media hype surrounding viruses and how they bring down the e-mail systems of many companies, you would think that the employees would know better than to disable their virus protection. I guess it just goes to show that no one is immune to computer viruses. Consider every file suspect until you've checked it out with an antivirus program that has the latest virus definitions installed, even if your best friend just gave it to you.

WordPerfect Office 11 (and 12) supports Digital Signatures in WordPerfect, Quattro Pro, and Presentations. You can use these signatures to sign and authenticate documents and macros. For Digital Signatures to function properly, you must have Microsoft Internet Explorer (IE) 5.5 or higher installed on your system. If you do not, the Setup program will install the browser components of IE 6.

**NOTE**

> WordPerfect Office 11 (and 12) include support for Entrust version 4.0 and later. Entrust is an upgrade component for WordPerfect that lets you encrypt and digitally sign documents in WordPerfect using the Entrust security system. You must have access to an Entrust server to use the WordPerfect Entrust integration.

For more detailed programming information on VBA, read through the macro online help file. Choose Help, Help Topics, Contents, Reference Information, WordPerfect and Visual Basic for Applications.

# TROUBLESHOOTING

### WHERE ARE THE REST OF THE SHIPPING MACROS?

*I want to play the* allfonts *macro, but it doesn't appear in the list of macros. Where are the rest of the files?*

Some of the macro files might have been accidentally deleted, or you might be looking in the wrong folder. First, look in Settings to see where macros are stored in your system. Choose Tools, Settings, Files and then click the Merge/Macros tab. Jot down the location of the default macro folder. Now, choose Tools, Macro, Play and verify that you are looking in the same folder that was noted in Settings. If not, browse to that folder and look for the macros. If you still don't see them, do a repair install, which will copy the macro files onto your system. Choose Start, Control Panel, Add/Remove Programs; then select WordPerfect Office 11 (or WordPerfect Office 12), and then choose Change. In the Program Maintenance window, choose Repair, and then click on Next. Click Next again, and then Install.

### I MADE A MISTAKE WHILE RECORDING A MACRO

*In the middle of recording a macro, I realized that I'd made a mistake. What should I do?*

Relax, it isn't the end of the world—the mistake is easily fixed. In fact, you might be surprised to learn that WordPerfect doesn't even record some of your mistakes in the macro.

You can stop recording the macro at this point and just start over, saving the new macro over the incomplete macro. Or, you can fix the mistake and go on. In most cases, the "fix" isn't recorded—only the final result of your actions.

## I GET AN INTERMITTENT ERROR MESSAGE WHEN I RUN MY MACRO

*I created a macro that changes the font and font size for selected text. When I run the macro, some-times I get an error that says the macro is being cancelled due to an error on line 3. Other times, the macro runs just fine. I've reviewed the macro and I can't find anything wrong. What now?*

Did you select text before you ran the macro? If not, the macro won't work. You've just run into a problem with states. If you record a macro that takes action on selected text, that macro expects a state of selected text when you run it. If it doesn't find that state, the macro can't run properly.

The same holds true for other conditions in WordPerfect. For example, if you write a macro that customizes graphics boxes, you need to make sure there is a graphics box in the docu-ment before you run the macro.

## I'M STUCK IN THE RECORD TEMPLATE MACRO DIALOG BOX

*I'm trying to create a template macro from scratch. When I enter a name for the macro and click Record, nothing happens. I have to cancel out of the dialog box.*

It sounds like the template file is damaged. If you're adding the template macro to the default template, you'll have to rename the default template and let WordPerfect create a new one when you start WordPerfect again. Unfortunately, this means you'll lose any cus-tomizations that have been made to the toolbars, keyboards, menus, styles, macros, and other objects that are stored in the default template.

Let me stop here and remind you how important it is to make a backup copy of your default template after you've done some customizing. It takes only a second, and it can save you hours. In fact, you might be able to recover by simply deleting the corrupted default tem-plate and renaming the backup copy. The name of the default template is wp11us.wpt (or wp12us.wpt) and you'll find it in the folder specified in Settings as the default template folder (choose Tools, Settings, Files, Template). The "us" stands for the US English version of the program. Those two letters will vary depending on the language and country version of WordPerfect that you use.

If you are adding a template macro to one of the project templates, try getting a fresh copy of the template from the WordPerfect Office CD. Insert the CD and when the Install Wizard starts, choose a Repair install.

## WARNING MESSAGES WHEN RUNNING MACROS

*I've just started using some of the macros that I wrote in previous versions of WordPerfect. When I run them for the first time, I get warning messages about obsolete commands. What's this all about?*

The first time you play a non-WP11 (or non-WP12) macro, the macro system recompiles the macro to make sure that the macro is using commands that still work in version 11 (and 12). If the macro is using commands that have become obsolete over releases of WordPerfect since version 5, you will get a warning message about the command. These commands will still work, though, and you can ignore the warnings—for now, at least. You should keep in mind that these commands can be removed in future versions of WordPerfect.

### Changing the Hypertext Style

*I just created a check box in my document, and that blue underline stands out like a sore thumb. Is there any way to change the appearance of the check box?*

Check boxes are created as hypertext, which by default appears underlined and in blue. Thankfully, you can modify the style used for hypertext. Keep in mind that if you alter the style, it will affect other hypertext codes in the document, so you might want the other hypertext codes to appear as buttons instead.

To modify the hypertext style, choose Format, Styles. In the Styles dialog box, choose Options, Settings. If necessary, place a check mark in the WordPerfect System Styles check box. Select WordPerfect heading styles and all other system styles, and then click OK. In the Available Styles list box, select Hypertext and then click Edit. In the Styles Editor dialog box, make sure there is a check mark in the Reveal Codes check box. In the Reveal Codes window, delete the [Color: Blue] code, the [Und] code, and the [Color: Black] code. Click OK and then click Close. The check box should now appear black and not be underlined.

# Project

I know I said I couldn't cover any of the programming commands as much as I would like to. I just don't have the space here to do justice to the information. However, there is one very simple thing you can do that opens all sorts of possibilities in your macros. You can insert a pause, which causes the macro to stop and wait for input. When you press Enter, the macro continues. You can insert as many pauses in a macro as you like. And you can type as much text as you like during the pause.

A pause in a macro is similar to the Keyboard Merge command, where you can pause the process to type something and then continue the process. A fill-in-the-blanks form is a perfect candidate, but so is any document with standard blocks of text and a few places where you need to type in something different.

Follow along with these steps to insert a pause in a macro:

1. Choose Tools, Macro, Record (or press Ctrl+F10).
2. Start recording the macro. Do everything up to the point where you want to pause for input.
3. Click the Pause While Recording/Executing a Macro button on the Macro toolbar.
4. If necessary, type some text or perform other tasks.
5. Click the Pause While Recording/Executing a Macro button again to resume recording the macro.
6. Repeat steps 2–5 to continue recording the macro.
7. Click the Stop Macro Play or Record button when you're finished.

Figure 26.28 shows a macro that creates a fax form. There is a pause to type the recipient's name, fax number, and subject. The rest is filled in automatically.

**Figure 26.28**

This macro creates a fax cover sheet form that enables you to type in the name of the recipient, the subject, and the number of pages.

Pause to type in the fax number.

Pause to type in the recipient's name.

# INDEX

backups, 123
Address Books, 795, 801
documents, 26
files, 98
templates, 720
Timed Document Backup feature, 26, 37-39

Balanced Newspaper columns, 250

Bar (Horizontal/Vertical) charts, 506

Bar series, 519

bars. *See also* property bar
application, cell locations, 300
Drop Cap Property, 222
Graphics Property, 363
Header/Footer Property, 238
Outline Property, 19
Reveal Codes, 64
Table Property, 19
Text Property, 19
Title, 653
Transcription feature, activating, 636

bases, 3D charts, 521

Basic Counts reports, 139

basic searches, QuickFinder, 110-112

Behind Text, wrap text option, 397

Bevel option (3D TextArt), 450

bibliographies. *See* table of authorities

bindings, margins, 229

bitmap editors, 443

bitmap graphics, 419
editing, 443-445
troubleshooting, 454

blank documents, 18, 22

blank lines (headers/footers), 245

Block Make It Fit feature, 256

block protect, keeping text together, 214

blue dashes, 23

blue formula indicators, 490

.bmp graphic file extension, 418-419

body text, defined, 344

bold, applying, 75-76

booklet feature, 187

Booklet Pages option, 179, 191

booklets
creating, 197-199, 242
divided pages, 188
margins, 188
printing, 187-191, 197-199
saving, 191
types, 188

Bookmark command (Tools menu), 564, 622-623, 626

Bookmark, Create command (Tools menu), 589

bookmarks
accessing, 623
case sensitivity, 627
creating, 564-565, 622-623
deleting, 566, 626
editing, 626
graphics, 665
hyperlinks, creating, 624-625
inserting, 564-566
Internet links, 631
jumping to, 624
moving, 566
naming, 565, 623, 626
QuickMarks, 566-567
renaming, 566
Reveal Codes, 626
screen shots, printing, 566
sections, linking, 622
selecting, 565-566
shapes, linking, 626
undeleting, 566

Border caption option, 408

Border Offset vertical line option, 381

Border palettes, 326

Border/Fill, QuickMenu, 367

borders
adding, 217-218, 256-258, 381
captions, 408
colors, 218
contoured graphics box, 397
dragging, dialog boxes, 101
fancy, 256
graphics, 218, 377
line styles, 218
options, 218, 365-369
paragraphs, removing, 218
round-cornered, 258
styles, changing, 326
tables, 673
changing, 320, 326-327
customizing, 326-327

thumbnails, 182
titles, charts, 514
troubleshooting, 260
turning off, 257

Borders/Fill command (QuickMenu), 328

Borders/Fill command (Table menu), 322, 326-328

Box Fields command (Format menu), 528

Box Properties command (Format menu), 529

Box Spacing command (Format menu), 530

boxes. *See also* dialog boxes
message boxes, PerfectScript macros, 714
organization charts
attributes, 529
connectors, 529
content, managing, 526-528
fields, adding, 527-528
modifying, 529
sizing, 529
spacing, 530
text, adding, 527
sticky note text boxes, 411-412

brackets ([]), 731

Branch Structure command (Format menu), 522

branches, organization charts, 531-532

breaks, pages, 231

Brightness, image tool, 416, 420

Brightness palette, 416

browsers. *See* Web browsers

browsing concordance files, 609

Bubble charts, 506

bubbles
comments, 543, 660
Footnote/Endnote, 661
margins, 79
tabs, 207

bulleted lists
creating, 82-83, 335-337
editing, 338-339
lines, 338-339
QuickBullets, 335
styles, changing, 339-341
Web documents, 658-659

bullets
menus, 25
QuickBullets, 82-84

demote, defined, 344

Demote, Outline Property Bar option, 345

Depth option (3D TextArt), 450

Depth option (pie charts), 512

Depth option (Quick 3-D), 437

descriptions, styles, 275

Desktop, creating shortcuts, 100

Details command (View menu), 91

Details view, 43, 91

dialog boxes
    Edit Skew, options, 315-316
    Open File, 43-44
    Publish to PDF, options, 678-680
    Review document, closing, 558
    Spell Checker/Grammatik/ Thesaurus/Dictionary, moving, 128
    Table Format, options, 312-320

.dib graphic file extension, 419

dictionaries
    *Oxford English Concise Dictionary*, 143, 146
    *Oxford English Pocket Dictionary*, 146
    *Pocket Oxford Dictionary*, upgrading, 143

Dictionary, 143-146. *See also* word lists

Dictionary command (Tools menu), 143

Digital Signatures, 841
    adding, 556-557
    certificates, viewing, 557
    documents, signing, 557
    implementing, 556
    keys, 556
    validity, 557-558

Digitals After Decimal option (Table Format dialog box), 317

Disable Locks in All Cells option (Table Format dialog box), 320

disabling writing tools, 147

Disconnect Network Drive command (Tools menu), 99

disconnecting network drives, 99

disks. *See* floppy disks

Display As Icon option (video), 638

Display Labels option (X-Axis labels), 516

Display Legend option (chart legends), 515

Display Legend Title option (chart legends), 515

DisplayWrite, WordPerfect conversion, 472

distributing XML documents, 700

document comments. *See* comments

Document Compare feature, 552-556

Document Compare Summary page, 553

Document Initial Styles, 269

Document Map feature, 592-593, 616

Document menu commands
    Cancel Printing, 174
    Pause Printing, 174
    Remove Printing, 174

Document on Disk, print option, 177

Document Options, Publish to PDF dialog box option, 680

Document Review feature
    margin markers, 546
    marked-up documents, 548-550
    revisions, 546-548
    usernames, 548

document styles, 268-270, 278

document summaries
    fields, customizing, 107-108
    filenames, 109
    filling out, 106-107
    information, 108
    options, 108
    printing, 108
    prompts, 109
    QuickFinder, 106
    settings, customizing, 109

Document Summary, print option, 176

Document Type Definitions (DTDs), 649, 687
    compiling, 701-703
    creating, 701
    overview, 701-702

Document, Current Document Style command (File menu), 244-246, 277

Document, Default Font command (File menu), 233

Document, Expand Master command (File menu), 583

Document, Redline Method command (File menu), 554-555

Document, Remove Markings command (File menu), 553

Document, Review command (File menu), 546

Document, Subdocument command (File menu), 581

documents. *See also* accessible documents; files; interactive documents; multimedia documents; Web documents; XML documents
    adapting for accessibility, 642
    backups, 26
    blank, 18, 22
    bookmarks
        creating, 564-565
        deleting, 566
        inserting, 564-566
        moving, 566
        naming, 565
        QuickMark, 566-567
        renaming, 566
        selecting, 565-566
        undeleting, 566
    closing, 28
    concepts, 622
    converting, 47, 475-476, 705-706
    copies, opening, 47
    copying and pasting between, 463-464
    creating, 20-25
        PerfectExpert Help, 35
        templates, 713
    cross-references
        automatic, generating, 579
        creating, 576-577
        graphics box counters, creating, 579-580
        marking, 575-577
        target names, 576
        targets, marking, 577-578

*How can we make this index more useful? Email us at indexes@quepublishing.com*